Personal Selling

The Wiley Marketing Series

WILLIAM LAZER, Advisory Editor
Michigan State University

MARTIN ZOBER, *Marketing Management*

ROBERT J. HOLLOWAY AND ROBERT S. HANCOCK
*The Environment of Marketing Behavior—
Selections from the Literature*

GEORGE SCHWARTZ, Editor
Science in Marketing

EDGAR CRANE
*Marketing Communications—
A Behavioral Approach to Men, Messages, and Media*

JOSEPH W. NEWMAN, Editor
On Knowing the Consumer

STEUART HENDERSON BRITT, Editor
*Consumer Behavior and the Behavioral Sciences—
Theories and Applications*

DONALD F. MULVIHILL AND STEPHEN PARANKA
Price Policies and Practices

DAVID CARSON
International Marketing: A Comparative Systems Approach

BRUCE E. MALLEN
The Marketing Channel: A Conceptual Viewpoint

RONALD R. GIST
Management Perspectives in Retailing

JOHN K. RYANS AND JAMES C. BAKER
World Marketing: A Multinational Approach

JOHN M. BRION
Corporate Marketing Planning

NORTON E. MARKS AND ROBERT M. TAYLOR
Marketing Logistics: Perspectives and Viewpoints

JAMES BEARDEN
Personal Selling: Behavioral Science Readings and Cases

Personal Selling

Behavioral Science Readings and Cases

JAMES H. BEARDEN

Professor of Marketing
East Carolina College

John Wiley & Sons, Inc.

NEW YORK · LONDON · SYDNEY

To my parents

Preface

This book provides a behavioral-science approach to the study of the personal selling function. It has been designed to serve as a supplementary textbook for courses in salesmanship, sales management, and other subject-matter areas dealing with the economics of personal selling in marketing.

The major goal of this book is to provide increased understanding, both theoretical and practical, of the personal selling function. In order to meet this goal it has been necessary to make a marked departure from the "traditional" approach usually developed in personal selling texts. Presentation of theories, concepts, and conceptual schema from multidisciplinary offerings is the framework through which increased theoretical understanding of personal selling is developed. Decision processes and decision-making aspects of the personal selling function are focused on by the use of case studies.

The group of readings selected for use in this book should do much to add to and enrich traditional texts presently being used. The readings have been taken from such disciplines as psychology, sociology, economics, and anthropology. For the convenience of instructors and students each is keyed to the chapters of all major salesmanship texts.

To develop an understanding of the various roles and demands of the salesman and the contribution that he makes to the marketing and economic systems, a group of twenty-six cases is provided. It is hoped that analytical skills and decision-making abilities can be exercised and enhanced by the use of these cases.

A great debt is owed to the host of people who made this book possible. Special appreciation is expressed to authors and publishers who have given permission to reproduce their materials. Many of the cases I have prepared were begun as student reports. To these contributing students and others who in using the cases as a basis for class discussion have been tolerant and critical much appreciation is due.

I am indebted to Dr. William R. Bennett, University of Alabama, who was instrumental in shaping my approach to personal selling; to Dr. Harry A. Lipson, University of Alabama, who as friend and mentor guided me through my dissertation and doctoral program; to Dr. E. R. Browning, East Carolina College, who provided me with opportunities necessary to pursue this endeavor; and to Dr. William Lazer, Michigan State University, who provided advice and direction in the early stages of this book.

My sincerest thanks to Mrs. Barbara Grimsley who, in addition to typing, assisted in the assembling and editing of the manuscript, and to my editor, Jack Young, John Wiley and Sons, for his faithful attention and support of my work.

Finally, I would particularly like to thank my wife and children who in so many ways contributed in this effort.

JAMES H. BEARDEN

Greenville, North Carolina
March 1967

Introduction

The publication of a text dealing with personal selling, especially at a time when intellectually and practically the core values of personal selling are being challenged, calls for more than usual justification. This book appears at a time when the validity of the salesmanship course within the School of Business is being questioned by business educators and nonbusiness educators. It comes at a time when, as Tosdal has pointed out, within the business community, "engineers, technical men, production men, and others are themselves not really convinced of the social and economic necessity of selling." Nevertheless, it is in the character of the times that justification of this book is found.

A basic question that stands out in the present state of personal selling is, "What is the role of personal selling in contemporary marketing?" At the present time, the question simply exists as an important question about which little has been said or done. While the question does not as yet have a satisfactory answer, it is one to which an answer must be found if progress in the whole field of marketing science is to advance at a healthy pace.

Although advancement in other areas of marketing has been rapid, no less an authority than the President of the Marketing Science Institute has stated: ". . . the area of *personal selling* is becoming one of the relatively dark corners in marketing. It stands in danger of being bypassed by the 'new breed' of mathematical and quantitative research specialists who are bringing excitement, increased precision, and more ambitious goals into other segments of the field." The result implicit in developing techniques of decision-making at the marketing management level, plus the emphasizing of alternative ways of performing the selling function, has been that scientific content of personal selling has suffered.

The time has come for academicians and practitioners alike to take a more intensive look at the personal selling function in marketing. To a great extent, it is the lot of marketing educators to reinstate or even establish for the first time the framework for approaching the study of personal selling. John Howard, in his book, *Marketing: Executive and Buyer Behavior,* has said: "It is probably true that the salesman has posed the most difficult problem for marketing teachers: the salesman existed and the company considered him a pretty important element (as indicated in the resources devoted to his activity), but the marketing teacher had little to say on the topic that he, the teacher, thought worth saying." Perhaps this lack of intellectual stimulation and motivation on the part of students and teachers has stemmed from the attempt of educators to do in the classroom what should be done "on the job," while neglecting the rational foundation of personal selling and the "why" of activities associated with it.

The traditional treatment of salesmanship has been strongly criticized because of its lack of emphasis on theories and concepts. The usual textbook approaches to the personal selling function have been regarded as a lapse into "how-to-do-it" exercises. An attempt to remedy this situation has been noticeable in proposals for new approaches and recent articles in various professional journals. In both instances emphasis has been on theoretical and conceptual material derived from some basic discipline (e.g., psychology, sociology, etc.), or some combination thereof. The result of these theoretical and conceptual abstractions has been the compartmentalization of topics obviously inadequate to cope with or provide an understanding of actual everyday sales situations. What appears to be needed in order to shed light on one of the "dark corners of marketing knowledge" is a blending of the practical and theoretical views.

Educators and practitioners in personal selling have typically been accustomed to dealing with "facts." Current literature and practice support this observation. While theories, concepts, and conceptual schema relating to personal selling have been generally criticized in the name of "reality" or "common-sense," salesmen themselves continue to use them in their everyday activities. Virtually every salesman has stored away in his mind a wealth of knowledge which he has acquired through experience, but which he has never systematized and verbalized. It is highly probable that this knowledge, even though uncommunicable, is the knowledge he falls back on when other guides are lacking. "Common-sense," after all, is an accumulation of concepts, hypotheses, and assumptions. Consequently, the material assembled in this text should not be regarded as an effort to challenge or discredit "common-sense" predictions and understanding of the prospect-salesman relationship.

Perhaps the blending of the "art" and "science" dimensions of personal selling would more accurately represent the goal of this book. Heretofore, the "art" dimension has prevailed in textbook treatment of personal selling.

A person who is "specially skilled in the practice of a manual art or occupation" is an artist. A "feel" for the materials with which he works is mandatory. His familiarity with these materials must go beyond "knowledge about them" to "knowledge by acquaintance with" them. As those who have studied the work of the artist have recognized, "the latter knowledge does not come to him by detached observation and theorizing primarily or alone but by direct 'handling' of his materials, by learning to appreciate their reluctances and readinesses, learning to guide his 'handling' by the qualitative reactions of his materials to the 'handling'." [1] Traditionally, the artist has learned through experience and apprenticeship rather than through academic training in theories and hypotheses pertaining to his craft.

The "art" dimension is clearly evident in the functioning and education of a variety of occupations. Certainly, evidence of the "art" dimension is found in the functioning and education of the salesman. Does this, however, rule out the need for seeking and studying conceptual tools to guide the functioning and education of salesmen? Does the mere mention of "conceptual" tools deny the "art" dimension in personal selling? More specifically, does the investigation of conceptual tools mean that an attempt is being made to substitute "scientific" knowledge relating to the salesman-prospect relationship for knowledge gained by acquaintance with and experience in the relationship?

Of course, a negative response is called for to each of the above questions. The purpose in suggesting that conceptual tools are needed in personal selling is to deny the gulf between the knowledge of the artist and the knowledge of

---

[1] Warren G. Bennis et al. (editors), *The Planning of Change* (New York: Holt, Rinehart and Winston, 1962), p. 188.

the scientist, which by assumption frequently appears in the functioning and education of salesmen. A widening of the gulf has been permitted because of (a) the de-emphasis of personal selling as a separate and valuable course in Schools of Business throughout the country, (b) failure to develop new approaches and to generate research in the area of personal selling, and (c) inaction and complacency toward personal selling as a subject matter. Academicians and practitioners alike have failed to provide the direction and leadership which would deny this gulf. Again, however, it is academicians who must assume a large share of the blame for the current status of personal selling as a discipline.

Hopefully, the material in this book will provide increased understanding, both practical and theoretical, of the personal selling function. It is not designed to provide a single self-contained body of knowledge of personal selling. Instead, it is meant to be an open-ended treatment—one that allows reflection and exploration by the student.

The major portion of this book is made up of thirty-seven readings. The readings have been selected to emphasize and prompt the consideration of theoretical information which can be brought to bear on the salesman-prospect relationship.

Borrowing and incorporating ideas and concepts from various disciplines into an existing field of practice have become fairly common of late. Seldom have these actions been taken to deny the uniqueness of a particular discipline or occupation; they have been attempts to invoke the knowledge, the skills, and the understanding of many disciplines in order to deal more adequately with the problems of a particular area. The collection of readings in this book has been compiled on the basis of this kind of reasoning.

Salesmen, perforce, are multidisciplinary. Up to now, this has not generally been true of personal selling as a field of study. Some exception to this lack of interdisciplinary effort has been in the area of associating personal selling with the functions and behavior of the individual. However, these occasional applications of psychological concepts and theories have been superficial at best. Taking this into account, along with the appearance of isolated articles in "Readings" books in marketing, the articles included here represent the first attempt to bring together material which will provide an interdisciplinary background and framework from which to study the personal selling function.

Data for thought, discussion, and sharpening of analytic skills are provided by an extensive list of cases which constitute the second part of the book. As most of those engaged in teaching or studying personal selling are aware, there is a paucity of case records which report the activities of salesmen. This text is designed to fill that vacuum, at least in part.

The cases reported here have been collected over several years of teaching at the University of Alabama and at East Carolina College and through the cooperation of several U.S. business firms. While some of the cases present detailed records, in most instances the term "episode" is perhaps a more accurate descriptive term than "case history." There are, however, advantages to the relative brevity of some of the cases. They are sufficiently brief to be read quickly, yet of adequate length to illustrate a number of important points and to stimulate discussion. On the whole, while the cases are of uneven quality, they can be useful and provocative in discussion of personal selling.

It is not suggested in any of the cases that what the salesman did is "right" or "good" or "desirable." This is left for those analyzing the cases to discuss and decide. Furthermore, what must be clearly realized is that there are numerous situations and consequently numerous approaches which are useful in selling.

Only when some decision has been made regarding objectives can decisions be made regarding the proper approach to be taken in a selling situation. These cases, it is hoped, will not only prove to be action-oriented but provide interest in and awareness of new directions in the teaching-learning process as it relates to personal selling.

Contents

PART I PERSONAL SELLING AND THE MARKETING MIX   1

    A. *The Sales-Marketing Relationship*   3

The Contactual Function in Marketing
EDMUND D. MC GARRY, *The Journal of Business*   3

The Role of Selling in Modern Marketing
WENDELL R. SMITH, *Emerging Concepts in Marketing*   17

Basic Duties of the Modern Sales Department
EUGENE J. KELLEY AND WILLIAM LAZER, *Managerial
Marketing: Perspectives and Viewpoints*   20

    B. *The Sales Challenge*   25

The Salesman Isn't Dead—He's Different
CARL RIESER, *Fortune*   25

Hewlett-Packard: "We don't sell hardware. We sell
solutions . . ."
WALL STREET JOURNAL, *How They Sell*   33

Electrolux: ". . . face those doorbells with that
up-and-at-'em spirit."
THE WALL STREET JOURNAL, *How They Sell*   38

    C. *Sales as Communication*   43

The Industrial Salesman as a Source of Market
Information
FREDERICK E. WEBSTER, JR., *Business Horizons*   43

The Diffusion of an Innovation Among Physicians
JAMES COLEMAN, ELIHU KATZ, AND HERBERT MENZEL,
Sociometry   48

Roles of Communicating Agents in Technological
Change in Agriculture
EUGENE A. WILKENING, *Social Forces*   58

Communication and Opinion Formation in a Medical
Community: The Significance of The Detail Man
ROBERT R. REHDER, *Academy of Management*   65

Cases   72

Establishing a New Sales Organization
(Procter & Gamble—A)   72

Fifty-Cents Deal   74

Michigan Chemical Distributors, Inc. (Dow Chemical
Company—A)   76

"London Fog"   77

People's National Bank (Burroughs Corporation—A)   79

PART II   BEHAVIORAL SCIENCES IN PERSONAL SELLING   81

A.   *Personal Selling from an Interdisciplinary Perspective*   85

The Application of Social Science Findings to Selling
and the Salesman
SAMUEL N. STEVENS, *Aspects of Modern Marketing,
AMA Management Report No. 15*   85

Interdisciplinary Horizons in Marketing
WILLIAM LAZER AND EUGENE J. KELLEY, *Journal of
Marketing*   92

Behavioral Science in Personal Selling Communication
STEVEN J. SHAW, *New Research in Marketing*   99

B.   *Psychological Dimensions of Personal Selling*   105

A Psychological Approach to Consumer Behavior Analysis
WARREN J. BILKEY, *Journal of Marketing*   105

Limits of Persuasion: The Hidden Persuaders Are Made
of Straw
RAYMOND A. BAUER, *Harvard Business Review*   112

Opportunities for Persuasion
EDWARD C. BURSK, *Harvard Business Review*   118

Motivation, Cognition, Learning—Basic Factors in
Consumer Behavior
JAMES A. BAYTON, *Journal of Marketing*   128

C.   *Sociological Concepts in Personal Selling*   135

The Significance of Social Stratification in Selling
RICHARD P. COLEMAN, *Marketing: A Maturing
Discipline*   135

Reference Groups as Perspectives
TAMOTSU SHIBUTANI, *American Journal of Sociology*   143

Group Influence in Marketing and Public Relations
FRANCIS S. BOURNE, *Some Applications of Behavioural
Research*   151

D. *Economics and Anthropology*   167

The Need for Sales to Match Productive Ability
ARNO H. JOHNSON, *Emerging Concepts in Marketing*   167

Anthropology's Contributions to Marketing
CHARLES WINICK, *Journal of Marketing*   185

Cases   191

Brown Milling Company   191

The Ferguson Lumber Company (Burroughs
Corporation–B)   192

Kamack Tanning and Manufacturing Company   194

Lacey-Harvey Toy Wholesaler   195

Lucky Liquid   196

Petrol Supply Company   197

Radio Station WXYZ   199

Taylor Steel Company (National Aluminum
Corporation–A)   200

Washington Sea Food   203

The Williams Products Company   204

PART III   PROCESS AND STRATEGY   207

Ways of Looking at Selling
HAROLD C. CASH AND W. J. E. CRISSY, *Psychology of
Selling*   209

Selling as a Dyadic Relationship—A New Approach
F. B. EVANS, *The American Behavioral Scientist*   213

Systems Selling: Industrial Marketing's New Tool
THOMAS J. MURRAY, *Dun's Review and Modern
Industry*   219

Cases   223

The Marion Bank (Burroughs Corporation–C)   223

The Kingsley Clothing Company   226

PART IV   PERSONAL SELLING IN INTERNATIONAL
MARKETS   229

The World Customer
ERNEST DICHTER, *Harvard Business Review*   231

The Silent Language in Overseas Business
EDWARD T. HALL, *Harvard Business Review*   239

Overseas Sales Grow for American Firms Peddling
Door-to-Door
JOHN A. PRESTBO, *The Wall Street Journal*   248

Do's and Don't's in Selling Abroad
ARTHUR C. NIELSEN, JR., *Journal of Marketing*   250

Selling the Tropical African Market
EDWARD MARCUS, *Journal of Marketing*   256

Cases   262

Distribution Channels in an Overseas Market—Italy
(Procter & Gamble—B)   262

Expansion of International Markets—Japan
(Procter & Gamble—C)   266

PART V   ETHICAL CONSIDERATIONS IN PERSONAL
SELLING   271

Ethical Theory, Societal Expectations, and Marketing
Practices
CLARENCE C. WALTON, *The Social Responsibilities of
Marketing*   273

Sales Ethics: Truth and Taste Needed?
Printers' Ink   283

Salesmanship and Professional Standards
DAVID J. SCHWARTZ, *Atlanta Economic Review*   288

Ethical Problems in Selling
FREDERIC A. RUSSELL, FRANK H. BEACH, AND
RICHARD H. BUSKIRK, *Textbook of Salesmanship*   294

Cases   304

Acme Furniture Company   304
City of Centerville (National Aluminum
Corporation—B)   307

Cranston Corporation (National Aluminum
Corporation—C)   308

Ace Paint and Varnish Company (Dow Chemical
Company—B)   309

PART VI   RESEARCH IN SELLING AND SALES
MANAGEMENT   311

Spatial Allocation of Selling Expense
J. A. NORDIN, *Journal of Marketing*   313

The Planning and Control of Personal Selling Effort
Directed at New Account Acquisition: A Markovian
Analysis
ABRAHAM SHUCHMAN, *New Research in Marketing*   321

The Measurement of Changes in Attitude Induced by
Personal Selling
G. DAVID HUGHES, *Toward Scientific Marketing*   329

Cases   334

Wade Weeks, Inc.   334

Sealright, Incorporated   339

Best-Yet Cake Mix Company   341

Personal Selling

I

Personal Selling and Marketing Mix

The readings presented in Part I are designed to provide the student with a broad perspective of the importance of personal selling in the American economy. Such a perspective may be gained by examining the relationship of the personal selling function to marketing, and by noting some of the tasks, responsibilities, and opportunities of salesmen.

THE SALES-MARKETING RELATIONSHIP

In his classic essay "The Contactual Function in Marketing," which "has to do with the searching-out of the market for the purpose of finding who the potential sources are and then of making and maintaining close connections between those who have goods to offer and those who may want them," Edmund D. McGarry provides the *raison d'etre* of personal selling. Evidence of this may be found in the author's statement, "The maintenance of these contactual relationships, however informal they may be, forms the framework for the structure of marketing which is necessary in any economy in which production is divorced from consumption."

In the second article, Wendell R. Smith ponders "The Role of Selling in Modern Marketing." He indicates that because of the extreme flexibility and adaptability of personal selling, it is often regarded as the *residual* element in the promotion or selling mix. The author suggests that it is now feasible and necessary to take a deeper look at the role of personal selling as a necessary prelude to the application of developing new techniques of research and analysis to this area of marketing.

Professors Kelley and Lazer discuss, in "Basic Duties of the Modern Sales Department," the effects of the marketing concept on the modern sales department. The application of the systems concept to personal selling, the strategic and innovative dimensions of the salesman's job, and the viewing of the salesman as a manager of a market area are examples of topics treated in this new conceptual outlook of personal selling.

THE SALES CHALLENGE

The articles in Section B of Part I deal with the nature of selling from an occupational viewpoint.

The first article illustrates the changing role of the salesman and some promises of even greater changes in the future. The demands placed on the salesman by his increasing duty of serving as a link between production and consumption are stressed.

Practical examples of the nature of the sales job are provided by the other two articles in this section. In an attempt to illustrate the diversity of personal selling activities, and the many consequences thereof, the two articles included have been selected to approximate the two polar extremes on a selling activity continuum. One pole is represented by a door-to-door salesman selling vacuum cleaners while the other pole represents a salesman whose product is scientific measuring devices.

SALES AS COMMUNICATION

In the first article, Webster discusses "The Industrial Salesman as a Source of Market Information."

Coleman, Katz, and Menzel report a study of interpersonal influences among physicians in the adoption of a new drug. The significance to the salesman of having understanding and awareness of such influences in the diffusion process is readily apparent.

The adoption of new products and services throughout the economy requires the communication of information about them. The role of a "commercial communicating agent," the salesman, in this process is indeed significant. Wilkening, in his article, "Roles of Communicating Agents in Technological Change in Agriculture" examines communication of information in farming.

As noted by Rehder in "Communication and Opinion Formation in a Medical Community: The Significance of the Detail Man," "communication and opinion formation have developed into major areas of interest for business and behavioral science studies. In recent years, research has pointed to the importance of interpersonal relations in communication and opinion formation processes. Studies indicate that individual decisions are strongly influenced by person to person relay networks and group norms which 'intervene' in the mass communication process." This article provides an in depth view of the part played by the detail man in "relaying both mass and interpersonal information in an effort to influence the physician's innovation behavior."

A. The Sales-Marketing Relationship

The Contactual Function in Marketing[1]

EDMUND D. McGARRY

The contactual function in marketing has to do with the searching-out of the market for the purpose of finding who the potential customers or the potential sources are and then of making and maintaining connections between those who have goods to offer and those who may want them.[2] Since the main task of marketing is to make the adjustment between what people desire and what it is practical for business to supply, it follows as a corollary that contacts must be made at each successive step in the marketing process. Through these contacts flow the information which consumers need regarding the goods available and their sources, on the one hand, and information which producers need concerning consumers and their wants, on the other. Even more important than the communication of information, however, is the allegiance built up between contacts, which affords a major means for this adjustment. The maintenance of these contactual relationships, however informal they may be, forms the framework for the structure of marketing which

is necessary in any economy in which production is divorced from consumption.

To those who are engaged in the work of marketing as part of their day-to-day activities, the subject is likely to appear as a simple process of buying and selling and of performing such other routines as are conventionally required for this work. But the process is one of infinite complexity and of profound significance when considered in its relationship to man's other activities and to the social structure in which he lives. In order to understand these relationships and to assess their implications in modern life, it is important that the process be considered at the level of its over-all operation and from the point of view of the part it plays in man's endeavors to adjust himself to his environment.

Marketing, when viewed in its broadest terms, as an essential part of man's adaptive behavior, can logically be broken down into a number of separate functions—essential elements which must be performed in order for the process to fulfill its purpose. These functions, as suggested by the writer in a previous article,[3] are (1) the contactual function (examined in this article); (2) the merchandise function, comprising the various activities undertaken to adapt the product to the user's ideas of what is wanted; (3) the pricing function, dealing with the prices at which goods are offered or at which they will be accepted; (4) the propaganda function, including all the methods used to persuade the potential users

◆ SOURCE: Reprinted by permission from *The Journal of Business* (The University of Chicago Press, 1951), April 1951, pp. 96–113.

[1] For the term and concept "contactual function" the writer is indebted to Ralph F. Breyer, *The Marketing Institution* (New York: McGraw-Hill Book Co., Inc., 1934), p. 6.

[2] The term "source" is used in the business sense to mean the available or potential sellers of a product. The present article is a further development of the thesis first presented in my essay, "Some Functions of Marketing Reconsidered," in Reavis Cox and Wroe Alderson (eds.), *Theory in Marketing* (Chicago: Richard D. Irwin, Inc., 1950).

[3] "Some Functions of Marketing Reconsidered," in Cox and Alderson, *op. cit.*, pp. 263–79.

to select the particular product and to make them satisfied with the product, once they have it; (5) the physical distribution function, covering transportation and storage of the goods; and (6) the termination function, embracing the actual change in custody of and responsibility for the goods and the culmination of the process.

THE NATURE OF THE CONTACTUAL FUNCTION

The contactual function consists of all those efforts in the marketing field the aim and purpose of which is to form a bond of mutual interest in the first instance between the marketer and his customers and, in a broader sense, between the producer and the consumer. Since these activities pervade the entire marketing system, the elements constituting the contactual function cannot ordinarily be isolated and made the basis for a division of labor but must rather be abstracted from the economic process as a whole and fitted into a scheme which will provide perspective and understanding of the major task of marketing.

The contactual function is usually performed along with the other functions of marketing.[4] The seller in making contacts is also trying to sell goods; he is performing the merchandising function, the pricing function, the propaganda function, and when the contact culminates in a business transaction, he has performed all the functions of marketing. From the short-range point of view, all the first four functions are aimed at an immediate sale; but, from the long-range point of view, it is the possibility of continuous trade that is the ultimate objective of all contacts.

The contactual function may be initiated either by the seller or by the buyer.[5] In cases where the seller takes the initiative, it consists of two phases. In the first place, he must define the particular segment of the general market he wishes to serve and determine the type of customers he wishes to serve. In this way he is able to concentrate his efforts on the cultivation of what, for him, is the most fertile part of the market. This segmentation of the general market may be made on the basis of mere spatial proximity, on the basis of economical physical distribution, or on the basis of various cultural patterns, such as those determined by income levels, educational backgrounds, habits of consumption, or any other set of common values which form a pattern that indicates a fertile and homogeneous market for the particular product.[6] In any event, once the segment desired has been defined and the characteristics of potential customers have been discovered, the marketer can proceed to analyze the possibilities of his market and, from such an analysis, can determine both the methods needed to cultivate the particular segment he has chosen and the agencies needed to reach it. Continuous studies of this kind enable the marketer to adjust his methods and his policies to the ever changing patterns of his market.

The second phase of the contactual function performed by the seller consists in actually making the contacts with potential customers. Usually the initial contact is made either by the seller himself or by his representative at the buyer's place of business. The immediate purpose of each contact is to become acquainted with the buyer, to learn his wants and attitudes, and to develop a relationship which the seller hopes will ripen into a more or less permanent business connection. Often, of course, some business is transacted on the first contact, but perhaps more frequently several preliminary contacts are necessary before any business of significance is undertaken. In the meantime the prospective buyer has learned to know the seller and what he has to offer, and the seller has become acquainted with

---

[4] "It must not be understood that the functions of marketing are separate and independent activities. Quite the contrary. Each is intimately interwoven with all the others" (Breyer, *op. cit.*, p. 17).

[5] For an extended treatment of buyer or seller initiative see Harry R. Tosdal, "The Advertising and Selling Process," *Annals of the American Academy of Political and Social Science*, May, 1940, pp. 62–70. Professor Tosdal makes this significant statement: Under no conceivable efficient arrangement of work would it be possible to have either buyers or sellers take the initiative exclusively without denying the premise upon which this paper is based, namely, that of free private enterprise" (p. 68).

[6] Concerning "segmentation of the market" see Alexander, Surface, and Alderson, *Marketing* (New York: Ginn & Co., 1949), pp. 376 ff. In economic terms, segmentation of the market is an attempt on the part of the entrepreneur to search out that part of the general market which will yield the greatest returns for the capital and labor applied to it.

the character of the buyer. They have, in short, become adjusted to each other in such a way as to communicate their ideas with mutual understanding.

In cases in which the buyer takes the initiative, the contactual function is performed in much the same way, except that the buyer searches out the more convenient and economical sources for the products he wants, goes to these sources, and tries to develop the confidence of the seller in his (the buyer's) integrity and ability to act either as an outlet for the seller's goods or as a user. In general, so long as goods are pressing upon the market for disposal, as is usual in the sale of manufactured products, sellers take the initiative; but in times of great scarcity there is a shift of initiative to the buyer. Moreover, buyer initiative is almost universal where the goods are of such a nature that they must be concentrated into economic quantities from large numbers of small producers, as is the case in the sale of farm produce. Regardless of which party takes the initiative, however, the result of the performance of the contactual function is the building of a structure for cooperative action.

Whether the seller or the buyer takes the initiative, the essence of the contactual function is the investigation of market potentials, the selection of the most suitable respondents (customers or sources), and the development of mutual confidence and respect between the initiator and the respondents. In doing this, there is a tendency for each party to adjust to the other. Thus an attachment grows up between the parties which makes it easier and more economical for each of them to do business with the other. The knowledge on the part of each of the other's needs, attitudes, and desires lays the basis for the development of a sympathetic understanding between them and tends to build within them a common interest.

The contactual relationship between buyers and sellers is essentially a human relationship, and, because of this, the function is most effectively carried out on a person-to-person basis. Although it is true that a considerable amount of business is carried on through nonpersonal contacts, such as the mail-order business, and there are strong incentives to impersonalize the sale of goods because of the economies available through such means, it is noteworthy that the performance of the contactual function still remains largely on a personal, man-to-man basis.[7]

The performance of the contactual function is perhaps the most costly element in marketing. When the contact is made on a person-to-person basis, the problems attendant on finding a time of meeting, learning the proper approach, adjusting personalities, and discovering a common ground for discussion all consume both time and effort. Furthermore, personnel adaptable to making contacts is relatively scarce and high priced and must usually undergo an extensive period of costly training before being able to carry on the function effectively.

Although it is convenient to describe the nature of the contactual function in terms of what happens under a free-enterprise system, in which marketing has had its greatest development, the fact must not be overlooked that this function is essential in any type of economy where production takes place on a mass basis and is thus divorced from consumption. In the case of a consumers' cooperative system, in which production is integrated with marketing, the initiative would theoretically be taken by the cooperators, that is, the consumers, who search out new members, on the one hand, and make the contact with producers, on the other. In the case of a government-controlled economy the contact-making is largely in the hands of the state. Needless to say, it is difficult to see how either of these systems could provide the flexibility of the contactual function which is found in the free-enterprise system and which, as will be shown later, is an essential part of high-level consumption.

HISTORICAL DEVELOPMENT OF CONTACTUAL FUNCTIONS

In a primitive society where man wrested directly from nature the means for his satisfactions, his chief concern was to adapt himself and his needs to what nature provided and to adapt what he found in nature to his needs either as an individual or as a group.[8] As soon,

[7] Julius Rosenwald is quoted as having said that, although he had built an extensive business by mail, people would never deal in that manner if they had an opportunity to get the same goods in a store.
[8] It is unnecessary to discuss here the various theories of the origins of trade. For an excellent

however, as he learned to depend upon the exchange of goods with his fellows, a new element emerged, for he then had not only to communicate his wants to those who possessed the means of satisfying them but also to induce these others to give up something they possessed for something he had to offer in return.[9] Both parties had to sacrifice something and to compromise their ideas. Neither could longer operate as a complete isolationist, for the survival of each depended upon his cooperation with the other. Each had to master the art of making himself congenial to others with whom he traded—to think in terms of the needs and desires of others as well as of his own.[10]

So long as only two individuals or groups were involved in trade, however, no elaborate economic machinery for making contacts was necessary.[11] Even in the handicraft economy, such as existed up until a hundred years ago and still exists in many parts of the world, there was little need for any special attention to the making of contacts between those who produced goods and those who were to use them. It was still a relatively simple matter for the consumer to go directly to the local shopkeeper, communicate his needs, and have what he wanted built to his order. Since most goods were made in small shops in close proximity to the customers whom they served, the shopkeeper was intimately acquainted with his customers, knowing the type of goods they required, the prices they could afford to pay,

and their numerous whims and idiosyncrasies to which he must cater.

However, the problem became vastly more complicated with the coming of the industrial revolution, when production was removed from the local shop and neighborhood and concentrated in distant factories, which produced for stock.[12] To bridge the widening gap in space, time, and interest between the producer and the consumer, there came into being an elaborate entrepreneurial division of labor, with numerous intermediaries specializing in different techniques at different stages of the marketing process. Thus, in place of the simple producer-consumer contact, there developed multicontactual systems in which several intermediaries bought and resold the products on their way from producer to consumer.

In the task of aiding the adjustment between what the consumer wants and what producers have to offer, the main objective of the contactual relationship is not simply to reach the intermediary at the first stage of the process (the wholesaler) but to reach through all the intermediaries to the final consumer. It is here that the ultimate market lies, and, unless the producer can devise methods by which goods move on to the consumer, his efforts are likely to be fruitless. Out of this fact has arisen the necessity for producers to make supplementary contact with consumers. The widespread use of missionary salesmen, samplers, detail men, and display specialists by producers to make contact directly with consumers indicates the importance of maintaining customer loyalty throughout the channels of distribution. The operational problem of welding together into a working organization the numerous intermediaries who take part in the selling of a manufacturer's product and thus making numerous chains of contacts with ultimate consumers is one of the most difficult in marketing.

CONFLICT AND COOPERATION

In considering the contact between buyers and sellers in developing a transaction, it must be recognized that there is an inevitable conflict between their respective interests. In order to appraise the value of an item, each party has to relate it to his own particular frame of reference, that is, his own situation. The seller is

summary of these theories see George W. Robbins, "Notions about the Origins of Trading," *Journal of Marketing*, January, 1947, p. 228; see also Morton Solomon, "The Structure of the Market in Undeveloped Economies," *Quarterly Journal of Economics*, August, 1948, pp. 519–41.

[9] Adam Smith thought rightly that it is unnecessary to inquire whether "the propensity to truck, barter and exchange one thing for another" was "one of the original principles of human nature, or whether, as seems more probable, it be the necessary consequence of the faculties of reason and speech" (Adam Smith, *The Wealth of Nations* [Everyman's ed. (New York: E. P. Dutton & Co., 1910)], Book I, chap. ii).

[10] "As contrasted with the other means of acquiring things, trading is by all odds the most complex. It is unique in that it alone is a two-way transaction" (Robbins, *op. cit.*, p. 230).

[11] This statement may be an oversimplification of the situation, because it is not known whether or not there was ever a time when all trade took place simply between producers and consumers. Moreover, in many primitive societies such trade as does occur is often accompanied by elaborate ceremonies.

[12] For a concise description of the changes brought about by the industrial revolution see Alexander, Surface, and Alderson, *op. cit.*, pp. 6 ff.

liquidating a specific concrete good into money, which has many alternative uses, while the buyer is accepting a specific concrete good in lieu of money which he might use for many other purposes. The seller, looking backward to the sacrifices he has put into the good and forward to the maximization of his profit, is prone to place a high valuation upon the item; on the other hand, the buyer, looking first to the money he must immediately sacrifice and then forward to the risks he must take in holding or using the item, is likely to discount the satisfactions he will derive from it and is therefore prone to place a low valuation upon it. This conflict of interest raises an inevitable barrier between the parties which can be resolved only through the give-and-take of compromise.[13]

Because of the conflict of interest between buyers and sellers, each is likely to feel that any advantage which the opposite party derives from the transaction is to be gained only at his expense. Within the area of bargaining this is, of course, true, but economists have long pointed out that both parties gain something in every transaction; otherwise they would not enter it. Moreover, since evaluations are subjective and are related to different situations, the extent of gain or loss in a bargain is, in a sense, indeterminate. For this reason each party must relate his estimate of loss or gain not only to the immediate effect on the opposing party but also to his own situation. Translated into their respective situations, this means an attitude of hostility toward the opposite party, and the transaction becomes an act of strategic importance, comparable to a move on a chess board or the deployment of troops in a battle.[14]

The interests of the parties are at variance not only because of different valuations placed upon the objects of the trade but also because, historically, the market place has always been the bloodless battleground where man could match his wits with other men for a material or psychic advantage. The victor, proud of his shrewdness as a bargainer, is usually rewarded also with high prestige in his community. One need only listen to the bragging of shoppers after a bargain sale to realize that such prestige is still among the predominant motives in many purchases in our modern highly sophisticated civilization.

Furthermore, the market place has always been the happy hunting ground for all sorts of shysters, mountebanks, and charlatans. Here the predatory of every age have looked for their victims among the innocent, the credulous, and the gullible. It is no accident that ancient law pronounced the maxim "Caveat emptor." But the prevalence of wooden nickels, counterfeit money, and bouncing checks is evidence that the blithe deceiver is as likely to be found among the buyers as among the sellers and that the seller must likewise beware. Suspicion, distrust, and misunderstanding have always been part and parcel of a free market.

The techniques of contact which tend to break down the barriers of distrust and suspicion between the parties are fairly well known to businessmen, although they are seldom formulated as such. First, they must talk the same language. This means not only that the words and phrases used must mean the same thing to each of them but also that they must have a clear understanding of all the qualities and characteristics of the goods traded in, as well as of the business techniques which they employ. Precision in communication is the major factor in agreement. Second, each must have confidence in the other's integrity and intentions. This involves not only common honesty at the level of business ethics prevailing but also a willingness on the part of each party to forego his own advantage and to take the consequences if the transaction happens to work out adversely to his interest. Third, each must have an intimate understanding of the other's background and status in the trade, so as to be able to interpret his point of view objectively and to see the opposite party's advantages and disadvantages in any undertaking. Fourth, and finally, each party must be able to make an intelligent evaluation of the entire situation, in order to see clearly the consequences of the action taken. When all these elements are favorable, it becomes possible to some extent to overcome suspicion and distrust and to build in their place the basis for trading.[15]

[13] For a clear and concise analysis of the psychology of consumer buying see Joseph Clawson, "Lewin's Vector Psychology and the Analysis of Motives in Marketing" in Cox and Alderson, op. cit.
[14] For an economic analysis of the strategies used by businessmen see K. W. Rothschild, "Price Theory and Oligopoly," Economic Journal, September, 1947, p. 299.

[15] "The transfer of ownership, the essential element in the selling function, involves the whole field of human relations and the whole field of human behavior; it concerns not only commodities

But even with the techniques of selling and buying known to both buyer and seller, the barrier between the two parties still remains, so long as each is thinking in the short-run perspective of a single transaction. The situation is entirely changed, however, when the attention of the parties is focused on the long-run welfare of their respective businesses and they are led to think in terms of a continuous business relationship between them. It then becomes clear that each is dependent upon the other and that cooperation between them is to their mutual advantage. The merchant buyer finds that his interest is, in part, the finding of goods for his customers and in part the distribution of the goods of his source. The manufacturer finds that it is to his interest to supply continuously the proper goods to his customers and not simply to liquidate his immediate stocks. The two thus become members of a team to supply consumers with the goods they want at prices they are willing to pay and to find a market for the goods which capital and labor have produced.

The development of the attitude of mutual interdependence between buyers and sellers throughout the chain of contacts requires that someone assume the leadership in the cooperative effort. Although this leadership is sometimes taken by the merchant at the retail end of the channel, as is the case when a chain store sponsors a brand, it is more usual for it to be assumed by the producer, whose competitive position is otherwise somewhat insecure, since it rests upon the whims of relatively few customers (merchants) who have numerous alternative sources. Because of this insecurity, the manufacturer whose product is acceptable to the public seeks a broader base for the intrenchment of his product among the vastly more numerous ultimate consumers who have an intimate knowledge of the product in use.[16] This leadership acts as a catalyst in welding together the chain of contacts between the producer and the consumer. It is the function of the leader of such a chain not only to prevent friction between the various links and to keep them in balance but also to furnish

the incentive and drive which will keep them operating effectively.

As the chain of contacts between the producer and the consumer develops, it tends to become institutionalized, that is to say, each agency tends to look upon itself less as an isolated and independent unit in the business world and more as a part of a greater entity which has an *esprit de corps* of its own. Thus it becomes the interest of each agency to preserve, protect, and defend every other element in the chain, in order to maintain the structure as a whole and thus provide continuously profitable business for all. The chain of contacts, once it has become established, provides the mechanism for a continuous two-way line of communication between the producer and the consumer and a linkage of their interests.

THE CONTACTUAL STRUCTURE OF MARKETING

The producing firm of any particular line of products can be visualized as a leader of a large number of chains of contacts, fanning out in different directions to reach his ultimate market. Marketing authorities tend to use the term "channel" or "channel group" to describe this system of contactual relationships, while businessmen call it their "distribution setup" or "organization." Perhaps a better term is that used by Lundburg, who calls it a constellation."[17] In a sense, all the different chains of contacts which a producer uses to distribute his product are linked together through the leader, who attempts to develop a community of interest among his chains of contacts and among the individual units (firms) which compose them. Thus the whole constellation or setup becomes a single working unit to distribute his goods.[18]

[16] For this reason he usually develops a brand and then attempts to secure brand insistence on the part of consumers through advertising.

and services but the tangible results of human acts and reactions. Salesmen deal with infinite variations of the human mind" (Harry R. Tosdal, *The Principles of Personal Selling* [New York: McGraw-Hill Book Co., Inc., 1926], p. 2).

[17] G. A. Lundburg, *Marketing and Social Organization* (Philadelphia: Curtis Publishing Co., 1945), p. 12.

[18] "As an example [of many cooperative entities in economic life], one may take the concept 'channel,' the combination and sequence of agencies that participate in bringing a good into existence and moving it into consumption.

"Only at the ultimate point of consumption does competition come into focus, and the true nature of this competition is as follows: first, that it takes place between entire channels rather than between individual entities along the channel; and second, that in each line of flow someone must take the responsibility for guiding the competition of the entire channel (for trade-marked

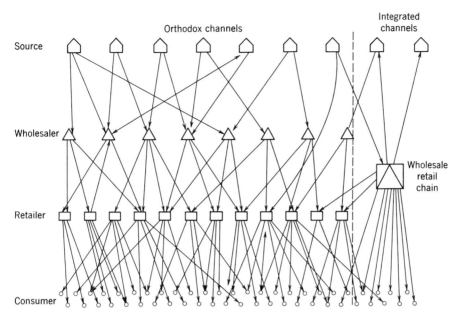

Chart I A schematic representation of the contactual marketing structures, showing orthodox and integrated channels.

The term "structure of marketing" is usually applied to the network of trade channels through which ownership of products moves from production to consumption. "A trade channel . . . consists of middlemen or other buyers or sellers involved in the process of moving a good from producer to consumer." [19] Since both these definitions treat only of the flow of products and leave out of consideration the fact that many contacts are made and maintained without any transactions taking place between the parties, it is necessary to qualify the term by calling it the "contactual structure." [20] It must be kept in mind that in this study our objective is to emphasize the relationships themselves and the part they play in effecting adjustments between goods which are produced and the people who are to use them. Actual physical distribution, while re-

lated, is subject to discussion as a separate function.

Chart I is a schematic device to indicate two types of contactual marketing structure—one an orthodox nonintegrated type and the other an integrated type. Needless to say, this representation is oversimplified not only because there are other types of structure but also because they leave out the so-called "functional middlemen." In this chart each agency (including the source and the consumer) is represented by a different symbol, and the contacts between the agencies are represented by arrows pointing from their respective initiating agency because the initiative may come from either the buyer or the seller. It will be noted that some of the arrows make full connection between the agencies, to indicate that the contacts have ripened into transactions, whereas others fall short of connecting, to indicate that, although contact is made, no transactions have resulted.

Under the orthodox or nonintegrated contactual structure a manufacturer must maintain contacts with his sources of material and with his wholesalers; the wholesalers must maintain contact with their sources (manufacturers) and with their customers (retailers); and the retailers must maintain contact with sources (wholesalers) and their customers (consumers). The use of these contacts in the sense

goods, this is usually the owner of the brand)" (Reavis Cox, "Quantity Limits and the Theory of Economic Opportunity," in Cox and Alderson, *op. cit.*, pp. 238–239).

[19] Charles F. Phillips and Delbert J. Duncan, *Marketing Principles and Methods* (Chicago: Richard D. Irwin, Inc., 1938), p. 37.

[20] Breyer, in his exhaustive study of channel and channel group costing, has differentiated a large number of channel types, none of which exactly fits the concept here defined (see Ralph F. Breyer, *Quantitative Systemic Analysis and Control: Study No. 1, Channel and Channel Group Costing* (Philadelphia: University of Pennsylvania, 1941).

of culminating transactions is usually intermittent, with frequencies varying from zero to many hundreds a year, depending principally upon the nature of the product and the volume of business done. In any case it is usually necessary that a firm maintain many contacts in addition to those which actually produce business. The maintenance of such contacts is not valueless, even though no transactions result from them, for through them each of the parties gains information and knowledge necessary to operate his business intelligently.[21]

In the case of the integrated agency the chart shows the chain store to which or from which all the contacts lead. It is noteworthy, however, that integrated institutions are seldom closed systems; that is to say, some of the units of the system buy from agencies outside the system, and other units sell to outside agencies. The reason for this, of course, is that the system's sources can seldom produce just enough for their outlets—they either produce more and have to sell outside the system or do not produce enough and have to go outside for other sources.[22]

The diagram as a whole represents a vast network of contactual relationships through which the goods that producers make and the goods that the consumers want are adjusted to each other or through which producers themselves are adjusted to consumers. Essentially, this adjustment takes place by means of selection from many alternatives.[23] Just as in a telephone switchboard the impulse of the signal moves to a selector, which makes contact with the proper reactor, which rings the proper bell or, as in the case of the response

mechanism of the human body, in which the afferent neurons seek out and make contact with the proper efferent neurons, so in the contactual structure consumers select the contact at the retail level which suits their particular and peculiar situation. The retailers, in turn, then the wholesalers, and, finally, the producers do the same thing. The action and reaction described may also operate in reverse order, in which the source selects its outlets and these outlets select their customers.

It must not be assumed from the graphic presentation of the contactual structure that it represents a static system. Quite the contrary, it is constantly changing. "There is a constant dissolution of old channels and creation of new ones."[24] If the buyer is dissatisfied with his old source or if he likes another one better, he shifts his business. If the seller wishes to expand his outlets, he may either solicit firms which have formerly patronized other sellers or promote the establishment of new firms to handle his product.

If it is assumed that the major task of marketing is to adjust goods produced to the consumers' needs and to adjust consumers' needs to the goods produced, it follows that an ideal contactual structure would provide, on the one hand, contact of the consumer with all the producers he wished to patronize and, on the other, of the producer with all the consumers he desired to serve. Theoretically, it is possible in a free economy for producers to deal directly with all the consumers they wish to deal with, and vice versa. It would be possible, for instance, for a soap manufacturer to provide enough contacts to reach every individual who might need soap. But obviously this would be impossible from a practical standpoint, because the number of contacts which can be provided is limited by the economic cost of making them.[25]

Nevertheless, our present system does provide a near-approximation to the ideal.

---

[21] Braithwaite and Dobbs indicate that the chief service of contacts is in the communication of information from one agency to another. The present author feels that this is too narrow a conception and that the affinity which grows up between the parties is far more important (see Dorothea Braithwaite and S. P. Dobbs, *The Distribution of Consumers Goods* [London: Routledge, 1932]).
[22] "Few if any vertically integrated firms are completely balanced. It is a safe rule that any given stage is producing somewhat more or less than is needed by the rest of the enterprise. Unless capacity is to be wasted, therefore, practically every integrated firm is continually buying from and selling to other firms, and often to its competitors" (M. A. Adelman, "Integration and Antitrust Policy," *Harvard Law Review*, LXIII [1949], 44).
[23] "The essence of the cultural process is selectivity" (Clyde Kluckhohn, *Mirror for Man* [New York: Whittlesey House, 1949], p. 26).

[24] Breyer, *Quantitative Systemic Analysis and Control*, p. 27.
[25] "Where the market is not perfect, there is a capital cost of transferring customers from one firm to another. The more imperfect the market, the higher will this capital cost be and the more of the customers of a firm it is sought to transfer, the higher the cost is likely to be for each additional customer, as we proceed from the less firmly attached customers to the more firmly attached customers" (E. A. G. Robinson, *The Structure of Competitive Industry* [London: Nisbit & Co., 1931], p. 120).

Through a division of labor by successive stages, the consumer is given a multiple choice of retailers; and retailers have a choice of wholesalers, as have wholesalers of producers or other sources. Or, to look at the structure from the other end, the manufacturer has a choice of wholesalers, who, in turn, have a choice of retailers, and retailers of final consumers. The structure thus provides not only a wide range of choice of products but also, and equally important, a wide range of sources from which the products may be procured.

STABILITY AND FLUIDITY

The contactual structure of marketing is in the nature of what sociologists call an "informal organization." It is held together by no formal organization or permanent agreement or arrangement of any kind. In fact, it is a structure only in the sense that its various constituent business units (firms) are interdependent and cooperate toward the common end of marketing goods. Actually, the only force which binds these units together is the loose, informal, and intangible relationships which businessmen call "contacts." The dealings which take place are individual transactions undertaken from day to day as the parties see fit. Beyond the particular transaction there are usually no formal commitments to continue to carry on business. However, these contactual relationships, when congealed and coagulated by continuous business trading, constitute a cohesive force which binds them together, and the successful contacts from level to level between producer and consumer together form a path through which information flows and attitudes are molded into adjustments.[26]

The nature of the contactual structure of marketing gives to it two seemingly incompatible characteristics. The structure has both a high degree of flexibility and a high degree of stability. The fact that any unit of the structure deals with its sources and its customers on a transaction basis, which is strictly temporary and immediate, and can change from one contact to another without notice and without embarrassment lends a fluidity to business which could not otherwise be attained. Because of this fluidity, any business firm is enabled to shift its purchases from one source to another or its sales from one customer to another without formal restriction. This is but another way of saying that a modern business firm is constantly adjusting its contacts to its own changing character; and, since its character is, in turn, dependent upon its total contacts, it is in a large sense adjusting itself to the fluid character of business itself. Thus the contactual relationships which make up the character of a firm tend constantly to adjust this character, on the one hand, to the requirements of the consumers and, on the other, to the requirements of the practical business situation of the hour.

However, in spite of the fluid structure of marketing under a free-enterprise system, there is a consistency in it—an element which enables it to persist, to grow, and to accumulate strength as it becomes older. This element consists of the continuity of contacts—the mutual affinity that grows up between two persons or firms in business which causes them to prefer to deal with each other rather than with someone else. The strength of this preference tends to accumulate with each transaction successfully completed. Almost any well-established firm can name dozens or hundreds of customers with whom it has dealt for years or even generations.[27]

The marketing contacts of a firm at any given time are likely to vary in strength all the way from those which are so tenaciously attached that they would not deal with a competitor unless powerful incentives were offered, through those which are completely indifferent as to whether they deal with this firm or some other, to those with such a negative attitude that they will deal elsewhere unless strong inducements are offered. For the well-established firm there is usually, as mentioned above, a hard core of contacts with strong preferences favoring it. These are the continuous contacts built up over the years on whose business the firm can usually count for support. They keep in close touch with one another, cooperate actively, and generally account for a major

[26] "When customers have learned through experiences that it [a firm] is worthy of confidence in fulfilling its promises and that its product is trustworthy, that firm can use 'reliability of seller' as a patronage motive in effecting sales. . . . Continuous business relationships growing out of such patronage motives often tend to establish durable buying habits and constitute good will for the seller" (Melvin T. Copeland, *The Principles of Merchandising* [New York: A. W. Shaw Co., 1924], p. 208).

[27] The word "customer," according to Webster, means "one who regularly or repeatedly deals in business with a tradesman or business house."

portion of the firm's sales.[28] In addition to these contacts (customers), there are a number of intermittent or casual contacts, which individually cannot be depended upon to buy or sell consistently and regularly but which, taken together, produce a sufficient amount of business to make their patronage essential. It is this backlog of intermittent but potentially regular customers with which any successful company must keep in contact in order to prevent its business from declining by natural attrition.[29]

It is clear that the cost of dealing with continuous contacts is far less than that of dealing with casual contacts. In dealing with regular customers it can be assumed that the parties already know each other. Neither party has to investigate the other. The transaction is more easily undertaken, and there is less inclination to haggle about terms. It is perhaps no exaggeration to say that, if a firm could confine its entire selling activities to regular and consistent customers, it could usually reduce its cost of marketing by from 10 to 20 per cent. On the other hand, the cost of making contact with the casual customer (or source) is usually high. Although the amount of business which any one selling firm can get from such contacts over a period is generally small, it requires as much or more time and effort to maintain them than it does to maintain regular customers. Since the dollar sales per contact in the case of intermittent customers are almost bound to be lower, the costs of making the contact as a percentage of sales are high.

Assuming that some type of cost-accounting system could be devised to show the differential cost between handling continuous contacts and casual contacts, it might well be argued

that, since a firm can handle the continuous contacts at a lower cost, it should grant these continuous customers a discount commensurate with its total saving.[30] Undoubtedly many firms do give a "break" to their regular customers, either in informal price arrangements or in cumulative quantity discounts. However, to charge higher prices to nonregular customers as a policy would be quite dangerous. The very fact that these casual customers do not buy consistently and regularly from this particular firm indicates that they probably also are in regular contact with numerous other sources and that it is not a matter of much importance which of the several sources they will patronize. Thus these firms may be regarded as being on the competitive margin and are in a strong strategic position to play one firm against another and thus force any firm that sells to them to give them the best possible terms.

The continuous dealing with certain customers lends a stability to the structure of contacts, while the dealing with casual customers or sources give it flexibility and forms the basis for the dynamic character of business. If a firm should limit its contacts to its regular customers, it would find itself subject to many of the vicissitudes of each and every customer and to accepting a risk on operations over which it has no control. The failure or interruption of any one contact, however, if there are other potentially regular customers available to take its place, is likely to have but little effect except in so far as it increases the effort necessary to change certain casual customers into regular customers.

It has been pointed out that, in so far as contacts are used continuously and uninterruptedly, they tend to reduce distribution costs. As long as true competition exists, this reduction is bound to be passed on to consumers in general. But this lower cost is often offset by

[28] "The bulk of goods is sold to purchasers who have purchased previously from the same seller, and who have previously purchased the same or similar goods. . . . The repeat sale and the type of selling which must be carried on in order that the cost of distribution as a whole be kept within reasonable limits are much more important than one time sales when the volume of total business transacted is considered" (Tosdal, *Principles of Personal Selling*, p. 7).

[29] "The footing of a firm is generally marked by a gradient running down from that part of the market on which it has the strongest hold to those customers who would just as soon buy from one of the firm's competitors. If the firm's position were pictured as a circle on a chart, it might show a dense core at the center and gradually shade off toward the fringe" (Wroe Alderson, "Survival and Adjustment in Behavior Systems," in Cox and Alderson, *op. cit.*, p. 76).

[30] It was the recognition of the high costs of continually changing contacts probably more than any other factor which led wholesalers to develop voluntary chains. By tying their customers to themselves with binding contracts, the wholesalers were able to secure continuous trading by a large body of customers, some of whom might otherwise have dealt only casually with them. The value of such continuous trading was such that the wholesale sponsor was able to "kick back" part of the profits accruing from the change, as an inducement to customers to enter the contracts. The practice of giving cumulative quantity discounts also represents an attempt to find a method of assuring continuous trade.

the higher costs of serving the new and casual customers, and the net effect may thus be regarded as negligible. In other words, the final consumer must pay for the flexibility in the system, but he gets a discount from its stability.

THE ECONOMICS OF CONTACTUAL RELATIONSHIPS

The highly fluid character of early business, with its small units operating under buyer initiative, led Adam Smith and other classical economists to a preoccupation with the quantity-price relationship in every transaction undertaken.[31] They assumed, perhaps correctly at that time, that the profit motive dominated practically every trade and that it was a matter of complete indifference who the parties to the trade were or what relationship existed between them.[32] A certain amount of this "rabble hypothesis" still remains in much of our economic thinking at the present time.[33] When questions are raised about matters such as contactual relationships, they are usually brushed off with the use of the term "other things being equal," which makes the logic of their argument simple and incontrovertible but still leaves untouched most of the human elements in trade.

Lately economists of the modern school, however, have greatly refined and expanded economic theory in the direction of exploring what they term "monopolistic competition" or "imperfect competition." Thus any factor which tends to prevent the purely competitive economic factors from working out to the logical conclusion of the lowest competitive price is regarded as a monopolistic element indicating an imperfection in competition. Whenever the product of any seller is "differentiated," its market becomes to some extent monopolistic, for it enables him to have some control over his market and makes it possible for him to secure (or at least to expect) an excess of profits over what they would be under pure competition. Although this theory has been developed chiefly to explain the effects of advertising and brand preferences, its exponents have usually lumped together with these the concept of "sticky" contactual relationships. Thus Chamberlin says: "Anything which makes buyers prefer one seller to another, be it personality, reputation, convenient location or the tone of his shop, differentiates the thing purchased to that degree, for what is bought is really a bundle of utilities of which these things are a part." [34] Established contactual relationships thus become one of many elements of product differentiation. The effect of this differentiation is that it allows the seller to increase his sales at a given price, maintain his sales at a higher price, or increase his sales at a higher price.

Following this analysis, Chamberlin and most of those who have accepted his line of reasoning have included the costs of developing and maintaining contactual relations in the category of selling costs, and "selling costs are defined as costs incurred in order to alter the position or shape of the demand curve for the product." [35] Thus he explains that "to the extent that he [the businessman] devotes his time and energies to building up his 'connections,' they are costs of selling." [36] In all this it is apparent that the possibility that it is just as important for the buyer to have "connections" with his sources as it is for sellers to have connections with their customers is either over-

[31] "The market price of every particular commodity is regulated by the proportion between the quantity which is actually brought to the market, and the demand of those who are willing to pay the natural price of the commodity, or the whole value of the rent, labor, and profit, which must be paid in order to bring it thither. . . . The price of monopoly is for every occasion the highest price which can be got" (Adam Smith, *op. cit.*, pp. 49, 54).

[32] "The traditional assumption of perfect competition . . . depends, in the first place, upon the existence of such a large number of producers that a change in the output of any one of them has a negligible effect upon the output of the commodity as a whole. . . . But in actual markets the customer takes into account a great deal besides the prices at which rival producers offer him their goods. . . . He has a number of good reasons for preferring one seller to another" (Joan Robinson, *The Economics of Imperfect Competition* [London: Macmillan & Co., Ltd., 1933], p. 88).

[33] The term "rabble hypothesis" is used by Professor Elton Mayo to describe "a sand heap of individuals all equal and undifferentiated," which he indicates is the basic but unrealistic premise of economic theory (Elton Mayo, *The Social Problems of Industrial Civilization* [Boston: Harvard Graduate School of Business Administration, 1945], chap. ii).

[34] Edward Chamberlin, *The Theory of Monopolistic Competition* (Cambridge: Harvard University Press, 1933), p. 8; see also p. 69.

[35] *Ibid.*, p. 117.

[36] *Ibid.*, p. 124.

looked or ignored.[37] If the seller did not maintain contacts, the buyer would necessarily have to do so.

Moreover, there appears to be a significant difference in the purpose of maintaining contacts from that of advertising (selling). The purpose of advertising is to sell more goods or to sell them at a higher price (or both) than could be sold without it, while the continued dealing of a firm with its established connections (either buyers or sellers) may be due to "the inertia or unwillingness of either party to make the effort necessary to substitute new customers for old ones," as Professor Kahn has suggested, or it may be based on the fact that it is more economical to deal with old customers than with new ones.[38] The continuous dealing with the same contacts reduces not only the effort necessary to make transactions but also the risks either party takes, since each party already knows the other and can fairly accurately forecast what he is likely to do under a given set of circumstances.

The cost of developing and maintaining contacts is somewhat more in the nature of the cost of a fixed asset than is the cost of advertising. Although the full effect of an outlay for advertising may not always be immediately reflected in sales, it is likely to diminish rapidly after the advertising has been discontinued. In the building of contacts, on the other hand, the costly element is involved primarily in the first transaction or previous to it (this is the cost of

getting the foot in the door, so to speak) and declines successively with each transaction after that. Consequently, a business with a large number of well-established contacts is likely to have lower costs of distribution than one which has fewer such contacts. The general principle is well recognized in the law, where the purchaser of a company with well-established connections is allowed to capitalize them as good will.[39]

If it is assumed that a number of firms, all having large numbers of well-established connections, are otherwise in competition with one another, it can well be argued that the price resulting from such competition will be lower than it would be if these firms lacked such established contacts—a generalization which follows from the fact that they have lower costs. The competitive element that is presumed to be lost through the propensity of firms to discriminate in favor of those buyers and sellers with whom they have had continuous contact may well be offset by the increased competition among groups of firms joined vertically in series from producer to consumer. This is but another way of saying that the competition takes place among channels rather than among firms horizontally considered.[40]

Despite the differences in costs and in the effect between the maintenance of proper contacts and the use of advertising mentioned above, the results of such actions appear similar when placed in terms of supply and demand curves. Effective contactual relationships tend to move the demand curve upward and to the right, and they do not affect supply in terms of goods offered for sale. It is only when we consider these changes in a larger frame of reference that the implications of the differences may be seen. Thus who can say that the use of proper contacts does not yield the consumer an income, psychic and subtle though it be, when he is enabled to choose between different sellers? And who can say that the use of proper contacts does not add to the supply, not in the

[37] The possibility also of buyers advertising and thus increasing supply is likewise overlooked in the Chamberlin analysis. Presumably in that case the cost of advertising would be a cost of production, for "cost of production includes all expenses which must be met in order to provide the commodity or service, transport it to the buyer, and put it into his hands ready to satisfy his wants," and "there are included in the manufacturer's price to the wholesaler charges to cover the expenses of building up his 'connections' and securing outlets, as well as similar charges of other producers who have sold him raw materials and supplies, and whose selling expenses he has recouped" (*ibid.*, pp. 123–24).

[38] Professor Kahn has intimated that the continuous dealings between two parties are due to inertia and unwillingness to make the effort necessary to make new sales contacts, and he attempts to prove that these motives are irrational when the consumer experiences no preference for the product of the old firm. However, he ignores the fact that the increased effort necessary to make the change is in itself an entirely rational basis for preferring old customers (R. F. Kahn, "Some Notes on Ideal Output," *Economic Journal*, March, 1935).

[39] The Supreme Court of the United States has defined good will as follows: "Good will is the disposition of a pleased customer to return to a place where he has been well-treated." Good will is usually measured by the unusual profits which accrue to a firm because of the buyers who habitually patronize it. It is the value, crudely capitalized, which businessmen put upon the contactual relationships which have been built up.

[40] See Cox, *op. cit.*

sense of the total stock offered for sale, but in the more realistic sense of making goods available for sale by those with whom others wish to deal?

However, if the real problem is not how prices behave but rather how people behave under certain circumstances, it is conceivable that some other approach than price analysis may be equally valid and equally constructive in understanding the process. In the last few years a number of writers with extensive business backgrounds have pointed out that, as modern business units have become larger, older, and more permanent, they are more and more motivated by the idea of security and permanence of the firm as an institution than by the amassing of greater profits.[41] It is, of course, conceded that profits are necessary for permanence, but situations often arise in which profits, both immediate and long-run, have to be foregone and decisions be based on what is best for the long-run stability of the firm. It is argued that the building of the prestige of a firm in the community and even its social justification have become major objectives in policy-making.

Whether or not there has been a fundamental change in the motivation of business, there is ample evidence to indicate a change in emphasis from pure price competition to competition based largely on what the businessman calls "service"; and the primary argument for this change is usually that it promotes the long-run prestige and maintains the status of the firms in the community. In other words, the trend in emphasis appears to be toward cooperation in sustaining the marketing structure rather than toward more vigorous inter-firm price competition. The tendency toward integration among large firms and, where this is not possible, the tendency to distribute through controlled outlets, such as exclusive agencies and contract sales agreements, are evidence of attempts to minimize price competition among the larger firms.

Smaller firms have likewise been active in their efforts to avoid price competition. Being weak economically, they have resorted to politics, where their very numbers give them enormous strength. They have put pressure on

legislatures for protective laws, such as price maintenance, unfair practices acts, anti-trade discrimination acts, and many others. Practices such as price-lining and guaranties against price decline are likewise evidences of attempts to get away from pure price competition.

If it is assumed that the desire for permanence and stability of its institutions have become the major objectives in our economy, the problem of developing and maintaining continuous contacts takes on great significance. Business cannot expect to shift its contacts from day to day and still attain the permanence necessary for an institution. It is clear that few large modern businesses could exist wholly upon casual contacts entered into for immediate profit with no thought of future business. Although business must continue fluid, it is essential that fluidity be in the form of a stiff matrix of relationships. If this argument is sound, then it follows that the whole concept of business regulation needs to be reviewed and possibly modified, to give consideration to this changing point of view.

SUMMARY AND CONCLUSION

It is the thesis of this article that the overall task of marketing is to make the adjustment between what the consumer conceives as his needs and what the producer finds practical to produce. One of the major functions involved in accomplishing this task is that of making contacts between those who want goods and those who produce them. These contacts between buyers and sellers at each step in the process from original sources of raw material to the ultimate consumers form the basis of marketing channels. These channels provide a vast network of contacts through which sources are enabled to discover suitable customers for their output and consumers are enabled to find suitable sources to fulfill their needs. In each case adjustments take place by the process of free selection of buyers by sellers and free selection of sellers by buyers.

The process of developing new contacts is one of the most costly elements of marketing. Because of this and because of a natural inclination of businessmen to deal with those whom they have dealt with before, the contactual relationships tend to become firmly established in what businessmen call "connections." This tendency to deal with established contacts gives to the structure a stability and

[41] Notable among these are Oswald Knauth and Chester Barnard, e.g., Oswald Knauth, *Managerial Enterprise* (New York: W. W. Norton & Co., 1948); Chester I. Barnard, *The Functions of the Executive* (Cambridge: Harvard University Press, 1947), and *Organization and Management* (1948).

consistency which decrease risks and reduce the costs of distribution. Without such established connections the entire process would be chaotic and unstable.

The thesis briefly outlined here must be considered in the nature of a hypothesis, not only because economists and business writers have given but scant attention to the phenomena, but also because much of the argument presented is based upon casual observation and conjecture. Before such a thesis can be accepted, the assumptions used must be verified by empirical evidence and the conclusions more precisely drawn. How strong are the attachments between buyers and sellers in a competitive market? How, if at all, can these attachments be measured? How many contacts are necessary before a firm can be considered established? What is the relationship between the number and strength of contacts and the success of a firm? These are questions which must be answered before a full understanding of the function is possible.

Even when the questions enumerated have been answered, there still remains the problem of the implications involved in this line of reasoning. Does a tendency toward continuous trading contacts affect the behavior of a firm through the business cycle? Does such trading make the economy less resilient, less flexible? Does such trading reduce competition? Does this type of trading lessen the degree of choice available to consumers? Would a system of trading in which price alone determined the choice of contacts be more desirable? The investigation of questions such as these might well lead to a considerable change in our conception of free markets.

The Role of Selling in Modern Marketing

WENDELL R. SMITH

We do not have an adequate answer to the question, "What is the role of selling in modern marketing?" Because of the extreme flexibility and adaptability of personal selling, it is often regarded as the residual element in the promotion or selling mix. It is now feasible and necessary to take a deeper look at the role of personal selling as a necessary prelude to the application of developing new techniques of research and analysis to this area of marketing.

The topic to which my remarks are to be addressed is perhaps better stated in the form of a question, "What is the role of selling in modern marketing?" I suggest that this is a question to which we do not have an adequate answer. However, it is a question of critical importance—a question to which an answer is urgently needed if the advancement of science in marketing is to continue in a logical and a balanced way.

To put it another way, the area of *personal selling* is becoming one of the relatively dark corners in marketing. It stands in danger of being bypassed by the "new breed" of mathematical and quantitative research specialists who are bringing excitement, increased precision, and more ambitious goals into other segments of the field. Most particularly they are concerning themselves with the measurement and analysis of other ways of performing the *selling function* in marketing—advertising and some forms of sales promotion.

Let's examine some of the reasons why this is happening and review the courses of action that are available to those who feel that effective, well planned and organized, ethical, personal selling is worth saving, and that its future has not been pre-empted by alternative ways of getting the selling function performed. Let me hasten to add that I am not one who believes that the quantitative approach—model

building, simulation techniques, and the use of computers—is going to take over. It seems clear, however, that this approach to marketing research and analysis will have a greater staying power and lasting impact upon the field than some other approaches that quickly skyrocketed into popularity by holding out false hopes to eager students, researchers, and businessmen. Now let's anticipate some semantic difficulties and get them out of the way.

As Arno Johnson has so effectively pointed out, "The coming changes in our labor force and productivity, accompanied by economic and social changes in the next ten years, will make the role of selling and advertising assume increasing importance in our economy." I think we will all agree that the *selling function* in marketing includes personal selling, advertising, sales promotion and related activity. Selling, or more properly *personal selling*, is concerned with direct, person-to-person persuasive communication. While this aspect of marketing is the oldest form of selling, its scientific content and development has lagged materially behind that of the newer, more impersonal ways of communicating persuasively with the market.

It overstates the case but slightly to conclude that marketing men have become preoccupied with increasing effectiveness in the management of *things* as opposed to the management of *people* or the human element involved in performance of the selling function.

As some of the people with whom I have discussed this matter put it, we have experienced a tremendous improvement in the development of education and training for the

◆ SOURCE: Reprinted by permission from *Emerging Concepts in Marketing*, edited by William S. Decker, Proceedings of the Winter Conference of the American Marketing Association, December 1962, pp. 174–78.

management of aspects of marketing other than personal selling. Much has been done in the development of research and advisory techniques designed to help managers of marketing make decisions with more confidence because they are based on better accumulations and analyses of facts. The danger implicit in this situation has been the temptation to emphasize education for staff activities as contrasted with line activities. As a result, personal selling has suffered. However, the future looks brighter by virtue of the fact that formal and specific attention is now being paid to the process of decision-making itself which is the essence of line activity and responsibility.

In my opinion, there are two major reasons why the "new breed" has deemed the personal selling area as less appropriate for the application of their techniques.

1. Because of the extreme flexibility and adaptability of personal selling effort, it is often regarded as the *residual* element in the promotional or selling mix. As a result of the greater ability and tendency of managers of advertising to develop specific plans and programs for the future, personal selling often comes to be regarded as the dependent variable. Admittedly, this generalization is dangerous because the relative rigidity or flexibility of the personal selling element of a marketing program varies significantly from product class to product class and even from company to company. Suffice it to say that newcomers to the field often interpret this residual status assigned to personal selling by management as an indication of relative weakness and unimportance.

2. For one reason or another, personal selling or *salesmanship* has not been too successful in establishing for itself a clearly defined role in the marketing curricula of schools of business. It is no secret that courses in salesmanship have all but disappeared from the offerings of many schools. In other institutions, they are little respected by the academic community and this lack of respect extends to some segments of the business community. The subject matter of many such courses lacked intellectual excitement from the point of view of students and faculty alike because they frequently attempted to do in the classroom what is better done on the job, while neglecting the rationale of selling and the "why" of activities associated with it. At the other end of the continuum, some courses in sales management became so broad and inclusive that only a title change

was necessary to follow the trend toward emphasis on the broader area of *marketing management.* An unfilled gap was thus created.

We should also admit that while marketing as an entity has had considerable difficulty in establishing itself as a candidate for designation as a science, the difficulty has been overwhelming in connection with selling. The roots of this are to be found deeply imbedded in the high-pressure selling tactics of the twenties. It appears that these activities occurred, not because marketing men thought this was the way to do the job, but because of inept production and general management that brought to the market unwanted or relatively undesired goods that had to be pushed through the channels of distribution if they were to be sold at all. In retrospect, this chastening experience was good for marketing in that it made crystal clear the role that marketing should assume in product planning and product development activities. However, it made personal selling or salesmanship the leading candidate for the role of "whipping boy."

Thus far I have been negative and critical of the way in which academicians and practitioners alike have responded to the continuing challenge of personal persuasive communication as an essential and productive marketing activity. I plead guilty to doing this as a means of preparing the ground for offering some constructive suggestions regarding the future.

There is an obvious case to be made for the re-establishment of personal selling as a full-ranking member of the family of activities that in total comprise the whole of marketing. Just as physical distribution has re-entered the spotlight by means of solid accomplishment in the application of new and more sophisticated techniques of inventory control and determining the logistics of product movement, a similar opportunity exists in the personal selling area. Even the most ardent critics of personal selling as we have known it in the past must concede that persuasive communication on a personal basis is essential as a catalyst to the process by means of which our productive capabilities can be translated into an improved standard of living and a more predictable and smoothly operating economic system. One needs only to look at many of the areas of industrial marketing to recognize the substantial payoff that can result from carefully planned and administered use of salesmen to accomplish sales, service, and two-way communication objectives. Substantial progress is observable in other areas of the economy. The selling of life insurance, for example, has made substantial progress as evidenced by its increased effectiveness, its increased acceptability to the general public, and its ability to attract able people. Much can be learned, too, from advertising's current response to criticism evidenced by the high level of interest in measurements of effectiveness as a step toward increased accountability to management.

It is now both feasible and necessary to take a more intensive look at the personal selling function in marketing: *feasible* because needed techniques and tools of investigation are now available, *necessary* because of a need to break with the past and to define and orient the activity anew within the context of an emerging science of marketing. What are the steps that will be necessary to attain this deeper understanding?

1. First it will be necessary to look at personal selling, not as a discrete activity, but as a part of a system by means of which the marketing job is accomplished. This spotlights the all-important allocation decision that commits the marketer to a specific mix of personal selling, advertising, and promotional effort. Put another way, it is imperative to discover, as a starting point, the irreducible minimum role of persuasive personal communication, taking fully into account the developments and advances that have been made in the impersonal methods of selling that have developed. It is unrealistic to assume that the role of personal selling can or should continue unchanged by technological progress. Just as the work of the agricultural segment of the economy is currently accomplished with a substantially lower human involvement than ever before, it is obvious that the substitution of capital for labor in the supermarket and similar developments will have an impact upon both the kind and quantity of personal selling required. While it was once reasonably correct to think of people employed in retailing as being primarily engaged in personal selling, this does not appear to be true today. It is imperative, then, to find and identify the hard core areas where personal selling does now and may be expected to continue to bear responsibility of such magnitude as to offer both challenge and opportunity to people professionally trained for the job. We need to do some market research to identify those situations where the need for tailored, personal selling is both substantial and rewarding.

2. Then we must review the exciting new developments in marketing, in the other business disciplines, and in the behavioral sciences for the purpose of developing an understanding of the task that can be performed by personal selling and discovering a technology that will enable this job to be performed in the most efficient and effective way. In this connection we may have to part with the very comfortable notion that "experience is the best teacher." It is well within the realm of feasibility that what is now going on in the development of search theory, decision theory, organization theory, game theory, and in other areas may have applicability to the selling situation.

Basic Duties of the Modern Sales Department

EUGENE J. KELLEY and WILLIAM LAZER

How *should* the marketing concept affect sales management and the field sales force? What *should* the modern sales department contribute to its company's success?

Sales department responsibilities increase under the marketing concept. Sales personnel, at both the managerial and field levels, are asked to broaden their area of interest and "raise their sights."

Under the marketing concept, salesmen are urged to look beyond quotas and calls per customer, and assist the other levels of the company in achieving clearly defined objectives. The marketing concept emphasizes this interaction and inter-relationship of selling and other marketing-related activities.

The sales manager *and field sales force* must now perform important management functions. An increasing number of companies are insisting that their sales managers demonstrate an ability to plan and execute creative field sales strategy and to integrate sales activities with the other elements of the marketing mix.

In short, the marketing concept is resulting in a re-evaluation of the nature and scope of the sales department.

SALES MANAGER'S DUTIES

Under the marketing concept, the sales manager is concerned with management of the

◆ SOURCE: Reprinted by permission from *Industrial Marketing*, April 1960. Note: Charts 1 and 2 did not appear in the original article but were later included in the article appearing in *Managerial Marketing: Perspectives and Viewpoints*, Revised Edition, William Lazer and Eugene J. Kelley (Homewood, Illinois: Richard D. Irwin, Inc., 1962), pp. 378–384.

total sales effort. His job consists of more than recruiting, selecting and training salesmen. His major responsibility is one of creating a growth atmosphere and planning and coordinating sales force strategy in order to achieve company objectives.

Sales management operating under the marketing concept recognizes innovation and experimentation as the essential ingredients of sales and marketing progress. Under this concept, sales management realizes that change not only produces problems, but also presents marketing opportunities.

The duties of sales managers operating under the marketing concept fall into two broad areas: (1) sales administration, and (2) sales force management. These are portrayed in Chart I.

Sales administration includes the planning and organizing functions, such as determining sales potentials, programming sales effort, coordinating sales inputs, and controlling sales outputs. In addition, the increasingly important functions of sales innovation, sales communication and sales research are sales administration responsibilities.

Sales force management includes the important functions of recruiting, selecting, training, supervising, compensating and motivating the field sales force.

Both sales administration and sales force management are of crucial importance. To date many sales managers have done a better job of recruiting, selecting, and training salesmen than they have of executing their sales administration responsibilities. In the future various pressures of competition, innovation, automation, high fixed costs and changing markets will force increased emphasis on sales administration.

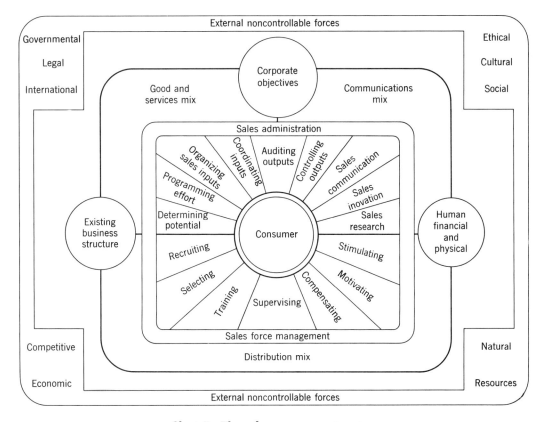

Chart I   The sales management system.

SALES STRATEGY EMPHASIS

The modern sales manager is concerned with the strategy inherent in a total approach to over-all sales. He still has the bread-and-butter tasks of achieving quotas and directing salesmen in the accomplishment of predetermined objectives; but he also is charged with helping to create market acceptance, establish brand or corporate images, provide research information, develop marketing manpower and establish harmonious dealer relationships.

The vital role of the sales manager in achieving corporate goals is emphasized in the marketing concept approach to sales strategy.

TWO DIMENSIONS

Marketing has two dimensions. First, marketing is an increasingly significant element in the total complex of business operation. Management makes a marketing decision after consideration of its effect on the whole business system and the over-all objectives.

Second, marketing is an integrated subsystem. The marketing program is comprised of a mix of communications, distribution elements and goods and services "inputs." The essence of an integrated marketing program is that managerial attention is given to coordinating the interacting elements of the marketing mix to achieve predetermined goals.

It is not possible for a sales manager to understand the true dimensions of marketing change if he thinks only in terms of traditional sales management functions. Thinking of marketing as a cooperative effort—as a "system"—enables him to understand the place of sales in the total marketing effort.

TOTAL SALES PERSPECTIVE

Actually, sales operates within a framework determined by various forces beyond the control of management. These include competitive, social and political forces. Sales managers will have to be more sensitive to the influence on sales strategy of these forces. Non-business disciplines such as psychology and sociology can be useful in supplying information on the external business environment.

A sales manager with a total sales perspective is less likely to see a particular problem as an isolated entity. For example, the problem of sales compensation is appraised in its relation to other components of sales, such as manpower development, selection, training, motivation, supervision and control.

Sales managers able to think in terms of how the field sales force is affected by the flows of information, money, and manpower are needed. These men will be in a better position to exe-cute the policies of marketing-minded corporate managements. Since sales management will be working under this "systems concept" approach, understanding it will be a prerequisite for advancement.

SALESMEN'S DUTIES

The systems concept should be important to salesmen as well as sales managers. This is particularly true if the salesman's job is seen as

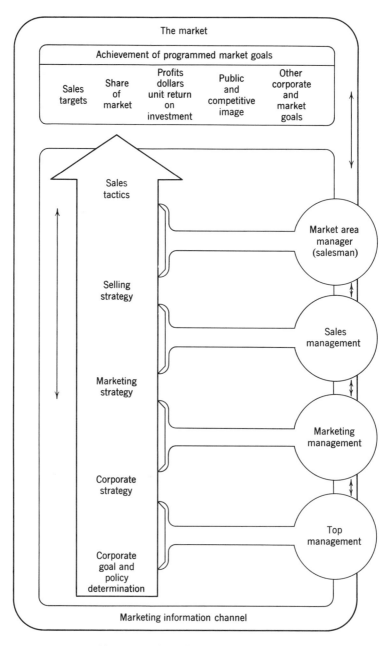

Chart II   The sales management system.

that of managing a market area as it is in Chart II. If, on the other hand, the salesman is looked upon as an order taker, the concept is not as applicable.

An increasing number of companies are realizing that the job of the salesman has strategic and innovative dimensions, just as does sales force management. Many salesmen are faced in their own territories with problems of goal determination, planning and long-run market development. Acting in these capacities, the field man is a manager of a market area.

The distinction between a salesman and a manager of a market area is important; it is the difference between viewing salesmen as employees or as members of management. More important, it affects the way the salesman sees his own job. Under the market area management concept, the creative, strategic, and innovative powers of the field sales force are more likely to be tapped and utilized. In short, the market area management concept of field selling can bring about a fundamental change in the character of the salesman's job.

This new conceptual outlook of the sales job is not easy for some managers, or some salesmen, to accept. Viewing salesmen as managers at first blush seems to de-emphasize the importance of present managers. Actually it does not. It raises the sights of managers to higher strategic and planning levels. It may be the means of greater understanding and growth for present managers as well as one way of releasing the inherent creative energy of a force of salesmen.

A man's ability to maintain this subtle but fundamental perspective in the management of his territory or his sales force is a basic criterion of his development potential for higher positions of managerial and administrative responsibility.

ELEMENTS OF TOTAL SALES

It is important for corporate success that sales personnel view the interaction of marketing elements as a single system. Many successful and sophisticated sales managers have been aware that change in one component of sales action has an impact on the rest of the system. But organized, systematic, and intensive attention to such interaction is relatively new in marketing and selling.

The three components of the over-all marketing effort which are particularly relevant to sales management are: input, communications and output.

1. *Inputs.* Market planners and field sales planners must recognize that such resources as manpower, money, information, products and service are the "inputs" of the sales action complex. The concept of assembling predetermined inputs to achieve specified sales objectives is a useful notion.

2. *Communications.* Communications with the customer and the company are key contributions of salesmen to total sales. The complexities of communications in sales are just beginning to be recognized. Salesmen must overcome the barriers of time, space and lack of knowledge to produce a sustained flow of meaningful information. Sales communication links the customer and his needs with the salesmen's firm.

The sales manager has the important assignment of coordinating this information flow. The sales manager links not only management to the sales force, but also the customer to higher management levels. This is one of the key concepts of the marketing management philosophy.

3. *Outputs.* Sales managers can be appraised in terms of a variety of measurable outputs. The most common, of course, are volume and profit standards. These criteria will always be fundamental, but others are being recognized as important. Such contributions as the type and quality of information provided for management planning are becoming more significant bases of evaluation.

Areas of mutual interest for all participants in the sales program can be identified and developed under the "systems" approach to sales. The salesman in the field is more likely to see how his efforts support and supplement the specialist in the home office. The headquarters specialist can be helped to see that it is the salesman who produces the markets which insure corporate survival and growth.

The idea of teamwork is easier to establish when all components of sales are recognized as contributing certain inputs which will be combined with other contributions to produce a predetermined set of sales outputs.

SCOPE OF CONCEPT

This concept of the sales action complex is also a way of looking at new areas of market opportunity.

In an era when technology is developing new products and new product applications at an accelerating rate, it behooves marketing and sales management to investigate the possibilities of "systems concept" selling.

In fact, many firms can view markets not only in terms of single companies but as complex business "systems." It is possible that a number of new products can be introduced simultaneously on a "systems" basis. The Air Force, for example, finds it necessary not only to buy individual products, but to purchase complete weapons systems including supporting service facilities.

And the same cooperative attitude should also carry through into manufacturer-dealer relations.

Many manufacturers do not recognize the mutual dependency aspects of their relations with suppliers and dealers. Frequently, distributors and manufacturers fail to recognize the community of interest involved in serving customers. How many manufacturers see their dealers as part of an extended sales system? Many say they do, but often unnecessary conflict exists where cooperation should prevail.

CONCLUSIONS

The specific benefits of the adoption of the systems approach to sales management are:

1. Coordination of corporate, marketing and sales efforts.

2. Integration of volume and profit targets established by the company with the operating activities of sales management.

3. Establishment of a circular and continuous relationship between corporate objectives and customer wants, needs and desires.

4. Combination of all sales inputs into an integrated marketing thrust. Through coordinated impact on the market place, effective and efficient sales action will result.

5. The systems concept approach requires sales management to achieve a perspective of marketing and corporate activities extending beyond the normal activities on such functions as production, purchasing and personnel.

6. The approach promotes teamwork. Decision makers at various corporate levels recognize the ramifications of their decisions at all levels. The salesman executing tactics in particular sales situations recognizes the contribution to the field sales team made by the men who devise sales strategy.

B. The Sales Challenge

The Salesman Isn't Dead—He's Different

CARL RIESER

There is no more abused figure in American life than the salesman. One group of critics scorns him for certain qualities that another group sneers at him for losing. To many novelists, playwrights, sociologists, college students, and many others, he is aggressively forcing on people goods that they don't want. He is the drummer, with a dubious set of social values—Willy Loman in the Arthur Miller play. The second group of critics, which includes the Secretary of Commerce and many business executives all over the U.S., charges the salesman with lacking good, old-fashioned, hardhitting salesmanship. He was spoiled by the postwar days when competition was easy. If only he would get up off his duff, and get out and *sell*, the goods would move and business would be in fine shape.

Both sets of critics are swatting at a target that doesn't matter much any more. The plain fact is that, as one Boston sales executive recently said, "The old drummer type of salesman has gone by the board." Nor are his talents especially needed in today's economy. To be sure, there are plenty of aggressive, hardhitting salesmen still around, and there will always be a place for their brand of selling. But this kind of man is no longer the archetype.

From bits and pieces of evidence in all sectors of U.S. business, it is now possible to discern the emergence of a new dominant type, a man with a softer touch and greater breadth,

a new kind of man to do a new—much more significant—kind of job. Whereas the old-time salesman devoted himself primarily to pushing a product, or a line of products, the new-era salesman is involved with the whole distribution pipeline, beginning with the tailoring of products to the customer's desire and extending through their promotion and advertising to final delivery to the ultimate consumer.

The salesman has been cast in his new role by "the marketing concept," a term that originated at General Electric around 1950 and has gained wide currency recently. It means essentially that companies are orienting their organization and effort toward the market, toward the ever changing needs of the customer, and the ever shifting calculations of their own production costs and opportunities. The emphasis is less concentrated on the isolated point-of-sale; it is spread forward, into the buyer's operations, and backward into the seller's operations. The profound consequences of this trend have been suggested by Orm Henning, marketing manager of industrial products at Texas Instruments:

"One should remind oneself that selling is only part of marketing—particularly in the scientific-industrial world. Marketing is communicating back to your factory your individual customer's needs and particular problems. When you realize and practice this, you open an entirely new vista in the area of sales. You cannot afford to sell a product, a static product—not in our business."

◆ SOURCE: Reprinted by permission from *Fortune*, **66** (Time Inc.), November 1962, pp. 124–127, 248, 252, 254, 259.

25

And what's true today in the electronics business—and many others—is going to be true of more and more businesses tomorrow.

The great change in selling affects practically all industries and all kinds of goods, whether they are what the marketing profession calls "pull-through" or "push-through" products. Pull-through refers generally to mass-produced consumer items, where a sort of siphon is already working. Pull-through products and services are pre-sold by the manufacturer to the final consumer by mass advertising and promotion, which in effect creates a demand that almost literally pulls the goods through the distribution pipeline. Push-through products are wholly new consumer goods for which the siphon has not yet begun to work or, more commonly, they are industrial materials and equipment. Since the latter are usually highly technical in nature, they must be explained to the buyer and they require more personal selling so as to generate in the buyer the idea that he needs the product.

The distinction between pull-through and push-through is becoming less important. The retailer now stocks Kleenex tissues, for example, because he is persuaded that Kimberly-Clark Corp. will maintain public recognition of the brand and will see to it that thousands of boxes are siphoned rapidly and profitably right through his warehouse and off his store shelves. The job of the Kimberly-Clark salesman is to service the account so that the buyer will keep buying. He expedites and consolidates the shipments, keeps track of the retailer's inventory, sees that the goods get the greatest display and promotion possible, keeps himself available in case of any trouble or emergency. The job of the man who sells computers is much the same. The computer is one element in a whole system of mechanical devices and programing techniques, which is sold on the basis of what the customer is persuaded it can do for him.

The salesman's responsibility becomes greater as technology advances and producers offer products of ever mounting complexity. "We are tending toward the marketing of systems and services," says James Jewell, marketing vice president of Westinghouse. "The customers want to buy greater production—not equipment. We take the full responsibility for engineering and installing, and we are moving further into servicing."

This orientation toward the customer's needs is pointed up in a recent book that has received wide attention in the trade—*Innovation in Marketing*, by Theodore Levitt, a management consultant and a member of the faculty of Harvard Business School. Levitt, who speaks for a new generation of believers in "the marketing concept," states flatly that

". . . a strictly sales-oriented approach to doing business can be suicidal. The difference between selling and marketing is more than semantic. Selling focuses on the needs of the seller, marketing on the needs of the buyer. Selling is preoccupied with the seller's need to convert his product or service into cash; marketing with the idea of satisfying the needs of the customer by means of the product or service and by the whole cluster of customer-getting value satisfactions associated with creating, delivering, and finally consuming it."

In this quotation Levitt seems to be over-simplifying the contrast between selling and marketing. Any implication that "the marketing concept" isn't motivated by the seller's desire for profits is, of course, mistaken. While his motives remain the same, the seller now sees marketing as a more elaborate link between production and consumption, a link that has to be carefully constructed and maintained.

Two situations may illustrate the change. In the past, a factory would over-produce the market and unload on the sales force the responsibility for unloading the goods on the customers. In the other situation, the salesmen kept their volume up by selling those products in their line that were easiest to sell—even those that were the least profitable. The incidence of both these cases tends to be diminished by the new trend with its more delicate alignment of markets and production, and its careful analysis of product profitability. The salesman is less often stuck with the necessity of a fast, hard sell. But he is steadily pressed to make the sales where the profit lies. Altogether, the marketing concept has played a vital role in developing the enormous velocity in the flow of goods, a phenomenon that has been described earlier in this series as the "short-order economy" (*Fortune*, August 1962).

THE MIRROR OF THE MARKETS

There is little doubt that the impact of "the marketing concept" has reduced the stature of the sales manager in scores of companies. He has lost his former autonomy and now reports to the marketing vice president rather than directly to the president. He has less say over such vital matters as pricing and credit policies. The sales force must fit its work into an over-all corporation marketing policy. Furthermore, over the decade, the autonomy of the sales manager has been further trimmed in many companies by the creation of the job of product manager, who has both line and staff authority for a given product or group of products and coordinates production with advertising, research, and field selling.

The marketing concept has had very decided and significant structural effects on sales forces. This can be seen very clearly at General Electric, father of the marketing concept. G.E.'s salesmen used to be essentially product specialists, each selling only the line of a specific manufacturing department, even though it went into a variety of markets. It took time for G.E. to orient its sales forces toward markets rather than products, but this process finally began seven years ago in the company's electrical-apparatus business. Instead of specializing in one product, e.g., cord sets, fan motors, push buttons, the salesman began selling a whole group of products to a particular market—for example, the air-conditioning industry. Early this year more than a dozen separate departments selling G.E.'s biggest single customer, the government, were reorganized into one defense sales force. In other words, instead of being product-oriented, the sales organizations have become "mirrors" of the markets G.E. serves.

Recently, Westinghouse reorganized its entire 13,600-man field sales organization along somewhat similar lines, in accord with what the company calls the "province concept." The company wants to be represented wherever possible by a "Mr. Westinghouse" rather than by a confusing bevy of different salesmen from various production divisions. (Significantly, in reorganizing, Westinghouse also seized the opportunity to put more salesmen in jobs where they actually meet customers and eliminated virtually an entire "staff" layer of some 104 sales managers who never called on customers.)

The same kind of reorganization has gone on in scores of companies in such diverse fields as motor trucks and optical equipment. At American Optical Co., for example, salesmen who used to be product specialists now sell a line that includes every piece of furniture and equipment for the doctor's office, from lenses to tables.

Thus the kind of man needed for this new kind of sales job has to be a generalist. The trend is away from the "sales engineer," the technically trained salesman, of a few years ago. His successor is a man capable of absorbing stacks of information churned out by the marketing department, and of applying it to his customers' problems. He goes forth armed with a tremendous amount of data on his customers' needs, their products, their corporate organizations, and their supply and delivery schedules.

He is also a man with more executive ability than the salesman of yesterday. A Boston sales manager describes the new salesmen as simply "businessmen who travel." One Milwaukee executive notes that increasingly the new salesman is being given the authority and stature to make important decisions in the field without having to go back to corporate headquarters for an O.K. General Foods has adopted a new title of prestige for its senior salesmen, each of whom lives with one food-chain customer and attends to its needs. They are called "account executives" and they command the services of junior salesmen, who do the routine housekeeping chores of servicing the customers' stores.

In the new order of things there is obviously still a need for hard-selling, aggressive salesmen to open up new accounts, to introduce new and untried products, to sell the wares of new companies that have no national reputation. Since the service-oriented sales staff has turned away from this kind of pioneering effort, the door has been opened to a new kind of specialist, typified by a New York firm called the George N. Kahn Co. This company provides a crew of highly aggressive young salesmen who open up new territories for companies that don't want to retrain their own sales forces for such sporadically necessary missions. (Kahn is not a manufacturer's representative; it works on a flat-fee basis rather than a commission and, after pioneering the sale of a product, expects that the manufacturer will take it back for handling by his own sales staff.) There is now some thought in the top management of a number of companies that the way to deal with this basic problem is to set up special sections of sales staffs with the specific function of going after new business. Thus what has been commonly thought of as the primary function of all salesmen is now becoming the specialty of a few.

THE SERVICE TROOPS

The new salesman has a tremendous advantage over his predecessors. Not only does he have access to much more information about his customers, but he is also backed up by formidable technical and other kinds of assistance. For example, in reshaping its inorganic-chemical sales recently, FMC Corp. (formerly Food Machinery & Chemical Corp.) has beefed up the number of its technical people directly behind the salesmen by some 20 per cent. The present ratio: one technical man to every four salesmen. The great pioneer in this development was du Pont, which years ago saw the close connection between selling and customer service. Today, at Chestnut Run, outside Wilmington, du Pont has an impressive $20-million, campus-like complex of laboratories and workshops, employing 1,700 scientists, technicians, and others devoted to providing sales literature, solving technical problems, providing all kinds of services for customers or potential buyers of du Pont products, and otherwise aiding the sales effort. Companies selling all kinds of goods have developed similar assistance, though, naturally, the more complex the technology, the more elaborate the technical backup.

The development of sophisticated electronic data-processing systems is revolutionizing inventory handling, ordering, warehousing, and other physical aspects of marketing. This, in turn, relieves the salesman of a great deal of detail that used to absorb valuable hours of his time—writing up orders and reports, checking whether goods are available and how soon they can be delivered, and performing other niggling drudgery.

At the same time, the computer also introduces an element of impersonality in the relations between a seller and a buyer. Much of today's ordering of goods and materials, from packaged foods to industrial chemicals, is done, as it were, by a computer, which tells the buyer when to reorder; the transaction is handled routinely and a salesman never enters into it. This disencumbering of the salesman releases him to function on a new level of performance, to use his time more creatively. At Allis-Chalmers, which has just set up a department of marketing, an executive says, "Now our salespeople won't get bogged down in a lot of detail that goes hand in hand with selling, like the preparation of presentations, charts, convention exhibits, and whatnot. We'll do all the work, including the training of salesmen, in cooperation with company divisions."

"YOU LOSE ONE OF THE BIG BABIES . . ."

The rise of the new salesman is the result of changes in the marketplace that have drastically altered the relationship of buyer to seller. One of the most significant developments has been the growing importance of the big customer. In almost every line of business, fewer and bigger customers are responsible for an increasingly large part of any given company's sales. Twenty-five years ago, when independent grocers were an important factor in food retailing, food processors did the bulk of their business with thousands upon thousands of chains and stores. Today, with the concentration of business in the hands of a relatively few big chains, some 300 buying offices throughout the U.S. account for 80 per cent of all food bought at wholesale. Preoccupation with the "key customer" affects every industry, from steel to office supplies. Sighs an officer of the Acme Chemical Co. in Milwaukee, "You lose one of the big babies and you're in trouble."

This whole trend is building up momentum as smaller buyers band together to increase their purchasing power and efficiency by buying cooperatively. It affects suppliers of school equipment, for example, because schools are consolidating on a county basis. Independent hardware stores and even hospitals are doing it.

How this has affected the food business has been fully explored in a new book with a provocative title, *The Vanishing Salesman*, by E. B. Weiss, a New York marketing specialist in the consumer-goods field. Actually, Weiss does not believe that the salesman is vanishing; his point is that the shift to the service-oriented sales function has so greatly altered the nature of personal selling that companies are faced with entirely new conditions in the hiring, training, and organization of salesmen. Weiss also notes that as retail food chains have become bigger and bigger, and their purchases have reached stupendous volume, the position of the individual buyer, once regarded as the salesman's opposite number, has greatly diminished. The buyer in a food chain used to be an important figure; he made the decisions on what the chain was going to buy. Now his power has been usurped by buying committees. The buyer has become merely a technician who interviews the salesmen from the food processor and passes on his findings to his superiors. Says Weiss:

"Members of the buying committee tend not to be buying specialists. Moreover, they make decisions covering the entire range of merchandise inventoried by the organization. Since they tend to be at executive levels considerably higher than that of the buyer who appears before them, they are more apt to depend on their own judgment than that of the buyer. And, by the same token, the buyer is not apt to put up much of a battle . . . In buying committee sessions, it is presumably the majority that rules. But since it is traditional in large organizations for so many committee members to vote with the head of the table, the majority rule prevails more in theory than in fact."

So the man that the seller must get to is the man at the head of the table. And this is true not only in the food field. Throughout U.S. industry, key buying power has steadily risen up through the corporate structure to higher echelons of authority. In industrial selling, an increasing number of purchasing decisions tend to involve bigger and bigger outlays of capital. In large part this is the result of the rise of what is now commonly called *systems selling*. Instead of buying components from many suppliers, a company often buys a whole integrated system, be it a system for heating and air conditioning, protecting a plant from theft and fire, automating a production line, or handling materials. As technology becomes more complex, users, intent on eliminating technical headaches, are ever more anxious to buy such systems, while suppliers, intent on greater profit, are ever more anxious to design and sell a whole package. Naturally, the final approval for such an expenditure or commitment moves up the line, from the plant superintendent or manager, to the corporate controller or treasurer, perhaps all the way to the president or board chairman.

"THE PRESIDENT'S PROJECT"

Not only has this created the need for salesmen with sufficient stature to talk to the customer's top management, but it has also drawn top executives more directly into the selling act. In company after company, higher officials now make a very determined effort to get out in the field and call on the big customers, and even to do considerable pioneer work with potential customers. This kind of thing, of course, is not new. Many companies were built by star salesmen at the top, a very good example being the late Thomas J. Watson, Sr., at I.B.M. ("What my father used to do when people began to talk about the great complexity of the products," says Tom Watson, Jr., the present head of the company, "would be to sweep his hand and say, 'It's all so simple. All it does is add, subtract, and multiply!'") And in industries where enormous capital investment is required, such as the utility business, intimate and continued contact between seller and buyer at a high level has always been important. But now personal selling by top executives is becoming much more common. Raytheon, for example, has divided up its list of big customers among managers and officers of the company, and assigned each the responsibility of keeping in touch with a few accounts, with a view to bolstering the salesman's efforts.

General Foods was one of the pioneers in this. When Charles Mortimer was president of the company, he started "The President's Project," a series of meetings with customers all over the country. "In the beginning the meetings started out 100 per cent social," explains Wayne Marks, now president of the company. "They were strictly for pleasure—and we invited more than one customer to a meeting. But we found that nothing *happened*. Except that we got acquainted. We didn't find out what to improve in our business operation. So the format was quickly changed."

Now Marks's office sets up his customer-visiting schedule at least a month in advance. The customer is requested to have all his key people at the meeting, and several weeks before the encounter, G.F. sends along a "questionnaire" to elicit comments on G.F.'s performance and suggestions for items to discuss. In the past eighteen months Marks, accompanied by a team of executives and salesmen, has visited fifty-four customers throughout the U.S.

Marks has found the customers "avid" for this kind of contact. Not only does G.F. come out of these encounters (some of them lasting for five or six hours over dinner and drinks) with a fuller idea of what it should be doing—but the customers learn a great deal about their own organizations that they weren't aware of. Says Marks:

"Many a meeting, at the end the boss man will say, 'Why don't *we* go out and find out what's happening in our own stores?' At the end of a recent meeting the top man told me, 'I've been frank with you and told you what I don't like about your operations. Would you be willing to report back to us on what you think of us?' "

THE "SELLINGEST" FIRM

Personal selling is now a company-wide endeavor, and the contact with the customer takes place at many levels in an organized, formal way. The best illustration of how this has changed fundamentally the relations between buyer and seller is offered by National Cash Register, long known as perhaps the "sellingest" firm in the country. N.C.R.'s founder, the late John H. Patterson, has been called the father of many of the standard techniques of modern selling. He established the first formal training courses for salesmen, the first yearly sales quotas, the first guaranteed sales territories for salesmen, the first annual sales convention. Patterson's earlier sales methods were comparatively crude; cash registers were sold to storekeepers by appealing to their fear that dishonest clerks were pocketing money out of the till. But over the years the company refined its appeals, and forty years ago, when it began selling accounting machines, it even evolved a primitive kind of systems selling. But its big leap came about five years ago when the company introduced, somewhat belatedly as compared with the competition, its first electronic computer.

N.C.R. had to set up a whole new sales force for the computer, and in doing so it made a profound discovery: it was not easy to make a salesman of accounting machinery into a computer salesman. Says one N.C.R. senior salesman: "It was the death of salesmen like Willy Loman. At N.C.R. a few were left behind. They couldn't make the switch. It wasn't that they were too old—some were in their forties. But men's intellectual capabilities get set at various ages, and some *were* too old at that age." The company also found that it had to alter its time-honored compensation system. Normally, the N.C.R. salesman collects an advance that is charged against the commission he makes on his sales. Says marketing director Harry Keesecker, "Computer selling is still incentive selling, but due to the kind of product—sometimes the long time between sales—

we have to compensate the salesmen by salary plus commission."

At the same time N.C.R. set up an elaborate organization to give the salesmen technical support. This now includes 325 mathematicians and technical people; the number has doubled in size in the past twelve months. They develop manuals and presentations, help the customer define his problems, train his computer operators for him, set up his E.D.P. system, and produce the programing for it. The support organization also trains the computer salesman, a departure for N.C.R., which years ago built its whole sales-training program around the use of experienced salesmen, borrowed from the field, as instructors. (The total computer sales and support staff numbers about 500 people, as against 2,100 in accounting machines, but the company is supplementing the small computer force by training as many of the accounting-machine men as possible to sell both kinds of equipment.)

THE WILLY LOMANS
ARE NO LONGER FEASIBLE

The difference between the old and new eras at N.C.R.—and in salesmanship in general—is dramatically illustrated by the story of how the company landed a rather sensational contract for the sale of a computer to the Dime Savings Bank of Brooklyn, New York, the country's second-largest mutual savings bank. The bank and the company had long-standing ties dating back to 1929, when the Dime bought its first N.C.R. posting machines for the tellers' windows. In subsequent decades the bank bought other N.C.R. equipment. In those years the chief link between the two was an N.C.R. salesman, Anthony de Florio, now district manager of sales for accounting and computer systems, and Karl Stad, who is now vice president of methods and systems at the Dime. The relationship was a cordial one, and N.C.R., which is mainly known for its experience in retailing and banking, was solidly in with the Dime.

In the late 1950's, however, there was a sudden change in the old easy-going ways. The bank decided, in 1957, that it was time to think about tying its entire bookkeeping operations into a computer to keep up with its bounding growth, and Stad was told to set up a task force to study the entire field and to recommend the "ideal" system. De Florio observes, "This was the beginning of group selling. The salesman had to understand the problems and systems of the customer. The staff at the bank had to define what was required, and we at N.C.R. had to be sure that the bank wasn't running away from us in know-how." (To N.C.R., as to many another company, the growing sophistication of the buyer has become an important factor to reckon with.) N.C.R. also had to reckon with competition; every other computer manufacturer came in for the kill at Dime. For the next two years Stad and his team studied the field and enlarged their expertise. By 1959 they had winnowed the choice down to four systems, including N.C.R.'s, and asked the competitors for feasibility studies. (Says de Florio: "By the time you get to feasibility studies, the Willy Lomans are no longer feasible.")

Now the contacts between the company and the bank multiplied. N.C.R. sent teams of technical people from Dayton headquarters to confer with Stad—they submitted a technical proposal two inches thick—and Stad went out to Dayton to talk to N.C.R.'s research people. He was put up at N.C.R.'s plush Moraine Farm, the estate of a former board chairman, which the company now uses to entertain groups of customers and potential customers. (Like du Pont and other companies, N.C.R. uses its factories and laboratories as a sales showcase.) By the end of 1959, Stad decided that N.C.R.'s 304 computer, then just being delivered to the first purchasers, was the one for the Dime.

Thereupon the Dime's board of trustees decided that Stad's decision ought to be second-guessed by an independent consultant in the electronic data-processing field. This, of course, opened up the whole matter again, and brought the competitors back in. Fortunately for N.C.R., the consultant confirmed the decision, and the affair between the bank and the company again resumed, in a deliberate and measured way. The Dime's board selected a committee of three trustees to study the proposal. They went out to Dayton—staying at an even more posh N.C.R. guest house, the old home of Orville Wright—and they talked with everyone from technicians to N.C.R.'s president, R. S. Oelman, and its then board chairman, S.C. Allyn. On the way back in the plane, the trustees decided to sign with N.C.R. It was an $800,000 decision, and it was a key one not only to the bank but to N.C.R., which closed some other bank contracts on the strength of the Dime's decision.

N.C.R. was in the middle of a training program for the Dime's employees when, early in 1960, a crisis arose. N.C.R.'s technicians reached the chilling conclusion that the 304 computer would not have the capacity to do what the Dime eventually would require—i.e., a direct linkage from the posting machines at the tellers' windows to the computer without the intermediate use of tabulating equipment. The next model in the design stage, the 315 random-access computer, would do the job— but not the 304. De Florio had to come clean with the bank. "I called up Karl and said, 'Let's have lunch at the Brooklyn Club,'" recalls de Florio, still wincing at the ensuing conversation. De Florio offered to tear up the contract for the 304. The Dime's board accepted the proposal, and the whole computer question was back in the soup again.

Rival manufacturers had another chance to make presentations, and N.C.R. had to start all over again selling its 315 model, then two years from delivery. De Florio kept pounding on one main point: the bank already was using N.C.R. machines at its windows, and any company that finally got the computer contract would have to tie in to N.C.R.'s equipment. In the end the argument prevailed; Stad recommended the 315 computer on the grounds that it would be "just as good" as other computers—though no better—and that N.C.R. had "window experience." Along with the computer, the bank also agreed to use other N.C.R. equipment in its integrated system, so the total package came to $2 million. Says de Florio, looking back on the whole transaction, "In this kind of selling you can't see everything you buy. A lot has to be bought on faith. Therefore a company likes to work with big companies. Come hell or high water, they have to deliver."

One of N.C.R.'s brightest and most successful young computer salesmen recently expanded this doctrine. "A salesman is important," he remarked, "because the policy makers today come from a previous generation of doing business. They don't have the technical equipment necessary to make a decision about a computer that requires technical sophistication. So the salesman has to take the language of the computer man and turn it into language his customer understands. I used to think that those decisions would be made on a scientific basis—but it's a gross act of faith." The salesman's job, he said, is "to create an environment in which an act of faith can take place."

THE "FOOT SOLDIERS"
NEED UPGRADING

There is doubtless still plenty of faith in sales transactions. But as the Dime Savings Bank affair shows, there is a great deal more. And this is the fact that salesmen do not seem to realize when they talk about their jobs. They are still trained to have a kind of emotionalism about their craft, and they carry with them a heavy load of outworn notions about their role. They view selling as both warfare and love, hostility and benevolence. They see themselves as "the men on the firing line," and "the foot soldiers of democracy." The combative nature of selling is stressed in almost every book on the subject, as in one of the most famous and widely sold of all books on selling, *Open the Mind and Close the Sale*, by John M. Wilson, who recently retired as N.C.R.'s sales manager. Wilson speaks of the "tension in every buyer-seller relationship," of the "challenge" in each encounter, of the need for "handling" the customer—though, of course, "in the way he wants to be handled."

This lag in the recognition of what has happened to selling is harmful, because the sales profession is still held in low esteem by the public. Just how low was indicated recently in a survey by *Sales Management* magazine of college students and their attitude toward selling. Selling ranked a very poor fourth, after teaching, law, and medicine, as a choice for a career. Only 6 per cent of the students favored it. (Of seventy-one students whose fathers are in sales, only *five* wanted to go into selling.)

The students did not particularly object to the working conditions in selling; relatively few said they were put off by too much travel-

ing, for example. Nor did many feel that the financial reward was inadequate. The chief objections to a selling career (some even denied that selling *is* a career) were these: "I don't want to force people to buy things they don't need." "Job security is poor." "I'm not extrovert enough." "Selling has no prestige."

One student unwittingly put his finger on the ironic predicament business faces. He remarked that selling simply does not require "a college education or intelligence." The main feature of the new kind of personal selling, of course, is that it does require men who are able and intelligent; the new salesmen, quite obviously, must be recruited from among the better college graduates. But how are they going to be recruited if the better college graduates think selling is beneath them? The experience of Scott Paper illustrates the difficulties business has in luring these men into selling. The company prides itself on the fact that 95 per cent of its sales staff are college graduates. Each year, to keep the staff replenished, it interviews some 2,000 students, invites about 100 of these men to visit its Philadelphia headquarters, makes offers to about seventy-five—and lands thirty-five or forty of them.

The trouble is that business has signally failed to get across the idea that there has been a tremendous change in selling. (The *Sales Management* poll shows that this generation of students has not grasped one of the simplest and most fundamental changes—i.e., that by and large salesmen are no longer paid on commission but are salaried.) Business has a massive educational job to do. Perhaps as a start it might throw away a lot of the old inspirational literature on selling and let the facts of the new situation do the inspiring.

Hewlett-Packard: "We don't sell hardware. We sell solutions. . . ."

While many companies speak of "educating" customers, Hewlett-Packard Co. is one of the few to take the saying literally. Each year it summons some 15,000 representatives of 1,500 companies to its headquarters in Palo Alto, California, for a "customer training program." The "trainees," who range from lab technicians to W. W. Eitel, president of Eitel-McCullough, Inc., a power transmission tube maker, spend two or three nine-hour days in HP classrooms learning the mysteries of the company's product line.

Small wonder. Hewlett-Packard's products—precision electronic measuring devices—are among the most intricate scientific instruments known. So its salesmen are hardly ever the jovial back-slappers of business tradition; they're engineers rather than drummers, and it often takes considerable schooling to know what on earth they're talking about. Part of a sample sales pitch: "It is well known the output of a linear filter is the integral of the product of the input wave and the impulse response reversed in time."

And this only begins the list of ways in which HP salesmen live in a different world from the one inhabited by sellers of beans, or steel, or motel rooms. To spout such a line, HP salesmen require even more education than their customers. So, though they're all college graduates to begin with, HP keeps them going to company classes throughout their careers, and constantly sends instructors to catch them on the road and brief them on the latest in measuring technology.

◆ SOURCE: Reprinted by permission from *How They Sell*, editors of *The Wall Street Journal* (Dow Jones & Company, Inc., 1965), pp. 3–17.

In the field, HP salesmen themselves turn teachers. They sometimes spend almost as much time patiently showing customers how to use and repair instruments already purchased as they do trying to sell new ones.

And salesmen—who HP prefers to call "field engineers"—are instructed to take the customer's side in any dispute with the company. If this means denouncing the shortcomings of an HP instrument to its makers rather than praising its good points to the customer, that's fine with Hewlett-Packard; it relies heavily on field engineers' reports for tips on how to change instruments to make them more efficient. As W. Noel Eldred, HP vice president for marketing, puts it to seminars of shirt-sleeved salesmen: "We don't want you to agree with us, we want you to fight us."

Mr. Eldred, a slim, slightly balding 56-year-old executive, explains: "We don't sell hardware. We sell solutions to measurement problems." Indeed, he goes on to decry the very word selling: "Selling is the technique of getting people to part with their cash, and is short term and selfish because it focuses on the needs of the seller." He prefers "marketing," which he defines as "an integrated effort to discover, create, arouse and satisfy customer needs."

Whatever it may be called, the success of HP's selling—or marketing—approach is beyond dispute. The company was born in 1939 when its founders pieced together seven sound measuring devices in a Palo Alto garage, and sold them to Walt Disney to control sound track volume in his movie Fantasia.

Now HP turns out some 1,250 different devices which about 10,000 customers buy at prices ranging from $50 to $40,000 each.

Among other jobs, its gray-painted, dial-studded instruments measure crankshaft speeds in Caterpillar Tractor Co. diesel engine tests, check out Lockheed Aircraft Corp. systems for keeping in touch with satellites, test the welter of instruments in United Air Lines jet cockpits, instruct engineering students at California State Polytechnic College, and monitor the administration of anesthetics to patients in a Boston hospital operating room.

In 1963, HP's sales took 28% of what the Electronic Industries Association figures was a $413 million test instruments market, up from 15% of a $32 million market in 1958. In whimsical tribute to this growing market share, salesmen of Moxon Electronics Corp., Los Angeles, passed out coffee coasters to a large missile parts maker, admonishing its executives to "Break the HP Habit." And Boonton Electronics Corp., Parsippany, New Jersey, put up posters at a big electronics trade show urging its sales force to "Help Stamp Out HP."

But such exhortations haven't had much effect. Hewlett-Packard sales of $116 million in the fiscal year ended Oct. 31, 1963, were up 82% from fiscal 1958, and 417% ahead of volume 10 years earlier. That's nearly two and a half times the 171% growth rate achieved by the whole electronics industry in the same 10 years.

The company's profits, though they dropped 6% in fiscal 1963 because of accounting changes and some non-recurring charges, have in general kept pace. They have averaged an 18% annual gain in the past five fiscal years. HP sales in the 1964 fiscal year were up about 8%, and profits more than 28%, from the 1963 period.

None of this means HP salesmen can now rest on their oars, though. However well they may have learned the more than 31,000 specifications on HP's current products, there will be new ones to learn tomorrow. More than half of HP's sales in 1963 came from products that didn't exist in 1959, and in the 1964 fiscal year HP spent a record $11.4 million to develop more than 100 new products. Moreover, not all HP's customers need training; some know a good deal about the product line and, as HP salesmen wryly report, delight in testing a field engineer's recall of an obscure performance specification.

So the schooling of HP's 250 salesmen is a never-ending process. As Noel Eldred tells them: "You're calling on smart people who are interested in picking your brains, so you have to try to know more about their job than they do. If your technical presentation is skillful enough to make them see a use for your product, generally you've got a sale made. If not, they're turned off completely."

The schooling, of course, begins even before salesmen arrive. HP hires only salesmen with bachelors' engineering degrees, and about 20% have masters' degrees—though Noel Eldred believes that "the type of person who makes a good salesman doesn't spend too much time polishing his academic career." They also must have three to five years' practical engineering experience. HP is choosy in considering even people with these qualifications; it hires only about one of every 20 applicants.

Once hired, a salesman attends five weeks of intensive product indoctrination classes. These are held in the same classrooms where customers are trained. Around the year, when not being used for customers, these rooms are filled with HP sales and service people: Small batches of the total 175 technicians and specialists who staff repair centers in Palo Alto and Rockaway, New Jersey; student salesmen laboriously memorizing the line and its brain-numbing nomenclature; rookie salesmen being checked out on their knowledge of new products; senior salesmen in to have their "motivation" reinforced. Only for two weeks at year-end are the classrooms closed for what amounts to a Christmas vacation.

"It's tough," says Bill Blum, a portly, 30-year-old salesman, speaking of this constant schooling. "But without it, I'm the loser."

After his initial HP schooling, a salesman serves a year's apprenticeship as an office-bound "staff engineer," taking phoned orders, handling customers' calls for information, and generally familiarizing himself with the line. For another year he works as a fledgling "field engineer," making sales calls under close supervision before finally being given his own territory.

That territory, incidentally, often isn't the large geographic slice of the country that field salesmen for other types of products get. HP salesmen can't call on too many companies, because they usually can't sell to central purchasing departments; these generally can't tell an oscilloscope from an inverter. "U.S. Steel's purchasing people can't be expected to know what our equipment does, it's so technical," says Noel Eldred. "So we have to send direct mailings, catalogs and such to maybe 30 different people in the company."

An HP salesman's "territory," therefore, is likely to be only a small group of companies, and sometimes only a single big company. Many customers, such as Lockheed, Douglas Aircraft Co. and Hughes Aircraft Co., "have so many different labs and projects that we have one man there full-time, making the rounds as if to 20 different companies," says Mr. Eldred.

Whatever the salesman's "territory," HP's schoolmen don't leave him alone when he gets it. Once a year he has to attend a week-long seminar in one of HP's 12 U.S. plants; he also must pay at least a brief annual visit to each of the other 11. Roving instructors also pop into each field territory once a month for day-long refresher courses.

Even when the instructors aren't after them, HP salesmen in local offices are pitted against each other at least one night a month in mock sales duels. They probe for weak spots in each other's presentations, and test ways to make selling points stronger. And when not attending some mandatory meeting salesmen often spend evenings cramming for tomorrow's "exam" from the customer.

As Hewlett-Packard's mostly young and ambitious salesmen readily admit, even this incessant education gives them only a "broad band with a low Q"—electronics jargon for a smattering of knowledge in many fields. To help them out, HP cloisters 10 "narrow band, high Q" wizards in its Palo Alto headquarters, and they're frequently called; the regular salesmen regard themselves as general practitioners of instrumentation and are quick to holler for the specialist when needed. "Getting caught wrong by some Ph.D. in a hairy mathematics discussion only has to happen once to convince you it's better to just say 'I don't know,'" says Bill Blum.

But, however broad their band or low their Q, HP's regular salesmen are schooled to give the customer all the service they can. They spend endless hours instructing customers in the servicing of instruments. An observer accompanying crew-cut Bill Blum on his rounds recently watched him spend an entire morning showing a small defense subcontractor the fine points of using a single inexpensive instrument the customer had bought the week before.

"I'm losing money doing this," says Bill, who like most HP salesmen is paid by a combination of base salary plus commissions, derived from sales. "But it's part of our service

reputation that we don't just sell an instrument and then forget it. We're out to help the customer, not just make the money. That's where we shine."

Customers large and small confirm that this attitude scores with them. "HP is a household word around here," says Ed C. Schaefer, a buyer for the Missile and Space Systems Division of Douglas Aircraft. "We prefer them because all you have to do is call their man to have him come in on any problem or service any complaint. Other companies haven't tried to give us an engineer who can move in and out of any project."

McCormick Selph Associates, Inc., Hollister, California, maker of detonators and other explosives for aerospace uses, sees an HP salesman only once every four months. But it still buys between $5,000 and $10,000 worth of equipment from him each year, because "he gives us particulars on what we're interested in and helps us with any problems we have," says test department manager Sal Cascino.

HP salesmen are more than salesmen in another way, too; the company uses them as new-product idea men. By siding with customer complaints about the inadequacies of existing instruments, salesmen often have prodded the company to come up with the new products vital to success in the fast-moving instrument field.

For example, Noel Eldred relates, a salesman calling on International Business Machines Corp. some time ago found that existing oscilloscopes (gadgets with a radar-like appearance that display electrical signals as blips on a round screen) were ineffective in testing high-speed computers. They couldn't keep up with the stream of electrical pulses the computers poured out. The salesman's relaying of these complaints prompted HP's design staff to come up with one of the company's largest-selling instruments—a sampling oscilloscope that records only every fourth or fifth pulse in a fast-moving train of electrical signals.

When completely new products aren't needed, HP salesmen often push the company to modify existing products to serve a customer's special need. Each of HP's nine manufacturing divisions maintains a "special handling" department to make good on field engineers' promises that the company will supply custom-made equipment, and salesmen keep these departments scrambling.

Six Palo Alto engineers, for example, worked nights for three months to cut the height of an

HP multi-instrument package to three inches from a foot so that Varian Associates, Inc., could deliver a shipboard instrument system before the deadline of a lucrative Navy contract.

For all this effort, HP liberally rewards its hard-driven salesmen both with money and recognition. Salesmen receive from $9,000 a year for a 26-to-28-year-old beginner to a maximum $18,000 for a six-to-eight-year veteran. Most of this is fixed base salary, but between 25% and 50% is commission income tied to fulfillment of sales quotas.

For the salesman who might feel unappreciated despite this high income, HP has a wide array of morale boosters: Service pins, seminar graduation certificates, mentions in company house organs, local salesman-of-the-month citations. Most prized are fairly frequent "good work" letters from Noel Eldred.

But HP doesn't shrink from using the stick as well as the carrot to keep salesmen hustling. For the type of salesman who runs hardest when being chased, "we spend an inordinate amount of time stressing the competition, discussing, evaluating, comparing even with some products where we have, say, 90% of a market and not much to worry about," says a marketing staffer.

HP supplements the salesmen's efforts by exhibiting at six national trade shows a year—plus innumerable regional shows, where it is represented by one of its local sales offices, and medical shows, where only one HP division shows its wares.

Noel Eldred attends each of the big six trade shows to hobnob personally with big customers, and seldom passes a work week without a couple of skirmishes in what subordinates describe as a "running battle" with HP's research and development men over the readiness of new products for introduction at these shows. In one year HP displayed more than 50 new products at each of the two biggest shows: The Institute of Electrical & Electronics Engineers (IEEE) Exhibit, held each March in New York, and the Western Electronics Show and Convention (WESCON), held in August in either San Francisco or Los Angeles.

Though mobilizing for major shows is a demanding and costly undertaking, HP considers them a bargain at the price. The company's booth at the IEEE show required $100,000 to construct and staff with 50 men. Yet it reached potential customers at a cost of $3 to $5 a head, one-tenth the cost of a field engineer's typical sales call. And there's little doubt it generates many sales. Hewlett-Packard's second-half sales traditionally jump about 10% over first-half volume almost entirely on the impetus of the IEEE exhibit.

HP used to get additional exposure for its products at trade shows by offering to lend its instruments to other companies to use in exhibiting their own products. But the company was stunned by the growing number of takers, and now grants such "loaners" by request only. Still, the company had about 100 brand new devices out on loan at one year's WESCON show, with one salesman detailed just to make the rounds of other booths checking on the operation of HP gear. Before tightening up, the company had as many as 500 instruments loaned out at an IEEE exposition, at a cost of $50,000 merely to renovate them when reclaimed.

Even more important than trade shows, Noel Eldred believes, is the company's dissemination of technical information—a mammoth mailing program that annually costs about $500,000 and distributes more than 6 million pieces of literature. Some 100,000 customers on the mailing list get a monthly, slick-paper Hewlett-Packard Journal of research advances in the general measurement field, as well as more partisan bi-monthly new product mailers, blizzards of instrument data sheets as substitutes for personal sales presentations, requested ad reproductions, instruction manuals, maintenance hints, and hypertechnical notes on applications of new techniques. In addition, every two years the company produces a ponderous, 400-plus-page comprehensive catalog that accounts for about half its total publishing bill.

And, in about its only approach to the flamboyant techniques of consumer-goods selling, HP sends 11 equipment-laden vans rolling to the doors of an average 22 customers a day for the electronic equivalent of the traveling medicine show. The vans range in size from delivery trucks to a mahogany paneled, $50,000 Scenicruiser bus carrying a $100,000 inventory.

Whether all these efforts will be able to keep HP growing at the blazing pace of the past few years remains to be seen. Since 1958 HP has plunged into a dizzying acquisition and expansion program. In one six-year period it acquired and made divisions out of six manufacturing concerns and has bought up 10 of 14 sales firms which formerly handled its products on an independent representative basis. It also has spread overseas, establishing six manufacturing and sales affiliates in Europe and a joint venture in Japan. It also has enlarged its sprawling hilltop headquarters in Stanford University's pastoral industrial preserve, and sees a need to expand in England "in a year or so."

Still, the company's sales growth, in percentage terms, has been slowing. Sales for the 1964 fiscal year were $124,909,724, a record but up only 8% from fiscal 1963; that trails the 19% average annual gain of the previous five fiscal years. "It's difficult to achieve as rapid growth as we did when we were smaller," concedes David Packard, chairman.

Noel Eldred expects a return to the 19% annual growth rate, but says "it will be done by spreading the breadth of our activity, not sim-

ply in the electronics business." The company's acquisition of Delcon Corp., a Palo Alto maker of ultrasonic industrial test devices and communications equipment, reflects this diversification-mindedness, Mr. Packard says.

In the electronics business, however, competitors see no signs HP will slow up enough to make their lot any easier. "They've got a darn good product, a great deal of initiative and drive, and one of the country's best sales executives," says Arthur Thiessen, chairman of General Radio Co., West Concord, Massachusetts. "There are no chinks in their marketing armor." And Edward T. Clare, marketing vice president of Cohu Electronics, Inc., San Diego, in a burst of startling frankness, describes his company's competitive prospects: "About all that's left open to us is to look for holes in HP's line."

Electrolux: ". . . face those doorbells with that up-and-at-'em spirit."

Mrs. Douglas Yerger, a Pottstown, Pennsylvania, housewife, thought she didn't need a new vacuum cleaner—much less one priced, with attachments, at $207.80. But Tony Rossi, knocking on her door just after supper, changed her mind. "He's a wonderful salesman," Mrs. Yerger beams.

Neighbors don't all share her enthusiasm, however. Before visiting Mrs. Yerger, Tony Rossi had got inside only three Pottstown doors to give a demonstration ("demo" as he calls it), and none had ended in a sale. Some 50 other doors were closed in his face that day, and not always softly."It's none of your business how I am," one woman snapped at Tony's polite opening line.

Tony has long since learned to take such experiences in stride. But he has done so only because Electrolux Corp. long ago learned it had to do two selling jobs. The one performed by Tony and 6,000 other canvassers on people like Mrs. Yerger is the more obvious. But the one performed by the company on the salesmen, to keep their confidence and enthusiasm high in the face of constant potential discouragement (Tony's one-sale-for-54-calls day in Pottstown is all too typical) is perhaps the more vital. For Electrolux, unlike any of its major vacuum cleaner competitors, lives almost entirely by door-to-door selling, and thus is largely at the mercy of Tony and his colleagues.

In both its selling jobs, Electrolux employs methods that would make sophisticates cringe. When knocking on doors, Mr. Rossi often greets housewives with humor of the most elementary but effective sort. "Mrs. Lazzeri—there's a good Irish name," he says to one lady. And he gravely tells a woman more than old enough to be his mother: "You can call me at home any time, Mrs. Lawson, and my wife won't know a thing."

On other calls Tony, an eight-year veteran, tries to arouse sympathy. If a trainee or partner is working the other side of the street, he may plead with a woman: "Please let me in. That man over there is my boss, and I haven't made a demonstration yet today."

To keep salesmen using such gimmicks with undiminished zeal visit after visit, Tony's superiors appeal to a curious mixture of acquisitiveness, altruism and ebullience. Salesmen's pay consists entirely of commissions and bonuses, but these are lavish. And they are supplemented by glittering sales-contest prizes, including trips, Cadillacs, color TV sets and cashmere overcoats; even the most modest accomplishments rate shirts or ties. In commissions and prizes, Tony Rossi makes about $20,000 a year on the $50,000 sales he rings up yearly for Electrolux.

Yet the salesman is urged to strive for the betterment of others, not himself. Many prizes, such as trips, fur coats and bicycles, are aimed at wives and children, and signs in the Upper Darby, Pennsylvania, sales office proclaim: "I pledge to my wife, my family and my organization a minimum of 5 selling demos daily." The salesman further is taught that however high his earnings climb, he hasn't fulfilled himself until he has brought "less fortunate" men into the organization and helped them to make as much.

Salesmen are further fired with enthusiasm at sales-talk rehearsals, self-analysis sessions re-

◆ SOURCE: Reprinted by permission from *How They Sell*, editors of *The Wall Street Journal* (Dow Jones & Company, Inc., 1965), pp. 175–190.

miniscent of group therapy, and branch meetings that take on the atmosphere of a New Year's Eve party crossed with a high school football rally. The rooms in which these meetings are held may be filled with balloons. An Electrolux house organ reported that one meeting at Easton, Pennsylvania, "got started with a big bang as those 10 hand-clapping, singing men made short work of the balloons."

Then the meeting may break into a company song. A visitor to a recent Upper Darby meeting heard salesmen bellowing this one, to the tune of "I've Been Working on the Railroad":

"We've been working with Eluxes, going out each day
If you want to sell in volume, show them 10 times a day
Ask them how the cleaner's working; sit inside and see
You can't sell them on the doorstep; inside you must be
Show the Model G, show the Model L
Show the Model G toda-a-ay . . ."

Difficult as it might seem to take some of this with a straight face, there's no questioning its success. Electrolux is generally ranked third in the vacuum cleaner business, behind Hoover Co. and General Electric Co. George Holmen, its Swedish-born president, says sales have risen every year since 1957, and in 1964 topped $103 million, compared to $95,078,131 in 1963.

Electrolux profits nearly doubled in the five years from 1959 through 1963, rising to $6 million that year and in 1964 rose to $7,702,016.

Electrolux's success is the more impressive in view of its unusual position as a door-to-door seller. When Gustaf Sahlin came to the U.S. 40 years ago to open an American branch of Electrolux Co. of Sweden, nearly all vacuum cleaners were sold door-to-door. But in the intervening years, as the company gradually became independent of Swedish control (the Swedish Electrolux now holds only about a one-third interest) its major rivals gradually gave up door-to-door selling.

The rivals had reason. Door-to-door selling is a giant business; the National Association of Direct Selling Companies, a trade group, estimates door-bell-ringers in 1964 chalked up sales of $3 billion. But the most successful and best-known companies in the field, such as Fuller Brush Co. and cosmetics-making Avon Products, Inc., mostly sell relatively small and inexpensive products.

95847

"Eluxes," in contrast, are expensive even for vacuum cleaners. Twelve competitive tank-type cleaners rated "acceptable" by Consumer Reports magazine list at retail for $59.95 to $89.95. But the Electrolux standard Model L is priced at $94.75. The "automatic" Model G, which stops itself when the dust bag is full, sells for $149.75. A wide array of attachments add to the cost. An Electrolux "power nozzle," with separately powered rotating brush for better rug cleaning, sells for $49.75; a rug shampooer costs $39.75.

Moreover, though many vacuum cleaner companies will shave list prices, if a discount house doesn't do it for them, Electrolux never does. Door-to-door salesmen never offer a housewife a special sale price, and cannot even shave commissions to build sales totals; they send the money or installment contracts they collect to the company and the company mails them commission checks. Some competitors believe Electrolux salesmen frequently give their customers cash rebates, but the company says it catches few doing this (they're fired immediately).

One reason for keeping prices up, Electrolux admits, is to protect salesmen's commissions, an important motivation factor. But its main contention is that its cleaners have to be the highest-priced on the market, because they're the highest quality. Consumer Reports rated Electrolux machines at the top of a list of 13 brands of tank-type cleaners. But it added: "There are good tank cleaners (at) less than half the cost of an Electrolux. While not equal to the latter in over-all quality, these lower-rated vacuums still offer fully satisfactory service."

Be that as it may, Electrolux says it finds price no great barrier in door-to-door selling (when it did try to sell a low-priced cleaner, in 1956 and 1957, its sales and profits actually fell). Its average sale now is $170, including an average $53 commission. But slightly more than half its machines are sold on credit. Thus Tony Rossi can close a sale for as little as $10 down, a figure he naturally stresses in his sales talk.

And Electrolux is firmly wedded to door-to-door selling for other reasons. If it sold through retailers, "we'd be just one more cleaner on Macy's floor, and that isn't the way to sell in volume," says A. J. Darnall, sales vice president. Electrolux salesmen don't avoid competition; they're eager to show a housewife that an Electrolux picks up dirt her old cleaner leaves behind. But the women they call on have a yes-or-no choice of buying an Electrolux, not a choice among several competing brands.

Selling door-to-door, Electrolux avoids many costs of selling through distributors and retailers. Getting full retail price, it can devote to salesmen's commissions and contest prizes the money that would otherwise become the profit of a retailer who would have no special reason to push Electrolux over the other brands. And its product advertising costs are held close to zero. The company's national advertising consists of one ad a year in Good Housekeeping magazine, entered to qualify for that magazine's prestigious Seal of Approval.

But if door-to-door selling makes some standard merchandising techniques unnecessary, it requires special techniques of its own. Most, of course, are familiar to consumers. But they look a bit different when seen from the other side of the door, through the eyes of a salesman like Tony Rossi.

Tony, a six-foot, 212-pounder and an outdoorsman who shoots one deer every year, grew up on his father's farm near Lionville, Pennsylvania, and originally was a farmer himself. But he made only $3,000 a year at farming, and had to supplement it by taking a night-time job as a toll collector on the Pennsylvania Turnpike. Dissatisfied, he began selling Electroluxes part-time, and made $8,000 his first year. That rose to $11,000 his first year of full-time selling.

He has been climbing in the company ever since, and has become manager of the West Chester, Pennsylvania, sales branch, charged with finding and training new salesmen. But he keeps up a daily schedule of full-time selling. "I like the money," he says bluntly. "Where else could a man who quit school in the tenth grade earn money like this?"

His preparation for his rounds begins with things that might seem far removed from selling. He drives a white Chrysler convertible which he chose over the Cadillac he could have afforded because he thinks a Cadillac would be too ostentatious for a salesman. If any customer asks "why should I buy something to help a guy who drives a Chrysler?" he has a ready reply: "Wouldn't you rather deal with a successful salesman with a fine product than with somebody who can't make any money at it?"

At the wheel, Tony heads for established, solid-looking, middle-class neighborhoods, with credit sales in mind. "You get so you can tell by how the house is kept, and what the car and the furnishings are like, whether the people will make an honest effort to keep up the payments," he says. He avoids not only poor neighborhoods, but brand-new housing developments and small homes likely to be owned by very young married couples. "They may be in the market for a cleaner, but very often they're already deep in debt, sometimes deeper than they realize," he says. If payments on a machine stop, and Electrolux has to repossess the cleaner, Tony has to return his commission on the sale to the company.

Parking his car at a corner and his cigar in the ash tray, Tony sets out for the first house. He doesn't smoke in a customer's home and never drinks during working hours, a rule for all salesmen.

On the doorstep, if no one answers his ring, he tucks a self-addressed postcard in the mailbox that can be used to request a later call. If a woman is on her way out, he fishes for an invitation to return, which he can take up on a rainy day when "blind" canvassing is unpleasant. He got such an invitation the other day from a stern-looking teacher in Downington, Pennsylvania, who greeted his opening pleasantries with sarcasm, after leading her into a rambling conversation about local school officials who have Electroluxes.

To women obviously not going anywhere, his approach is direct: "How are you? How's your vacuum cleaner doing? I'm in the neighborhood showing the new Electrolux, and I'd like very much to give you a demonstration at no cost or obligation to you." If the woman already has an Electrolux, he volunteers to give it a free check; he might sell a package of dust bags or even an attachment.

At the slightest sign of welcome Tony rushes to his car and hauls a cleaner out of the trunk. Inside, he asks permission to remove his coat, and begins "piling dirt." This is the essence of the demo. The salesman cleans a patch of carpet, opens the machine, and dumps the dirt back on the rug, talking all the time about the machine until he has made a row of 20 or so piles.

"You wouldn't believe all that dirt could hide in that carpet you swept just the other day, would you, Mrs. Willensky?" he asks. He shows how the cleaner can pick up three heavy steel balls, and how it can clean furniture and draperies as well as carpets.

If the customer is plainly uninterested, Tony

sweeps up the piles of dirt, gets permission to wash his hands, and departs without pressing, though leaving a card. He did this in Pottstown with a young baker's wife who, between attending to her newborn baby, told him she liked the Electrolux but didn't see how she could afford it. "They really can't afford it," he said outside. "If I go back in six months to a year, though, I may get a good sale."

But if the customer is still interested, Tony shifts gradually from the demo into the selling "close." In one home recently it went like this: "You can see that you need an Electrolux; the cleaner you have is all right, but see how much dirt it left." In response to some murmurs about the price: "If you could afford it right now, wouldn't you take it? Of course, you would. So all you have to give me is $10, and I'll leave this machine right here."

Then, with great sincerity: "Look, Mrs. Willensky, I'm going to do something for you. I'm going to give you the maximum allowance on your old machine ($20 for a competing brand, $29 for an Electrolux) to help you out. I know you want this machine, and I really want to make this sale. You talk it over with your husband. Tell him about the trade-in and the 18 months to pay. I'm so sure he'll want you to have it that I'll come back this evening when he's here, and you can sign the contract then."

Such tactics make the door-to-door salesman's hours unorthodox. Tony usually canvasses from 10 A.M. to noon, from 1 to 5, and from 6 to 8 P.M. weekdays, and from 10 A.M. to 5 P.M. on Saturday. He may work later or on Sunday to close a sale or win a contest. Contests, he finds, interest customers as well as salesmen. "You tell people that you can win a suit or a trip to Florida for your family if you make so many sales by Monday, and they really want to help you," he says.

Tony himself has won trips not only to Florida but to Colorado; his willowy wife, Alice, went on all of them, and on some took their children: daughters Bonita and Toni, and son Mark. Tony also has won diamond rings for Alice and himself, a mink jacket for Alice, a rifle, a shotgun and a stereophonic phonograph. The Rossis live in a $25,000 ranch house Tony had a builder put up on his father's farm; sitting in their recently purchased "Spanish modern" furniture they can gaze through the glass west wall at wooded hills.

Tony finds all this ample reward for the long hours, the night calls, and the doors slammed in his face. But not all salesmen have his natural drive and optimism—and not all achieve his average of one sale for every three demos; they're supposed to make up for it by steadily pushing themselves to ring more bells and make more demos.

To keep them doing so, Electrolux management at all levels has to devote most of its time to pumping up their loyalty and ambition.

The principal requirements for salesmen are that they be bondable and of good character. Background doesn't count: Sam Rodbard, a 67-year-old former Chicago tailor, and Jimmy Uyeshima, a blind Californian, have become highly successful salesmen; and Dewey Howard, a former minister from Boise, Idaho, was crowned national Electrolux sales champion in 1963, with volume in the preceding 12 months of $94,209. "We don't have trouble hiring people, it's holding them," says Mr. Darnall, the sales vice president. He concedes turnover is high, though he won't disclose the rate.

To hold men, Electrolux has made them employes, instead of independent contractors, as most door-to-door salesmen are. Thus, it deducts Social Security payments from commission checks and provides health insurance and a pension plan. And it appeals incessantly to their desires for money and recognition.

"You have so much to talk about when you're talking to your neighbors, friends and others about this business," Mr. Darnall told one of the sales conventions Electrolux holds thrice yearly. "Talk about your earnings! Talk about your prizes! Talk about the automobiles that are won! You'll find they can hardly believe it." Sales managers set something of an example in this regard; several are rumored to be millionaires, and they're careful never to do anything to discourage such talk.

Salesmen get recognition from the company as well as their neighbors. A vice president of another door-to-door selling firm comments: "Countless millions of people go through life with no recognition, but Electrolux puts their names and pictures in company newspapers, and they just love it. Adults seek recognition like children who want Sunday school medals."

An important source of recognition is the frequent banquets and meetings held by Electrolux's seven sales regions, 42 divisions and 367 branches to present sales awards. These gatherings, says the official Electrolux history, "are strictly black-tie events, to point up the dignity of the affair and of the salesman's calling." Wives are required to attend, for a wife is a "valued and welcome" member of the Electrolux "family."

Electrolux tries in other ways to get the salesman's wife to fulfill what the book calls "her No. 1 responsibility"—to keep her husband "in a cheerful frame of mind so that he can face those doorbells each day with that up-and-at-'em spirit." Wives are informed directly about contests and the prizes at stake, so they can prod their husbands. It's not unknown for the boss of a slipping salesman to approach his wife directly to ask her to give him more encouragement, or even to discuss family problems, if these seem to be distracting her man from his job.

Among the salesmen themselves, the regular branch meeting is the focus for both inspirational and prodding efforts. Most offices meet every morning for a half hour or so and, in between the balloon-breaking and singing, conduct some business. On some mornings, this will be a sales rehearsal. One man plays the part of a reluctant housewife, another tries his best selling approach on "her," and the rest kibitz.

Other sessions feature an odd combination of boasting and revival-meeting-style confession. First each successful salesman describes a recent sale—how he won a housewife's confidence, how he overcame her objections. Then a man who hasn't made a sale in a week gets the floor, and is interrogated: Did he allow himself to get discouraged? Did he take an afternoon off to play golf? Did he skip a morning meeting and start the day with a sour face? Did he forget to ring every bell on the street, to think of his wife and children, to demonstrate the power nozzle? The meeting doesn't end until he has re-examined his attitude, confessed his mistakes, accepted the counsel of his brethren, and sworn to make a sale that day.

Whatever an outsider might make of such antics, they have made enough money for Electrolux to provide the funds for a sharp expansion. In a diversification move, the company bought White Mop Wringer Co., which makes janitor supplies for factories and office buildings.

To expand its door-to-door operation, Electrolux in one year has opened 31 branch offices, including Tony Rossi's, and plans to keep up the pace. "We haven't begun to cover the U.S.," says Mr. Darnall. It hopes to staff the offices with salesmen who will bawl lustily, to the tune of "Hey, Look Me Over":

"Hey, look us over, when we ring your bell
We have something for you we know you'll
*   think is swell*
The cost is really low; you ought to see it go
You press on the button and move your arm
Away the dirt will go . . ."

C. Sales as Communication

The Industrial Salesman as a Source of Market Information

FREDERICK E. WEBSTER, JR.

The central element in the promotional strategy of the majority of companies is the salesman—not advertising. Investigation suggests that few firms are using salesmen to the best advantage. By limiting, either explicitly or implicitly, the salesman's role to that of a promotional agent, the company minimizes his opportunity to function as a source of market information.

VALUE OF MARKET INFORMATION

In the past decade especially, managers and educators have been exposed to a large quantity of literature expounding the so-called marketing concept. The various interpretations of the marketing concept have at least one common ingredient—emphasis on the importance of information about customers' needs and wants as an essential basis for management decisions. Under this concept, the marketing task is to direct the firm's operations toward the product and service requirements of customers. Marketing starts with the customer, not the product. In fact, the whole course of business starts with the customer by first learning what his needs are and then determining whether and how the company is able to provide a commodity that can contribute to the customer's satisfaction.

◆ SOURCE: Reprinted by permission from *Business Horizons* (Indiana University), Spring 1965.

Gathering information and using it to make decisions are most visible in customer survey marketing research. A different kind of information gathering is represented by the day-to-day reports of market information by the sales force. As compared with survey research, salesmen's information about customers, competitors, and other market factors offers the following advantages:

1. The incremental costs are low
2. The salesman tends to have well-established relationships with customers and a familiarity with their needs and wants
3. Customers, to the extent that they perceive the salesman and his company as a potential supplier of problem-solving products and services, will be more willing to provide information to salesmen than to an unknown questioner
4. Salesmen can collect and report information with little additional effort, submitting it with their regular call reports.

Because the research for this article exclusively concerned technical industrial products, the following discussion pertains primarily to industrial companies characterized by:

Heavy reliance upon salesmen as opposed to advertising

A product line that changes continually as the result of technological developments

Flexibility in adapting product designs to fit customer requirements, which also change

43

rapidly as the result of technological developments

Markets consisting of easily identified customers, actual and potential, in terms of numbers, size, and location.

It should be stressed that these are factual observations, not assumptions, about companies selling technical products to industrial producers. With the exception of the changing product line, these characteristics pertain to most firms selling in industrial markets. The industrial supplier probably needs more and better information about customer requirements than the consumer goods producer because of the relatively greater importance of the individual customer to the firm's operations. While the industrial salesman is still important as a promotional agent, he must operate within the constraints established by the customer's production requirements.

USING SALESMEN'S INFORMATION

Use of the salesman for gathering information can be much more critical than his use for promotion. While this generalization obviously does not hold for every company and every industry, the practices of several electronics firms suggest that industrial marketing efficiency can be greatly improved through increased reliance upon the salesman as a source of market information. This article will focus upon four principal uses of information provided by salesmen: product planning, sales forecasting, competitive strategy, and pricing. These are not the only areas where the salesman can provide essential information, nor are they independent. For example, pricing and competitive strategy involve wide areas of interdependence. Also, the salesman is certainly an important source of information on matters relating to sales force management. In the following discussion, however, only these four functions will be considered.

Product Planning

The company supplying industrial manufacturers must frequently adapt or modify its product line to fit customers' needs. To be effective each change must be based on sound information about what the customers require. While salesmen may have substantial bias with respect to product development needs, just as engineers do, the salesman gains information about the market more easily than does the development engineer. Thus, the salesman's bias can provide a necessary offset for the engineer's bias.

For the industrial producer, product planning frequently involves anticipation of changing customer product requirements with a carefully planned technical development program. As one moves along the continuum of nontechnical to technical products, anticipating the changing customer requirements becomes more complex. The development process can only be efficient to the extent that it is based on current, complete, and correct information about customers' requirements and plans. Although prediction can never be entirely accurate, it is possible to develop a more direct approach if accurate information is available. Specific development targets can replace such generalized developmental research goals as "to advance the state-of-the-art," which are more appropriate for basic research. A rifle can be substituted for a shotgun in R&D efforts, with the payoff of increased results and lower costs.

Although this point of view seems obvious, the author's research suggests that it is not always obvious to engineering groups, to management in general, or even to marketing management in the companies that were studied. All too frequently, marketing has defined too narrowly its role in company operations. Technically-oriented firms in particular have been slow to recognize the need for defining marketing in terms broader than selling. One result has been inefficiency in the product development program; all companies studied could report at least one instance of developing a product for which there was virtually no market demand, and many marketing opportunities have been foregone because the company did not have a product to meet the new requirements of its customers.

To define the salesman as a selling agent exclusively is to ignore the opportunity for significant improvement in product planning efficiency. Salesmen in industrial companies are usually sufficiently well trained (many have at least a bachelor's degree in engineering) to be able to perform an initial evaluation of the feasibility of a customer's requests for a product modification or development. The risk is not great, therefore, if salesmen are given the task of providing new product ideas, of generating too many irresponsible development ideas. Furthermore, the salesman is particularly sensitive to the adequacy of his company's product offerings in respect to market demands. He is sensitive to obsolescence and gaps in the company's product line because they make his selling job more difficult.

Sales Forecasting

Information supplied by salesmen is more commonly used for sales forecasting than for product planning. They frequently provide estimates of the size of the market in their assigned territories and occasionally break down these estimates into product groupings. The estimates are used to compute sales forecasts, which in turn are used for sales force evaluation and control, sales budgeting, and production planning. Different forecasts are frequently used for each purpose.

A unique dimension of forecasting presents itself to companies that rely on competitive bidding for most of their sales volume. Here the problem is to estimate the likelihood of winning a particular contract, rather than the size of the market. This is the major forecasting problem for the defense contractor, although it is typical of any firm relying on competitive bidding. One approach to forecasting bidding success defines a unique role for the salesman.

A company asked its salesmen to assign probabilities to the event of winning contracts on which it had bid. The dollar value of the potential contract, multiplied by this probability, provided an expected value for the contract. By adding expected values for each outstanding bid, the company obtained a sales forecast they could use as the basis for production planning in the current period. (This will be recognized as a simple application of Bayesian decision theory.)

An example will make the procedure clear. Assume that the company has four outstanding bids to be opened during the current period, and that these bids are for $100,000; $200,000; $50,000; and $500,000. If the company were certain of success in each of these bidding competitions, the sales forecast would be $850,- 000. But because of competitive bidding the company cannot be certain of winning each contract award, so the sales forecast should be less than $850,000. Salesmen assigned to each of these four accounts provided the following estimates of the chance of winning each contract: 25 per cent, 50 per cent, 10 per cent, and 30 per cent respectively. The table summa- rizes the calculations necessary to arrive at a forecast.

Contract	Bid Price	Probability of Winning Award	Expected Revenue from Each Award
A	$100,000	.25	$ 25,000
B	200,000	.50	100,000
C	50,000	.10	5,000
D	500,000	.30	150,000
Sales Forecast = Total Expected Revenue =			$280,000

This example is somewhat unrealistic because the small number of contracts introduces a great deal of variability in estimates. When the number of outstanding bids is large, however, and salesmen do not exhibit consistent bias, very accurate estimates can result. The company using this method reported an enviable average variability of 1.5 per cent on a monthly basis.

The "probability of winning award" is really a very complex statistic summarizing information about the conditions surrounding the bidding competition, including: the strength of the company with the particular customer, compared with competition; an estimate of competitive bid prices; the acceptability of the company's bid in terms of product offering; and, if available, the salesman's evaluation of the effectiveness of the presentation. Each of these factors is likely to be significant in the customer's final award decision, especially if there are differences in the "technical proposals" or product offerings submitted by competing bidders. Of course, if the procurement is strictly a "nuts and bolts affair" and all products precisely meet rigorous specification requirements, then the decision is likely to be influenced solely by price. In many industrial procurement situations, however, bidders vary considerably in their product offerings and nonprice factors become important.

In these complex procurement situations, the salesman is in the best position to estimate the company's various strengths and weaknesses. The assignment of probabilities forces the salesman to think explicitly and to quantify his judgment of his company's competitive strength. The probability figure summarizes the influence of a host of competitive factors upon revenue expectations. Because of his familiarity with the customer and with the local competitive situation, the salesman can make this estimate with greater accuracy than a less well-informed observer.

The preceding discussion has concentrated on one aspect of the salesman's potential contribution to sales forecasting; the competitive bidding situation defines a special role for the salesman. Extension of this basic approach to other estimates of market potential and market share, using probability notions, is fairly straightforward. The arguments in favor of using salesmen as sources of information for sales forecasting in general are well known and will not be repeated here.

Competitive Strategy

It is somewhat unrealistic to separate competitive strategy from other marketing considerations since each decision, whether in the area of product, price, promotion, or marketing-channels policies, cannot be realistically separated from the over-all competitive strategy and marketing mix. Nonetheless, to explore competitive strategy as a separate area highlights the need for information about competitors' actions. Proximity to the market gives the salesman an opportunity to provide information about competitors' actions.

The industrial market is dynamic because of changing customer requirements and is made increasingly dynamic by the variability in competitors' reactions to changing customer requirements and to each other. Any marketing decision that does not take competitors' behavior into account is likely to lead up a blind alley.

The salesman once again has an important role to play in providing information on competitors' offerings and plans, not only in terms of products, but also such diverse elements of the marketing mix as pricing, delivery commitments, call frequency, credit terms, warranties, follow-up services, and trade relations. The salesman has access to two sources of information about competitors' plans and activities—competitors' salesmen and customers. Most certainly, customers represent the better source of information, since competitors will obviously try to keep important strategic activities confidential. Customers are frequently willing to talk about promises and commitments made by competitors, however, hoping for a more favorable commitment from the salesman.

Information about competitors can be used effectively by the company in planning competitive strategy and in modifying the marketing mix. Trade journals, trade shows, and the inevitable grapevine are all very useful supplements—but the salesman has the best access to current and continuous information about competitors' behavior. He can provide it routinely as part of his reporting procedures, or he can provide specific information about a course of action being contemplated by the company. For example, he can solicit customers' reactions to a planned product modification, a change in billing procedures, or virtually any other element of the marketing program that is likely to affect the customer's decisions about suppliers. The salesman might find, for example, that competitors had recently begun promoting a new product similar to one being contemplated by his company. Thus, the salesman can be used to provide information about competitors' activities, customers' reactions to competitors' offerings, and customers' probable reaction to changes in company strategy. Each kind of information is significant in evaluating potential changes in the company's competitive strategy.

Pricing Decisions

Nowhere is the need for information about competitors' practices and customer reaction made clearer than in the pricing decision. Salesmen are quite frequently asked to determine what the market will bear. In many industrial market segments, product offerings are diverse and there is no established market price for a product, although there may be many close substitutes. Often, the nub of the problem is to predict how much extra the market is willing to pay for a particular product feature. The salesman may be able to provide a good estimate of an appropriate selling price.

In the competitive bidding situation, the salesman's conversations with a buyer may reveal, within narrow limits, the prices being quoted by competitors. While several ethical issues are involved that we cannot explore here, many of our respondents reported that the critical function of the salesman in a competitive bidding procedure is to find out what the competition has bid. A common practice, often referred to as the Chinese auction, consists of the buyer telling each salesman that his company's bid is higher than another company's bid in an attempt to force the price as low as possible. The salesman must then estimate the truthfulness of the buyer's statement in order to determine what price quotation to recommend to his company.

In the more general pricing situation, the salesman has access to three types of information that are necessary inputs to the pricing decision: the value of the product in the customer's planned application or end-use; the prices being quoted by competitors for similar products; and the customer's expectations about the price he will have to pay. Because each type of information is likely to be peculiar to the individual customer, and because the salesman is closest to the customer, the salesman is in the best position to estimate the price the customer is willing to pay for a given product.

IMPLEMENTING THE SALESMAN'S INFORMATION RESPONSIBILITY

The task of holding the salesman responsible for supplying information is easier if it is carefully planned, has clearly defined objectives, and makes specific provision for evaluation and control. Many companies studied recognized the potential contribution of their sales force, but had been frustrated in their attempts to make the plan operational. The major problems appear to be training salesmen to provide information and making effective use of the information in company planning. Because the task places increased demands upon the salesman, he will probably not perform it unless he is specifically ordered to. And the information will be of little value unless the company has specific procedures for summarizing and evaluating it. One of the companies studied required that the salesman fill out a report on each call. This generated more than two hundred call reports per day, which the marketing manager's secretary screened. She filed the reports that were not of more than routine interest, and the company made no further use of the information in them.

The salesman must be informed as to what kinds of information are useful to, and required by, the company which will use it. The R&D group will want one kind of information, the production department another, and the sales manager yet a third kind. Information required and requested by each department should be evaluated to determine whether the potential contribution warrants the cost and effort of obtaining it. Specific procedures must then be established for collection, summarization, and evaluation. Finally, some method of evaluating the salesman's collection efforts must be established for control purposes. Most frequently, this evaluation is best performed by the person or group using the information, in conjunction with the sales manager.

Doesn't this informational role place a tremendous burden upon the salesman, a burden he will resist and resent? Unfortunately, the answer is affirmative unless the salesman sees results that increase his effectiveness. Whether or not he sees these results depends strongly upon the ability of the organization to use the information efficiently and intelligently. If the company is using the salesman's information to keep its product and marketing strategy optimally tuned to the ever-changing requirements of the market, selling the product will be a much easier job.

The customer contact function is useful as both a source and a use of information. In his contact with customers, the salesman obtains information that is used as an input for strategy decisions; the output of these decisions is a set of strategy directives designed to increase the promotional efficiency of the salesman in his contact with customers. If the company is making proper use of the salesman as a source of information, and is using that information effectively, product offerings will be optimally fitted to market requirements, as will the company's other services and terms of sale.

Furthermore, the salesman will find satisfaction in being asked to play a critical function in the company's planning efforts. If this contributes to his selling effectiveness, the salesman is going to see the importance of the information that he provided. Inherent in the intelligent use of salesmen as a source of market information, therefore, is a strong motivational element to stimulate salesmen to stronger selling effort.

The Diffusion of an Innovation Among Physicians *

JAMES COLEMAN, ELIHU KATZ and HERBERT MENZEL

Anthropologists and sociologists have long been concerned with the processes through which customs, practices, attitudes, or messages spread. Traditionally, these processes have been studied by examining the ecological distribution of the trait at successive points in time. In a few cases, the actual transmission of messages from person to person has been traced out (e.g., 1, 3, 4, 5, 10). A still different approach to the study of this problem is reported in this paper. The population is physicians in four cities; the item whose use was spreading was a new drug; and the study focused on the on-going social processes which finally led to widespread adoption of the drug by these physicians.

Data were collected 15 months after a new drug with wide potential use, here called "gammanym," had been placed on the market. By this time almost all the doctors in relevant specialties in the four cities studied had used

◆ SOURCE: Reprinted by permission from *Sociometry*, Vol. 20 (American Sociological Association), December 1957, pp. 253–270.

* This article may be identified as Publication No. A 239 of the Bureau of Applied Social Research, Columbia University. An earlier version was read at the annual meeting of the American Sociological Society, Detroit, Michigan, September 8, 1956. We are indebted to Helmut Guttenberg for creative assistance throughout the project. Philip Ennis, Marjorie Fiske, Rolf Meyersohn, and Joseph A. Precker participated in the design of this study. The preparation of this paper was facilitated by funds obtained from a grant made to the Bureau of Applied Social Research by the Eda K. Loeb Fund.

the drug, some almost immediately, others only after a considerable interval of time. The research problem, stated most concretely, is this: What were the social processes which intervened between the initial trials of the drug by a few local innovators and its final use by virtually the whole medical community? The results reported below concern the effectiveness of networks of interpersonal relations at each stage of the diffusion process. The study is to be reported in full elsewhere (2); a pilot study has already been reported upon (9). A separate article by one of us describes the cumulative research experiences which led to the decision to focus explicitly upon interpersonal relations, using sociometric techniques (6).

METHODS—I

The method of survey research, involving structured interviews with a sample of physicians, was used. But since the problem as defined concerned the social structure which linked these doctors together, it was necessary to deviate in two important ways from the customary survey design which, in effect, treats individuals as so many independent units of observation. (a) Each doctor interviewed was asked three sociometric questions: To whom did he most often turn for advice and information? With whom did he most often discuss his cases in the course of an ordinary week? Who were the friends, among his colleagues, whom he saw most often socially? In response to each of these questions, the names of three doctors were requested. This made it possible to trace out the links by which each doctor was connected with the rest of the medical community. (b) It was decided to include in the sample, as nearly as possible, *all* the local doctors in whose specialties the new drug was of major potential significance. This assured that the "others" named by each doctor in answer to the sociometric questions were included in the sample, so that it became possible to characterize pairs or chains of socially connected doctors. Accordingly, 125 general practitioners, internists, and pediatricians were interviewed; they constituted 85 per cent of the doctors practicing in these fields in four Midwestern cities, ranging in population from 30,000 to 110,000.[1]

The dependent variable of the analysis which follows is the month during which each doctor first used the drug. This information was *not* obtained in the interviews; it was obtained through a search of the prescription records of the local pharmacies for three-day sampling periods at approximately monthly intervals over the 15 months following the release date of gammanym. In this way, the month during which each doctor first used the drug was ascertained.[2] The research is thus based on three kinds of data: the month of each doctor's first prescription for the new drug, obtained through a search of pharmacists' files; data about the informal social structure of the medical community, derived from doctors' replies to sociometric questions in an interview; and many individual attributes of each doctor, likewise obtained by interview.

RESULTS—I

Before presenting the results concerning interpersonal relations, the results concerning

other ("individual") determinants will be briefly characterized. As expected, the date on which a doctor first prescribed the new drug was related to a large number of his *individual* attributes, e.g., his age, the number of medical journals he subscribed to, his attachments to medical institutions outside his community, and certain attitudinal characteristics. To illustrate the relationship of drug introduction date to such individual attributes, one of the latter will be singled out: the doctor's relative orientation to his professional colleagues and to patients, inferred from his answer to the following question:

How would you rank the importance of these characteristics in recognizing a good doctor in a town like this?

a. The respect in which he is held by his own patients
b. His general standing in the community
c. The recognition given him by his local colleagues
d. The research and publications he has to his credit

The following rankings were classified as "profession-oriented": cdab, cadb, cbda, cabd; the following rankings were classified as "patient-oriented": abcd, acbd, acdb, bacd. The 14 doctors who gave other rankings were assigned to one group or another by a rank-order scaling procedure which will be described in detail elsewhere (2).

Figure 1 shows the relationship of the resulting classification to the date of introduction of the new drug. The solid curve represents those doctors who were classified as profession-oriented, and shows the cumulative proportion of gammanym users among them for each month. Thus, for example, by the fourth month 40 per cent of these doctors had used gammanym; by the sixth month over 50 per cent. The lower curve similarly represents the doctors who were classified as patient-oriented; by the sixth month only 42 per cent had used the drug. Thus the more profession-oriented doctors in these cities generally used the drug earlier than the less profession-oriented ones.[3] Similar

[1] In addition, 103 doctors in other specialties were also interviewed, thus making a total sample of 228, or 64 per cent of all doctors in active private practice in these cities. The analysis presented here is based only on the 125 general practitioners, internists, and pediatricians, except that sociometric designations accorded them by the remaining 103 doctors were included when measuring the sociometric status of the 125.

[2] The date so ascertained will tend to be slightly later than the doctor's actual introduction date, due to the sampling of days. The interval between sampling periods was made to alternate between 32 and 25 days, so that each two successive sampling periods included all 6 days of the working week. Records were obtained from 64 of the 84 drug stores in the four cities. Of the remaining 20,

only two had any significant pharmaceutical business.
[3] The difference between the mean adoption dates of the two groups in Figure 1 is 2.8 months, which is significant at the .01 level, using a standard two-tailed test of difference between means of normally distributed variables. It should be pointed out, however, that the argument of this report

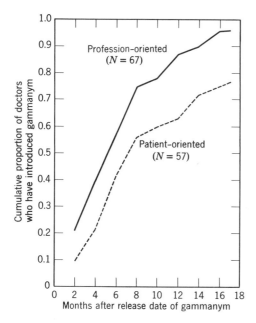

Figure 1 Cumulative proportion of doctors introducing gammanym: profession-oriented versus patient-oriented.

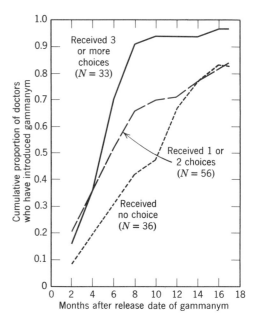

Figure 2 Cumulative proportion of doctors introducing gammanym: differences in integration on friendship criterion.

results were obtained for many other individual attributes—i.e., attributes describing individuals without reference to their social relations with one another.

But even stronger relations were found when we turned to *social* attributes—those characterizing a doctor's ties to his local colleagues. Doctors who were mentioned by many of their colleagues in answer to any of the three sociometric questions used the drug, on the average, earlier than those who were named by few or none of their colleagues. More generally speaking, the degree of a doctor's integration among his local colleagues was strongly and positively related to the date of his first use of the new drug. Figure 2 shows, for example, the results with regard to the network of friendships. The "integrated" doctors—those named as "friends" by three or more of their colleagues—were much faster to introduce gammanym into their practices than the rest. The networks of discussion and of advisorship yielded similar findings.

does not rest on the statistical significance of isolated findings so much as on the consistency of the results of several diverse approaches with one another and with prior theoretical notions. It is doubtful that significance tests in the usual sense are meaningful in situations like the present. For a detailed statement of our position in this matter, see (8, p. 427).

Two important contrasts differentiate Figure 2 from Figure 1, and, more generally, social attributes from individual ones, in their relation to gammanym introduction. First, the relationship in Figure 2 (as measured, for example, by the difference between the mean drug introduction dates of the extreme groups) is greater than that in Figure 1; greater, in fact, than the relationship of the introduction date of gammanym to all but one of the many individual characteristics which were examined. (The single exception is the doctor's total prescription volume for the general class of drugs which includes gammanym: the greater his use of drugs of this type, the earlier did he introduce gammanym.) [4] This emphasizes the importance of social contacts among doctors as a crucial determinant of their early use of the new drug.

But it may reasonably be questioned whether the relationship shown in Figure 2 may not arise merely because the measures of social

[4] The difference between the mean drug introduction dates of those high and low on integration according to the 3 sociometric questions used is 3.1, 4.1, and 4.3 months. The difference between those with high and low total prescription volume for this general class of drugs is 5.0 months. Only one other individual characteristic (number of journals read) produced a mean difference of as much as 4.0 months.

Table 1. The Average Relation of Twelve "Individual" Variables and of Three Measures of Social Integration to the Rate of Gammanym Introduction at Two Points in Time

	Average Difference in Per Cent of Gammanym Users between High and Low Groups		Ratio of Differences
	After 1 Month	After 7 Months	
Individual variables	9.2	27.4	2.98
Social integration	8.7	40.3	4.64

integration are themselves associated with some personality or other individual differences which predispose a doctor to early introduction. It is in answer to this question that a second contrast between Figures 1 and 2 is relevant.

Notice that the two curves in Figure 1 are roughly parallel, differing from one another only in vertical displacement. This is true as well in most of the remaining charts (not shown) which relate individual characteristics to gammanym introduction. The curves in Figure 2, by contrast, differ from each other in shape as well as location: the curve for the more integrated doctors, although not starting out much higher than the other curves, rises steeply upward with a slight gain in slope at the fourth month, while the curve for the more isolated doctors rises at a moderate and almost constant slope. To put it differently, the integrated doctors were little different from their isolated colleagues at the very beginning; but then their rate accelerated to produce an increasing gap between the curves. In contrast, the profession-oriented doctors in Figure 1 differed from the patient-oriented from the very start almost as much as later on.

The constant difference between the profession-oriented and patient-oriented doctors suggests that they differ individually in their receptivity to new developments in medicine. On the other hand, the accelerating difference between the integrated and isolated doctors suggests a kind of "snowball" or "chain-reaction" process for the integrated: They are individually little different in receptivity from their more isolated colleagues, but as their fellows come to use the drug, they pick it up from these doctors themselves; and as more of their fellows come to use it, their chances of picking it up are greater.

The difference between the two kinds of relationship to drug introduction is also shown

by Table 1, which compares the individual variables and the social variables in their relation to gammanym introduction at two points in time: 1 month and 7 months after the drug was introduced. For each of these dates, the table shows the average difference in per cent of gammanym users (a) between those measuring "high" and "low" on each of twelve individual variables and (b) between those measuring "high" and "low" on three measures of social integration. The latter are based on choices received in response to the three sociometric questions mentioned earlier. The twelve individual variables include all those examined which showed a difference of two or more months in mean date of introduction between the high and the low groups.

The size of these differences measures the size of the relationship at the two times. As is evident, the social integration measures show a slightly *smaller* relationship than do the individual variables after 1 month, but a much *larger* relationship after 7 months. Thus, as exemplified by the comparison between Figures 1 and 2, the socially integrated doctors "pull away" from their isolated colleagues, while the doctors differing in some individual attribute simply maintain their intrinsically different receptivity as time goes on.

Figures 3 and 4 show the difference between two corresponding theoretical "models" of the introduction process. In Figure 3, the upper and lower curves both express a model of "individual innovation"; the difference between the two is simply that the receptivity is greater for the upper. This difference in individual innovation rate or receptivity corresponds, we suggest, to the difference between profession-oriented and patient-oriented doctors (and between doctors who differ in other individual attributes as well). In contrast, in Figure 4 the upper curve (which is roughly similar in shape to the curve for the integrated doctors) represents a snowball process in which those who have introduced pass on the innovation to their colleagues. (This curve is described by an equation which has been used to characterize rates of population growth, certain chemical reactions, and other phenomena which obey a chain-reaction process.) The lower curve in Figure 4 is still the individual innovation process. (Technically, the individual and snowball processes are described by equations on the graphs, which can be paraphrased as follows: *Individual process*—the number of doctors introducing the new drug each month would remain a constant percentage of those who have not already adopted the drug. *Snowball process*—the number of doctors introducing the new drug each month would increase in proportion to those who have already been converted.)

In short, these comparisons suggest that the process of introduction for those doctors who were deeply embedded in their professional community was in fact different from the process for those who were relatively isolated from it. The highly integrated doctors seem to have learned from *one another,* while the less integrated ones, it seems, had each to learn afresh from the journals, the detail man (drug salesman), and other media of information.

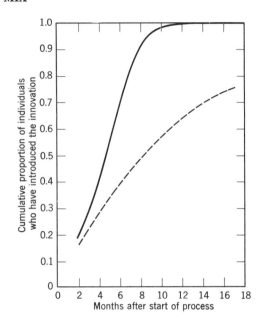

Figure 4   Comparison of model of "chain-reaction" innovation with model of individual innovation: $dy/dt = ky(1-y)t$.

METHODS—II

This result called for a more detailed investigation into the ways in which the networks of relations among the doctors affected their introduction of the new drug. Such an investigation required a shift of focus from doctors to relationships among doctors or to the networks themselves as the units of analysis. Various methods could have been devised to do this. We chose to record the behavior of *pairs* of doctors who were sociometrically related to one another, reasoning that if the networks of relations were effective, then pairs of doctors who were in contact must have been more *alike* in their behavior than pairs assorted at random. That is, if there was a snowball or chain-reaction process of drug introduction from one doctor to another, then adjacent links in the chain—pairs of socially related doctors—should have introduced the drug about the same time.

In order to test this hypothesis for the discussion network, Figure 5 was constructed. (Similar figures were constructed for the networks of friendship and advisorship.) Each sociometric pair was assigned to a column of this matrix according to the gammanym introduction date of the chooser, and to a row according to the gammanym introduction date of the doctor chosen. (A mutual choice con-

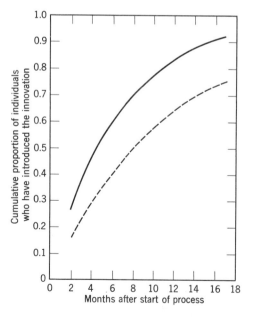

Figure 3   Model of individual innovation showing effects of differences in individual receptivity k: $dy/dt = k(1-y)t$.

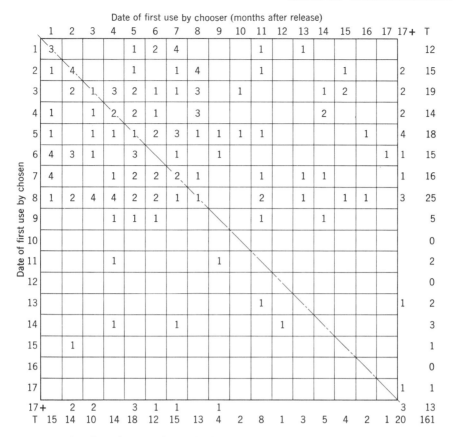

Date of first use by chooser (months after release)

Date of first use by chosen	1	2	3	4	5	6	7	8	9	10	11	12	13	14	15	16	17	17+	T
1	3			1	2	4					1		1						12
2	1	4		1		1	4				1				1			2	15
3		2	1	3	2	1	1	3		1				1	2			2	19
4	1		1	2	2	1		3						2				2	14
5	1		1	1	1	2	3	1	1	1	1					1		4	18
6	4	3	1		3		1		1								1	1	15
7	4			1	2	2	2	1			1		1	1				1	16
8	1	2	4	4	2	2	1	1			2		1		1	1		3	25
9			1	1	1						1			1					5
10																			0
11			1					1											2
12																			0
13											1							1	2
14			1			1						1							3
15		1																	1
16																			0
17																		1	1
17+		2	2		3	1	1		1									3	13
T	15	14	10	14	18	12	15	13	4	2	8	1	3	5	4	2	1	20	161

Figure 5   Chart showing dates of adoption of each member of discussion pairs.

stitutes two pairs in this tabulation, since any chooser and his choice constitute a pair.) Pairs of doctors who introduced the drug during the same month (interval zero) fall in the main diagonal; pairs of doctors who differed in introducing the drug by an interval of one month fall into cells adjoining the diagonal; and so on.

The resulting distribution of these intervals for the sociometric pairs was then compared to the corresponding distribution of intervals for a set of "random pairs" which has the following characteristics. If a pair is selected at random: (a) the probability that the chooser-member of the pair introduced gammanym during a particular month is the same as in the actual sample but is independent of the introduction date of the doctor chosen; (b) the probability that the chosen member introduced gammanym during a particular month is the same as in the actual sample but is independent of the introduction date of the doctor making the choice. Thus, for example, among the random pairs, those who introduced gammanym in the first month and those who

did so in the seventh gave equal portions of their choices to other first-month introducers. Similarly, those who introduced gammanym in the first month and those who introduced it in the seventh *received* equal portions of their choices from first-month introducers. Operationally, a set of "chance" frequencies satisfying these criteria can easily be obtained by computing for each cell of Figure 5 the product of the associated marginal totals, divided, for convenience, by the grand total.[5]

Contrary to expectations, the proportion of pairs whose members had introduced gammanym during the same month, one month

[5] A complication arose from the fact that the study was carried on in four different cities, with sociometric choices between cities excluded. This could spuriously raise any measure of pair-wise similarity of behavior, if there are large differences in behavior between the cities. (This fact was called to our attention by Jack Feldman of NORC.) In order to avoid such a spurious relation, "chance" frequencies, as above described, were calculated separately from the marginal totals for each city, and only then summed over the cities.

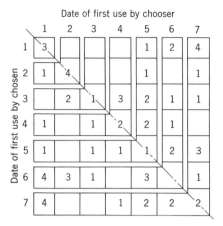

Date of first use by chooser

Figure 6 Exploded view of portion of Figure 5 showing monthly segments.

apart, two months apart, and so on, according to the chance model proved to be almost identical to the proportion of actual discussion pairs who had introduced gammanym simultaneously or with varying intervals. The results for pairs of friends and for advisor-advisee pairs were similarly disappointing. This meant the rejection of our original hypothesis that pairs of doctors in contact would introduce the drug more nearly simultaneously than pairs of doctors assorted at random.

There was, on the other hand, the earlier evidence that the doctor's integration was important to his introduction of gammanym. This dictated a more intensive look at the behavior of pairs of doctors. Accordingly, we raised the question whether the networks, though ineffective for the *whole* period studied, may have been effective for the *early* period, immediately after the drug was marketed. An inspection of Figure 5 suggests that this could easily be the case. If only the upper left-hand portion of the matrix, representing the first two, three, or four months, is considered, then there appears to be a tendency for both members of a pair to introduce the drug in the same month.

In order to describe this tendency more precisely, it was decided to eliminate from consideration those associates of each doctor who used the drug only after *he* did. That is to say, the following question was now asked of the data: How closely did the drug introduction of each doctor follow upon the drug introductions of those of his associates who had introduced the drug before him? The answer is: very closely, for early introducers of the drug; not at all closely, for late introducers of the drug.

This result is based on a measure for each month, obtained by dividing up the total matrix of pairs of doctors as shown in Figure 6. The single cell in the upper left-hand corner represents those pairs both of whose members introduced the drug in the first month. The L-shaped section next to it contains the pairs which consist of one doctor who introduced the drug in the second month and one who introduced it in the first *or* second. The next L-shaped section contains all pairs which consist of one third-month adopter and one third-month-or-earlier adopter, and so on. It was now possible to determine the average interval for the sociometric pairs in each L-shaped section; likewise the average interval for the corresponding random pairs. On this basis, a measure of simultaneity was computed for each section, according to the formula:

Measure of Simultaneity (positive) =

$$\frac{(\text{avge. interval for random pairs}) - (\text{avge. interval for sociometric pairs})}{\text{avge. interval for random pairs}}.$$

This measure expresses the difference between the random and actual intervals as a fraction of the difference between the random interval and complete simultaneity (i.e., an interval of zero). The measure thus has a maximum of 1, and is zero when pairs are no closer than chance. In those cases where the actual interval exceeded the random interval, a different denominator was used.[6]

RESULTS—II

The values of the index are plotted in Figure 7 for the second through the sixth months. Separate curves are plotted for pairs of friends, discussion pairs, and advisor-advisee pairs. The interpretation of these results must be tentative because of the small numbers of cases; on the other hand, the patterns which emerge are rather consistent.

[6] Measure of simultaneity (negative) =

$$\frac{(\text{avge. interval for random pairs}) - (\text{avge. interval for sociometric pairs})}{(s - 1) - (\text{avge. interval for random pairs})}$$

s being defined as the number of the latest month included in the particular L-shaped section. (E.g., $s = 4$ in the case of pairs consisting of one fourth-month adopter and one fourth-month-or-earlier adopter.) When the index has a negative value, it therefore expresses the difference between the random and actual intervals as a fraction of the difference between the random interval and the maximum interval that is possible.

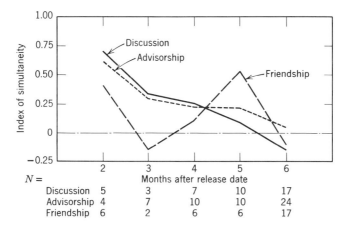

$N =$	2	3	4	5	6
		Months after release date			
Discussion	5	3	7	10	17
Advisorship	4	7	10	10	24
Friendship	6	2	6	6	17

Figure 7   Index of pair-simultaneity for three networks at different times.

Figure 7 suggests, first of all, that the networks of doctor-to-doctor contacts operated most powerfully during the first 5 months after the release of the new drug: such influence as any doctor's drug introduction had upon his immediate associates evidently occurred soon after the drug became available. (Figure 7 omits the later months during which the index is negative or very small.) Second, the three networks did not behave identically.[7] The discussion network and the advisor network showed most pair-simultaneity at the very beginning and then progressively declined. The friendship network shows initially less pair-simultaneity than the other two, but—with some instability—appears to reach its maximum effectiveness later. Finally, after the fifth or sixth month following the release of the new drug, none of the networks any longer showed pair-simultaneity beyond chance.

These results, however tentative, suggest that there may be successive stages in the diffusion of this innovation through the community of doctors. The first networks to be operative as chains of influence appear to be those which connect the doctors in the professional relationships of advisors and discussion partners. Only then, it seems, does the friendship network become operative—among those doctors who are influenced in their decisions more by the

colleagues they meet as friends than by those whom they look to as advisors or engage in discussion during working hours. Finally, for those doctors who have not yet introduced the drug by about 6 months after the drug's release these networks seem completely *inoperative* as chains of influence. The social structure seems to have exhausted its effect; those doctors who have not responded to its influence by this time are apparently unresponsive to it. When they finally use gammanym, they presumably do so in response to influences outside the social network, such as detail men, ads, journal articles, and so on, and not in response to their relations with other doctors.

But one further phase in the social diffusion of gammanym can be discerned by examining separately the sociometrically integrated and the relatively isolated doctors. One would expect the networks of doctor-to-doctor contact to show their effectiveness first among the more integrated doctors and only then among those who are less integrated in their medical community. It has already been seen (Figure 2 and text) that the more isolated doctors, on the average, introduced gammanym considerably later than the socially more integrated doctors. We now propose, however, that when more isolated doctors *did* introduce the drug early, it was not with the help of the social networks. While the networks were operative as channels of influence *early* for the integrated doctors, they were operative only later for the more isolated ones. This is what seems to have occurred. Figure 8 plots the index of simultaneity separately for more and less integrated doctors. (The graphs show weighted averages for all three networks; separately the numbers

[7] Many of the sociometric ties reappear in two or three of the networks. The three sociometric questions yielded a total of 958 "pairs" within the sample of 125 doctors; but since some of these pairs were identical in answer to two or all three of the questions, there were only 704 *different* pairs. This overlap is still small enough to allow differences in patterns to emerge, as shown in the text.

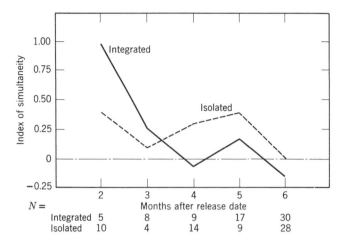

Figure 8   Index of pair-simultaneity at different times for doctors differing in integration.

of cases would be so small as to produce erratic trends.)

The peak of effectiveness of doctor-to-doctor contacts for the well-integrated doctors appeared in the earliest month for which it can be plotted—the second month—after which effectiveness sharply declined. For the relatively isolated doctors, by contrast, the networks were not so effective at first as were those for the integrated doctors, but they maintained their effectiveness longer. Thus it appears that the networks of relations were effective not only for the more integrated doctors but also for the relatively isolated doctors who introduced the drug during the first 5 months of the drug's availability.

CONCLUSION

The above results, taken together, suggest a process which may be summarized as follows: At first the influence of these social networks operated only among the doctors who were integrated into the community of their colleagues through ties of a professional nature—as advisors or as discussion partners. Then it spread through the friendship network to doctors who were closely tied to the medical community through their friendship relations. By this time, social influence had also become operative in the more "open" parts of the social structure—i.e., among the relatively isolated doctors. Finally, there came a phase during which most of the remaining doctors introduced gammanym but did so in complete independence of the time at which their associates had introduced it: the networks now showed

no effect. For the integrated doctors, this phase began about 4 months after the drug's release; for the isolated doctors, it began about 6 months after the drug's release. This picture is of course a tentative one, for the small size of the sample introduces variability, and there may be factors which produce spurious results.

There remains the question: Why should these sociometric ties to colleagues who have used the drug be influential during the first months of the drug's availability, but not later? One possible answer lies in the greater uncertainty about the drug that must have prevailed when it was new. (Data not reported here show that those doctors who introduced gammanym early did so far more tentatively than those who introduced it later.) We know from work in the tradition of Sherif that it is precisely in situations which are objectively unclear that social validation of judgments becomes most important.

More generally, this explanation implies that a doctor will be influenced more by what his colleagues say and do in uncertain situations, whenever and wherever they may occur, than in clear-cut situations. This explanation was confirmed by further data from the study which show that doctors influence each other more in treatments whose effects are unclear than in treatments whose effects are clear-cut. This topic will be dealt with in detail elsewhere (7).

CONCLUDING METHODOLOGICAL NOTE

A word should be added about the significance of research of this kind, aside from the possible interest in its specific substantive findings. It exemplifies a methodological approach which will, we feel, assume a larger role in the social research of the next decade: namely, making social relationships and social structures the units of statistical analysis. To be sure, the analysis of social relations has always been the sociologist's business. Nevertheless, most empirical studies have either treated and described a community, a factory, a hospital ward, or any other large grouping of people as a single unit, or else they have statistically analyzed data collected on hundreds or thousands of single individuals, as in the typical "survey" study. What has been missing until recently is study designs which would explicitly take into account the structuring of single persons into larger units, and yet allow sophisticated quantitative treatment. The techniques of sociometry can meet this purpose, but have, with some notable exceptions (e.g., 4, 11), been applied chiefly to small closed groups and primarily for descriptive purposes.

The attempt reported here has been to carry out a design and analysis which would effect a marriage between sociometric techniques and survey research, in order to investigate quantitatively problems of the sort which community studies have ordinarily investigated by qualitative means. The attempt, of course, points up many more problems than it even partially solves: e.g., how to integrate an analysis of formal social structures with an analysis of informal ones; how to proceed from pair-analysis to the analysis of longer chains and complex networks; and so on. A set of methodological and substantive problems awaits the researcher. It is suggested that the solution will give sociologists important new tools with which to investigate social dynamics.

REFERENCES

1. Back, K., et al., "A Method of Studying Rumor Transmission," in L. Festinger et al., *Theory and Experiment in Social Communication,* Ann Arbor, Michigan: Research Center for Group Dynamics, University of Michigan, 1950, 307–312.
2. Coleman, J. S., E. Katz, and H. Menzel, "The Diffusion of a Medical Innovation" (tentative title), Glencoe, Illinois: The Free Press (in preparation).
3. Dodd, S. C., "Diffusion Is Predictable," *American Sociological Review,* 1955, **20**, 392–401.
4. Festinger, L., S. Schachter, and K. Back, *Social Pressures in Informal Groups,* New York: Harper, 1950, Chap. 7.
5. Jennings, H. H., "Leadership and Isolation," in G. E. Swanson, T. M. Newcomb, and E. L. Hartley, eds., *Readings in Social Psychology,* New York: Holt, 1952.
6. Katz, E., "The Two-Step Flow of Communication: An Up-to-Date Report on an Hypothesis," *Public Opinion Quarterly,* 1957, **21**, 61–78.
7. Katz, E., J. S. Coleman, and H. Menzel, "Social Influence on Decision-Making in Ambiguous Situations—Some Data from a Survey among Physicians" (unpublished).
8. Lipset, S. M., M. A. Trow, and J. S. Coleman, *Union Democracy,* Glencoe, Illinois: The Free Press, 1956.
9. Menzel, H., and E. Katz, "Social Relations and Innovation in the Medical Profession: The Epidemiology of a New Drug," *Public Opinion Quarterly,* 1956, **19**, 337–352.
10. Moreno, J. L., *Who Shall Survive?,* Beacon, New York: Beacon House, 1953, 440–450.
11. Riley, M. W., J. W. Riley, Jr., and J. Toby, *Sociological Studies in Scale Analysis,* New Brunswick, New Jersey: Rutgers University Press, 1954.

Roles of Communicating Agents in Technological Change in Agriculture*

EUGENE A. WILKENING

The adoption of new techniques in farming requires the communication of information about them. When viewed as a process the adoption of a new technique requires several different kinds of information. These range from initial knowledge about the technique to an understanding of how it can be made more effective after it is adopted.

The main assumption of this paper is that the type of information transmitted about new farm techniques or practices is related to the primary functions and to the structural and operational features of the transmitting agents. Stated another way, different sources are utilized for different types of information. The particular sources utilized will depend upon the way in which they are perceived by the *individual seeking the information* [1] and thus upon the functions performed by those sources for that individual.

Lazarsfeld, Berelson and Gaudet found differential influences of communication media in influencing voters' decisions.[2] Merton de-

scribes the role of a national news magazine among different occupational groups in a community.[3] Eisenstadt has shown how the orientation of immigrants in Israel by officials is influenced by the degree of identification with them and by certain situational factors.[4] These studies suggest that the communication of information is a function of perceptions of the communicating media and of the relationship of the media to the receiver. Moreover, there is evidence in the study of voters' choices and in the study of immigrants in Israel that the influence of different communicating media varies with the type of information obtained.

Information about technological change in farming is transmitted by a number of sources or communicating agents. The communication of farm information is a primary function of some and a secondary function of others. For example, the main functions of the neighborhood group are status giving, mutual aid, response, etc., and not the dissemination of information about new farm practices. Communicating agents also operate differently. Some provide personal contact, others impersonal; some individual and some group contacts;

♦ SOURCE: Reprinted by permission from *Social Forces*, Vol. 34, No. 4 (University of North Carolina Press), May 1956, pp. 361–367.

* Data were obtained from a research project supported by the Wisconsin Agricultural Experiment Station and Extension Service.
[1] Franklin Fearing, "Toward a Psychological Theory of Human Communication," *Journal of Personality* XXII (Sept. 1953), 71–88.
[2] Paul F. Lazarsfeld, Bernard Berelson and Hazel Gaudet, *The People's Choice: How the Voter Makes Up His Mind* (New York: Duell, Sloan and Pearce, 1944).

[3] P. K. Merton, "Patterns of Influence: A Study of Interpersonal Influence and of Communication Behavior in a Local Community," in Paul F. Lazarsfeld and F. N. Stanton (eds.), *Communications Research 1948–49* (New York: Harper & Bros., 1949).
[4] S. M. Eisenstadt, "Conditions of Communication Receptivity," *Public Opinion Quarterly*, XVII (Fall 1953), 363–373; and "Processes of Communication Among Immigrants in Israel," *Public Opinion Quarterly*, XVI (Spring 1952), 42–58.

some occur daily and others weekly, monthly or less often; and some are locally oriented while others are regionally or nationally oriented. The problem of this paper is to determine the role of different types of communicating agents in the process of accepting technological changes in farming.

Previous studies have attempted to distinguish between the sources of first hearing about new farm practices and sources for most information about those practices.[5] Ryan and Gross found that commercial salesmen were the most frequent source of first knowledge about hybrid corn while other farmers were of most help in deciding to try it out. The author's studies in North Carolina and Wisconsin show that mass media, agricultural agencies, and other farmers are important sources of "first knowledge," depending upon the practice. In general, other farmers and the agricultural agencies were more frequent sources for "most information" about new farm practices.

The development of testable hypotheses requires that the sources of farm information be distinguished first on the basis of their primary functions and secondly on the basis of the structural and operational characteristics growing out of these functions. These are summarized in Table 1. While there are differences in functions and structural features of specific sources under each of the major types, these differences are largely in degree and not in kind.

The last column of the table indicates the expected type of information provided in the acceptance of changes in farming. The three types of information are: (1) hearing about the change, (2) information of help in deciding whether to try out the change, and (3) instructions in how to put the change into effect. These different types of information are usually obtained at different stages with respect to the adoption of changes. The stages corresponding to the types of information are the *awareness,* the *decision-making,* and the *action* stages, respectively. This is supported by the idea that the acceptance of technological change is a process which occurs over time. In the case of hybrid corn in Iowa, an average of five years elapsed between the time hybrid corn was first heard about and the first trial. This time varies with the particular type of innovation.[6]

SOURCE OF DATA

Data for this paper were obtained as part of a study involving changes in farming of 636 young farm operators in six Wisconsin counties. The sample includes all farm operators in randomly selected townships who had started farming within ten years previous to the survey, who were under 45 years of age, and who had made most of their income from farming in 1953. The six counties were chosen at random from among 26 in which an extension program for young farm families was initiated in 1954.

Questions were asked as a part of this study to determine the primary sources of farm information of three different kinds. The questions are:

"Where or from whom do you usually *first hear about* new ideas in farming?"

"After you first hear about some new idea, where or from whom do you get information that *helps you decide* whether to try it out on *your farm?*"

"If you decide to try out a new idea, where or from whom do you get most help on *how much* material to use, *when* to use it, *how* to go about it, etc.?"

The intent of these three questions was to determine the major sources of information at the three different stages in the acceptance of new ideas or changes in farming. Another approach would have been to ask which of the three types of information are obtained from each of the major sources. It is felt that such an approach would have led more likely to

[5] Bryce Ryan and Neal C. Gross, "The Diffusion of Hybrid Seed Corn in Two Iowa Communities," *Rural Sociology,* VIII (May 1943), 15–24; E. A. Wilkening, *Acceptance of Improved Farm Practices in Three Coastal Plain Counties,* North Carolina Agricultural Experiment Station, Technical Bulletin 98, May 1952; and E. A. Wilkening, *Adoption of Improved Farm Practices as Related to Family Factors,* Wisconsin Agr'l Exp. Station Research Bulletin 183, December 1953.

[6] For example, the average time between "first hearing about" and "first adopting" improved permanent pastures in North Carolina was seven years. (E. A. Wilkening and F. A. Santopolo, "The Diffusion of Improved Farm Practices from Unit Test-Demonstration Farms in the Tennessee Valley Counties of North Carolina," N. C. State College, Raleigh, N. C. and Tennessee Valley Authority, 1952. Mimeographed.)

Table 1. Major Functions and Structural Features of Four Types of Communicating Agents for Farm Information and Expected Roles of These Types in the Acceptance of Changes in Farming

Type of Communicating Agent	Major Functions	Structural and Operational Features	Major Expected Role with Respect to Change
Mass Media (farm papers, farm magazines, newspapers, radio and television)	a. providing information of widespread interest b. selling advertising	a. impersonal contact b. frequent contact easily accessible c. content of general interest d. one-way communication	a. first knowledge
Other Farmers (neighbors, friends, relatives)	a. social status b. solidarity c. mutual aid d. response e. recreation	a. personal contact b. frequent contact is usually incidental to primary group functions c. content oriented to local and personal experiences d. two-way communication	a. help in decision-making b. instruction in putting change into effect
Agricultural Agencies (county agent, vocational agriculture instructor, College of Agriculture, Soil Conservation Service, etc.)	a. disseminating information on specific practices b. teaching basic principle of farming c. providing special and technical services	a. personal and impersonal contact b. contact limited primarily to those seeking information c. content of general and of specific and local interest d. two-way communication	a. instruction in putting change into effect b. help in decision-making
Commercial Sources (business firms and private professionals)	a. buying and selling materials and equipment b. professional services	a. personal and impersonal contact b. contact incidental to buying, selling and special services c. content oriented to economic and to special interests d. two-way communication	a. instruction in putting change into effect b. first knowledge *

* This expected role of commercial firms is not supported by the findings of this study.

biases arising from favorable or unfavorable attitudes toward the sources themselves. Nevertheless, such an approach should be attempted as a further test of the hypotheses set forth here.

In obtaining responses to the questions used here there was some difficulty in getting respondents to distinguish between the three different types of information. This was particularly true for the second and third questions. Their validity could be tested by asking similar questions about specific changes or innovations in farming as in certain of the studies referred to above. This was not feasible in the present study.

THE MASS MEDIA

It was expected that the mass media, including magazines, newspapers and radio programs, would be the most frequent sources for first hearing about new farm practices. The mass media provide frequent contact with most farm families. They cost little and their use is not highly influenced by one's social status or group membership. Hence, their convenience and availability make them efficient dispensers of information at the stage of *initial awareness*.

The findings are in keeping with expectations. Seven out of ten gave one of the mass media—farm papers, farm magazines, news-

Table 2. Percentage Distribution of Responses with Respect to Communicating Agents from Which 630 Young Farmers "Usually Hear First about New Ideas in Farming," That Help Decide Whether to Try New Ideas on Their Farms, and "From Which Get Most Help on How Much Material to Use, When to Use It, How to Go about It, etc."

Type of Communicating Agent	Type of Help or Information			Significance of Difference Between Percentages		
	From which "usually first learn about new ideas in farming"	That help decide whether to try out new ideas after hearing about them	"From which get most help on how much material to use, when to use it, how to go about it, etc."	Column 1 and Column 2	Column 1 and Column 3	Column 2 and Column 3
	Column 1	Column 2	Column 3	Column 4	Column 5	Column 6
Total	100	100	100			
Farm papers, farm magazines and newspapers	62.7	3.8	2.2	P < .01	P < .01	—
Radio and television	8.0	.02	—	P < .01	P < .01	—
County agent and university	7.4	21.1	34.7	P < .01	P < .01	P < .01
Vocational agriculture instructor	6.6	5.2	4.9	—	—	—
Special agencies (SCS, ASC, etc.)	0.9	2.0	4.1	—	P < .01	P < .05
Commercial sources	2.2	8.2	21.2	P < .01	P < .01	P < .01
Other farmers	11.0	47.0	23.7	P < .01	P < .01	P < .01
Self, no outside source given	0.5	8.6	4.2	P < .01	P < .01	P < .01
No response	0.6	3.9	5.1	—	—	—

papers, radio or television—as the usual contact for first hearing about new ideas in farming. Of these, the printed page was most frequently mentioned, with three-fifths giving this type of source for initial knowledge about new ideas. Of the printed sources, farm papers and magazines, as compared with newspapers, make a ratio of six to one.

Only 4 percent and 2 percent respectively gave one of the mass media as a source of help in deciding whether to try out "new ideas" after hearing about them, as a source of help in learning "how much material to use, when to use it, how to go about it, etc." The difference between the percentages giving either type of mass media as the usual source from which new ideas are first heard and as the usual source for each of the other two types of information are highly significant.

The difference between the percentages giving either type of mass media for the latter two types of information is not significant at the .05 level. However, the evidence is in the direction of the mass media aiding more in the *decision-making* stage than in the *action* stage. Differences between the mass media might be expected here. Newspapers or farm papers carrying columns of agricultural specialists are likely to be utilized more for instructions in carrying out new practices than are farm magazines appealing to wider audiences. Also, television is better adapted to the role of instruction in how to perform certain techniques than is radio. The low percentages giving the mass media for help in *decision-making* and in the *action* stages of adopting changes does not mean that farmers do not obtain some help from them. The question elicits responses with respect to the *most usual source* for the different types of information and not with respect to any use of a source of information.

The extent to which radio or television was given as the source of first hearing about new ideas in farming varies greatly by counties. Only 1.1 percent and 1.3 percent of the sub-samples of two counties gave radio or television programs in response to this question, while 15.3 percent of the sample of the county in which the College of Agriculture is located gave one of these media. This reflects the wide variation in availability of informational programs of certain types to farmers by geographical area.

OTHER FARMERS

The major role of other farmers in communicating information about changes in farming is in the *decision-making* stage. Almost half (47 percent) gave neighbors, relatives, or other farmers as the main source of help in deciding whether to try out a new idea on their own farms. While the percentage giving this type of response ranged from 34 to 60 percent among the six-county sub-samples, other farmers were given more frequently than either of the other major types of sources for this type of information in each county. The percentage giving other farmers as the main source of help in the *decision-making* stage for the total sample is significantly higher than the percentages giving this type of source for either of the other two stages.

The second most important role of other farmers in the process of accepting changes in farming—as a source of help in taking the action—is when and how to put new practices into effect. Almost one-fourth gave other farmers as the most usual source of help in this stage. This proportion is significantly higher than the proportion giving other farmers as the source of first knowledge about new ideas. The variation by county in the proportion giving other farmers as a source of help in putting the practice into effect is not great. With the exception of one county in which 17 percent gave this response, the range is only 6 percent between highest and lowest.

That other farmers play an important role in first informing one about "new ideas in farming" is indicated by the fact that about one-ninth fell in this category. This varied from 5.01 percent in one county to 14.6 percent in another, although there was little variation among the other four counties in this respect. For those changes not promoted as much by other agencies, the influence of other farmers at this stage is likely to be much higher.

EDUCATIONAL AND SERVICE AGENCIES

It was expected that the county agent and other agricultural agencies would be given most frequently as the source of help for learning about the techniques of putting new practices into operation. They have the combination of personal contact (two-way exchange), professional training, and access to reliable information essential for this role. Persons who may not look to outside agencies for help in deciding whether to try a new practice might do so when they get to the point of wanting to know *how to go about it.*

The findings are generally in keeping with the expectations. One of the educational or action agencies was given by 43.7 percent of the total sample for this type of help. This is significantly higher than the proportion giving this type of source for help in the *initial awareness* or in the *decision-making* stages. The proportion giving agency sources for most help in this stage is fairly consistent with the exception of one county in which only one-third gave this type of source for most help in learning how to put new practices into effect.

The county agent is relied upon most for learning how to put new ideas into operation according to this survey of young farm operators. About one-third said they would go to the county agent for this type of help. This includes personal advice, meetings, circular letters, and university bulletins obtained through his office. The validity of this type of response is supported by the fact that over one-third had contacted the county agent or his assistant within the past year.

The second most important role of the educational and service agencies is that of help in deciding whether to try out new practices. Over one-fourth gave one of the agencies in response to this question. Next to other farmers, the agencies are most important in this role. They are also important in the role of being the first to inform about new ideas in farming, although second to the mass media in this respect. Their mention in first informing about new practices is significantly less than their mention as help in deciding whether to try out new ideas.

There is considerable variation by county in the extent to which agricultural agencies were given as a source of help in decision-making as well as a source of first knowledge about new ideas in farming. This reflects a variation in number of personnel, in types of media used by the agencies, and in the content of their programs. For example, in one county only 6.7 percent of the sample gave one of the agencies as the usual source of first hearing about new ideas as compared with another in which 22.6 percent gave this type of source. The proportion giving one of the agricultural

agencies for most help in the *decision-making* stage ranges from 21.0 percent to 35.5 percent.

There is evidence that the roles of the agricultural agencies in the dissemination of information about changes in farming differ. All agencies tend to follow the pattern as presented above except vocational agriculture instructors (including veterans farmer-training instructors). There is no significant difference between the proportion giving this source for the three types of information. Furthermore, there is wide variation between counties in the proportion giving agriculture instructors for all three types of information, indicating that a great deal depends upon the number and types of instructors in the counties.

COMMERCIAL SOURCES

Commercial firms perform a major role in providing helpful information in the action stage. This is in keeping with their hypothesized role and with the findings of previous studies. Of course, their influence is limited to those innovations which require the use of materials or equipment. For certain practices of this type their influence may be very great as in the acceptance of hybrid seed corn in Iowa, new oat varieties in Wisconsin, new analyses of fertilizer and chemicals for disease, insect, and weed control. The dealer is in a strategic position to supply this type of information in that his major function is selling farm materials and equipment.

About one-fifth gave commercial dealers as the main source of information on the *when* and *how* of putting new practices into operation, a significantly higher proportion than for either of the other two types of information. The proportion giving this type of source for help in the *action* stage varies from 15 percent to 27 percent in the county sub-samples, and from 2.5 percent to 13.3 percent in the *decision-making* stage.

Commercial firms are more influential in the *decision-making* stage than in the *awareness* stage, according to the findings of this study. This is somewhat contrary to expectations based upon the findings of previous studies. Ryan and Gross's study of hybrid corn acceptance in Iowa shows salesmen to be most influential in first informing about the innovation. Perhaps this reflects the high-pressure tactics used in the promotion of certain commercially profitable changes. For most changes, however, the commercial dealer plays a less aggressive role in disseminating information in the early stages. However, if credit were given to commercial firms for the advertising of new products over the radio, in newspapers and in farm magazines, perhaps they would rate higher in the *initial awareness* stage.

DISCUSSION

The findings of this study support the general assumption that the type of information transmitted about farm technology is related to the characteristics and functions of the transmitting agents, as well as the specific hypotheses of the study. The only major variation in hypothesized and actual findings is that commercial firms play a less important role in first informing about changes than in decision-making and in putting changes into operation. An explanation of this finding may be in the failure to give credit to commercial sources utilizing farm magazines, newspapers, and radio programs.

The mass media combine the functions of communicating information to a wide audience and selling advertising; hence, they utilize techniques for widespread and timely dissemination of information. This enables them to perform most effectively the role of providing initial awareness of new ideas and techniques in farming. Direct contact with the educational agencies also performs the role of informing persons about innovations in farming. There is evidence that this is particularly true for certain types of practices—those which represent essentially new operations or techniques as compared with changes in materials or slight modifications of existing operations.[7]

Friends, neighbors, and other personal contacts perform a major role in evaluating changes in farming. Evaluation of new ideas requires that they not only be considered with respect to local conditions but also that they be considered as they affect one's family and relationship with others. Awareness of and the general soundness of an innovation may be obtained from an impersonal source, but its suitability for the potential adopter and the

effect upon his personal relationships is most likely to be determined by personal communication with persons who are aware of his situation and who are involved in these relationships. This may be the county agent or agriculture instructor for those who have developed personal contacts with such persons. For most, however, sanction of a new practice is likely to be sought from neighbors, friends, relatives, or others with whom the farmer has continuing relationships. In other words, the most appropriate contacts for evaluating the new practice are those which serve other functions—friendship, mutual aid, status, etc.—for the farmer.

Learning the techniques of putting new practices into operation is a task-oriented function. It is expected therefore that this role is performed by those sources having the technical "know-how" and who communicate it effectively. Most instruction in techniques requires two-way communication and personal demonstration with actual materials and equipment. The agricultural agencies with professionally trained personnel are best equipped to perform this role, although other farmers and commercial dealers also perform this role for many persons not having established contacts with the agencies. It is not likely, therefore, as some seem to imply, that the day has arrived when it is sufficient to utilize the mass media in disseminating information about new ideas in farming. The possibilities for television in this respect remain to be demonstrated. Yet, it is unlikely that even it can replace the interpersonal exchange between the farmer and the expert or between the farmer and other farmers or dealers in learning about how to put new practices into effect, many of which are rather complex and intricate.

While the findings of this study may not hold true for farmers of older age and for farmers of other regions, they do substantiate for the most part the findings of previous studies. Both form and content of information appear to be associated with the nature of the communicating agent as a social system with its set of functions, norms, and operational features. Greater refinement in the roles of the communicating agents might be obtained (a) by a series of questions pertaining to each type of agent, and (b) by questions pertaining to different types of changes or practices.

[7] E. A. Wilkening, "Sources of Information for Improved Farm Practices," *Rural Sociology*, XV (March 1950), 19–30.

Communication and Opinion Formation in a Medical Community: The Significance of the Detail Man

ROBERT R. REHDER

Communication and opinion formation have developed into major areas of interest for business and behavioral science studies. In recent years, research has pointed to the importance of interpersonal relations in communication and opinion formation processes. Studies indicate that individual decisions are strongly influenced by person to person relay networks and group norms which "intervene" in the mass communication process.[1]

THE MEDICAL COMMUNITY

The American medical profession's highly structured organization, sophisticated social controls and increasing reliance on an innovation-oriented pharmaceutical industry make this a particularly attractive research area. Further, given the current innovation rate of the pharmaceutical industry, it is not altogether surprising to find considerable interest by both business and the behavioral sciences in the communication and opinion formation processes within the medical profession.

The pharmaceutical industry is reputedly spending approximately three times the average for all United States industry research expenditures.[2] Its high innovation rate is making old products and markets obsolete at an accelerated rate. One of several important developments is the rapidly increasing shift to *ethical* pharmaceuticals.[3] Between 1939 and 1959 the pharmaceutical manufacturer's sale of drugs has increased from $300 million to $2.3 billion, with ethical drugs accounting for all but approximately $4 million of this rapid growth.[4] Control of the over $2 billion ethical drug market is therefore exercised by approximately 170,000 practicing physicians through prescriptions.

The objective of this paper is to analyze the detail man's role in the diffusion and adoption of a new ethical pharmaceutical within a single medical community. For the purposes of this study, the medical community was defined

◆ SOURCE: Reprinted by permission from the *Academy of Management*, December 1965, pp. 282–291.

[1] Elihu Katz and Paul F. Lazarsfeld, *Personal Influence* (Glencoe, Illinois: The Free Press, 1955). This book is one of the most complete and authoritative works in this field and contains an extensive bibliography of related studies.

[2] Pharmaceutical Manufacturer's Association Staff Survey as presented by Austin Smith, President of the Association, before the U.S. Senate Sub-Committee on Antitrust and Monopoly Legislation, February 23, 1960. "All Industry" figures are from the American Management Association, Sept., 1959. (Made available by the Pharmaceutical Manufacturer's Association.)

[3] An *ethical* pharmaceutical is one promoted to the physician or another licensed medical or dental practitioner for his administration or prescribed use.

[4] Charles E. Silberman, "Drugs: The Pace Is Getting Furious," *Fortune*, May, 1960, p. 139.

as the population of people utilizing the services and facilities of a common medical center. The medical center would normally be comprised of a central hospital, with various combinations of medical and paramedical education facilities, surrounded by clinics, research institutions and various allied medical groups.

THE ROLE OF THE DETAIL MAN

A review of the literature in the field of medical communication and opinion formation indicates that the ethical pharmaceutical company's service representative, the *detail man*,[5] plays an important role in physician innovative behavior. However, there is little research centered on the detail man.

Previous studies have largely relied on physican responses to questions concerning his drug adoption influencing sources.[6–10] Several have noted that a physician's response to a question posed by a non-medical profession member will be influenced by what the doctor believes his medical colleagues would expect him to say. [11, 12]

The physician in the United States is looked

upon as being a model of ethical and scientific behavior. He is expected to make rational decisions based on the identification and evaluation of all the available, relevant evidence. The importance of reference group behavior in the evaluation of a physician's response concerning factors influencing his innovative behavior was emphasized by Hawkins and Hall.[13] The authors stated that the responses of the physician would probably vary according to the interviewers, as a physician desires to perpetuate his profession's stereotype to non-members. Dr. Hawkins related his experiences representing himself as a sociologist and later as a health scientist when questioning physicians. He stated that the role of the health scientist, as an in-group member, elicited greater spontaneity and frankness. The authors further noted that to date, even in research conducted by professional research agencies, apparently no one has attempted to gain these underlying in-group innovation factors by medical identification or sponsorship.

THE INTRODUCTION OF INNOVATION INTO THE MEDICAL COMMUNITY

This paper draws upon data from a study of a large pharmaceutical company's introduction of a new ethical pharmaceutical product in 1959. The study centered on one West Coast medical community in order to analyze the many variables interacting within a single medical community any of which may influence innovation behavior.

In order to gain a comparative understanding of the major ethical pharmaceutical firms, ten companies were selected for a two month pilot study. Such areas as clinical research and the new product introduction program, including field travel with detail men, were given special attention. Particular effort was made in the research design to avoid the distortion of physician reference group behavior.

Then a single well-established and highly diversified ethical pharmaceutical company was selected from the pilot study for further study. The selection procedure was of considerable importance as a pharmaceutical company's standing with the medical profession greatly affects its marketing program and, in particu-

[5] U.S. Department of Labor, *Dictionary of Occupational Titles*, 2d ed. (Washington, D.C.: 1949). The *detail man* "introduces new pharmaceutical products and their methods of use to physicians, dentists, hospitals, and public health officials, promoting the use of the product rather than selling it. This requires a thorough familiarity with the application of the medical preparations and a general knowledge of medical practice." Perceptive professors may liken the activity to that of the book publisher's representative at its best, especially as the story unfolds.

[6] Theodore Caplow, "Market Attitudes: A Research Report from the Medical Field," *Harvard Business Review*, XXX (November, 1952), pp. 105–112.

[7] Theodore Caplow and John J. Raymond, "Factors Influencing the Selection of Pharmaceutical Products," *Journal of Marketing*, XIX (1954), pp. 18–23.

[8] American Medical Association, *Effectiveness of Promotion in a Medical Marketing Area*, A Study Conducted by Ben Gaffin and Associates (Chicago: American Medical Association, 1956).

[9] Robert Ferber and Hugh G. Wales, *The Effectiveness of Pharmaceutical Promotion* (Urbana, Illinois: University of Illinois Press, 1958).

[10] American Medical Association, *Attitudes of U.S. Physicians Toward the American Pharmaceutical Industry*, A Study Conducted By Ben Gaffin and Associates (Chicago: American Medical Association, 1958).

[11] Pharmaceutical Advertising Club, *Pharmaceutical Advertising* (New York: Pharmaceutical Advertising Club, 1955), pp. 3, 17.

[12] Caplow, *loc cit.*

[13] Norman Hawkins and Esther Hall, "The Social Psychology of Prescription Writing," *American Journal of Hospital Pharmacy*, XVII (March, 1960), p. 146.

lar, its detail men's access to the physician. The selection of the new medical product and the medical community further involved many considerations.

The new product selected was available only by prescription and would be advertised only to the medical profession. In addition, for obvious reasons, the new product selected (hereafter referred to as the innovation) was not a long-awaited wonder drug nor a product of limited or highly questionable need and effectiveness. As this study involved the detail man's interactions within a medical community, both the characteristics of the medical community and the company's detail men servicing that community were evaluated together in the selection procedure.

The population of the West Coast community selected was 180,000 people, including approximately 400 American Medical Association registered physicians. This medical community was serviced by four experienced detail men from the cooperating company, all having been with that company for at least five years. The cooperating firms' central and area management provided complete information regarding the research and introduction program for the innovation, including all the communication channels involved and budgets. Records were kept of all medical journal advertising, direct mail, research articles, abstracts, product samples and other promotion material concerning the innovation and its distribution. In addition, verbatim notes were taken of all area marketing meetings involving the medical community and its detail men when the new product was involved.

The pilot study revealed that detail men will occasionally travel in pairs and that medical personnel normally assume the silent observer to be another company representative. If the researcher's identity happened to be revealed during the physician visit, the material was excluded from the study. Verbatim notes were taken of 75 physician details [14] introducing the innovation within the medical community. This information was supplemented with notes concerning the detail men's professional and social relationship with the physician as related by the detail men. Fifteen physician details were eliminated because the researcher's

identity was revealed during the visit. Attention was also given to minimizing undesirable observer interaction with the four detail men servicing the medical community and their supervisors.[15] During the first weeks of field study, however, some observer influence was apparent with the detail men. The detail men were at first more formal and cautious, and responses concerning methods and practices were inclined to be guarded.

The limited number of detail men from one company servicing the single medical community is not assumed to be representative of nation-wide detail men's professional or social relationships with the medical profession. However, the pilot study with ten major companies, and numerous discussions with the management and detail men from these companies who had previously worked in various parts of the country, did suggest a general similarity in detailing methods and professional relationships among the major ethical pharmaceutical companies. The cooperating company employs a nation-wide training and development program for its large detail force. To that extent the formal detailing methods and procedures, as well as detailing aids and supporting promotional methods, were generally uniform throughout the United States. The company's marketing program for the selected innovation was the same throughout the United States and was launched simultaneously.

INTERPERSONAL RELATIONSHIPS AND RECIPROCITY

Each of the four detail men servicing the medical community was seen to have a variety of territories and detailing characteristics. However, a continuing established relationship with territory medical personnel was common to all of these men. The relationships established with medical personnel appeared to be a most significant factor in the introduction and diffusion of the innovation within the medical community.

Each detail man had his list of physicians, referred to as "good writers," with whom he had developed a favorable relationship and who regularly wrote prescriptions specifying his company's products. The significance of this

[14] The terms "detail" and "detailing" are commonly used in the pharmaceutical industry and, in general, refer to the promotion methods and efforts of the detail man previously defined.

[15] The four detail men introducing the innovation to the medical community under study are not identified or further described for disguise purposes.

interpersonal relationship was indicated by several physicians who were quite apologetic for not writing a detail man's product after they had been detailed on it during the last visit. They promised to switch to it. One of the significant functions of the norm of reciprocity, as defined by Alvin W. Goulder, is its facilitation of social interaction.[16] The norm provides realistic grounds for mutual trust by imposing obligations on the person who has received a benefit to repay it at some time.

The *samples, professional services* and *social communication* provided by the detail man and the physician's reciprocal prescription patronage were factors contributing to the development of a favorable detail man–physician relationship. The provision of samples, gifts, and entertainment to the medical profession has been one of the more highly publicized functions of detail men, as a result of congressional investigations.[17] In the introduction of the innovation under study, samples of the innovation, vitamins and other high value pharmaceuticals were widely and regularly distributed. Samples of specific drugs were also frequently requested by the physician for his family and paramedical staff.

Another service directly related to the latter is the detail man's *ability to economize the physician's time.* There are two major aspects to the detail man's function in time economy.

One is his potential ability to reduce the time lag between the availability of a new therapeutic agent and its application by the physician. Significant factors appeared to be:

a. The detail men's established knowledge of the medical personnel in their territories allowed them to concentrate their promotion information on those specialists who would have the greatest potential need for such innovations.

b. Their various degrees of established interrelationships with the medical personnel facilitated both their access to, and promotion efforts with, the local physician.

c. They directed the physician's attention to selected professional information from all major local and national sources supporting their product, and immediately answered particular questions concerning it.

The second related aspect of the detail man's function in time economy is his potential ability to increase the physician's personal current therapy education time. Time is a most precious commodity to the successful physician and keeping current on a steady procession of new therapeutic agents alone requires a significant portion of his time.[18] The pharmaceutical industry is quite aware of the premium the physician places on this dimension and expends considerable effort to educate and help their detail men economize the physician's time. Raymond Bauer and Mark Field in a study of the Soviet Pharmaceutical System discuss Soviet new product information dissemination problems.[19] They cite State arrangements encouraging the use of personal representatives of pharmacies or pharmaceutical sub-depots to communicate new drug product information to the physician.

The preliminary activities, as well as the presentations of the detail men, were planned to further the physician's time economy. The detail men observed were quite proficient at adapting their schedules to coincide with the physician's free time, canceled appointments, or breaks between patients.

The detail presentations were further designed to provide a maximum amount of specialized information in a short period of time. In general, the detailing time devoted exclusively to the discussion of the innovation under study ranged between three to six minutes. In the short period of time devoted to the innovation, the medical syndrome involved and

[16] Alvin W. Goulder, "The Norm of Reciprocity: A Preliminary Statement," *American Sociological Review,* XXV (April, 1960), p. 161. Mr. Goulder states that the norm of reciprocity is one of the universal "principal components" of moral codes. He further suggests that the norm of reciprocity makes a minimal demand that people should help those who have helped them.

[17] U.S. Senate, Statement by Dr. A. Console before the U.S. Senate Subcommittee on Antitrust and Monopoly, April 13, 1960, p. 14 (made available by the Committee on the Judiciary 86th Congress). ". . . not to mention the added inducement of the free cocktail party and the golf outing complete with three golf balls stamped with the name of the doctor and the company in contrasting colors."

[18] For further analysis of the physician's problems involving available time for new product education see Bauer, Raymond A. "Risk Handling in Drug Adoption," *Public Opinion Quarterly,* Vol. 25 (Winter, 1961).

[19] "Ironic Contrast: U.S. and USSR Drug Industries," *Harvard Business Review,* September–October, 1962.

the new product indicated for its treatment were reviewed and a printed file card containing this information was given to the physician. Local and national professional sources of information concerning the syndrome and the innovation were drawn to the physician's attention and frequently discussed. Questions concerning the product were answered or referred to the company's medical staff. Samples of the product were shown and given to the physician for his trial use. In addition to therapeutic information, the detail men, having mobility and breadth of continuing medical associations, were seen to be a major channel of medical community social information. The topics regularly discussed during the details were recent local changes in hospital and group practice affiliation as well as professional and social meetings.

The detail men's established relationships with the pharmacists, nurses, and receptionists also facilitated new product introduction within the medical community. The willingness of the pharmacist to cooperate in the detail man's search of the physician's prescription file was seen to be of great importance. The local pharmacy prescription file [20] provided the detail men with a certain indicator of their detailing effectiveness and very helpful control information regarding changing prescription habits. The relationships established by the detail men with the medical community nurses and receptionists enchanced the detail men's access to their physicians and greatly increased the detail man's effectiveness. The physician's trial use of the innovation samples on the nurses was not uncommon, and their trial satisfaction provided local testimonials of the product's effectiveness.

With growing competition from similar or virtually indentical products manufactured by different companies, the importance of favorable interpersonal relationships has become increasingly important. Only the Dichter study, where projective interview techniques were used, indicates that a favorable interpersonal relationship between the detail man and the physician might influence the prescription brand preference of the phy-

sician.[21] This inference was underscored by the study's finding that 45% of the physicians indicated that a "good" detail man was more like a friend than a salesman.

The influence of reference group behavior is strongly indicated in the responses of physicians to questions posed by non-medical outsiders concerning the physician's attitudes toward individual companies. The Ben Gaffin study, for example, revealed that nearly one-half of all the doctors interviewed indicated that they had a favorite company whose products they tended to prescribe.[22] When questioned further, however, as to why they preferred these companies and their products, the physicians indicated that it was the "reliability of product, competency of detail men, quality and quantity of research, and truthfulness and low-pressure of its advertising," implying the absence of non-objective decision-making influence. A large number and variety of non-stereotyped physician responses recorded by the observer during his assumed identity as a detail man during this project would strongly suggest significant non-objective factors influencing the physician's prescription decisions. The influence of limited trial results on family or staff personnel, and favored pharmaceutical companies and detail men were frequently recorded.

THE DETAIL MAN AS A COMMUNICATIONS RELAY

The importance of interpersonal relations as an intervening variable in the mass communications process has been indicated by numerous studies outside of a specialized scientific community.[23, 24]

The detail men in this study exposed the medical community physicians to information from the following sources in support of the innovation (see Table 1):

a. Professional journals—the innovation's advertisements and clinical research articles

[20] Pharmacy prescription files are required by law in the United States and contain the name of the physician, the name of the product and how it was designated (trade or generic name) as well as the date it was written.

[21] Pharmaceutical Advertising Club, *Pharmaceutical Advertising* (New York: The Pharmaceutical Advertising Club, 1955).
[22] American Medical Association, *Effectiveness of Promotion in a Medical Marketing Area* (Chicago: American Medical Association, 1956).
[23] For example, see Paul F. Lazarsfeld, Bernard Berelson, and Hazel Gaudet, *The People's Choice* (New York: Columbia University Press, 1948).
[24] Bernard R. Berelson, Paul F. Lazarsfeld, and William N. McPhee, *Voting* (Chicago: University of Chicago Press, 1954).

including local patient research by community physicians.

b. Direct mail and house organ advertising.
c. Promotion material and samples of the innovation.
d. Unpublished local innovation research conducted in cooperation with the company in order to establish its clinical acceptability for mass distribution.
e. Local medical current therapeutic and product cost information concerning the innovation.

The innovation introductory marketing programs included advertisements in seven different medical journals over a twelve-week period. Abstracts of company journal advertisements were regularly made available to the detail men for incorporation into their detail presentations and distribution to the physician. Another frequently cited journal reference in this study was a professional article reporting the clinical results of the innovation with 60 patients. This article was also abstracted by the company and regularly used in the innovation detail presentations. It contained several references to national medical leaders in support of the product and favorable passages were underlined and specifically directed to the physician's attention.

The detail men in addition frequently distributed and drew the physician's attention to both the innovation direct mail physician announcement letter and the company house organ. The latter is mailed weekly to 139,000 physicians and contained twenty consecutive weekly half page advertisements of the innovation.

The promotion material, in addition to the samples previously discussed, consisted of a

Table 1. The Innovation Introductory Program

Promotion Method	January Week 1	2	3	4	February Week 1	2	3	4	March Week 1	2	3	4	April Week 1	2	3	4	Budget [b]
Detailing	X	X	X	X	X	X	X	X									$600,000 [c]
Promotion literature	X	X	X	X	X	X	X	X									16,000
Samples	X	X	X	X	X	X	X	X	X	X	X	X	X	X	X	X	211,200 [d]
Announcement letter [a]	X																7,200
House organ advertising	X	X	X	X	X	X	X	X	X	X	X	X	X	X	X	X	64,000
Professional journal advertising																	
Journal #1		X				X			X				X				
Journal #2			X				X				X				X		
Journal #3	X				X				X				X				
Journal #4	X				X				X				X				
Journal #5	X				X				X				X				
Journal #6	X				X								X				
Journal #7	X				X								X				
Total journal budget																	48,000
Total budget estimate																	$898,400

[a] Announcement letters sent to all retail pharmacists having accounts with the Company and to physicians practicing in the following specialties: obstetrics, gynecology, internal medicine, general practice, industrial physicians, and resident physicians.

[b] Denotes total budget appropriations as estimated by the Company multiplied by a constant figure.

[c] The innovation detailing figure was estimated from single detail call costs and average number of calls per day estimates supplied by the Company, in addition to the author's medical community results regarding the per cent of physician detailing time received by the innovation.

[d] Sample budget is based on manufacturer's wholesale price.

ten page booklet on the innovation and its indications, and a set of notebook size flip-cards for use by the detail man. In addition, 3×5 file cards summarizing the product's key uses, dosages, etc., and innovation printed prescription blanks ready for the physician's signature were regularly distributed.

Unpublished local innovation clinical research also played an important part in the introduction of the new product. One detail man was requested by the company to recommend a specialist in the medical community to conduct final phase clinical research on the innovation six months prior to the introduction date. A well-known community specialist agreed to undertake the study and the results were eventually sent to the company medical department. Similar local clinical research studies were carried out in various parts of the United States and are a regular part of the industry's new product research program. The detail man stopped by regularly to express his interest in the research physician's results. He received a satisfactory report from the doctor but an enthusiastic endorsement from his nurse who was trying the product. The reports of this clinical innovation study were reviewed during its introduction to the community detail men and were thereafter regularly cited by the detail men in their visits to community physicians.

Another significant facet of the detail men's communications relay function was the use of therapeutic and product cost comparisons in support of the innovation. The physician is currently confronted with a large and constantly growing number of specific and potent therapeutic agents generally available in many forms, strengths, and combinations from a number of competing companies. This state of affairs has greatly increased the opportunities for incompatibilities and dangerous side effects. Countless questions are raised that cannot all be anticipated and printed; or, because of legal complications, they are preferably left unprinted.

It was observed in the pilot study that subtle product comparisons were regularly used by detail men from the ten major ethical pharmaceutical companies involved in the study. Through the use of subtle product comparisons and direct answers to the more specific questions frequently posed by the physicians, the detail men can treat awkward and controversial material. The detail man appeared to be a preferred channel of communication for such information. For example, one detail man made 35 specific references to local physicians' opinions and/or results in his 26 innovation details. In addition, the traditional Journal advertising policy followed by the ethical pharmaceutical house avoids product comparison advertising and the legal complications arising from its use.

Comparative economic information was seen to play a particularly important part in the introduction of the new product within the community. Physician interest in this area, as indicated by the high frequency of their inquiries and responses, was also significant. The detail men regularly utilized the local prices of competing products to support the economic advantage of the innovation. The detail men are again the only media regularly providing comparative economic product information.

The importance of the therapeutic information made available by the detail men to the physician was also indicated by an analysis of the physician's inquiry and response participation in the calls. A tabulation of the physician's therapeutic inquiries revealed a high interest in the composition of the product, strength, dosage indications and precautions advisable.

Of major significance was the part played by the detail man in relaying both mass and interpersonal information in an effort to influence the physician's innovation behavior. The studies of Menzel and Katz further indicate that interpersonal channels are also important as mediators of influence in the medical profession.[25, 26] There is some indication that the detail man is able to by-pass opinion leaders who might interfere with mass media innovation information relay via social channels. The detail man's established medical relationships and good prescription writers further appear to facilitate his acquiring group member endorsement.

In addition, the detail men also filtered both mass and interpersonal information to support the new product. Lazarsfeld and Katz indicate that if interpersonal communication agrees with the mass media, there will be a "reinforcing" effect which will facilitate the influence

[25] Herbert Menzel and Elihu Katz, "Social Relations and Innovation in the Medical Profession: The Epidemiology of a New Drug," *Public Opinion Quarterly*, XIX (1955–56), pp. 337–352.
[26] Herbert Menzel, Elihu Katz, and James Coleman, "The Diffusion of an Innovation Among Physicians," *Sociometry*, XX (1957), pp. 253–270.

attempt.[27] The fact that the detail man is recognized by the physician as a professional representative of his company and advocate of its products might, however, affect this reinforcement.

The detail men's unique interaction with both mass and interpersonal communication channels suggests that factors influencing medical opinion formation cannot be effectively evaluated by statistical sampling of respondents treated as isolated individuals. The considerable hiatus between the American medical stereotype and the individual physician's human cognitive limitations, as well as the indications cited above, indicate the need for gaining additional medical in-group identification in future research.

CASES

Establishing a New Sales Organization (Procter & Gamble—A)

Procter & Gamble was founded in 1837 as a partnership to manufacture and sell soaps and candles. Later in the century, the development of other lighting methods greatly reduced the demand for candles, whereas improved national cleanliness habits increased the use of soap. As a consequence, soap became considerably more important to the business than candles. Eventually, the Company stopped manufacturing candles altogether.

Shortly after the turn of the century, a development occurred which was far-reaching because it placed the Company in the food business. P&G had formed a subsidiary in 1901 to acquire and build seed crushing mills in southern cotton states to assure a constant supply of cottonseed oil for use in the manufacture of soap. The Company refined some of the higher grades of the cottonseed oil and sold them to other manufacturers to be used in making salad oils. The experience gained working with this raw material prompted the Company chemists to search for a way to use these vegetable oils in a shortening product which would be superior to lard. The development of an entirely new manufacturing process was the answer to this problem. The new process made it possible to convert cottonseed oil to a creamy form which appears to be solid at room temperature and has almost indefinite keeping qualities. Crisco—the first creamy, white, all-vegetable shortening—was introduced in 1911, establishing P&G in the food field.

Since Procter & Gamble at that time was known solely as a manufacturer of soaps, the introduction of its first food .product required thoughtful preparation in manufacturing, selling and advertising. Because cooking fats were sold through the same outlets as soap, it was important to educate the dealer that Crisco was a fine edible product—not a by-product of soap. Because Crisco represented an entirely new type of cooking fat, there would be an advantage to packing it differently from lard, which was sold at that time in cartons and in bulk. The packaging problem was solved by packing Crisco in cans, thus providing a visible form of differentiation and, also, giving the product itself added protection. Aside from helping the education of the dealer, these actions also helped educate the consumer on the existence of this new concept in food.

At the time of Crisco's introduction, P&G sold only to grocery wholesalers—not directly to retailers. To avoid confusion, the Company initially used separate salesmen to sell Crisco to the wholesalers. After Crisco had been introduced, however, it was added to the line of products sold by the Company's Case Goods Sales Department. This, of course, required careful training and indoctrination of the salesmen.

In the early 1920's, P&G decided to sell directly to retailers as well as to wholesalers. The Company had been concerned for some time about the cyclical buying of soap by wholesalers because of their awareness of the fluctuation in the market for tallow, then a principal ingredient in soap manufacture and an important cost factor. (Tallow, like other commodities, often ranges widely in price. For example, during the 1919–21 period, tallow sold for as low as 5¢ a pound and as high as 21¢ a pound.) Whenever the wholesaler felt that a rise in the price of tallow was imminent, he would be inclined to order soap heavily. On the other hand, if he anticipated a price drop, he would resist ordering as long as possible. This resulted in wide swings in manufacturing schedules, with factories running day and night for certain periods and then being forced to close at other times of the year.

◆ SOURCE: Reprinted by permission from The Procter & Gamble Company, c. 1961.

[27] Elihu Katz and Paul F. Lazarsfeld, *Personal Influence* (Glencoe, Illinois: The Free Press, 1955), pp. 82–83.

Thus, at the manufacturing level workmen faced periods of unemployment, and at the retail level stores frequently ran out of stock and consumers were unable to buy P&G products, because wholesalers sometimes waited too long to order.

A Company study revealed that consumers used soap fairly constantly throughout the year. The solution, therefore, appeared to be to sell directly to retailers as well as to wholesalers and insure an even flow of P&G products to the public. This meant the development of a much larger field sales organization and the reorientation of the members of the existing force. The results, however, were worth the effort. By eliminating the reasons for cyclical buying, P&G was able to plan production schedules at a fairly even rate throughout the year, which provided many operating economies and stabilized employment. As a direct result, in 1923, only two years after direct retail selling was inaugurated, the Company was able to initiate a plan of guaranteed annual employment under which hourly paid employees are guaranteed at least 48 weeks of work each year.

The work on synthetic detergents in Germany in the early 1920's made it possible for Procter & Gamble to diversify in another direction. Based on this work, P&G in the early 1930's developed a synthetic detergent, Dreft, which, unlike soap, did not combine with the minerals present in hard water to produce a film, or deposit, often referred to as "soap film." From this work, it became apparent to P&G management that synthetic detergents should provide an excellent base for a shampoo product which would not leave a film deposit on the hair, and thus would give hair a better luster than a soap base shampoo could. Procter & Gamble, therefore, introduced Drene detergent shampoo in 1934 as its first entry in the beauty field.

The distribution pattern for shampoo products was different from that of soap and shortening products. At the time of the Drene introduction, the largest percentage of shampoo sales occurred in drug and department stores rather than in grocery outlets. Soap and shortening, on the other hand, were sold almost 100% in grocery stores.

P&G decided, therefore, to set up a special Drene sales force to sell only this one product. This group grew until after the war it became the Toilet Goods Sales Department, within an entirely separate Toilet Goods Division set up by P&G to concentrate on health, beauty and toiletry products. With the increased importance of the supermarkets after the war, the Toilet Goods Sales Department in many instances called on the same dealers and buyers as the Case Goods Sales Department.

P&G adheres to a policy of promotion from within the Company; consequently, practically all management personnel for the Toilet Goods Sales Department came from either the Drene sales force or the Case Goods Sales Department. After World War II, the Toilet Goods Sales Department was called upon to introduce many new brands in quick succession, including Prell and Shasta shampoos, Lilt and Party Curl home permanents, Gleem and Crest toothpaste, and Secret deodorant.

Following the war, the Company also experienced substantial growth in its soap and detergent business, due primarily to the introduction of new synthetic detergent brands such as Tide, Joy and Cheer. These new brands were added to an already substantial line of cleaning products. Crisco, however, remained the only food product sold by the Case Goods Sales Department until 1955 when the Company introduced golden Fluffo shortening nationally. Ten years after World War II, the Case Goods Sales Department was selling 17 large-volume soap, detergent and food brands. The line was so large the Company began to consider the desirability of establishing another sales force to handle several of these products.

Recognizing the tremendous growth potential in the food business which would result from a burgeoning population together with higher per capita incomes and standards of living, the Company began considering the establishment of a Case Food Sales Department to sell Crisco and Fluffo, as well as to handle the introduction of other food products on which the Company had been doing considerable research for a number of years. This food sales department, if established, would be part of a P&G Food Products Division which would operate separately from the Soap Division and the Toilet Goods Division.

QUESTION

1. Should a separate food sales department be established? Please give reasons to substantiate your decision.

Fifty-Cents Deal

Good Foods Company is a nationally known manufacturing and marketing corporation. Good Foods manufactures toilet soaps, toothpastes, shampoos, packaged household detergents, and dozens of different food products. These many products are marketed under a policy of intra-company competition. This means that each product has its own brand name and must compete with other related products made by Good Foods. Of the many merits of this type of marketing, possibly the most important is that by having several different brands of a related product on the market, Good Foods can obtain a greater percentage of the total market for this product than it could if it only marketed one brand of this product.

Good Foods Company has an excellent marketing team. The marketing functions of this company are broken up into three main divisions of which the Foods Division is one of the largest. On July 1, Chuck Sellers became salesman for Good Foods Company in the large Foods Division. He was assigned a nine-county area in Eastern Texas in which to sell the food products of Good Foods.

Prior to joining this company, Chuck had majored in Business Administration at Texas State College. Upon his graduation in May of 1962, he started teaching accounting in a large high school. Recently, Chuck's wife Betty had a baby girl. With the new addition to the family, Chuck decided to stop teaching and enter into a career of selling. He had always heard that salesmen were well paid but other than having taken several courses in salesmanship and advertising while in college, he had absolutely no knowledge of how to sell or even if he could sell.

Chuck wrote to several large companies about a job in selling, and one of the first to answer was Good Foods Company. After talking with their representatives, Chuck decided to take a job with them. When Chuck had mentioned that he had no selling experience, the Good Foods representative laughed and told him that teaching was excellent preparation for entering into a selling job.

When Chuck started to work on July 1, a Good Foods representative came down to show him the basic methods of selling. At the end of three days, the Good Foods representative, who was also the District Manager for Eastern Texas and Chuck's supervisor, returned to his office in Dallas and left Chuck to learn his job on his own.

Chuck, although a little unsure of himself, started out on his route to sell Good Foods products to food wholesalers and food jobbers. When he entered the office of the first jobber, Chuck tried out the selling methods that his supervisor had shown him. The selling worked, but Chuck found that he did not even know how to fill out the order blank. The jobber had to show him how to fill out the orders. In the brief three-day training period, there had not been enough time for the District Manager to teach him how to do any of the vast amount of paperwork that had to be sent to the main office of Good Foods in Atlanta, Georgia.

Each night after having spent approximately eleven hours traveling from one jobber's warehouse to another, Chuck returned home to face two to three hours of paperwork for the Atlanta office. Having had no instruction on how to do this paperwork, he had to continuously call his supervisor in Dallas for assistance. One result of this was a phone bill amounting to $300 the first month he worked for Good Foods. He believes that seventy-five per cent of this amount could easily have been saved if he had been given just a one-week training period.

As the days passed, Chuck liked his job more and more. He enjoyed selling and he had decided from the very beginning that he was going to be a salesman rather than just an order taker. As a salesman, it was his job to show the food wholesalers and jobbers the opportunities for savings if they would buy in carload lots, the percentages of markup they could obtain from the Good Foods products, and the deals and allowances that Good Foods offered occasionally.

After selling the products to the jobbers in carload lots, Chuck would then go to the retail stores that the jobbers supply and attempt to get these retailers to buy enough of the Good Foods products from the jobbers to be able to set up a good display. Chuck believes that more of his products will be sold if they are displayed prominently and in volume. Another reason Chuck visits the retailers is to try to convince them to feature Good Foods products in their advertisements on radio, television, and in the newspaper. Local advertising, Chuck believes, is one of the most important methods of obtaining sales for his products.

On July 21, Chuck received a letter from the Good Foods office in Atlanta. The letter stated:

"We are giving $0.50 allowance per case on Bake Brite cake mix on either 'purchase' or 'count and recount' basis. Your accounts may purchase on this deal during any consecutive two weeks between July 24 and September 2. The performance date will be September 16."

Chuck, having been with the company for only three weeks, had no idea what the letter meant and called the supervisor in Dallas for an explanation. The supervisor explained that the letter meant that Good Foods was giving a discount of $0.50 for each case of Bake Brite cake mix that is sold during any consecutive two-week period between July 24 and September 2 on either a "purchase" or a "count and recount" basis. If the "purchase" basis is used, a jobber will be given a discount on all of the Bake Brite cake mix that he buys during the consecutive two-week period, provided the jobber offers this mix to the retailer at the discounted price for any two weeks which must end on or before September 16. The jobber will pay the regular price for the cake mix and will be mailed a check from Good Foods for the discount of $0.50 per case on all Bake Brite cake mix that he purchases.

If the "count and recount" method is used, Chuck must count the cases of Bake Brite that the jobber has in stock on the first day of the two-week period. Then Chuck must count the cases of Bake Brite that the jobber has on his shelves on the last day of the two-week period. The jobber is then mailed a check for the discount of $0.50 per case for all of the Bake Brite cake mix that he sells during the two-week period. If a jobber had a large stock of Bake Brite, he would probably prefer the "count and recount" method. However, if the jobber uses the purchase method, he might be able to purchase more than his retailers would require for the two-week period. In this case the jobber could keep the discount for himself.

Many of the jobbers were quite pleased with the offer, and all of them tried to take full advantage of it. On August 1, Chuck presented the offer to John Brown, the owner-manager of Brown Wholesale Company. Chuck and Mr. Brown had become good friends in the short time that he had been working for Good Foods, and Mr. Brown had helped him fill out many of the order forms required by Good Foods.

After deciding to buy on the "purchase" method, Mr. Brown ordered 110 cases of Bake Brite cake mix. Two weeks later, on August 15, Chuck returned to Brown Wholesale Company and asked Mr. Brown if he wanted to purchase any more Bake Brite cake mix before the two-week period ran out. In answer to the question, Mr. Brown ordered 170 additional cases of cake mix.

While in the office Chuck asked to see invoices in order to confirm that Brown Wholesale Company had made the discount available to its retail customers for a two-week period. Subsequently, Chuck sent a request to the Atlanta office for them to send to Brown Wholesale the $0.50 discount per case or a total of $140 for the 280 cases of Bake Brite cake mix that had been purchased.

On Chuck's next visit to Brown Wholesale Company, he was met at the door by Mr. Brown who had the check from Good Foods. The check was made out for only $55 instead of the $140 that had been requested. By receiving the discount of only $55, this made Mr. Brown have a loss of $26.20 on the sale of the 280 cases of Bake Brite cake mix instead of the $58.80 profit that he had anticipated. Upon questioning, Chuck received the following information from Mr. Brown.

Mr. Brown told Chuck that he makes only 5 per cent profit on his sales of Bake Brite cake mix. Good Foods sold the mix to him at $4.12 per case. At 5 per cent profit per case, Mr. Brown normally sells the mix at $4.33 per case to the retailers. This gives Mr. Brown a gross profit of $0.21 per case or $58.80 gross profit on the entire sales of the 280 cases that he purchased during the two-week period. Mr. Brown had, however, granted the retailers the $0.50 discount per case which resulted in his selling the mix to them at $3.83 per case or a total of $1,072.40 for the 280 cases. Because he purchased the 280 cases for $1,153.60, there was a loss of $81.20. However, when Mr. Brown received the check from Good Foods for the discount of $140, he would have a gross profit of $58.80 which would be exactly the 5 per cent gross profit that Mr. Brown wanted.

Since the check was not for $140, Chuck immediately wrote to the Atlanta office and asked why Mr. Brown hadn't been sent the full amount of the discount that had been requested. Several days later, the answer came that the check was for the 110 cases that Mr. Brown had purchased on August 1, 1964. Mr. Brown's order for 170 cases on August 15, 1964, had not occurred within the prescribed two-week period. In order for a discount to have been granted on the second order, it must have been placed on or before August 14, 1964.

Because Chuck had never been told anything about this dating policy, he had assumed that the consecutive two-week period meant that he should take the date of the first order which was August 1 in this case and add two weeks or fourteen days to this initial date. This would mean that the last order must fall on or before August 15.

Chuck called Mr. Brown and told him what the Good Foods office in Atlanta had said. Mr. Brown was extremely nice and understanding about the whole matter; but Chuck, knowing he himself was to blame, doesn't think that Mr. Brown should have to take the loss. Chuck believes that because Good Foods had not explained this dating policy to him, they should back him up and honor the discount.

QUESTIONS

1. Should Chuck Sellers challenge the home office's decision in this matter? If so, how?
2. Write a letter to the home office explaining in detail why you think an additional check should be forwarded to Brown Wholesale Company.
3. What kind and how much training is required for this salesman's job? How can this training be best accomplished?

Michigan Chemical Distributors, Inc.
(Dow Chemical Company—A)

On December 5, Jim Bender, chemical salesman assigned to the Detroit Sales Office, received a telephone call from George Shepherd, the chief purchasing agent for the Michigan Automobile Company.

Michigan Automobile Company was one of the three largest car and truck manufacturers in the United States with annual sales in excess of a billion dollars. It was located in a large city in Michigan. The company was currently purchasing $3,000,000 of Dow materials annually.

Shepherd advised that for the last ten years his company had been buying carbon tetrachloride for bucket and dip degreasing of metal parts from Michigan Chemical Distributors, Inc., a Dow distributor. Purchases in the early

◆ SOURCE: Reprinted by permission from W. R. Bennett and L. T. Reeves, Jr., *Salesmanship: Selected Cases* (University, Alabama: National Society of Sales Training Executives, 1963).

years had been at the rate of a drum or two per month but had reached the truckload per month level.

Shepherd continued by stating that he desired to purchase the material directly from Dow for the following reasons:

1. That his company would be in a stronger position in the event of a shortage having purchased carbon tetrachloride direct rather than through a distributor.
2. That better technical service would be provided by Dow on problems arising from the use of carbon tetrachloride than could be provided by the distributor.
3. That the place of the distributor was in the less than truckload business, while the manufacturer should handle the truckload business.
4. That he personally disliked the new distributor salesman who called on him and too aggressively sought the carbon tetrachloride business.

Shepherd concluded by stating that he would like to discuss the matter with Bender when he next called on the Michigan Automobile Company on the tenth of December.

Michigan Chemical Distributors, Inc., was the most important Dow distributor in the State of Michigan. It was located in the city of Lansing and employed six salesmen to cover its territory, which included the State of Michigan except the city of Detroit. This distributor handled a limited line of industrial chemicals and annually sold $800,000 of Dow materials to all types of industrial firms. Michigan Chemical had worked for many years building a close relationship with Michigan Automobile. The distributor had always given service and speedy delivery on even the smallest orders. The distributor felt that this close relationship and excellent service had finally begun to pay off, since the size of orders for various chemicals had been increasing at a substantial rate.

Mr. Ralph King, the president of Michigan Chemical, was a man about fifty. He had made a good living in this business and had built a sizeable estate from its earnings. He was very aggressive and very easily upset. He liked to do business with Dow and was very friendly with the Dow salesman, Jim Bender, the various product managers in Midland, and top-level sales management. He had been a distributor for Dow for 25 years and had always approached Dow first when he was considering the addition of a new line of chemicals.

QUESTIONS

1. What kind of salesman is Jim Bender? What must he do in order to be successful?
2. What is the problem in this case as you see it?
3. Why should a company like Dow want to sell through a distributor?
4. How does a company determine at what point it should begin to sell direct?
5. Are the reasons given by Shepherd fabricated or real?
6. How much should personalities enter into a decision concerning this problem?
7. To what extent can Jim Bender dictate the distributor's policy?
8. How close a personal relationship should the Dow salesman have with the distributor?
9. How would you suggest that Bender handle this problem, assuming that Dow can change its policy?

"London Fog"

Londontown Manufacturing Company of Baltimore, Maryland, was incorporated in 1930 to manufacture men's custom tailored suits, sports coats, and top coats. Early in the 1950's the president of Londontown conceived the idea of a combination raincoat and top coat that would have utility as well as style. At this time the majority of raincoats on the market were plastic coats that retailed for $2.95 or less. The only "quality" raincoats on the market were imported from Europe. By 1954 the company had developed an all-purpose coat (combination raincoat-top coat). They mar-keted their cotton coat under the brand name "London Fog."

The advent of "Dacron" in 1956 provided the company with an opportunity for increased quality and variety in their products. Thus, with the growing popularity of the raincoat line, Londontown phased out of the custom tailored suit line and began to concentrate on raincoats and jackets. The "London Fog" coat, retailing at approximately $37.50, gained widespread acceptance and popularity from the outset.

The company's experience up to now has been that certain types of communities have greater potential as market areas for "London Fog" than others. For example, "white-collar" towns and "college" towns have generally provided easy and successful entry without a great amount of pioneering work by the company. The selection of a city or town has not presented nearly the problem that selection of the particular retail outlets in a community has. A general rule followed by Londontown is to have one store for every 10,000 people in a city (see Exhibit 1). While some latitude is available for selecting the specific type of outlet which will handle "London Fogs," the company attempts to find retail stores which meet certain criteria.

One of the characteristics Londontown looks for in searching out a "London Fog" dealer is whether or not the prospect has a downtown outlet and a shopping center outlet. The company feels that a branch store operation makes possible double distribution with only one merchandising effort. Following the same reasoning, a retailer is sought who handles both ladies' and men's wearing apparel.

The third characteristic looked for in a "London Fog" dealer stems from the company's

EXHIBIT 1

Average Towns and Relationship Between Population and London Fog Approved Stores

Town	Population (approx.)	London Fog Approved Stores	
		Specialty	Department
Wilmington	50,000	4	1
Wilson	30,000	2	1
Rocky Mount	35,000	2	1
Goldsboro	30,000	1	2

Note. A goal set by Londontown is to sell $1.00 for every person in the state.

belief that "people who shop specialty shops do not shop department stores and the result is very little crossover." Thus, several specialty shops (shops that sell quality clothes) are selected initially, followed by the selection of a quality department store.

Finally, a check on the financial status of likely prospects is made in *Dun and Bradstreet,* through local banks, or through other local sources.

Once a retail store has been selected as a prospective dealer, a Londontown representative contacts the store with an offer to make the "London Fog" line available. The company has encountered only a very small number of retailers who have rejected the offer.

After a retailer indicates his willingness and desire to handle the line, the Londontown representative explains the conditions and terms of a "London Fog" franchise. This verbal agreement as to conditions and stipulations establishes the franchise. Some of the requirements of a dealer who accepts the franchise are:

1. "London Fog" is to be sold at a suggested price. The owner must agree not to cut price or put "London Fog" on sale.

2. "London Fog" is not to be transshipped (shipping "London Fog" coats to stores not authorized to sell them).

3. "London Fog" requires certain action by the store manager in regard to advertising.

National advertising of "London Fog" is handled by the Gilbert Advertising Agency in New York. This agency is given a sizeable budget for a fall season campaign. The advertising program is devoted primarily to magazine and newspaper space. The major magazines and newspapers selected for "London Fog" advertisements are: *The New York Times; The New Yorker; Ebony; Esquire; Los Angeles Times; Sports Illustrated; Playboy; Off to College;* and *Holiday.* Recently, two of "London Fog's" advertisements won first and third places as the best advertisements in the apparel industry.

Advertising on a local level is carried out through a cooperative advertising plan. Londontown will supply mats and equipment for advertising in local newspapers. The owner of the store may, however, use his own art in local advertising. If he does, he must have the words "London Fog" in bold plain print and devote the complete advertisement to "London Fog." Londontown will match dollar for dollar up to five per cent of the shop's yearly

wholesale purchases from Londontown on amounts spent on local advertising.

Mr. Holly Wayneman is the Eastern North Carolina sales representative for Londontown. His duties include:

1. Soliciting as many orders as possible with careful regard to the needs of the shop. He must not sell more coats to a shop than the shop is likely to sell or handle. On the other hand, he must sell more to a shop if he feels they can handle more than they are presently handling.

2. Screening new dealers. This involves a survey of the market and shops, a credit check on the selected shops, and contacting the owner and explaining the verbal contract.

3. Terminating the franchise if the dealer is not performing satisfactorily. If the dealer is not selling as many "London Fog" coats as is believed within his capacity or if he is violating the verbal agreement, the Londontown representative could conceivably cancel his franchise.

4. Assisting in advertising. He provides mats and materials and approves local advertisements that are prepared by local artists.

5. Assisting with the merchandising. He must help the store owners arrange their orders over a period of time which will facilitate their making payments promptly.

6. Being constantly on the alert for unauthorized stores either selling "London Fog" coats or capitalizing on the name in some other way.

One of the biggest problems that confronts Mr. Wayneman has to do with the last duty mentioned above. In spite of the care and expense that goes into selecting the shops to handle "London Fog" coats, there is a constant problem involving unauthorized shops. The company believes that because of their extensive advertising program and complete capture of the market, others want to step in and get some share of this market, even if it means resorting to unethical practices. The following situation confronting Mr. Wayneman provides evidence of one way in which stores have tried to use the name "London Fog."

Store A in Wilson was not selected to represent "London Fog." This store is a member of a large chain that sells ladies' clothes at cut-rate prices. This type of store is never selected by Londontown as a dealer. One of Wayneman's Wilson customers, Store B, contacted him and said that he had come across a rack

EXHIBIT 2

in Store A that advertised "London Fog type" coats at a much cheaper price (see Exhibit 2).

QUESTIONS

1. What action, if any, would you take as the "London Fog" salesman?
2. Assume that the owner of Store B has indicated that he wants the situation, as reported in the case, corrected immediately, would a different type of strategy be called for?
3. What additional information would you like to have?
4. Define the job of a salesman for London-town.

People's National Bank
(Burroughs Corporation—A) *

Edward Ray has been employed by Burroughs Corporation as a salesman since June, 1957. Prior to joining the company, Ray was a student at Middleville College where he received a BS degree in Commerce and Business Administration with a major in accounting. After being hired by Burroughs, he was given trainee

◆ SOURCE: Reprinted by permission from Bennett and Reeves, *op. cit.*

* CASES prepared by James H. Bearden.

status for one year. During this period he received a monthly salary while attending training classes and receiving on-the-job instruction from a senior salesman.

After completing this training program, Ray was assigned to the Marion area as a salesman. This area was composed of the city of Marion, population 75,000, and several outlying towns with populations varying from 2,000 to 6,000. His compensation plan was changed to a commission basis upon the assumption of his new duties.

In this territory, Burroughs also employed two full-time service and maintenance personnel.

Ray owned his home in Marion where he and Mrs. Ray lived with their four children.

In order to keep pace with the expansion of American industry in recent years, business machine companies have undergone sweeping changes in their product offerings. Companies that a few years ago were thought of as merchandisers of adding machines, cash registers and accounting machines, have expanded their product lines to include "electronic brains" and "giant computers." Burroughs Corporation was one of these companies.

Burroughs' management recognized that changes and innovations in their product line called for constant changes in their selling program. They recognized that the highly technical and complex nature of computers and computer equipment required special knowledge and selling skills over and above those of a regular office machine salesman. Recognition of this situation resulted in a company-sponsored training course for the Burroughs' sales force. Two five-day sessions, one month apart, were offered on a voluntary basis. These classes were scheduled for April 25, 1961, and May 25, 1961. In addition, self-training material was provided for the sales force.

The Burroughs Corporation had computers on the drawing boards as early as 1950 and effected delivery in test areas in 1954. However, the first real job of passing literature on to the sales force did not begin until early 1959. Edward Ray became interested in the new product soon after he began to get information about them. He developed a special interest in the applications to banking organizations. Once he felt that he was familiar enough to answer questions and point out benefits of the computer, he began to discuss the product briefly in his contacts with banking accounts.

In November, 1960, he began a serious effort to interest the People's National Bank in a computer.

People's National, over the years, had been one of Ray's most steady accounts. Sales to People's National were among the first sales Ray had made after joining Burroughs. The person responsible for the bank's purchase of supplies and equipment was the senior vice-president, Mr. Hardy Davis, age 63. Throughout their association Ray had found Davis receptive to and interested in new ideas and suggestions regarding new types of equipment. Ray regarded Davis as a good business man who was deliberate and conservative in his purchasing role.

The attempts by Ray to arouse Davis' interest in Burroughs' Visible Record Computer, a $217,000 electronic data processing system, had been unsuccessful. Ray had gone so far as to prepare a detailed time study for the bank, showing that use of the computer would cut down employment and reduce certain other expenditures, while at the same time it would provide the bank with better information. This study was brought to Davis' attention on three separate visits by Ray, each time with no successful result.

In February, Ray, accompanied by his sales supervisor, Mr. J. O. Tremore, made another call on Davis. Again Davis resisted any notion of a purchase or even the initial step of submitting it to the president for his opinion. While the discussion was taking place, the president of the bank, William Denmark, entered Davis' office. Ray and Tremore both were acquainted with Denmark, although neither had had previous business dealings with him. After exchanging greetings with Ray, Mr. Denmark said, "What's the matter—can't you get him to buy?"

Ray replied in a half-joking tone, "I just can't seem to interest him in a real money-saving proposition for People's National."

"Don't tell me you're trying to replace these machines we just purchased last year!"

"No sir. What I'm trying to do is make it possible for you to sell us back those as well as most of your other office machines and let us substitute one compact unit which will handle the present work plus much more. You know— we are in the computer business now."

"Oh yes, that's right—while I was in Los Angeles at the banking conference last month, I saw the exhibit your company had set up in the lobby of our hotel. There was quite a bit of talk about the revolution in bank accounting systems. As a matter of fact, I made a note to call one of your business machine boys to give us a rundown on some of these developments, but somehow I just haven't gotten around to it yet. Tell you what—why don't you drop around this afternoon and bring me up to date?"

After a brief word with Davis on another matter, Denmark turned and moved toward the door—"Well, Ray, I'll see you around 3:00, if that's convenient with you."

"That will be fine, Mr. Denmark," replied Ray.

QUESTIONS

1. How should Ray handle the situation at the end of the case? Did Ray handle the matter properly up to the end of the case?
2. How should he handle the interview with Mr. Denmark?
3. How can a salesman handle resistance to change? Why is Davis reluctant to change?
4. How would a knowledge of General Semantics help the salesman?
5. What is the influence of Tremore on Ray's handling of the situation? Does Tremore's presence make the problem more difficult?
6. What do you think Davis expects of Ray? Does Ray's behavior conform to these expectations?

PART

II

Behavioral Sciences in Personal Selling

It is easy, in a single college or university, to find students who are being prepared in the various professional schools with widely different and sometimes strongly contrasting assumptions about the nature of and approach to this matter of human behavior. Students of political science, economics and business administration, psychology, sociology, and anthropology are each being presented with different beliefs, assumptions, and expectations about people and their behavioral patterns. Once in practice many of these "specialists," confident of their own knowledge and beliefs tend to ignore the insight and awareness which could be gained by borrowing from other disciplines. The "specialist" fails to recognize, as is so obviously the case in personal selling, that problems in the world of practical affairs are seldom purely "economic," purely "psychological," or purely "sociological."

It might well be proposed that the student of personal selling would be better off in a course in "human relations," "social relations," or some other course name applied to the provisional mergers of knowledge and research methodologies that deal with human behavior. This development is highly unlikely in the near future. Evidence of it may be found in the isolation and estrangement of the personal selling function currently espoused by most writers in the area.

What can and needs to be accomplished at this time, however, is a type of "borrowing" of material and ideas from various disciplines. The disciplines generally known as the "behavioral sciences" contain a tremendous inventory of material relevant to personal selling.

One of the major problems in making use of the knowledge relevant to personal selling issuing from the behavioral sciences is the sheer volume of material which has been developed. Should salesmanship be concerned with personality mechanisms of the individuals? Are "role" problems most urgent in the salesman-prospect relationship? Should the salesman concentrate on the "power" structure of the prospect system? What material should be brought to bear on the salesman-prospect relationship from the many offerings in the social sciences?

The discussions of which ideas or concepts should be used by the salesman may best be approached by an anecdotal illustration.

A group of spectators sat watching a football game. They saw two groups of eleven men facing each other, heard a whistle blow, then suddenly action erupted, followed by another blast of the whistle, whereupon everyone stopped. One of the spectators said, "That was a good draw play, we gained eight yards." When questioned about his jargon, he said, "Well, the quarterback handed the ball to the fullback, who counted off several seconds, waiting for the opposition to be drawn in, and then crashed into the middle of the line and advanced eight yards before being tackled and stopped. That's what is called a 'draw play.' " Someone asked a second spectator, "What did you see?" "Well," he replied, "I saw the acting out in different degrees of the needs for aggression and achievement in the players and the effects of how each views himself in relation to the other twenty-one men." A third spectator said, "I saw eleven men on either side engage in a pattern of coordinated behavior with very well worked out expectations of action for each position in regard to other positions, until these patterns were disrupted by the other side." A fourth spectator said, "I also saw your role relationship and integrations. But additionally, I saw a leadership structure, which included a man in one position calling signals during the play and a captain exercising some limited authority. I saw a social system of eleven men opposing another social system, each of which was composed of many subsystems and structures like leadership, conflict, plus a coach attached to each system." A fifth spectator said, "I saw two kinds of traditions: the ritualistic and emotional meaning of a game of this sort and the heightened excitement and tension of this particular game due to the traditional rivalry between these two teams. Both traditions reflect the competitive and peer values of our young adult culture."

Here we have a football fan's description and analysis of his "jargon." He has learned the concepts and conceptual schemas of football, and finds that it is a useful shorthand for describing a set of events. Also, we find an analysis of motives and self by the second spectator (perhaps an individual psychologist); a role analysis of expectations in a small task group by the third spectator (perhaps a small-group man); a portrayal of social structures and social systems by the fourth (no doubt a sociologist); and a statement of how the traditions and values of the culture affect behavior by the fifth (a cultural anthropologist).[1]

The observations and analyses of each observer utilize a different set of concepts and terms. The point to be made is that no one concept is the "only" one. Each has application in calling to attention a particular aspect of the situation. Just as a football coach or player might find one, two, or all of these interpretations useful in accomplishing his goals or tasks, so it is with the salesman as he investigates the various concepts dealing with human behavior.

In the final analysis, the question of which are the most relevant concepts, the most appropriate and useful concepts for a particular salesman-prospect relationship must be answered by the salesman. His own selective judgment must be used. No matter how many "how-to-do-it" sources or "cookbook" approaches he has consulted *he* must select and combine from the existing tools the ones which can be useful in performing his job.

PERSONAL SELLING FROM AN INTERDISCIPLINARY PERSPECTIVE

According to Stevens, in his article "The Application of Social Science Findings to Selling and the Salesman," psychologists and sociologists, through research and consultation, can greatly assist in achieving increased understanding of the

---

[1] Warren G. Bennis et al., *The Planning of Change* (New York: Holt, Rinehart and Winston, 1962), pp. 195–196.

role of the salesman in the marketing process. Findings on the sociopsychological characteristics of salesmen and the sociopsychological nature of the sales environment are stated.

Lazer and Kelley appraise the present and potential contributions of behavioral science findings and quantitative measurement methods to marketing in their article "Interdisciplinary Horizons in Marketing."

"Behavioral Science in Personal Selling Communication" deals with concepts that contribute to a better understanding of the face-to-face communication phase in the salesman-prospect relationship.

PSYCHOLOGICAL DIMENSIONS OF PERSONAL SELLING

An intriguing approach in recent efforts to obtain a theory of consumer behavior is presented in Bilkey's article "A Psychological Approach to Consumer Behavior Analysis." The figure and description below illustrate the nature of the article and its treatment of the vector hypothesis.

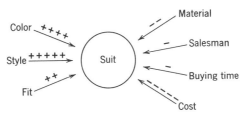

Figure 1

Recent developments emerging from gains in knowledge of the social sciences and particularly psychology have received a great amount of publicity. This in turn has led to a great amount of fear and anxiety in the general public concerning manipulation and persuasion. In the second article, "Limits of Persuasion: The Hidden Persuaders Are Made of Straw," a psychologist discusses many of these fears and places them in better perspective.

In a companion article to the preceding one, another way of looking at persuasion—at its opportunities rather than its limitations—is discussed. The theme of "Opportunities for Persuasion" is that "selling is a process of increasing wants, or even better creating new wants." And this is what keeps our economy dynamic.

The article, "Motivation, Cognition, Learning—Basic Factors in Consumer Behavior," presents an integration of concepts in contemporary psychology which the author, James A. Bayton, believes is necessary for a comprehensive explanation and analysis of human behavior. Bayton describes the interrelationships among the motivation, the weighing and rationalizing mind, and the learning behavior which influence the individual to repeat some acts and discard others. The concepts are drawn from diverse areas of psychology—from psychoanalysis to reinforcement theory.

SOCIOLOGICAL CONCEPTS IN PERSONAL SELLING

"The Significance of Social Stratification in Selling" is a treatment of the application of Lloyd Warner's well-known concept of social classes to selling and marketing problems. The author, Richard P. Coleman, states the purpose of the article thus: ". . . the purpose of this paper is to clarify *when* and *in what ways* social class concepts are significant in selling, and to suggest when they might not be as significant as other concepts, or at least need to be used in concert with other analytic categories."

The principles of group influence have long been recognized as instrumental in individual decision-making. In the two articles, "Reference Groups as Perspectives," and "Group Influence in Marketing and Public Relations," the significance of the concept of reference-group is considered. Shibutani's article is a broad treatment of the intricacies of reference-group analysis, while Bourne's study illustrates its relevance to a practical situation. The salesman's need to understand this concept is readily discernable by even the most casual observer of Bourne's definition of the concept: "On the common-sense level, the concept says in effect that man's behavior is influenced in different ways and in varying degrees by other people."

ECONOMICS AND ANTHROPOLOGY

In the first article Johnson discusses the coming changes in our labor force and productivity and the resultant effects on the economic role of selling. In his article, he notes that selling must receive increased recognition as an educational and stimulating force in the upgrading of the over-all standard of living. "The Need for Sales to Match Productive Ability" is clearly spelled out: "Supplying the 20 million new non-agricultural jobs in the next ten years, which we must have to satisfy the probable demands of our labor force of 1973, and to increase our total sales level to consumers by some $200 billion, will require both an expansion of selling efforts and rapid progress in increasing and measuring the effectiveness of selling."

Charles Winick, in "Anthropology's Contributions to Marketing," discusses some reasons for the infrequent use of anthropology and some thoughts of how it might be employed to the mutual benefit of marketing people and anthropologists.

A. Personal Selling from an Interdisciplinary Perspective

The Application of Social Science Findings to Selling and the Salesman

SAMUEL N. STEVENS

In one of the most penetrating studies of America as a civilization,[1] Max Lerner defines the distinguishing characteristic of our American tradition as "the emphasis placed on dynamism." "This dynamism," he observes, "cannot be chastely selective, with its elements chosen or rejected on the basis of class outlook and political belief. . . . The fact is that the American experience has operated in every area. There has been the dynamism of the pioneer and the mechanic, the independent farmer and the trade-union worker; of the toolmaker, the inventor, the financier. There has been the dynamism of the 'company men'—the managers, the factory organizers, the salesmen who have made the irrepressible practical imagination of Americans world-famous."

The psychologist, the sociologist, and the economist have all recognized that the saga of American success is vested in the willingness of men of vision to dare to dream and of hard-headed entrepreneurs to take the calculated risk. At the center of our business enterprise has been the man who sold the products of our mines, rivers, forests, and factories. Since the early days of the twentieth century, when the American people began to develop needs beyond the most primitive, it has been the peddler, wandering over the countryside with his cart of wares; the drummer, traveling by horse and buggy to visit the general stores along the highways and byways of our country; and the fast-talking, lone-wolf specialty salesman who, even as they sold their goods, created expanding needs and opened up ever larger markets. It is no exaggeration to say that, from an economic point of view, selling has been the most dramatic symbol of American dynamism. And the salesman has been called the last but most enduring social symbol of a restless, hungry, growing American culture.

A HISTORICAL PERSPECTIVE

In the early years of the twentieth century, the psychologist and the economist were the social scientists most interested in selling as a social phenomenon and the salesman as an economic factor in modern society. From 1900 to 1925, the psychologist's interest in these areas was focused primarily upon three problems:

1. The selection of men who would succeed as salesmen.
2. The psychological nature of selling as a form of behavior.

◆ SOURCE: Reprinted by permission from *Aspects of Modern Marketing, AMA Management Report* No. 15 (New York: American Management Association, Inc., 1958), pp. 85–94.

[1] Max Lerner, *America as a Civilization* (New York: Simon & Schuster, 1957).

3. The training and supervision of the salesman as aspects of learning and motivation.

During these years, advertising, sales promotion, and what there was of market research were thought of primarily as supporting mechanisms for the payoff work of the face-to-face salesman. In 1907 Walter Dill Scott [2] published the first systematic analysis of the problems of advertising and selling from the psychological point of view. From that time until the present, the books and articles written on the subject have been legion. The fact that much of this literature has been superficial, trite, and sterile need not cause us to overlook the important facts which underlie the problems as they were defined by both the psychologist and the economist.

The first important research in the selection of salesmen was carried on by Walter Dill Scott for the American Tobacco Company. Scott's search for important differences in the psychological characteristics of good and poor salesmen and of salesmen and non-salesmen was a pioneering effort. The fact that no significant results were achieved should surprise no one with any time perspective, for instruments capable of the precise measurement of individual differences in areas of sales significance did not then exist. Since that time, of course, the persistent quest for psychological understanding in this area has met with more success. Gradually we have developed a valid analytic concept of the sales environment and reliable instruments for the measurement of most of the important differences which distinguish the persuasive, hyperkinetic individual who can sell from the more analytical, less aggressive person who will find more stable occupational patterns more congenial.

The interest of psychologists in the problems of training and motivation began to be expressed in research form after World War I. The impressive psychological instruments and the greater understanding of the psychology of learning developed through research on military problems during the war led both professional and business men to be overly optimistic about the successful application of these tools and insights to the sales training situation. Yet continued research in the field of communication has since produced a body of technical and scientific knowledge which has taken most of the guesswork out of the organization of materials for sales training purposes. And the growth of clinical psychology, with its intensive studies of the personalities and social motivations of individuals, has made the supervision of salesmen a much more creative management function than it had been possible to achieve through the purely statistical and analytical approach taken prior to World War I.

SOCIOPSYCHOLOGICAL CHARACTERISTICS OF SALESMEN

At this point, let us consider, in rather general terms, the major conclusions which social scientists have reached in regard to the social and psychological characteristics of salesmen; later, we shall deal in the same manner with conclusions reached in regard to the sales environment.

1. *There is no significant relationship between intelligence-test scores and sales success.* The requirements for ability to learn, to solve problems, and to adjust quickly to the sales situation obviously differ widely in practice, depending upon the nature of the product, the type of selling involved, the competitive nature of the market, and many other such factors. Specialty selling and engineering selling, for example, make such different demands of the salesman that they can hardly be classified as being of the same order of experience.

2. *No significant relationship has been found between independent measures of personality traits and sales success.* Many of our "classical" notions of what makes a salesman do not appear to have any validity when put to psychological test. As selling has become more professional, the successful salesman has become less of a stereotype.

3. *No correlation exists between age and sales success.* Many research studies have revealed that, in companies which have established fairly rigid age ranges for the selection of salesmen, these standards have been almost as frequently ignored by the field sales managers as they have been recognized. The simple fact is that age, although theoretically related to maturity, is not absolutely correlated with it. In short, many young men are more mature than older men.

4. *There is no correlation between measurable character traits and sales success.* Many "typical" character traits ascribed to salesmen

[2] Walter Dill Scott, *The Psychology of Advertising* (Boston: Small, Maynard & Co., 1907).

since the early days of the hard sell have been found to have little basis in reality. We find that the traits which make for success in selling are the same as those which win the approval of employers in other occupations.

5. *There is no significant correlation between level of education and sales success.* Respect for education as an important tool in selling has grown by leaps and bounds. There has, in fact, been a tendency to set artificial levels of educational achievement for many sales positions. Yet careful statistical analysis of the educational backgrounds of individuals who are succeeding as salesmen reveals no such firm relationship between the amount of formal learning and the strict educational requirements for success in a given sales job. This does not mean that education is of no importance; it simply re-emphasizes the fact that there are many factors other than education which ultimately determine the success or failure of the salesman.

6. *No significant correlation exists between level of sales activity and sales success among individual salesmen.* This finding may be very difficult for many sales managers to accept. By tradition as well as by inclination there has been an understandable tendency for managers to believe that increased day-to-day activity will more or less inevitably produce increased sales volume. Theoretically, this is, of course, correct: A given man with a given selling method will produce more through sustained activity. Yet the fact is that attempts to increase the level of sales activity generally contribute less to increased sales volume than an equal amount of attention directed toward improving the selling method. Research clearly indicates that better selling techniques applied to carefully selected prospects are more likely to produce results.

7. *Each of the above factors has significance when studied in relation to all of the others in individual salesmen.* While no one of the factors cited above—age, education, personality, level of activity, and the rest—seems to have predictive significance, research indicates that when such social and psychological variables are studied in relation to one another the resulting profiles are valid guides for the selection of men who are likely to become successful salesmen. It was not until a very large number of important psychological instruments had been developed and more sophisticated statisti-

cal methods for the treatment of data had come into being that we were able to secure significantly useful results from our research in the evaluation of sales potential. Today it is possible to combine the social and psychological factors in such a way as to determine with considerable accuracy, in advance of employment, the likelihood of success in selling.

8. *Such study as that indicated in point 7 above can provide a useful tool for selection and development.* When, on the basis of research which compares the successful with the unsuccessful salesmen, a profile is built which reflects the unique characteristics of the successful men, it becomes possible to upgrade the sales force progressively through the use of the profile as a critical standard for the selection of new men.

9. *Salesmen are more likely to succeed when chosen with regard to the kinds of customers they will deal with than in terms of the types of products sold.* We must recognize that the salesman does not operate in a vacuum. He works in a sales environment in which he and the potential customer are important factors. When the salesman is compatible with his customer, he has a much greater chance of success than when he is not. Therefore, an important part of the analysis upon which a sales profile is based should be a study of the kinds of customers the potential or prospective salesman will deal with.

10. *Salesmen differ from non-salesmen in four important ways:*
   a. Salesmen are persuasive rather than critical.
   b. Salesmen are intuitive rather than analytical.
   c. Salesmen have higher average energy levels (expressed in activity).
   d. Salesmen are more strongly motivated by the desire for prestige, power, and material gain than by a service ideal or the need for security.

11. *Salesmen's interests cluster around a dominantly persuasive common core.* Almost all of the important research into the interests of salesmen and marketing people substantiates this finding. The role of secondary interests varies with the nature of the products sold and the peculiarities of the sales environment itself. For instance, people engaged in technical and scientific selling almost always have a secondary interest that is either engineering or

scientific, or both, while a man who is successful as a feed salesman will have a range of interests of relatively minor strength compared with his persuasive interest. In both cases the product and the sales environment give validity to the interest pattern.

These points represent the major findings of research on the sociopsychological characteristics of salesmen. The extent to which a manager of salesmen can creatively and imaginatively apply this knowledge in finding and developing men who can sell is the measure of his managerial success.

NATURE OF THE SALES ENVIRONMENT

Turning our attention now to the environment in which the salesman works, let us consider those environmental characteristics which psychological research indicates contribute most strongly to successful selling.

1. *An atmosphere of mutual compatibility must be achieved.* As we have already indicated, it is wise to select the salesman with primary consideration for the kind of customer he will deal with. When this is done, one of the most important aspects of natural environmental compatibility is realized. When the salesman knowingly plans his call to meet the convenience of the customer and makes his presentation in terms of known customer needs, a further development of a compatible environment takes place. Finally, the achievement of a mutually agreed-upon sales decision involves the realization by both the customer and the salesman of an increased sense of personal worth. Compatibility therefore begins with a sense of community between salesman and customer based on congenial personality factors; it develops as a skilled salesman molds the sales environment; and it achieves its climax through the experience of a heightened sense of personal worth as a sales decision is mutually arrived at.

2. *The customer's attention must be focused on the salesman and his message.* The psychological factors involved in the making of a sale have long been recognized. The structuring of the sales environment so that the salesman and his message become the focal points for the attention of the prospective customer is one of the most widely acknowledged fundamentals of sales training.

3. *An atmosphere of permissiveness must be established by evoking a felt need on the part of the customer.* Successful selling results when the sales environment is permissive rather than hostile or indifferent. Usually, such a positive, permissive environment is achieved as a direct result of felt need on the part of the customer.

4. *The natural aggressiveness of the salesman must be channeled to enhance the customer's ego; it should not be allowed to express itself in self-assertion, dominance, or hostility.* We must recognize that in any sales situation there is an element of psychological competition and a striving for ego-dominance on the part of both the salesman and the customer. That salesman is most likely to be successful who is able to achieve control by enhancing the ego of the customer rather than by asserting his own dominance.

5. *An atmosphere conducive to decision and action toward the resolution of the customer's felt need must be established through the development of feelings of satisfaction and profit.* The closing of a sale has long been considered the central problem in sales training. A great deal of research has been devoted to determining the most effective techniques by which the customer can be led to sign on the dotted line. Whatever the techniques recommended by the professional experts in the field, one essential psychological condition must be achieved. This may be described as the resolution of felt need through the development of feelings of satisfaction and profit. The psychological as well as the economic benefits of affirmative action in line with the desires and recommendations of the salesman become compelling conditioning factors to direct action.

The good salesman is aware, implicitly, of these things. He has an intuitive feel for them. A subtle aspect of sales training is the development of an *explicit* understanding of these factors, so that the salesman can manipulate the sales environment with more sureness and awareness.

BASIC SELLING TOOLS

There are a number of basic tools with which the salesman must be equipped in order to implement the social science findings described above in the way that will be most productive for his particular company and its particular products. In general, these basic tools are of three major types, as described below.

1. *Technical product knowledge.* Tangible and concrete information concerning his company's products, processes, and services constitutes the salesman's basic tool. This type of knowledge can be effectively communicated to salesmen in groups by means of demonstrations and discussion, or individually by means of well-prepared brochures, booklets, and the like. Adequacy and correctness of product knowledge must be constantly checked and evaluated by the sales supervisor. Research has revealed that many times the failure of the salesman is the result of inadequate or incorrect product knowledge. It cannot be assumed that because a salesman is told once he will remember forever.

2. *Administrative techniques* (organization of territory, development of call pattern, record keeping, etc.). Good sales management today attempts to develop wisdom and know-how in this area through extremely concentrated training and close face-to-face supervision. It is not natural for a salesman to consistently reorganize his detailed knowledge of territory changes; neither will he readily accept the discipline of highly structured call patterns; and he simply is not temperamentally suited to the correct maintenance of a large number of records. The better the man is as a salesman, in fact, the less congenial he is likely to find the necessity for close and constant record keeping. Management, therefore, must develop a number of highly effective motivational methods to secure the kind of cooperation from the salesman that good sales control requires.

3. *Group training* (face-to-face sales strategy and motivation, demonstration, directed practice, side-by-side field practice). Many studies have been carried on to determine the relative effectiveness of field demonstration and role playing in teaching selling strategy. The consensus at the present time is that both of these methods are highly effective. In view of the central psychological principles we have discussed, it is clear that the salesman must *do* in order to learn. Listening and observing are, of course, forms of doing, yet they do not have the same efficiency-producing effect as actual field performance under observation. It does not seem likely that there will ever be an effective substitute for side-by-side field practice

carried on sympathetically by the sales manager and his salesman.

CHANGING TIMES, CHANGING NEEDS

Today, only a small segment of the total sales environment presents a congenial condition for direct selling. The needs and wants of the consuming public are being predetermined through the use of advertising and sales promotion in magazines and on radio and television. In the consumer area, for example, the sales merchandiser no longer deals directly with a customer; instead, he deals with a buyer or a buying panel. His problem is not to influence the ultimate consumer to buy, but rather to convince the professional buyer that the other functions of marketing have already created a demand for the product, and that he can profitably make precious shelf space available. This situation presents the consumer salesman with an entirely different challenge, to meet which he requires an entirely different selling approach. He must be able to talk technically in terms of frontages, shelf space, product movement, supporting promotions, the economic effects of couponing, the secondary services which the manufacturer will render the distributor, and the influence of displays on the impulse buyer.

In the industrial field the same kind of problem exists, although it has a slightly different psychological context. The industrial salesman must sell to a professional purchasing agent who has received his product specifications from some other company official. As a result, the industrial salesman must establish friendly relations with management users in order that they will specify his product when requisitioning through the purchasing office. With regard to the psychology of selling, this means that the industrial salesman must be a good public relations man and a good service engineer far in advance of the occasion of actual felt need on the part of the business.

It becomes obvious that today's salesmen are not entrepreneurs but professional communicators, working within the framework of a fairly rigid management system. Thus, they are not wholly dependent on individual performance or productivity for income or economic advantage. The psychological problems, therefore, not only continue to be related to the selection of the kind of man who will accept the challenge of professional persuasiveness in a highly structured situation but also have to do with the development of techniques by which the use of incentives and internal and external motivations can be rationalized and made effective. The salesman must be able not only to understand his product and his customer but to relate this understanding to the economics of marketing and to such institutional problems as pricing and profit.

The typical problems which interest the psychologist and the sociologist today derive from an appreciation of the dynamic elements which comprise the marketing complex. "Motivation research" is a phrase symbolic of the new focus of interest. Projective techniques, as applied to both the salesman and the customer, are new devices. The nature of the corporate image, the power of the brand name, and the maintenance of a consumer franchise are all attracting the research time and interest of the social scientist. Morale studies, as they reveal the attitudes of salesmen toward the sales process and the company product, are assuming new and increased significance. The professionalization of sales training—with its highly operational definitions, its use of double and sometimes triple stimuli as learning facilitators, and its dynamic implementation of other incentives than money alone—is of increasing sociopsychological importance.

Hovering over these more highly individualistic problems are many which have to do with the sheer economics of distribution. The costs of doing business today threaten to eat up the ever-narrowing margin of profitability. Basic and applied research on products, packaging, and production techniques take an increasing toll from the consumer's dollar. Fringe benefits, pensions, and unemployment compensation involve added administrative costs which throw the traditional corporate concepts of doing business out of balance. These considerations cannot fail to affect the salesman and his selling effort.

TOWARD A PSYCHOLOGY OF MARKETING

Clearly, great changes have occurred in our economy during the past 15 years. The impact of these changes must be appreciated if sales management is to meet the challenge. The economic and social character of the mid-twentieth-century marketplace is the direct result of the fact that American dynamism has continued to work steadily toward the adaptation of our capitalistic, competitive society to the increasing complexities of a world-wide revolution. The more complex our economic society becomes, the more unstable it is. The greater our economic resources to meet our expanding needs are, the more fierce competition becomes and the more critical the role of selling appears to be in the marketing complex.

Free enterprise, symbolized by the free-wheeling entrepreneur of an earlier day, has been subject to many social and political controls. Government has assumed the role of the father-protector of the consumer. Sheer economic power is no longer looked upon with approval by many highly placed government officials. Efforts to place limitations on competition through the use of arbitrary economic power have been most vigorous at the very time when competition itself has been most bitter. The very tentative and uncertain balance between demonstrated need and capacity to produce is in constant danger of being lost. We observe, with a growing sense of frustration and concern, a spiraling gross national product and a tightening margin of gross profit.

It is in the light of these dynamic changes that mid-century selling has been forced to become an integral part of a larger and more complex economic process. We call this larger process "marketing." In an earlier day, advertising, sales promotion, credit and deferred-payment plans, and product development were supplementary aids to direct selling. Today these functions of marketing are themselves aspects of a total sales effort, and face-to-face selling is no longer the dominant causative factor in the distribution of goods.

This transformation is not entirely accepted by salesmen and their sales managers. Many of the frustrations now being experienced are the direct result of the failure of sales management realistically to adjust the role of the salesman to the changing patterns of modern marketing. Unless new insights are quickly gained, we may find ourselves in a declining economy. We may see a depression in the midst of plenty—a "profitless prosperity," as some have ominously called it.

Because selling has become marketing and because the entrepreneur salesman has of necessity become a professional, the need for more exact and more discriminating selection of sales personnel has become more pressing than ever. Our research into the characteristics of the "new" mid-twentieth-century sales-marketer has produced results which are most encouraging. The selection profiles which we have developed, in both the consumer and the industrial fields, reflect the changes in the sales job and in the characteristics of the successful salesman.

We are sure that, at most levels of selling, the sales-marketer must be more educable and have a higher intelligence potential than the salesman of the past. He must be less of an individualist and more of a team player. He must be as strongly motivated for personal success as salesmen ever were. He must be a more disciplined person, with greater control over his energy output. He must be more of a student, using his fund of marketing and sales knowledge with greater intuitional skill. He must be capable of more precise analysis of the marketing variables which affect his sales effort, and he must acquire additional skills in organizing, planning, and scheduling his sales work.

It will be obvious to all thoughtful sales managers that this type of salesman will require more guidance and will profit more from well-scheduled training. His economic requirements will be greater. His chances for professional growth will have to be more carefully spelled out. Sales supervision will require a higher degree of real managerial leadership. From every point of view it is reasonable to suggest that, *as selling becomes marketing, it also comes of age.* An expanding economy and an enlarged opportunity for personal financial achievement go hand in hand.

The psychologist and the sociologist may become true servants of management as they assist it, through research and consultation, in achieving increased understanding of the nature of the marketing process and the role of the salesman in it.

Interdisciplinary Horizons in Marketing

WILLIAM LAZER and EUGENE J. KELLEY

Marketing has reached a stage in its development as a discipline where critical evaluation of research findings and theories from other fields can add new dimensions to the field of marketing. More materials of other disciplines are likely to be incorporated in marketing in the future.

This article surveys some of the present and potential contributions of behavioral science findings and quantitative measurement methods to marketing.

The interdisciplinary approach to marketing includes utilization of contributions of the social and behavioral sciences, the physical sciences, and various areas of business administration and economics. The strength of the total approach lies in the addition of new dimensions and more meaningful perspectives to various marketing concepts, development of improved techniques for solving marketing problems, integration of findings and theories with marketing practice, and the development of a more widely applicable and generally useful body of marketing knowledge.

The potential promise of an interdisciplinary approach to the development of marketing theory was discussed by Wroe Alderson and Reavis Cox a decade ago. They wrote "that here and there in the literature of several intellectual disciplines are appearing the elements from which an adequate theory of marketing will be constructed." [1]

There has not yet been, however, any substantial acceptance of the development of a truly interdisciplinary approach to marketing knowledge. The use of other disciplines in marketing to date may be characterized as multidisciplinary.

Individual marketers have brought specific

problems to psychologists, sociologists, anthropologists, social psychologists, and other behavioral scientists. In many instances these specialists were able to find solutions. The problems were studied, however, from the limited perspectives of particular subject-matter areas. As a result, the needed cross-fertilization of ideas and the integration necessary to obtain more widely applicable generalizations and marketing concepts has not occurred on any large scale.

The point of departure and the focus of study differ with each of the disciplines underlying marketing. But there are frequently great similarities in the methodology and content of marketing and that of other disciplines. Marketing progress can be furthered by studying the similarities among disciplines rather than emphasizing the differences.

BEHAVIORAL SCIENCE CONTRIBUTIONS TO MARKETING

Table 1 relates specific behavioral science concepts to particular problems being faced by marketing management. It illustrates the value of the interdisciplinary approach in extending the frontiers of marketing knowledge and in helping to solve marketing problems. For example, such concepts as communication and information, motivation and behavior, creativity, problem solving, and decision making have significant implications for effective marketing management. They are being investigated from different vantage points by

◆ SOURCE: Reprinted by permission from *Journal of Marketing* (National Quarterly Publication of the American Marketing Association), Vol. 25, No. 2, October 1960, pp. 24–30.

[1] Wroe Alderson and Reavis Cox, "Toward a Theory of Marketing," *Journal of Marketing*, Vol. 13 (October, 1948), pp. 137–152, p. 142.

such disciplines as psychology, sociology, social psychology, anthropology, and political science.

Topics of interest to marketing managers are grouped according to four major marketing problem areas in Table 1. These areas are marketing administration and the three major components of an integrated marketing program. A unified goal-directed marketing program and its resulting marketing mix is comprised of three submixes. These are the *goods-and-service mix,* which includes product and pricing elements; the *communications mix,* which includes the functional areas of advertising, sales promotion, and personal selling; and the *distribution mix,* which is comprised of channels of distribution and physical distribution activities. The table illustrates the significance of the findings of several behavioral sciences to marketing management in solving specific problems within each of these areas.

These rankings are an attempt to relate in broad terms the degree of significance of the concepts. They were determined after an investigation of the literature of psychology, sociology, social psychology, anthropology, and several business administration areas. Specialists in these disciplines were consulted to substanti-

Table 1. Behavioral Science Contributions to Selected Marketing Management Problems

	Psychology	Sociology	Social psychology	Anthropology	Political science
Marketing administration					
Creativity, problem solving and decision making	Considerable	Some	Some	Some	Little
Leadership and administration	Some	Considerable	Considerable	Little	Some
Organization	Some	Considerable	Considerable	Some	Some
Systems—survival and growth	Little	Considerable	Some	Considerable	Some
Goods and services mix					
Adjustment and change	Considerable	Some	Considerable	Some	Little
Consumers and consumption	Considerable	Some	Some	Little	Little
Innovation	Some	Some	Some	Considerable	Some
Products, packages, brands and images	Considerable	Some	Some	Little	Little
Role, status, and symbols	Some	Considerable	Considerable	Some	Some
Communications mix					
Attitudes and opinions	Considerable	Considerable	Considerable	Considerable	Some
Communications and information	Some	Some	Considerable	Some	Some
Individuals and group relations	Considerable	Considerable	Considerable	Some	Some
Motivations and behavior	Considerable	Some	Considerable	Some	Some
Persuasion and influence	Some	Some	Considerable	Little	Some
Distribution complex: channels and physical					
Centralization, decentralization and integration	Little	Considerable	Little	Some	Little
Institutional structure	Little	Considerable	Some	Considerable	Considerable
Wealth and income	Little	Little	Little	Some	Some
Wants, needs, and goals	Considerable	Some	Considerable	Some	Little

Key:
- ▨ Considerable significance
- ▢ Some significance
- ☐ Little significance

ate the rankings. The rankings are necessarily subjective. Further research may result in modifications.

Many of the concepts cannot be conveniently classfied as belonging to only one discipline. As intensive investigations are conducted into specific topics from an interdisciplinary perspective and as the multidimensional nature of concepts becomes more apparent, such tables will become more complex.

Psychologists, sociologists, anthropologists, and other social and behavioral scientists are not necessarily any more unified in the concepts they hold of their disciplines than are marketers. Complete agreement does not exist among these scientists as to the most promising lines of development for particular aspects of their subject-matter areas. The important marketing-subject area of motivation is an example. Motivation has been studied at considerable length by psychologists and other behavioral scientists. Rather than any one unified approach emerging, at least three major directions are being followed by psychologists studying motivation.[2]

First, there is the approach of laboratory psychologists who have tended to focus upon the physiological aspects of psychology. Then, there are clinical psychologists who have concentrated on the role of certain psychological factors in motivation. This group tends to minimize the biological drives as influencing human motivation and behavior. The third approach is represented by Gestalt psychologists, particularly Kurt Lewin and his followers. Of the three, this latter approach may have the greatest significance for marketing people in studying human motives and other related questions.

This Gestalt approach is essentially socio-psychological in nature. It stresses the thesis that people do react to environmental factors. From the Gestalt viewpoint, motivations and behavior are analyzed as a function of the particular person, his inherent drives, and of the immediate environment of which he is a part.

These three different psychological approaches are cited to indicate that in the disciplines underlying marketing a variety of theories and avenues to the understanding of human behavior may exist. The basic problems in utilizing behavioral science concepts in marketing management are to evaluate and reconcile the various theoretical explanations and research findings relating to a subject. The attempt to integrate numerous, and often conflicting, explanations of behavioral scientists into a practicable solution can become a highly perplexing experience.

Also, for many of the problems facing marketing management, the behavioral sciences do not as yet offer useful concepts or methods. Indeed, "the behavioral sciences as they now stand do not provide a large reservoir of immediately useful analytical concepts and models."[3] This is not a reason for ignoring the promise of these disciplines. It is a challenge to begin realizing the potential.

INTERDISCIPLINARY CONTRIBUTIONS TO MEASUREMENT IN MARKETING

Marketing practitioners and teachers are aware of the numerous measurement methods that have been developed by various subject-matter areas. The interdisciplinary approach has been used by many measurement tools such as scaling and ranking techniques, personnel tests, various projective techniques, interviewing and questionnaire methods, statistical sampling and measurements, and mathematical models and programming.

Figure 1 specifies some of the more promising contributions to measurement in marketing by five disciplines: sociology, psychology, social psychology, statistics, and operations research. It lists specific measurement techniques from each discipline which have been, or may be, profitably applied to marketing research. These techniques may be useful in solving problems in such marketing areas as: advertising, product and price analysis, sales forecasting, locational problems, competitive strategy, and estimating market potentials. They contribute to more precise cardinal and ordinal measurements in marketing and facilitate the planning and controlling of marketing operations.

In many instances tools borrowed from behavioral sciences are adapted and modified by marketing researchers. Through refinements

[2] Herta Herzog, "Behavioral Science Concepts for Analyzing the Consumer," paper given at the Conference of Marketing Teachers from Pacific Coast States held at the University of California, Berkeley, September 9, 1958.

[3] G. L. Bach, "Some Observations on the Business School of Tomorrow," *Management Science*, Vol. 4 (July, 1958), pp. 351–364 at pp. 354–355.

in application, the basic measurement techniques themselves are improved and marketing research thereby contributes to other disciplines.

This classification of measurement techniques merely suggests topics of interest. It is not comprehensive, and the categories are not necessarily comparable. There are a number of other important contributing subject-matter areas. Many of these techniques could be classified under several of the disciplines cited.

In the figure this has been done only in a limited number of cases to avoid much duplication, but still to indicate the interdisciplinary overlapping of many of the methods of measuring specific aspects of human behavior.

THE INTERDISCIPLINARY CONCEPT
AND SYSTEMS ANALYSIS

The integration of the functional areas of business administration is an area where the

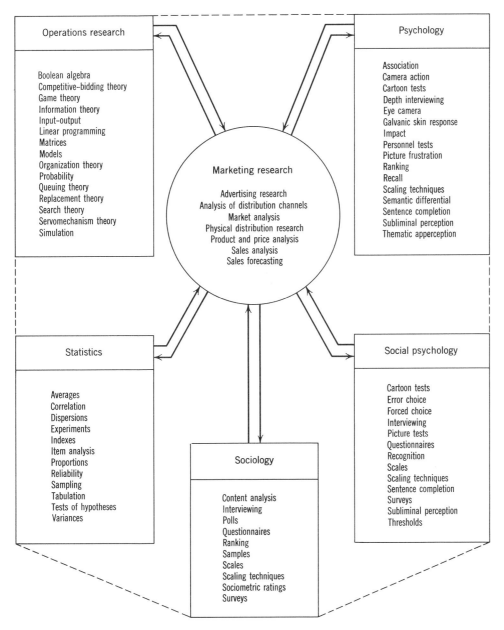

Figure 1 Measurement in marketing.

interdisciplinary approach may be helpful. The problem is one of viewing a business enterprise as an operating system, as a whole. The impact of marketing, finance, production, or human-relations decisions on other aspects of company operations and on the business as a whole must be considered in a total cross-functional view of business enterprise.

Marketing administrators may be on the verge of a new level of sophistication in understanding marketing's role in the total system of business action. Managers are becoming increasingly interested in the interaction between the components of business enterprise. Forrester has pointed out that business achievement depends on the successful interaction among five subsystems, the flows of information, materials, money, manpower, and capital equipment within the firm.[4]

These five subsystems interlock to amplify one another within the total business complex. Conventional functional thinking may not be adequate for an understanding of the effects of these interactions. It does not allow for anticipated impacts on decisions, policies, organizational forms, and investment choices within the firm.

Figure 2 indicates the relationship of interdisciplinary activity to a marketing management system. The disciplines listed in the area bordering the external non-controllable forces can be useful in providing information and insights about marketing.

Consumers are the focal point of the entire system of business action. They are separated from firms attempting to serve them in space, time, ownership, valuation, and knowledge. These separations tend to increase in complex socio-economic systems. Sellers attempt to overcome the barriers of space and time by communicating to the consumer the want-satisfying characteristics of the product offered through the marketing program.

The marketing program is but one significant element in the total business system. Marketing decisions should be made in terms of their impact on the company as a whole and their contributions to over-all objectives. The human, financial, and physical resources of the firm should be factors in marketing decision making since the marketing program

[4] J. W. Forrester, "Industrial Dynamics, A Major Breakthrough for Decision Makers," *Harvard Business Review,* Vol. 36 (July–August, 1958), pp. 37–66 at p. 37.

affects these factors. This corporate complex also includes the interrelationships and coordination of the activities of the manufacturing firm with distributors and dealers as part of their joint effort to serve the consumer.

The interdisciplinary approach can be useful in understanding and even predicting the influence of these external forces on marketing decisions. Figure 2 emphasizes that marketing and corporate decisions are influenced, perhaps determined, by various forces which are largely beyond the control of the management of an individual enterprise. These include competitive, social, political, legal, ethical, and international forces. Change is represented in the figure by arrows. As business systems become more complex, the rate of change increases with corresponding increases in the complexity of business analysis and decision.

The systems approach to business action is particularly important to marketing executives and educators. They have a unique opportunity to integrate business-management functions into a meaningful whole and to take leadership in advancing systems thinking in business administration.

This opportunity stems from two related developments. First, businesses in the future will become more marketing oriented. Second, the total marketing concept will be adopted in which marketing is viewed as an integral subsystem within the total system of business action.

The greatest long-run contribution of the interdisciplinary approach to the study of marketing and business systems may be that of influencing the ways of thinking about marketing and business problems. Marketing students and practitioners using the interdisciplinary approach should gain added insights into the nature and scope of marketing management activities. This is because a person's concept of marketing, or any other subject, depends largely upon the knowledge of the area gained through his own or vicarious experiences.

Marketing problems may be viewed as problems arising from the gratification of human wants and needs. As such, particular marketing activities become a part of the more general problem of raising the standard of living through satisfying the needs of human beings. The discipline of marketing in this perspective is seen as a contributing component of a broader science which encompasses man and his culture.

Acceptance of the interdisciplinary approach

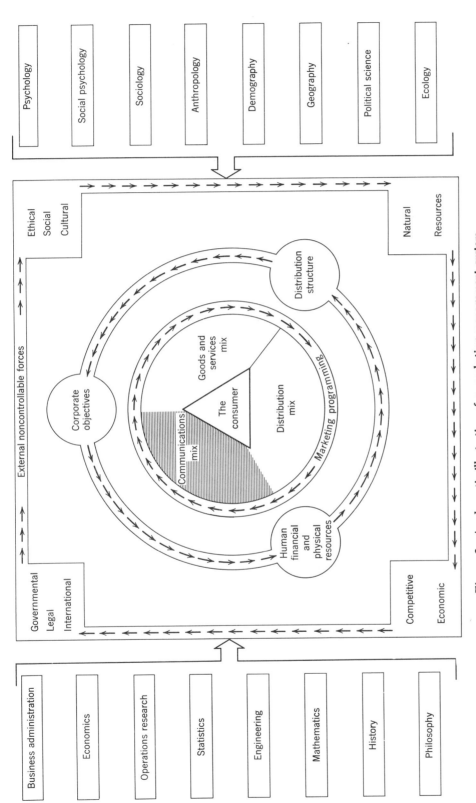

Figure 2 A schematic illustration of a marketing management system.

The boxes and labels in the figure read:

Psychology
Social psychology
Sociology
Anthropology
Demography
Geography
Political science
Ecology

External noncontrollable forces

Ethical
Social
Cultural

Natural
Resources

Distribution structure

Corporate objectives

Goods and services mix

The consumer

Distribution mix

Communications mix

Marketing programming

Human financial and physical resources

Governmental
Legal
International

Competitive
Economic

Business administration
Economics
Operations research
Statistics
Engineering
Mathematics
History
Philosophy

97

does not mean that marketing men must become psychologists or sociologists, nor does it mean that men trained in the behavioral sciences should move over completely to marketing. The relationship between marketing and other disciplines is a reciprocal one. Marketing is concerned with the study of human action in the market place, the study of the process of exchange and economic transaction and of the interacting efforts and responses of buyers and sellers in the market. This sphere of human action is essential to our economic system and the study of it is growing in importance. The field of marketing provides a testing ground on which to verify, modify, and extend the hypotheses and relationships which have been described by various behavioral sciences.

The interdisciplinary approach can contribute greatly to a more penetrating and rigorous analysis of consumers in their socio-economic environment. As the body of knowledge about human behavior increases and is incorporated into marketing thought and practice, marketing management should be enabled to serve the needs of consumers more effectively.

The application of the interdisciplinary approach to marketing, however, is not a simple matter. Social scientists themselves experience great difficulty in communicating about and bridging disciplines. We are still a long way from a general science of human behavior which could be applied in marketing.

In the last analysis, it is likely to be the marketing men rather than pure behavioral scientists who will contribute most to the solution of difficult marketing problems and the development of marketing thought. In the future, as in the past, the major advances in marketing knowledge probably will come from people who have a marketing background and who possess an intense professional interest in advancing science in marketing.

Behavioral Science in Personal Selling Communication

STEVEN J. SHAW

The consummation of many purchase decisions depends upon a two-way exchange of ideas between buyer and seller. This paper deals with behavioral science concepts that contribute to a better understanding of the face-to-face communication phase in the buyer-seller relationship.

SEMANTIC AND OTHER PROBLEMS

Some of the problems faced by the researcher in the application of behavioral science concepts to specialized areas of marketing were pointed out by Bennett [3:77] at the 1962 Ford Foundation Seminar at Williams College on "New Developments in Business Administration." One of the difficulties, according to Bennett, is that findings most important to the behavioral sciences are frequently of very little importance to marketing. An even more serious impediment is the problem of terminology. In his "Sociological Reflections on Business," Lazarsfeld deplores the semantic confusion which results from different usages of a given term. In developing a definition of motivation, he found it necessary first to define and distinguish eight types of dispositions—preferences, traits, wants or needs, directional traits, expectations, tendencies, intentions, and the ubiquitous, undifferentiated "motivation" itself.

◆ SOURCE: Reprinted by permission from *New Research in Marketing* (Institute of Business and Economic Research, University of California, Berkeley, 1965), by the Regents of the University of California, Berkeley.

In this study specific usages of behavioral terms are spelled out wherever necessary in order to reduce the semantic confusion.

MIND OF THE PROSPECT

Since people are the focus of the salesman's efforts, it is logical to start an analysis of the buyer-seller relationship with a meaningful diagram of the physiological apparatus that makes up the human mind. Neuropsychologists, biochemists, and other specialists have recently made great advances in the study of man's mental mechanism, and their discoveries may make it possible within the next decade or two to exercise some control over human behavior through electrical techniques, the use of drugs, and other devices [24:101–111].

Leonhard's model [17:43] shown in Figure 1 gives a useful conceptualization of the human mind. It divides the mind into three levels—two conscious and one unconscious or subconscious. When we speak of a person as being friendly or quiet, we are talking about the outer level of the mind which he shows to the world, and which is perhaps the smallest part of himself. Within every person there is also a conscious level which is completely private. This is the area of daydreams and wishful thinking and secret plans. Below this is the unconscious level.

If I were to redraw Leonhard's diagram, I would give more emphasis to the gray middle area, for it is an important key to a better understanding of a prospect's conscious but

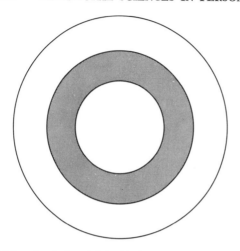

White: rationalizations, beliefs, attitudes, existing in verbal form
Gray: concepts, feelings, emotions which can be verbalized
Black: nonverbal, unconscious emotions

Figure 1   White and gray: top of the mind conscious. Black: unconscious or subconscious.

completely private world. With regard to this second level, Smith [28:20–21] says:

"At the second level, the individual has difficulty in 'facing up to' and discussing his motives, emotions, and attitudes. . . . Examples in this zone are the desire to impress one's neighbors with a bigger T.V. set, moving into a better neighborhood as a means of social climbing, reading a certain newspaper in order to feel like a big shot, driving a high-powered car rapidly in order to let off aggressive impulses, drinking a coke as a reward after frustrating circumstances and smoking cigars in order to feel masculine.

"The motives at this second level are only slightly outside awareness, and psychologically sophisticated people can penetrate to them easily enough. Yet, for most interviewees, this is not the case. They conceal these motives behind a mask of rationalizations, intellectual discussions, and half-truths. They act on the nineteenth-century assumption that their behavior is always reasonable.

They insist that they buy the new T.V. because the old one has a flicker, move into a new neighborhood because it represents a better real-estate investment, read the uppity newspaper because it contains more news, drive rapidly in order to save time, drink the coke because it 'tastes good,' and smoke the cigar because it has a pleasant aroma."

Salesmen cannot probe prospects' minds through projective tests, but they should be aware of the degree to which prospects live in a private world of hopes, fears, and dreams. They need to be perceptive, to read between the lines and recognize that prospect feelings expressed as objections and stalls may only be rationalizations masking true motives and reasons.

PURPOSIVE BEHAVIOR

The practice of classifying behavior as rational or irrational has little if any usefulness. For some time now, behavioral scientists [21: 52; 22:95–102] have been suggesting that it might be more useful to think of a prospect's behavior as being purposeful and in tune with his self-image or a socially approved image.

In many situations it might help the salesman to seek the specific purpose(s) behind prospect behavior. Skillful observation, questioning, and listening could all contribute. For instance, a female customer-acquaintance of a retail salesman might walk into his store and ask for an expensive hat. Knowing that this customer has to provide for the needs of a family of six on a limited budget, he might arbitrarily judge her behavior as irrational and be tempted to suggest a more modest purchase. However, a tactful series of questions might reveal a changed situation—the head of the household might just have been promoted to an executive position. Viewed in this new light, the woman's action would appear to be purposeful and consistent with her family's enhanced status.

NEEDS AND WANTS—BASIS OF PROSPECT MOTIVATIONS

Related to this concept of purposive behavior is the idea that prospects have many needs and wants and that satisfaction of these needs and wants is the basis of motivation. The interaction and influence of several motivational forces may lie behind a prospect's decision. Often a prospect can come to a decision only after long and deliberate weighing of two or more conflicting urges. For example, in his deliberations about the amount of money to spend for a new automobile, a prospect may be torn between desire for economy and craving for status enhancement.

Although the lists of motives presented by

contemporary psychologists differ somewhat, they also have much in common. According to Clawson's survey [9:89] of the motives revealed in actual marketing and motivation research studies conducted by scores of organizations throughout the country, consumers are influenced at some time, to some degree, and for some products by at least 600 "motives." These include not only a host of biological, psychological, and social motives, but a great variety of others—artistic, political, religious, intellectual, and economic types.

In personal selling communication, it might be helpful for the salesman to think of his prospect as having some of the following types of needs and wants:

Biological needs are the basic physical needs in the food, clothing, and shelter category that a prospect has to satisfy. Until these essentials of survival are met, other needs are pushed into the background.

Economic needs—with per capita income so high today, one might think that economizing must be of lesser importance than it was in the past. However, consumer wants are unlimited. Education and travel give prospects new experiences and wants multiply faster than income, so choices are still dictated to a considerable degree on the basis of such economic considerations as cost, dependability, durability, convenience, economy in use.

Psychological needs stem from the prospect's personal make-up. Alderson [1:188–193] discusses this individual psychology, which results from heredity and differences in background and experiences. Individuals experience infinitely varied sources of fears, hopes, anger, and happiness. Even for prospects in the same social stratum, individual differences may be important. What frightens one person may please another. Thus, in the sale of a tire, fear might be a key motivator with one prospect, but not with another.

Social needs—social psychologists, cultural anthropologists, and sociologists agree that a prospect's behavior is greatly influenced by his associations within the various small formal and informal groups which make up his life-environment. He conforms to certain powerful group modes and taboos. Thus, the college coed may decide to wear culottes because the leaders on campus wear them.

As a motive, conformity implies social pressure to follow the leader or the boss, while emulation suggests a more voluntary copying— for example, the voluntary imitation by some coeds of the hair style of an outstanding national personality. Belongingness and esteem are two other social needs which can be satisfied only through group interactions.

Aesthetic needs—prospects have artistic natures. They are attracted to beautiful things and abhor the ugly and commonplace. People work better in beautiful surroundings. To a considerable extent, new fashions are purchased in order to satisfy aesthetic needs. The woman who frequently rearranges her living room appointments may well be motivated by aesthetic and creative urges as much as by conscious or unconscious desire to emulate another member of her social circle.

Political needs—C. Wright Mills [20:37–39] has probably done more than any other social science researcher to bring into the open the frequently camouflaged power drive. The salesman who calls on purchasing agents and other executives of industrial firms must be particularly aware of the influence and interplay of power politics. Politics and power are especially important in the creation and maintenance of reciprocal buying arrangements in industrial selling.

Religious needs are quite frequently important in the market place, as when religious background influences a prospect to avoid certain foods completely or to use other foods only during religious holiday periods.

Intellectual needs—level of education is one index of social standing, and certain types of training are necessary as door openers to professional and skilled occupations. Intellectual improvement is a key direct-appeal salesmen can use in marketing encyclopedias and such travel-facilitating products as automobiles, cameras, and wash-and-wear clothing. Even in the sale of insurance, the salesman can appeal to a middle- or upper-class parent's wish to protect his children's future education.

PSYCHOLOGY IN PERSONAL SELLING COMMUNICATION

The application of psychology to personal selling is not new. In the 1920's and 1930's, Strong and Snow [30 and 29] did some pioneer work on the integration of psychology into sales theory. AIDA theory (attention, interest, desire, and action) was formulated as a method of improving buyer-seller communications. The use of suggestion in closing the sale and the idea of getting all the senses (especially sight and touch) into the sales demonstration are practical examples of the effective application of psychology to personal selling.

Unfortunately, during the 1920's "psychology" had unpleasant connotations. Psychologists were thought of as "head-shrinkers" and people did not want to accept the ideas they developed. To meet this resistance, Snow divided his lengthy textbook, *Psychology in Personal Selling*, into three smaller volumes and renamed them *Effective Selling*. The ideas remained those of the original, technical volume. Until recently, writers have tended to avoid referring to psychological concepts as originating from psychology.

In a series of pamphlets on the psychology of selling, psychologists Cash and Crissy [7] have contributed many suggestions on how theories and ideas from their discipline apply to sales training and to broadening the understanding of the behavior and motivation of prospects. Among other things, they explain how a salesman's familiarity with such concepts as perception (which they break down into sympathy, empathy, and recipathy), summation, and homeostasis can improve his communication with prospects.

In order to develop their sales trainees into more perceptive communicators, General Electric is making use of applied psychology [19]. Also, the research findings of Nichols and Stevens [23] on listening are exerting a healthy influence on the improvement of the prospect-salesman communication aspect of company sales training programs. The following outline on listening is used in a new sales training program of the National Starch and Chemical Company:

LISTENING [1]

(1) Keep Mind Alert
    Control impatience
    Mentally summarize
    Listen between lines
    Question evidence being presented
(2) Identify Purpose
    Try to anticipate
    What's he trying to get at?
    Minimize emotional deaf spots

[1] J. D. Staunton, "Applying Behavioral Science Information to Sales Training," a research paper presented before the 1960 Convention of the National Society of Sales Training Executives.

(3) Establish Mind-to-Mind Contact
    Encourage listener physically
    Use confirming interjections without interrupting listener's thought
(4) Look for a Pattern of Organization
    Try to construct a mental outline of what is said
    Listen before preparing answer
    Avoid trying to trap listener into a corner

The Yale Communication Research Program also has made significant discoveries [15] about learning and other communication techniques pertinent to salesmanship theory, but much of the work of application still needs to be developed.

The writings of Hayakawa [13] in the area of general semantics have done much to alert sales managers and sales trainees to some of the semantic pitfalls in personal communication. For one thing, many words have a variety of meanings, and prospects' responses to word symbols are conditioned to a great extent by their subjective experiences, memories, likes and dislikes.

SOCIOLOGY IN PERSONAL SELLING COMMUNICATION

Among other things, sociologists have contributed some useful theories on the behavior of social classes. Warner [31] at Chicago, Hollingshead [14] at Yale, and Centers [8] at Princeton have pioneered studies on social class structure. Recent consumer research studies [11:108] have confirmed the theory that a prospect's social class background—his attitudes, beliefs, customs, and tastes—has a great influence on his pattern of spending. Many of the studies on the buying habits of social classes conducted by social researchers have direct application to personal selling. For instance, Coleman's studies [10:171] of the buying behavior of "overprivileged" prospects contain some useful ideas.

INFLUENCE OF SMALL GROUP LEADERS AS TASTEMAKERS

A number of significant studies on the influence of group and interpersonal influences have been completed at Columbia University's Bureau of Applied Social Research [16]. In small groups of close associates in business and community life, there are frequently leaders whose opinions are influential in the purchase of goods. These opinion leaders are tastemakers who pave the way for the acceptance of many new products. Whyte [32:140; 4:61–63] has analyzed the influence of these tastemakers on individual air conditioner buying decisions in a middle-class community of younger white-collar workers in a suburb of Philadelphia.

The perceptive salesman who cultivates the friendship of tastemakers in his community and uses them as centers of influence should be able to increase his sales productivity. The endorsement of the salesman and his product by these tastemakers could start an endless chain of sales through emulation and conformity.

Before a salesman can use tastemakers as centers of influence, he must first distinguish who they are. In order to develop a set of criteria for identifying tastemakers, Opinion Research Corporation (ORC) conducted several studies [2] of households in Ridgewood, New Jersey. ORC found that tastemakers tended to rate high on mobility. The typical high mobiles on ORC's scale were found to be families who traveled extensively, read for intellectual experience, had advanced in their jobs, rose to higher income levels, moved around and met many different types of people, valued independence in family relations, stressed education for their children, and tried to improve their own. Extent of travel and reading showed up as particularly critical selectors. Awareness of these mobility characteristics should increase a salesman's success with the center-of-influence method of prospecting.

STAGES IN THE ADOPTION PROCESS

In an analysis of the communication aspects in personal selling, it might be helpful to visualize the process by which a prospect accepts a new product as consisting of a series of distinct but related stages. In studies of the diffusion of new products, behavioral scientists [e.g., 18:3–4] typically conceptualize the adoption process as consisting of five stages: awareness, interest, evaluation, trial, and adoption or rejection.

Using this classification, Rogers [25:311–314] has developed some generalizations which could prove of considerable value to sales managers. For instance, following study of several case histories he concluded that in the evaluation and trial phases of the process, the personal contact of informed salesmen is more effective than advertising since it permits a two-way exchange of ideas about the product and the prospect's needs.

Using the studies of Katz, Lazarsfeld, Whyte, and Rogers, Brooks [5 and 6] has developed some important generalizations which might enable the firm to improve its sales promotion efforts. Specifically, he points out how the sales or marketing manager can relate his firm's selling effort to patterns of purchasing behavior. Like Rogers before him, Brooks concludes that personal selling may be superior to advertising in its ability to change attitudes toward a product. A plausible reason for this alleged superiority is that face-to-face representation facilitates a two-way exchange of ideas between buyer and seller. The buyer can talk back, giving the salesman valuable information about his special needs.

More detailed development of this two-way communication aspect of personal selling is contained in the other sources [12:3; 27; 26:47].

REFERENCES CITED

1. Alderson, Wroe. *Marketing Behavior and Executive Action.* Homewood, Ill.: Irwin, 1957.
2. *America's Tastemakers,* Parts I and II. Princeton, N.J.: Opinion Research Corporation, April–June 1959.
3. Bennett, William R. "Extending Capacities in the Behavioral Sciences," *Proceedings of the Winter Conference of the American Marketing Association.* Pittsburgh, December 27–29, 1962.
4. Brink, Edward L., and Kelley, William T. *The Management of Promotion.* Englewood Cliffs, N.J.: Prentice-Hall, 1963.
5. Brooks, Robert C. "Relating the Selling Effort to Patterns of Purchase Behavior," *Business Topics,* Winter 1963.
6. ———. "Word-of-Mouth Advertising in Selling New Products," *The Journal of Marketing,* October 1957.
7. Cash, C. W., and Crissy, W. J. E. *Psychology of Selling Series.* New York: Personnel Development Associates, 1958–1964.
8. Centers, Richard. *The Psychology of Social Classes.* New York: Russell and Russell, 1961.
9. Clawson, C. Joseph. "The Coming Breakthrough in Motivation Research," in S. George Walters, Max D. Snider, and Morris L. Sweet (eds.), *Readings in Marketing.* Cincinnati: Southwestern Publishing, 1962.
10. Coleman, Richard P. "The Significance of Social Stratification in Selling," in Martin L. Bell (ed.), *Marketing: A Maturing Discipline.* Chicago: American Marketing Association, December 1960.

11. Dahl, Robert A., Haire, Mason, and Lazarsfeld, Paul F. *Social Science Research on Business: Product and Potential.* New York: Columbia University Press, 1959.
12. Francisco, L. Mercer. "Sees Personal Selling Reshaped by Social Sciences, As Advertising Has Been," in Steven J. Shaw and Joseph W. Thompson (eds.), *Salesmanship: Modern Viewpoints on Personal Communication.* New York: Holt, Rinehart, and Winston, 1960.
13. Hayakawa, S. I. (ed.). *Our Language and Our World,* Part IV. New York: Harper, 1959.
14. Hollingshead, August B., and Redlick, Frederick C. *Social Class and Mental Illness: A Community Study.* New York: Wiley, 1958.
15. Hovland, C. I., Janis, Irving, and Kelley, Harold. *Communication and Persuasion.* New Haven: Yale University Press, 1953.
16. Katz, Elihu, and Lazarsfeld, Paul F. *Personal Influence.* Glencoe, Ill.: The Free Press, 1955.
17. Leonhard, Dietrich. *Consumer Research with Projective Techniques.* Chicago: George Fry and Associates, 1955.
18. Lionberger, Herbert F. *Adoption of New Ideas and Practices.* Ames: The Iowa State University Press, 1960.
19. McCarthy, John. *Psychological Aspects of Selling,* Parts I, II, and III. New York: General Electric, 1958.
20. Mills, C. Wright. *The Power Elite.* New York: Oxford University Press, 1956.
21. Newman, Joseph W. *Motivation Research and Marketing Management.* Boston: Harvard University, Graduate School of Business Administration, 1957.
22. ———. "New Insight, New Progress for Marketing," *Harvard Business Review,* November–December 1957.
23. Nichols, Ralph G., and Stevens, Leonard A. *Are You Listening?* New York: McGraw-Hill, 1957.
24. Pribram, Karl H. "Neuropsychology in America," in Bernard Berelson (ed.), *The Behavioral Sciences Today.* New York: Basic Books, 1963.
25. Rogers, Everett M. *Diffusion of Innovations.* New York: The Free Press of Glencoe, 1962.
26. Shaw, Steven J. "Behavioral Principles in Salesmanship Courses," *Journal of Marketing,* April 1961.
27. ———, and Gittinger, C. McGerron. *Marketing in Business Management.* New York: Macmillan, 1963, Ch. 8.
28. Smith, George H. *Motivation Research in Advertising and Marketing.* New York: McGraw-Hill, 1954.
29. Snow, A. J. *Psychology in Personal Selling.* Chicago: Shaw, 1926.
30. Strong, Edward K. *Psychology of Advertising and Selling.* New York: McGraw-Hill, 1925.
31. Warner, W. Lloyd, Meeker, Marchia, and Eells, Kenneth. *Social Class in America.* Chicago: Science Research Associates, 1949.
32. Whyte, William H. "The Web of Word of Mouth," *Fortune,* November 1954.

B. Psychological Dimensions of Personal Selling

A Psychological Approach to Consumer Behavior Analysis [1]

WARREN J. BILKEY

During recent years there has been considerable interest in obtaining a scientifically verifiable theory of consumer behavior. One of the most recent attempts at such a formulation is the vector hypothesis which is an application of Lewinian vector psychology to consumer analysis. The purpose of this article is to summarize briefly the main features of the vector hypothesis, to describe the techniques thus far advanced for measuring the psychic tensions involved, and finally to present some of the author's findings in his exploratory attempt to apply one of these measuring techniques in a small consumer study.

SUMMARY OF THE VECTOR HYPOTHESIS

Since the theoretical aspects of the vector hypothesis have been described in an earlier issue of *The Journal of Marketing* its basic features merely will be summarized by means of the following four postulates.[2]

(1) *Consumption is but one aspect of a person's total pattern of activities.*[3] For this reason an analysis of his purchasing behavior should take account of his entire situation, e.g., of the limitation of his time and of his unwillingness to devote thought and energy to buying, as well as of the limitation of his funds. Interview findings indicate that people do seek to achieve a *satisfactory* allocation of their funds among the various alternatives available to them, but whether this involves a deliberate attempt at maximization has not yet been determined.

(2) *A person's actual (as distinguished from his planned) disbursement pattern is the end resultant of many separate disbursement acts.*[4] Typically there is no single all-inclusive decision point for a consumer's disbursement pattern. Rather, he buys or fails to buy whenever a disbursement opportunity presents itself. The reason for this is that all purchases do not occur at the same time nor at the same fre-

♦ SOURCE: Reprinted by permission from *Journal of Marketing* (National Quarterly Publication of the American Marketing Association), Vol. 18, No. 1, July 1953, pp. 18–25.

[1] The research upon which this article is based was financed by funds received under the Research and Marketing Act of 1946, administered by the B.A.E., U.S. Department of Agriculture. A complete report of this study is to be published as a U.S.D.A. bulletin. Helpful suggestions were received from the author's wife, Angelica, and from Profs. W. H. Carter, Jr. and W. P. Snavely of the University of Connecticut.

[2] See W. J. Bilkey, "The Vector Hypothesis of Consumer Behavior," *The Journal of Marketing,* Oct., 1951.

[3] This postulate is derived from Gestalt psychology, and is confirmed by interview findings.

[4] This postulate is based upon empirical observation, and the analysis of family expenditure records.

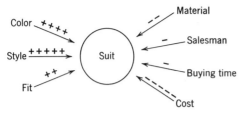

Figure 1

quency so as to permit an effective weighing of alternatives when making a particular disbursement act. That is, for some categories (e.g., food) purchases occur at a regular rate, but for other categories (e.g., furniture and automobiles) purchases occur very infrequently and cannot be accurately anticipated. For this reason a separate choice is required for each purchasing act. Thus, particular purchasing acts occur throughout the course of the consumer's income period, and the choices made are affected by circumstances existing or believed to be existing at the moments in question. The sum total of the disbursements made then constitute the person's disbursement pattern.

(3) *A person's disbursement acts are the net outcome of his psychic tensions regarding each item or activity involved, together with habits, carryovers of past commitments and external impositions such as taxes.*[5] According to Lewinian vector psychology, the underlying basis for an actively made consumer choice is an internal psychic conflict between the person's attraction toward (positive valences) certain attributes of the item or service in question, and his repulsion against (negative valences) other attributes regarding that good or service, including its cost. If his positive valences for it are greater than his negative valences against it the purchase will be made, and vice versa (see Figure 1). Thus, an active psychic conflict is regarded as being a person's way of achieving a desirable over-all disbursement pattern. This, however, places him in a dilemma, for an active psychic conflict involves psychic effort which is undesirable to him. For this reason there is a tendency for a person to attempt wherever possible to avoid such conflict by impulse-buy-

ing or by reducing many of his purchasing decisions to routines or habit patterns—however, such attempts to avoid psychic conflict can be followed only within limits, or his income utilization would eventually become intolerably inefficient.[6]

(4) *If a homogeneous group of consumers all have an identical likelihood of making a particular purchase, a frequency distribution of their psychic tensions regarding the purchase in question will tend to form a normal probability curve.*[7] This postulate is the theoretical basis for applying the vector hypothesis to the analysis of a large number of families—as was done in this study.

The above four postulates are the pillars upon which the vector hypothesis rests. Taken together, they point to the conclusion that a person's (or group's) disbursement behavior for any given item can be analyzed in terms of his (or their) psychic tensions regarding it—when due consideration is given to impulse behavior, habits, past commitments and impositions.[8] Before turning to the author's study

---

[5] This postulate is based upon Lewinian vector psychology. See Kurt Lewin, "Group Decision and Social Change" in T. M. Newcomb, E. L. Hartley and others, *Readings in Social Psychology* (N.Y.: Henry Holt and Co., 1947).

[6] Two methods used by housewives to side-step psychic tensions for food purchasing are: (1) to buy in constant physical terms, i.e., to follow certain menu routines and then simply to maintain the inventory of the pantry shelf (thus, as food prices change, their total food expenditures change), or (2) to buy in constant monetary terms, i.e., to allocate and spend a certain amount of money per time period for food (thus, as food prices change the quantity or quality of their food purchases varies). By following habit patterns, by obeying impulses, or by employing arbitrary guides, active decision making can be avoided, but the achievement of such simplification is generally done at the expense of efficient buying. (Both habit and impulse behavior may be conditioned.) See W. J. Bilkey, "The Basic Relationships in Consumer Expenditure Behavior," *Harvard Studies in Marketing* No. 4-H (bulletin), Cambridge, Mass., 1951.

[7] This postulate is adapted from Abba P. Lerner, *The Economics of Control* (N.Y.: The Macmillan Co., 1946), pp. 29–32. The main evidence supporting it is that in each of two independent studies when the psychic tensions for a group of consumers were averaged, the data behaved in a regular and consistent manner as if the postulate were true. This occurred with Professor Lewin's data as well as with the author's. Essentially the same principle also is involved implicitly in the consumer buying anticipation studies of the University of Michigan Survey Research Center.

[8] During the course of the study which will be described shortly, the interviewees experienced no changes in external impositions, and the individual variations in impulse buying, habits and past commitments tended to cancel out. For this reason, an

Table 1. Conflict Ratings of High, Middle and Low Economic Groups for Specified Food Items
—as Presented by Kurt Lewin

Food	High Group	Middle Group	Low Group
Vegetables	.89	1.44	.57
Milk	.70	.89	.33
Meat	.65	1.28	.95
Butter	.30	.94	.67
Fruits	.43	.94	.62
Potatoes	—	.33	.76

From Kurt Lewin, "Group Decision and Social Change," T. M. Newcomb & E. L. Hartley, eds., *Reading in Social Psychology* (1947), p. 332, by permission of Henry Holt and Co., Inc., publishers.

The higher the numerical value, the greater the average psychic tension regarding the food. Values less than 1.00 mean that some interviewees never mentioned the food in reply to any of Lewin's three questions.

which was an exploratory attempt at such an analysis, we now will discuss briefly the techniques available for measuring these psychic tentions.

MEASURING TECHNIQUES

Thus far two techniques have been devised for approximating the magnitude of consumers' psychic tensions: (1) the self-rating method which involves having the persons rate their own tensions on a "0–100 centigrade thermometer scale," and (2) the inferential method which involves asking consumers particular questions and then having the analyst rate their psychic tensions on the basis of the answers received. The self-rating method will be described in detail later in this article. The inferential method may be illustrated by a study performed by the psychologist, Prof. Kurt Lewin.[9] In it he asked a sample of consumers the following three questions (it should be noted that food prices were rising at the time): (a) "Which foods are you already cutting because of the increase in the price of food?", (b) "If prices continue to rise, which foods might you cut?" and (c) "Even if food prices continue to rise, which foods are you particu-

larly anxious not to cut?" He then assigned arbitrary weights to the replies as follows: a weight of one to foods mentioned in answer to only one of these three questions, a weight of two to foods mentioned in answer to both questions (a) and (b), a weight of three to foods mentioned in answer to both questions (b) and (c), and a weight of four to foods mentioned in answer to both questions (a) and (c). He then classified the respondents according to their income, and averaged the scores obtained. His results are shown in Table 1. Considering that frozen foods were becoming popular around the time his study was made, Lewin's results are quite in accord with what one might expect on strictly *a priori* grounds. Unfortunately, he made no attempt to compare these psychic tensions with the respondents' actual purchases.

In that study Professor Lewin was concerned merely with the general level of the consumers' psychic tensions, i.e., their conflict rating for various foods. In terms of Figure 2, he was concerned only with the question of whether their positive valences and negative valences were both high or both low, not with the values of each.

As we compare the self-rating and the inferential measuring techniques it appears that both have strong and weak points. First let us consider the inferential method. Its advantages are: (1) interviewees don't have to evaluate their psychic tensions, they need only answer specific questions, and (2) it can be administered reasonably easily. Its shortcomings

averaging of the data for the 63 families studied resulted in their expenditure behavior apparently being almost exclusively a function of variations in their psychic tensions for the items in question.
[9] Kurt Lewin, "Forces Behind Food Habits and Methods of Change," *National Research Council Bulletin*, No. 108, 1943.

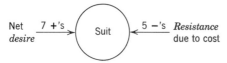

Figure 2 Simplified *desire-resistance* relationship as used for this project; the tension relationships are taken from Figure 1. The *desires* (+ valences) indicate the net total of all liked attributes minus all disliked attributes except those relating to cost. The *resistances* (− valences) indicate only the resistance due to cost. This relationship yields a net excess of 2 +'s (the same as for Figure 1). Note the general similarity of *desire* to the marginal utility of a good and of *resistance* to the marginal utility of money.

are: (1) there is no adequate objective criterion available to the analyst to determine what values to assign to the answers obtained,[10] and (2) interviewees often dislike repeating statements which they feel can be logically inferred from their earlier answers. The latter difficulty seems to be of considerable practical importance.

The advantages of the self-rating method described below are: (1) it can be easily administered, and (2) answers are taken at face value without having to assign arbitrary values to them. Its shortcomings are: (1) the interviewee has no objective criterion upon which to base his answers and (2) there is no *a priori* evidence to indicate the degree to which the answers are interpersonally comparable.

Fortunately, these two measuring techniques are not mutually exclusive. Both methods may be employed in a single study, and there is a possibility that the results obtained will be complementary. Another possibility is to develop a hybrid of these two techniques.

DESCRIPTIONS OF STUDY

The research now to be described was intended as a pilot study to discover whether any significant relationship seemed to exist between the interviewees' purchases of particular items and their measured psychic tensions regarding those items. A secondary objective, to ascertain whether these measured psychic tensions seemed to be influenced by variables which are economically meaningful, will be reported upon in a subsequent paper.

Because of the exploratory nature of this

study, the author wished to work only with persons who would actively cooperate in it, hence a random sampling technique of selection was not used. Instead, mimeographed leaflets explaining the nature of the study were distributed. Persons interested in helping with it then submitted their names, and from these names 63 interviewees were selected as randomly as possible.[11]

The purchasing head of each family was interviewed once every month during the course of the study (each interview being made as near to the middle of the month as circumstances permitted), and the family's expenditures for the month in question then were recorded during the following month's visit. Thus, the psychic tension data for each month were obtained prior to the completion of that month's expenditures. That is why psychic tensions (*net valences*) are shown as the independent variable in Figure 4.[12]

To minimize the possibility that the families might deliberately adjust their purchases to harmonize with their interview statements, the following precautions were taken: (1) most of the questions called for numerical responses, the full significance of which was not explained to the interviewees, (2) the interviewees never were shown their preceding month's answers, and (3) a large number of questions were asked so as to make memorization of their numerical responses difficult—each interview lasted about one and one-half hours and covered all of the family's major disbursement categories.

To be theoretically precise, the interviews for this study should have been made in terms of the vector relationship as illustrated in Figure 1; however, during this pilot study phase of the analysis a more easily workable concept was wanted. For this practical reason, the model shown in Figure 1 was reduced to the simpler desire-resistance relationship in Figure

[10] For an appraisal of the various methods for determining scoring weights see L. W. Ferguson, *Personality Measurement* (N.Y.: McGraw-Hill, 1952), pp. 128–132.

[11] Of the 63 interviewees, 45 were interviewed once a month for 12 months, 8 for 6–11 months, and 10 for 1–5 months. In terms of occupation: 46 were on the faculty or staff of this University, 14 were small businessmen or laborers and 3 were married university students. In terms of location: 12 were from New London, Connecticut, and the remainder were from the Storrs-Willimantic area. No significant differences in tension-purchasing relationships were found between any of these groups.

[12] *Net valences* are merely the net difference between the person's positive valences for a given item (or category) and his negative valences regarding it. E.g., in Figure 1 the person has 11 positive valences for the suit and 9 negative valences against its purchase, or 2 positive *net valences* regarding its purchase.

2. This was accomplished by letting *desire* constitute the arithmetic total of the person's valences regarding all of the attributes shown in Figure 1 except cost. *Resistance* then involved only the person's unwillingness to incur the money cost of the item in question. The interviewees were asked to rate their *desires* and *resistances* for each of their disbursement categories on a modified Allport-Vernon value scale—see Figure 3. The numerical answers which they gave then were treated as if they were the person's psychic tensions for the categories or items in question.

INTERVIEW FINDINGS

Consumer Durables

Several of the interviewees indicated that they were giving some consideration to the purchase of a consumer durable good such as a car, washing machine, sewing machine, rug, etc. During each interview they then were asked to rate their psychic tensions (in the sense as illustrated in Figure 2) for the item in question. Using the self-rating scale shown in Figure 3, they were asked: (1) "How strong is your desire for the (good)?" and (2) "How

strong is your desire to avoid the expense which the (good) would entail?" Table 2 illustrates the responses obtained for an item

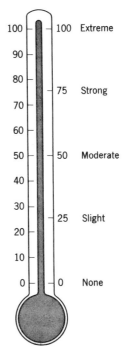

Figure 3   Self-rating scale.

Table 2.   Valence Relationships Which Culminated in a Purchase—a Rug. Data as Obtained from Interviewee No. 4; Comments Made by Her During the Interviews Are Given Below

The Vector	Feb.	Mar.	Apr.	May	June	July	Aug.	Sept.	Oct.
Desire for rug (+valences)	75	—	50	25	25	—	75	90	fin
Resistance to expenditure for rug (−valences)	0	—	25	0	100	—	50	50	fin
Net valences	75+	—	25+	25+	75−	—	25+	40+	fin

Feb.—Had an even stronger desire for a new stove (100+'s and 0−'s). The interviewer failed to ask resistance against expenditures for a stove plus a rug.

Mar.—Bought a new electric range. Missed March interview because of sickness in the family.

Apr.—No comment.

May—Interviewee commented: "Now that I have a new stove I'm so satisfied that I have no desire for a new rug. Also there's the fact that I got new shoes and a dress." (She had been clothes shopping a few days before the May interview.)

June—Prior to the interview she had priced rugs and found that the kind she wanted would cost around $300; her earlier estimates had been that such a rug might cost around $150. She stated, "I simply won't pay that."

July—Missed interview because family was vacationing.

Aug.—Interviewee commented: "Now I have a desire for a rug."

Sept.—No comment.

Oct.—Interviewee had purchased a rug shortly before the October interview. She commented: "Now I want a new refrigerator." (75+'s and 50−'s.)

Table 3. Valence Relationships Which did not Culminate in a Purchase—a Car. Data as Obtained from Interviewee No. 69; Comments Made by Him During the Interviews are Given Below

The Vector	July	Aug.	Sept.	Oct.	Nov.	Dec.	Jan.
Desire for car (+valences)	50	50	50	50	50 to 75	50	50
Resistance to expenditure for car (−valences)	50	50	50	75	25 to 50	75	75
Net valences	0	0	0	25−	25+	25−	25−

July—No comment.

Aug.—No comment.

Sept.—Interviewee commented that he might buy a car within a month or he might not do so for two years, and that he was watching ads conscientiously. His present car had been repaired a few months earlier and he expected no further trouble for a couple of years.

Oct.—Interviewee commented: "A new car looks more hopeless than ever." He had committed $500 to his wife for the purchase of furniture, and there was a possibility that she also might need an operation.

Nov.—Interviewee commented that he was now thinking more about a car; that he had been inconvenienced a few days earlier by a brake-down with his present car.

Dec.—The interviewee stated that his wife had been taken to a hospital shortly before the interview, and had had an expensive operation.

Jan.—No comment; no purchase.

which finally was purchased—a rug. Note the general tendency after June for the *desire* (+ valences) answers to increase relative to the *resistance* (− valences) answers. In every case which finally culminated in a purchase, the responses obtained behaved in this general manner. Table 3 illustrates the responses obtained for an item which was not purchased—a car. Note the general tendency over time for the *desire* (+ valences) answers to decrease relative to the *resistance* (− valences) answers. In every case where the interviewee failed to purchase the item in question, the responses obtained all followed this general pattern.

Food

Since food is bought continuously, it was analyzed in terms of whether or not changes in its rate of purchase might occur. This involved asking the following four questions, each to be answered in terms of the scale shown in Figure 3:

Desire questions:

1. "How strong is your desire to increase your food items consumed (in quality or quantity) by 10% from last month's amount?"

2. "How strong is your desire to avoid cutting your food items consumed (in quality or quantity) by 10% from last month's amount?"

Resistance questions:

3. "How strong is your desire to reduce your food expenditures by 10% from last month's amount?"

4. "How strong is your desire to avoid increasing your food expenditures by 10% from last month's amount?"

To obtain the psychic tension ratings for food, answers to the two *desire* questions were averaged and answers to the two *resistance* questions were averaged; the difference between these two magnitudes then being referred to as *net valences*.

Figure 4 shows the relationship between the *net valences* for food averaged for all families by months with the corresponding averages of their food expenditures for the same months. Note that the April relationship in Figure 4 seems to be out of place. That apparently was due to a general tendency on the part of many of these families to have reduced their food inventories during that month. A considerable number of the interviewees stated that their food expenditures were unusually low then because they had cleaned out their frozen food lockers in April. Most of them commented that they had eaten unusually well then. The conclusion drawn from the data shown in Figure 4 is that there was a rather close quantitative relationship between the interviewees' psychic tensions for food and their corresponding food expenditures when allowance is made for inventory variation.

Food Components

The analysis presented thus far has indicated the existence of a relationship (presumably causal) between net valences and purchases for both consumer durables and for food. The question then arose whether such a relationship might also hold for the components within a category, e.g., for particular food items. To test this, the interviewees were requested during the course of the study to maintain purchasing records for meat and eggs. Only a portion of the interviewees complied with this request; however, the results from those who did keep records indicate that a valence-expenditure relationship does exist for these items as well as for food as a whole, although it was less close. When cast in the form shown in Figure 4, the following relationships were obtained between the interviewees' psychic tensions and their corresponding monthly expenditures: for meat r = +.761 and the regression line was Y = 15.27 + .13X, for eggs r = +.635 and the regression line was Y = 4.73 + .05X.

CONCLUSIONS FROM STUDY

As indicated earlier, the research project described above was intended as a pilot study to ascertain: (1) whether a significant relationship appears to exist between people's psychic tensions regarding particular items and their purchases of those items, and (2) whether these postulated psychic tensions in turn are influenced by considerations which are economically meaningful. It should be recalled that only 63 families were studied, that they were not randomly selected, that the families in question were aware that they were being studied and that techniques for measuring psychic tensions are barely in process of development. Under these circumstances we can conclude only that the results obtained suggest an affirmative answer to the above two questions, and that further research seems definitely to be warranted. On the basis of his experience with this and with other studies, the author is convinced that the vector hypothesis provides a useful theoretical framework for consumer analysis, even with the measuring techniques currently available.

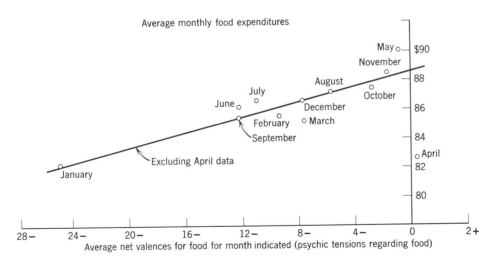

Figure 4 Relationship between monthly averages of net valences for food and average net food expenditures for the same months. April data seem to be out of place because of inventory de-accumulation; many of the families stated that they closed out their lockers and finished eating their canned goods in April, so that their food consumption then was greater than their expenditures indicate. Excluding April data: Y = 88.87 + 0.27X, and r = +0.910. Including April data: Y = 87.51 + 0.17X, and r = +0.550.

Limits of Persuasion: The Hidden Persuaders Are Made of Straw

RAYMOND A. BAUER

In recent years the public has developed an exaggerated fear of the possibility of their behavior being controlled and manipulated by others. Some of this fear probably traces back to the "technique of the big lie," which seemed to delude the masses in dictator countries, as well as to the "brainwashing" stories that came out of the Korean War. These fears have been played upon by popular writers until half-truths are accepted as verified facts. In this article a psychologist takes a sober look at many of these unreasoned fears and puts them in better perspective.

Man seems to live in perpetual hope and horror that infallible means have been developed whereby one man can control another's behavior. As usual, the hope and the horror are opposite sides of the same coin:

On the hopeful side, some selfishly see the possibility of advantage for themselves in gaining control over their fellow men. Others, more idealistically, look to a "science of man" as the basis for establishing a Utopia which will be optimally efficient in the production of both material goods and human happiness.

On the side of horror, some fear that they themselves will be "manipulated" to the advantage of someone else. Others fear the motives for their own relations to their fellow men. The image of a potential Utopia gets turned inside out and we see that the reverse image is that of 1984—the totalitarian state of George Orwell's novel—in which the best qualities of man are lost.

Recent developments in the science of psychology, and the publicity given to some of its more sensational applications—such as "subliminal advertising" or "brainwashing"—have strengthened our anxiety. The significance of these developments is of particular concern to

♦ SOURCE: Reprinted by permission from *Harvard Business Review*, Vol. 36, No. 5, September–October 1958, pp. 105–110.

businessmen, for they, along with politicians, will be responsible for the use of the new techniques. But there is no reason for panic. Anxiety stems, in part, from ignorance of the causal relations between the "persuaders" and the "persuaded." To show this relationship, and the limitations it imposes on the techniques, we must consider three broad areas of application:

Propaganda and human relations.
Appeals to "noneconomic" motives.
Appeals to "unconscious" motives.

With a better understanding of the functioning of these techniques, we will be in a stronger position to evaluate them realistically.

NEW FEAR OR OLD SCARE?

The specter of "manipulation" and "hidden persuasion" has stalked all the lands that man has ever inhabited. The most primitive manifestation of the deep anixiety which we feel on this issue is represented by Nightmare Alice, the witch of Li'l Abner Land. From time to time, Nightmare Alice makes an effigy of one of the "good people" of Dogpatch and places this person under her hidden control. Black magic is found among most nonliterate peoples, and the fear of it persists. In the Middle Ages, people were "possessed by the devil"; in our own colonial times we went back to "witches."

In recent decades, to be sure, we have done away with such superstitions and become more "scientific." Or have we simply dressed up our old fears in modern fashions? Remember how during the 1920's and 1930's we worried about the mysterious powers of the mass media, particularly as manipulated by such practitioners as George Creel and Ivy L. Lee? My point is that although this century has led to tremendous progress in our knowledge of the human mind, our fear that this knowledge will be misused is as old as the history of man.

But what are the facts? Does modern psychology give us the tools to control each other? The full range of considerations is, of course, beyond our purview here. Moreover, any discussion of psychological techniques of persuasion and manipulation must, of course, be done without knowing what new knowledge may be developed. It is my belief, however, that what I have to say must hold in principle for almost any conceivable situation that may develop.

RATIO OF RESISTANCE

Let me begin my positive assertions with what may seem like a paradoxical statement. Without doubt we have, largely on the basis of improved social science knowledge in the fields of psychology, sociology, and anthropology, developed increasingly refined and effective means of persuasion. It does not follow, however, that even in the field of advertising we are able to effect more persuasion. How can this be? Simply because the increased knowledge benefits not only the persuader but also the target of persuasion. As the persuaders become more sophisticated, so do the people to be persuaded.

One way of reading the history of the development of techniques of persuasion is that the persuaders have been in a race to keep abreast of the developing resistance of the people to be persuaded. Thus:

In the decades following World War I, we were very excited about the power of propaganda. We came close to saying that if it were possible to get a story in the newspapers or on the radio, people would automatically believe it and act on it. But what happened? Many people became so suspicious of propaganda that they would scarcely believe the news on the sports page.

As a result, World War II propaganda in the Western countries was markedly different from that of World War I. Propagandists—that is, "persuaders"—were scrupulously careful not to test the credulity of their readers and listeners; they also avoided more blatant emotional appeals.

Why? People had become more sophisticated, and more resistant to "persuasion." Social science research on the effects of communications, by the beginning of World War II, had pretty well destroyed the myth of propaganda's omnipotence.

We see today similar developments in advertising. There is still some advertising that is reminiscent of the old-fashioned pitchman selling snake oil. However, the development of the "soft sell" seems to me a tacit acknowledgment of the developing resistance of the potential consumer.

Manipulation More Difficult

Within business and industry we have witnessed the evolving concern with human relations and communication. These events also have been viewed with horror as evidence of the growth of manipulation. But the viewers-with-horror naively assume that the knowledge on which this presumed manipulation is based is limited to the manipulators. Without in any way deprecating the desirability of the human relations approach—I not only favor it but even try to practice it—I doubt if it has produced any increase in manipulation.

As a matter of fact, all this new concern must have made the process of interpersonal communications more complicated. It is traditional that, as people become more diplomatic, their communications become more subtle. Perhaps we are all reaching the point of the diplomat who, on being informed of the death of his opposite number, queried: "I wonder what he meant by that." So in the absence of any long-run trend statistics on the number of effective persuasive and manipulative acts in business and industry, I shall remain content with pointing to the obvious mechanisms of resistance to persuasion; noting that manipulation has become more difficult; and suggesting there is no more reason to believe that the actual practice of manipulation has increased than that it has lessened. The data to prove me wrong are unobtainable.

HIDDEN PERSUADERS?

Our main fear, however, is not that we will be taken in by the persuasive logic of a Madison Avenue salesman but that, through appeals to deep, unconscious motives, we can be manipulated without even knowing it.

A book such as Vance Packard's *Hidden Persuaders* [1] generates a good deal of soul searching, both among the general public and within professional circles. This book, for the benefit of the fortunate few who are not familiar with it, tells a story, though certainly not *the* story, of how psychology has been applied in market research. By determining people's unconscious motives "via the principles of modern dynamic psychology," researchers are able to devise methods whereby mysterious and miraculous marketing results are produced. The consumer is powerless to resist these techniques, and he just buys and buys without knowing why. From this it is, of course, only one step to applying these techniques in politics, and 1984 will arrive at least twenty years ahead of schedule. Packard's picture, needless to say, is a trifle stylized.

Packard wrote his book to warn the public. The net impact of the volume is that there has been a complete revolution in market research in the form of motivation research, the term for the intensive exploration of the psychological factors involved in consumer behavior and product usage. But it is only the *intensity of concern* that is new. So far as I can see, the major practical result has been—as one might expect—an increased and unrealistic demand for motivation research. Packard succeeded in painting the picture of psychological demonology so persuasively that motivation researchers are now concerned with giving their clients a more realistic notion of what they can do.

But Packard also succeeded in creating again the primitive anxiety that we are on the verge of being able to establish complete control over human behavior to the extent that the victims of this control will not have a chance to resist it because they do not realize it is there.

Noneconomic Motives

In the first place, people *do* have some chance to resist the motives associated with the new techniques. People buy many things

[1] New York, David McKay Company, Inc., 1957.

for *noneconomic* reasons, but such motives are not necessarily *unconscious*. It is a serious mistake to equate the two; and the use of the term *irrational* makes the confusion even worse. Once you label noneconomic motives irrational, you imply they are unreasonable, and you are well on the way to assuming they are unconscious.

When I say that people do things for noneconomic reasons (what others might call "irrational"), I am talking about the fact that people may buy a particular automobile because they desire status, the esteem of themselves and others; because they like products which fit their own self-image; or even because a man likes the feeling of potency which comes from driving an overhorsepowered vehicle. But I can see no reason to say a man is more "rational" to want transportation than to want self-respect and the esteem of others—though if it helps you to understand why he is doing what he is doing, you can say he is being less economic.

It is true that most of the motives I have just mentioned are not usually cited in reponse to the direct question: "Why did you buy that product?" In our culture, the accepted reasons for buying a product bear on its primary economic function: for instance, the cost of transportation provided by the car, the cleaning effectiveness of a soap, and so on. Accordingly, we are not as likely to think of the noneconomic motives as reasons for buying, bearing as they do on the secondary functions (or "added value") of products. Or, if we do, perhaps we feel a little ashamed and so are reticent about them. But in no meaningful sense are these motives unconscious. With a little stimulation almost every one of us recognizes their existence.

Practical Consequences

This is no mere quibble. The fact that people can and do acknowledge the existence of these motives has considerable practical consequence. The use of appeals directed to such motives—as well as the widespread discussion, which we have already witnessed, of the concern given such motives in product design and merchandising—is bringing them into the center of consciousness as buying motives even if they were not there before. Some people will come to accept these as proper buying motives, and will probably learn to shop as astutely for the product that gives them the most prestige as for the product that has the lowest price, best mechanical qualities, and so on. Other people will resist these appeals, not accepting the secondary functions as a legitimate reason for buying.

Appeal to such motives may still serve, as in the past, to win the merchandiser a temporary advantage. However, as such appeals become customary and the public becomes generally aware of them, they will leave the merchandiser just about where he was to start with as far as his "persuasive advantage" is concerned.

Just because marketing and product design are based increasingly on psychologically oriented market research, it does not follow that products will continue to be sold increasingly on the basis of their secondary functions or "added value." At this time merchandisers are becoming more and more alert to the power of the secondary characteristics of products to satisfy consumer wants. As a psychologist I can have no conceivable objection in principle to people's noneconomic wants being satisfied. But we must look seriously at the possibility that this trend may reach the point of saturation.

Even now, the "irrationality"—a word I detest—of the consumer may be grossly overestimated. In few, if any, of the discussions of consumer motivation is there any mention of the growth of such consumer information services as Consumer's Research and Consumer's Union. The notion that people are not concerned with and do not understand the technical aspects of the products they buy may have to be tempered in the future. Today's consumers are almost certainly more interested and better informed on the technical features of products than they have been in the past.

There is something ironical in depicting the housewife shopping in the supermart as being indifferent to economy, being cozened by hidden persuaders into spending 15% more for her market basket than some stringent criterion says is necessary. Remember, the corner grocery store offers the housewife psychological rewards that the supermart does not. Yet in the interests of economy housewives have deserted the corner grocery store for the more impersonal, but more economical, supermart. This very same group of housewives has patronized discount houses, which scarcely give them the same psychological satisfactions as do department and high-class specialty stores.

One of the established arguments for stressing the secondary functions of a product is that all products in a given line are virtually identical with respect to their primary economic function. But suppose all automobiles in a given price range became virtually identical with regard to their symbolic value: this might drive the manufacturers to strive again for differentiation on the basis of the primary function of transportation. This notion is far from facetious. While Chrysler may indeed have gotten into difficulty a few years ago by deemphasizing styling, today it is the small economical car—American Rambler or a foreign make—that is making inroads into the market, not the cars with "sex appeal."

This is not to brush aside the importance of the motives that the motivation researchers have stressed. I am merely suggesting that we keep our image of the consumer in somewhat clearer perspective. The merchandiser who concentrates too much on the secondary characteristics of products will find himself in as much difficulty as the one who ignores them completely. Motivation research may indeed become indispensable *because* of the very trends in the population I have been describing. The merchandiser will probably need increasingly detailed psychological knowledge of consumers as the years go on, if only to know what difficulties he is up against and how far he must stay away from noneconomic appeals.

UNCONSCIOUS MOTIVES

This is not the whole picture. All that I have said to this point is that many of the motives with which motivation research deals are not unconscious in *any meaningful sense;* and that, as these particular motives are appealed to, the consumer recognizes them more explicitly as motives linked to consumer behavior, and develops the capacity for a critical appraisal of appeals to such motives.

But there *are* some truly unconscious motives—that is, motives which the individual would not acknowledge consciously to *himself* even if, or especially if, they are called explicitly to his attention. To illustrate:

One of the most spectacular of the claims for the exploitation of unconscious motives is the development of the hardtop convertible. The hardtop is labeled as a compromise between the male buyer's dual attachment to the stable, reliable wife, symbolized by the sedan, and the flashy, unreliable mistress, symbolized by the convertible.

Certainly, in psychoanalytic thinking, it is accepted that the male child has conflict over thinking of his mother as a sexual object, and develops a split image of women. But I cannot conceivably take a stand on whether or not this is the complete story of the hardtop, or what substantial portion of the story it may comprise. I use it only as an example of appealing to a motive that is meaningfully referred to as unconscious.

There is something very plausible in the notion that if we understand another person's unconscious motivation, then we can appeal to his motives and get him to do something without his knowing why he did it. Certainly, he ought to be powerless to resist. To some extent this is true. But the entire picture is more complicated. Remember that there is a reason for certain motives remaining unconscious; in general, conscious acknowledgment of these motives would produce intolerable anxiety. Hence, appeal to such motives may backfire, and backfire violently. Thus, on an *a priori* basis, combining the "mistress and the wife" in the form of the hardtop convertible *could* have aroused anxiety and caused people to stay away from this model in droves.

POWER TO RESIST

I am not arguing for or against the effectiveness of any of these techniques of persuasion. I have merely indicated that individuals have the capacity to resist even on the unconscious level. I *am* arguing that the individual's resistance to persuasion probably increases in proportion to the efforts made to persuade him against his own perceived interest. We may even go further than that. Our primitive anxiety concerning the possibility of being manipulated leads us to resist persuasion by others, even in some instances where it may be *in our own interest*. Thus we have the automatic response, "Nobody's going to tell me what's good for me."

My guess is that over the years the American people have developed resistance to manipulation at about the same rate that our techniques of persuasion have become more sophisticated and effective. I mean, of course, that if *the audience had remained the same*, our new techniques would be more effective than our old ones. But the audience has not remained the same. The pace of the race has grown

swifter, but it is difficult to say who has gained on whom.

Another point to remember is that merchandising is a competitive activity, and any technique of research or persuasion is about equally available to anyone who wants to make use of it. Even the vaunted subliminal advertisements would tend to cancel out each other if all refrigerator manufacturers, for example, were to use them on television. Competition among persuaders, indeed, is very much like that between the persuader and the object of his persuasion. Adoption of a new technique may well give a momentary competitive advantage, but this advantage lasts only until competitors have also adopted that technique. As long as there is a multiplicity of advertisers, it is difficult to see how the public at large can become the passive puppets of "hidden persuaders."

Omnipotent Control?

But there is still one other dread possibility to dispose of, if we can. Let us consider what might happen if there were *no* competition—if the tools of manipulation were in one group's hands. This would be 1984, the society in which an elite group will direct the behavior of everyone else in so subtle a way that no one is aware that it is happening. Perhaps it has already happened? How could we tell when it began?

I would not say for a moment that there are no situations in which one person can exercise absolute control over another. Give one man a gun (known in the vernacular as a "persuader"), and he can do a pretty good job of directing the activities of an unarmed man. True, some people in such a situation have escaped, taken the gun from the man, or got themselves shot. But I would not like to quibble about such a small minority, particularly in view of the fact that the effectiveness of this persuader depends on its presence being known, not hidden.

Accounts of brainwashing and similar phenomena indicate that—with a considerable expenditure of effort, careful control of a man's environment (which includes isolating him and getting him in a state of fatigue), good intuitive psychological insight, and a great deal of patience—it *is* possible to change the beliefs of a large proportion of one's victims. There is even some threat in the offing that the use of drugs and of electrodes implanted in the brain may make such procedures more effective.

Although I have some modicum of competence on such subjects, I frankly do not know exactly how far one can go now or in the immediate future with such procedures of influencing people. But look at how remote this is from the notion of controlling *a large society* via psychological techniques. Not only is it doubtful if strictly psychological practices would effect a considerable amount of brainwashing in the absence of all the other factors of control over the individual's environment, but there is the very practical matter that the amount of time and energy expended on each individual must be at least equal to his own time and energy. In short, the influencing of a single individual in a confined situation and by a large number of people is an entirely different case from that of a small number of people influencing a large number of people on a societal level. The Soviet Union is the closest approximation to this latter circumstance that we have seen, and I can say from my own studies of that society that the persuasion was far from hidden, far from total, and, possibly, far from desirable for the efficient functioning of the society.[2]

To be quite realistic, I do not see how anyone who has observed or operated any large-scale organization can take seriously the notion of complete control of behavior. In particular, social science has taught us at least as much

[2] See, for example, Raymond A. Bauer, "Brainwashing, Psychology or Demonology," *Journal of Social Issues,* Vol. 13, No. 3, 1957, p. 41.

about the *necessity* of permitting initiative—which a 1984 society by definition cannot do—as it has taught us about directing behavior.

CONCLUSION

In sum, I am skeptical about the extreme pictures of "hidden persuasion" that have been drawn for either the present or future of business or politics. This does not mean I am indifferent to the prospects of individual instances of the unscrupulous use of psychological or other social science knowledge. What I have been attacking is the notion of the possibility of omnipotent control over the behavior of large numbers of human beings. That such a notion rears its head repeatedly comes, I believe, from our primitive anxiety over manipulation. This anxiety is caused, on the one hand, by our fear that other people may be doing it to *us*, and therefore that we have lost control over our own destiny. It comes, on the other hand from the notion that *we* may be doing it to others; and here we have a sense of guilt concerning our own motives and behavior toward those others.

I may be fighting a straw man in the sense that this particular *object* of people's fears is not real. But the *fears* exist; they are real. To date most people have not recognized that the threat of omnipotent control over man's behavior *is* a straw man. It may be that my contribution here is that of pointing out that the "hidden persuaders" in their exaggerated form are, in fact, made of straw.

Opportunities for Persuasion

EDWARD C. BURSK

It is helpful to know the limits of persuasion: to realize that gains in motivation research techniques are accompanied by gains in individuals' discernment and ability to resist; and to learn that it is difficult, if not impossible, to exert mass control of people through subconscious manipulation. Raymond A. Bauer's article makes this clear.[1] But there is another way of looking at persuasion—at its opportunities rather than its limitations, particularly when it is practiced openly and rationally.

In fact, I think it can be argued that psychological limitations come into operation only to the extent that persuasion is misapplied. Resistance may be a reaction to attempts at persuasion; however, persuasion does not always produce resistance. I have seen plenty of instances where persuasion is effective largely because it reduces resistance. Sometimes buyers even take positive delight in being sold. And then other times they react unfavorably to too much persuasion or too little persuasion or the wrong kind of persuasion.

What is the right amount and kind of persuasion? That is a difficult question, since different ideas (or different products and brand features) have different reaction factors in people's minds. The potentialities for securing acceptance, as well as the difficulties of overcoming resistance, vary over a wide range. So it is useful to have the clearest possible understanding of why consumers buy or do not buy.

♦ SOURCE: Reprinted by permission from *Harvard Business Review*, Vol. 36, No. 5, September–October 1958, pp. 111–119.

[1] Raymond A. Bauer, "Limits of Persuasion," *Harvard Business Review*, September–October 1958, pp. 105–10.

CONSUMER MOTIVATIONS

The mistake is to think that knowing consumer motivations means being able to shape them to specific ends, such as getting people to go out and buy a particular product or reach for this brand in preference to that brand. I claim that persuasion is more a matter of strategy than of manipulation; that it is a process of arraying logical forces so that people themselves decide to do what you want them to, rather than of actually changing people's minds; and that any effort to get action by tampering with people's emotions not only runs up against the psychological limitations of resistance but also can be prohibitively time-consuming and expensive.

The way a seller deploys his forces depends of course on the buyer's forces, which include his motives. So the seller needs to take the buyer's motives into account in order to outmaneuver him and get him to move in the desired direction. Here is where the opportunities are; and ironically, they will not be realized until the new motivation research knowledge which makes them such opportunities is reduced to its proper, limited role. I feel it is important to make this crystal-clear before going on to tackle the problem of constructing strategies.

Decision vs. Diagnosis

It is always a temptation for managers to abdicate the functions of analysis and decision-making when some "magical" technique promises to do the work for them. The new techniques we are learning from the mathematical and behavioral sciences do provide a stronger basis of information for understanding situations on which action is to be taken, and more accurate devices for measuring the results of action once it has been taken; but they cannot prescribe action. Moreover, even for those purposes, management itself must think through its problems, formulate its specific needs, and make explicit its purposes; otherwise the techniques are likely to be pointless, and only fruitful by accident. So it is good to be reminded that motivation research, with all its ballyhoo, is far from providing the "answers" to everything.

The very existence of limitations adds a positive opportunity. Managers should be glad that they must work with imperfect tools—for then other managers, in competing companies, will face the same impossibility of securing perfect results, and the premium will be to those who use the tools more skillfully. Indeed, it is the essence of aggressive management to take up imperfect tools and *make* them work! And the fact that the availability of new techniques may reduce the range of decision-making simply means that, in the narrowing area where judgment and initiative *are* still needed, the effect of relative degree of skill is magnified: the more costly are the mistakes, and the greater is the edge over competitors gained by correct decisions.

So, as we now turn our attention to the *opportunities* for persuasion, the clue is that, however valuable the new research techniques may be for purposes of diagnosis, they are inept for decision-making. It is management that must do the creative part of the selling job. This applies both to products and to ideas; but I shall carry the discussion forward in terms of products, since this area not only is important in its own right but serves to illustrate more concretely the principles that are involved.

Lessons of Experience

I do not think you can discount the lessons of experience. There are certain things that any man who has done much selling knows; he may not understand the reasons, but he can tell you what works. The points that I intend to make are drawn from observation of many salesmen's activities, including my own for a number of years. I have found that the advertising men who have been most successful in *selling* products (in the sense of building

consumer demand or brand preference) also subscribe to the same general philosophy.

The fact that consumer motivation experts often disagree violently among themselves (particularly when it comes to recommending action based on their findings) does not make them wrong, but it certainly does not make me wrong in advocating a more direct and realistic view of selling, either. Indeed, it is because I recognize motives as being both so important and so difficult to deal with that I believe we need to approach selling from the practical viewpoint of strategy.

In short, I am convinced that the best way to sell is along the following lines:

It is normal and healthy for people to like to buy, just as it is abnormal and unhealthy for them to dislike to buy; and in selling we should deal with people as if we expected them to be normal and healthy rather than in need of mental hygiene—or at least predominantly on that side of the balance, so they have it *in their own power* to resolve any emotional conflict over buying.

Whether the urge to buy is realized and/or any resistance is overcome depends on management's selling efforts (both on the broad economic scale and for individual companies); and more effort—just plain effort—may be almost as important as new skill.

The way for management to secure the desired results is to employ a strategy that makes use of our best understanding of the psychology of the selling-buying relationship—both as to specific motivations in different situations and, even more important, as to the general phenomenon of people wanting to buy, yet being wary of pressure or trickery, which applies in all situations.

The essence of such a strategy would be to minimize resistance and maximize the urge to buy through selling conducted on the *rational* level—namely, planning and presenting rational goals for people which will lead them to the particular product or brand, in such a way that they satisfy their motivations and even act as their own psychiatrists in the event of any conflict.

Selling of this kind is more effective than deliberate attempts at psychological influencing because it is more in line with the needs and capacities of salesmen, advertising copy writers, and top management; it is more likely to be psychologically sound for the mass of people on the buying end of the relationship; and so secures greater results at less expense.

Apart from the efficiency of the strategy, intensification of selling efforts along lines like these furthers the long-run objectives of both business and society; for it both serves to keep the economy dynamic and contributes to the standard of living of normal, healthy people.

If these concepts hold—and I think those people who have had much firsthand experience in selling would heartily agree—then it is possible to construct a simple (but intensive) strategy for a particular product in a particular market which will handle the complexity and subtlety of the particular motivations involved. In trying to "sell" my ideas in this article I shall make use of some of the same kind of direct, enthusiastic drive.

URGE AND RESISTANCE

It hardly needs to be demonstrated that people like to buy. There is a sheer enjoyment in acquiring things, which goes far back to primitive roots. The act of buying is an expression of power, of mastery. Also, people generally like to be nice to people; and if the other person is a salesman, then the inclination is to be nice to him—and the way to be nice to a salesman is to buy from him.

Now, as I understand it, the person who is normal and healthy minded tends to do what society approves of. The purchase of goods and services—not just food and clothing but education, and not just *a* car but a car *of modern fashion*—is part and parcel of our way of life. And it is not only socially right to buy certain kinds of individual products and services; it also is right to buy lots of things in general. Indeed, this is how people's success is usually measured—as individuals or as families, in their own self-opinion or in the eyes of society. Or, at least, this is how *most* people feel, which is what counts.

So there is a positive urge to buy—to buy in general and to buy specific products. But there is also a negative counterforce that can cause resistance—resistance in general and resistance to specific purchases. Right now we are concerned with the general dimensions—with the underlying strategy (which of course then has to be adapted to more specific motivations).

Underlying Strategy

Just as it is socially acceptable to buy, so it is *not* socially acceptable to *overbuy*, that is, to the point where a person appears reckless, improvident, a poor manager of his finances; or to buy *unwisely*, that is, without due regard for price and quality. Admittedly, these are vague terms; in fact they shift with time, and at any one time mean different things to different people. But the idea that there is a point beyond which it is not right to buy is nonetheless very real in every individual's mind, and people are uneasy lest they go beyond it without realizing they are doing so. As far as sellers are concerned, it is the existence of the resistance that is important, not the particular shading of individual buyers' ideas. It will always be operative, and strategy must be pointed to overcome it regardless of how strong it is.

Thus, no matter what that shading, there is the one, single, and over-all fact that for every selling situation the buyer must have some self-approved reason for saying *yes*—whether the affirmation is in terms of handing over the money or signing on the dotted line, or just feeling agreement with an advertising message. For example, a man may want to buy a new car because it is new and sleek and shiny, but he also needs some rationalization like: "I'll get a better trade-in if I buy now." Or a woman may want a particular brand of soap because she thinks it will make her seductive to all mankind, but she also must be able to think something like: "If I look prettier, my husband will be pleased"; or more simply, "It will protect my skin"; or still more simply, "It cleans."

This is why it sometimes is difficult for a salesman to close a sale, even though the prospect may seem favorably disposed: the right kind of rationalization has not been offered, even though the actual motivation for buying may have been amply satisfied. The same thing is true in direct-mail selling; a man may want to subscribe to a magazine because it makes him feel important, but the promotional piece must also assure him that by filling out and mailing the subscription order form he will receive some practical help in improving his professional skills or solving his business problems.

I am convinced this is also true in advertising; that of two ads, both of which apply to a product mainly bought for *irrational* reasons, the one that provides in addition some cogent *rational* reason should produce a stronger reaction than the one that does not. I suspect that one explanation of why the combination of an advertising appeal to the image of masculinity *and* a new crush-proof box worked so well for Marlboro cigarettes is that the box offered a generally acceptable rationalization.

Rational *vs.* Irrational

I should like to rescue the terms *rational* and *irrational* from the confusion they seem to have fallen into. If applied carefully, they pose a distinction that can be very useful for selling and advertising:

Rational applies to reasons for buying (or not buying) which are *self-approved*—that is, which the buyer feels to be right and reasonable because they are in line with his own expectations of himself as a thinking man and/or his understanding of what other people (society) would consider to be right and reasonable on the part of a thinking man.

By the same token, *irrational* applies to reasons for buying (or for not buying) which are *not* self-approved and socially acceptable, as just defined.

Not that a buyer thinks this all out, or ever formulates it explicitly, but as a result of all his experiences and the current mores of society he just feels some reasons are "all right" for him, and others are not. Completely independent of this distinction is the distinction between conscious and unconscious, or between economic and noneconomic. The trouble is that the terms do sometimes coincide—e.g., *irrational* with *unconscious*, *economic* with *rational*,·and so on—and that is why a careless tendency to equate them has developed.

True, rational reasons are more *likely* to be conscious than reasons which are not self-approved, because there is no cause for shame or anxiety about them and hence no tendency to push them into the unconscious. This is fortunate, because it means that rational motives are that much easier to identify for selling strategy. However, the fact remains that rational motives *can* be unconscious, particularly when conflicting motives toward a purchase are involved, as in this example:

A man may want to buy a new labor-saving device for his wife, but be very concerned about the money outlay. Prudence in spending money is a rational motive, but the man also likes to think of himself as being good to his wife. So what does he do? He finds fault with the machinery of the proposed new washing machine (or whatever it is)—and does not admit to his wife *or to himself* that a technical defect is *not* the real reason, and he is simply holding back because he doesn't feel right about spending the money.

Even more important, a rational motive may apply also to noneconomic or intangible values, *if* it is self-approved. Most men would consider it reasonable that a man should buy helpful things for his wife, as in the example just cited; the fact that he and society think that it is one of his responsibilities makes it reasonable— even though it may be a self-pleasure, too. Similarly, in this sense, it is rational to want to live in a good neighborhood, to have a modern-style car, to own a television set.

In fact, one of the great buying phenomena of modern times is the way it became almost obligatory to buy a television set so the children of a family could hold their own in their relationships with other children—an intangible but very rational reason. My interpretation is that people already strongly desired TV sets for unapproved, selfish reasons, and it was the overwhelming availability of a good rational reason for justifying the purchase which triggered the buying wave. (Note that the same combination of circumstances does not apply to *color* TV, which has of course not swept in anywhere near so readily.)

It is because of the overlapping of terms that it is absolutely essential to have a separate concept, like rationality, which makes a clear-cut distinction between what is approved and what is not approved, and thus pinpoints the crucial factor in selling strategy. To illustrate:

Suppose a man honestly wants to buy a small car for the sake of economy, but he is afraid he will look like an odd-ball. So he pretends, to the rest of the world *and to himself*, that he is thinking of how easy it will be for his wife to park. Being kind to the weaker sex is his only course; he cannot follow the economic motive because it is not self-approved. At this time and in this neighborhood there is something wrong with a man who doesn't have a big car like everybody else's.

But what is socially acceptable is always changing, and we will do well to keep this in mind as market researchers report "changing" consumer preferences. In fact, I wonder if some of the "changes" recently reported may not simply be due to differences in the freedom with which consumers feel they can *talk* about specific products and advertisements. Thus, in certain regions of the country it now is beginning to be popular to *boast* about the economies offered by small cars.

This does not mean that economy is becoming a more important motive than it used to be. It only means that here and there economy is becoming an accepted or self-approved reason for buying a small car. And the key to understanding the difference between the new and the old situation is not in whether motives have become more or less conscious or more or less economic, but in that change of rationality.

Cause and Effect

We must recognize, too, that a rationalization often is nothing more than a convenient reason for action that actually reflects other motives. To illustrate:

I would agree that it is rational for a woman to patronize a supermarket or a discount house for the sake of economy, but I would argue that this is not altogether her real reason. Certainly she is also influenced by her desire to *appear* (to herself and to the world) as a careful buyer or a shrewd bargainer—perhaps even more so than by her desire for actual money savings. And if she does *not* patronize such outlets, she can always find equally rational reasons—"The meats are so much better where I shop"; or, "They stand back of their products at my store."

There is no doubt that, no matter how rational people pretend to be, very often they buy (or do not buy) things for irrational reasons. But it does not follow that the best way to sell them is by appeals to those irrational motives. The very fact that people insist on devising some rationalization for themselves suggests that it may be effective to supply them with a strong rational reason, so they can follow their irrational bent to the seller's product more surely and speedily. On the other hand, it may actually be ineffective to use irrational appeals because they have more difficulty in securing positive attention rather than just momentary, vague reaction; or, if they do get across, only serve to point out motives the buyer cannot be proud of as the thinking man he wants to be.

There is much discussion these days about brand images and consumers' self-images. I am sure this is a useful way of *describing* relationships between product and buyer, but not necessarily of *creating* such relationships. Is a brand image the cause of buying, or just the effect of selling? Is a self-image a coherent unit, or just a bundle of unsorted, unweighed, and unweighable motivations? Whether behavioral scientists can answer these questions or not, a large part of the job of making the brand image fit the consumer's self-image can be done, and may have to be done, at the rational level. After all, one of the biggest components of a person's self-image is the picture of himself as a reasonable, thinking man.

I know I am doing injustice to the scope and subtlety of psychological analysis, but such oversimplification is basic to the construction of efficient selling strategy. I am convinced that, *no matter what else is done or what other motivations are involved,* to close a sale or make a telling advertising impression the buyer *must* be given a self-approved reason for purchasing the product or preferring the brand. And, as we shall see subsequently, there is still plenty of opportunity, and indeed need, for understanding just what the specific motivations are in specific situations, and whether they are in fact rational or irrational.

OUT IN THE OPEN

It is on the score of the general dimensions of urge and resistance that I advocate more open selling. People are hard to fool—increasingly so. But there is not just the danger that sly selling will be detected and boomerang—thus ruining that particular attempt *and* impairing all other, more honest attempts. Rather, the trouble is that such selling may be inefficient because it does not make use of the *positive* effect of openly helping people to buy.

Certainly, any apprehension on the part of buyers that someone is trying to sell them something without letting them know it and giving them a fair chance to make their own buying decisions will create almost insurmountable resistance. By the same token, selling that does not try to hide itself or pretend to be something different is reassuring—so long, of course, as it does not go over to the opposite extreme of pushing people to buy through blatant high-pressure techniques, which again will make them feel they do not have a chance to make their own decisions *on the rational basis that is so necessary to them.* There is as much difference between high-pressure selling and good low-pressure selling [2]—open purposeful, low-pressure selling—as there is between such open selling and hidden selling.

Positive Selling

People expect that a seller who has something to sell will want to sell it; that is rooted in our culture. Further, they respect sellers who have enthusiasm for their products; that too is natural. Indeed it is cause for alarm, and thus for resistance, if a seller apparently is *not* convinced he has a good product. And since the essence of the low-pressure technique is to present the product as the solution to some problem or need of the buyer, the more purposeful the approach, the more the buyer feels he counts.

It is criminal waste of the buyer's own self-interest not to use it to lead him to the product or the brand. Actually, he is likely to be happier if he is so led. I have observed many selling situations where a hopeless seller lost sales while a hopeful buyer in fact wanted to be persuaded to buy. For example:

A middle-aged couple came into an appliance store, asked about a color TV set, and in general showed by the models they looked at and the remarks they made that, without realizing it, they had already made up their minds to spend a large amount of money. But every time they raised a question about price, the salesman quickly exhibited a cheaper model, not realizing that what they were asking for was not a better bargain but some assurance there was a rational reason for them to pay the amount in question.

At least three times they were on the verge of saying, "We'll take it." At least three times the salesman lost them by not trying to sell them. They left the store without buying. Although they said—and by this time perhaps thought—that they could not afford the money for one of the small sets, it was obvious that they were completely unhappy because they had not been sold the big set they really wanted.[3]

In Advertising Too

Again, I think this idea also applies to advertising. To illustrate from the extreme: offbeat copy themes which deprecate the product, or act coy or cute, have proved singularly ineffective. Sometimes they achieve some temporary success just because they attract attention by their oddity, but usually people resent the lack of dignity; sellers who take justifiable pride in their products could not possibly talk or think like that.

If anything, the need for open selling is even greater in advertising, which has to depend on fleeting impressions amid the competition of a multitude of sights and sounds. People have developed a defense mechanism against even noticing ads which do not bear on some problem or want they already have in some degree. Today a picture of a refrigerator and a headline of a new feature will attract the attention of those who are refrigerator-minded, while the John-loves-Mary theme where the refrigerator only comes in subsequently is literally passed by.[4] It makes sense that people will see or hear the message that speaks to them in the terms of their own specific everyday interests—and one of the most important of these is the buying of specific products or services. So why not at least try to make a definite selling impact?

The utmost in waste of good dollars and glossy paper would seem to be the *nonselling* that is characteristic of much advertising of industrial products or services. It may be true that here the burden is on the salesman in the field; but even in the secondary role of seeking inquiries or paving the way for the salesman, the message will come through stronger if it has at least enough "sell" to be pointed specifically and purposefully to the prospective buyer's problems. Why waste the opportunity to do *some* selling, when that must have more meaning to the buyer than any dull "institutional" generalizations?

Increased Effort

Even if sellers and advertisers do not sharpen their skills, just doing more selling can be effective because it is actually in line with the general psychology of the buying-selling situation. Indeed, many sellers may be so far short

[2] See Edward C. Bursk, "Low-Pressure Selling," *Harvard Business Review*, Winter 1947, p. 227; "Thinking Ahead: Drift to No-Pressure Selling," *Harvard Business Review*, September–October 1956, p. 25.
[3] Reported in "Northeastern Distributors, Inc., Recording—Part II," a case prepared and copyrighted, 1954, by Harbridge House, Inc., Cambridge, Massachusetts.

[4] See Richard D. Crisp, "Thinking Ahead: Advertising Research," *Harvard Business Review*, March–April 1953, p. 30.

of utilizing the full potential of their present selling approaches that *initially* they can gain more by straightforward increase in effort than by putting the same amount of money and time into new skills. There is a *continuing* gain, too. Increased effort usually brings about a clearer focus on buyers' motivations; it helps the seller to seek the right course instinctively, and so to improve the skill of his selling.

In sum, when a seller approaches a buyer more purposefully, there are two results: (*1*) The effort itself has a general effect on the buyer's attitude that is favorable. (2) This in turn makes the buyer more receptive to sales strategy designed for the specific situation—and here is where increased skill has its greatest opportunity.

SINGULAR STRATEGY

People's minds are complex, and every individual's self-image is different from every other individual's self-image. But selling must be a concentrated, focused action. One of the advantages of the open selling just discussed is that it provides a general setting in which the individual—any and every healthy individual—will tend to move himself toward the purchase—any and every approved purchase. Now, it is also possible to take another big step to lead the customer toward the purchase of specific goods and services. It is possible to devise a singular strategy which will be effective in a plural market—plural in the sense of many individuals, and also in the sense that each individual has multiple, varying, and even conflicting motives.

Not that all products or services will have the same strategy. Far from it; each will be different, and this is why it is so important to know what particular motives are involved. So it is wise to make the best possible use of consumer motivation experts. The only question is: "What is the best possible use?" and I do not intend to go into that.[5]

But let me note, just so it does not get left out of the picture, that a good common-sense analysis of consumer motives is much better than nothing, can be better sometimes than a *poor* expert approach, and always is a helpful check against the findings of the social scientists. Let me also note that beyond the *fairly ele-* mentary point of identifying the major motives involved, further research is likely to be marginal for the purpose under discussion here; the essence of the singular strategy is a single, central motive (or core of closely related motives), and it therefore avails little to know all the subsidiary, marginal motives in detail.

However—and this is important—that "fairly elementary point" calls for *much more* analysis and investigation than the usual seller employs. It is all too easy to assume that consumers are logical rather than psychological—and especially that they are logical with the seller's identical logic. They just may happen to have their own way of thinking and feeling. So there is always danger that without the stimulus of an objective, inquiring point of view the seller can overlook some *important* motive that could make or break the whole strategy. In selling there must be nothing taken "for granted"—or somebody else will do the taking "for real," such as a competitor out after the same consumers' dollars.

Design for Buying

Once the motivations are known, the design of the strategy is simple: the seller concentrates on the strongest (or most effectively communicable) *rational* buying motive for the particular consumers he plans to sell to. This is calculated to work in all possible combinations of urge and resistance, on the theory that in every instance where there are reasons both for buying and for not buying the most effective procedure is to maximize the urge and/or minimize the resistance. Thus:

Suppose there is a rational buying motive in your favor and no real resistance beyond the routine desire to be sure to make a good buy—as, for example, when a man honestly wants a car that will provide the most economical transportation to work. You just plow ahead and sell—you just demonstrate to him that your car will give him that transportation, reinforcing his existing rational motive.

But suppose the prospect's buying urge is irrational—as, for example, in the case of the "sexy" convertible mentioned by Bauer.[6] You do not aim at the irrational motive. It is in your favor, so why tamper with it? Why run the danger of making the prospect aware of his irrationality (or wickedness, if a sexual drive

[5] See Joseph W. Newman, "Working With Behavioral Scientists," *Harvard Business Review,* July–August 1958, p. 67.

[6] *Op. cit.,* p. 108.

is in fact operative here), stirring up a conflict in his mind, and actually causing resistance? You just give him a strong rational reason to latch onto—service, trade-in, or sunshine and health—and free his already existing urge to lead him to it.

If, however, there is a strong negative reason present, the problem becomes more subtle. Go back a few years in imagination to the days when the automatic washing machine was first introduced; and take the case of a woman who wants to buy one for the straightforward reason that it will make life easier for her, but for whom this is not a self-approved reason. Moreover, such motivation is sharply in conflict with her unconscious picture of herself as a martyr to drudgery. She hesitates to ask for the product—that is, to ask her husband for it and/or even to ask *herself* for it; hence, resistance.

There are two possible courses of action here: (*1*) You can present a rational reason that will give strength to her irrational desire for a joyful Monday—such as "washes clothes cleaner" or "less harmful to fabrics"—which will overcome the irrational resistance, and off she will go (with her husband) to buy it. This is just about what happened, and it happened quickly. (*2*) You also can try to change the non-self-approved to self-approved—in other words, to make it rational. This is a longer, slower process, yet by now I suspect that hundreds of advertisers promoting hundreds of appliances have actually made labor saving for the housewife quite respectable.

The difficulty is compounded when there is no strong motivation already existent and working for you. Negative reasons become correspondingly more significant. If the resistance is on the rational side, it can usually be met rationally. Most rational objections, if anticipated and met head-on, can be turned to advantage by a good salesman operating on the rational level.

This is particularly true in business selling. In the case of a storekeeper hesitating to buy because he has a heavy inventory, the strategy is to show him that the turnover rate of the new product will decrease his investment per dollar of sales. Or, in the case of industrial equipment purchases, the quality or service features that add to price can almost always be translated into long-run dollar savings.

The toughest situation of all is where the cause of resistance is irrational. Usually, it will be expressed rationally, and no amount of meeting the prospect on this ground will change the picture. Even if you win the argument, he simply will shift from one meaningless position to another.

The surest course is, again, the long-run one of changing the irrationality of the resistance to rationality—making it socially acceptable, and thus self-approved. Take this situation: people may hesitate to make more long-distance telephone calls because of a feeling of uneasiness engendered by association with sickness, death, emergency, delayed arrival, and other unpleasant news conveyed by such calls—although they usually explain their reluctance on the ground of expensiveness. This may be one of those situations where irrational resistance is unconscious just because it is irrational and hence at odds with a person's picture of himself.

But the telephone companies by their advertising over a period of time have begun to make the telephoning of friends and members of the family appear a friendly, natural, constructive process—just witness the ease with which today's young people pick up the phone and place a call (usually collect). For the new generation it *is* rational.

My hunch is that this telephone advertising would have been still more effective if all mention of cost had been omitted. Even the claim that "it costs less than you think" calls attention to the fact that there is such a convenient rationalization for having an irrational feeling about long-distance calls. If so, this is a situation where only a long-range rational approach will make a good strategy; and an immediate rational appeal may actually reduce effectiveness. The moral is obvious: even though the selling strategy does not incorporate an irrational appeal, it is necessary to know that a strong irrational motivation is at work against you in order to select the proper rational approach. In other words, here is one more demonstration that motivation research does provide a valuable service when used for diagnostic purposes.

Of course, the strategy will vary for different markets; and where the market is made up of quite varied segments, each segment may have to have its own singular strategy. But, in general, there will be only one rational motive big enough to dominate the other forces involved. The appeals which are built around it may be manifold, but they represent the creative job of translating the motive into selling language, which is another question entirely.

Design for Selling

Note that in all the above examples a rational motive turns out to be the best vehicle for carrying the prospect to the purchase. It is assumed that the prospect will provide some exertion himself, but of course something has to be done to get him started. Now I want to show why basing appeals on a rational motive also provides the best mechanism for the salesman's *action*, so necessary to get the prospect off dead center and actually moving toward the purchase.

For one thing, the salesman can use the rational approach more easily. It is more simple for him to understand, more natural for him to plan, more direct for him to follow. Further, by concentrating on one goal for the prospect and moving toward it purposely, he is likely to end up with an attractive presentation. Since he is thinking in terms of a need or want, rather than a product feature or advantage, he is necessarily concentrating on the prospect as a human being with thoughts and feelings, and will therefore instinctively tend to act so as to *please* the prospect. (That may well be a safer way to get the help of irrational appeals than by deliberately trying to use them; if appropriate, they will come through in gestures, in choice of words, in art work, without undermining the rationality of the approach.)

The fact that the goal is a rational need or want is even more helpful. Since it is acceptable, it gives the salesman the self-respect and confidence he must have if he is to keep on selling. Since it makes sense, he does not become embarrassed or confused. Not being a trained psychologist, he can be very wrong if he tries to figure out all the nuances of irrational motivations; and, even if by chance he is right, he will act self-consciously, and spoil the sincerity that is so essential for good low-pressure selling.

Some of the same demands prevail in mass selling programs and advertising. Sales managers and advertising executives are likely to function more effectively—more spontaneously and more aggressively—if they set out to sell on the basis of the best rational motive and do not get all tangled up with hidden persuaders.

The straightforward effort to sell will stimulate their thinking processes, and will add punch to their messages. For example:

The advertising firm of Doyle Dane Bernbach has been attracting much attention lately. It has built its billings to 20 million dollars in less than ten years, eschewing research and emphasizing copy. According to the agency president, William Bernbach, "We get people to look and listen by being good artists and writers. We don't expect of research what it is unable to do. It won't give you a great idea."

The agency stresses a simple but striking idea, a specific selling point. For bread: pictures of nibbled slices, and the message that "New York is eating it up." For an airline: a map of the Atlantic Ocean one-fifth torn away, and the message that "Starting December 23, the Atlantic Ocean will be twenty per cent smaller." And apparently clients have had big increases in sales.[7]

But there is an even more fundamental reason for depending on rational appeals if one is aiming for a plural market—as most sellers are, whether it be a specialized group or the mass market. Everybody's self-images or bundles of motives are a little different, and the trick is to pick an appeal that will best cover the particular market being sought—that will have great positive strength for most of the individuals, moderate to little weight for the balance (it is too much to expect 100 per cent aim), and no deterring effect on any. For these purposes a rational motivation usually serves best. Irrational wants and feelings are diverse and subtle, but rational desires are necessarily shared by a large part of the market since they reflect the norms and customs of society. By the same token, they are unlikely to restrict the market by any deterrent of embarrassment or confusion.

CONCLUSION

Most people have healthy minds; they like to buy. There is no need to dig into their subconscious to free them from blocks and tensions before they buy. (Indeed, such an effort may be dangerous—may stir up conflict without enough time or skill to remove it—something even psychiatrists worry about.) Irrational resistances, even if in the subconscious, can be

[7] See *Time*, March 31, 1958, p. 78.

handled by the healthy prospect himself—and *will* be, if he is provided with a sufficient *rational* motive as incentive.

But selling is not just satisfying present wants or playing up to old desires. Selling is a process of increasing wants, or even better, creating new wants. This is what keeps our economy dynamic. Further, the more business gets consumers to consider the pursuit of non-economic values as approved and rational, the more it is building people's potential for a higher, less materialistic way of life. And it is up to education to see to it that consumers say *no* to the more meretricious forms of satisfaction.

The danger of consumer motivation research is that business may rely on "scientific" techniques and forget to go out and sell. As far as getting buying action is concerned, the actual psychological subtleties may just be too tenuous for the hit-and-run of daily life. But we can use our understanding of how people buy to build a lot of little strategies for persuading people to want specific products and services, and one grand strategy of giving people continually bigger and better goals for themselves.

In either case, there is one big, uncomplex psychology at work—the interaction of enthusiastic seller and eager buyer, out in the open where they belong. And whatever irrational forces there are will be released if they are in your favor, contained if they are against you. Such selling is not manipulating people behind their backs; it is giving them rational motives for doing what is in their own best interests as individuals and as society-at-large.

Motivation, Cognition, Learning— Basic Factors in Consumer Behavior

JAMES A. BAYTON

This is a comprehensive application of contemporary psychological theories to the analysis of consumer behavior. Although modern marketing is drawing heavily upon psychology, there is a tendency for the emphasis to become somewhat "one-sided," as observed in the stress on motivation research. The danger is that concentration upon only one aspect of behavior will obscure other important psychological dimensions necessary to understanding the behavior of consumers.

MOTIVATION, COGNITION, LEARNING

The analysis of consumer behavior presented here is derived from diverse concepts of several schools of psychology—from psychoanalysis to reinforcement theory.

Human behavior can be grouped into three categories—motivation, cognition, and learning. Motivation refers to the drives, urges, wishes, or desires which initiate the sequence of events known as "behavior." Cognition is the area in which all of the mental phenomena (perception, memory, judging, thinking, etc.) are grouped. Learning refers to those changes in behavior which occur through time relative to external stimulus conditions.

Each broad area is pertinent to particular problems of consumer behavior. All three together are pertinent to a comprehensive understanding of consumer behavior.

MOTIVATION

Human Needs

Behavior is initiated through needs. Some psychologists claim that words such as "motives," "needs," "urges," "wishes," and "drives"

should not be used as synonyms; others are content to use them interchangeably. There is one virtue in the term "drive" in that it carries the connotation of a force pushing the individual into action.

Motivation arises out of tension-systems which create a state of disequilibrium for the individual. This triggers a sequence of psychological events directed toward the selection of a goal which the individual *anticipates* will bring about release from the tensions and the selection of patterns of action which he *anticipates* will bring him to the goal.

One problem in motivation theory is deriving a basic list of the human needs. Psychologists agree that needs fall into two general categories—those arising from tension-systems physiological in nature (biogenic needs such as hunger, thirst, and sex), and those based upon tension-systems existing in the individual's subjective psychological state and in his relations with others (psychogenic needs).

Although there is not much disagreement as to the list of specific biogenic needs, there is considerable difference of opinion as to the list of specific psychogenic needs. However, the various lists of psychogenic needs can be grouped into three broad categories:

1. *Affectional needs*—the needs to form and maintain warm, harmonious, and emotionally satisfying relations with others.

◆ SOURCE: Reprinted by permission from *Journal of Marketing* (National Quarterly Publication of the American Marketing Association), Vol. 22, No. 3, January 1958, pp. 282–289.

2. *Ego-bolstering needs*—the needs to enhance or promote the personality; to achieve; to gain prestige and recognition; to satisfy the ego through domination of others.

3. *Ego-defensive needs*—the needs to protect the personality; to avoid physical and psychological harm; to avoid ridicule and "loss of face"; to prevent loss of prestige; to avoid or to obtain relief from anxiety.

One pitfall in the analysis of motivation is the assumption that a particular situation involves just one specific need. In most instances the individual is driven by a combination of needs. It seems likely that "love" brings into play a combination of affectional, ego-bolstering, and ego-defensive needs as well as biogenic needs. Within the combination some needs will be relatively strong, others relatively weak. The strongest need within the combination can be called the "prepotent" need. A given consumer product can be defined in terms of the specific need-combination involved and the relative strengths of these needs.

Another pitfall is the assumption that identical behaviors have identical motivational backgrounds. This pitfall is present whether we are thinking of two different individuals or the same individual at two different points in time. John and Harry can be different in the motivational patterns leading to the purchase of their suits. Each could have one motivational pattern influencing such a purchase at age twenty and another at age forty.

Ego-Involvement

One important dimension of motivation is the degree of ego-involvement. The various specific need-patterns are not equal in significance to the individual. Some are superficial in meaning; others represent (for the individual) tremendous challenges to the very essence of existence. There is some evidence that one of the positive correlates of degree of ego-involvement is the amount of cognitive activity (judging, thinking, etc.) involved. This means that consumer goods which tap low degrees of ego-involvement will be purchased with a relatively lower degree of conscious decision-making activity than goods which tap higher degrees of ego-involvement. Such a factor must be considered when decisions are made on advertising and marketing tactics.

At times the ego-involvement factor is a source of conflict between client and researcher. This can occur when research reveals that the product taps a low degree of ego-involvement within consumers. The result is difficult for a client to accept; because *he* is ego-involved and, therefore, cognitively active about his product, consumers must certainly be also. It is hard for such a client to believe that consumers simply do not engage in a great deal of cognitive activity when they make purchases within his product class. One way to ease this particular client-researcher conflict would be for the researcher to point out this implication of the ego-involvement dimension.

"True" and Rationalized Motives

A particular difficulty in the study of motivation is the possibility that there can be a difference between "true" motives and rationalized motives. Individuals sometimes are unaware of the exact nature of drives initiating their behavior patterns. When this occurs, they attempt to account for their behavior through "rationalization" by assigning motivations to their behavior which are acceptable to their personality structures. They may do this with no awareness that they are rationalizing. There can be other instances, however, in which individuals are keenly aware of their motivations, but feel it would be harmful or socially unacceptable to reveal them. When this is the case, they deliberately conceal their motivations.

These possibilities create a problem for the researcher. Must he assume that every behavior pattern is based upon unconscious motivation? If not, what criteria are to be used in deciding whether to be alert to unconscious motivation for this behavior pattern and not that one? What is the relative importance of unconscious motives, if present, and rationalized motives? Should rationalized motives be ignored? After all, rationalized motives have a certain validity for the individual—they are the "real" motives insofar as he is aware of the situation.

The situation is even more complicated than this—what about the dissembler? When the individual actually is dissembling, the researcher must attempt to determine the true motives. But, how shall we determine whether we are faced with a situation where the respondent is rationalizing or dissembling? In a given case, did a projective technique reveal an unconscious motive or the true motive of a dissembler? Conceptually, rationalized motives and dissembled motives are not equal in psychological implication; but it is rare, if ever, that one finds attempts to segregate the two in consumer research directed toward the analysis of motivation. This failure is understandable, to some extent, because of the lack of valid criteria upon which to base the distinction.

COGNITION

Need-Arousal

Motivation, thus, refers to a state of need-arousal—a condition exerting "push" on the individual to engage in those activities which he anticipates will have the highest probability of bringing him gratification of a particular need-pattern. Whether gratification actually will be attained or not is a matter of future events. Central to the psychological activities which now must be considered in the sequence are the complex of "mental" operations and forces known as the cognitive processes. We can view these cognitive processes as being *purposive* in that they serve the individual in his attempts to achieve satisfaction of his needs. These cognitive processes are *regulatory* in that they determine in large measure the direction and particular steps taken in his attempt to attain satisfaction of the initiating needs.

The Ego-Superego Concept

The ego-superego concept is pertinent to a discussion of cognitive activities which have been triggered by needs. Discussions of the ego-superego concept usually come under the heading of motivation as an aspect of personality. It is our feeling that motivation and the consequences of motivation should be kept systematically "clean." In the broadest sense, ego and superego are mental entities in that they involve memory, perceiving, judging, and thinking.

The ego. The ego is the "executive," determining how the individual shall seek satisfaction of his needs. Through perception, memory, judging, and thinking the ego attempts to integrate the needs, on the one hand, and the conditions of the external world, on the other, in such manner that needs can be satisfied without danger or harm to the individual. Often this means that gratification must be postponed until a situation has developed, or

has been encountered, which does not contain harm or danger. The turnpike driver who does not exceed the speed limit because he sees signs saying there are radar checks is under the influence of the ego. So is the driver who sees no cars on a straight stretch and takes the opportunity to drive at excessive speed.

The superego. The superego involves the ego-ideal and conscience. The ego-ideal represents the positive standards of ethical and moral conduct the individual has developed for himself. Conscience is, in a sense, the "judge," evaluating the ethics and morality of behavior and, through guilt-feelings, administering punishment when these are violated. If a driver obeys the speed limit because he would feel guilty in doing otherwise, he is under the influence of the superego. (The first driver above is under the influence of the ego because he is avoiding a fine, not guilt feelings.)

Specific Examples

Credit is a form of economic behavior based to some extent upon ego-superego considerations. It is generally felt that one cause of consumer-credit expansion has been a shift away from the superego's role in attitudes toward credit. The past ego-ideal was to build savings; debt was immoral—something to feel guilty about, to avoid, to hide. These two superego influences restrained the use of credit. For some cultural reason, credit and debt have shifted away from superego dominance and are now more under the control of the ego—the primary concern now seems to be how much of it can be used without risking financial danger.

The purchasing of specific consumer goods can be considered from the point of view of these two influences. Certain goods (necessities, perhaps) carry little superego influence, and the individual is psychologically free to try to maximize the probability of obtaining satisfaction of his needs while minimizing the probability of encountering harm in so doing. Other goods, however, tap the superego. When a product represents an aspect of the ego-ideal there is a strong positive force to possess it. Conversely, when a product involves violation of the conscience, a strong negative force is generated against its purchase.

Let us assume that, when the need-push asserts itself, a variety of goal-objects come into awareness as potential sources of gratification. In consumer behavior these goal-objects may be different brand names. The fact that a particular set of goal-objects come into awareness indicates the generic character of this stage in the cognitive process—a class of goal-objects is seen as containing the possible satisfier. What the class of goal-objects and the specific goal-objects within the class "promise" in terms of gratification are known as "expectations."

There are, then, two orders of expectation: generic expectancies, and object-expectancies. Suppose the needs were such that the individual "thought" of brands of frozen orange juice. Some of the generic expectations for frozen orange juice are a certain taste, quality, source of vitamin C, protection against colds, and ease of preparation. The particular brands carry expectations specifically associated with one brand as against another. The expectation might be that brand A has a more refreshing taste than brand B.

In many instances, cognitive competition occurs between two or more generic categories before it does between goal-objects within a generic category. Much consumer-behavior research is directed toward the investigation of generic categories—tires, automobiles, appliances, etc. But perhaps not enough attention has been given to the psychological analysis of cognitive competition between generic categories. An example of a problem being studied is the competition between television viewing, movie going, and magazine reading. For a particular producer, cognitive competition within the pertinent generic category is usually of more concern than cognitive competition between his generic category and others. The producer usually wants only an intensive analysis of consumer psychology with respect to the particular generic category of which his product is a member.

Let us now assume that under need-push four alternative goal-objects (brands A, B, C, and D) came into awareness. Why these particular brands and not others? Why are brands E and F absent? An obvious reason for brand E's absence might be that the individual had never been exposed to the fact that brand E exists. He had been exposed to brand F, however. Why is it absent? The problem here is one of memory—a key cognitive process. The producers of brands E and F obviously are faced with different problems.

Two sets of circumstances contain the independent variables that determine whether a given item will be remembered. One is the nature of the experience resulting from actual consumption or utilization of the goal-object. This will be discussed later when we come to the reinforcement theory of learning. The other is the circumstances present on what might be called vicarious exposures to the goal-object— vicarious in that at the time of exposure actual consumption or utilization of the goal-object does not occur. The most obvious example would be an advertisement of the goal-object. Of course, the essential purpose of an advertisement is to expose the individual to the goal-object in such a manner that at some subsequent time it will be remembered readily. The search for the most effective methods of doing this by manipulation of the physical aspects of the advertisement and the appeals used in it is a continuing effort in consumer-behavior research. Finally, for many consumers these two sets of circumstances will be jointly operative. Experiences with the goal-object and subsequent vicarious exposures can coalesce to heighten the memory potential for an item.

Making a Choice

With, say, four brands in awareness, the individual must now make a choice. What psychological factors underlie this choice? The four brands could be in awareness due to the memory factor because they are immediately present in the environment; or some because they are in the environment, and the others because of memory.

The first problem is the extent to which the items are differentiated. The various goal-objects have attributes which permit the individual to differentiate between them. The brand name is one attribute; package another; design still another. These differentiating attributes (from the point of view of the consumer's perceptions) can be called signs or cues. All such signs are not equally important in consumer decisions. Certain of them are depended upon much more than others. For example, in a study of how housewives select fresh oranges, the critical or key signs were thickness of skin, color of skin, firmness of the orange, and presence or absence of "spots" on the skin.

The signs have expectancies associated with them. Package (a sign) can carry the expectancy of quality. Thin-skin oranges carry the expectancy of juice; spots carry the expectancy of poor taste quality and insufficient amount of juice. Often sign-expectancies determined through consumer research are irrelevant or invalid. Signs are irrelevant when they do not represent a critical differentiating attribute of a goal-object. Certain discolorations on oranges have nothing to do with their intrinsic quality. Expectancies are invalid when they refer to qualities that do not in fact exist in association with a particular sign.

The different goal-objects in awareness can be assessed in terms of the extent to which they arouse similar expectancies. This phenomenon of similarity of expectations within a set of different goal-objects is known as generalization. One goal-object (brand A, perhaps), because of its associated expectancies, can be assumed to have maximum appeal within the set of alternative goal-objects. The alternates then can be ordered in terms of how their associated expectancies approximate those of brand A. Is this ordering and the psychological distances between the items of the nature of:

Brand A		Brand A
Brand B		
	or	
		Brand B
Brand C		Brand C

These differences in ordering and psychological distance are referred to as generalization gradients. In the first case, the expectancies associated with brand B are quite similar to those for brand A, but are not quite as powerful in appeal. Brand C has relatively little of this. In the second case, the generalization gradient is of a different form, showing that brand B offers relatively little psychological competition to brand A. (There will also be generalization gradients with respect to cognitive competition between generic categories.) In addition to the individual producer being concerned about the memory potential of his particular brand, he needs to determine the nature of the generalization gradient for his product and the products of his competitors. Mere ordering is not enough—the "psychological distances" between positions must be determined, also, and the factor determining these distances is similarity of expectancy.

The discussion above was concerned with cognitive processes as they relate to mental representation of goal-objects under the instigation of need-arousal. The items brought into awareness, the differentiating sign-expectancies, and the generalization gradient are

the central factors in the particular cognitive field aroused under a given "need-push." One important dimension has not yet been mentioned—instrumental acts. These are acts necessary in obtaining the goal-object and the acts involved in consuming or utilizing it. Examples are: "going downtown" to get to a department store, squeezing the orange to get its juice, ease of entry into service stations, and the operations involved in do-it-yourself house painting.

Instrumental acts can have positive or negative value for the individual. One who makes fewer shopping trips to downtown stores because of traffic and parking conditions displays an instrumental act with negative value. Frozen foods are products for which much of the appeal lies in the area of instrumental acts. The development of automatic transmissions and of power-steering in automobiles are examples of product changes concerned with instrumental acts. The point is that concentration upon cognitive reactions to the goal-object, *per se*, could be masking critical aspects of the situation based upon cognitive reactions to the instrumental acts involved in obtaining or utilizing the goal-object.

LEARNING

Goal-Object

Starting with need-arousal, continuing under the influence of cognitive processes, and engaging in the necessary action, the individual arrives at consumption or utilization of a goal-object. Using our consumer-behavior illustration, let us say that the consumer bought brand A and is now in the process of consuming or utilizing it. We have now arrived at one of the most critical aspects of the entire psychological sequence. It is with use of the goal-object that degree of gratification of the initial needs will occur.

Reinforcement

When consumption or utilization of the goal-object leads to gratification of the initiating needs there is "reinforcement." If at some later date the same needs are aroused, the individual will tend to repeat the process of selecting and getting to the same goal-object. If brand A yields a high degree of gratification, then at some subsequent time, when the same needs arise, the consumer will have an increased tendency to select brand A once again. Each succeeding time that brand A brings gratification, further reinforcement occurs, thus further increasing the likelihood that in the future, with the given needs, brand A will be selected.

This type of behavioral change—increasing likelihood that an act will be repeated—is learning; and reinforcement is necessary for learning to take place. Continued reinforcement will influence the cognitive processes. Memory of the goal-object will be increasingly enhanced; particular sign-expectancies will be more and more firmly established; and the generalization gradient will be changed in that the psychological distance on this gradient between brand A and the competing brands will be increased.

Habit

One of the most important consequences of continued reinforcement is the influence this has on the extent to which cognitive processes enter the picture at the times of subsequent need-arousal. With continued reinforcement, the amount of cognitive activity decreases; the individual engages less and less in decision-making mental activities. This can continue until, upon need-arousal, the goal-obtaining activities are practically automatic. At this stage there is a habit.

Note this use of the term "habit." One frequently hears that a person does certain things by "force of habit," that habit is an initiator of behavioral sequences. Actually habits are not initiating forces in themselves; habits are repeated response patterns accompanied by a minimum of cognitive activity. There must be some condition of need-arousal before the habit-type response occurs. This has serious implications in the field of consumer behavior. The promotional and marketing problems faced by a competitor of brand A will be of one type if purchase behavior for brand A is habitual, of another if this is not true. If the purchase is largely a habit, there is little cognitive activity available for the competitor to "work on."

Frequency of repeating a response is not a valid criterion for determining whether or not a habit exists. An act repeated once a week can be just as much a habit as one repeated several times a day. The frequency of a response is but an index of the frequency with which the particular need-patterns are aroused. Frequency of response also is often used as a

measure of the *strength* of a habit. The test of the strength of a habit is the extent to which an individual will persist in an act after it has ceased providing need gratification. The greater this persistence, the stronger was the habit in the first place.

PROBLEM—CONCEPT—RESEARCH

The above views integrate concepts in contemporary psychology which seem necessary for a comprehensive explanation of human behavior, and apply these concepts to the analysis of consumer behavior. Each psychological process touched upon contains areas for further analysis and specification.

Some type of comprehensive theory of human behavior is necessary as a *working tool* to avoid a lack of discipline in attacking problems in consumer behavior. Too frequently a client with a practical problem approaches a researcher with an indication that all that is needed is a certain methodology—depth interviewing, scaling, or projective devices, for example.

The first step should be to take the practical problem and translate it into its pertinent conceptual entities. This phase of the problem raises the question of motivations. Here is a question involving relevance and validity of sign-expectancies. There is a question dealing with a generalization gradient, etc. Once the pertinent conceptual entities have been identified, and only then, we arrive at the stage of hypothesis formulation. Within each conceptual entity, a relationship between independent and dependent variables is established as a hypothesis to be tested.

Often the relation between conceptual entities must be investigated. For example, what is the effect of continuing reinforcement on a specific generalization gradient? Within the same research project, one psychological entity can be a dependent variable at one phase of the research and an independent variable at another. At one time we might be concerned with establishing the factors associated with differential memory of sign-expectancies. At another time we could be concerned with the influence of remembered sign-expectancies upon subsequent purchase-behavior.

Discipline requires that one turn to methodology only when the pertinent conceptual entities have been identified and the relationships between independent and dependent variables have been expressed in the form of hypotheses. Fundamentally this sequence in the analysis of a problem serves to delimit the methodological possibilities. In any event, the methodologies demanded are those which will produce unambiguous tests of each particular hypothesis put forth. Finally, the results must be translated into the terms of the original practical problem.

We have used the term "discipline" in this phase of our discussion. The researcher must discipline himself to follow the above steps. Some find this a difficult thing to do and inevitably their data become ambiguous. They must resort to improvisation in order to make sense of the results *after* the project is completed. A research project is truly a work of art when the conceptual analysis, the determination of the hypotheses, and the methodologies have been developed in such an "air-tight" sequence that practically all that is necessary is to let the facts speak for themselves.

C. Sociological Concepts in Personal Selling

The Significance of Social Stratification in Selling

RICHARD P. COLEMAN

Dating back to the late 1940's, advertisers and marketers have alternately flirted with and cooled on the notion that W. Lloyd Warner's social class concept [1] is an important analytic tool for their profession. The Warnerian idea that six social classes constitute the basic division of American Society has offered many attractions to marketing analysts when they have grown dissatisfied with simple income categories or census-type occupational categories and felt a need for more meaningful classifications, for categorizations of the citizenry which could prove more relevant to advertising and marketing problems. However, in the course of their attempts to apply the class concept, marketers have not always found it immediately and obviously relevant. Sometimes it has seemed to shed light on advertising and merchandising problems and at other times it hasn't—with the result that many analysts have gone away disenchanted, deciding that social classes are not much more useful than income categories and procedurally far more difficult to employ.

It is the thesis of this writer that the role of social class has too often been misunderstood or oversimplified, and that if the concept is applied in a more sophisticated and realistic fashion, it will shed light on a great many problems to which, at first glance, it has not seemed particularly relevant. What we propose to do here, then, is discuss and illustrate a few of these more subtle, more refined and (it must be acknowledged) more complicated ways of applying social class analyses to marketing and advertising problems. In other words, the purpose of this paper is to clarify *when* and *in what ways* social class concepts are significant in selling, and to suggest when they might not be as significant as other concepts, or at least need to be used in concert with other analytic categories.

THE WARNERIAN SOCIAL CLASSES

The six social classes which are referred to in this paper are those which W. Lloyd Warner and his associates have observed in their analyses of such diverse communities as Newburyport, Massachusetts;[2] Natchez, Mississippi;[3]

◆ SOURCE: Reprinted by permission from *Marketing: A Maturing Discipline*, edited by Martin L. Bell, Proceedings of the Winter Conference of the American Marketing Association, December 1960, pp. 171–184.

[1] See W. Lloyd Warner, Marchia Meeker, Kenneth Eells, *Social Class in America* (Chicago: Science Research Associates, 1949).

[2] See W. Lloyd Warner and Paul Lunt, *The Social Life of a Modern Community* (New Haven: Yale University Press, 1941).

[3] See Allison Davis, Burleigh B. Gardner and Mary R. Gardner, *Deep South* (Chicago: University of Chicago Press, 1941).

Morris, Illinois;[4] Kansas City, Missouri;[5] and Chicago. These social classes are groups of people who are more or less equal to one another in prestige and community status; they are people who readily and regularly interact among themselves in both formal and informal ways; they form a "class" also to the extent that they share the same goals and ways of looking at life. It is this latter fact about social classes which makes them significant to marketers and advertisers.

Briefly characterized, the six classes are as follows, starting from the highest one and going down.[6]

1. The Upper-Upper or "Social Register" Class is composed of locally prominent families, usually with at least second or third generation wealth. Almost inevitably, this is the smallest of the six classes—with probably no more than one-half of one per cent of the population able to claim membership in this class. The basic values of these people might be summarized in these phrases: living graciously, upholding the family reputation, reflecting the excellence of one's breeding, and displaying a sense of community responsibility.

2. The Lower-Upper or "Nouveau Riche" Class is made up of the more recently arrived and never-quite-accepted wealthy families. Included in this class are members of each city's "executive elite," as well as founders of large businesses and the newly well-to-do doctors and lawyers. At best only one and one-half per cent of Americans rank at this level—so that all told, no more than 2 per cent of the population can be counted as belonging to one layer or the other of our Upper Class. The goals of people at this particular level are a blend of the Upper-Upper pursuit of gracious living and the Upper-Middle Class's drive for success.

3. In the Upper-Middle Class are moderately successful professional men and women, owners of medium-sized businesses and "organi-

zation men" at the managerial level; also included are those younger people in their twenties or very early thirties who are expected to arrive at this occupational status level—and possibly higher—by their middle or late thirties (that is, they are today's "junior executives" and "apprentice professionals" who grew up in such families and/or went to the "better" colleges). Ten per cent of Americans are part of this social class and the great majority of them are college educated.

The motivating concerns of people in this class are success at career (which is the husband's contribution to the family's status) and tastefully reflecting this success in social participation and home decor (which is the wife's primary responsibility). Cultivating charm and polish, plus a broad range of interests—either civic or cultural, or both—are also goals of the people in this class, just as in the Lower-Upper. For most marketing and advertising purposes, this class and the two above it can be linked together into a single category of "upper status people." The major differences between them—particularly between the Upper-Middle and the Lower-Upper—are in degree of "success" and the extent to which this has been translated into gracious living.

4. At the top of the "Average Man World" is the Lower-Middle Class. Approximately 30 per cent or 35 per cent of our citizenry can be considered members of this social class. For the most part they are drawn from the ranks of non-managerial office workers, small business owners, and those highly-paid blue-collar families who are concerned with being accepted and respected in white-collar dominated clubs, churches, and neighborhoods. The key word in understanding the motivations and goals of this class is Respectability, and a second important word is Striving. The men of this class are continually striving, within their limitations, to "do a good job" at their work, and both men and women are determined to be judged "respectable" in their personal behavior by their fellow citizens. Being "respectable" means that they live in well-maintained homes, neatly furnished, in neighborhoods which are more-or-less on the "right side of town." It also means that they will clothe themselves in coats, suits, and dresses from "nice stores" and save for a college education for their children.

5. At the lower half of the "Average Man World" is the Upper-Lower Class, sometimes

[4] See W. Lloyd Warner and Associates, *Democracy in Jonesville* (New York: Harper & Brothers, 1949).
[5] The writer's observation on the Kansas City social class system will be included in a forthcoming volume on middle age in Kansas City, currently being prepared for publication by the Committee on Human Development of the University of Chicago.
[6] Some of the phrases and ideas in this characterization have been borrowed from Joseph A. Kahl's excellent synthesizing textbook, *The American Class Structure* (New York: Rinehart & Company, Inc., 1957).

referred to as "The Ordinary Working Class." Nearly 40 per cent of all Americans are in this class, making it the biggest. The prototypical member of this class is a semi-skilled worker on one of the nation's assembly lines. Many of these "Ordinary Working Class" people make very good money, but do not bother with using it to become "respectable" in a middle-class way. Whether they just "get by" at work, or moonlight to make extra, Upper-Lowers are oriented more toward enjoying life and living well from day to day than saving for the future or caring what the middle class world thinks of them. They try to "keep in step with the times" (indeed, one might say the "times" are more important than the "Joneses" to this class), because they want to be at least Modern, if not Middle Class. That is, they try to take advantage of progress to live more comfortably and they work hard enough to keep themselves safely away from a slum level of existence.

6. The Lower-Lower Class of unskilled workers, unassimilated ethnics, and the sporadically employed comprises about 15 per cent of the population, but this class has less than 7 or 8 per cent of the purchasing power, and will not concern us further here. Apathy, fatalism, and a point of view which justifies "getting your kicks whenever you can" characterize the approach toward life, and toward spending money, found among the people of this class.

Now, we do not mean to imply by these characterizations that the members of each class are always homogeneous in behavior. To suggest such would be to exaggerate greatly the meaning of social classes. To properly understand them, it must be recognized that there is a considerable variation in the way individual members of a class realize these class goals and express these values.

For example, within the Upper-Middle and Lower-Upper Class, there is one group—called Upper Bohemians [7] by Russell Lynes—for whom cultural pursuits are more important than belonging to a "good" country club. As a result, the tastes in furniture, housing accommodations, and recreations exhibited by the men and women of this "issues-and-culture set"—leaning toward the avant garde and eclectic, as they do—are apt to be very different from those practiced by the more conventional, bourgeois members of these status levels. Nevertheless, to both the Upper Bohemians and the Upper Conventionals, displaying "good taste" is quite important, with the differences between them not so much a question of good-versus-bad taste as one of whose form of good taste is preferred (though, to be sure, the Upper Bohemians are usually quite certain theirs is better).

Other sub-categories can be found in these higher classes and parallel kinds of sub-categories can be found in the Lower-Middle and Upper-Lower classes. Within the Upper-Lower Class, for instance, there is a large number of people who are quite concerned with their respectability and spend much of their spare time in church trying to do something about it. Their respectability concerns are not quite like those of the Lower-Middle Class, however, for they seem to care more about The Almighty's view of them than of their fellow man's. Thus, the Upper-Lower Class might, for certain analytic purposes, be subdivided into Church-Going and Tavern-Hopping segments, although this would by no means exhaust all possibilities of sub-categorization here.

All of this is by way of indicating that the millions of individuals who compose each social class are not necessarily similar or identical in their consumption patterns, even though they are of equal status socially and share a set of goals and points of view which are class-wide. Thus far, the literature on social class in both marketing journals and sociological publications has emphasized the similarities of people within classes and rarely pointed out these variations. This has been necessary, of course, in order to properly introduce the concept and educate social scientists and marketers to its utility, but it has led on occasion to naive misuse of the concept and ultimate disillusion. In my view, it has come time for us to advance into a more sophisticated application of social class to marketing problems, which involves awareness of the differences as well as similarities within each class.

SOCIAL CLASS VERSUS INCOME

Let us proceed now to stating the basic significance of this class concept for people in the selling field. In the first place, it explains why income categories or divisions of Americans are quite often irrelevant in analyz-

[7] See Russell Lynes, *A Surfeit of Honey* (New York: Harper & Brothers, 1957).

ing product markets, consumers' shopping habits and store preferences, and media consumption. For example, if you take three families, all earning around $8,000 a year, but each from a different social class, a radical difference in their ways of spending money will be observed.

An Upper-Middle Class family in this income bracket, which in this case might be a young lawyer and his wife or perhaps a college professor, is apt to be found spending a relatively large share of its resources on housing (in a "prestige" neighborhood), on rather expensive pieces of furniture, on clothing from quality stores, and on cultural amusements or club memberships. Meanwhile, the Lower-Middle Class family—headed, we will say, by an insurance salesman or a fairly successful grocery store owner, perhaps even a Diesel engineer—probably has a better house, but in not so fancy a neighborhood; it is apt to have as full a wardrobe though not so expensive, and probably more furniture though none by name designers. These people almost certainly have a much bigger savings account in the bank.

Finally, the Working Class family—with a cross-country truck driver or a highly-paid welder as its chief wage-earner—is apt to have less house and less neighborhood than the Lower-Middle or Upper-Middle family; but it will have a bigger, later model car, plus more expensive appliances in its kitchen and a bigger TV set in its living room. This family will spend less on clothing and furniture, but more on food if the number of children is greater, as is likely. One further difference: the man of the house probably spends much more on sports, attending baseball games (for example), going hunting and bowling, and perhaps owning a boat of some description.

The wives in these three families will be quite noticeably different in the kind of department stores they patronize, in the magazines they read, and in the advertising to which they pay attention. The clothing and furniture they select for themselves and their families will differ accordingly, and also because they are seeking quite different goals. This has become very clear in studies Social Research, Inc., has done for the *Chicago Tribune* on the clothing tastes of Chicagoland women, for the Kroehler Company on the place of furniture in American homes, and for MacFadden Publications on the purchasing patterns and motivations of their romance magazines' Working

Class readers.[8] (These have been contrasted in turn with the motivations of Middle Class women who read service magazines.)

The Upper-Middle Class wife—even of the struggling young lawyer—usually buys all her public-appearance clothes at specialty shops or in the specialty departments of her community's best department stores; she feels constrained to choose her wardrobe according to rather carefully prescribed standards of appropriateness. In furnishing her home, she thoughtfully considers whether a given piece or a combination of pieces will serve as adequate testament to her aesthetic sensitivities, plus doing credit in turn to her husband's taste in wife-choosing. She pays careful attention to the dictates of the best shelter magazines, the "smart" interior decorators in town, the homes of other women in her class, and maybe that of the boss's wife.

The Lower-Middle Class woman is more single-mindedly concerned with furnishing her home so that it will be "pretty" in a way that suits her and hopefully might win praise from her friends and neighbors. She tries to get ideas from the medium-level shelter and service magazines and is perpetually depressed because her home isn't furnished as much like a dream house as she would like it to be. In this she is quite different from the Upper-Lower wife who is apt to care more about having a full array of expensive, gleaming white appliances in her kitchen than a doll's house of a living room. Where the Lower-Middle housewife usually has a definite style in mind which she's striving to follow, the Upper-Lower woman simply follows the lead of newspaper furniture advertising (and what she sees when window shopping) toward furniture which is "modern-looking," by which she means the "latest thing" that has hit the mass market.

A great many more examples of differences in consumption patterns by class levels could be given, but the principal ones have been well reported already—facetiously by Vance Packard and seriously by Pierre Martineau;[9] for further amplification on this point the latter source is recommended. The significance to

[8] This study has been published under the name *Workingman's Wife* (Oceana Press: New York City, 1959), by Lee Rainwater, Richard P. Coleman, and Gerald Handel.
[9] See Pierre Martineau, *Motivation in Advertising* (New York: McGraw-Hill Book Company, 1957), and "Social Classes and Spending Behavior," *The Journal of Marketing*, Vol. 23, No. 2, October 1958, pp. 121–130.

merchandisers and advertisers of these findings about motivational differences between classes is fairly obvious, the major idea being that for many products, advertising appeals and merchandising techniques must be differentially geared to the points of view reflected in these three main social classes. Advertising of brands or goods aimed at a specific class must take into account the motivations of that class, and not try to sell everything as if it were an Upper Class or Upper-Middle status symbol.

Up to now, we've been talking about product areas—clothing, furniture, and residential neighborhoods—where the relationship between social class and quality of goods purchased is highest. In these things the so-called "Quality Market" and the Upper-Middle (and higher) markets coincide. That is, the purchasers of highest quality clothing and highest quality furniture are more nearly from the Upper-Middle and Upper social classes than from the highest income categories, and so on it goes down the hierarchy. The correlation between price of goods purchased and social class is relatively quite high in these product areas while the correlation between price paid and annual income is lower than one might expect.

There is another group of products which are not linked in such a direct way with social class, but neither are they linked with income categories in any obvious relationship. The current car market provides an instructive example of this situation, for the nature of the market cannot be grasped by using one or the other concept exclusively. What is happening in today's car market can only be understood when income categories are placed into a social class framework.

THE "OVERPRIVILEGED" AS "QUALITY MARKET"

Within each social class group there are families and individuals whose incomes are above average for their class. The Upper-Lower family with an income above $7,000 a year—sometimes a product of both husband and wife working, and sometimes not—is an example of this. So, too, is the Lower-Middle Class business owner or salesman who makes more than $10,000 a year, but has no interest in either the concerts or country clubs of Upper-Middledom and hence is still Lower-Middle Class. The Upper-Middle Class couple with more than $25,000 a year at its disposal but no desire to play the "society game" of subscription balls

or private schools is also in this category. These are what might be called the "overprivileged" segments of each class. They are not "overprivileged" in the absolute sense, of course; they are "overprivileged," however, relative to what is required or needed by families in their class. After they have met the basic expectations and standards of their group in the housing, food, furnishing, and clothing areas, they have quite a bit of money left over which is their equivalent of "discretionary income."

In much the same way, each class has its "underprivileged" members; in the Upper-Middle Class these are the younger couples who haven't made the managerial ranks yet, the college professors, the genteel professionals, and a few downwardly mobile people from high-status backgrounds who are trying to hang on to what fragments of status they have left—for the most part these people are below the $12,000-a-year mark and they can barely meet some of the basic requirements of Upper-Middle life, much less experience any of its little luxuries; in the Lower-Middle Class these are the poorly paid bank tellers, the rows of bookkeepers in railroad offices, the school teachers with considerably more status aspiration than income; and in the Upper-Lower Class it is almost any family earning less than $4,500 or $5,000 a year, at today's rates of pay in metropolitan areas.

In the middle of each class's income range are its "average" members, families who are neither underprivileged nor overprivileged by the standards of their class. You might think of this as the Upper-Middle Class family between $12,000 and $20,000 a year, the Lower-Middle family in the $7,000–$9,000 range, and the Upper-Lower family near $6,000 per annum. However, this word of caution is necessary: a lot of people in the middle income range of their class see themselves as underprivileged because they are aspiring to become one of the "overprivileged" in their class or to move on up the ladder to a higher class.

The relevance of all this to the car market is that when you look at this particular market today, you find it is the "average" members of each class, whether Upper-Middle, Lower-Middle, or Upper-Lower, who constitute the heart of the Low-Priced Three's audience; these are the people who are buying Fords and Chevrolets this year and last, and probably next. No longer is the Ford and Chevrolet market just a lower-middle income market, or (in class terms) a Lower-Middle or a Lower

Class market. Rather, it is recruited from the middle income group *within each* social class. Indeed, the $15,000-a-year Upper-Middle "organization man" is apt to choose a Ford or Chevy from the Impala-Galaxie level or else a top-price station wagon once he ventures into this market, whereas the average-income Lower-Middle man will settle for a middle-series Bel Air or Fairlane 500, and the "average-income" Upper-Lower guy either splurges for an Impala or "sensibly" contents himself with the spartan Biscayne.

While this has been happening to the Low-Priced Three makes, the heart of the medium-price car market has relocated in the "overprivileged" segments of each class. Today, rich blue-collar workers are joining prosperous Lower-Middle Class salesmen and well-to-do Upper-Middle Class business owners in buying Pontiacs, Buicks, Oldsmobiles, Chryslers, and even Cadillacs. In fact, what there is left of big-car lust in our society is found at peak strength among the "overprivileged" Upper-Lowers or else among men who have achieved higher status, but grew up as kids in the Upper-Lower class and have not forgotten their wide-eyed envy of the big car owner.

Finally, as you may have guessed by now, the compact car market's heart is to be found in the "underprivileged" segments of each class (here we are speaking of the market for a compact as a first car). The overwhelming majority of Rambler purchasers, Falcon buyers, and foreign economy car owners come from this socio-economic territory. Thus, it is not the really poor who are buying these cheapest, most economical cars—rather it is those who think of themselves as poor relative to their status aspirations and to their needs for a certain level of clothing, furniture, and housing which they could not afford if they bought a more expensive car.

The market for compacts as second cars is somewhat more complicated in its socio-economic geography, being located in the middle range of the Upper-Middle Class, and the "overprivileged" segment of the Lower-Middle. The "overprivileged" Upper-Middle may have one as a third car, but he prefers either a T-Bird, a foreign sports car, a Pontiac convertible, or a beat-up station wagon as his second car, while the "overprivileged" Upper-Lower is apt to go for a used standard if he wants a second car.

If marketers and advertisers had assumed that the market for compacts was going to be the lowest-income or lowest-status members of our society, they would have seriously miscalculated in their merchandising and advertising approach. Rambler, for one, did not make this mistake. American Motors advertised its cars as "bringing sense into the auto market" and thus enabled people who bought one to pride themselves on the high-minded rationality they had displayed. Rambler owners, as they drive down the street, are not ashamed that they couldn't afford better—instead, as the company has told them to be, they are proud that they did not yield, like their neighbors, to base emotional desires for a car bloated in size beyond necessity and loaded in gadgetry beyond reason. Compact car owners have their own form of snobbery—what might be called "sensibility snobbery"—with which to content themselves and justify their purchase.

This analysis of the car market is one example of what I mean by the sophisticated application of social class concepts to marketing and advertising problems. There are many products and many brands which, like cars, are more nearly symbols of high status class within class than symbols of higher status per se. A color television set is such a product, or at least it was two years ago when Social Research, Inc., studied its market. At the time color television manufacturers were puzzled because sales were thinly spread throughout the income scale, without any noticeable increase in concentration until an extremely high level was reached. Furthermore, they were unable to see any particular relationship between social class and color set ownership, since about as many Upper-Lower Class people owned them as did Upper-Middles. However, when the two factors of income and class were put together, in the manner described above, it became clear that the color television market was concentrated among high-income or "overprivileged" members of each social class. Other products which bear this complicated relationship to class and income are the more costly brands and larger sizes of home appliances. Fairly expensive recreational equipment like outboard motor boats also tend to be in this category.

In summary, today's market for quality goods and quality brands is not necessarily drawn from what has historically been described as the "Quality Market" of Upper-Middle and Upper Class people, nor even necessarily from the highest income categories. Rather, in many instances, it is drawn from those people within each social level who have the most discretionary income available for enjoying life's little extras above and beyond the requirements of their class. Every merchandiser and advertiser ought to take a good hard look at what he is selling and ask himself if it bears this particular relationship to the class and income picture. If his product does, and if his brand is one of the more expensive, then he should merchandise it not as if it were just for social climbers or for the upper classes, but rather as part of the Better Life, U.S.A. If, on the other hand, his brand is one of the least expensive, then he is not just selling to the poor, but rather to those in all classes who feel it is only sensible on their part to settle for a brand such as his and save the difference for other things which are more important in their statement of social class aspiration and identity.

SOCIAL CLASS ISN'T ALWAYS IMPORTANT

Now, to make the picture complete, it must be pointed out that Social Research, Inc., has found some products in which the income factor is all-important and the social class variable is relevant only to the extent that it is correlated with income. Perhaps the most perfect example of this is the market for air conditioners in Southwestern cities. There, everybody—except the sickly and the extremely old-fashioned—agree that air conditioning one's home is imperative if summer is to be survived with any degree of comfort. Consequently the expensiveness of a family's air conditioning equipment—whether centrally installed, or window units to the number of four, three, two, or one—is directly correlated with family income. It is not merely a function of discretionary income—as in our example about purchase of medium-priced cars; it is instead almost completely a function of total annual income. If more Upper-Middles than Upper-Lowers are fully air-conditioned it is only because more of them can afford to be; it is not because Upper-Middles as a group are placing higher priority on the air-conditioned existence.

Undoubtedly air conditioners are not alone in being classless—so that one more thing the marketer who uses social class in a truly sophisticated way needs to understand is that there can be occasions when it is an irrelevant variable. Realizing this, he will not become disenchanted with social class when he finds a marketing problem where it does not shed

light or where it does not seem pertinent. Of course, he will want to make sure that in advertising such a product there is indeed no need to take class into account. After all, some apparently classless products are properly sold to the market in a segmental approach, appealing first on one ground to one class, then on other grounds to another.

There are other products—and probably air conditioning is one of them and children's play clothes may be another—where this is not necessary. For such products some factor, such as physical comfort (in the one case) or simple durability (in the other), is so basic in the consumer's consideration that all other motivations pale into insignificance beside it. There are even products, like beer, where the democratic approach—that is, a tone of "let's-all-be-good-fellows-together" is exactly right and segmental appeals or snob stories are all wrong.

Another aspect to the sophisticated employment of social class refers back to the point made earlier that social class groups are not always homogeneous. It must be recognized that at times a product's market is formed by "highbrows" from the Upper-Upper Class on down to the Lower-Middle, or by "suburbanites" and suburban-minded people of all classes—in which case the social class variable may confuse a market analysis more than clarify it.

Particularly must merchandisers and market analysts beware of equating "Class" with "Brow"; for they are not synonymous. For example, the Upper-Middle Class and those above it are mainly middle brow in taste (veering toward an all-American lower-middlebrow level of preferences in television shows and advertising messages) even though the majority of highbrows are found at this level. At times advertisers have made the mistake of assuming that the Upper-Middle Class should be appealed to in a highly sophisticated fashion—and though this is just fine if the product itself is likely to appeal primarily to the Manhattanized type of Upper-Middle, it is not correct if it is expected to sell to the kind of doctor in Dubuque who enjoys a visit to New York every now and then but would never want to live there.

In short, not only must the sophisticated marketer abandon social class in favor of income categories on occasion in his analysis and interpretation of a market, he must recognize that at times both income and class are superseded in importance by divisions of the public into brow levels, by divisions into "high mobiles" and "low mobiles," innovators and non-innovators, inner-directed and other-directed, urbanites, suburbanites, exurbanites, ruralites, and Floridians, or what have you. Usually, of course, fullest understanding of a market will require that social class be linked in with whichever sub-categorization proves pertinent from among those in the catalogue just recited, much as income and class were linked together for fullest comprehension of the car market.

As a final point, let it be noted that the way of life and the goals of people in each social class are in perpetual flux. Neither the "who" of each class nor "what motivates them" are constants to be assumed without continual re-evaluation. Right now, particularly, it is very clear that our society is changing. Every year the collar-color line is breaking down further. More blue-collar workers are becoming Middle Class as well as middle income and Modern, and a white-collar position is less and less a guarantee of Lower-Middle status. As a consequence of this, the Lower-Middle Class is perhaps somewhat more "materialistic" in outlook and slightly less "respectability" con-scious than it was 25 years ago, or even 8. Meanwhile, for men and women to achieve Upper-Middle status without college backgrounds is becoming more and more difficult, so that this class is turning much more worldly-wise and well-read, much less conventionally bourgeois than it was in the zenith of Babbitt's day.

In short, the form of our society and its division into social classes is not fixed as of Yankee City in 1931, Jonesville in 1944, Kansas City in 1952, or St. Louis in 1960. We won't be able to say exactly the same things about either the classes themselves or their relationships to specific markets by next year at this time. This fact about the American class structure, that it is not static, that it is in the process of change, is in itself important to merchandisers, to advertisers, to anyone in selling. Among other things, it means that undoubtedly they have played a part in past changes and can play a leading role in directing future changes. But of more direct concern here, to the marketing analyst it means that if he allows his stratification concept to become dated, his use of it will cease as of that moment to be sophisticated.

Reference Groups as Perspectives

TAMOTSU SHIBUTANI

In spite of ambiguity, reference group has become an increasingly popular concept, utilized in hypotheses concerning a variety of social phenomena. The restriction of this concept to a single referent, namely, group whose perspective is used as a frame of reference by the actor, will increase its usefulness as an analytic tool. Shared perspectives arise through participation in common communication channels, and the cultural pluralism of modern mass societies arises from the easy accessibility of a multiplicity of channels. The concept of reference group, if defined with greater precision, can greatly facilitate research on the manner in which each actor's orientation toward his world is structured.

Although Hyman coined the term scarcely more than a decade ago, the concept of reference group has become one of the central analytic tools in social psychology, being used in the construction of hypotheses concerning a variety of social phenomena. The inconsistency in behavior as a person moves from one social context to another is accounted for in terms of a change in reference groups; the exploits of juvenile delinquents, especially in interstitial areas, are being explained by the expectations of peer-group gangs; modifications in social attitudes are found to be related to changes in associations. The concept has been particularly useful in accounting for the choices made among apparent alternatives, particularly where the selections seem to be contrary to the "best interests" of the actor. Status problems—aspirations of social climbers, conflicts in group loyalty, the dilemmas of marginal men—have also been analyzed in terms of reference groups, as have the differential sensitivity and reaction of various segments of an audience to mass communication. It is recognized that the same generic processes are involved in these phenomenally diverse events, and the increasing popularity of the concept attests to its utility in analysis.

As might be expected during the exploratory phases in any field of inquiry, however,

◆ SOURCE: Reprinted by permission from *American Journal of Sociology*, Vol. 20, No. 3, May 1955, pp. 562–569.

there is some confusion involved in the use of this concept, arising largely from vagueness of signification. The available formal definitions are inconsistent, and sometimes formal definitions are contradicted in usage. The fact that social psychologists can understand one another in spite of these ambiguities, however, implies an intuitive recognition of some central meaning, and an explicit statement of this will enhance the utility of the concept as an analytic tool. The literature reveals that all discussions of reference groups involve some identifiable grouping to which an actor is related in some manner and the norms and values shared in that group. However, the relationship between these three terms is not always clear. Our initial task, then, is to examine the conceptions of reference group implicit in actual usage, irrespective of formal definitions.

One common usage of the concept is in the designation of that group which serves as the point of reference in making comparisons or contrasts, especially in forming judgments about one's self. In the original use of the concept Hyman spoke of reference groups as points of comparison in evaluating one's own status, and he found that the estimates varied according to the group with which the respondent compared himself. Merton and Kitt, in their reformulation of Stouffer's theory of relative deprivation, also use the concept in this manner; the judgments of rear-echelon soldiers overseas concerning their fate varied, depending upon whether they compared themselves to soldiers who were still at home or men in combat. They also propose concrete research operations in which respondents are to be asked to compare themselves with various groups. The study of aspiration levels by Chapman and Volkmann, frequently cited in discussions of reference-group theory, also involves variations in judgment arising from a comparision of one's own group with others.[1] In this mode of application, then, a reference group is a standard or check point which an actor uses in forming his estimate of the situation, particularly his own position within it. Logically, then, *any* group with which an actor is familiar may become a reference group.

A second referent of the concept is that group in which the actor aspires to gain or maintain acceptance: hence, a group whose claims are paramount in situations requiring choice. The reference group of the socially ambitious is said to consist of people of higher strata whose status symbols are imitated. Merton and Kitt interpret the expressions of willingness and felt readiness for combat on the part of inexperienced troops, as opposed to the humility of battle-hardened veterans, as the efforts of newcomers to identify themselves with veterans to whom they had mistakenly imputed certain values.[2] Thus, the concept is used to point to an association of human beings among whom one seeks to gain, maintain, or enhance his status; a reference group is that group in which one desires to participate.

In a third usage the concept signifies that group whose perspective constitutes the frame of reference of the actor. Thus, Sherif speaks of reference groups as groups whose norms are used as anchoring points in structuring the perceptual field,[3] and Merton and Kitt speak of a "social frame of reference" for interpreta-

tions.[4] Through direct or vicarious participation in a group one comes to perceive the world from its standpoint. Yet this group need not be one in which he aspires for acceptance; a member of some minority group may despise it but still see the world largely through its eyes. When used in this manner, the concept of reference group points more to a psychological phenomenon than to an objectively existing group of men; it refers to an organization of the actor's experience. That is to say, it is a structuring of his perceptual field. In this usage a reference group becomes any collectivity, real or imagined, envied or despised, whose perspective is assumed by the actor.

Thus, an examination of current usage discloses three distinct referents for a single concept: (1) groups which serve as comparison points; (2) groups to which men aspire; and (3) groups whose perspectives are assumed by the actor. Although these terms may be related, treating together what should be clearly delineated as generically different can lead only to further confusion. It is the contention of this paper that the restriction of the concept of reference group to the third alternative —that group whose perspective constitutes the frame of reference of the actor—will increase its usefulness in research. Any group or object may be used for comparisons, and one need not assume the role of those with whom he compares his fate; hence, the first usage serves a quite different purpose and may be eliminated from further consideration. Under some circumstances, however, group loyalties and aspirations are related to perspectives assumed, and the character of this relationship calls for further exploration. Such a discussion necessitates a restatement of the familiar, but, in view of the difficulties in some of the work on reference groups, repetition may not be entirely out of order. In spite of the enthusiasm of some proponents there is actually nothing new in reference-group theory.

CULTURE AND PERSONAL CONTROLS

Thomas pointed out many years ago that what a man does depends largely upon his definition of the situation. One may add that the manner in which one consistently defines a succession of situations depends upon his organized perspective. A perspective is an ordered view of one's world—what is taken

[1] H. H. Hyman, "The Psychology of Status," *Archives of Psychology*, XXXVIII (1942), 15; R. K. Merton and A. Kitt, "Contributions to the Theory of Reference Group Behavior," in R. K. Merton and P. F. Lazarsfeld (eds.), *Studies in the Scope and Method of "The American Soldier"* (Glencoe, Ill.: Free Press, 1950), pp. 42–53, 69; D. W. Chapman and J. Volkmann, "A Social Determinant of the Level of Aspiration," *Journal of Abnormal and Social Psychology*, XXXIV (1939), 225–38.
[2] *Op. cit.*, pp. 75–76.
[3] M. Sherif, "The Concept of Reference Groups in Human Relations," in M. Sherif and M. O. Wilson (eds.), *Group Relations at the Crossroads* (New York: Harper & Bros., 1953), pp. 203–31.
[4] *Op. cit.*, pp. 49–50.

for granted about the attributes of various objects, events, and human nature. It is an order of things remembered and expected as well as things actually perceived, an organized conception of what is plausible and what is possible; it constitutes the matrix through which one perceives his environment. The fact that men have such ordered perspectives enables them to conceive of their ever changing world as relatively stable, orderly, and predictable. As Riezler puts it, one's perspective is an outline scheme which, running ahead of experience, defines and guides it.

There is abundant experimental evidence to show that perception is selective; that the organization of perceptual experience depends in part upon what is anticipated and what is taken for granted. Judgments rest upon perspectives, and people with different outlooks define identical situations differently, responding selectively to the environment. Thus, a prostitute and a social worker walking through a slum area notice different things; a sociologist should perceive relationships that others fail to observe. Any change of perspectives—becoming a parent for the first time, learning that one will die in a few months, or suffering the failure of well-laid plans—leads one to notice things previously overlooked and to see the familiar world in a different light. As Goethe contended, history is continually rewritten, not so much because of the discovery of new documentary evidence, but because the changing perspectives of historians lead to new selections from the data.

Culture, as the concept is used by Redfield, refers to a perspective that is shared by those in a particular group; it consists of those "conventional understandings, manifest in act and artifact, that characterize societies." [5] Since these conventional understandings are the premises of action, those who share a common culture engage in common modes of action. Culture is not a static entity but a continuing process; norms are creatively reaffirmed from day to day in social interaction. Those taking part in collective transactions approach one another with set expectations, and the realization of what is anticipated successively confirms and reinforces their perspectives. In this way, people in each cultural group are continuously supporting one another's perspectives, each by responding to the others in expected ways. In this sense culture is a product of communication.

In his discussion of endopsychic social control Mead spoke of men "taking the role of the generalized other," meaning by that that each person approaches his world from the standpoint of the culture of his group. Each perceives, thinks, forms judgments, and controls himself according to the frame of reference of the group in which he is participating. Since he defines objects, other people, the world, and himself from the perspective that he shares with others, he can visualize his proposed line of action from this generalized standpoint, anticipate the reactions of others, inhibit undesirable impulses, and thus guide his conduct. The socialized person is a society in miniature; he sets the same standards of conduct for himself as he sets for others, and he judges himself in the same terms. He can define situations properly and meet his obligations, even in the absence of other people, because, as already noted, his perspective always takes into account the expectations of others. Thus, it is the ability to define situations from the same standpoint as others that makes personal controls possible. [6] When Mead spoke of assuming the role of the generalized other, he was not referring to people but to perspectives shared with others in a transaction.

The consistency in the behavior of a man in a wide variety of social contexts is to be accounted for, then, in terms of his organized perspective. Once one has incorporated a particular outlook from his group, it becomes his orientation toward the world, and he brings this frame of reference to bear on all new situations. Thus, immigrants and tourists often misinterpret the strange things they see, and a disciplined Communist would define each situation differently from the non-Communist. Although reference-group behavior is generally studied in situations where choices seem possible, the actor himself is often unaware that there are alternatives.

[5] R. Redfield, *The Folk Culture of Yucatan* (Chicago: University of Chicago Press, 1941), p. 132. For a more explicit presentation of a behavioristic theory of culture see *The Selected Writings of Edward Sapir in Language, Culture and Personality*, ed. D. G. Mandelbaum (Berkeley: University of California Press, 1949), pp. 104–9, 308–31, 544–59.

[6] G. H. Mead, "The Genesis of the Self and Social Control," *International Journal of Ethics*, XXXV (1925), 251–77, and *Mind, Self and Society* (Chicago: University of Chicago Press, 1934), pp. 152–64. Cf. T. Parsons, "The Superego and the Theory of Social Systems," *Psychiatry*, XV (1952), 15–25.

The proposition that men think, feel, and see things from a standpoint peculiar to the group in which they participate is an old one, repeatedly emphasized by students of anthropology and of the sociology of knowledge. Why, then, the sudden concern with reference-group theory during the past decade? The concept of reference group actually introduces a minor refinement in the long familiar theory, made necessary by the special characteristics of modern mass societies. First of all, in modern societies special problems arise from the fact that men sometimes use the standards of groups in which they are *not* recognized members, sometimes of groups in which they have never participated directly, and sometimes of groups that do not exist at all. Second, in our mass society, characterized as it is by cultural pluralism, each person internalizes several perspectives, and this occasionally gives rise to embarrassing dilemmas which call for systematic study. Finally, the development of reference-group theory has been facilitated by the increasing interest in social psychology and the subjective aspects of group life, a shift from a predominant concern with objective social structures to an interest in the experiences of the participants whose regularized activities make such structures discernible.

A reference group, then, is that group whose outlook is used by the actor as the frame of reference in the organization of his perceptual field. All kinds of groupings, with great variations in size, composition, and structure, may become reference groups. Of greatest importance for most people are those groups in which they participate directly—what have been called membership groups—especially those containing a number of persons with whom one stands in a primary relationship. But in some transactions one may assume the perspective attributed to some social category— a social class, an ethnic group, those in a given community, or those concerned with some special interest. On the other hand, reference groups may be imaginary, as in the case of artists who are "born ahead of their times," scientists who work for "humanity," or philanthropists who give for "posterity." Such persons estimate their endeavors from a postulated perspective imputed to people who have not yet been born. There are others who live for a distant past, idealizing some period in history and longing for "the good old days," criticizing current events from a standpoint imputed to people long since dead. Reference groups,

then, arise through the internalization of norms; they constitute the structure of expectations imputed to some audience for whom one organizes his conduct.

THE CONSTRUCTION OF SOCIAL WORLDS

As Dewey emphasized, society exists in and through communication; common perspectives —common cultures—emerge through participation in common communication channels. It is through social participation that perspectives shared in a group are internalized. Despite the frequent recitation of this proposition, its full implications, especially for the analysis of mass societies, are not often appreciated. Variations in outlook arise through differential contact and association; the maintenance of social distance—through segregation, conflict, or simply the reading of different literature—leads to the formation of distinct cultures. Thus, people in different social classes develop different modes of life and outlook, not because of anything inherent in economic position, but because similarity of occupation and limitations set by income level dispose them to certain restricted communication channels. Those in different ethnic groups form their own distinctive cultures because their identifications incline them to interact intimately with each other and to maintain reserve before outsiders. Different intellectual traditions within social psychology—psychoanalysis, scale analysis, *Gestalt*, pragmatism—will remain separated as long as those in each tradition restrict their sympathetic attention to works of their own school and view others with contempt or hostility. Some social scientists are out of touch with the masses of the American people because they eschew the mass media, especially television, or expose themselves only condescendingly. Even the outlook that the *avant-garde* regards as "cosmopolitan" is culture-bound, for it also is a product of participation in restricted communication channels—books, magazines, meetings, exhibits, and taverns which are out of bounds for most people in the middle classes. Social participation may even be vicarious, as it is in the case of a medievalist who acquires his perspective solely through books.

Even casual observation reveals the amazing variety of standards by which Americans live. The inconsistencies and contradictions which characterize modern mass societies are products of the multitude of communication channels and the ease of participation in them. Studying relatively isolated societies, anthroplogists can speak meaningfully of "culture areas" in geographical terms; in such societies common cultures have a territorial base, for only those who live together can interact. In modern industrial societies, however, because of the development of rapid transportation and the media of mass communication, people who are geographically dispersed can communicate effectively. Culture areas are coterminous with communication channels; since communication networks are no longer coterminous with territorial boundaries, culture areas overlap and have lost their territorial bases. Thus, next-door neighbors may be complete strangers; even in common parlance there is an intuitive recognition of the diversity of perspectives, and we speak meaningfully of people living in different social worlds—the academic world, the world of children, the world of fashion.

Modern mass societies, indeed, are made up of a bewildering variety of social worlds. Each is an organized outlook, built up by people in their interaction with one another; hence, each communication channel gives rise to a separate world. Probably the greatest sense of identification and solidarity is to be found in the various communal structures—the underworld, ethnic minorities, the social elite. Such communities are frequently spatially segregated, which isolates them further from the outer world, while the "grapevine" and foreign-language presses provide internal contacts. Another common type of social world consists of the associational structures—the world of medicine, of organized labor, of the theater, of café society. These are held together not only by various voluntary associations within each locality but also by periodicals like *Variety*, specialized journals, and feature sections in newspapers. Finally, there are the loosely connected universes of special interest—the world of sports, of the stamp collector, of the daytime serial—serviced by mass media programs and magazines like *Field and Stream*. Each of these worlds is a unity of order, a universe of regularized mutual response. Each is an area in which there is some structure which permits reasonable anticipation of the behavior of others, hence, an area in which one may act with a sense of security and confidence.[7] Each social

world, then, is a culture area, the boundaries of which are set neither by territory nor by formal group membership but by the limits of effective communication.

Since there is a variety of communication channels, differing in stability and extent, social worlds differ in composition, size, and the territorial distribution of the participants. Some, like local cults, are small and concentrated; others, like the intellectual world, are vast and the participants dispersed. Worlds differ in the extent and clarity of their boundaries; each is confined by some kind of horizon, but this may be wide or narrow, clear or vague. The fact that social worlds are not coterminous with the universe of men is recognized; those in the underworld are well aware of the fact that outsiders do not share their values. Worlds differ in exclusiveness and in the extent to which they demand the loyalty of their participants. Most important of all, social worlds are not static entities; shared perspectives are continually being reconstituted. Worlds come into existence with the establishment of communication channels; when life conditions change, social relationships may also change, and these worlds may disappear.

Every social world has some kind of communication system—often nothing more than differential association—in which there develops a special universe of discourse, sometimes an argot. Special meanings and symbols further accentuate differences and increase social distance from outsiders. In each world there are special norms of conduct, a set of values, a special prestige ladder, characteristic career lines, and a common outlook toward life—a Weltanschauung. In the case of elites there may even arise a code of honor which holds only for those who belong, while others are dismissed as beings somewhat less than human from whom bad manners may be expected. A social world, then, is an order conceived which serves as the stage on which each participant seeks to carve out his career and to maintain and enhance his status.

One of the characteristics of life in modern mass societies is simultaneous participation in a variety of social worlds. Because of the ease with which the individual may expose himself

---

[7] Cf. K. Riezler, *Man: Mutable and Immutable* (Chicago: Henry Regnery Co., 1950), pp. 62–72; L. Landgrebe, "The World as a Phenomenological Problem," *Philosophy and Phenomenological Research*, I (1940), 38–58; and A. Schuetz, "The Stranger: An Essay in Social Psychology," *American Journal of Sociology*, XLIX (1944), 499–507.

to a number of communication channels, he may lead a segmentalized life, participating successively in a number of unrelated activities. Furthermore, the particular combination of social worlds differs from person to person; this is what led Simmel to declare that each stands at that point at which a unique combination of social circles intersects. The geometric analogy is a happy one, for it enables us to conceive the numerous possibilities of combinations and the different degrees of participation in each circle. To understand what a man does, we must get at his unique perspective—what he takes for granted and how he defines the situation—but in mass societies we must learn in addition the social world in which he is participating in a given act.

LOYALTY AND SELECTIVE RESPONSIVENESS

In a mass society where each person internalizes numerous perspectives there are bound to be some incongruities and conflicts. The overlapping of group affiliation and participation, however, need not lead to difficulties and is usually unnoticed. The reference groups of most persons are mutually sustaining. Thus, the soldier who volunteers for hazardous duty on the battlefield may provoke anxiety in his family but is not acting contrary to their values; both his family and his comrades admire courage and disdain cowardice. Behavior may be inconsistent, as in the case of the proverbial office tyrant who is meek before his wife, but it is not noticed if the transactions occur in dissociated contexts. Most people live more or less compartmentalized lives, shifting from one social world to another as they participate in a succession of transactions. In each world their roles are different, their relations to other participants are different, and they reveal a different facet of their personalities. Men have become so accustomed to this mode of life that they manage to conceive of themselves as reasonably consistent human beings in spite of this segmentalization and are generally not aware of the fact that their acts do not fit into a coherent pattern.

People become acutely aware of the existence of different outlooks only when they are successively caught in situations in which conflicting demands are made upon them, all of which cannot possibly be satisfied. While men generally avoid making difficult decisions, these dilemmas and contradictions of status may force a choice between two social worlds. These conflicts are essentially alternative ways of defining the same situation, arising from several possible perspectives. In the words of William James, "As a man I pity you, but as an official I must show you no mercy; as a politician I regard him as an ally, but as a moralist I loathe him." In playing roles in different social worlds, one imputes different expectations to others whose differences cannot always be compromised. The problem is that of selecting the perspective for defining the situation. In Mead's terminology, which generalized other's role is to be taken? It is only in situations where alternative definitions are possible that problems of loyalty arise.

Generally such conflicts are ephemeral; in critical situations contradictions otherwise unnoticed are brought into the open, and painful choices are forced. In poorly integrated societies, however, some people find themselves continually beset with such conflicts. The Negro intellectual, children of mixed marriages or of immigrants, the foreman in a factory, the professional woman, the military chaplain—all live in the interstices of well-organized structures and are marginal men.[8] In most instances they manage to make their way through their compartmentalized lives, although personal maladjustments are apparently frequent. In extreme cases amnesia and dissociation of personality can occur.

Much of the interest in reference groups arises out of concern with situations in which a person is confronted with the necessity of choosing between two or more organized perspectives. The hypothesis has been advanced that the choice of reference groups—conformity to the norms of the group whose perspective is assumed—is a function of one's interpersonal relations; to what extent the culture of a group serves as the matrix for the organization of perceptual experience depends upon one's relationship and personal loyalty to others who share that outlook. Thus, when personal relations to others in the group deteriorate, as sometimes happens in a military unit after continued defeat, the norms become less binding, and the unit may disintegrate in panic. Similarly, with the transformation of personal relationships between parent and

[8] Cf. E. C. Hughes, "Dilemmas and Contradictions of Status," *American Journal of Sociology*, L (1945), 353–59; and E. V. Stonequist, *The Marginal Man* (New York: Charles Scribner's Sons, 1937).

child in late adolescence, the desires and standards of the parents often become less obligatory.

It has been suggested further that choice of reference groups rests upon personal loyalty to significant others of that social world. "Significant others," for Sullivan, are those persons directly responsible for the internalization of norms. Socialization is a product of a gradual accumulation of experiences with certain people, particularly those with whom we stand in primary relations, and significant others are those who are actually involved in the cultivation of abilities, values, and outlook.[9] Crucial, apparently, is the character of one's emotional ties with them. Those who think the significant others have treated them with affection and consideration have a sense of personal obligation that is binding under all circumstances, and they will be loyal even at great personal sacrifice. Since primary relations are not necessarily satisfactory, however, the reactions may be negative. A person who is well aware of the expectations of significant others may go out of his way to reject them. This may account for the bifurcation of orientation in minority groups, where some remain loyal to the parental culture while others seek desperately to become assimilated in the larger world. Some who withdraw from the uncertainties of real life may establish loyalties to perspectives acquired through vicarious relationships with characters encountered in books.[10]

Perspectives are continually subjected to the test of reality. All perception is hypothetical. Because of what is taken for granted from each standpoint, each situation is approached with a set of expectations; if transactions actually take place as anticipated, the perspective itself is reinforced. It is thus the confirming responses of other people that provide support for perspectives.[11] But in mass societies the responses of others vary, and in the study of reference groups the problem is that of ascertaining *whose* confirming responses will sustain a given point of view.

THE STUDY OF MASS SOCIETIES

Because of the differentiated character of modern mass societies, the concept of reference group, or some suitable substitute, will always have a central place in any realistic conceptual scheme for its analysis. As is pointed out above, it will be most useful if it is used to designate that group whose perspective is assumed by the actor as the frame of reference for the organization of his perceptual experience. Organized perspectives arise in and become shared through participation in common communication channels, and the diversity of mass societies arises from the multiplicity of channels and the ease with which one may participate in them.

Mass societies are not only diversified and pluralistic but also continually changing. The successive modification of life-conditions compels changes in social relationships, and any adequate analysis requires a study of these transformational processes themselves. Here the concept of reference group can be of crucial importance. For example, all forms of social mobility, from sudden conversions to gradual assimilation, may be regarded essentially as displacements of reference groups, for they involve a loss of responsiveness to the demands of one social world and the adoption of the perspective of another. It may be hypothesized that the disaffection occurs first on the level of personal relations, followed by a weakening sense of obligation, a rejection of old claims, and the establishment of new loyalties and incorporation of a new perspective. The conflicts that characterize all persons in marginal roles are of special interest in that they provide opportunities for cross-sectional analyses of the processes of social change.

In the analysis of the behavior of men in mass societies the crucial problem is that of ascertaining how a person defines the situation, which perspective he uses in arriving at such a definition, and who constitutes the audience whose responses provide the necessary confirmation and support for his position. This calls for focusing attention upon the expectations the actor imputes to others, the communication channels in which he participates,

[9] H. S. Sullivan, *Conceptions of Modern Psychiatry* (Washington, D.C.: W. H. White Psychiatric Foundation, 1947), pp. 18–22.

[10] Cf. R. R. Grinker and J. P. Spiegel, *Men under Stress* (Philadelphia: Blakiston Co., 1945), pp. 122–26; and E. A. Shils and M. Janowitz, "Cohesion and Disintegration in the Wehrmacht in World War II," *Public Opinion Quarterly*, XII (1948), 280–315.

[11] Cf. G. H. Mead, *The Philosophy of the Act* (Chicago: University of Chicago Press, 1938), pp. 107–73; and L. Postman, "Toward a General Theory of Cognition," in J. H. Rohrer and M. Sherif (eds.), *Social Psychology at the Crossroads* (New York: Harper & Bros., 1951), pp. 242–72.

and his relations with those with whom he identifies himself. In the study of conflict, imagery provides a fertile source of data. At moments of indecision, when in doubt and confusion, who appears in imagery? In this manner the significant other can be identified.

An adequate analysis of modern mass societies requires the development of concepts and operations for the description of the manner in which each actor's orientation toward his world is successively reconstituted. Since perception is selective and perspectives differ, different items are noticed and a progressively diverse set of images arises, even among those exposed to the same media of mass communication. The concept of reference group summarizes differential associations and loyalties and thus facilitates the study of selective perception. It becomes, therefore, an indispensable tool for comprehending the diversity and dynamic character of the kind of society in which we live.

Group Influence in Marketing and Public Relations

FRANCIS S. BOURNE

The principles of group influence, postulated by sociologists and social psychologists particularly during the last two decades, are potentially useful in marketing. Here is an attempt to relate these concepts to some practical marketing problems.

THE CONCEPT OF REFERENCE-GROUP INFLUENCE

Much of the discussion group influence in these seminars was organized around the reference-group concept. Basically, the concept is a very simple one, and it has been recognized both by social scientists and, on a common-sense basis, by practical men for as long as people have been concerned with human behaviour.

On the common-sense level, the concept says in effect that man's behaviour is influenced in different ways and in varying degrees by other people. Comparing one's own success with that of others is a frequent source of satisfaction or disappointment. Similarly, before making a decision one often considers what such and such a person or such and such a group (whose opinion one has *some* reason to follow) would do in these circumstances, or what they would think of one for making a certain decision rather than another. Put in these ways, of course, reference-group influence represents an unanalysed truism which has long been recognized. The problem to which social scientists have been addressing themselves intensively only for the last two decades, however, concerns the refinement of this common-sense notion to the end that it might be effectively applied to concrete situations.

◆ SOURCE: Reprinted from Rensis Likert and Samuel P. Hayes, Jr. (Editors), *Some Applications of Behavioural Research*. Paris: UNESCO, 1957.

The real problems are those of determining which kinds of groups are likely to be referred to by which kinds of individuals under which kinds of circumstances in the process of making which decisions, and of measuring the extent of this reference-group influence. Towards this end, empirical researches have been conducted in recent years which have at least made a start in the process of refining the reference-group concept.

Reference-group theory, as it has developed, has become broad enough to cover a wide range of social phenomena, both with respect to the relation of the individual to the group and with respect to the type of influence exerted upon the individual by the group in question.

Reference groups against which an individual evaluates his own status and behaviour may be of several kinds:

1. They may be membership groups to which a person actually belongs and may involve either: (a) Small face-to-face groups in which actual association is the rule, such as families or organizations, whether business, social, religious, or political, or (b) groups in which actual membership is held but in which personal association is absent. (For example, membership in a political party, none of whose meetings are personally attended.) These groups may be of the same kinds as the former but differ only in the lack of face-to-face association with other members.

2. They may be groups or categories to

which a person automatically belongs by virtue of age, sex, education, marital status and so on. This sort of reference-group relationship involves the concept of role. For example, before taking a certain action an individual might consider whether this action would be regarded as appropriate in his role as a man or husband or educated person or older person or a combination of all these roles. What is involved here is an individual's perception of what society—either in general or that part of it with which he has any contact—expects people of his age, sex, education or marital status to do in given circumstances.

3. They may be anticipatory rather than actual membership groups. Thus a person who aspires to membership in a group to which he does *not* belong may be more likely to refer to it or compare himself with its standards when making a decision than he is to refer to the standards of the group in which he actually belongs but would like to leave. This involves the concept of upward mobility. When such upward mobility is sought in the social or business world, it is ordinarily accompanied by a sensitivity to the attitudes of those in the groups to which one aspires, whether it involves the attitudes of country-club members in the eyes of the aspiring non-member or the attitudes of management in the eyes of the ambitious wage-earner or junior executive.

4. They may be negative, dissociative reference groups. These constitute the opposite side of the coin from the anticipatory membership groups. Thus an individual sometimes avoids a certain action because it is associated with a group (to which the individual may or may not in fact belong) from which he would like to dissociate himself.

Reference groups influence behaviour in two main ways. First, they influence *aspiration levels*, and thus play a part in producing satisfaction or frustration. If the other members of one's reference group (for example, the neighbours) are wealthier, more famous, better gardeners, etc., one may be dissatisfied with one's own achievements and may strive to do as well as the others.

Secondly, reference groups influence *kinds* of behaviour. They establish approved patterns of using one's wealth, of wearing one's fame, of designing one's garden. They also lay down taboos, and may have the power to apply actual sanctions (for example, exclusion from

the group). They thus produce *conformity* as well as *contentment* (or discontent).

These two kinds of influence have, however, a good deal in common. Both imply certain perceptions on the part of the individual, who attributes to the reference group characteristics it may or may not actually have. Both involve psychological, rewards and punishment. . . .

THE PRACTICAL VALUE OF THE REFERENCE-GROUP CONCEPT IN MARKETING AND PUBLIC RELATIONS

In applying the reference-group concept to practical problems in marketing and public relations, three basic questions arise:

Reference-group relevance. How do you determine whether and to what extent reference-group influence is operating in a given situation? The reference group is, after all, only one of many influences in decision-making, varying greatly in prominence from situation to situation.

Reference-group identification. How do you identify the particular reference group or groups, or individuals, who are most relevant in influencing decisions under given circumstances? This is perhaps the most difficult question to answer in many cases, particularly where multiple reference groups are involved.

Reference-group identification and effective communication. Once having identified the nature of the group influence operating in a given situation, how do you then most effectively *communicate* with the groups or individuals you desire to influence?

This, of course, is the crux of the matter, since the answers to the first two questions are of value only to the extent that they can be translated into more pertinent and effective communication, designed to influence purchasing behaviour or the attitudes of various publics towards a firm or industry.

Experimental evidence is now available which sheds light on each of these three questions. From this evidence, and from the general advancement in the methodology of social research in recent years, there have emerged some very tentative generalizations. These can be applied only with the most careful attention to the special circumstances operating in individual instances, and serve more as guides to fruitful ways of examining problems as they arise than as simple answers to problems.

Reference-Group Relevance in Decision-making

Whether or not reference-group influence is likely to come into play in the decisions of individuals depends on many interrelated factors. For descriptive purposes, however, it is convenient to consider some of these factors under two main headings:

Influence determinants which vary primarily according to the individual making the decision, such as the feeling of security or insecurity with respect to potential reference-groups, the perception of the positions of these groups concerning kinds of behaviour expected or attitudes to specific issues, and the extent of knowledge about the matter on which a decision must be made.

Influence determinants which vary primarily according to the matter to be decided, such as the attributes of the product, in a marketing situation, or the nature of the organization and issue at stake in a public relations situation.

In marketing, it is rarely practical to utilize information about individual differences (the first class above), because products must be designed and appeals made with large groups in mind.[1] In public relations, on the other hand, individual differences may be very important. In this area the *general* level of attention with respect to a particular issue is often low. In these circumstances the relevant public may be confined to a few individuals, and in such cases knowledge of the relation between these individuals and potential reference groups would certainly be to the point.

Individual Differences and Reference-Group Influence.

THE RELATION OF SECURITY LEVEL AND CONFORMITY TO REFERENCE-GROUP INFLUENCE. A tentative generalization which has emerged in this area, and which has been supported by some experimental evidence, is this:

Individuals enjoying the greatest amount of security by virtue of their prestige and status within a group will generally conform (both publicly and privately) to the standards of that group, but are also freest to deviate from these standards on occasions when, to their minds, particular circumstances seem to justify such deviations. On the other hand, those with the weakest feelings of security and least status in a group are most likely *publicly* to conform to its standards on all occasions, even though harbouring private opposition and resentment. The latter holds, of course, only if there are penalties associated with loss of membership in the particular group. Conformity then serves the purpose of maintaining membership in that group. . . .

THE INDIVIDUAL'S PERCEPTION OF NORMS OF POTENTIAL REFERENCE GROUP. Perhaps one of the more obvious limitations to the relevance of a potential reference group in influencing a decision is an individual's lack of knowledge or incorrect perception of the group's actual position on an issue, even where he values the group's views or at least its acceptance of him. Thus, for example, the American Legion may be an effective reference group for a substantial number of veterans with respect to veterans' legislation. It may be much less so, however, in connexion with views on international affairs. The Legion has a position on such matters, but the average veteran is much less likely to know exactly what that position is. Along this line, a study conducted for a church council found issues on which the church's national policy was not followed by a considerable portion of the church's members. The study revealed that these differences between that church's policy and the opinions of its individual members were not necessarily conscious nonconformity with group norms but, in many cases, reflected ignorance of what those norms were.

One practical implication from these studies is that the effective influence of a reference group, even one known to command a substantial following, may be increased by giving special publicity to the position of the group on a specific issue.

INDEPENDENT KNOWLEDGE ABOUT THE MATTER TO BE DECIDED. Experimental evidence has indicated that reference-group influence is particularly potent in an informational vacuum. Where the individual has little or no knowledge about the attributes of a product or the issues involved in a public relations campaign, reference-group influence is at its strongest. On the other hand, when the individual has per-

---

[1] An exception to this generalization may be found in the case of personal selling, where knowledge of the individual's specific relation to and perception of certain groups would be highly relevant.

sonal knowledge and experience, the reference-group influence is likely to be *less* relevant, other things being equal. Thus in the study of a church and its parishioners alluded to above, it was found that uninformed parishioners tended to have the same attitudes towards secular issues as did their clergymen, but that, among those parishioners who were politically-informed and had other sources of information on these issues, there was a tendency more often to ignore the positions taken by their clergymen.

Different Kinds of Decisions and Reference-Group Influence.

MARKETING AND REFERENCE-GROUP RELE-VANCE. As already suggested, the reference group constitutes only one of the many influences in buying-decisions, and this influence varies from product to product. How then does one determine whether reference-group influence is likely to be a factor in buying-behaviour in connexion with a given product or brand? Research has been conducted on the various factors that influence buying-behaviour with reference to several products, and out of this have emerged some general ideas about how reference-group influences may enter into purchasing.

Buying may be a completely individualistic activity or very much socially conditioned. Consumers are often influenced by what others buy, especially those persons with whom they compare themselves or use as reference groups.

The conspicuousness of a product is perhaps the most general attribute bearing on its susceptibility to reference-group influence. There are two aspects to conspicuousness in this particular context that help to determine reference-group influence. First, the article must be conspicuous in the most obvious sense that it can be seen and identified by others. Secondly, it must be conspicuous in the sense of standing out and being noticed. In other words, no matter how visible a product is, if virtually everyone owns it, it is not conspicuous in the second sense of the word. This leads to a further distinction: reference groups may influence either (a) the purchase of a product, or (b) the choice of a particular brand or type, or (c) both.

The possible susceptibility of various product and brand-buying to reference-group influence is suggested in Table 1. According to this classification, a particular item might be sus-ceptible to reference-group influence in its purchase in three different ways, corresponding to three of the four cells in the table. Reference-group influence may operate with respect to brand or type but not with respect to product (Brand + Product −) as in the upper left cell, or it may operate both with respect to brand and product (Brand + Product +) as in the upper right cell, or it may operate with respect to product but not brand (Brand − Product +) as in the lower right cell.

Only the 'minus-minus' items of the kind illustrated (Brand − Product −) in the lower left cell are not likely to involve any significant reference-group influence in their purchase *at the present time.*

What are some of the characteristics that place an item in a given category, and what significance do such placements have for marketing and advertising policy?

"Product plus, Brand plus" Items. Cars are a case in which both the product and the brand are socially conspicuous. Whether or not a person buys a car, and also what particular brand he buys, is likely to be influenced by what others do. This also holds true for cigarettes and drugs (decisions made by M.D.'s as to what to prescribe) and for beer with respect to type (premium versus regular) as opposed to brand. Cigarettes and drugs, however, qualify as 'plus-plus' items in a manner different from cars.

For example, while the car belongs to a class of products where brand differentiation is based at least substantially on real differences in attributes, the cigarette belongs to a class of product in which it is hard to differentiate one brand from another by attributes; hence attributes are ascribed largely through reference-group appeal built up by advertising. Popular images of the kinds of people who smoke various brands have been created at great cost, and in some cases additional images are being created to broaden a particular brand's market. In the case of drugs, it was found that the reference-group influencing *whether* the product was used was different from that influencing the particular *brand* selected. Reference-group influence was found to be prominent in determining whether or not beer was purchased at all, and also in determining whether regular or premium beer was selected. It did not appear strongly to influence choice of a particular brand.

"Product plus, Brand minus" Items. Instant coffee is one of the best examples of this class of item. Whether it is served in a household depends in considerable part on whether the housewife, in view of her own reference groups and the image she has of their attitudes toward this product, considers it appropriate to serve it. The brand itself, in this instance, is not conspicuous or socially important and is a matter largely for individual choice. In the case of air-conditioners, it was found that little prestige is attached to the particular brand used, and reference-group influence related largely to the idea of purchasing the product itself. Analysis in one city revealed that the purchase of this often "visible from the outside" product was concentrated in small areas. Clusters of conditioners were frequently located in certain rows and blocks. In many cases, clusters did not even cross streets. Immediate neighbours apparently served as a powerfully influential reference group in the purchase of these appliances. In this general class may also be found the black and white TV set, with its antenna often visible from outside the house. As the saturation point in black and white TV set ownership rapidly approaches, however, the influence of reference groups may soon become unimportant, and the product can then be put in the 'brand minus, product minus' quadrant, beside refrigerators. Colour TV may remain in the 'brand plus, product minus' quadrant, with type (colour) rather than brand *per se* as the element strongly related to reference groups.

"Product minus, Brand plus" Items. This group is essentially made up of products that

Table 1.   Products and Brands of Consumer-Goods May Be Classified by Extent to Which Reference-Groups Influence Their Purchase [1]

	Weak − Reference-Group Influence Relatively Strong +	
Reference-Group Influence Relatively Strong + (+)	− Clothing Furniture Magazines Refrigerator (type) Toilet soap	+ Cars* Cigarettes* Beer (prem. v. reg.)* Drugs* +
Weak − (−)	Soap Canned peaches Laundry soap Refrigerator (brand) Radios	Air-conditioners* Instant coffee* TV (black and white) −
	− Product +	**Brand or Type**

[1] The classification of all products marked with an asterisk (*) is based on actual experimental evidence. Other products in this table are classified speculatively on the basis of generalizations derived from the sum of research in this area and confirmed by the judgement of seminar participants.

SOURCE: Bureau of Applied Social Research, Columbia University (Glock, unpublished).

all people or at least a very high proportion of people use, although differing as to type or brand.

Perhaps the leading example in this field is clothing. There could hardly be a more socially visible product than this, but the fact that everyone in our society wears clothing takes the *product* out of the area of reference-group influence. The *type* of clothing purchased is, however, very heavily influenced by reference groups, with each subculture in the population (teenagers, zootsuiters, Ivy League Collegians, Western Collegians, workers, bankers, advertising men, etc.) setting its own standards and often prescribing, within fairly narrow limits, what those who feel related to these groups can wear. Similarly, though not quite as dramatically, articles like furniture, magazines, refrigerators and toilet soap are seen in almost all homes, causing their purchase in general to fall outside the orbit of reference-group influence. The visibility of these items, however, coupled with the wide variety of styles and types among them, makes the selection of particular kinds highly susceptible to reference-group influence.

"Product minus, Brand minus" Items. Purchasing behaviour in this class of items is governed by product attributes rather than by the nature of the presumed users. In this group, neither the products nor the brands tend to be socially conspicuous. This is not to say that personal influence cannot operate with respect to purchasing the kind of items included in this group. As with all products, some people tend to exert personal influence and others tend to be influenced by individual persons. Reference groups as such, however, exert relatively little influence on buying behaviour in this class of items, examples of which are salt, canned peaches, laundry soap and radios. It is apparent that placement in this category is not *necessarily* inherent in the product itself and hence is not a static placement. Items can move in and out of this category.

While it is true that items which are essentially socially inconspicuous, like salt and laundry soap, are natural candidates for this category, it is not entirely impossible that, through large-scale advertising and other promotional efforts, images of the kind of people who use certain brands of salt or laundry soap could be built up so as to bring reference-group influence into play on such items, much as in the case of cigarettes. The task would be more difficult, however, since the cigarette is already socially visible. On the other hand, items such as radios and refrigerators, which are conspicuously visible and whose purchase was once subject to considerable reference-group influence, have now slipped into this category through near-saturation in ownership.

IMPLICATIONS OF STRONG AND WEAK REFERENCE-GROUP INFLUENCE FOR ADVERTISING AND MARKETING

It should be stressed again that this scheme of analysis is introduced to show how reference-group influence might enter into purchasing behaviour in certain cases. It cannot be regarded as generally applicable to marketing problems on all levels. There is still a need to know more precisely where many different products or brands fit into this scheme. Attempts to fit products and brands into the preceding classification suggest that research needs to be done in order to obtain more relevant information about each product.

Assuming, however, that a product or brand has been correctly placed with respect to the part played by reference groups in influencing its purchase, how can this help in marketing the product in question?

1. Where neither product nor brand appear to be associated strongly with reference-group influence, advertising should emphasize the product's attributes, intrinsic qualities, price, and advantages over competing products.

2. Where reference-group influence is operative, the advertiser should stress the kinds of people who buy the product, reinforcing and broadening where possible the existing stereotypes of users. The strategy of the advertiser should involve learning what the stereotypes are and what specific reference groups enter into the picture, so that appeals can be 'tailored' to each main group reached by the different media employed.

Although it is important to see that the 'right' kind of people use a product, a crucial problem is to make sure that the popular image of the product's users is as broad as possible without alienating any important part of the product's present or potential market in the process. Mistakes have been made in creating or reinforcing a stereotype of consumers which was too small and exclusive for a mass-produced item; this strategy excluded a significant portion of the potential market. On the other hand, some attempts to appeal to new groups through advertising in mass media have resulted in the loss of existing groups of purchasers whose previous (favourable) image of the product-user was adversely affected. A possible strategy for increasing the base of the market for a product by enlarging the image of its users is to use separate advertising media through which a new group can be reached without reducing the product's appeal to the original group of users. Another method might be to appeal to a new group through co-operative advertising by a number of companies producing the product, possibly through a trade association. This would minimize the risk to an individual producer who, trying to reach a new group of users through his own advertising (women as opposed to men or wealthy as opposed to average people, for example), might antagonize people who had a strong need to identify with the *original* image of the product's kind of user.

PRODUCT ATTRIBUTES VERSUS REFERENCE-GROUP INFLUENCE. A technique which could serve to assess the relative influence of reference groups, as compared with product attributes, on the purchase of a given product was employed in research on a food product which will be referred to as product 'X.'

A cross-section of 'X' users was asked several questions relating to particular attributes of 'X,' such as whether it was more harmful or beneficial to one's health, whether or not it was considered fattening, whether it was considered extravagant or economical, whether or not it tasted good, and so on. These same people were also asked a reference-group-oriented question about 'X,' to determine whether or not 'X' was popular with most of their friends. It was found that there was usually more 'X' eating among people who reacted negatively to the attributes of 'X' but admitted to its popularity among most of their friends, than among those who reacted positively to the attributes of 'X' but indicated that it was not popular with their friends.

These relationships are shown in Table 2. In this table, the scores in parentheses are those of people whose replies showed both attribute influence and reference-group influence exerting pressure in the same direction.

Special attention should be directed toward the other scores. These represent situations in which people are under cross-pressures. For each of the four attributes considered, the reference-group influence is stronger than the attribute influence, in the use of 'X.' This is brought out by the arrows, which point toward the cross-pressure situations where the reference-group influence is negative. In all these, consumption frequency is less than where attribute influence alone is negative. Or, put another way, positive perception of reference-group behaviour with respect to the food product ('X' is very popular) coupled with negative perception of its actual attribute value ('X' does more harm than good, is fattening, etc.) leads to more consumption than negative perception of reference-group behaviour ('X' not very popular) coupled with positive perception of actual attribute value ('X' does more good than harm, not fattening, economical).

As can be seen from the comparisons indicated by the arrows, reference-group influence is markedly stronger than attribute influence for three of the four attributes. Only for 'taste' does the attribute influence come close to competing with reference-group influence in determining consumption of 'X.'

One implication of this finding would be that advertising by the 'X' industry might stress the *social* aspects of the product, and the extent to which it is enjoyed by many groups of people like the audience being appealed to, rather than basing its advertising on the *actual attributes* of the product.

In a study of a beverage, it was found that, of those who drank the beverage in question, 95 per cent claimed that their friends also drank it, while of those who did not drink this beverage 85 per cent also claimed that their friends did *not* drink it.

Some products, then, must be sold to whole social groups rather than primarily to individuals.

RELEVANCE OF REFERENCE GROUPS IN AREA OF PUBLIC RELATIONS. Can the same type of classification of reference-group influence, previously applied to products and brands in the marketing field, be applied to companies and industries in the public relations area? Some such classification could conceivably be made in a general manner. For example, popular attitudes toward certain industries, which have come under political scrutiny and in reference to which political parties have taken definite stands, such as the power industry, may well be influenced by reference-group thinking. Similarly, popular attitudes toward a particular company may be influenced by trade

Table 2. Relation Between Reference-Group and Attribute Influence in Use of Food Product 'X'

Product Attribute	INDEX OF FREQUENCY OF EATING 'X' [1] + REFERENCE-GROUP − WITH MOST OF RESPONDENT'S FRIENDS 'X' IS:	
	Very Popular	Not Very Popular
Effects of 'X' on health		
+ More good than harm	(.41)	−.10
− More harm than good	.08	(−.51)
+ Do not avoid fattening food and/or feel 'X' is not really or a little fattening	(.30)	−.21
− Try to avoid fattening food and feel 'X' is really or a little fattening	.14	(−.29)
Economic value judgement		
+ Fairly economical	(.29)	−.20
− Sort of an extravagance	.11	(−.33)
Taste judgement		
+ Tastes good	(.42)	.05
− No reference to good taste [2]	.09	(−.38)

[1] All scores in the above table constitute an index of the frequency of 'X' eating among respondents falling into the given cell. The scoring procedure used was: frequent 'X' users—score +1; medium 'X' users—score 0; occasional 'X' users—score −1.

The final score is derived by subtracting the number of occasional 'X' users in a given cell from the number of frequent users and dividing the remainder by the total number of respondents in the cell. For example, the index score .41 was obtained as follows: 329 respondents felt that a moderate amount of 'X' does more good than harm AND report that 'X' is very popular with most of their friends. Of these 329 respondents 178 are frequent 'X' users, 97 are medium 'X' users and 43 are occasional 'X' users.

The score: 178 − 43 = 135. The *Index* value: 135/329 = +.41.

[2] 'Tastes good' represents the selection of this phrase from a word list of various attributes that might be applied to 'X.' 'No reference to good taste' refers to those respondents who did not select 'Tastes good' from the word list.

SOURCE: Bureau of Applied Social Research, Columbia University.

union reactions to the company's specific policies in labour relations. This could take place either in an industry which itself was in the public eye and hence more susceptible to reference-group influence, or in an industry relatively little in the public eye. Using a classification analogous to that presented above, the first of these two hypothetical cases would fall into a 'Company plus, Industry plus' classification with respect to reference-group influence on attitudes towards the industry, while the second would fall into a 'Company plus, Industry minus' category. In the first category might be a company in the steel or coal or railway industry that has had a prolonged and

highly-publicized strike, whereas in the latter category might be found a well-known company with a similar experience, let us say in the hat industry, an industry with which public interest is not particularly involved. Finally, to round off this classification scheme, industries not visibly related to an important public interest and made up of many relatively small companies which have not been involved in serious disputes with particular groups would tend to fall into the 'Company minus, Industry minus' category with respect to reference-group influence.

The factor of social visibility is an important clue to reference-group influence both in marketing and public relations. However, the value of the above classification by reference-group influence appears to be much more limited for public relations than for marketing. Public relations problems are far more varied and complex, and these complexities limit the value of such a gross classification scheme as that advanced above.

Some of the limitations on the usefulness of such a classification scheme are:

1. Little if any relevant research is available in the public relations field to support such speculative classification.

2. Relatively few industries and companies, nationally speaking, elicit stable images of great force of one kind or another among the general public.

3. While a *generally* favourable image of a company is, of course, highly desirable, a company's public relations problems usually break down into several component parts, and can best be measured along several separate dimensions. In fact, one national survey organization, which conducts a biannual audit of company public relations, uses twelve separate components on which attitudes toward the company are based.

4. Just as the attitudes toward a company must be broken down functionally, they must often be considered separately on a geographical basis. The same industry and even the same company may have different public relations problems in the different places where its plants are situated. Local problems can best be evaluated in their specific contexts, and lend themselves to a minimum of generalization at the present stage of knowledge in this field.

5. From a public relations standpoint, the general public is only one of many publics with which a company or industry is concerned at various times and with respect to various aspects of its operation. Other special publics which may be of concern, depending upon the particular problem at hand, include customers, employees, suppliers, stockholders, associates in the industry, Government officials (either local or national), and so on. Each of these groups may constitute a reference group influencing company action at one time or another, and each of them has, in turn, its own reference groups, through which the company may seek to influence it.

6. Finally, whereas in marketing the implications of reference-group influence are often quite clear, because they can be evaluated

against a measurable criterion—the act of buying or not buying—there is rarely in public relations any equivalently unambiguous criterion against which reference-group influence can be measured. Except when the issues at stake are of very direct and great importance to the public concerned, it is difficult to tell what the significance of a particular attitude toward a company or industry may be. Is a widely held superficial attitude more or less important to a company than a deep-seated feeling held by a smaller group, and what implications does each have for action? These are researchable questions, but more difficult than those in the marketing field, where buying behaviour provides, in most cases, a more convenient test.

An example of how varied the possibilities are for reference-group influence in the public relations area is provided in the experience of a large utilities company. The company was seeking a rate increase in a state and this, of course, required government action at the state level. At first, an attempt was made to exert direct influence on the special 'public' which was in a position to grant the raise in rate. Negotiations between the company's top management and members of the state commission, however, failed to achieve this aim. The company next began a campaign in which it was explained to company employees in each local community what the rate increase would mean to them in terms of new equipment, jobs, and so on. These local employees at all levels undertook to make this information known to the members of their communities. In each community, some local company employee talked personally to each important opponent of the rate increase. When the Commission met again, it authorized an increase in rate, and company earnings went up. Had the rate increase not been justifiable, it is likely that the public relations of this company would eventually have suffered. Resentment is created when people feel that they have been influenced through reference groups or otherwise, to act against their own interests. . . .

Identifying Influence Groups

Once it has been established that reference-group influence is relevant to people's decisions in a given situation, it is still necessary to identify which of several possible reference groups is most relevant in actual practice. The discussion that follows will first summarize some of the methodological approaches generally available in the investigation of this problem, and then present some specific researches designed to help in identifying influence and reference groups.

Methods of Identification.

DIRECT QUESTIONING OF THE PUBLIC. This involves asking the respondent directly about the groups that may be influencing his opinions or actions in a given situation. This is sometimes successful, but more often this approach cannot be relied upon by itself. Frequently people are not actually aware of the source of influence for a particular action of theirs. Where a person's ego is strongly involved, moreover, a direct question may lead to concealment of real reasons for behaviour.

ASSOCIATIVE-PROJECTIVE TECHNIQUES. These techniques are designed to elicit responses from people in such a way that they are not aware that they are committing themselves *personally* to any specific point of view or attitude. This technique is regarded as being of special value where the direct technique falters, because it is designed to counteract both conscious and unconscious concealment of attitudes.

Projective tests may be used both to identify relevant reference groups and to ascertain the image held of them. The respondent is asked to react to a situation indirectly through asking his opinion of *someone else* behaving in a given fashion. This can be achieved entirely on a verbal level. It may also involve the use of a picture (thematic apperception test) which the respondent is asked to characterize or interpret, or he may be asked to tell a story illustrated by it. What is achieved at best is to place in a less threatening context a question which might otherwise present some threat to a person's ego. It may also serve to help the respondent formulate answers in a relatively vague situation, bringing to the surface dormant reactions which might not be at once prompted by a direct question.

An illustration of the use of this projective-associative technique in the field of marketing is to be found in a survey of consumer reactions to instant coffee. When people were asked directly why they didn't use this product they were most likely to react in terms of the product's attributes. More oblique inquiry was required to bring to the surface other potential influences on a person's attitude toward the

product. In this case, housewives were shown two shopping lists represented as belonging to two different women. All items on these lists were identical except that one of the lists contained regular coffee and the other instant coffee. The respondents were then asked to characterize the kind of women who were likely to have each of these shopping lists. A fairly consistent image emerged from this test, revealing that most housewives saw the users of instant coffee as lazy, and as poor homemakers.

The implication was that housewives shied away from instant coffee because they feared that other housewives (an important reference group in such a situation) would regard them as inferior homemakers. This suggested an advertising approach directed toward building up a positive image of the type of people who used instant coffee as busy, active, capable people of affairs, rather than primarily stressing the attributes of the product itself.

Indirect approaches of this kind have yielded valuable insights for the marketer and copywriter, but a caution must be introduced with regard to the reliability of interpretation of projective test results. Alone, the responses to indirect questions can no more be taken at their face value than can direct questions. Corroborative evidence is always desirable. As an example of the possible difficulties in interpretation in this area, a study of attitudes towards Negroes conducted at a women's college in New England was cited. When the girls in a dormitory were asked directly if they would mind having a Negro girl as a roommate in the dormitory, the majority of them said they would not mind. When asked if they thought the other girls in the dormitory would mind, the majority reported that they thought the others would mind. The partisan of projective techniques might regard the latter as an expression of the true feelings of the girls involved. This indirect question, they would maintain, shielded the girls from having to express personal prejudice. This could be a plausible explanation of the discrepancy in answers. However, it is also possible that the response to the indirect question involved a mere misunderstanding of the attitudes of the other girls, and hence should be discounted on that score. Actually, other evidence would be required before one could assess with confidence the attitudes of these girls on the question.

Valuable as projective tests undoubtedly are,

techniques for their interpretation are still in their infancy. Confirmation from other tests is still needed.

CHECK OF ACTUAL HOMOGENEITY OF ATTITUDES WITHIN A GROUP. If most of a group are believed to manifest the same attitude, this is usually taken as evidence that their attitude is at least partly the result of their group membership. This should be checked, however, by actually canvassing the group to see if the attitude attributed to it is in fact held by a substantial majority of its members and not held by a substantial majority of non-members. Thus, for example, if people were asked to characterize 'a teacher who advocated progressive education,' and if a frequent response was a 'graduate of a teachers' college,' this would supply a *clue* as to a possible reference group for progressive education. However, it would then be necessary to check whether the given teachers' college did in fact number among its graduates a substantially larger proportion of progressive education advocates than did other institutions or whether this was merely a case of a misunderstanding on the part of many people.

CHECK THE DIFFERENCE IN ATTITUDES BETWEEN OLD AND NEW MEMBERS OF A GROUP. Another kind of evidence helping to identify a reference group on a particular subject can be obtained by comparing the attitudes of people who have just joined the group with those of older members. This gets at the influence of membership on attitudes directed toward the subject in question. For example, if seniors at the teachers' college exhibited significantly greater leanings toward progressive education than did freshmen, and if this was not the case at some other college, it might be fair to conclude that the teachers' college did to some extent serve as a reference group for students on this particular question.

COMPARE THE ATTITUDES OF PRESTIGEFUL, ACCEPTED MEMBERS OF AN ORGANIZATION WITH THOSE OF PERIPHERAL MEMBERS. If the influential members of a group are more generally and strongly committed to a particular viewpoint than are the peripheral members, this is good evidence that the viewpoint depends heavily on membership in that group. In general, determining whether a group serves as a reference for its members on a particular subject is relatively easy when the given group is a formal one, but considerably more difficult

when the group represents an informal relationship. This calls for other techniques.

SOCIOMETRIC TECHNIQUE. This technique can be used to locate informal social groups which serve as reference groups for individuals. Since no formal membership is involved in such groups, personal relationships must be traced by detailed questioning of an entire group of people who are in significant association with each other. People are asked a whole battery of questions about their social relationships. Whom do they associate with? Whom do they like and respect? To whom do they look to for advice on subject A, on subject B, on subject C, etc.? To what extent do people turn to them for advice on given subjects, and so on? Ideally, the sociometric technique requires an exhaustive tracing of association patterns until the entire community of people with whom one is concerned have been questioned. In this way, distinctive groups can be identified which have no formal identity but which can be observed to behave and think with a certain uniformity with respect to certain questions. Furthermore, the flow of influence within these clusters can be traced, and the more influential members with respect to certain subjects can be identified.

DIRECT OBSERVATION OF BEHAVIOUR. In studying buying behaviour, clues to the influences (including reference-group influences) which affect purchases can sometimes be obtained by direct observation of the act of buying and the interchange between purchaser and salesman.

Examples of Identifying Relevant Reference Groups. When an individual's own attitudes and those of all the groups to which he may belong are similar with regard to any decision, whether it be in the field of voting or purchasing behaviour, there is no great difficulty in predicting his action, nor is there any need for identifying one reference group as having greater relevance or influence than another. When, however, large numbers of individuals belong to several groups and have friends whose attitudes to certain ideas differ from one to another or from those of the individual himself, the problem of cross-pressures appears. It is in this normal type of real-life situation that research is required, to indicate which of several potential reference groups appears to carry the greatest weight in influencing a *particular* decision.

. . . the various groups of which consumers are members may set up cross-pressures on purchasing behaviour. The final nature of this behaviour might depend upon: (a) the particular groups that have greatest relevance for the kind of purchasing behaviour in question, or (b) the ability of the marketer to recognize these cross-pressures and to develop effective promotion that takes advantage of their influence.

In the consumer field, for example, the attitudes of various groups of one's associates toward television-ownership may markedly influence the purchase of television sets. Whereas one's neighbours and children probably serve as positive reference groups favouring the purchase of a set or of a new kind of set (colour), there are situations where business or professional colleagues, especially the latter, apparently serve as a negative reference group. Research could be conducted to determine, for various classes of people, which groups have norms that are closely associated with ownership of television or colour television. If the more influential groups are found to be opposed to television-ownership, then efforts might be made to change the images held by those negative groups as to the kind of people who would buy television or colour television sets.

Personal Influence.

SOCIOMETRIC STUDIES OF INFLUENCE PATTERNS IN MARKETING FIELD. A substantial number of studies have now been made which trace the *patterns of influence* in the purchase of various products and in the adoption of new practices. Some of the earlier community sociometric studies, such as that conducted at Decatur, Illinois, in 1945, established certain generalizations about the role of personal influence in decision-making and the nature of those who exert influence in various areas. In this study, a panel of women was interviewed and, later, re-interviewed. Those who changed their opinions or their purchasing habits, or adopted new products between the two waves of interviews, were singled out for special questioning as to what influenced the changes in their behaviour.

These studies suggested that the importance of personal influence, relative to that of mass media, was considerably greater than had been commonly accepted. Also established was the notion that different individuals are the opinion-leaders or 'influentials' in different situations or for different decisions. These opinion-leaders are not necessarily distinguished by special characteristics of wealth or social status. Marketing influentials appeared to be distinguished more by their positions in the life cycle (size of family, age of children, etc.) than by their socio-economic status, and their contacts tended to be with those on the same socio-economic level. Only in the case of political influence did there appear to be considerable vertical contact in the social scale, with opinion-leaders higher in the scale than those influenced. In order to obtain practical marketing guidance, it is evidently necessary to find out who are the opinion-leaders for each product, how they can be reached, and what attributes of the product should be emphasized.

Considerable interest has been shown recently in tracing the patterns of influence in the adoption of new commercial, professional and agricultural products and practices.

Adoption of a New Professional Practice.

One study of innovation of new practices in a professional area, based in part on sociometric analysis, traced the process by which these professionals decided to accept innovations. Diffusion of information was studied by interviewing all the professionals, numbering slightly over 200, in four small urban communities in which the practice in question had been introduced for a period of about two years. The normal network of social relations among the professionals in each of these communities was first determined by the following three sociometric questions:

1. (Purely social) 'Could you name the three or four professionals you meet most frequently on social occasions?'
2. (Discuss professional affairs with) 'Who are the three or four professionals in your conversations with whom the subject of the practice in question comes up?'
3. (Seek professional advice) 'When you need added information or advice about the practice in question where do you usually turn?'

Then, each professional who had recently decided to adopt the new practice was asked questions to bring out the channels of information and influence which entered into this recent decision. The replies were compared with the professional's position in the social network. The sources are shown in Table 3.

It should be noted that the first sources of exposure were largely commercial in nature but that subsequent exposure tended increasingly to be professional.

The pattern of adoptions of the new practice was then related to the social networks identified by the replies to the questions above. All the professionals were placed in four different categories on the basis of the stage at which they adopted the new practice. The first adopters are referred to as 'innovators.' They took the lead in adopting the new practice, but their action did not result in a great rush to follow their example. The next group of professionals adopting the practice were called the 'influentials,' since their action was followed shortly by similar behaviour among most of the other professionals in the community. Next came the largest group, the 'followers' who adopted the new practice shortly after the so-called 'influential' group, from whom they took their cue. Finally, after a long pause, the remaining small group, termed 'diehards,' adopted the new practice. This pattern of adoption is shown in Figure 1.

AGRICULTURAL INNOVATION.   Agricultural sociologists have been conducting parallel research on the acceptance of innovation in farm machinery, new seeds, wheat sprays, etc. In much of this research the S-curve of adoption noted above in the professional study was closely approximated.

Stages in Adoption of New Products or Practices. In adopting new farm products or procedures, five stages have been noted. The time it takes to get from the original stage to final adoption naturally varies. For instance, the average time span from awareness to adoption of hybrid seed corn in Iowa was seven

Table 3.   Sources of Information Used by Professional Men in Adopting a New Practice

	SOURCES		
	First %	Second %	Third %
Commercial			
Salesmen	57	26	6
Commercial mail	18	16	14
Commercial periodical	4	11	21
Journal advertisements	1	3	2
Non-commercial			
Colleagues and professional journals	20	44	57

Source: Bureau of Applied Social Research, Columbia University.

years. But however long the span, the five stages generally observed are: Awareness, Interest, Evaluation, Trial, and Adoption. . . .

IDENTIFYING REFERENCE GROUPS IN INDUSTRIAL MARKETING.   The industrial consumer or purchasing agent has his own reference groups. These have not, however, been subjected to much systematic examination. Some of these potential reference groups are:

1. Other buyers—what they think of him; his relation to professional associations of buyers.

2. Company influentials—the known or imagined preferences of the president of the company or of other influential senior officers.

3. Company technicians—the attitudes of other company departments, such as the en-

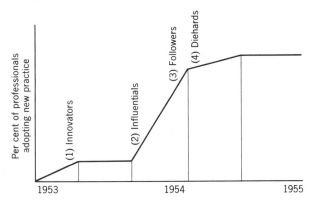

Figure 1   Adoption of a new practice by professionals follows a distinctive pattern. Source: Bureau of Applied Social Research, Columbia University.

gineering department, which writes the specifications.

4. Customers—the factor of reciprocity as it affects the desire to do business with one's customers if possible.

5. Community pressures—for example, business or community pressures to 'Buy American,' or to buy local rather than outside products.

Data on reference-group influence in the behaviour of industrial purchasers might be obtained in the following ways.

First, select a locality and observe the behaviour of purchasing agents in that locality. Determine whether there are any regularities in the pattern of purchasing behaviour displayed by these industrial consumers in particular companies. Are there companies which are opinion-leaders and others which are followers in this activity? Are there differences between small, medium and large companies in purchasing patterns?

Secondly, interview purchasing agents directly, to find out their own criteria for their buying behavior. Let the purchasing agent describe his own sources of information and explain what considerations entered into his decision in specific buying situations. One might find that the purchasing agent's behaviour could be explained simply by the attributes of the product. Alternately, one might find that it could be explained by certain predispositions on his part, such as ambition for promotion within the company and his perception of how that could best be achieved. Or it might turn out that his behaviour was due to his following a leader or a reference group which had importance for him.

Again, one might collect case history or qualitative but concrete information by asking the best buyers or salesmen what factors influence buyers. From this initial qualitative study, a pattern might emerge which would indicate the importance of particular reference groups. Salesmen and buyers know much about these matters but may not have verbalized it. This initial look at the problem would show whether more information could be obtained, and would give some 'leads' to the important variables in a variety of situations. One of the difficulties in getting to the core of reference-group influence in this area, however, is the fact that companies and individuals often regard industrial purchasing behaviour as a trade secret.

PROBLEMS IN IDENTIFYING 'INFLUENTIALS' IN PUBLIC RELATIONS. One of the basic principles derived from the study of leadership is that there are no universal qualities that determine leadership in general nor are there any fixed official positions in a community which can be counted on to represent real influence in that community. There is considerable variation in both aspects, from situation to situation. Usually, the type of leader to look for will depend on the particular kind of public relations question involved.

Two of the important functions associated with leadership are: (a) the creating, initiating function (analogous to the 'innovator'); (b) the moderating, judiciary function (analogous to the 'influential'). Many experiments have shown that the idea man and the moderator are rarely the same person. In a given community, it may be necessary to reach both kinds of leader in order to put over a particular position.

Sometimes both kinds of people are initially opposed to a new idea. It is then necessary to identify and neutralize the aggressive opponents. Even though they do not have ultimate veto power, they may have substantial nuisance-value. It is often also necessary to identify the more silent individuals in the background whose strategic position, frequently in the financial structure of the community, gives them a final say in what shall and what shall not be done. Usually, both these types of men must either be in favour of the idea or, at least, neutralized if the idea is to be successfully introduced into the community.

This oversimplified model, of course, applies primarily to a small community. As pointed out above, identification of significant leaders can only be usefully discussed in terms of an actual situation in an actual community. Studies of racial tensions, community health and educational problems clearly reveal that the initiators and legitimizers of ideas differ from one problem to another. . . .

The Audience as a Reference Group

Distortion of Communication. An important communication phenomenon, which had, until recently, received little research attention, is that of the influence of the perceived audience on the communicator. . . .

A practical implication . . . in the area of selling and public relations is that many valuable prospects are often passed by because of the natural tendency to avoid those who are perceived, even if mistakenly, to be unfriendly. Too often, organizations talk only to those already converted and do little to seek out possibly valuable allies who might be receptive to their message.

Communicating with a less-than-friendly audience, of course, raises certain special problems in communication. The fact that people tend to expose themselves more to, and retain more of, material toward which they are already favourably disposed should induce the communicator to associate the material he desires to get across with ideas that are already familiar and acceptable to the audience and with subject matter that is known to be of interest to them.

Deciding Whether to Present Both Sides. Experiments which have been conducted on the relative effectiveness of various ways of presenting an idea have far-reaching implications, both for advertising and public relations. One of these experiments was designed to bring out the factors determining the relative effectiveness of one-sided versus two-sided arguments.

Whether a one-sided or two-sided presentation of a case is more effective depends on at least four considerations:

1. Whether the audience is initially favourable or unfavourable to the communicator's position.
2. Education level of the audience.
3. Whether a counter-attack is anticipated.
4. Whether short-run or long-run effects are being considered.

With respect to these conditions the findings of the research in question may be summarized as shown in Table 4.

In general, the one-sided argument is most effective when presented to an initially favourable audience, of less education, where counter-arguments are not anticipated, and where short-run effects are sought. On the other hand, the two-sided argument proves to be more effective among people who are initially unfavourable to the communicator's point of view, who are better educated, who are likely to be exposed to a counter-argument, and where long-run effects are sought. . . .

How does one decide in a given public relations situation whether to concentrate on one side of an issue or to present both sides? Should

advertising, for example, deal only with the advantages of one's product?

Among the considerations are the education and sophistication of the public to be reached, and the likelihood that the public will be exposed to conflicting claims or an opposing point of view. Another consideration is whether an immediate reaction by members of the public is desired (a buying decision) or whether a more-or-less permanent attitude or opinion is the objective (a position on an issue).

In relation to product advertising and marketing of a mass-produced article, the research findings described above tentatively suggest that an approach emphasizing only the positive features of the product is usually sufficient. Competing products are normally advertised on their own merits, rather than on directly conflicting claims. Unless the public to which the advertising is directed is made up primarily of well-educated and sophisticated individuals, an approach introducing both sides is apt to raise doubts. The direct approach stressing only the product's merits is more likely to lead to a buying decision; once the consumer has tried the product, he will, if it is of the expected good quality, be favourably inclined toward it and somewhat resistant to change. If the purchase is a substantial one, he may also, to some extent, actually welcome arguments that justify the wisdom of the decision he has made. If the advertising claims have been misleading, however, the purchaser will of course be resentful and more resistant to subsequent messages from this source.

In the rather special cases where information

Table 4. Relative Effectiveness of One-Sided and Two-Sided Arguments

One-sided Argument More Effective	Two-sided Argument More Effective
With initially favourable audience	With initially unfavourable audience
Among less educated	Among more educated
When no counter-argument is anticipated	When counter-argument is anticipated
Over short-run (Little significant difference)	Over long-run

Source: Department of Psychology, Yale University.

derogatory to the product has been released or likely to emerge (from medical sources, safety groups, competitors, etc.), questions of whether and how the criticisms should be answered would depend upon the seriousness of the adverse claims, the attention they receive, the importance of the reference groups involved, and other relevant factors in the particular situation. Deciding between a one-sided and a two-sided selling approach may involve game theory, in which one attempts to anticipate the opponent's next move.

Where public relations issues are involved, on the other hand, these research findings tentatively suggest that presenting both sides

would normally be more effective. In most situations, it can be anticipated that the public will be exposed to differing points of view or claims by opposing groups. Taking account of these views by presenting both sides seems more likely to establish firm opinions and support within reference groups significant to the particular issue, than would be the case with a one-sided presentation. Presenting both sides will also reduce the possibility of creating underlying resistance which people develop if they feel or learn that reference-group influence is being utilized in ways that conflict with their own judgement or that work against their own best interests.

D. Economics and Anthropology

The Need for Sales to Match Productive Ability

ARNO H. JOHNSON

How much additional sales of goods and services to consumers will be needed to create the 20 million additional non-agricultural jobs our labor force will demand in the next ten years? This article discusses the probable impact of our growing labor force and growing productivity per worker on the economic role of selling and on improvement of the American standard of living. It documents, also, the probable influence of basic economic and social changes such as are taking place in income and discretionary spending power, education, age distribution, family life, suburban living, and retail distribution.

A basic factor affecting the economic role of selling in the American economy is the growth of our labor force, both in numbers and in productivity. Within ten years—by 1973—our labor force will demand some 20 million additional non-agricultural jobs. This implies the creation of an average of 1,800,000 to 2,000,000 net new job opportunities each year during the next decade. Compare this needed growth with the fact that in the twelve years from 1950 to 1962 inclusive, our average annual addition to non-agricultural employment was about 900,000, or only half as much.

To provide these jobs will require a substantial expansion of sales of goods and services—an expansion of demand and markets far greater than the population growth itself. It means an opportunity and need for an upgrading of living standards in line with increased productive ability. The role of selling and advertising in expanding markets and overcoming the "habit-lag" or inertia to change in living customs and desires, can hardly be overemphasized.

◆ SOURCE: Reprinted by permission from *Emerging Concepts in Marketing*, edited by William S. Decker, Proceedings of the Winter Conference of the American Marketing Association, December 1962, pp. 145–173.

The magnitude of the task facing selling can be judged from the estimate that, in the total standard of living area of personal consumption alone, about $200 billion in annual sales will need to be added on top of the 1962 level of $355 billion by 1973.

In addition to the impact of the increasing productivity of an enlarged labor force on needs for selling a better standard of living, there are some other economic and social changes that will enhance the role of selling in our economy.

1. The rapid movement upward in income groups—with an increasing need for the educational force of selling and advertising to overcome "habit-lag."

2. Movement upward in education—with an opportunity to upgrade concepts and ways of life.

3. Changing age distribution of the population—affecting new family formations, housing, and job requirements.

4. Changing mobility of the population and movement to the suburbs—resulting in major changes in distribution.

Let's study in more detail the forces that may have an important impact on the economic role of selling in the next decade.

THE UNITED STATES NEEDS 20 MILLION NEW NON-AGRICULTURAL JOBS BY 1973

The increasingly important economic role of sales as well as investment in the United States is emphasized by the indicated need for the creation of 20 million new non-agricultural jobs in the next decade—by 1973. An increase in non-agricultural employment from the level of 63 million in mid-1962 to 83 million by 1973 is basic to any plans for optimum opportunity and utilization of our labor force. See Figure 1.

To provide the tools and environment of production for 83 million non-agricultural employment will require substantially increased capital investments. Also, this level of employ-ment over the next decade can be justified only by a rapid expansion of markets to utilize the increased production of goods and services. This, of course, points directly to an upgrading of our standard of living as measured by total personal consumption of goods and services. The educational force of selling and advertising will be required to encourage changes in habits and desires of consumers rapidly enough to provide the needed employment of our in-creased labor force.

It is estimated that our total labor force in 1973 will be about 92 million or 40.7% of our projected population of 226 million. The labor force share of population was 42.5% in 1940, 42.7% in 1950, and dropped to 40.2% in 1962

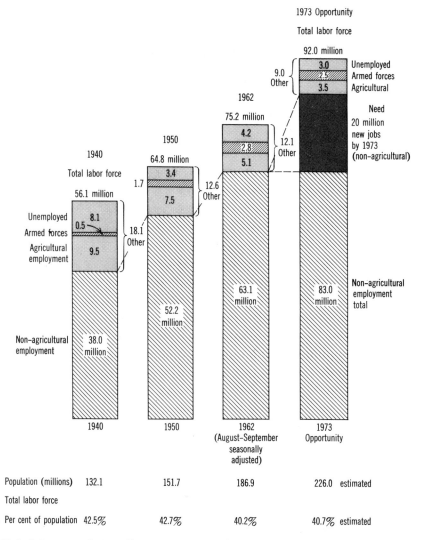

Figure 1   United States needs 20 million new non-agricultural jobs by 1973. Source: J. Walter Thompson Company.

during the period of unusual age distribution of our population with a high proportion under 15 and over 65 being outside the normal employment ages. Considering some probable reverse changes in age distribution by 1973, the estimated 40.7% desiring to participate in the labor force then seems a conservative figure.

With 92 million expected in the total labor force, and with a continued decline expected in agricultural employment, and an arbitrary estimate of 2½ million needed in the Armed Forces, we will need 20 million more non-agricultural jobs by 1973 if we are to keep unemployment down to a level of around three million.

The magnitude of the impact of the expanded need for new non-agricultural jobs in the United States can be visualized by comparison with the growth since 1950. In the 12 years between 1950 and mid-1962 our average increase was about 900,000 in non-agricultural employment—in the next 11 years to 1973, we must add about 1,800,000 jobs annually, or twice as fast as our record of the last 12 years! And these workers will be better educated and capable of greater productivity. So the investment needs and opportunities and the needs for rapid expansion of consumer markets must be recognized and encouraged.

$200 BILLION MORE SALES OF GOODS AND SERVICES ANNUALLY NEEDED BY 1973

We need to increase our total annual sales of goods and services to consumers by about $200 billion in the next decade to keep pace with our increasing productive ability and employment needs.

It is possible that, by 1973, the total gross national product in the United States may grow to over $870 billion. Such a growth in production would make possible a 56% increase in total living standard or personal consumption expenditures of the total population. See Figure 2.

$870 billion by 1973, in terms of 1962 prices, is a conservative measure of our total productive ability since it allows for a gain of only 2.4% per year in per capita productivity—a rate of gain no larger than we have demonstrated since prewar. Actually, in the 22 years between 1940 and 1962, total physical production per capita (in terms of constant dollars) increased by about 2.4% per year. Projections from the Bureau of the Census estimates indicate a possible growth of population to 226 million by 1973 from the level of 186 million in 1962.

So $870 billion of productive ability for 1973 should be looked upon as a minimum level for a long-range planning. If any allowance were made for an increase in rate of improvement of per capita productivity, or for the much discussed "5% growth rate," the productive ability in the next ten years would be in the neighborhood of $950 billion.

To support an $870 billion production economy in the United States by 1973, which is the minimum to anticipate if we are to avoid serious unemployment and under-utilization of our productive ability, we in the United States alone must add to our annual level of personal consumption expenditures the huge amount of about $200 billion (up to a total personal consumption of over $555 billion by 1973 compared with the $355 billion level in mid-1962).

Even after allowing for a rapid growth in government needs to $185 billion (versus $116 billion in 1962) and an expansion of private investment needs from $81 billion in 1962 to $130 billion by 1973, there still remains the startling conclusion that *personal consumption* in the United States must be *expanded by at least 56%* to about $555 billion in 1973, if we are to match a productive ability of $870 billion. That means adding $200 billion of personal consumption to the $355 billion level of mid-1962.

The velocity of change in living standards of the population needed to match the most conservative estimates of future productive ability nearly staggers the imagination. To add $200 billion to the U.S. standard of living means adding, in the next *ten years*, on top of the present high level of consumption the equivalent of more than the entire growth in consumption in the *320 years* from the landing of the *Mayflower* at Plymouth in 1620 to the best prewar year of 1940! Total consumption in 1940 was only $163 billion in terms of 1962 dollars.

In the *33 years* from 1929 to 1962 we added $211 billion to total personal consumption (in June 1962 prices), so even talking modern times the United States must add as much to consumption and total standard of living in the next *ten years* as in the previous *33 years* if it is to keep up with minimum estimates of production growth.

This possibility of rapid expansion in total

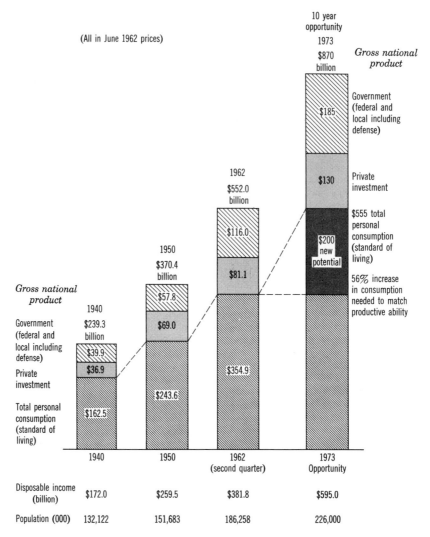

(All in June 1962 prices)

Figure 2   United States production in the amount of $870 billion by 1973 adds $200 billion to consumer needs. Opportunity for 56% higher living standards. Source: J. Walter Thompson Company.

consumption and markets has real implications for study by leaders in marketing and finance since both consumption and savings and investment play such an important part in over-all improvement in living standards and in providing the tools of production.

An $870 billion economy, for example, would indicate a growth in personal savings to a level of over $45 billion annually by 1973, or to nearly 8% of disposable income, compared with $12½ billion in 1950 and $27 billion in 1962. In prewar 1939 personal savings represented only $3 billion, or 4% of the then available disposable income.

There are some basic economic and social changes that are favorable to the expansion of consumption and the utilization of our labor force. These are factors, too, that will empha-

size the economic role of selling in our economy of the next decade.

DISCRETIONARY SPENDING POWER POTENTIAL UP 125% SINCE 1950 COULD GROW ANOTHER 90% BY 1973

An important factor in changing and expanding our standard of living is the rapid growth in *discretionary spending power* of our population resulting from our increased productivity per capita. See Figure 3.

This chart shows that discretionary spending power based on a 1950 standard of living concept grew 125% between 1950 and 1962. It could grow another 90% over 1962 to an impressive total of about $370 billion by 1973 if we reach our minimum production opportunity of $870 billion and succeed in keeping consumer prices reasonably near the present range with an index around 106. There is a likelihood of a 45% growth in discretionary spending power in the next five years—by 1968.

Discretionary spending power is defined here as the surplus spending power over and above what would be required to supply the same per capita standard of living for the basic necessities of food, clothing, and shelter as equivalent to the *1950* actual standard of living after taking into account present prices. The discretionary spending power just since 1950 has increased from 42% of total disposable income after taxes to 51% in 1962, and by 1973 its share of the greatly increased income could grow to 62%!

That means that families moving up to better income groups could take on the greater physical consumption of many products, for example, that was found prewar in similar income groups if they desired. They could upgrade their diets and health and their homes as well as their cultural interests and leisure-time activities. But these desires will have to be encouraged and activated by the educational forces of selling and advertising to overcome the "habit lag" or inherent inertia and resistance to change or improvement.

FAMILY REAL INCOME EXPANDING—
REVOLUTIONARY CHANGE IN TEN
YEARS 1950–1960

In the ten years, 1950 to 1960, the number of families in the United States with *real* in-

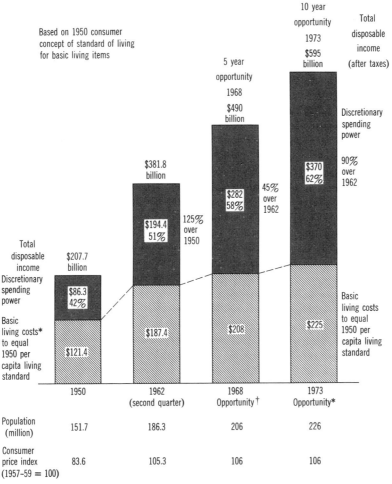

	1950	1962 (second quarter)	1968 Opportunity †	1973 Opportunity*
Population (million)	151.7	186.3	206	226
Consumer price index (1957–59 = 100)	83.6	105.3	106	106

*Basic living costs of food, clothing, shelter

†Based on production potential of $700 billion in 1968 and $870 billion in 1973

Figure 3   Discretionary spending power growth 125% in 1950–1962. Opportunity for 90% further growth in 10 years in United States. Source: J. Walter Thompson Company.

comes over $10,000 increased 167%. This is in terms of constant 1960 dollars. In other words, by 1960 there were two-and-two-thirds times as many families (of two or more persons) with a real purchasing power of over $10,000 annually as existed ten years before. See Figure 4.

The number of families with a real purchasing power between $7,000 and $10,000 jumped 107%! Thus the number over $7,000 jumped to 2½ times the number in 1950 (15.5 million families in 1960 versus 6.8 million in 1950).

The total of families with over $5,000 of real purchasing power (in terms of income in constant 1960 dollars with inflation removed) nearly doubled from 14.4 million or 36% of the total in 1950 to 26.4 million or 58% of the total in 1960; while those with under $5,000 real

income dropped from 23.5 million to 19.0 million—a decline of 25% in numbers.

The median average real income per family grew 37% from $4,093 in 1950 (in 1960 dollars) to $5,620 in 1960. Without correction for inflation the median family income grew 70% from $3,319 in 1950, and the number of families with incomes over $5,000 jumped from 10.2 million in 1950 to 26.4 million in 1960. This movement upward in family income groups is expected to continue as productivity increases, resulting in a rapid expansion in potential purchasing power.

The National Industrial Conference Board has projected the number of families with over $10,000 annual incomes (in constant 1960 dollars) as increasing from the 2½ million in 1950 and 6½ million in 1960 to over 16 million in

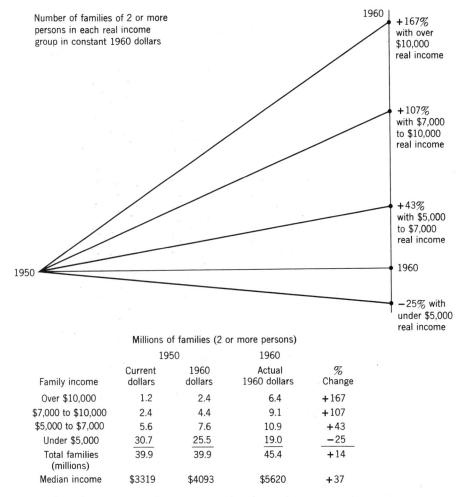

Millions of families (2 or more persons)

Family income	1950		1960	% Change
	Current dollars	1960 dollars	Actual 1960 dollars	
Over $10,000	1.2	2.4	6.4	+167
$7,000 to $10,000	2.4	4.4	9.1	+107
$5,000 to $7,000	5.6	7.6	10.9	+43
Under $5,000	30.7	25.5	19.0	−25
Total families (millions)	39.9	39.9	45.4	+14
Median income	$3319	$4093	$5620	+37

Figure 4   Family real income expanding. Revolutionary change in 10 years 1950–1960. Source: Bureau of the Census Series, p. 60, No. 37, January 17, 1962, J. Walter Thompson Company.

1970. This means that before the decade ends about three-fifths of all buying will be accounted for by families earning over $10,000 a year.

This movement upward in income groups can be expected to have an important impact on investment potentials as well as on other areas of the standard of living.

The 1962 Census of Shareholders In America by the New York Stock Exchange indicated, for example, that 24% of the individuals with incomes above $10,000 were shareholders compared with 12½% of the $7,500–$10,000 group, 8% of the $5,000–$7,500 group, and only 4% of those under $5,000. In the small group above $25,000 the share ownership was 45%.

With the possibility of the average total personal income per household in the United States reaching over $10,300 when our production level reaches $870 billion ten years from now, the climb upward in income groups will continue to expand the opportunities for upgrading the standard of living by consumers and expansion of interest in stock ownership and investment.

AVERAGE FAMILY INCOME SHOULD GROW TO OVER $10,300 BY 1973

$870 billion of production by 1973 should provide about $690 billion of personal income for consumers—an average of $10,300 per household for the 67 million households we are expected to have in 1973. This average income per family would be about 27% above the average of $8,100 in 1962.

The following table shows how our increased productivity could expand personal income and purchasing power over the next decade.

RAPID RISE IN EDUCATION LEVEL POINTS TO NEW LIVING STANDARDS

Another rapidly changing characteristic of our population that points to new ways of life and upgraded living standards is that of education level. By July 1961 the number of adults (over 20) with a full high school education was 5½ times as great as in 1930 and 126% greater even than in 1940. This adult population, containing about 52½ million high school graduates in 1961, contrasted with an adult population of 23 million graduates in 1940 or a population of about 4½ million graduates shortly after World War I, in 1920. See Figure 5.

This indicated that, by 1961, we had quite a different population in terms of education than we had prewar and that this change could have a significant influence on living and reading habits and on "social mobility" of the population. It could offer favorable opportunities for expansion of consumption of items that fit into an upgraded standard of living in terms of quality, convenience, variety, and cultural tastes.

The rapid change in educational composition of our population will continue. In ten years the probable 71 million high school graduates in our adult population will represent about 55% of the total persons 20 years and over. That is a numerical increase of 35% over 1961 while the adult population grows 13%. Total college graduates increased from 3.9 million in 1940 to 8.4 million in 1961, and in the next ten years they should total 11.2 million—or nearly three times the number in 1940.

By 1972 we can expect a 32% increase in school enrollments—a 20% increase in the elementary schools, a 41% increase in the high

In Current Dollars (not corrected for inflation between 1940 and 1962)	Total Production (Billions)	Personal Income (Billions)	Households (Thousands)	Average Income Per Household (Before Taxes)
1940	$100.6	$ 78.7	34,949	$ 2,250
1950	284.6	228.5	43,554	5,250
1962 (2nd Quarter)	552.0	439.5	54,200	8,100
Opportunity (in terms of June 1962 prices)				
1963–64	$585.0	$470.0	56,000	$ 8,400
1968 (in 5 years)	700.0	565.0	61,000	9,250
1973 (in 10 years)	870.0	690.0	67,000	10,300

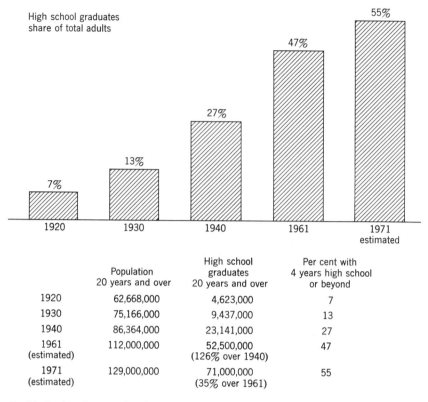

	Population 20 years and over	High school graduates 20 years and over	Per cent with 4 years high school or beyond
1920	62,668,000	4,623,000	7
1930	75,166,000	9,437,000	13
1940	86,364,000	23,141,000	27
1961 (estimated)	112,000,000	52,500,000 (126% over 1940)	47
1971 (estimated)	129,000,000	71,000,000 (35% over 1961)	55

Figure 5   Rapid rise in education level; 126% increase since 1940 in number of high school graduates in United States adult population; 35% additional increase by 1971. Source: J. Walter Thompson Company.

schools and more than twice as many in colleges (105% increase). See Figure 6.

This rapid improvement in education level will help to accelerate the movement upward in income groups in the next decade. The Census Bureau analysis of income in 1961 related to education indicated that education is an important factor in America's increased productive ability—since, by and large, income received must bear some relationship to one's contribution in total production. On the average a man's income in 1961 stepped up with each step up in level of education. See Figure 7.

For example, men with four years of high school enjoyed median incomes about 2½ times as large as those with less than eight years of elementary school. And where the man had received four years of college training his income averaged 44% above the high school graduate.

With the very rapid movement of our population into education levels of high school graduates and above, we should anticipate even more rapid increases in productive ability

and income and in the urge to upgrade the standard of living and social concepts and goals. Likewise, this rise in education level can prove a real impact in investments. Some 61% of college graduates were shareholders in 1962 compared with 16% of those with four years of high school and 5% of those with three years or less of high school.

The changing character of our population is shown by the changing pattern of living and expenditures for personal consumption.

CHANGING PATTERN OF LIVING IN THE UNITED STATES

Even though the present consumption standards in the United States are high relative to many other areas of the world there is increasing recognition that they could be vastly upgraded for the mass of the population without being excessively luxurious—and that expansion of this latent demand can stimulate the increased productivity for profitable expansion of production.

A change toward better family living and home life is reflected in the trend of consumer expenditures in the United States since 1947. Total personal consumption expenditures increased 105% between 1947 and 1961, but those items having to do with family living and health and personal care have gone up since 1947 considerably more than average. See Figure 8.

Sales of drug preparations, for example, grew to over three times the 1947 level. Hospital expenditures, life insurance, medical and hospitalization insurance grew rapidly. Expenditures for dental care, physicians, personal care, and toilet articles and preparations all increased more than the total standard of living as measured by personal consumption expenditures.

Consumer expenditures for foreign travel in 1961 were nearly four times as great as in 1947. Expenditures for home use of gas, electricity and telephone, and for owner-occupied housing increased more than threefold. User-operated transportation expenditures were three times greater.

Education expenditures as a part of the improved living standards grew to a level over 3½ times as great, along with a rapid expansion of expenditures for TV, radio, records, musical instruments and reading.

Higher living standards also were reflected in the resurgence of religious worship and

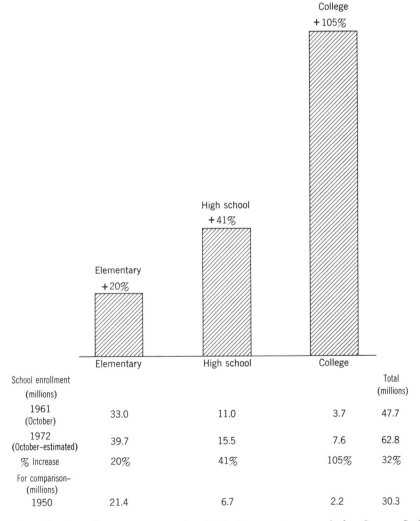

School enrollment (millions)	Elementary	High school	College	Total (millions)
1961 (October)	33.0	11.0	3.7	47.7
1972 (October–estimated)	39.7	15.5	7.6	62.8
% Increase	20%	41%	105%	32%
For comparison– (millions)				
1950	21.4	6.7	2.2	30.3

Figure 6 How school enrollment may grow by 1972. Source: Bureau of the Census Series, p. 25, No. 232, June 22, 1961, and p. 20, No. 117, July 11, 1962, J. Walter Thompson Company.

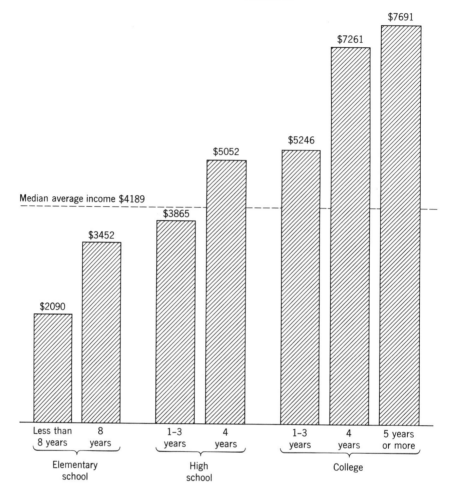

Figure 7   How education expands income: 1961 median average income—males over 14 by years of school completed. Source: Bureau of the Census Series, p. 60, No. 38, August 28, 1962, J. Walter Thompson Company.

church membership as shown by a jump of 54% in church membership between 1947 and 1961 —twice as fast as the 27% population growth. In the same period consumer expenditures for religious and welfare activities expanded 145% or to a level nearly 2½ times as great as in 1947.

Leisure time available for home and travel and recreation activities has more than doubled in thirteen years. Total weeks of vacation of workers jumped from 34.4 million weeks in 1946 to 77.7 million weeks in 1959. It is estimated that over 85% of vacations now are with pay. With the increase in leisure time the total visitors to areas administered by the National Park Service tripled, from 21.8 million in 1946 to 62.6 million in 1959.

A significant difference in interests in sports is evident as people move up in income and standard of living concepts. Consumer expenditures for spectator sports admissions increased only 26% between 1947 and 1961. That was far below the 105% growth in total personal consumption expenditures. On the other hand, consumer expenditures for participant sports and activities increased 150%—well above the 105% growth in total personal consumption expenditures and nearly six times as rapidly as spectator sports.

"THE BABY BOOM" SINCE 1940

The "baby boom" since 1940 in the United States has been of such proportions that it will have a pronounced effect on sales potentials and population characteristics over the next ten to fifteen years. See Figure 9.

The number of births in the United States

has continued at a level far above earlier predictions by population experts. The total births may reach 4½ million in 1963–64 compared with about 2½ million in 1940. This is changing the composition of families and the age distribution of the United States population.

Add 22 years to the dates shown in Figure 9 and it is easy to follow the rapid increase to be expected from 1962 on, in the number of young people reaching the family-formation age and the working-force level.

Our population has grown by over 34 million in the last 12 years from 151.7 million in 1950 (April) to over 186 million in 1962 (including Alaska and Hawaii in both periods). It is expected to reach 226 million by the middle of 1973. This is the equivalent of add-

ing a Metropolitan Market the size of Detroit or Boston every year over the next decade—a yearly growth in population averaging above 3½ million.

IN TEN YEARS—A 47% INCREASE IN FAMILIES WITH TWO OR MORE CHILDREN

The trend to families with two or more children at home has been pronounced. In the ten years between 1951 and 1961 the number of families with two or more of their own children at home increased 47% while total families increased only 15%. Thus families with two or more children have increased three times as fast as the total growth in families.

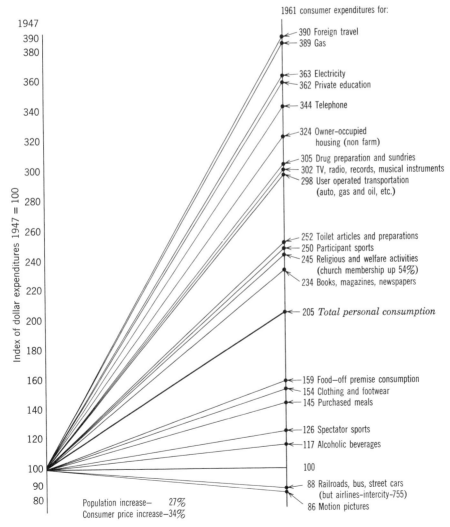

Figure 8   Changes in consumer expenditures since 1947 reflect changing home life. Source: Office of Business Economics, U.S. Dept. of Commerce, July 1962, J. Walter Thompson Company.

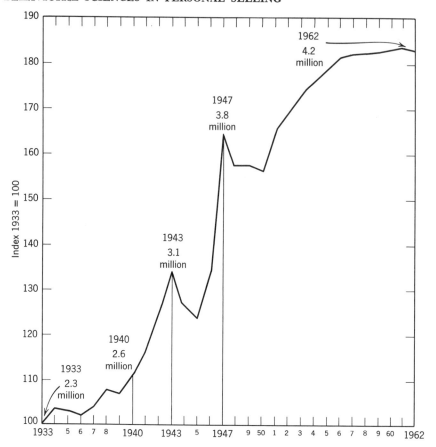

Figure 9   The baby boom since 1940. Source: J. Walter Thompson Company.

For many years American families de-creased in size. Now there are indications that this trend is reversing because of the greater number of children per family.

Now some 61% of all families of two or more related persons have related children under 18 in the home. This is an important factor influencing the family's market for food, for housing and household appliances and services, and many other items. In particular, it is put-ting increased pressure on housing since many of the homes in existence have only one bath or too few bedrooms. And it greatly increases the family need for hospital and medical pro-tection as well as for recreation opportuni-ties.

SIGNIFICANT SHIFT IN AGE GROUPS COMING

As of July 1962 it was estimated that there were 86% more children under 10 years of age in our population than in 1940. See Figure 10.

This huge increase in the number of children soon will cause public outcry against inade-quate school facilities and shortage of teachers, as well as juvenile delinquency. It will affect housing requirements, food consumption, rec-reation, and many phases of family living. During the next five years, by 1968 and be-yond, there will be a huge movement of chil-dren into the adolescent age groups where food consumption is high and where interest in many products starts. See Table 1.

The 22-year period from 1940 to 1962 was characterized by the rapid increase in popula-tion of the two extremes of age groups—the very young under 10, and those over 60. There was an actual decrease of −2% in the number of young adults in the prime family-formation age group of 20–29.

The *next decade will be different*. It will be characterized by a rapid increase in the family-formation age group 20 to 29, and adolescents 10 to 19, and a −10% decline in the middle executive group 30 to 39.

Age Group	Past 22 Years 1940–1962 % Change	Next 10 Years 1962–1972 % Change
Under 10	+86	+28
10–19	+31	+30
20–29	− 2	+43
30–39	+26	−10
40–59	+39	+ 9
60 and over	+76	+23
Total	+40	+20

The increase in births may continue at levels above our previous history because a Census study (Bureau of the Census—Series P-20, No. 108—July 12, 1961) has indicated increasing fertility—particularly a rapid increase in the number of children being born to women in the age groups under 35.

This is of significance when combined with the fact that in the next ten years the fastest-growing segment of the population will be the 20–24 age group—a 57% increase between 1962 and 1972.

Age of Women	Average Number of Children Ever Born Per Woman—by Age Groups		
	1940	1959	% Increase
20–24	0.52	1.08	108
25–29	1.13	2.04	81
30–34	1.68	2.45	46

Past 22 years 1940-1962

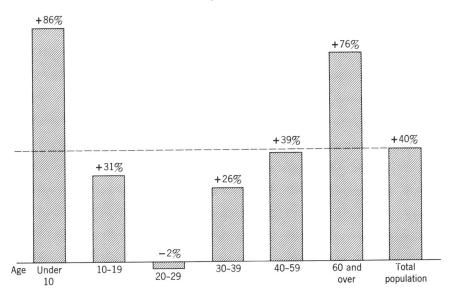

Next 10 years 1962-1972

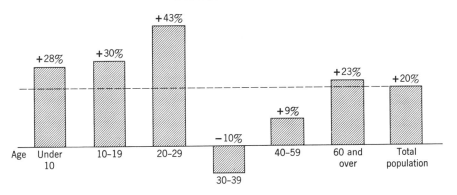

Figure 10   Changing United States age pattern. Source: J. Walter Thompson Company.

Table 1.   Changing U.S. Age Pattern—1940–1972

| | Distribution of U.S. Population by Age (Millions) | | | | |
| | | | | | % Increase | |
	1940	1950	1962 (Estimated)	1972 (Estimated)	1940–1962	1962–1972
Under 5*	11.4	17.1	21.5	27.5	89	28
5–9	10.7	13.3	19.5	25.0	82	28
Total Under 10	22.1	30.4	41.0	52.5	86	28
10–14	11.8	11.1	17.6	21.7	49	23
15–19	12.3	10.7	14.0	19.5	14	39
Total 10–19	24.1	21.8	31.6	41.2	31	30
20–24	11.6	11.6	11.2	17.6	−3	57
25–29	11.1	12.3	11.1	14.2	—	28
Total 20–29	22.7	23.9	22.3	31.8	−2	43
30–34	10.2	11.6	12.2	11.3	20	−7
35–39	9.6	11.3	12.8	11.1	33	−13
Total 30–39	19.8	22.9	25.0	22.4	26	−10
40–44	8.8	10.3	11.9	11.9	35	—
45–49	8.2	9.1	11.2	12.2	37	9
50–54	7.2	8.3	10.0	11.1	39	11
55–59	5.9	7.3	8.7	10.3	47	18
Total 40–59	30.1	35.0	41.8	45.5	39	9
60–64	4.8	6.1	7.2	8.8	50	22
65–69	3.7	5.0	6.4	7.6	73	19
70–74	2.6	3.4	4.8	5.7	85	19
75 and over	2.6	3.9	5.7	7.5	119	32
Total 60 and over	13.7	18.4	24.1	29.6	76	23
Grand Total *	132.5	152.4	185.8	223.0	40	20

* Adjusted for Census under-enumeration of children under 5 years.
Figures relate to July 1. Population includes Armed Forces abroad. 1962 projected from 1960 Census. 1972 projected from Census estimates for 1970.

The percentage of white women having a child within 12 months after the first marriage has increased rapidly:

When First Married:
1930–1934   24% had child within 12 months
1950–1954   35% had child within 12 months
1955–1959   44% had child within 12 months

Married women in the last few years have represented the major part of the addition to the labor force in the United States. Although the presence of children formerly kept many women from entering or re-entering the labor force this now seems to be much less of a deterrent. In 1959, for example, as compared with 1950 there was a 57% increase in the number of children ever born per 1,000 women 15 to 44 years old in the labor force compared with a 24% increase in the rate of childbirth among women not in the labor force. The rapid increase in the number of women in the labor force and the increased fertility of this group could be of considerable significance to industry.

MOBILITY OF OUR POPULATION

The coming trend to young adults will probably emphasize another characteristic of our population by increasing the already high mobility of the U.S. population—particularly among the younger half of our married couples.

Within any five-year period the equivalent of our entire civilian population over the age of one year changes place of residence. In the year March 1960 to March 1961, for example, the number moving totaled 36½ million or 21% of the 177 million civilian population over the

age of one year. The greatest mobility was among young adults of 20–24 years—46% of these moved place of residence within the year. All of the group from 18 to 34 were well above average in shifting. See Figure 11.

The new homemakers, young married females, were far above average in changing place of residence. 56% of these housewives between 18 to 24, and 25% of the ones between 25 to 34, moved during the year. This group of the young-married who were under 35 years old represented about 37% of all married females between 18 to 64 in 1961. With the large increase to be expected soon in the number of young homemakers this mobility will become an increasingly important marketing factor.

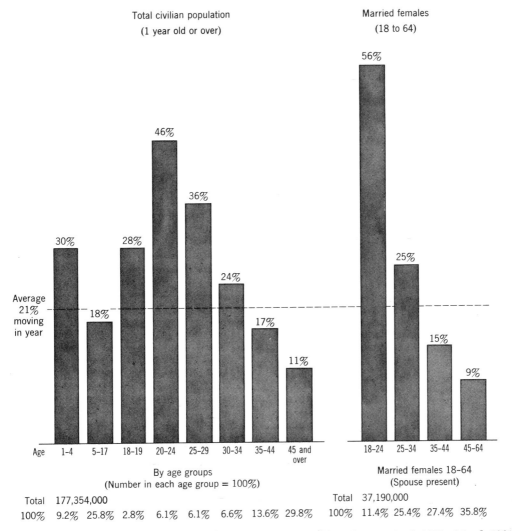

Figure 11 Mobility of our population: per cent moving to different house, March 1960—March 1961.
Source: Bureau of the Census Series, p. 20, No. 118, August 9, 1962, J. Walter Thompson Company.

POPULATION SHIFT TO THE SUBURBS—
DROP IN FARM POPULATION—RAPID
GROWTH OF NON-WHITE POPULATION
IN CENTRAL CITIES

Between 1950 and 1960 population in the suburban portion of 199 Metropolitan Areas grew 61% while the central cities grew only 1% and the rest of the United States, outside of the 199 Metropolitan Areas, increased 7%. The farm population declined 20%. See Figure 12.

Farm population dropped from 30.5 million or 23.1% of the total in 1940 to 25.1 million or 16.6% in 1950, and on April 1, 1960, at an estimated 20 million, the farm population was approximately 11% of the total population of 180 million. This was on the old Census definition of a farm. Under the new 1960 Census definition rural farm population totaled only 15.7 million or less than 9% of the total U.S. population. However, with productivity per man hour increasing much more rapidly on

the farm than in industry, the average purchasing power of the remaining farm families is growing substantially—a selective market not to be ignored.

The full impact of the shift to the suburbs in the last ten years was obscured by the official reports of the 1960 Census in tables showing the breakdown of population within Standard Metropolitan Statistical Areas between central city population and population of the area outside central cities. These reports did not take into account areas annexed to central cities between 1950 and 1960. The reported increase in population for many of the central cities was far too large since the growth was by annexation of territory which, in 1950, had been classed as outside the central city—in most cases essentially "suburban" in character. A total of 4.9 million of the population growth of central cities was by annexation.

When corrected to the same corporate limits or minor civil divisions as in 1950, the 1960

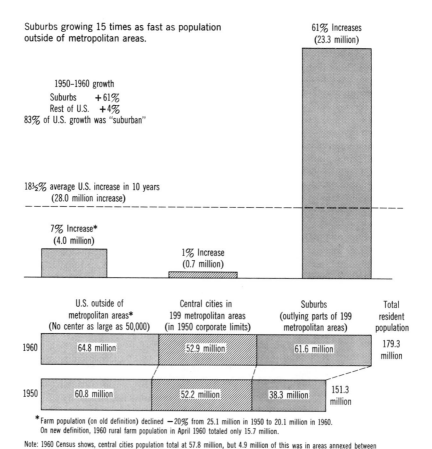

Figure 12   Population shift to suburbs reflects changing living standards. Source: J. Walter Thompson Company.

Census showed increases in the Metropolitan Areas outside the central cities far greater than had been generally realized—and a correspondingly greater drop in population in the old central cities.

83% of the total U.S. growth in population between 1950 and 1960 was in the suburban parts of Metropolitan Areas outside the corporate limits of central cities as defined in 1950. The "suburbs" grew 61% while the entire rest of the U.S. grew only 4%—a suburban growth 15 times as rapid as in the rest of the United States.

A significant feature of the population shift to the suburbs has been the changed character of the population of the central cities. There has been a rapid movement of rural population of marginal income to the urban centers and into industrial and non-farm jobs where the resulting income increase has greatly improved this population as a market. This trend has been particularly significant in the rapid growth of the non-white population in central cities.

The Bureau of the Census released a study of the great "Supermetropolis" forming in the Eastern United States (release CB-61-100 August 13, 1961). This supermetropolitan area of 31.5 million inhabitants consists of 32 contiguous Standard Metropolitan Statistical Areas stretching through 10 Northeastern and Middle Atlantic States from New Hampshire to Virginia.

In the 40 central cities of this "supermetropolis" the non-white population increased 50% between 1950 and 1960 to an average of 22% of the total population. In the same period the white population decreased −10%.

In the suburban areas outside the central cities the white population increased 44% while the non-white population grew 49% (from a much smaller base in 1950).

Examples of the rapidly growing non-white market in central cities were New Haven 131% increase in non-white versus −16% decrease in white; Bridgeport 127% increase in non-white versus −7% decrease in white; Hartford 97% increase in non-white versus −17% decrease in white; Newark 84% increase in non-white versus −27% decrease in white; and Trenton 78% increase in non-white versus −22% decrease in white population.

With a population shifting as rapidly as this, the importance of advertised brands, quickly identified by their packaging or symbols, is obvious. The newcomers' ability to find the familiar and preferred brand at once in the new supermarket or shopping center outlet smooths the process of distribution.

REVOLUTION IN DISTRIBUTION—SHIFT TO SELF-SERVICE SUPERMARKETS AND SHOPPING CENTERS

Along with the climb in incomes, the shift to the suburbs, and the growth of shopping centers since 1950, there has been a revolutionary change in distribution to match the changing population. Rapid growth of discount merchandising and of self-service in supermarkets, drug stores, and other outlets is increasing the importance of advertised products with well-developed consumer preference. As an example of the revolution in distribution consider the changes in grocery-store distribution in the last ten years.

30,000 supermarkets in 1961, with total sales of $38.2 billion, had an $8 billion greater total volume of business than all the 394,000 grocery stores in existence in 1951—only ten years earlier.

Representing only 12% of the stores today, the supermarkets have 70% of the volume of sales. An additional group of 55,000 superettes, representing 22% of the stores, account for 22% of the volume so that two classes of stores that are almost entirely self-service—supermarkets and superettes—with only 34% of the stores, handle 92% of the grocery volume. The total number of grocery stores dropped from 394,000 in 1951 to 249,000 in 1961, but total grocery store retail sales volume increased from $30.4 billion to $54.5 billion.

SELLING WILL ASSUME A MORE IMPORTANT ROLE IN OUR ECONOMY

The coming changes in our labor force and productivity, accompanied by economic and social changes in the next ten years, will make the role of selling and advertising assume increasing importance in our economy. To provide the markets necessary for an adequate level of employment will require a consumption-oriented economy with a substantial upgrading of the over-all standard of living.

Selling and advertising must receive increased recognition as an educational and stimulating force needed to overcome the "habit-lag," to change latent needs into insistent demand, and to build awareness of needs that are inherent in a better standard of living.

It has been characteristic of our American economy that many of the "luxuries" of one period become "necessities" as concepts of living advance. Now it has become almost impossible to define "necessities" or "needs" since our current standards for even the so-called basic "necessities" of food, clothing, and shelter are so far above bare subsistence. The further expansion of our economy, and standard of living, therefore, depends increasingly on the development of the latent needs or "wants." Wants can be created as we become educated to new concepts and goals and these created wants become expanded markets for goods and services as our increased productivity provides the purchasing power.

Supplying the 20 million new non-agricultural jobs in the next ten years, which we must have to satisfy the probable demands of our labor force of 1973, and to increase our total sales level to consumers by some $200 billion, will require both an expansion of selling efforts and rapid progress in increasing and measuring the effectiveness of selling.

Anthropology's Contributions to Marketing

CHARLES WINICK

Of the social sciences which deal with man and society, only economics, psychology, and sociology have been widely used in marketing. Economics is at the core of much of the content of marketing; psychology has yielded a variety of interviewing and projective testing procedures; sociology has contributed concepts like social class.

Marketers have been relatively slow in using anthropological insights and approaches, even though anthropology is also concerned with man and society. This article considers why anthropology has been used relatively seldom, and how it has been and might be employed.

The relative slowness of anthropologists and marketers in finding common ground is surprising.[1] Anthropologists have served as colonial administrators, in foreign-aid programs, and in other situations requiring a special sensitivity to foreign cultures. They have also developed sales-training procedures which involve the analysis of the rate of speech of salesmen with potential customers, through devices which measure the rate of interaction between people talking.[2] Another specialized industrial situation in which anthropologists have worked involves the application of their knowledge of the field of anthropometry or measurement of the body, in the design of products like chairs and knobs.[3]

Other anthropologists have worked in applied fields such as: reactions to disaster, the operation of internment and relocation centers, mental health, medical care, labor-management

relations,[4] the culture of a factory,[5] community organization, social work,[6] military government, the cultural change associated with economic development,[7] contact between cultures, the nature of small-town life, behavior in extreme situations, the study of culture at a distance,[8] the reconstruction of the themes of a culture, relations among minority groups, the social structure of a hospital,[9] American national character,[10] and television.[11]

Although anthropologists have published their findings on America in very accessible formats,[12] there has been little discussion of

◆ SOURCE: Reprinted by permission from *Journal of Marketing* (National Quarterly Publication of the American Marketing Association), Vol. 25, No. 5, July 1961, pp. 53–60.

[1] John Gillin, "The Application of Anthropological Knowledge to Modern Mass Society," *Human Organization,* Vol. 15 (Winter, 1957), pp. 24–30.
[2] Eliot D. Chapple, "The Interaction Chronograph," *Personnel,* Vol. 25 (January, 1949), pp. 295–307.
[3] Earnest A. Hooton, *A Survey in Seating* (Cambridge: Harvard Department of Anthropology, 1945).
[4] Charles R. Walker, *The Man on the Assembly Line* (Cambridge: Harvard University Press, 1952).
[5] Eliot Jaques, *The Changing Culture of a Factory* (New York: Dryden Press, 1953).
[6] Franklin K. Patterson, Irving Lukoff, and Charles Winick, "Is Society the Patient," *Journal of Educational Sociology,* Vol. 30 (October, 1956), pp. 106–112.
[7] Almost every issue of *Economic Development and Cultural Change* carries relevant articles.
[8] Margaret Mead and Rhoda Metraux, *The Study of Culture at a Distance* (Chicago: University of Chicago Press, 1952).
[9] Charles Winick, "The Hospital as a Social System," *New York State Nurse,* Vol. 26 (January, 1954), pp. 9–13.
[10] David M. Potter, *People of Plenty* (Chicago: University of Chicago Press, 1954).
[11] Charles Winick, *Taste and the Censor in Television* (New York: Fund For the Republic, 1959).
[12] Margaret Lantis, editor, "The U.S.A. As Anthro-

how their findings could be applied to marketing problems.[13] One advertising publication has published an article on the possibility of using anthropology in advertising.[14] The journal of applied anthropology, formerly called *Applied Anthropology* and now called *Human Organization,* almost never carries any material on marketing; and the national journal, *American Anthropologist,* also ignores the subject.

ANTHROPOLOGY, SOCIOLOGY, AND PSYCHOLOGY

Anthropology is usually defined as the study of man. Such a definition is so all-inclusive that the field is generally divided into four subfields: archeology, cultural anthropology, linguistics, and physical anthropology. Archeology is concerned with the historical reconstruction of cultures which no longer exist. Cultural anthropology examines all the behaviors of man which have been learned, including social, linguistic, technical, and familiar behaviors; often it is defined as the study of man and his works. Linguistics is the comparative study of the structure, interrelationships, and development of languages. Physical anthropology is concerned with human biology and the development of the human organism, with special interest in race differences.

When anthropology is employed in marketing, it is usually cultural anthropology which is relevant. Cultural anthropology began with the study of primitive cultures, and its comparative analyses documented the different ways in which cultures have solved their problems of living.

Cultural anthropology has much in common with psychology and sociology. All three are concerned with the examination of man in his cultural setting. They differ in the emphases which they place on different elements of the relationship between a person and his environment. It can be said that all human behavior essentially is a function of the interrelations of personality, the social system, and culture.

Oversimplifying, psychology is concerned with personality, sociology addresses itself to the social system, and anthropology explores the culture. The interdisciplinary field of social psychology may draw on all three of these fields, and there are integrated social psychology texts which do so.[15]

A sharper focus on the differences among these three social sciences may be obtained by speculating on how each of the three might look at a family.

The psychologist would be interested in the personal adjustment and emotional health of each member of the family. He would want to examine their attitudes, mutual perceptions, and motivational systems. Their happiness or lack of it would interest him.

The sociologist would be concerned primarily with the dimensions of role and status within the family and with the number of different kinds of families. He would examine how the social structure created various kinds of internal arrangements which made it possible for the family to exist. He would be interested in the norms of behavior and the stresses and strains shown by the deviations from the norm and resulting from role conflict. He would study class membership as well as the rates of various kinds of behavior, such as the birth rate.

The cultural anthropologist would examine the technological level which the culture had reached and the interrelations of technology with culture. He would scrutinize the procedures for inheritance of property and how kinship was reckoned and described, and how the spouses got to know each other. He would study the family's food and housing. He would be interested in the language level and dialects and in who talked to whom. He would be concerned with how the age of different members of the family affected their behavior, and with trends in illnesses. He would study how the culture "rubbed off" on the family unit. The anthropologist thus does not have information which it would be impossible for the sociologist or psychologist to obtain, but he has a special sensitivity to certain facets of social life.

The sociologist and psychologist bring a powerful and varied arsenal of concepts and approaches to the study of social life. In what

pologists See It," *American Anthropologist,* Vol. 57 (December, 1955), pp. 1113–1380.
[13] Richard C. Sheldon, "How the Anthropologist Can Help the Marketing Practitioner" in W. David Robbins, editor, *Successful Marketing at Home and Abroad* (Chicago: American Marketing Association, 1958), pp. 209–304.
[14] Alan S. Marcus, "How Agencies Can Use Anthropology in Advertising," *Advertising Agency,* Vol. 49 (September 14, 1956), pp. 87–91.

[15] Steuart Henderson Britt, *Social Psychology of Modern Life* (New York: Rinehart & Company, 1949 revised edition); S. Stanfeld Sargent and Robert C. Williamson, *Social Psychology* (New York: The Ronald Press Company, 1958).

ways is the anthropologist able to contribute insights and experience toward the science of "marketology," and to what extent may they not be immediately accessible, for example, to the sociologist?[16] The anthropologist is especially trained to have empathy with groups other than his own and to "tune in" on their patterns of culture. Inasmuch as his training has exposed him to a wide variety of cultures, he can take a global view of a situation and see it in the context of a larger background. His training makes him sensitive to cross-cultural differences which may be of crucial importance in many different situations, because his entire training is geared toward awareness of such differences.

Anthropology has less of the factionalism which characterizes psychology and sociology. This is not to suggest that all is serene in anthropology or that it has never been troubled by theoretical or methodological issues. However, even though anthropologists may disagree on something like the exact value of the contribution of a particular anthropologist, they would generally agree on what the cultural anthropologist looks for, and there are standardized check lists on how to view a culture.[17] In contrast, a psychologist's allegiance to the Gestalt, behaviorist, psychoanalytic, learning-theory, or perception schools is likely to influence what he does with a given problem. A sociologist's commitment to the structure-function, historical, ecological, "middle range," environmental-determinism, or demographic schools would largely determine the emphases of his approach to a problem. Since such divergent schools are less likely to exist in cultural anthropology, it is probable that anthropological guidance on a given marketing problem would be relatively consistent.

WHAT THE ANTHROPOLOGIST KNOWS

The anthropologist is specifically trained to study national character, or the differences which distinguish our national group from another. He should be able to provide measures for distinguishing the subtle differences among

a Swede, a Dane, and a Norwegian; or between a Frenchman and an Englishman; or a Brazilian and an Argentinian; or between a typical resident of Montreal and one of Toronto. The anthropologist is also a specialist in the study of subcultures. He would be able, in a city like New York, to differentiate the patterns of living of such disparate but rapidly homogenizing groups as Puerto Ricans, Negroes, Italo-Americans, Jews, Polish-Americans, and Irish-Americans.

Because almost any large community consists of a variety of subcultures, this awareness of subcultural trends can be especially useful. A more subtle area of special interest to anthropologists is the silent language of gesture, posture, food and drink preferences, and other nonverbal cues to behavior.[18]

Related to this is the anthropologist's professional interest in languages and symbols. He might, for example, be especially concerned about why a particular shape has special significance as a symbol in a society, or how the structure of a language or a regional speech pattern was related to how people think.[19]

Another area of concern to the anthropologist, because of its symbolic meanings has to do with "rites de passage" or the central points in a person's life at which he may ritually be helped to go from one status to another, for example, birth, puberty, or marriage.[20]

Taboos represent a continuing area of interest to the anthropologist.[21] Every culture has taboos or prohibitions about various things, such as the use of a given color, or of a given phrase or symbol. The anthropologist is aware of the larger values of a culture, which represent the substratum of custom which is taken for granted and the violation of which represents a taboo.

The anthropologist's method is primarily the exposure of his highly developed sensitivity to the area in which he is working, via observation and extended interviews with informants. Projective tests have also been widely used in anthropological studies. The anthropologist can

[16] Robert Bartels, "Sociologist and Marketologists," *Journal of Marketing,* Vol. 24 (October, 1959), pp. 37–40; Christen T. Jonassen, "Contributions of Sociology to Marketing," *Journal of Marketing,* Vol. 24 (October, 1959), pp. 29–35.
[17] Royal Anthropological Institute, *Notes and Queries on Anthropology* (London: The Institute, 1956).

[18] Edward T. Hall, *The Silent Language* (New York: Doubleday & Co., 1959).
[19] Benjamin Lee Whorf, *Collected Papers on Metalinguistics* (Washington: Department of State Foreign Service Institute, 1952).
[20] Jan Wit, *Rites De Passage* (Amsterdam: De Windroos, 1959).
[21] Franz Steiner, *Taboo* (London: Cohen and West, Ltd., 1957).

bring a wealth of insight to marketing situations.

USE OF ANTHROPOLOGY IN MARKETING

There are at least three kinds of situations in which the knowledge of the anthropologist has been employed in marketing: specific knowledge; awareness of themes of a culture; sensitivity to taboos.

Specific Knowledge

Here are a few cases in which the specific knowledge of an anthropologist was applied to marketing situations.

A manufacturer of central heating equipment was planning to introduce central heating to an area which previously had used other heating. Since people generally grow up to accept a certain approach to heating which they take for granted, introduction of the new central heating posed marketing problems in coping with deeply imbedded consumer resistance to what would be a major innovation. An anthropologist was able to draw on his knowledge of the folklore and symbolism of heat and fire in order to suggest methods of presenting the new system, so as to make it as consonant as possible with the connotations of heat, even though the nature of the heating method had changed radically. There was considerable consumer resistance to the central heating, but it decreased substantially after the first year.

In addition to a marketing problem, the introduction of central heating also posed problems of public policy which the manufacturer had to overcome before he could obtain approval for the introduction of the heating equipment. The area was one which suffered from a declining birth rate, and officials were concerned about the extent to which central heating might cause the birth rate to decline further, because of their belief that heated bedrooms would cause a decline in sexual activity and ultimately in births.

The anthropologist was able to point to some cultures in which the birth rate had declined and some in which it had not done so after the introduction of central heating. The anthropologist's data made it possible for the manufacturer of the central-heating equipment to discuss its probable effects realistically with the appropriate officials.

Another field in which the anthropologist has

specific knowledge that other social scientists are not likely to have is that of clothing and fashion. The only empirical study of the fashion cycle in woman's clothing which has successfully been used for predictive purposes by clothing manufacturers was conducted by anthropologists.[22] In marketing situations, the anthropologist has often been able to combine his special knowledge of the needs of the body for clothing of various kinds at different ages, his sensitivity to what technology makes possible and his awareness of fashion.

For example, an anthropologist was consulted by a leading manufacturer of overalls for young children, a product which had remained unchanged for decades. He examined the product in the light of the special needs of children who wear overalls, the growing use of washing machines to launder the overalls, their relative frequency of laundering, and contemporary technology. He suggested that the overall straps have a series of sets of metal grippers instead of buttons, thus making it possible to use different sets of grippers as the child grew instead of tying or knotting the straps. Noting that the straps often fall off the shoulders when children played, he suggested that the shirts which children wore under the overalls have either a loop for the straps to pass through or a synthetic fastener which faced matching material on the strap, so that the shoulder of the shirt could be pressed against the strap and remain attached to it until shoulder strap and shirt were pulled apart.

He also recommended that the seams of the overalls, previously single stitched, be double stitched like those of men's shirts, which have to withstand frequent launderings. The double-stitched overalls would be less likely to come apart as a result of frequent launderings in a washing machine. These recommendations were adopted, and within a few years substantially changed and expanded the nature of the overall market for young children. The children's parents were more pleased with the overalls because they lasted longer and looked better on the children, and they were far more functional than before.

The special knowledge of the anthropologist has been called into play where there are special subcultural groups to which the marketer wishes to address himself. One beer

[22] Jane Richardson and Alfred L. Kroeber, *Three Centuries of Women's Dress Fashions* (Berkeley: University of California Press, 1940).

manufacturer wished to extend his market share among Negroes in a large eastern city in the United States. He was advised about reaching this group by an anthropologist who was familiar with the special subculture of Negroes, and who pointed to the profound effects of Negroes' caste membership on their purchasing behavior. The ambiguity of their role has led many Negroes to be especially aware of articles that have status connotations and of whether a brand symbolizes racial progress. Examination of the manufacturer's marketing program by the anthropologist led to several recommendations for change. The manufacturer began to help in the support of several major social events related to the arts in Negro communities, and to stress that the beer was a national brand with quality-control procedures. He changed the content of his advertising in the direction of enhancing its status and quality connotations. These changes were all directed toward improving the status connotations of the beer to Negroes.

Guidance on related problems with respect to the Puerto Rican and Jewish markets has also been used constructively. Since 35 to 40 per cent of the population of the United States consists of minority subcultures, the anthropologist's contributions may be considerable.

Another situation had to do with the selection of specific symbols for various purposes. A major manufacturer of women's products was uncertain about whether to continue using the Fleur de Lis emblem on his package. Anthropological analysis of the symbol suggested that its association with French kings and other cultural connotations of maleness made it more masculine than feminine. The anthropologist's recommendations were confirmed by subsequent field testing.

In a related case, a manufacturer of women's cosmetics conducted an anthropological study of the comparative symbolism in our culture of women's eyes and mouth, which suggested that the eye tends to be experienced as a relatively protecting organ while the mouth tends to be experienced as more nurturing. This knowledge of the differences between the special meanings of eye and mouth could constructively be used in marketing the products, and especially in advertising. The advertising explicitly and implicitly mentioned the role of the eye in protection of the woman. It stressed the role of the mouth as the organ which both symbolically and literally gives love. This replaced the manufacturer's previous advertising, in which both eye and mouth were treated in the same way, as organs which could be made beautiful.

Awareness of Themes

The anthropologist has functioned in situations in which he can use his special understanding of themes of a culture, oftentimes taken for granted.

A major chain of candy shops was suffering a decline in sales. A marketing-research study had established that the brand was usually bought as a gift, either for others or as a gift for the purchaser. The chain was unable to develop any ways of using this finding that were not hackneyed. Anthropological guidance on the symbolism of gift-giving enabled the chain to develop merchandising, packaging, and advertising formats for the gift theme. Anthropological study of the connotations of the major holidays suggested themes for window displays, and advertising of the candy in conjunction with the holidays. The chain's marketing strategy was revised on the basis of the anthropological interpretation and clarification of the marketing-research study. Anthropologists are the only social scientists who have systematically studied gift-giving and gift-receiving.[23]

Another example of anthropological interpretation of a marketing-research study was provided by a shirt manufacturer. The study had established that women buy more than half of men's shirts in a particular price range. The anthropologist was able to interpret this finding in the light of several anthropological studies of the relations between husbands and wives in America. The manufacturer had been thinking of placing advertising for his men's shirts in selected women's magazines. The anthropologist was able to point to a number of studies of husband-wife relations which suggested growing resentment by men over the extent to which women had been borrowing and buying men's clothing, and which suggested that the proposed advertising campaign might not be propitious.

Another anthropologist's special sensitivity to the "rites de passage" helped a shoe manufacturer whose sales were declining because of aggressive foreign and domestic competition. The anthropologist was able to point to the

[23] Marcel Mauss, *The Gift* (London: Cohen & West, Ltd., 1954).

extent to which shoes represent major symbols of our going from one stage of life to another, and to assist the manufacturer in developing methods for using the relationship between shoes and "rites de passage." [24]

A landmark along the road of an infant becoming a child usually is found between the ages of 4 and 6 when he can tie his own shoelaces. The manufacturer developed some pamphlets and other instructional material for parents on how to help children to learn to tie their shoelaces. Distribution by local retailers contributed toward making parents favorably aware of the brand's line for children in this age group.

The teenager signalizes her entrance into a new social world by her first high heels. Window displays and advertising which explicitly stressed the new social activities of the teenager wearing her high heels, and naming specific shoe models after teenage social events ("The Prom") contributed toward associating the manufacturer's name with the excitement of the new world symbolized by the high heels.

Older people see the wearing of special "old people's shoes" as the ultimate reminder that they are becoming old. The manufacturer was able to redesign his line for older people so that it retained its special health features but still looked as stylish as any adult shoe, and had no visible stigma of "old people's shoes."

Sensitivity to Taboos

Marketers may unwittingly violate a taboo, whether cultural, religious, or political, especially in selling overseas. Blue, for example, is the color for mourning in Iran and is not likely to be favorably received on a commercial product. Green is the nationalist color of Egypt and Syria and is frowned on for use in packages. Showing pairs of anything on the Gold Coast of Africa is disapproved. White is the color of mourning in Japan and, therefore, not likely to be popular on a product. Brown and gray are disapproved colors in Nicaragua. Purple is generally disapproved in most Latin American markets because of its association with death. Feet are regarded as despicable in Thailand, where any object and package showing feet is likely to be unfavorably received.

The anthropologist can cast light on taboos

and on their opposite: favored colors and symbols. The reason for the people in a country or an area liking or not liking a particular color or symbol may be a function of political, nationalist, religious, cultural, or other reasons.

SOME APPLICATIONS IN CANADA

Canada represents a special opportunity for the application of anthropology in marketing situations. Twenty-nine per cent of the country's entire population is in French-speaking Quebec, and over half of this number know no English. Canada thus offers a changing kind of bilingual and culture contact situation with major cross-cultural differences for anthropological analysis.

Both the farm community and the industrial community of Quebec have been studied by anthropologists. [25] The re-evaluation of the nature of Quebec family and community life sparked by Dean Phillipe Garigue of the University of Montreal and a team at Laval University has led to renewed interest in Quebec on the part of anthropologists. Their studies have produced considerable information on styles of life in Quebec which should be translatable into marketing data on pricing policies, colors, package size, flavor and taste of various food items, texture of fabrics, automobile symbolism, product scents, and related subjects.

Specific Knowledge

Perhaps the most frequent occasion for the anthropologist to demonstrate specific knowledge in Canada has to do with language. One laundry-soap company had point-of-sale material on its soap describing it as extra strong and the best one to use on especially dirty parts of wash ("les parts de sale"). After sales of the soap had declined, an anthropologist who was called in by the company pointed out that the phrase is comparable to the American slang phrase "private parts." This kind of mistake might have been avoided if anthropological guidance had been available before sales declined.

Some products do not sell well in Quebec because the English name may be almost un-

---

[24] Charles Winick, "Status, Shoes, and the Life Cycle," *Boot and Shoe Recorder,* Vol. 156 (October 15, 1959), pp. 100–202.

[25] Horace Miner, *St. Denis* (Chicago: University of Chicago Press, 1939); Everett C. Hughes, *French Canada In Transition* (Chicago: University of Chicago Press, 1943).

pronounceable to a French speaker, or the name of the product may be meaningless even when translated idiomatically. Even the English spoken in Montreal differs somewhat from the English spoken in Toronto, creating potential hazards for the marketers who may not know, for example, that a "tap" in a "flat" in Toronto is likely to be a "faucet" in a Montreal "apartment."

Awareness of Themes

A study done by an anthropologist for a food manufacturer demonstrated the relationship between the purchases of certain food items and the gradual decline of the wood-burning stove which used to be a staple of Quebec farm kitchens. The wood stove would almost always have a stew pot ("pot au feu") simmering all day. Various ingredients were put into the pot to provide flavor. With the introduction of gas and electric kitchen ranges, it not only became relatively expensive to keep the stew pot going but the simmering could not be sustained because the pot would tend to boil rather than simmer.

This change was accompanied by some radical adjustments in food consumption which were of great relevance to food marketing. The manufacturer was able to begin distribution of canned soups and stews which soon found a very large market and rapidly replaced the "pot au feu."

Taboos

Alertness to taboos was illustrated by an anthropologist's suggestion to a manufacturer of canned fish for changing a series of advertisements which were appearing in Quebec magazines and newspapers. The same advertisement was run repeatedly. The advertisements showed a woman in shorts playing golf with her husband. The caption read that the woman would be able to be on the golf links all day and still prepare a delicious dinner that evening if she used the product. Every element in the advertisement represented a violation of some underlying theme of French Canadian life; the wife would not be likely to be playing golf with her husband, she would not wear shorts, and she would not be serving the particular kind of fish as a main course. In this case, the anthropologist was consulted *after* the series had been running for awhile.

THE MARKETER AS AN ANTHROPOLOGIST

A good case could be made for the thesis that marketing researchers do more anthropological research on modern cultures than do anthropologists. Marketing researchers are studying national character, subcultures, themes, and ways of life. The kind of information which marketing-research studies seek on how people live and what products they use represent first-rate material for the cultural anthropologist.

The questionnaire, panel, audit, sales analysis, and other methods of modern marketing differ in degree but not in kind from the trained observations of the anthropologist, but there is no reason why the two methods cannot complement each other. Greater communication between these two fields can and should lead to mutual enrichment of both.

CASES

Brown Milling Company

Brown Milling Company began operating in 1953. During the past twelve years, this company has grown from a meager existence into a very large, diversified milling company. Its main business is grinding and mixing feed for producers of hogs, cattle, and chickens. However, the company has a large grain business and has facilities for the storage of over 200,000 bushels of corn. Some of the corn is sold directly to other grain dealers, but most of it is used in the business. Recently, the company has started operating a small swine market which caters mainly to the customers of Brown Milling Company.

John Ray is the only salesman working for Brown Milling Company. He was employed by the company as a mill clerk in 1957. As he learned the business, he gradually moved into the selling position which he now holds. John is paid a salary plus a commission. The commission is based on a certain percentage of the net profit of the business.

John describes his job as one of order taking, advising, trouble shooting, and, in general, insuring satisfaction. He visits large producers once every two weeks. During these visits, he discusses with the producer various problems. He takes orders from the producers, but most of these are small and miscellaneous items. The producers generally phone direct to the mill for large orders whenever their feed supply gets low. Immediate free delivery service is available at all times.

During the summer of 1964, John received information that Ben Fields, Farm Supervisor of the Farmer's Bank, had developed a large swine farm on one of the estates that he was managing for the bank. Realizing that this swine farm had the potential of becoming a $100,000 business, John went to see Mr. Fields. Mr. Fields treated him very courteously but did not agree to use Brown Milling Company as a feed supplier. During the following year, John called upon Mr. Fields occasionally, but he never received any orders. One day Mr. Fields called John, stating that he wanted to talk with him. Immediately, John went to see him. The story that Mr. Fields told John was one of troubles on top of troubles. He was having trouble with disease in his herd of sows. His pigs were being born dead or too small. In general, his swine farm had not been successful, and he was under pressure to make it successful. Mr. Fields told John that if Brown Milling Company would guarantee to solve his disease problem, he would purchase all his feed from them. John could not guarantee this, but he told Mr. Fields that he was certain that Brown Milling Company could help solve his problems. With hesitation, Mr. Fields agreed to start using Brown Milling Company as his feed supplier.

During the following year, Mr. Fields depended entirely upon Brown Milling Company to furnish all of his feed requirements which amounted to over $30,000. John made weekly visits to the swine farm and made suggestions to Mr. Fields concerning the use of feed additives and other problems. By the year's end, the swine farm was operating at a profit and most of the disease problem had been solved.

This friendly and profitable relationship existed for eighteen months. Recently while John was visiting the swine farm, Mr. Fields announced abruptly that he was going to stop buying feed from Brown Milling Company. He told John that it was nothing that the company had or had not done and that he was not dissatisfied at anyone or anything.

Shocked and disappointed, John set out to do a little investigating. He found that the new feed suppliers, James Brothers Milling Company, were also the beneficiaries of the estate which was being held in trust and on which the swine farm was located. John feels that the

beneficiaries, in order to gain the feed business of the swine farm, applied pressure on the bank officials and Mr. Fields. John's main reason for thinking this is a statement that Mr. Fields made in which he said, "If I start having disease troubles again, despite what anyone says, I will start buying feed from you again."

QUESTIONS

1. Develop a plan which you think John Ray should follow in handling the present situation.
2. What problems do you foresee in executing the plan you have suggested?
3. How would you deal with these problems?

The Ferguson Lumber Company
(Burroughs Corporation—B)

As a salesman of office machines, Edward Ray recognized that one of his best sources of locating prospective customers was through professional accountants working in and around his sales territory. He knew that an accountant was in a strategic position in knowing what types of equipment particular firms used in their offices. The accountant came by this information through his close association with clients and their bookkeeping departments. Ray also was aware that in many cases the management of firms called on their retained accountants to provide them with additional information, more accurate information, and more up-to-date information. In such situations the accountants frequently pointed out to management that in order to make such information available, new equipment would probably be needed in the firm's bookkeeping procedures. In certain cases a decision to purchase office equipment stemmed from the accountant's recognition of a need for better information in handling a firm's books. In other cases the management sought the advice and recommendation of the accountant as to what type of replacement or new equipment might meet the requirements and needs of the firm. In either case the accountant had to have a good knowledge of the types of office equipment in general use and any new developments forthcoming in the field.

♦ SOURCE: Reprinted by permission from Bennett and Reeves, *op. cit.* Case prepared by James H. Bearden.

Ray felt he had generally maintained a good working relationship with local accountants, several of whom he knew quite well. In the past he had secured many orders through his contacts with these men. On the other hand, Ray felt that he had reciprocated for the many leads accountants had given him by giving them information on new equipment and answering specific queries as to what kind of equipment would yield specified information. However, in those cases in which the information given to the accountant led to a purchase of office equipment, Ray estimated that he had received more orders than his competitors.

Several months ago Ray was having coffee with Harvey Allen, a young accountant who had been practicing in Marion for five years. During the ensuing discussion, Allen mentioned that he was working with a local lumber company and that he had a problem with which Ray might help him. He told Ray that the president of the lumber company was interested in measuring the profitability of certain segments of the company's business. He pointed out that the firm's present accounting procedures would not yield a sufficient breakdown of accounts to make the desired evaluation. The two men exchanged questions and ideas for some thirty minutes concerning what accounting procedures would yield the desired data and what types of office equipment would be compatible with the accounting procedures employed.

Finally, Ray suggested that he had no appointments set up for the rest of the afternoon and that he would like to call on the president of the firm and acquaint him with the Burroughs Sensimatic, a $4,000 machine, which would provide the desired break-down of sales. However, Allen pointed out that since the man knew very little about the accounting end of the business, perhaps it would be best to hold off on any sales presentation of the Sensimatic, at least until such time as he could gauge the president's feeling toward a complete overhauling of the firm's accounting procedures and a $4,000 outlay on new office equipment. At this point in the discussion a friend of Ray's joined them for coffee and the conversation shifted to a boating trip that was to take place shortly. Allen excused himself and departed.

Several days later Ray received a telephone call from Allen indicating that he had talked with Mr. John Ferguson, President of The Ferguson Lumber Company, on the matter

they had discussed earlier. Allen told Ray that Ferguson remained steadfast in his desire to get a break-down on the profitability of the various segments of the business and was willing to go along with the change in accounting as well as the added investment of several thousand dollars for office equipment. Allen also mentioned that he had given his personal endorsement that the Sensimatic would do the job satisfactorily. Allen then suggested that Ray call on Ferguson the following day.

At The Ferguson Lumber Company the next day, Ray introduced himself to Mr. John Ferguson. Ray indicated that he was the office equipment salesman Allen had recommended.

"Oh yes, Mr. Ray. You have the $4,000 machine that my accountant wants me to get. That's a lot of money for a bookkeeping machine; but since Allen says it will get us results and he will personally vouch for you and your machine, I suppose I will go along. My sisters handle all the bookkeeping out here. You go talk to them and see what they think about it," Mr. Ferguson commented.

Ray met with the two ladies and briefly discussed the Sensimatic and its benefits. The majority of his conversation was with Mrs. James Howard, since her sister left the office shortly after he arrived. Ray spent some time inquiring into the number of invoices the company handled per day, the number of lines per invoice, and in securing samples of forms the company used in the office operation. After satisfying himself that Mrs. Howard was favorably impressed with the Sensimatic, Ray left the office with the understanding that he would return to the firm the following day.

The next morning Ray called on Mr. Ferguson. Ray told him that he had made a brief survey of the office work load and was sure that Burroughs Sensimatic would do a good job for the company. After assuring him that he would personally conduct the training of the Sensimatic operator, Ray received Ferguson's order for the machine.

The office personnel consisted of Mrs. James Howard, age 37 and a commerce graduate of State University, and her sister, Mrs. Edith Primrose, age 35. Mrs. Howard was in charge of accounts payable, posting to general ledger, payroll, check writing, and in general served as office manager. She was capable of performing all of the office work and had done so on occasions when her sister was absent.

Mrs. Primrose's duties consisted mainly of sorting and verifying invoices and posting accounts receivable. Mrs. Primrose had received no formal training beyond high school. Her bookkeeping knowledge had been achieved largely through on-the-job training commencing some ten years earlier when she began working at the lumber company. Even though the two sisters and their brother were co-owners of The Ferguson Lumber Company, Mr. Ferguson, as president, made virtually all of the major decisions of the company, while the sisters served primarily as office personnel.

During the next eight weeks Ray spent approximately 75 hours at the lumber company designing the new accounting system and preparing new forms to be used with the Sensimatic. At the end of this two-month period the machine was delivered and Ray began to train Mrs. Primrose in the operation of the Sensimatic. In designing the accounting system, Ray had combined the sales journal, now more elaborately broken down, and the cash receipts journal in with the accounts receivable. In designing this phase, Ray had frequently talked with Mrs. Primrose about how he was setting it up, since this was Mrs. Primrose's area of responsibility. However, any actual machine instruction was delayed until the Sensimatic was installed.

Normally, in instruction of this type, Ray would sit with the operator one full day and go through step-by-step procedures. The second day, the operator would take over the operation with Ray standing by to answer questions and clarify procedural aspects. Ray generally had short visits with the new operator for two or three more days, after which the operator had usually attained competency.

With Mrs. Primrose, however, Ray had to spend the major part of a week in the office before he was able to get out for any length of time. Even after this, Mrs. Primrose called three or four times a week concerning some problem with which she needed help. This went on for several weeks. Ray concluded that it was the non-routine situations that were giving Mrs. Primrose so much trouble. Every time a situation arose that Ray had not specifically gone over with Mrs. Primrose or had not covered in the step-by-step written outline he had prepared for her, she could not handle it and consequently called on him. Still, in this situation, Ray had not accomplished in seven weeks what he had usually accomplished in one week. This was the general situation as it existed in November.

As it stood, Ray was being forced to give up good leads on other prospects because of the amount of time he was having to spend with the training of Mrs. Primrose. In addition, he was faced with the problem of not having the company ready to make the shift to the new accounting system by the first of the year, the time Ray, Allen, and Ferguson had agreed upon for the complete changeover of operation.

QUESTIONS

1. What is the relationship between the Burroughs salesman and the public accountant?
2. What is the salesman's obligation in this case? Is his concept of this obligation the same as that of Mr. Ferguson?
3. How should the salesman handle the problem? Did he make any mistakes as the case developed?

Kamack Tanning and Manufacturing Company

The Kamack Company was organized in the 1900's mainly as a tanning company concerned primarily with the manufacture of heavy duty work shoes. Since these early days, the company has grown to one of the largest tanners in the United States and has also become one of the nation's largest producers of shoes. Not only does the company produce the number one selling shoe in the nation, but they also manufacture and market various other products such as pigskin coats for sportswear and men's pigskin hats. All of the company's products are sold under the brand name "Slip Shod." These products are manufactured from a relatively new material, pigskin. This hide, often considered to be leather, has "come into its own" as any shoe dealer will readily admit.

The Ohio salesman for Kamack Tanning and Manufacturing Company is Bob Mason.

The newest product in the Kamack line is the "Slip Shod" Hat. A sports hat, the "Slip Shod" is usually worn to sporting events such as football games and other outdoor events. It may also be worn for semi-casual wear. It comes in a variety of colors and has a rather narrow brim. The pigskin material from which it is constructed makes it a very versatile piece of wearing apparel in that rain will not damage or discolor it. Stiff brushing with a firm clothes brush will bring a "fuzz" up on the surface of the pigskin to help it maintain its water repellency and appearance.

Recently, Mason was considering the desirability of placing his line of hats in a store that was already one of his two largest shoe accounts. The store was carrying an inventory of some fifteen hundred pairs of men's shoes and another four hundred pairs of women's and children's shoes. He decided to approach the buyer in the men's department with the suggestion that he take a look at his line of "Slip Shod" Hats. After a lengthy presentation, Mr. Mason realized that the buyer was very disinterested.

The following day Mason had lunch with the manager of the store, a close personal friend. In the course of conversation, Mason mentioned that he had been trying to sell the men's department a new line of hats. At this point the manager became interested in the hats and asked to see the sample line that Mason had in the car. As soon as lunch was concluded, the two of them looked over the sample line. The manager liked the hats and said that he personally would like to have one of them. He felt that the hats would sell and that there would be a justified market for them. With this comment, another executive came by on the way back from lunch and the three men walked back to the store. Nothing further was said about placing the line in the store.

Later in the day, Mason once again interviewed the buyer for the men's department. The subject of hats was again brought up. Even though a different method of sales presentation was used and finer points brought out about the hats, he still found no acceptance on the part of the buyer. Once again, he allowed the subject to change and nothing further was said about the hats.

The following day it was necessary for Mr. Mason to again be in the store to work with his shoe stock. He was approached by the store manager who asked him if he had talked with the buyer as to the handling of the hat line. He replied that he was not sure as to the intentions of the buyer and the conversation was again changed.

Mr. Mason realizes that he will not visit this store again in three weeks, and thus has a problem of whether or not to push the buyer by telling him that the store manager definitely likes the product or whether to go directly to the store manager for assistance. He knows, too, that he is being pushed by his sales manager to install the "Slip Shod" Hat line in large and thriving department stores in order that the public might become more familiar with the product and the "Slip Shod" name as associated with something other than shoes.

QUESTION

1. What is the problem in this case? How should it be handled?

Lacey-Harvey Toy Wholesaler

Lacey-Harvey, a toy wholesale and distributing company, has its main office in Maysville, New Jersey. The company sells all types of toys, games, and novelty items to drugstores, toy specialty stores, and their largest customers, department store chains. Their market covers the three-state area of New Jersey, Delaware, and Virginia. Their business is seasonal in that Christmas is the busiest time of the year; however, they maintain salesmen to visit their retail accounts, as well as maintain television advertising in the territory.

Robert Pal, who works out of the Maysville office, has been with the firm for twenty-three years. Mr. Pal's income is on a salary plus a commission of sales basis. His territory stretches from Rapids to Wilmington. A special effort is made by Robert to visit his larger accounts every two weeks, and others at least once a month. He tries to visit each account at the same time each month so that they will hold their orders for him. Also, each customer has been provided with his home phone number for placing orders between visits, if necessary.

Mr. Pal occasionally makes large sales, but the majority of his sales are "small" in nature. A great deal of his time is spent in promoting special items at reduced prices, taking inventory for his buyers, and in general trying to build a better traffic through the store.

Lacey-Harvey gives Robert the right to deal with each individual account on the specific discount that he will receive; however, the standard discount used on sales is 40 per cent of list price. In instances when the warehouse is overstocked with a specific item, an extra discount will be given with a large purchase.

This extra discount never exceeds 10 per cent, which will bring the total discount to 50 per cent of list price.

Recently Robert visited Bedds Drugstore in Rockingham. The store is owned by Robert Bedds, who also owns similar drugstores in Andrews and Wilmington. These stores carry a very complete line of toys and novelty items and Robert has been trying for two years to secure this account. Bedds has never made a purchase from him. On this visit, Bedds related to Pal that he felt that his drugstore was entitled to the same discount on toys that his neighbor, a unit of a large department store chain, was receiving from Lacey-Harvey. Pal explained to him several times that the department stores only received the standard 40 per cent discount plus transportation of all purchases to the store. Bedds insisted that the department store was receiving 40 per cent plus a 10 per cent extra discount. Mr. Bedds' words were, "If you give me their price, I'll buy."

Several weeks later, Walter Dame, sales manager for Lacey-Harvey, was in the area presenting a toy show for buyers. Dame and Pal visited Bedds. Dame explained to Bedds that the department store was receiving the same discount and privileges that all customers received, but Bedds' attitude was the same.

Pal continued to visit Bedds once a month and whenever he was near enough to stop by without losing much time. However, the reply always remained the same. Toward the end of the summer, Pal learned that Bedds intended to open another large drugstore in Ravon.

Then on his next visit to the department store in Rockingham, Pal asked the store's toy buyer, Bill Bailey, if he would like to step around the corner to Bedds Drugstore for a cup of coffee. The two men were seated when Bedds walked over and asked Bailey what discount he was receiving from Pal on Lacey-Harvey toys. Bailey replied 40 per cent. Bedds laughed and said, "Boy, he sure has you trained."

The following week while visiting a buyer in Ravon, Pal noticed Bedds there making arrangements for the opening of his new store. Pal feeling that everything else had failed, stopped by to see Bedds once more. In his order book, he has a duplicate of the order placed the day before by the department store in Rockingham. The discount of 40 per cent

is plainly evident, and he wonders if it would do any good to show Bedds such "proof."

QUESTIONS

1. How would you advise the salesman in this situation?
2. What alternative strategies could be employed by the salesman?

Lucky Liquid

The Snow Flake Manufacturing Company, one of the country's leading producers of household cleaners, had a product line made up of sixteen different items. The line consisted of four all-purpose cleaners, three starches, three bleaches, three liquid detergents (dishes, etc.), two clothes washing detergents, and a disinfectant.

Fred Jones has been employed by the Snow Flake Manufacturing Company since June, 1958. Before joining the company, Fred attended Clemson College where he received a B.S. degree in Business Administration with a major in management. After being hired by the company, Fred was given trainee status for thirty days. He attended training classes in addition to accompanying a salesman on customer calls. During this training period, Fred was placed on a monthly salary.

After Fred had completed the training program, he was assigned to the Eastern Tennessee district as a salesman. This district was composed of fifteen cities with a population range of 25,000 to 60,000 and many smaller towns with populations varying from 2,000 to 8,000. Fred established residence in Renfroe primarily because of its central location in his district. His plan of compensation was changed to a base salary—plus commission basis at the time of his new assignment.

Fred's job consisted primarily of selling Snow Flake products to grocery wholesalers. One of the key sales techniques used by the Snow Flake Manufacturing Company was a plan whereby "free goods" were made available for the wholesaler to pass along to his retailer customers. The plan consisted of establishing an inventory of "Lucky Liquid," one of Snow Flake's sixteen products and the most popular brand all-purpose cleaner, at the wholesaler's place of business at no cost to the wholesaler. The wholesaler in turn was allowed to pass along the "Lucky Liquid" free of charge to his retailer accounts provided the retailer met one stipulation. Specifically, the plan made it possible for the wholesaler to give a free case of "Lucky Liquid" to any of his retailer customers who gave him an order of ten cases of Snow Flake products.

The free goods plan was viewed as a very effective merchandising technique both by the manufacturer, who saw the plan as a good method of getting wholesalers to push Snow Flake products, and by the wholesalers, who used the plan to appeal to cost conscious retailers. Much of its effectiveness was based on the premise that since the Snow Flake Manufacturing Company had a fairly extensive product line, and since the retailer could mix his order (this is, the ten-case order could be made up of any combination of Snow Flake products) the wholesalers' salesmen would find it easy to secure a ten-case order.

The mechanics of this plan provided that the Snow Flake salesman would receive copies of the orders secured by the wholesalers' salesmen from retailers. In addition, the wholesaler was required, upon the Snow Flake salesman's request, to provide invoices to substantiate the issuance of "free goods" to his retailer accounts. This procedure allowed Snow Flake Manufacturing Company to check invoices and orders against the wholesaler's physical inventory of "Lucky Liquid." Thus it could be determined if the plan was being properly administered by the wholesaler.

Two of Fred's largest accounts were the C and O Wholesale Grocery Company and the Black and Carson Company. These two grocery wholesalers each had annual sales volumes of between four and five million dollars, and each employed a sales force ranging from six to eight salesmen. Fred's annual sales to C and O and Black and Carson were $35,000 and $40,000, respectively.

In an attempt to offset declines in their sales volume attributable to the growth of large corporate chains, each of the two wholesalers, as true with a great many others throughout the country, organized independent retail grocery merchants into a voluntary chain. In return for various benefits which included favorable buying opportunities, advice, advertising and promotional aid, and in certain instances, a common name for all members, the retailers agreed to concentrate their purchases with the sponsoring wholesaler. The C and O Company sponsored a voluntary chain of Red and White Stores. The Black and Carson Company sponsored Shopworth Stores.

On a recent sales call on the C and O Company, Fred was approached by C and O president, John Walker. Mr. Walker told Fred that he was disturbed over a situation regarding the "free goods" plan of the Snow Flake Company. Mr. Walker explained that he had just added a new retail merchant, Howey Lambert, to his Red and White voluntary chain. He noted that Lambert was switching his affiliation to Red and White from the Black and Carson sponsored Shopworth chain. Mr. Walker pointed out that on the first visit to Lambert by a C and O salesman the following problem occurred:

"Lambert ordered five cases of Snow Flake products from the C and O salesman. He indicated that he would like to get the free case of Lucky Liquid delivered at the same time and that he would order the other five cases of Snow Flake products the following week. The salesman explained to Mr. Lambert that the 'free goods' plan required that a free case of 'Lucky Liquid' could be given only with a ten-case order and that he would not be able to comply with this request. Mr. Lambert became quite angry and pointed out to the salesman that he had been receiving a free case with an order of five while he was affiliated with Black and Carson. He wanted to know why the plan of 'free goods' had been changed."

QUESTIONS

1. What are the salesman's major problems?
2. In deciding how to solve these problems, what are the major considerations that must be taken into account?
3. If you were the salesman, what immediate steps would you take?

Petrol Supply Company

Petrol Supply Company, a manufacturing and marketing company, has its central offices in Bainbridge, West Virginia. The company fabricates petroleum storage tanks of all types, both sheet metal and plastic. In addition to the tanks, Petrol Supply Company manufactures several types of gauges used in the measuring of liquid petroleum products. While manufacturing is limited to petroleum storage tanks, the company markets a much broader line of products. Not only do they sell the products they manufacture, but they also sell a complete line of equipment used in the petroleum industry. Their market includes most of the mid-Atlantic and Southern states.

George M. Summer, who works out of the Bainbridge office, has been an industrial salesman with the company for fifteen years. Prior to this, he worked as a plant supervisor for a major oil company. Mr. Summer's income is based on a straight commission on sales. He prefers this compensation plan because he believes it enables him to earn much more than he could on a salary basis. He also likes the feeling that he is actually earning every dollar that he gets.

Mr. Summer travels from ten to eighteen days each month in eastern North Carolina and northeastern South Carolina. He has a secretary in his office who takes telephone orders from petroleum dealers while he is on the road.

His main duty is to visit every petroleum agent, jobber, commissioned agent, and dealer in his territory at least once every three months. He does, however, check on the larger dealers once each month. On these visits he carries several catalogs containing thousands of products which are needed and used by petroleum sellers, even though the petroleum dealers usually have a previously prepared list of the products they want to order. Upon receipt of an order, he immediately sends it to the Bainbridge office which in turn has the ordered products shipped from one of its several storage warehouses directly to the customer. If the ordered item is not in stock or is rather bulky and large, it is shipped directly from its place of manufacture. The bill for the order is sent to the buyer immediately after the goods are shipped. The usual terms of credit are payment within sixty days with a discount of two per cent if paid within twenty days. However, if the order is extremely large, longer payment plans are available.

While Mr. Summer occasionally makes a large sale, the bulk of his sales are small orders from large numbers of petroleum dealers. He continues to call on even the very small dealers who buy only small cost items in the hope that the goodwill he is building up will pay off when the dealer starts replenishing old equipment and buying new. This happens often enough to keep Mr. Summer optimistic about the idea. Between visits, many of the dealers who need products immediately call Mr. Summer's office collect and give the order to the secretary. She in turn has these rush orders processed immediately and shipped the same day if possible.

Several months ago Mr. Summer decided to add a new sales technique to his presentations. He decided to offer his time to the larger petroleum dealers for the purpose of going through their equipment inventories and helping them decide which items should be eliminated, which should be replaced, and what new items were needed.

His sales supervisor, upon hearing of his plan, was impressed with the idea and encouraged him to test it in the field. Summer pondered the idea for several days and decided to give it a try. The first two dealers on his route seemed impressed with the idea but did not feel that they needed an equipment inventory at the present time. The third dealer told him that he did not want him "sticking his nose in places where it didn't belong." Though rather discouraged, Summer decided to try once more. This time the dealer was not only impressed, but he seemed overjoyed to have someone assist in an equipment inventory. Summer spent part of the afternoon and most of the next day going through this dealer's equipment. After finishing the inventory, he presented his findings and suggestions to the dealer. After examining the report for about thirty minutes, the dealer circled all of the equipment he wanted to order from Petrol Supply Company. Summer then made up the order which amounted to approximately $32,-000. The dealer, to Summer's surprise, signed an order for immediate delivery and thanked him for his generous assistance. This was the largest single order Summer had received during the fifteen years that he had been with Petrol Supply Company. It amounted to what he would normally sell during a whole month of traveling.

Summer continued to offer to help the petroleum dealers bring their equipment inventories up to date. Many dealers refused flatly while others said they had rather wait until a future date. However, in the months that followed several dealers did accept the offer and it always resulted in larger than usual sales to those dealers.

After much persuasive effort, one of Summer's largest accounts, John Poole, a petroleum marketer in South Carolina, agreed for him to make a study of his equipment. Because Poole's market area was quite large and also because he had a tremendous amount of equipment, the study took four full days during which time Summer was accompanied by Poole himself. Upon completion of the inventory, Summer presented his suggestions for new equipment. Mr. Poole seemed to be well pleased. He then asked Summer to go through the extensive list of needed equipment, quote a price by each item, and then to get the total price of the equipment. Mr. Summer, certain that a large order was forthcoming, spent that evening in pricing the equipment. The total price amounted to $121,000. The next morning he presented the finished report to Poole. Mr. Poole politely thanked him for spending his valuable time in making the study, invited him to stop in to see him the next time he came into the South Carolina area and told him that if he decided to order anything he would give his Bainbridge office a call.

Mr. Summer, very disappointed that an immediate order was not being made, assured Mr. Poole that he was glad to have helped him and that he hoped to be able to help him even more in the future.

Two weeks passed and no order was received from the South Carolina dealer. Summer decided to make another visit to see Mr. Poole. At Poole's office he had a two-hour wait prior to getting in to see him. After receiving Summer, Poole thanked him for helping them to determine their equipment needs. He added that the inventory was so complete that he acted upon the suggestions and purchased most of the needed equipment from a local petroleum equipment firm. Poole stated that he hoped in the future he could place a big order with Petrol Supply.

QUESTIONS

1. Is the strategy developed by the salesman sound? What, if any, are its weaknesses?
2. How can the problem confronting the salesman in this case be prevented from occurring in the future?

Radio Station WXYZ

Ted Jacobs is employed by Radio Station WXYZ as a sales representative. WXYZ is one of three radio stations in a town of approximately 30,000 population. Prior to his present job, selling radio commercials, Ted worked as a used car salesman and as a salesman of ad-

vertising space for the local telephone company's yellow pages.

In his present job Ted is furnished with a list of accounts to call on and encouraged to pick up any new accounts as he can. The list of accounts consists of small business firms such as service stations, heating and air conditioning firms, and small retail concerns. Ted has many accounts which require weekly servicing for new advertising material.

Even though station WXYZ is the oldest in the market, the strongest in terms of power, and programmed to attract a mature or adult listening audience, many of the prospects visited by Ted cannot be convinced that these attributes justify the price per commercial differential between WXYZ and its generally less experienced competitors.

Ted has been calling on Hyman's Department Store, one of the leading downtown department stores, for approximately six months. Hyman's is a strong newspaper advertiser and uses commercials regularly on competitive stations. Bill Jones, manager of the department store, originally lived in Walkertown, North Carolina. Ted had worked at a large used car dealer's when he lived in Walkertown. By associating names of people and events, Ted gained acceptance of Mr. Jones and finally persuaded him to use WXYZ for a large advertising promotion. The promotion proved very successful for the store, and Jones was pleased with the results the radio commercials had brought. Thereafter, Mr. Jones began to buy "spots" on WXYZ often.

Recently a new shopping center developed in the city, and Ted canvassed all the business tenants in the center. He quickly picked up two small accounts that bought approximately $30 per week in advertising. The largest firm there was the Giant Discount Store, and Ted called on the manager hoping to get his commercial time. However, the manager refused to talk further to Ted after seeing the station's rates. Subsequently, the sales manager for WXYZ assigned another salesman by the name of Tom Bailey to attempt to cultivate the Giant Discount Store account. Since Bailey had been in radio sales for twelve years, it was the sales manager's opinion that Bailey's past experience would be to his advantage in dealing with some of the newcomers to the WXYZ market area.

Several weeks ago, on a routine visit to Hyman's Department Store, Ted found Mr. Jones in conversation with Henry Burton, owner of a small hardware store that Ted called on. The men asked if Giant Discount Store was using WXYZ as an advertising medium, and Ted told the men that he had given up on them as a prospect. Jones and Burton expressed great concern that Giant Discount Store would be a serious threat to their respective businesses. Ted invited the two men to have lunch with him since it was nearly noon.

During lunch, Ted convinced the two that they should advertise on WXYZ in order to effectively compete with the discount store. For more dynamic advertising, Ted suggested that he be allowed to have a clever musical jingle prepared that would promote their respective stores. Both men agreed to the suggestion. After leaving the restaurant, Ted walked back to Hyman's with Mr. Jones and related how the short jingle could be used in conjunction with a selling message and further explained that by agreeing to use as many as 250 selling commercials during the year, that his rates would decrease by 25 per cent.

Ted had the jingles prepared and took them to each store for the men to hear. Both men liked the jingles and placed a two week saturation order with WXYZ. Mr. Jones told Ted that he and Burton had discussed the possibility of taking advantage of the 25 per cent decrease by planning on the 250 commercials during the next twelve months, but that they would let him know on his next visit. Jones added that he and Burton had considered the proposal based on the assumption that WXYZ would not solicit Giant Discount Store's business, in view of the competitive interests of the concerns.

Ted related this information to his sales manager, who in turn stated that Bailey hadn't made any progress with selling the discount store.

Ted prepared rough advertising schedules and returned to Hyman's Department Store the next week. He found Mr. Jones in the Appliance Department. Jones appeared to be in an unusually bad mood and when Ted presented him with the schedules, he told Ted that he could forget their previous talk since he had heard several Giant Discount Store commercials on WXYZ. He further stated that Burton had telephoned him, calling his attention to these commercials. Ted asked permission to use the telephone and immediately called the radio station. He found that Bailey had signed a contract between the station and

the discount store. Upon asking to speak to his sales manager, Ted was told that he had gone out of town.

Ted turned to Mr. Jones and explained that his sales manager was out of town, but that he would discuss the situation with him as soon as possible. Jones told Ted that he was leaving for New York at six o'clock that evening and he needed to know before he left since he was taking the store's proposed budget to the New York office for approval. He further stated that if the discount store was to be a regular user, he would place his advertising dollar in television.

When Ted returned to the office, he received a telephone message that Henry Burton of the local hardware store had decided against any further use of the station and had canceled his current order. At 5:30 P.M. Ted telephoned Jones in order to inform him that his sales manager had not returned. However, he was told that Mr. Jones had left just minutes before. As Ted looked over the papers on his desk, he spotted a memo his sales manager had written to all salesmen pointing out a list of merchants using competitive stations and inferred that their own selling efforts were not yielding as much results as the competition. He ended the memo with "the game is called sales."

QUESTIONS

1. Evaluate the strategy employed by the salesman. What changes would you have suggested in such a strategy? Why?
2. What would you advise the salesman to do now?

Taylor Steel Company
(*National Aluminum Corporation—A*)

Jack West, age forty-three, was a sales engineer for the National Aluminum Corporation, a concern which manufactured and sold a wide range of aluminum products for industrial and home use. He held an engineering degree, had attended the eight-month National Aluminum school, and had twenty years' selling experience with the corporation. He reported to the district sales manager of the Industrial Products

◆ SOURCE: Reprinted by permission from Bennett and Reeves, *op. cit.* Case prepared by Walter Gorman.

Division which was responsible for sales of such industrial items as connectors, high voltage cable, wiring of all types, fittings, and substation structures to utilities and related industries. Jack was paid a straight salary and "incentive." The incentive bonus was based on management's evaluation of his over-all performance and his sales volume in relation to his quota.

Jack's job had changed with company policy within the last few years. Before the Korean War, Jack made independent calls on utilities, construction firms, and other large industrial concerns requiring his equipment while traveling a one-state territory. At this time his entire sales quota was based on "named accounts" (customers judged by potential sales volume to be important enough to merit direct personal attention by a National Aluminum sales engineer). Less important regular-account customers were assigned to distributors, whose salesmen sold National Aluminum products along with other non-competing lines used by large industry. National Aluminum subsequently promoted Jack to a higher position and reclassified some of the named-account customers to regular-account customers coming under the distributor's jurisdiction. This was done because the distributors who could stock all of the supply needs of a utility could afford to call on accounts more frequently and still obtain sizeable orders, and because of the high premium on a sales engineer's time. Jack's territory had been expanded geographically to cover a three-state area, and his main purpose was to act as a missionary salesman for the distributors. He traveled with distributor salesmen, trained them to sell National Aluminum products, and maintained only eight "named accounts."

Two types of distributors were assisted by National Aluminum salesmen. The Cranston Corporation, which operated in the three states comprising Jack's territory, was an example of a privately-owned firm. National Aluminum had two contracts with Cranston Corporation: an industrial distributor contract for small wiring, fittings, and connector items, and an agency contract (an agent does not take title and is subject to the manufacturer's terms on price and territory) for the expensive items such as high-voltage cable and substation structures. Under the agency contract, National Aluminum had a great deal of area and price policy control; while under the distributor con-

tract Cranston Corporation could sell anywhere at their own prices since they purchased from the manufacturer, and control passed with title to the goods. Cranston Corporation maintained a large National Aluminum inventory of products under each contract. Cranston had an electrical equipment department consisting of eight salesmen who spent approximately one-third of their time on the National Aluminum line. Jack assisted this department in several ways. He helped the manager with technical, sales, and inventory problems; he made calls on the road with individual salesmen; and he held motivational and product knowledge sales meetings.

The second type of distributor was National Aluminum owned, but it operated in essentially the same manner as Cranston Corporation. It was assisted by a salesman comparable to Jack, and it realized the same commissions and margins on products. It was shown no partiality in National Aluminum policy. Although it specialized in the National Aluminum line, it also carried other non-competing industrial products. National Aluminum-owned distributors had been established primarily in those areas where satisfactory distributors had not been available.

Sometimes in fringe areas, territory coverage of distributors tended to overlap. Usually the distributor who had traditionally served the fringe-area account maintained the business, but in some instances the new distributor gained the fringe account. This was within company policy when the traditional distributor either preferred not to, or could not, handle the account. In this situation, the National Aluminum sales engineer who held quota for the account through the traditional distributor was instructed to consider first that National Aluminum should keep the business, and that his quota and distributor were secondary consideration.

Jack made both selling and installation calls with Cranston salesmen. He was usually requested to aid the salesman when a call was considered particularly important. Most often he went to help convince a key prospect or solve a technical problem in an installation. As he traveled with these salesmen, he frequently discussed sales strategy or gave them product information helpful in maintaining specific accounts. Generally, the sales interviews involved a technical discussion with the superintendent of engineering of the utility company. Information had to be obtained from the superintendent before custom-tailored proposals featuring detailed specifications could be prepared, and the superintendent had to be sold on recommending National Aluminum products over competition. In this regard three major competitors were anticipated. The superintendent, once convinced, made recommendations to the purchasing authority (the mayor or city clerk usually for municipal utilities). If the call, on the other hand, was not a sales call and involved an installation problem, Jack solved it himself or saw to it that the problem was brought to the attention of the National Aluminum staff engineer. The Cranston Corporation salesman could, therefore, use Jack's support in every aspect of the sale.

At the outset of the Korean War, Taylor Steel Company of Smithton obtained a contract for producing war munitions. Through a contact in Smithton, Jack West learned of Taylor's award of this contract immediately after it was negotiated. He called upon the president of Taylor Steel Company, Mr. J. L. Taylor, promptly and advised him that the National Aluminum Corporation offered its complete facilities in furnishing all of the wiring and structures which would be required for the shell plant. Mr. Taylor advised Jack that he was the first supplier to call on him, and he appreciated it very much. He went on to outline to Jack in detail that much work had to be done before he would have any idea what would be required. He pointed out that first of all he had to get an organization together and then proceed to work out all engineering details. He told Jack to stay in touch with him; and that as soon as an organization was established, Jack could work with his men.

In about a week, Mr. Taylor had established offices and had hired personnel. Jack immediately contacted the chief engineer and the man who would be in charge of the electrical department. Over a period of one month to six weeks, he assisted in working out details with Mr. Taylor's people as to the components which would be required. From time to time Jack spoke to Mr. Taylor. He tried not to bother Mr. Taylor, however, because he knew Mr. Taylor was busy with the over-all management problems of getting an organization together, renovating a plant, and working with government officials.

At the end of six weeks to two months, the electrical layout had been completed, the bill of material established, and Jack was in a position to quote prices. He then called on Mr. Taylor and told him that he was in this position. Mr. Taylor stated at that time that he was not quite ready to "move."

In keeping up with the production date as scheduled and the schedule of erection of equipment, it became apparent to Jack that his deliveries were going to be long and, therefore, that he would need to get Mr. Taylor to act. He went back to Mr. Taylor and advised him that it would be to his best interest to "move" on the electrical purchases as soon as possible. Mr. Taylor stated that he still was not quite ready. Jack continued to work with his people, and they were concerned about meeting their construction schedule. They, too, were pushing Mr. Taylor to go ahead and turn them loose on ordering this specific aluminum equipment. Jack was calling on these people several times a week. He finally got to the point at which there was no further work to be done, and the only thing left was for Mr. Taylor to act.

Jack continued then to see Mr. Taylor personally from time to time. After several contacts he became aware that he was disturbing Mr. Taylor with his continued persistence. He felt justified in pushing for a decision because he believed further delay would prevent completion of the plant in time for it to meet its initial production schedule. After several unproductive contacts, Mr. Taylor outlined to Jack in detail what his plans were and said he felt that he could get the plant in production in plenty of time. Jack stated that he did not think the plans would work because of insufficient lead time allowance. With some indication of exasperation, Mr. Taylor terminated the interview and told Jack that he would get in touch with him when he was ready to act. Mr. Taylor was emphatic in telling Jack not to make any further contacts. "Don't call me. I'll call you," he said.

About a week after Mr. Taylor had given Jack these instructions, Jack was in Cannonville. His sales assistant in the office called him long distance. He advised Jack that he had just received a call from Smithton and that he had taken it in Jack's absence. The call was from Taylor Steel, and he told Jack that Mr. Taylor had requested that Jack now come to Smithton to go over the job with him. Jack received this call in Cannonville at approximately 9:00 A.M. He immediately checked out of his hotel and proceeded to Smithton. He arrived there during the lunch hour and was told that Mr. Taylor was out to lunch. At 1:00

P.M. he was sitting in the reception room outside of Mr. Taylor's office. He saw Mr. Taylor drive up and he opened the front door to let him in.

Jack spoke to Mr. Taylor and said that he was ready to do business with him. At the time there were several other people of Mr. Taylor's employment standing in the office. Mr. Taylor looked at Jack with a severely cold look and hesitated a minute. Jack shook hands with him and told him that he was ready, willing, and able to perform for him on his aluminum requirements. Mr. Taylor took one or two steps and turned around to Jack in what appeared to be utter rage. He asked Jack coldly if he recalled his last meeting. Jack replied that he certainly did and that the meeting was to the effect that when Mr. Taylor got ready for him, he would call him. Mr. Taylor then told Jack that these instructions still remained and proceeded to "dress him down." He terminated his tirade with the comment, "I doubt that I will really need your assistance at all." According to Jack, this whole action was so fast moving, and Mr. Taylor's apparent rage was so great, that he could not make rebuttal or ask intelligent questions. He was embarrassed, humiliated, and at a complete loss for words.

Jack immediately went to a telephone, called his sales assistant, and asked why he had been notified that Mr. Taylor had called for him when Mr. Taylor denied having called. The sales assistant stated that, as far as he knew, Mr. Taylor had called, and that he could not understand the situation either.

QUESTIONS

1. Did Jack handle the situation well? Should the salesman press the prospect for a decision if he feels he is acting in the best interest of the prospect?
2. How can the salesman prevent being backed into the corner, "Don't call me, I'll call you"? What can the salesman do when the prospect says "Don't call me, I'll call you"?
3. How should the salesman proceed at the end of the case?

Washington Sea Food

The Washington Sea Food Company is located in Richmond, Virginia. The company is family owned and has been in operation for the past fifteen years. The company's main product is processed chickens, but it also handles sea food and portion-controlled meat products. Customers of the Washington Sea Food Company include restaurants, school, and college cafeterias.

Mr. Walter Brown has been working for the Washington Sea Food Company for eight years. For the past six years, Brown has had as a customer Mr. John Greene, a restaurant owner in Blytheville, Virginia.

Mr. Greene owns and operates three restaurants: The Smoke House, The Green Light, and The Beef House. The approximate seating capacity of each restaurant is 75–100 persons. Recently, Mr. Greene has turned the operation of The Beef House over to his wife. Although Mrs. Greene operates The Beef House, Mr. Greene has continued to do the buying for all three restaurants through one restaurant, The Green Light.

Six years ago when Mr. Brown first called on Mr. Greene, he had to sell each product on the basis of price and quality. From all indications Mr. Greene has been completely satisfied with the results.

Currently, Brown's route enables him to call on Mr. Greene twice a week. Through these frequent visits, the men have built a very good working relationship. This relationship has developed to the extent that Mr. Greene made it a practice to leave the keys to his frozen food locker at the cash register for Mr. Brown. With keys to the frozen food locker available, Mr. Brown could enter the locker unaccompanied to take an inventory of the meat products. After the inventory, Brown would write out an order for the needed merchandise, and then present it to Mr. Greene who would sign the order without question.

Three months ago, Brown called on Mr. Greene at The Green Light restaurant. As always, he entered the restaurant and went to the cash register for the keys to the frozen food locker. Instead of finding the keys, he was given a note by the cashier. The note from Mr. Greene informed him not to enter the frozen food locker because no merchandise was needed. Brown felt that this was very unusual, and decided to stop by The Beef House. Here he was told that Mr. Greene had just called and left a message asking him to return to The Green Light restaurant for an order. When he returned to The Green Light restaurant, he was met by Mr. Greene who did not offer his keys as usual, but instead accompanied him on his tour of the frozen food locker. During the tour of the food locker, Brown noticed that Mr. Greene had been buying merchandise from another company. He immediately inquired about the new products in the food locker. Mr. Greene answered, "They are cheaper than yours." The new products found in the locker were cheaper, so Brown agreed with Mr. Greene. Mr. Brown received a small order on this call.

On the next few calls, Brown never had the chance to inventory the food locker because Mr. Greene would leave a list of merchandise he wanted to buy at the cash register. Each order was smaller than the previous order. Since this was one of Mr. Brown's better accounts, he decided to ask some of the restaurant employees what was wrong with Mr. Greene. After inquiring among the employees, Mr. Brown learned that Mrs. Greene had been recently elected to a position on the executive committee of the Virginia Restaurant Association. Upon further investigation, Mr. Brown found that the competitor who had been getting much of his lost business also belonged to this association.

On Brown's most recent visit to The Green Light restaurant, he was met by Mr. Greene at the cash register. When Mr. Greene rendered his order for merchandise, he asked Brown if the Washington Sea Food Company was a member of the Virginia Restaurant Association. Brown replied that his company did not belong to the Association. Receiving a small order as usual, he ended the discussion and left the restaurant.

Brown speculated that the following events in some way were causing him to lose the Greene account: First, Mrs. Greene's election to a post in the Virginia Restaurant Association; second, the fact that the competitor gaining a good share of Greene's business was an active member in the Restaurant Association; and finally, the fact that Mr. Greene had asked about Washington Sea Food's membership status in the Restaurant Association.

As a result of the foregoing, Brown brought membership in the Virginia Restaurant Association to the attention of his company. The following letter was sent to Mr. Greene from the Washington Sea Food Company:

Dear Sir:

It was recently brought to my attention that you are losing faith in Washington Sea Food as a supplier, due to our laxness in participation in the activities of the Virginia Restaurant Association.

In 1963, we attended the Virginia Restaurant Association's convention in Norfolk. Then, this year, we participated in the convention held in Richmond. Both times, a booth was featured, samples were available, and attendants stood by. These two endeavors involved an expense of nearly $1,000.

I hope the above information will prove reassuring that Washington Sea Food is active in the aforementioned organization. May our business with your restaurants continue on a mutually satisfactory basis.

Sincerely,

John Still, President
Washington Sea Food Company

QUESTIONS

1. What should be the next step taken by the salesman?
2. How valid are the assumptions made by the salesman regarding the events leading to his losing this account?
3. Of what value are such assumptions to a salesman?

The Williams Products Company

The Williams Products Company, a large producer of rubber belts, produces custom-made and mass production belting items. Under the custom-made service which they offer, belts are designed to solve special problems manufacturers might have in conveying materials from place to place. These belts are designed by the company engineers to meet the conditions of the problem, and therefore, face very little competition.

The mass production items are manufactured to a standard set by the belting industry. These belts are produced to a certain width, length and load specification. This type of belt is used to transmit power from motors to a shaft or machine. This market is very competitive due to the standardization of the industry.

In May, 1966, a sales office was located in Southern California. The more competitive type products were to be maintained in a warehouse located at the sales office in order to provide fast delivery on orders. From this branch office, three salesmen were to call on prospective manufacturers and food processing companies in Southern California.

Henry Franklin, a salesman with six years' experience with the company, accepted a transfer into this territory. He had a reputation in the Williams Company of being one of the top salesmen, always developing his territory well. After being in the new territory twenty-one months, Henry had a major growth of sales underway. He had been successful in getting the Williams Belts in all major areas except one—The Cole Company—a processor of pickles. (Major areas are those areas where tremendous quantities of the competitive type product are used.) This was one of the best prospects for this type of product because of the vast quantity of belts used in conveying pickles.

Henry called regularly on the Cole Company's Purchasing Manager, Vernon Stokes. He was always very amiable to Henry but did not seem particularly interested in the Williams Belt. On one occasion Mr. Stokes explained to Henry that the problem at the Cole Company was not machine efficiency but the risk of spoiling a vat of pickles and the subsequent loss of several hundred dollars during a breakdown.

Mr. Stokes invited Henry to look over the operation. After closely examining the machine in operation, Henry explained in detail to Mr. Stokes the best quality cleated Williams Belt, a belt which recently had been perfected by the Williams Company engineers. Henry convinced Stokes that this new type of belt would be ideally suited for this particular situation. The result was an order for the belt amounting to approximately $350. The size of the order was not what Henry had hoped for, but he felt it would perhaps develop into a situation in which tremendous quantities of the product would be used.

Several weeks later, Henry called on Mr. Stokes, confident he was going to receive a large order. After the usual greeting, Henry inquired how the Williams Cleated Belt was performing. To his dismay, Mr. Stokes replied, "Well, our normal replacement is about every twelve weeks; however, your expensive quality belt, ideally suited for the situation, had to be replaced after six weeks."

QUESTIONS

1. If you were the salesman, what would be your reply to Mr. Stokes?
2. Review the actions taken by the salesman from the first call on this account. Fill in missing stages with what you think should have happened.
3. What course of action is required of the salesman now?

PART

III

Process and Strategy

The salesman faces an incessant demand for strategies. What is the proper action for him to take and what shall he say at this particular moment? He must reach into his reservoir of sales techniques and choose the precise means to deal with each progressing stage of a situation. Some salesmen depend, to a great extent, on the behavior of the prospect system; the progressive responses of the prospect regulate his choice of strategies. For other salesmen, it is a matter of taking the next step in a prepared sequence of techniques.

One way to define selling strategy is to say that it is "what salesmen do." It is obvious, however, that "what salesmen do" varies greatly and, thus, it would be ill-conceived to present all of the selling activities and approaches as having similar philosophy, method, or result. This is not to suggest that the achievements of one salesman are better or more effective or more valuable than those of a salesman using a different approach. It is simply to suggest that there are a variety of ways of selling. These variations in selling have found their way into common parlance. When we hear terms such as "door-to-door," "peddler," "clerk," "sales engineer," and the like, we immediately assume distinctions among each of the corresponding realities. Analysis of these distinctions would reveal significant differences in the depth of diagnosis, in the degree of involvement of both parties in the relationship, in the subtlety of factors and feelings explored, in the complexity of methods used by salesmen.

Salesmen, whether they are aware of it or not, operate in terms of a theoretical orientation. They use such tools as hypotheses, assumptions, and postulates. Without theory, salesmen lack clear-cut guides for planning and performance. Therefore the three readings selected for treatment of selling strategy have not been made on the basis of "how-to-do-it" but rather against the background of theory.

The traditional view in science is that one has an understanding of a process if one can predict the outcome accurately. It is highly unlikely that a complete understanding of the sales process is being approached. The first two articles included in this section make no claim to enable prediction. They merely represent an old and a new way of looking at selling.

In the article, "Ways of Looking at Selling," Cash and Crissy describe the three theories that over the years have been proposed to explain the sales process.

In the second article, Evans proposes that, in order to understand the sales process, it is necessary to look to both parties to the sale as a dyad, not individually. "Specifically the hypothesis is: the sale is a product of the particular dyadic interaction of a given salesman and prospect rather than a result of the individual qualities of either alone."

In the article, "Systems Selling: Industrial Marketing's New Tool," an approach which is just getting off the ground is discussed.

Ways of Looking at Selling

HAROLD C. CASH and W. J. E. CRISSY

If a salesman is asked to describe his job he is likely to mention the company he works for, the products he sells, and the kinds of customers he has. If he is questioned about how he does his work he may tell the claims he makes for his products and how they can be used. He is apt to relate one or more of his interesting sales experiences. He will find it more difficult to discuss selling as a process. He can talk readily about the parts or phases but he finds it difficult to describe the whole. The discussion which follows is focused on the sales process viewed as an integrated whole involving the salesman and the prospect or customer in an intimate, inter-personal relationship.

Three theories have been proposed for describing the sales process:

1. Stimulus-response
2. Selling formula—attention, interest, desire, action (AIDA)
3. Need-satisfaction

There are proponents of each of these among salesmen and sales managers. Even when a salesman is not consciously aware of it, his selling methods can often be interpreted in terms of one of these three theories. It is beneficial for the reader to review each of them so that he can then guide his selling efforts by the one most appropriate to his immediate situation.

STIMULUS-RESPONSE

This is the simplest of the three theories. It has its psychological origin in early experiments with animals. Investigators found that a

◆ SOURCE: Reprinted by permission from *Psychology of Selling*, Vol. 1 (Flushing 58, New York, Personnel Development Associates, 1958).

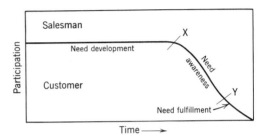

Figure 1   Need-satisfaction theory.

given stimulus, for example, food, would cause a given response, for example, in the case of food, salivation. In summary, associated with each stimulus there is a particular response.

Applying this to selling, the salesman needs to have a repertoire of things to say and do (stimuli) in order to bring about buying (response). Implied in this theory is that if a salesman says and does the right things, an order will follow (Figure 1).

For a very simple situation, where the unit sale is low and the time that can be devoted to the sales effort is very brief, it may be feasible to operate on this basis. However, every salesman has found from experience that a stimulus which works with one customer does not necessarily work with another. As a result, he is in the dark when he attempts to analyze the reasons for his success or failure. It also becomes apparent that the salesman who works on this basis has little likelihood of improving his performance as a result of his experience.

SELLING FORMULA

This theory implies that it is necessary and desirable to treat all customers alike. Sales are

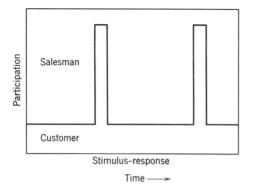

Figure 2

made by taking the customer through a series of mental states, attention—interest—desire—action. Sometimes the additional steps of satisfaction and conviction are included. The salesman using this approach will develop a standard presentation or "canned" sales talk, if he has not already been supplied one by his management. He will, in each sales presentation, make statements designed to attract attention, arouse interest, create desire, and obtain action. He tends to ignore the thoughts of the customer and tries to develop these mental states in sequence. Proponents of this method claim that it insures that all important product information will be presented to each customer, and that it is necessary for salesmen to use this approach in order to make a sale (Figure 2).

Opponents of the method point out that it is an analysis of the situation from the salesman's point of view rather than the customer's, and that use of the formula tends to make the salesman feel that he is some sort of an engineer who by following a standard procedure can persuade the customer to make a purchase. They also point out that a customer may not experience these states in any given order and that they are not of equal importance.

This method would appear to have value when the customers have identical or at least similar needs, and where salesmen lack the ability to develop a sales approach based on each customer's individual needs. It is also to be noted that the formula has considerable utility to a writer or teacher of salesmanship. It provides a framework within which most ideas on selling can be presented.

This approach runs into difficulty when the customer wants to get the answer to a specific question. If the salesman fails to preceive this,

he continues making the presentation and may thereby literally talk himself out of a sale.

NEED-SATISFACTION THEORY

In this theory it is assumed that purchases are made to satisfy needs. Therefore, in order to make a sale the salesman must discover the prospect's needs and show how his products or services will fill those needs. This is a customer-oriented approach as compared with the two previous theories which are, primarily, salesman-oriented approaches.

To be useful in application this theory requires greater skill and maturity on the part of the salesman because he is prevented from talking about his product until he has discovered the customer's needs. This is a sharp contrast to the selling formula, where the salesman is encouraged to point out all the important features of his product. It also requires that the salesman be sufficiently self-confident to undertake control of the sales interview through questioning rather than by dominating the conversation.

For more serious and complex sales situations this approach is preferred to the two previously described theories. It is obviously more time-consuming, but the increased likelihood of making a sale by matching the customer's needs with the appropriate product features and benefits makes this approach more attractive, particularly in situations where the potential commissions and/or profits are great enough to warrant the extra expenditure of time.

AN ELABORATION OF THE NEED-SATISFACTION THEORY

The need-satisfaction theory is definitely preferable as a basis for all selling above the canvassing level. The form in which it is presented above is too brief to be meaningful. Accordingly, there follows an elaboration and interpretation of the basic premises of the theory, extensive enough so that anyone can adopt it for his own use. Figure 1 is used to facilitate the task.

The Three Phases

The chart can be read as follows. At the beginning of the sales interview the salesman asks questions which elicit conversation on the part of the customer or prospect. Each reply should trigger off the next question. This results in the salesman talking a much smaller percentage of time than the customer. This is portrayed by assigning the space above the curve to the salesman and the space below the curve to the customer. The goal of the salesman is to get the customer to talk about his needs. This is called the "need development" phase of the sales interview.

At point X the salesman gets insight into the customer's needs and, as can be seen, starts to take over more and more of the conversation. This is seen in the change of the curve in the chart. Now, the salesman, recognizing the customer's needs, should set out to get the customer to see his own needs. The term applied to this phase is "need awareness." When the salesman gets the customer to see his needs clearly, point Y has been reached.

The final phase, "need fulfillment," consists of the salesman showing the customer how the product will meet his needs. To do this he necessarily monopolizes the conversation, and it is seen that the curve approaches the bottom of the chart, zero per cent of the talking then being done by the customer.

To contrast the three theories on the single variable of salesman-buyer participation in the sales interview examine Figures 2 and 3. In the stimulus-response situation the salesman makes a point, then allows the customer to reply. If the answer is "no" the salesman again takes over the conversation. In the selling formula the salesman dominates conversation except during interest and desire stages.

Need Development. While there are many reasons why customers might buy a product, each customer has his own peculiar ideas as to his needs and the uses he will make of the product. The salesman is generally equipped with all the sales points in terms of uses and benefits that will show how his product or service will meet the needs of any customer in any situation. The temptation is strong for the salesman to explain all points to each customer. It is suggested that in the beginning of the sales interview the salesman refrain from telling what his product will do and concentrate on finding out what the customer needs or thinks he needs. Once the customer's needs are understood, the product features and benefits which will meet these needs constitute the basis of the sales presentation for that customer. The salesman must ask questions which will bring out the customer's needs, and to do

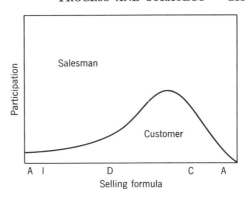

Figure 3

this he must ask questions that will keep the customer talking freely. In Figure 1 it is seen that in the need development phase the customer does far more talking than the salesman. However, once the salesman sees how the product will meet the customer's needs he has reached point X, and the course of the sales interview changes.

Need Awareness. Even though the salesman understands the customer's needs, it does not follow that the customer fully realizes his own needs. It may be necessary for the salesman to go back over some of the ground covered in the need development phase to bring out more clearly to the customer just what his needs are. If he will focus the conversation on those areas where he detects needs, the customer will eventually see such needs himself; but the salesman should not start to close until point Y has been reached. At that point both the salesman and the customer have a clear picture of the needs.

It will be argued that if the salesman already knows the customer's needs there is no point in putting off the closing. It is entirely possible, of course, that the salesman has found out what the customer's needs are before he makes his call on that customer. Even though the salesman knows the customer's needs from previous calls or other sources or deduces them very quickly in the sales interview, he should not try to close until the customer has a full understanding of his needs. When the customer realizes that the salesman knows his needs and has gained his knowledge of them from the immediate conversation, he is likely to feel a mutual understanding has been reached. If, on the other hand, the salesman tries to close too quickly it will build up resentment in the customer. Therefore, the best preparation for closing consists of the salesman and the customer developing the needs together.

Need Fulfillment. Once both the customer and the salesman agree on the customer's needs, the salesman can in his own mind select those product features which will meet the customer's needs. In other words, he shows the customer how his needs can be filled by purchasing the product. This is the meaning of need fulfillment.

The reader will recognize that the traditional course or book on salesmanship usually starts at this point. The problem of understanding needs is treated lightly or skipped, and the salesman is limited to telling the customer what the product will do. The point of view expressed here is that it is better for the salesman to understand the customer's needs and be sure that the customer understands how the salesman obtained his information.

SUMMARY

Three theories of selling have been described. The need-satisfaction theory appears to be most valuable for higher level selling and accordingly it has been elaborated to the point where the salesman can apply it.

Selling as a Dyadic Relationship— A New Approach

F. B. EVANS

The proposal is made that the phenomenon of selling should be analyzed both psychologically and sociologically. In this study, consequently, the research unit is taken to be the interactive dyad. Some results of an exploratory study of life insurance agents and their prospects are reported. Dr. Evans is on the faculty of the Graduate School of Business at the University of Chicago.

Very little is known about what takes place when the salesman and his prospect meet. The two parties meet in a highly structured situation, and the outcome of the meeting depends upon the resulting interaction. In this sense, the "sale" is a social situation involving two persons. The interaction of the two persons, in turn, depends upon the economic, social, physical, and personality characteristics of each of them. To understand the process, however, it is necessary to look at both parties to the sale as a dyad,[1] not individually. Specifically the hypothesis is: the sale is a product of the particular dyadic interaction of a given salesman and prospect rather than a result of the individual qualities of either alone. This approach to the selling situation is quite different from the ones typically found in business practice.

THE TRADITIONAL VIEW OF SELLING

Although salesman selection and evaluation cannot be undertaken with any significant degree of certainty (in spite of the large investments made in psychological test procedures), the emphasis in business is still placed upon finding ideal sales types. The salesman is thought of as outgoing, bluff, hardy, and ag-

gressive.[2] Salesmen, themselves, feel that the stereotype fits. Raymond W. Mack has suggested that salesmen are "money" oriented as opposed to technical people who are "work" oriented.[3] There is very little commitment to the job and no fixed behavior patterns. Mack further suggests that selling is an occupation one enters for status maintenance; a job into which are filtered the sons of managers, professionals, and proprietors who are unable to keep up with the standards set by their fathers.[4] It is also said that unlike many other professions even moderate success in selling depends upon a real liking for the job.[5]

Literally thousands of books and articles have been written about sales techniques but invariably these deal only with the salesman's point of view. Three approaches are common to these works. They are:

1. *The Sales Personality*—what the salesman must be. The salesman must develop a "sales personality" by self-appraisal and self-development.[6] The salesman must be mentally tough but he must have more tact, diplomacy, and social poise than most other employees. He must be ambitious, self-confident, like people, thrive on responsibility, like to travel and want to be his own boss.[7]

2. *The Persuasive Salesman*—how to persuade or manipulate prospects. Some writers suggest a general approach, for example: a. Establish need for the product. b. Believability.

◆ SOURCE: Reprinted by permission from *The American Behavioral Scientist* (Division of Sage Publications), Vol. VI, May 1963, pp. 76–79.

213

c. Make materials attractive and positive. d. Repetition. e. Offer a variety of products or services.[8] Other writers concentrate on finding different ways to handle the various kinds of prospects. For example: regardless of type, all true prospects will buy from someone. Will it be you? It could be if you will learn to classify prospects and then use the methods, principles, and techniques that will permit you to handle the various prospects in the most profitable manner.[9]

3. *The Adaptable Salesman*—be whatever the prospect wants. For example: the good salesman is a chameleon and likes being one. He must be what the client wants, to make the client feel that he (the salesman) understands him,[10] and, the salesman must find a man's wave length and tune in.[11]

INTERACTION STUDIES

Business Studies

Two sociological studies have dealt with retail saleswomen and restaurant waitresses. Both have recognized the importance of the interaction between the client and the salesperson. Lombard studied twenty saleswomen in the children's clothing department of a large department store.[12] He found that salesgirls perceive customers who reject the merchandise as rejecting them and vice versa,[13] that customers in a hurry perceive salesgirls as not being interested in them,[14] and that the salesgirl who feels secure in beliefs about herself perceives the customer as someone who needs help.[15] She feels she has done her best when she helps the customer.

Whyte similarly pointed out the importance of the interaction between the restaurant waitress and her customers, and the waitress and the cook.[16] He found that the behavior of the waitress varies with the social status of the customer she serves.[17] The higher the social status of the restaurant's clientele, the less friendly and personal the waitress must act. The well-adjusted waitress did not react to her customer's moods, etc. She controlled her behavior.[18] Whyte also noted, "if the cook and waitress have a fight or if the waitress clashes with her supervisor, then that waitress is likely to take out her aroused feelings on the customer through poor service or discourtesy. . . ."[19]

Interviewing

As opposed to selling, most studies of interviewing in social research have dealt with the interaction problems of interviewer and respondent. The general assumption is that the more freely the information is given the more valid it is likely to be.[20] Anything that hinders the communication may bias the answers. The fewer such characteristics as age, sociometric status, and education the interviewer and respondent have in common, the more difficult the interview.[21] Similarly the interviewer's role expectations of the interviewee can bias the survey results.[22] The interviewer may record the answers that he thinks the respondent should (wants to) give rather than the correct ones.

The September, 1956, issue of the *American Journal of Sociology* was devoted to the problems of interviewer and respondent interaction. It showed that the relative ages and sex of the respondent and the interviewer affect the answers to questions used.[23] The least inhibited communication took place between young people of the same sex, the most inhibited between people of the same age but different sex.[24] Similarly a study of over 2,400 interviews showed that 90% of the respondents reacted favorably to being interviewed and found pleasure in the relationship with the interviewer.[25]

It has also been shown that interview results can be biased by many other factors. Hyman has said that excessive social orientation of the interviewer is not conducive to superior performance.[26] In other words, too much rapport with the respondent is as bad as too little. And a study of 40 telephone interviews showed that the results were biased if the interviewer said "good" after certain answers as opposed to saying "mm-hmm."[27]

Medicine and Psychotherapy

A doctor's speech and manner are often an important part of his treatment of patients. Many patients are susceptible to *iatrogenicity*, doctor-induced illness.[28] In medical school the prospective doctor is taught the importance of not communicating his own anxieties to the patient.[29] What the doctor says and what the doctor *is* is an important part of the pattern of treatment.[30]

In psychotherapy, communication with the patient *is* the treatment, and every action of the therapist is an important part of the pattern. There is, accordingly, considerable discussion of the interaction situation in the psychoanalytic literature.[31]

Other Interaction Studies

Besides the areas of interviewing and medicine, many other studies in sociology and social psychology have dealt with variables which are important to two-person interaction systems.

It is a common psychological assumption that the average person will often forego a wanted article if he has to face a negative emotional situation to get it, and if the emotional situation is pleasing and gratifying to him, he is likely to purchase articles which he would not otherwise buy.[32] Homans has pointed out that the more frequent the interaction between people, the stronger in general their affection or liking for one another, provided the relationship is mutually rewarding.[33] Similarly, studies have shown that an individual will prefer to interact with someone like himself rather than different if the interaction situation allows for mutual gain.[34]

Studies of military personnel have shown that there is less intense aggression directed towards an instigator of higher status (rank) than toward one of lower status.[35] And in social case work it has been noted that when the client's problems arouse anxiety in the caseworker, there is a risk that the worker will respond in relation to his own anxiety, and not to the client's needs.[36]

SELLING LIFE INSURANCE

Life insurance selling is considered to be one of the higher types of "creative" selling. It is highly rated among sales occupations. The life insurance agent is better liked and thought to be better trained, more honest, less aggressive, and less high pressured than the automobile or real estate salesman.[37] It is also an occupation where relatively few succeed in the long run; less than a quarter of the new inexperienced agents last through the first four years.

Rarely does the life insurance purchaser seek out either the agent or the company. The agent must locate the prospect and sell him upon his need for (more) insurance. Also, few people discriminate among the major life insurance companies in the United States. The typical view is that all the large companies are equally good and that their prices and services

are identical.[38] The particular life insurance agent who contacts a prospect is the critical factor in determining whether or not a sale is made. Little life insurance would be sold without the actions of the salesmen.

DYADIC INTERACTION IN LIFE INSURANCE SELLING

In spite of the recognized importance of the relationship between the life insurance agent and his prospect almost no research has been done which focuses upon them as an interacting pair.[39] A study is now being conducted to examine the interaction situation of particular salesman-prospect dyads. The sample consists of approximately 125 established and successful salesmen and some 500 of their particular prospects, half of whom purchased from the agents and half of whom did not. The analysis will focus upon the dyads, successful outcomes versus unsuccessful outcomes.

The main hypothesis of this study is that the interaction in the dyad determines the results. The more similar the parties in the dyad are, the more likely a favorable outcome, a sale. The areas being studied include the social, economic, physical, personality, and communicative characteristics of both parties. Also included are the salesman's role and the prospect's view of it, sales techniques, product and company knowledge, and the influence of third parties to the selling situation.

Although this study is only about one-third completed at this time, comparisons of the sold and unsold prospects (alone) indicate the importance of their reactions to the particular salesman who called upon them. Table 1 shows that prospects who purchase insurance know more about the salesman and his company and feel more positively towards them than prospects who do not buy.

The salesmen in this study have shown a high degree of role involvement. Most feel that they are salesmen 24 hours a day, not just for working hours; they feel they work no harder than people with office jobs, and are satisfied with the way their lives have turned out. They enjoy talking to prospects and typically discuss things other than insurance with the prospects.

Half of the agents view their job as being like that of a minister; the other half think it is more like a teacher's. None believe it is like other sales jobs. They say that they hold the clients' interests higher than either a lawyer

Table 1. Comparison of Sold and Unsold Prospects' Recall and Attitudes Towards Sales Agent Who Called on Them

Interaction indicator	Sold (Percentage)	Unsold (Percentage)
Consider salesman a friend	31	6
Consider salesman an expert	67	55
Salesman liked me as a person	78	60
Salesman enjoys his job	95	75
Salesman enjoyed talking to me	98	71
Prospect knew salesman's name	76	32
Would introduce salesman to my business friends	92	78
Would introduce salesman to my social friends	89	79
Salesman represents the best company	20	10
Denied agent's call	0	20
Company A, not represented by salesman, is best	18	17
Total Dyads	(45)	(104)

or tax accountant does. They do not feel that they are intruders upon the prospect's privacy and they claim not to be personally upset by a prospect's refusal to buy. Also they conform to rigid standards of dress which they think the role requires.

In spite of their role involvement these salesmen exhibited many conflicting attitudes. Less than 10% of them would like to see their sons follow in their footsteps. They claimed that they enjoyed meeting new people, yet over two-thirds of them said they would quit selling if they had to make only cold canvas calls. They feel they need introductions or referrals from past clients. Three-quarters of the agents indicated no interest in the professional C.L.U. degree, nor did they believe it would in any way help their selling.

Although the agents realize that they must please their prospects, they tend to deny the importance of the interpersonal relations. They say that their prospects are the kind of people they'd like to know better as friends, the kind they'd invite to a family party or to their church's picnic. Still they claim that a prospect's age, religion, ethnic background, appearance, or whether he has children makes no difference to them. It seems quite unselective. The agents in the study are all married men with children, and the majority do not smoke.

The agents equate hard work with success. They want to tell the prospect what's best for him. They prefer to call on prospects at home, in the evening, and to talk to them in either the dining room or kitchen. A table is a handy sales tool. Some agents like to have the wife present when the sales presentation is made but most are indifferent on this point. In carrying out his role the salesman believes he knows the expectations and reactions of his prospects. In this he is only partially right.

The agent's training and his job expectations make him believe (or want to believe) that he can sell everyone. The agents tend to deny the importance of their interaction with particular kinds of prospects. However, analysis of the dyads available so far in this study points to the importance of certain similarities between the salesman and his prospect. Table 2 indicates that the successful dyads are more alike internally than the unsuccessful ones. The differences are small, but they are consistent.

The more alike the salesman and his prospect are, the greater the likelihood for a sale. This is true for physical characteristics (age, height), other objective factors (income, religion, education) and variables that may be related to personality factors (politics, smoking). It is also important to note that the perceived similarity for religion and politics is much higher and of greater importance to the sales than the true similarity.

SUMMARY AND CONCLUSION

Life insurance selling is commonly conceived of as depending upon the relationship between the salesman and his prospect, yet the salesman-prospect dyad has rarely been studied. The traditional marketing approach to selling has been contrasted with interaction studies in sociology and medicine. Research is now being done on the salesman-prospect dyad. Some early results of this study indicate differences in the ways sold and unsold prospects viewed the particular salesman who called upon them, how the salesman views his role, and differences in pair similarity between sold and unsold dyads. Similarity of attributes within the dyad appears to increase the likelihood of a sale.

Much more basic research into various

Table 2.   Internal Pair Similarity of Sold and Unsold Dyads

Characteristic	Sold Dyads (Percentage)	Unsold Dyads (Percentage)	Total (Percentage)
Salesman same height or taller than Prospect	32	68	100
Salesman shorter than Prospect	28	72	100
Salesman same or better educated than Prospect	35	65	100
Salesman less educated than Prospect	23	77	100
Salesman and Prospect less than nine years apart in age	33	67	100
Salesman and Prospect more than nine years apart in age	25	75	100
Salesman earns same or more than Prospect	33	67	100
Salesman earns less than Prospect	20	80	100
Salesman and Prospect either both smokers or both non-smokers	32	68	100
Salesman and Prospect have different smoking habits	26	74	100
Salesman and Prospect have same religion	32	68	100
Salesman and Prospect have different religions	28	72	100
Salesman and Prospect have same political party	35	65	100
Salesman and Prospect have different political party	27	73	100
Prospect perceives Salesman's religion the same as his own	36	64	100
Prospect perceives Salesman's religion different from his own	28	72	100
Prospect perceives Salesman's political party the same as his own	48	52	100
Prospect perceives Salesman's political party different from his own	20	80	100
Total Dyads	30(45)	70(104)	100(149)

aspects of the selling situation will be needed before any definitive and practical results may be expected.

NOTES AND REFERENCES

[1] For a general discussion of dyad analysis, see M. W. Riley, et al., Sociological Studies in Scale Analysis (New Brunswick, N.J.: Rutgers University, 1954).

[2] W. K. Kirchner and M. D. Dunnette, "How Salesmen and Technical Men Differ in Describing Themselves," Personnel Journal, 37, No. 11 (April, 1959), p. 418.

[3] Raymond W. Mack, Northwestern University, in an unpublished speech, "Who Is the Salesman?," 1955.

[4] Ibid.

[5] Anne Roe, The Psychology of Occupations (New York: John Wiley & Sons, 1956), pp. 178–79.

[6] R. W. Husband, The Psychology of Successful

Selling (New York: Harper & Brothers, 1953), pp. 260–270.

[7] W. J. Stanton and R. H. Buskirk, *Management of the Sales Force* (Homewood, Ill.: Richard D. Irwin, 1959), pp. 126 ff.

[8] W. E. Robinson, President, The Coca-Cola Company, "Fundamental Factors in Persuasion," *Industrial Medicine and Surgery*, June, 1956, pp. 269–72.

[9] J. W. Thompson, "A Strategy of Selling," *Salesmanship*, edited by S. J. Shaw and J. W. Thompson (New York: Henry Holt, 1960), p. 18.

[10] H. J. Leavitt, "Selling and the Social Scientist," *Journal of Business*, XXVII (April, 1954), pp. 41–43.

[11] H. S. Bell, *Championship Selling* (Englewood Cliffs, N.J.: Prentice-Hall, 1959), p. 45.

[12] George F. F. Lombard, *Behavior in a Selling Group* (Boston: Harvard, 1955).

[13] *Ibid.*, p. 207.

[14] *Ibid.*, p. 209.

[15] *Ibid.*, p. 227.

[16] William F. Whyte, *Human Relations in the Restaurant Industry* (New York: McGraw-Hill, 1948).

[17] *Ibid.*, p. 92.

[18] *Ibid.*, p. 109.

[19] *Ibid.*, p. 18.

[20] Mark Benny and Everett C. Hughes, "Of Sociology and the Interview," *American Journal of Sociology*, LXII (September, 1956), p. 139.

[21] Robert L. Kahn and Charles F. Cannell, *The Dynamics of Interviewing* (New York: John Wiley, 1957), p. 11.

[22] Herbert Hyman, *et al.*, *Interviewing in Social Research* (Chicago: University of Chicago, 1954), pp. 83–117.

[23] Mark Benny, David Reisman, and Shirley A. Star, "Age and Sex in the Interview," *American Journal of Sociology*, LXII (September, 1956), pp. 143–52.

[24] *Ibid.*, p. 152.

[25] Charles F. Cannell and Morris Axelrod, "The Respondent Reports on the Interview," *American Journal of Sociology*, LXII (September, 1956), p. 177.

[26] Hyman, *et al., op. cit.*, p. 282.

[27] Donald C. Hildam and Roger W. Brown, "Verbal Reinforcement and Interviewer Bias," *Journal of Abnormal and Social Psychology*, 53 (1956), p. 111.

[28] Robert P. Goldman, "Do Doctors Make You Sick?" *Custom and Crises in Communication*, edited by Irving J. Lee (New York: Harper, 1954), pp. 257–61.

[29] Brian Bird, *Talking with Patients* (Philadelphia: J. B. Lippincott, 1955), p. 63.

[30] Fillmore H. Sanford, "Interpersonal Communication," *Industrial Medicine and Surgery*, 25 (June, 1956), pp. 261–65.

[31] Harry Stack Sullivan, *The Psychiatric Interview* (New York: W. W. Norton, 1954); Dominick A. Barbara, "The Value of Non-Verbal Communication in Personality Understanding," *The Journal of Nervous and Mental Diseases*, 123, No. 3 (March, 1956); and H. L. Lennard, *et al.*, *The Anatomy of Psychotherapy: Systems of Communication and Expectation* (New York: Columbia University, 1960).

[32] Charles Berg, *The First Interview* (London: George Allen and Unwin, 1955), p. 31.

[33] George C. Homans, *Social Behavior: Its Elementary Forms* (New York: Harcourt, Brace & World, 1961), pp. 186–187.

[34] Selwyn Becker (unpublished research report, Stanford University, 1959).

[35] John W. Thibaut and Henry W. Riecken, "Authoritarianism, Status, and the Communication of Aggression," *Human Relations*, No. 8 (May, 1955), p. 119.

[36] Francis B. Stark, "Barriers to Client-Worker Communication at Intake," *Social Case Work*, XL, No. 4 (April, 1959), p. 183.

[37] R. K. Bain, "The Process of Professionalization: Life Insurance Selling" (unpublished doctoral dissertation, University of Chicago, 1959, p. 342).

[38] Unpublished data, by the writer, 1959.

[39] Research on life insurance selling is commonplace but it has followed the traditional marketing methodologies. *Supra.*

Systems Selling: Industrial Marketing's New Tool

THOMAS J. MURRAY

When C. Ray Harmon was brought in as assistant to the president of Los Angeles' Electronic Specialty Co. in 1955, he found the firm floundering along with a few components on its production lines, a meager $1.6 million in sales and only $72,000 in profits. The company had just gone public after an erratic eleven-year existence, and its growth prospects in the electronics market were not particularly bright. Harmon, however, came armed with a reputation as a "hatchet man" whose specialty was chopping off operating inefficiencies. More important, he brought with him a plan to change the entire profile of the concern.

In just nine years, Harmon's idea has transformed a sluggish outfit into a thriving operation. Sales are expected to top $85 million this year, and earnings will probably exceed $1.6 million. And what was Harmon's plan? It was to develop full lines of compatible products and services that could be tied together and marketed in packages called "systems." His method: spin off all unrelated items and build a full "systems" capability for the firm through acquisitions.

Electronic Specialty's experience, while unusually successful, is by no means an isolated case. The systems approach to industrial marketing has sent a quiet revolution rippling through the ranks of American business. Scores of companies have placed their marketing em-

phasis on selling systems, or, as they are often described, combinations of products and services designed to perform a complete function for the customer. The upshot is a dimming of the traditional role of many suppliers as mere vendors of off-the-shelf items and a concomitant growth in their ambitions to act as project contractors who move in and solve problems.

Big firms such as Allis-Chalmers, Honeywell and General Precision, as well as medium-sized and small concerns, such as Dorr-Oliver, Taylor Instrument, Ajax Magnethermic, Hobart Manufacturing and Rohr Corp. to name but a few, are trying to become all things to their customers. From their wide range of goods and services, these companies are now providing start-to-finish systems designed, engineered and packaged to perform integrated functions ranging from manufacturing to material handling and from data processing to distribution.

Among the more complex systems are General Precision's fully automatic pressure pumping and inventory measuring system for huge petroleum tank farms and Ajax Magnethermic's fully integrated continuous-casting system for the processing of nonferrous metals from raw materials to finished product. Somewhat simpler systems include the total power propulsion package engineered for and installed in commercial jet transports by Rohr Corp. and the full refrigeration, heating, ventilating and air-conditioning package designed and sold by Hussmann Refrigeration to supermarkets.

For most of these firms, the big push toward systems selling in the industrial market is of very recent vintage and in many cases involves some of the same corporate integration achieved at Electronic Specialty. Thus, with companies such as Allis-Chalmers, which began its drive about four years ago through the acquisition of a joint interest in a systems company, or with General Precision, which combined two hardware companies in 1962 to enhance its systems capability, or with Ajax, which bought two concerns with compatible product lines in 1958, the shift to this approach has involved a step-by-step development of their capabilities. Says William Terry, general manager of Allis-Chalmers' electrical apparatus and systems division: "Every expansion of our plants is geared in some way to further development of this systems concept."

Why is everybody getting on the systems-selling bandwagon? For the most part, it is due to an emerging awareness among marketing men that industrial buyers are searching for greater value for every puchasing dollar. Says Conrad Jones, vice president at the well-known management consulting firm Booz, Allen & Hamilton: "In the future, you'll find more customers thinking in terms of doing more business with fewer suppliers. You can't satisfy a customer with just a product. We think selling a total package of satisfaction is the way of the future."

More specifically, the reasons for the upsurge of interest in this marketing strategy range over the full spectrum of recent industrial developments:

Intensifying competition has caused suppliers to search out new ways to market their goods, hence the accent on selling whole packages of products and services with its promise of more sales, fuller use of capacity and greater turnover.

An increasing awareness on the part of industrial firms that the machinery and techniques required for a modern plant are so complex, they can rarely understand all their own needs, much less buy and install the equipment on their own.

The need for greater reliability of technical machinery and processes is forcing industrial buyers to lean heavily on the quality of equipment purchased, hence the demand for greater supplier responsibility.

The realization of small industrial firms, caught in a competitive squeeze, that they can no longer afford to think in terms of individual components.

Spurred on by these developments, vendors have been promoting, advertising and selling this systems concept with ever-widening emphasis. And yet, for all the hoopla surrounding the trend, there is really nothing new about it at all. Its origins can probably be found in the approach of the Bell System more than fifty years ago when American Telephone & Telegraph President Theodore Vail looked upon the telephone not as a product to be sold but as a total communications system with a variety of integrated services. Similarly, heavy-equipment manufacturers such as General Electric and Allis-Chalmers decades ago were putting together combinations of their equipment and services to perform complete cycles on production lines.

What is new, however, is the increasing integration of automation with manufacturing and processing functions and all the allied operations of a contemporary industrial facility. Suppliers view the possibilities of applying some form of automation to their products as virtually endless. "In ten years," says George W. Downs, director of systems sales at General Telephone's Automatic Electric Co., "it will be fantastic. Soon all processes will be automated."

Moreover, applications of the systems approach in the military market have provided a powerful impetus to its growth in the industrial field. The skills, advanced technology and marketing ability acquired in servicing defense contracts have begun to give many companies new outlets to the commercial market. "In one case about two years ago," points out Electronic Specialty President William H. Burgess, "we discovered that a system we had been building for a defense contract was applicable to the industrial area."

But for all the emphasis on the term *systems*, there is considerable objection in some quarters to the glibness with which it is used. To Harold A. Wolff of Booz, Allen & Hamilton, the packages being sold by most suppliers are not, despite their claims, systems. "They're just selling related products," insists Wolff. "There's nothing new about that. It's just fundamental marketing know-how."

And certainly there is no unanimity among suppliers themselves on a precise definition of the term they have begun to use so freely. In fact, at a seminar organized by the American Management Association, representatives of several leading manufacturers found themselves at odds about what systems selling is. Finally, after much wrangling, says Lester M. Gottlieb, manager of marketing plans for IBM's data-processing division, a consensus was reached. The definition: "It is marketing based on the consideration of a customer or prospect's needs together with a proposal of a solution for his problem," relates Gottlieb. "This is opposed to coming in with a product and creating a need for it. Or to put it simply, it's really just problem-solving." Nevertheless, until a more precise term is coined, the prevailing trend among suppliers is to describe the concept they are using as systems selling.

WHITHER OBJECTIVITY?

There is, of course, some question about whether a company selling its own equipment in the design and installation of a system can be truly objective in its solution to a customer problem. "The nub of this thing is objectivity," asserts President Allan Harvey of Dasol Corp., New York management consultant firm. "There is a fundamental conflict of interest here and a question of whether a firm has developed the best solution to a client's problem."

By way of answering this charge, most firms assert that they are staking far too much of their reputation on such sales to chance such a risk. To George F. Lambeth, Dorr-Oliver marketing manager, for example, project responsibility means that the firm can insure the quality and performance of its product and thus enhance its prestige. Moreover, management likes the fuller corporate identity that goes with the sale of a system rather than a mere product, and regards its installations as a showcase to spur further sales.

The advantages accruing from this marketing tool do not stop there. Right off the top is the obvious boost it gives to sales. "Ours have grown by one-third," claims Ralph L. Shapcott, president of General Precision's industrial controls division. Adds Donald T. Gregg, manager of Taylor Instrument Co.'s contract and construction division: "Over several years now it has added an appreciable portion to our volume, perhaps as much as 10%." And reports Nathaniel T. Holzer, vice president of marketing at Los Angeles' Redcor Corp.: "You might say that our climb from just $300,000 in sales just two years ago to over $4.5 million this year is largely a result of this approach."

Equally heart-warming to its practitioners is the broader line of products the systems approach can spawn. A vendor's capabilities can be stretched to produce new items for integration in more elaborate systems or in further improvements to an original installation. Also, the competitive edge it gives a firm is so compelling, it is almost sufficient reason in itself for switching to a systems approach. Since sale of a total system involves a long-term marriage between vendor and buyer, the supplier is virtually assured of being the one continuing source of parts and service. Says one marketing executive, with an almost diabolical grin: "It's positively Machiavellian, isn't it?"

For all firms marketing such packaged programs, the one enduring benefit is an over-all improvement in customer relations. The intimate relationship that develops between both parties, together with the solution that a supplier brings (hopefully) to his client's problems, molds a special tie that is unlike anything in more conventional vendor-customer relationships.

Organizing a company for the systems approach to marketing involves, in many cases, a thoroughgoing overhaul of its operations—from management outlook to sales procedures in the field. At Electronic Specialty, the basic decision started at the very top and was predicated on the belief that an acquisition program was the essential route to building up the required product lines. The firm has since picked up some twenty firms with compatible products, including a complete marketing organization for its selling, and has developed a full engineering capability to handle its design and application programs.

One major problem that can trouble the multidivisional company getting into the systems business is coordinating the various activities of each division. This problem has been solved at Electronic Specialty by the creation of a position called system project manager, an outgrowth of military and aerospace marketing practices. Notes IBM's Lester Gottlieb: "This is a fairly prevalent solution among systems companies. Making him [the system project manager] responsible for the whole project is one of the most efficient ways to coordinate the activities of each group and to optimize the total corporate point of view."

The actual selling process also calls for a radically different approach. For one thing, sales personnel must completely revamp their thinking away from the traditional product orientation. Says Taylor Instrument's Donald Gregg: "You're working on higher echelons, perhaps even with corporate officials. You rarely discuss the comparative merits of your hardware. You focus on your competence, your reputation and your ability to perform."

For most companies this has meant the establishment of special training programs for sales personnel. At Allis-Chalmers, says William Terry, sales people are brought into headquarters four times a year for special seminars that continuously build up their technical competence and familiarity with new developments.

But not every company agrees with the training approach. At Dorr-Oliver, for example, an official says the company does not contemplate any special training for its salesmen. "For those still oriented in their thinking toward equipment rather than a process," he explains, "we have to convince them to change their approach themselves. It won't happen overnight, of course, but they just have to learn to educate themselves."

Still another development is the increasing use of team selling. Involving as it does in most cases a very high price tag and a relatively complex package of equipment, a systems sale calls for presentation by at least a systems engineer in addition to the regular sales personnel. At Ajax Magnethermic, says marketing manager Marvin E. Hackstedde, the field sales people, all of whom are graduate engineers, are backed up by specialized inside salesmen who follow through on an assigned product area all the way from the initial approach to the prospect to the final installation of a complete continuous-casting system.

But, as more than one observer has pointed out, the systems approach is still so relatively new in its expanded use that there is really no genuinely adequate training ground for systems engineers. "There is an extreme lack of qualification in this field and it is dangerous," warns John W. Field, director of the management information services department for The Diebold Group, a leading management consultant specializing in automation problems. "Words can be sold, but not performance. An intimate knowledge of many disciplines is required for this kind of work, but the demand for trained people hasn't been gratified with adequately trained personnel. What we need are analytical generalists."

In at least one case, that of General Precision's industrial controls division, a likely spawning ground for this new breed of technician is in the customer's own engineering department. According to one General Precision spokesman, the division has found that the man in an equipment user's engineering department who has already been responsible for putting together machinery to solve problems and is familiar with all the functions of the firm's technical operations is, in effect, a systems engineer. "Getting him on our side, however, is the problem," said the official.

IDENTIFY THE PROBLEM!

While this problem is certainly a knotty one for suppliers, an even more critical one is the very heart of any system sale: identifying the problem to be solved for a customer. In many cases, prospects are not even aware of the exact trouble they are having and throw the full responsibility on the supplier. Depending on the relative complexity of the problem, sales engineers steeped in the lore of production and technology may be able to pinpoint the trouble at an initial session. Or, as in most of today's highly complex situations, the customer will have to provide the supplier with all the knowledge about his process for a full study and evaluation. "When you go into a customer's plant, you have to know every step of his process," says Allis-Chalmers' Terry. "You can't apply computers and controls until you have an intimate knowledge of the whole process."

To most suppliers, this initial step is the most crucial moment in a potential sale. Embroiled as they are in bidding for many contracts, they feel that an early foothold in determining a customer's requirements is absolutely imperative; otherwise, as some vendors complain, they may spend thousands doing the groundwork only to find the prospect using someone else's specifications and purchasing the equipment from a competitor. "We have met situations," claims a Dorr-Oliver official, "where our preliminary engineering for a proposal was taken by the prospect and used to purchase equipment elsewhere."

To minimize the chance of such occurrences, systems sellers must carefully size up each prospect. At Allis-Chalmers, for example, where proposal costs run from $10,000 to as much as $50,000, marketing people calculate their risks very carefully. Says Terry: "We have to decide if we have a reasonable chance of getting the contract. This is very selective selling." Agrees IBM's Gottlieb: "To stay profitable, there is one overriding guideline: propose only when there is a reasonable chance of getting the order."

If proposals have proven costly to some firms, so too has the development of the systems themselves. Notes Taylor Instrument's Gregg: "This is high-risk stuff. Many of these things have never been done before, and it's awfully difficult to cost them out. We've been too prone to base prices on customer intent; yet this has been too obscure in many cases." Adds David P. Wilkinson, Electronic Associates vice president of planning: "If you can sell some stock solution over and over again via a system, then it's possible to make a profit out of this systems business. Otherwise, a systems company really has a tough time of it."

No less pressing a problem is the need to educate the customer in the limits and potentials of his system. Lack of comprehension has frequently led to misuse of an installation and consequent complaints to the supplier about the quality and performance of his equipment. "Many clients simply don't understand what their system is, what it does and what it can do," laments Redcor's Nat Holzer. "We have launched a customer education program and are beefing it up with a continuing documentation program. As far as we are concerned, it's becoming more and more the responsibility of the manufacturer to teach the customer completely about his system."

One further ramification of this education process, says George M. Muschamp, vice president for engineering at Honeywell's industrial products group, is fully informing the customer that if he is to take on a complete system he may have to accept some reorganization that goes deep into company operations.

Obviously, then, systems selling is not in any way a simple undertaking. For, as one marketing executive points out with almost painful memory: "It usually takes about three years of hard, hard work to convert fully to the systems approach to selling. Moreover, it calls for an unlimited amount of patience, conviction and perseverance."

Left unsaid in that statement are many obstacles. Among them: the enormous task of pulling together products and services that relate; the costly job of gearing production to meet neatly dovetailed schedules; the tough problem of finding or training adequate engineering and sales forces; the backbreaking effort of coordinating autonomous divisional activities; and the continuing task of keeping customers satisfied with a full line of services.

Despite these obstacles, the trend to systems selling is gathering strength and spreading. In fact, some marketing authorities, such as Roger Ball of Chicago's Roger Ball & Associates and Booz, Allen's Conrad Jones, predict that it will eventually move into the consumer market. Ball envisions companies selling housewives complete storage and maintenance systems for their households. Jones points to the upcoming S. C. Johnson & Son (Johnson Wax) nationwide car-wash chain, with its complete wash and wax capability, as a variation on the systems-selling theme.

But it is to the industrial market that most companies look for the most advanced strides. Just getting off the ground as it is in most cases, the systems approach has already endowed its practitioners with a rewarding glimpse of what it can do for a host of industries, from chemicals to transportation. More important, as Automatic Electric's George Downs puts it: "This is really the infancy of something new in industry. Its future will be fabulous."

CASES

The Marion Bank
(Burrough Corporation—C)

Marion Bank was the smallest of three banks serving the city of Marion and surrounding territory. It was also the newest bank in the city, having been established in 1957. The two other banks serving this area were City Federal and People's National, both founded prior to the turn of the century.

Marion Bank was founded by a group headed by Harry Kessler, a businessman with widespread business interests throughout the state. Kessler was well known for his ability to establish or purchase small businesses and build them into thriving firms of substantial size. In preparing and equipping the bank for operations, Mr. Kessler purchased a minimum of banking equipment, almost all of which was second hand. This situation added more authority to a common rumor around Marion that Mr. Kessler was more interested in using the bank as a speculative venture than in the actual founding of a sound banking operation. Within a year from the time the charter was granted, Kessler sold Marion Bank to a group of local civic-minded businessmen. The local

◆ SOURCE: Reprinted by permission from Bennett and Reeves, op. cit. Case prepared by James H. Bearden.

group appointed Harvey Jackson, age 45, to head the newly acquired bank.

Shortly after this change occurred, Edward Ray, who had recently come to Marion, began making calls on Mr. Jackson in order to introduce him to the Burroughs' line of banking equipment. After numerous visits and presentations of various types of supplies and equipment, Ray received an order from Mr. Jackson, the bank's sole purchaser of supplies and equipment for a $2,800 micro-film unit. In the process of delivering and installing this unit, Ray came to know Jackson quite well. Ray had recognized earlier that the bank was operating with used and outmoded equipment; and through this close contact with Jackson, he was able to emphasize frequently that much of the bank's equipment needed replacing. Jackson agreed with Ray that before too long the bank would be forced to purchase newer equipment. However, Jackson's contention, and his main line of resistance to Ray's proposals for replacing old equipment, was that currently the bank's major problem stemmed from personnel problems in the Accounting Department. Jackson believed that this department was performing at a substandard level as a result of the large turnover of personnel, especially machine operators.

Training of personnel in the Accounting Department was the responsibility of the head bookkeeper. However, because of the press of other duties, the head bookkeeper was able to devote little time to actual training. In fact, Ray was of the opinion that the head bookkeeper, aside from lack of time, did not have a strong enough background to do a thorough job of training. Ray had observed that the most prevalent method of training new machine operators in the department was for the leaving operator to train her own replacement. Through his association with the bank and its employees during the past month, Ray was aware of this situation and some of the problems it created. Ray felt that such an arrangement was permitting bad practices to creep into the operation of the office machines. It was his opinion that the operator, through lack of time and interest prior to leaving, was not as attentive to the training of a replacement as was necessary to bring about efficient office practice.

Ray suggested to Jackson that he would be glad to assist in the training of new machine operators. Jackson accepted the offer and proposed that Ray compute the amount he would

charge for this assistance and present it to him.

Ray concluded that once the bank president was satisfied that his Accounting Department was operating at a more efficient level, a replacement order for the outdated equipment would be forthcoming. Therefore, he rejected the idea of accepting payment for his assistance to the bank in the training of new machine operators.

During the next six months Ray was called upon to train five machine operators, two of whom were hired and consequently trained concurrently. Ray had not anticipated that the number of new operators in this department would be as large as it was. However, increased business and promotions, in addition to two resignations, required a considerable amount of training time on Ray's part. He became concerned over the amount of time he was having to devote to this activity. During this same period there were several occasions on which Mr. Jackson called Ray at his home to ask for assistance on various bookkeeping matters. On one such occasion, Ray was asked to come to the bank one evening and help find and error that was causing the bank to be out of balance by $75,000. Even in matters of this nature, Ray was cooperative and gave whatever assistance he could.

In January, one year after his first call on Mr. Jackson and the Marion Bank, Ray's repeated and continual efforts to get Jackson to replace and add to the bank's office machines met with substantial results. Ray, even though failing to get an order for replacing old machinery, convinced Jackson that the bank needed additional equipment to handle its actual and expected work load and subsequently secured an order for two accounting machines, each at a cost of $4,700. At the time of the signing of this order contract, Ray advised Jackson that, due to a heavy demand for this type of equipment, the company had a backlog of orders on this machine and delivery would more than likely not be made until the first of July. Mr. Jackson was agreeable to this arrangement.

In March the largest of Marion's three banks changed ownership. At the same time that the buying group bought City Federal, they also bought the Marion Bank for operation as a City Federal branch. Ray heard about this change of events via a telephone call from Mr. J. O. Tremore, his sales supervisor in the home office. Mr. Tremore told Ray that John Richie was scheduled to take over as new president of City Federal. Mr. Tremore also related the following information in regards to Mr. Richie:

"Richie had been a strong advocate and user of Burroughs' banking equipment throughout his banking career. In 1944 he moved to Smithfield to head a new bank opening in that city. On the opening of this new bank, Richie sought to purchase some new accounting machines through the Burroughs' agent in the Smithfield area. Due to the wartime situation in 1944 the War Production Board directed about 90 per cent of Burroughs' business to the defense effort. Consequently, with Burroughs' first effort pointed toward defense, their production of banking equipment was curtailed sharply. Burroughs made an effort to do what they could for their civilian customers, but it was a virtual impossibility to supply any new equipment. Actually, it was difficult to meet the civilian demand with second-hand equipment, but on occasion, through a real effort to be of service to their customers, Burroughs was able to place some older equipment. This was the situation with Richie. Delivery of second-hand equipment was made to Richie, but Burroughs was not able to furnish personnel to assist in the installation of the equipment. Richie was highly displeased with this situation. Since then, Burroughs' salesmen have been received by Richie but not one order has been received."

During the conversation between Tremore and Ray, the subject of the two accounting machines scheduled for delivery to Marion Bank in July came up. Tremore pointed out that Ray could handle this situation in any manner he thought best. He indicated that Ray, by virtue of his close contact with the actual situation, was probably in a much better position to decide on what action should be taken. However, Tremore suggested that his on-the-surface opinion was that Ray should call on Richie and inform him that delivery of the two accounting machines was in process and would be made around July 1 as scheduled.

City Federal was the largest account Ray had in his entire sales territory. Practically all of the office equipment in the bank had been placed by Burroughs, most of it by Ray himself. Ray was fully aware of the importance of this account and had always paid particular attention to it. He was on good terms with the executives and enjoyed a first name relationship with most of the employees.

Aside from a normal routine of placing one or two orders every six months, Ray's current major project with City Federal consisted of preparing and laying the groundwork for a major replacement of equipment some two years hence. Also included as a current major project was an effort to place a $5,000 machine in the Commercial Loan Department. This machine had been placed in the department on a trial basis in February. At the time of the change in ownership in March, City Federal had made no formal decision on the final purchase of the machine. However, Ray was of the opinion that purchase would take place shortly because operators had been trained and procedures were being adapted to use of the machine.

Ray wasted no time in requesting an interview with the new president. The interview was granted during Richie's first week in his new office. At this interview, Ray introduced himself as the Burroughs' representative in the area. After a few minutes of conversation and mutual sharing of previous work experience and locations, Ray presented to Richie a carefully prepared written list of Burroughs' equipment currently owned by the bank. The list included information regarding the purchase date and age of the equipment (in some cases used equipment had been purchased), what equipment needed replacing, and the trade-in value of old equipment. Also included was a brief indication of some new items of equipment that the bank needed at present. Ray brought out that, in addition to the equipment noted on the list, the bank currently had on trial a commercial loan machine for which no final contract had been signed. Richie replied that he understood that the machine was already being used and that he had really not had a chance to look into its operation at this time.

During their conversation Ray brought up the subject of the two accounting machines which were scheduled for delivery to Marion Bank in July. Richie said he knew about this order and it was of some concern to him. He pointed out that he was planning to consolidate the new branch bank bookkeeping system with that of the parent organization and that he certainly wished that the two $4,700 machines had not been purchased. He indicated, however, that he could possibly use one of the machines. Ray's immediate reaction and reply to this comment was that he could certainly understand how this might be of concern to the new president and he would be glad to cancel delivery on one of the machines. He further pointed out that Burroughs wanted to work with City Federal and they would certainly not push any equipment on them, even though it had been previously ordered. Ray was taken aback when Richie retorted with the statement that he certainly appreciated Burroughs' attitude in this matter and that actually he would like to have delivery on both machines canceled.

QUESTIONS

1. Is Ray a good observer? Did he make incorrect inferences?
2. What is the obligation of the salesman in giving service? What is his obligation in correcting poor management practices?
3. What should Ray do when he is offered pay for his services? Did Ray promise too much in the case?
4. Did Ray handle himself properly in his relations with Richie? Was Tremore's advice to Ray sound?
5. What should Ray do as the case ends?

The Kingsley Clothing Company

Mr. Bob Baker has been a sales representative for Ajax Sewing Machine Company for six years. Ajax is actually a subsidiary of Ringer Sewing Machine Company. Ajax is primarily a manufactural supplier of sewing machines. The biggest customers are clothing plants located throughout the United States and Canada. While operating as a subsidiary of Ringer, Ajax sells a machine very similar to that of the parent company. In fact many parts of various machines are interchangeable between the two makes. Bob is a company representative who works out of the Portsmouth, South Carolina, branch of Ajax. Sales have been good and are increasing due to the fact that many Northern manufacturers are moving South to open new plants. Bob has many sources for developing leads, but his best results have been with the local Chamber of Commerce in each city of his territory. Bob spends as much time as possible visiting members of the various Chambers in hopes of discovering a lead.

Several months ago, Bob was visiting with some members of the Chamber of Commerce of Garristown. Bob's good friend, Jim Butler, mentioned that there was a good possibility that Kingsley Clothing Company out of Pittsburgh, Pennsylvania, was going to lease a new plant in Garristown. Butler informed Bob that A. J. Mizelle was the representative handling initial negotiations for Kingsley and that he had set up a temporary office in the Hickston Building. He further noted that Mr. Mizelle was to meet with the Chamber the following day to give his final decision on Kingsley's proposed move to Garristown. Butler told Bob that he would be in touch with him as to the results of the meeting.

The following day Bob received a call from Butler telling him that Kingsley had decided to lease the plant in Garristown. Bob was especially pleased to hear this because of the promising sales possibility for Ajax machines. Bob obtained the exact address of the new plant from Butler.

Immediately he called for an appointment with Mr. Mizelle for Monday of the following week. The remainder of the weekend, Bob studied as much as he could about the operations of Kingsley Company. From the booklet that Mr. Mizelle had given to Butler, Bob learned that Kingsley used Ringer and Fairlir sewing machines in all of their plants.

Monday morning Bob was waiting in Mr. Mizelle's office for his appointment. He introduced himself as a representative for Ajax Sewing Machines, a subsidiary of Ringer. He called attention to the fact that they had a mutual friend in Jim Butler.

Bob went through his usual presentation and answered all the questions that Mr. Mizelle asked. Bob found the conference to be very pleasant and informative. However, Bob was not prepared when Mr. Mizelle stated, "Although I am not the final decision maker for this type of purchase, I will do everything I can to see that Kingsley purchases Ajax machines from you." Further discussion showed that Kingsley would need around 235 to 250 machines for their new plant. Bob was completely shocked at the size of the possible order. He told Mr. Mizelle that he would contact his branch office in Portsmouth immediately, thus making sure that they could handle such a large order. Mr. Mizelle said that he would contact Bill Jones, head purchasing officer for Kingsley in the Pittsburgh office, and then get in touch with Bob afterwards.

Bob went home and began to make plans

for placement of the order and subsequent delivery of the Ajax machines to Kingsley. After four days went by and there was still no word from Mr. Mizelle, Bob dropped by Mr. Mizelle's office to present the order for approval. Bob found that Mr. Mizelle was no longer in Garristown. Instead he was interviewed by a Mr. Hassell, who had begun duties three days ago as local plant manager for Kingsley. He indicated he had no knowledge of any agreement made by Mr. Mizelle.

QUESTION

1. What are the various problems that the salesman must resolve in this case? Which problems should he deal with first?

PART
IV

Personal Selling in International Markets

World trade is just beginning. Barriers are being broken by great strides in transportation, communication, and economic thinking. In order to participate effectively in this new development, it is essential that students of the personal selling function prepare to serve in this new arena. The readings selected for this section emphasize this challenge.

An examination of individual differences among cultures and markets in international trade is made by Ernest Dichter in "The World Customer."

In the second article, "The Silent Language in Overseas Business," Hall shows how "five key topics—time, space, material possessions, friendship patterns, and business agreements—offer a starting point from which companies can begin to acquire the understanding necessary to do business in foreign countries."

The third article illustrates a current development in selling in world markets.

In Nielsen's article, some of the dangers in selling in foreign markets are discussed. Coupled with these warnings are suggestions for positive actions. "Selling the Tropical African Market" provides a discussion of such problems as "sales representation," "use of itinerant salesmen," and "selection of sales personnel" as they pertain to a specific foreign market.

The World Customer

ERNEST DICHTER

Only one Frenchman out of three brushes his teeth.

Automobiles have become a must for the self-esteem of even the lowliest postal clerk in Naples or the Bantu street cleaner in Durban.

There is a supermarket in Apia, the capital of Western Samoa (which received its independence in January of this year). I found can openers and the cans to go with them in a remote village on the island of Upolu.

Four out of five Germans change their shirts but once a week.

Amazon Indians use outboard motors in deep green water alleyways.

What do these facts, and many others like them, portend for the future marketing manager? For top management in companies with foresight to capitalize on international opportunities? They mean that an understanding of cultural anthropology will be an important tool of competitive marketing. They mean that knowledge of the basic differences, as well as basic similarities, among consumers in different parts of the world will be essential. They mean that the successful marketer of the future will have to think not of a United States customer, nor even of a Western European or Atlantic community customer, but of *a world customer.*

For Western European countries, it is specific marketing facts and consumer purchasing behavior patterns which are of moment to today's businessman seeking new customers. At

present, these countries comprise the biggest potential overseas market for most products. They are also the countries about whose consumers the most research information has been gathered. However, as some of the above examples illustrate, other parts of the world too are becoming potential markets, as human desires break the barricades of centuries in South America, Africa, and Asia.

Emergence of the European Common Market has forced businessmen and philosophers alike to take a look at the European as a distinct species. We now see the European as more than a Frenchman or an Austrian. The Atlantic community market and the world market may make us yet take a fresh look at what is alike and what is really different in humans, their desires, hopes, fears—in short, their motivations. Close observation of customers, and potential customers, all over the world reveals that there *are* some striking similarities, yet at the same time a considerable degree of permanent difference. From objective examination of these basic cultural similarities and differences, one may discern clues for serving the World Customer today.

In this article, I shall first point to a number of consumer behavior patterns relevant to international marketing, particularly within the Western European market but also in some of the less developed areas. Then I shall examine the differential role of national pride, which obviously affects and will affect the success of American-made products in Western European and other countries in the Atlantic market. Finally, in an effort to define and interpret the economic and psychological differences among world customers, I shall postulate six world

♦ SOURCE: Reprinted by permission from *Harvard Business Review,* Vol. 40, No. 4, July–August 1962, pp. 113–122.

market groups of nations, measured by the yardstick of middle class development.

THE DISTINCTIVE EUROPEAN

The U.S. company going into Europe has to study the culture and the psychology of the people of the country, not just its manufacturing facilities and markets in the technological sense. The advertising and sales managers have to learn that reaching customers in a given country involves a real understanding of the basic motivations which operate within that country.

In dealing with various European markets, the American businessman must open his eyes to certain paradoxes, stereotypes, and hidden competitors.

Apparent Paradoxes

There are paradoxes between the way in which American products are perceived and the way they are used. Thus, anti-Americanism is strongly coupled with a desire for many U.S. products, often out of pure snobbery, often because they are symbols of an affluent society. The Italian housewife considers her American sister a poor cook and a lady of leisure, but dreams day and night of owning a Hollywood kitchen.

A similar paradox is that of the West German businessman who scoffs at American know-how, pointing out the technical superiority of many of his national products, but proudly puts his elegantly uniformed chauffeur in a Ford, polished up to the last fold of its lacquered steel hull tuxedo.

Ingrained Stereotypes

The American businessman must cast off deeply ingrained stereotypes in analyzing the purchasing behavior of European consumers, in reference to product meaning, "purchasing morality," and quality consciousness.

We all "know" that French women are very fashion conscious. Yet a study recently showed that this was exactly one of those glib stereotypes that have little if any basis in reality. The purchase of a dress or coat is much more of an investment for the Frenchwoman than for the American woman. This results from differences both in income and in prices of fashion products. It is not enough, therefore, to tell a French shopper that a garment is fashionable.

She also wants to know, in a way, the "trade-in value" of the dress or blouse. How long will the fabric last? How many years will she be able to wear it? These are promises and appeals which have to a very large extent lost their attraction to the American woman.

The European is very conscious of preservation. He collects and retains things. The only parallel that we have had in this country was during the period of World War II, when we developed a new kind of pride, a pride in doing without, a pride in not having bought a new car for several years, for example. This pride did not last very long. Just as soon as cars became available again, we reverted to our somewhat affluent American habit of replacing models quite rapidly. Yet this concept of "purchasing morality" still exerts influence in the United States for some products. For example, the average male still hesitates to buy two or three suits at one time because he feels that suits, together with many other articles of clothing, are highly overvalued, and therefore it is extravagant to buy more than one at the same time. On the other hand, most of us have learned that it no longer pays to resole shoes more than twice.

As for quality consciousness, as well as confidence in the trustworthiness of the manufacturer, this is quite different in different countries. In Australia or South Africa—and for that matter in England—you find on most toilet tissues the reassuring message that the manufacturer guarantees that the paper was not made out of secondhand rags, but only new rags and new raw materials.

Such a promise has become completely unnecessary in North America. Whatever advertising may be accused of, in many areas it provides the consumer, particularly in branded merchandise, with an assurance that he will not be cheated as long as he buys a well-known brand. It is true today that whether we buy a Westinghouse, a General Electric, or a Kelvinator refrigerator, we get more or less equal values as long as we pay about the same amount of money. What we have learned to buy is the freedom of individual choice. We buy images; we buy the sizzle because we have been reassured that the steak itself is of generally good quality. *In many European countries this confidence*, this almost blind reliance on the promise of the manufacturer, *has not yet been established*. Therefore, advertising approaches have to be based much more on definite proofs of quality.

Hidden Competitors

Another problem facing Atlantic marketers is that in many areas they are still dealing with hidden competitors, lurking in places unfamiliar in domestic marketing. Taking toilet tissue again, in some recent motivational research done in West Germany I found it was much too premature to promise the German consumer luxury softness or colors compatible with the bathroom fixtures. Instead, the hidden but real competitor with which the toilet tissue manufacturer has to contend is the newspaper and the old standby of the German equivalent of the Sears, Roebuck catalog. The West German family feels that toilet tissue, particularly the American luxury type, is wasteful and unnecessary. The advertising approach, then, has to deal much more with providing absolution and selling the concept that good quality toilet tissue is a part of modern life.

ETHOS OF NATIONALISM

Nationalism obviously plays a major role in determining consumer acceptance of nondomestically made products. Understanding its manifold aspects is a *sine qua non* for U.S. businessmen operating overseas.

National feeling manifests itself in many ways. Some of these have already been touched on briefly before. In this section, I shall show in greater detail how: (1) national pride can be a motivating sales factor employable by the astute overseas marketer as an asset; (2) longstanding cultural traditions in one nation can dictate the *discard* of advertising approaches proven successful in another nation; (3) stereotyped national *self*-illusions can alter the direction of marketing strategy.

National Pride

Admiration of foreign products often goes together with *hidden inferiority feelings* which are overcompensated by tearing the foreigner down. These products are the tangible symbols of foreign superiority. For example:

In Venezuela, despite various forms of anti-Yankee sentiment, it is considered chic to smoke U.S. cigarettes. Even when the American brand name is used and the Venezuelan smoker can discover the little phrase "Hecho en Venezuela" on his package, the almost completely identical cigarette suffers at least a 50% prestige loss. A successful approach used in overcoming this problem was to convince Venezuelans that the people they secretly admired in a form of love-hatred—the Americans—indeed liked Venezuelan tobacco, used it for their own cigarettes, and had no negative feeling toward Venezuelan cigarettes.

A similar solution was found in connection with Venezuelan rum by serving this rum in hotels in Caracas frequented by U.S. businessmen and tourists. The Venezuelan could be convinced that if it was good enough for the supposed foreign connoisseur, then it certainly ought to be good enough for him.

The French gasoline, *Total*, had a domestic marketing problem arising from a national inferiority complex. Gasoline, to the Frenchman, was for a long time represented by American and British companies. Gasoline and oil (to a lesser extent) are symbols of power. The Frenchman was not convinced that his own gasoline would have the same power as the foreign brands. The approach calculated to overcome this sentiment was to present *Total* as an international brand that happened to originate in France and the Sahara, but was accepted and well-liked in many other countries.

In Morocco, sales of French pasteurized milk had dropped considerably with the advent of Morocco's independence. This stemmed partly from the exodus of the French army with its families, and also from Moroccan unfamiliarity with drinking pasteurized milk.

But the drop in milk sales was also due to other factors, psychological in nature. One was the lack of confidence in the quality of pasteurized milk—Moroccan women were accustomed to buying from street vendors who milked the cows in front of their own eyes and then ladled the milk out of the pail. The soulless, odorless, clean pasteurized milk in bottles was simply too far removed from the original natural source of milk for the women to realize that they were still receiving the same quality of product.

But even more interesting was a factor dealing again with the phenomenon of national pride. The company had changed the lettering on its milk bottles and milk cartons from French to Arabic. The purpose was to please the newly independent consumers. Research showed, however, that instead of being pleased, consumers reacted negatively to this attempt at flattery. They stated it in the following way:

"What is good enough for the French people is good enough for us. We don't want Arab milk. We want good French milk that the Frenchmen drink themselves."

For *marketing purposes* it thus was necessary to re-establish confidence in the naturalness of pasteurized bottled milk by showing cows and having street vendors also peddle pasteurized milk. A second measure was to change the lettering on the milk bottles back to French. Both steps resulted in increased sales.

The little phrase "Made in—" can have a tremendous influence on the acceptance and success of products over and above the specific advertising techniques used by themselves.

In a recent study in West Germany, this query was posed as part of a projective test: "An important discovery has been made in the technical field which has a great influence on our daily life. Which country has made this discovery?" As many as 78% answered: "Germany." (The study is being repeated in other countries. It will be interesting to examine the answers.) We also asked the Germans to think of a new product which through an error in production caused the death of several hundred people. The task of the respondents was to indicate which country would be most likely to manufacture such a product. We found that Germans considered this most likely to happen in the East zone, Russia, or the satellite countries, and then up to 30% in Italy or France.

The strong positive attitude evidenced by Germans toward their own technical product influenced an advertising approach developed for Ford in Germany. Research showed that the name Ford had a strong American association. The reaction of Germans was: "Americans drive our cars, Volkswagen and Mercedes; therefore they must be convinced that German cars are better than their own; so why should we buy their cars?" When the German Ford was presented as an example of cooperation between American ingenuity and know-how and German thoroughness and efficiency, considerable sales success was achieved.

"Inverted Morality"

The influence of cultural traditions permeates a host of consumer behavior patterns.

The fact that 64% of Frenchmen don't brush their teeth is in part caused by the lack of running water in many communities. But a far more interesting aspect of this behavior could be explained on the basis of what I call "inverted morality." Here is an illustration of what can happen:

In Puritanical cultures it is customary to think of cleanliness as being next to godliness. The body and its functions are covered up as much as possible.

But, in Catholic and Latin countries, to fool too much with one's body, to overindulge in bathing or toiletries, has the opposite meaning. It is *that* type of behavior which is considered immoral and improper. Accordingly, an advertising approach based on Puritanical principles, threatening Frenchmen that if they didn't brush their teeth regularly, they would develop cavities or would not find a lover, failed to impress.

To fit the accepted concept of morality, the French advertising agency changed this approach to a permissive one. The new approach presented the brushing of teeth as modern and chic but not as an absolute necessity which when neglected would result in dire consequences.

In line with the "inverted morality" notion is the fact that deodorant sales in France are lower than in most other countries. The majority, up to 80% of French housewives, use laundry soap instead of toilet soap. Only 20% of them have discovered perfumed, feminine soap which in the United States is frequently referred to as a "French type" of soap.

Self-Illusions

Often nationals of a particular country are completely mistaken themselves about their own main characteristics. Successful marketers must be as cognizant of these national self-illusions as they must be aware of the mistaken stereotypes noted earlier. For example:

Germans still refer to themselves as a nation of poets and thinkers; yet the largest selling newspaper, *The Bildzeitung*, has a circulation of 2½ million based largely on sensationalism and tabloid treatment of news. Even German *advertisers* had to be shown that this circulation, although proven by audits, was indeed psychologically possible. The only way this could be done was to force the German advertiser to look at his own people, including himself, without hypocrisy and in the harsh light of reality.

All references to economy, comfort, and warmth had only a minimal effect in getting Englishmen to install central heating. They all ran up against a barrier of traditional self-illusion that Englishmen are of a hardy race that does not need the softening and effeminate effect of central heating. Inroads could be made only when the health of babies was used as a rationalization and after reassurance was given to the English "he-man" that to feel comfortably warm would not be detrimental to his self-image of virility.

Most Europeans are convinced that they are individualists and nonconformists. Studies have shown that this is to a very large extent an illusion. There is a widely expressed fear of losing individuality, but right now it is the European who is becoming the representative of the mass market while it is the American market which in turn relies more and more on psychological segmentations. U.S. manufacturers may produce individuality on a mass scale, but individuality has become the decisive appeal in many products and services.

National self-illusions are hardly restricted to other nations. In the United States, as in quite a few other countries, many of our ethical principles are still based on the concept that we have to work by the sweat of our brow. In Germany, this is even more so. *The more you work, the more moral you feel.* Yet at the same time our modern psychological development and automation have resulted in a situation where fewer and fewer people work with their hands. Service fields are increasing, and we have more and more leisure time. The recent victory of the electricians' union in New York introducing a five-hour day aroused the nation for many reasons. Particularly pertinent here is that it clashed with most of our cherished beliefs of the importance of achieving happiness through work.

We are now confronted with increasing leisure time. Our discomfort results to a large extent from a lack of hedonistic morality such as prevailed among the Greeks for whom life was here to be enjoyed by a few people who did not have to work and did not have to feel guilty about it.

Leisure pursuits are spreading rapidly. Labor-saving devices are multiplying, and they are being adopted all over the world. The major difference lies in the degree of manifest or latent guilt feelings which are aroused:

Instant coffee is used by the Dutch housewife accompanied by the verbal protest that she only uses it in an emergency. What happens, however, is that the number of emergencies has increased amazingly.

French farmwives are inclined to say that they need large kitchen stoves in order to do the cooking for their large farm families. Young farmwives, however, have begun to admire and gradually buy the smaller units used by their city sisters. They have discovered that they do not have to stay as long behind the stove, and so are finding interests in other roles than that of a kitchen slave.

BREAKING BOUNDARIES

Politically, in recent years we have watched a host of new nations emerge from erstwhile colonial status. It may be argued that many colonies would have been better off staying under the protection of enlightened colonial powers. Yet their desire for independence, no matter how premature we consider it to be, is so impulsive, explosive, and uncontrollable that no other solution remains than to satisfy this emotionally, humanly understandable hunger.

More important to the marketer is the fact that the same desire which spurred these political events has another dimension—viz., *in terms of consumption, whole centuries are being skipped in a world revolution of human expectations.*

Thus, from the viewpoint of the international psychologist's concern with the people still living in national units, we see the gradual development of the World Customer who breaks all boundaries:

When a South African clothing manufacturer asks how to sell more long pants to previously half-naked Bantus, he is the first one to smash the barrier of apartheid, no matter how segregationistic his views may be. The moment one starts thinking of 10 million natives as consumers, one has to concern himself with their emotions and motivations.

Research revealed a greater psychological parallel between the emancipated Zulu and the emancipated white worker than between the nonemancipated Zulu and his emancipated tribal brother. The latter is ashamed when visited by his former ethnic peers. He has learned to speak English Afrikaans, has started to wear long pants, and often owns a car—a second-hand, dilapidated car, but nevertheless a car. He represents in many ways the same emotional conflict as that which existed between the first- and second-generation immigrants during the period of heavy immigration in the United States.

In Australia until a few years ago 10% of the population was represented each year by newcomers, migrants, or—more euphemistically—"new Australians." These new Australians will change the basic Australian character in unrecognizable fashion within another ten years or so. As consumers, on the one hand, they want to eat, drink, and use the same products as the established Australians; on the other hand, they bring in their own customs and often superimpose Italian, German, or Spanish culture on the Australians.

Six Market Groups

How can we locate the World Customer at various stages of development? How can we measure nations?

The "consumer revolution" which we are witnessing is basically not a proletarian one, but is *a revolution of the middle class*. It is the degree of development of a large middle class which makes the difference between a backward and a modern country both economically and psychologically. That is the clue for appraising and interpreting different cultures, for measuring their achievement.

The most important symbol of middle class development in the world today is the automobile. It is the automobile which represents achievement and personal freedom for the middle class. And this restless middle class is the most important factor in the constructive discontent which motivates people's desires and truly moves them forward. In some countries, like the United States, West Germany, Switzerland, Sweden, and Norway, most people have enough to eat and are reasonably well housed. Having achieved this thousand-year-old dream of humanity, they now reach out for further satisfactions. They want to travel, discover, be at least physically independent. The automobile is the symbol of mobility; the auto-mobile has become the self-mobile!

Using middle class development as a measure of achievement, if we were to visualize the social composition of each country in terms of a scale showing the size of its middle class,

upper class, and lower class, we could probably define some six groups.

Group One: The Almost Classless Society, Contented Countries. In this group we would include primarily the Scandinavian countries. The middle class takes up almost all of the scale, with very few people left who could be considered really poor and few who are really rich. We are dealing with a socialistic security and equalization which sounds like paradise, but often leads to loss of incentives.

In these countries, products are viewed in a rather sober fashion. The car, for instance, is strictly utilitarian, and showing off with one's auto is not considered correct.

Studies have shown that reliability and economy are very important. Attitudes toward products are rational: they do not represent a special status value. There is generally a conservative attitude toward new gadgets and styles. Second cars are practically nonexistent.

Group Two: The Affluent Countries. This group includes the United States, West Germany, Switzerland, Holland, and Canada. Few people starve, and there is still some room at the top. The top of the middle class itself, however, often is high and desirable enough so that there is no need to break through and trespass into the unpopular and threatened class of financial aristocracy.

Among these countries the most advanced is the United States. What happens in many areas in the United States represents the latest and leading trends and permits us to predict what will happen in the next few years in the other affluent countries. People in affluent countries want greater individuality in their products. They dream of high-quality, repair-proof, almost custom-tailored articles.

While the German still uses his car for prestige purposes, in the United States the status value of cars has substantially diminished and has been shifted to other products and services such as swimming pools, travel, and education. The average American considers his car more like an appliance than a status symbol. Conspicuous cars like the Cadillac or the Lincoln try to emphasize their quiet elegance to avoid being considered cars for show-offs. There is increased attention to functional values and integration in car designs. Cars are not pampered; they are expected to do their job.

Group Three: Countries in Transition. In this group we may place England, France,

Italy, Australia, South Africa, and Japan. These countries still have a working class in the nineteenth century sense. But this class is trying to break out of its bondage and join the comfortable middle class. The upper classes still have privileges and can afford maids, Rolls-Royces, and castles; but their privileges are being rapidly whittled away. These countries have not had complete social revolutions. (The Labor government in England represented such an attempt but failed.) Servants are still cheap but rapidly getting more expensive and less easily available. Many wage-earning groups suffer from low wages. Living standards are behind those of the United States and West Germany. The white-collar worker often makes less money than the factory worker, but he has not integrated yet with the developing labor-based middle class. Prestige still plays an important role.

Cars are pampered in these countries. They are an extension of one's personality. They are given pet names. They represent major investments. Cars are outward symbols of success. There are still many first-car people, who have only now bought their first proof of "having arrived." Price plays an important role as an invitation to enter the automobile world—upgrading the buyer from bicycles and motorcycles. For top classes, some very expensive cars are available. Style plays a role with certain groups; there is much experimentation, curiosity, and desire for product adventure. Markets are still fluid, have not stabilized yet. There is resistance in all these countries against planned obsolescence. A lot of people hold onto their cars for six to ten years or more. American cars are considered to be too flashy and also too expensive.

Group Four: Revolutionary Countries. Venezuela, Mexico, Argentina, Brazil, Spain, India, China, and the Philippines are in this group. In these areas large groups of people are just emerging from near-starvation and are discovering industrialization. Relatively speaking, there are more extremely rich people, a small but expanding middle class, and a very large body of depressed economic groups that are beginning to discover the possibilities of enjoying life through the revolution in industry.

In these countries large sections of the population have not even reached the level of being consumers. These are the Indians living in many South American countries, the people living in villages in India and Indonesia, and so on.

Automobiles are available only to a relatively small group. They are expensive and considered a luxury. They are taxed so highly that they are beyond the reach of most people. American cars are considered the ideal. People want to show off. Small cars are bought as a way to get started. As the middle class develops, there should be an even further increase in the sale of small and compact cars, with the really rich people preferring big American cars.

Group Five: Primitive Countries. The newly liberated countries of Africa and the remaining colonies comprise the fifth group. In these countries there exists only a very small group of wealthy indigenous and foreign businessmen, new political leaders, and foreign advisers. The rest of the population is most often illiterate and ignorant and exists in a preconsumer stage, characterized either by barter or by almost complete primitive "self-sufficiency." The few cars that are sold are primarily for the government bureaucracy. There is no real car market as yet.

Group Six: The New Class Society. In Russia and its satellite countries, there is emerging a class of bureaucrats who represent a new form of aristocracy, while everybody else represents a slowly improving, low middle class. True, in these countries the extremely low income and the starving proletarians have disappeared.

The automobile, the modern home with its mechanized kitchen and mass-produced food items, and supermarket distribution represent the symbols of a new industrial society. By understanding the basic position of a country on this scale of development one can understand the role of products at present and one can also predict their future possibilities.

There is an interest in prestige cars. All the bourgeois symbols of capitalist countries are being copied—particularly those of the United States.

Our Greatest Opportunity

Many recent stories in the press—most of them picked up in foreign countries—make it appear that we ought to be ashamed of the good life we are leading. This recanting has its origin in a deep-seated guilt feeling which is unhealthy and dangerous. Some of the recanting is directed against a number of specific products, such as electrical gadgets, big cars, luxury and leisure time, and merchandise.

The real measuring rod of the success of one system over another should be based on the happiness of the citizens, their creativeness, and their constructive discontent. The desire to grow, to improve oneself, and to enjoy life to the fullest is at least equal, if not decidedly superior, to the goal of being ahead in a missile or a satellite program.

Our present life, therefore, should be presented as a challenge to the outside world—not in a boastful way, but as a life attainable by everyone through democratic and peaceful pursuits.

CONCLUSION

In most countries I have visited, I find that human desires are pretty much alike. The big difference lies in the level of achievement, in its many different forms.

In Iquitos, on the Amazon River, I recently visited an Indian tribe. They live in blissful fashion, hunting and planting bananas and yuccas. Who is smarter—we, the hard-working "civilized people"—or the contented Indians?

Part of the answer was provided by the fact that our guide complained that there were fewer and fewer Indians for tourists to see. They were becoming "too civilized." In other words, these primitive people who were supposed to be happy are caught in the inevitable maelstrom of development. They smoke cigarettes and are beginning to wear jeans and shirts.

Growth and progress are the only possible goals of life. I believe that the clue to man's destiny lies in his relentless training toward independence, not only politically, but also in the psychological sense. We are beset by fears, by inhibitions, by narrow-minded routine thinking. Step by step, year by year, we free ourselves more and more. Jets reduce physical distances; international trade and mass communications break down barriers. The world is opening up. The Common Market will broaden into an Atlantic Market and finally into a World Market. In order to participate effectively in this progressive development of mankind, it is essential to have a creative awareness of human desire and its strategy throughout the world—to understand and prepare to serve the new World Customer.

The Silent Language in Overseas Business

EDWARD T. HALL

With few exceptions, Americans are relative newcomers on the international business scene. Today, as in Mark Twain's time, we are all too often "innocents abroad," in an era when naiveté and blundering in foreign business dealings may have serious political repercussions.

When the American executive travels abroad to do business, he is frequently shocked to discover to what extent the many variables of foreign behavior and custom complicate his efforts. Although the American has recognized, certainly, that even the man next door has many minor traits which make him somewhat peculiar, for some reason he has failed to appreciate how different foreign businessmen and their practices will seem to him.

He should understand that the various peoples around the world have worked out and integrated into their subconscious literally thousands of behavior patterns that they take for granted in each other.[1] Then, when the stranger enters, and behaves differently from the local norm, he often quite unintentionally insults, annoys, or amuses the native with whom he is attempting to do business. For example:

In the United States, a corporation executive knows what is meant when a client lets a month go by before replying to a business proposal. On the other hand, he senses an eagerness to do business if he is immediately ushered into the client's office. In both instances, he is re-

acting to subtle cues in the timing of interaction, cues which he depends on to chart his course of action.

Abroad, however, all this changes. The American executive learns that the Latin Americans are casual about time and that if he waits an hour in the outer office before seeing the Deputy Minister of Finance, it does not necessarily mean he is not getting anywhere. There people are so important that nobody can bear to tear himself away; because of the resultant interruptions and conversational detours, everybody is constantly getting behind. What the American does not know is the point at which the waiting becomes significant.

In another instance, after traveling 7,000 miles an American walks into the office of a highly recommended Arab businessman on whom he will have to depend completely. What he sees does not breed confidence. The office is reached by walking through a suspicious-looking coffeehouse in an old, dilapidated building situated in a crowded non-European section of town. The elevator, rising from dark, smelly corridors, is rickety and equally foul. When he gets to the office itself, he is shocked to find it small, crowded, and confused. Papers are stacked all over the desk and table tops—even scattered on the floor in irregular piles.

The Arab merchant he has come to see had met him at the airport the night before and sent his driver to the hotel this morning to pick him up. But now, after the American's rush, the Arab is tied up with something else. Even when they finally start talking business, there are constant interruptions. If the American is at all sensitive to his environment, everything

◆ SOURCE: Reprinted by permission from *Harvard Business Review*, Vol. 38, No. 3, May–June 1960, pp. 87–96.

[1] For details, see my book, *The Silent Language* (New York: Doubleday & Company, Inc., 1959).

around him signals, "What am I getting into?"

Before leaving home he was told that things would be different, but how different? The hotel is modern enough. The shops in the new part of town have many more American and European trade goods than he had anticipated. His first impression was that doing business in the Middle East would not present any new problems. Now he is beginning to have doubts. One minute everything looks familiar and he is on firm ground; the next, familiar landmarks are gone. His greatest problem is that so much assails his senses all at once that he does not know where to start looking for something that will tell him where he stands. He needs a frame of reference—a way of sorting out what is significant and relevant.

That is why it is so important for American businessmen to have a real understanding of the various social, cultural, and economic differences they will face when they attempt to do business in foreign countries. To help give some frame of reference, this article will map out a few areas of human activity that have largely been unstudied.

The topics I will discuss are certainly not presented as the last word on the subject, but they have proved to be highly reliable points at which to begin to gain an undertanding of foreign cultures. While additional research will undoubtedly turn up other items just as relevant, at present I think the businessman can do well to begin by appreciating cultural differences in matters concerning the language of time, of space, of material possessions, of friendship patterns, and of agreements.

LANGUAGE OF TIME

Everywhere in the world people use time to communicate with each other. There are different languages of time just as there are different spoken languages. The unspoken languages are informal; yet the rules governing their interpretation are surprisingly *ironbound.*

In the United States, a delay in answering a communication can result from a large volume of business causing the request to be postponed until the backlog is cleared away, from poor organization, or possibly from technical complexity requiring deep analysis. But if the person awaiting the answer or decision rules out these reasons, then the delay means to him that the matter has low priority on the part of the other person—lack of interest. On the other

hand, a similar delay in a foreign country may mean something altogether different. Thus:

In Ethiopia, the time required for a decision is directly proportional to its importance. This is so much the case that low-level bureaucrats there have a way of trying to elevate the prestige of their work by taking a long time to make up their minds. (Americans in that part of the world are innocently prone to downgrade their work in the local people's eyes by trying to speed things up.)

In the Arab East, time does not generally include schedules as Americans know and use them. The time required to get something accomplished depends on the relationship. More important people get fast service from less important people, and conversely. Close relatives take absolute priority; nonrelatives are kept waiting.

In the United States, giving a person a deadline is a way of indicating the degree of urgency or relative importance of the work. But in the Middle East, the American runs into a cultural trap the minute he opens his mouth. "Mr. Aziz will have to make up his mind in a hurry because my board meets next week and I have to have an answer by then," is taken as indicating the American is overly demanding and is exerting undue pressure. "I am going to Damascus tomorrow morning and will have to have my car tonight," is a sure way to get the mechanic to stop work, because to give another person a deadline in this part of the world is to be rude, pushy, and demanding.

An Arab's evasiveness as to when something is going to happen does not mean he does not want to do business; it only means he is avoiding unpleasantness and is side-stepping possible commitments which he takes more seriously than we do. For example:

The Arabs themselves at times find it impossible to communicate even to each other that some processes cannot be hurried, and are controlled by built-in schedules. This is obvious enough to the Westerner but not to the Arab. A highly placed public official in Baghdad precipitated a bitter family dispute because his nephew, a biochemist, could not speed up the complete analysis of the uncle's blood. He accused the nephew of putting other less important people before him and of not caring. Nothing could sway the uncle, who could not grasp the fact that there is such a thing as an *inherent* schedule.

With us the more important an event is, the further ahead we schedule it, which is why we find it insulting to be asked to a party at the last minute. In planning future events with Arabs, it pays to hold the lead time to a week or less because other factors may intervene or take precedence.

Again, time spent waiting in an American's outer office is a sure indicator of what one person thinks of another or how important he feels the other's business to be. This is so much the case that most Americans cannot help getting angry after waiting 30 minutes; one may even feel such a delay is an insult, and will walk out. In Latin America, on the other hand, one learns that it does not mean anything to wait in an outer office. An American businessman with years of experience in Mexico once told me, "You know, I have spent two hours cooling my heels in an executive's outer office. It took me a long time to learn to keep my blood pressure down. Even now, I find it hard to convince myself they are still interested when they keep me waiting."

The Japanese handle time in ways which are almost inexplicable to the Western European and particularly the American. A delay of years with them does not mean that they have lost interest. It only means that they are building up to something. They have learned that Americans are vulnerable to long waits. One of them expressed it, "You Americans have one terrible weakness. If we make you wait long enough, you will agree to anything."

Indians of South Asia have an elastic view of time as compared to our own. Delays do not, therefore, have the same meaning to them. Nor does indefiniteness in pinpointing appointments mean that they are evasive. Two Americans meeting will say, "We should get together sometime," thereby setting a low priority on the meeting. The Indian who says, "Come over and see me, see me anytime," means just that. Americans make a place at the table which may or may not mean a place made in the heart. But when the Indian makes a place in his time, it is yours to fill in every sense of the word if you realize that by so doing you have crossed a boundary and are now friends with him. The point of all this is that time communicates just as surely as do words and that the vocabulary of time is different around

the world. The principle to be remembered is that time has different meanings in each country.

LANGUAGE OF SPACE

Like time, the language of space is different wherever one goes. The American businessman, familiar with the pattern of American corporate life, has no difficulty in appraising the relative importance of someone else, simply by noting the size of his office in relation to other offices around him:

Our pattern calls for the president or the chairman of the board to have the biggest office. The executive vice president will have the next largest, and so on down the line until you end up in the "bull pen." More important offices are usually located at the corners of buildings and on the upper floors. Executive suites will be on the top floor. The relative rank of vice presidents will be reflected in where they are placed along "Executive Row."

The French, on the other hand, are much more likely to lay out space as a network of connecting points of influence, activity, or interest. The French supervisor will ordinarily be found in the middle of his subordinates where he can control them.

Americans who are crowded will often feel that their status in the organization is suffering. As one would expect in the Arab world, the location of an office and its size constitute a poor index of the importance of the man who occupies it. What we experience as crowded, the Arab will often regard as spacious. The same is true in Spanish cultures. A Latin American official illustrated the Spanish view of this point while showing me around a plant. Opening the door to an 18-by-20-foot office in which seventeen clerks and their desks were placed, he said, "See, we have nice spacious offices. Lots of space for everyone."

The American will look at a Japanese room and remark how bare it is. Similarly, the Japanese look at our rooms and comment, "How bare!" Furniture in the American home tends to be placed along the walls (around the edge). Japanese have their charcoal pit where the family gathers in the *middle* of the room. The top floor of Japanese department stores is not reserved for the chief executive—it is the bargain roof!

In the Middle East and Latin America, the businessman is likely to feel left out in time and overcrowded in space. People get too close to him, lay their hands on him, and generally crowd his physical being. In Scandinavia and Germany, he feels more at home, but at the same time the people are a little cold and distant. It is space itself that conveys this feeling.

In the United States, because of our tendency to zone activities, nearness carries rights of familiarity so that the neighbor can borrow material possessions and invade time. This is not true in England. Propinquity entitles you to nothing. American Air Force personnel stationed there complain because they have to make an appointment for their children to play with the neighbor's child next door.

Conversation distance between two people is learned early in life by copying elders. Its controlling patterns operate almost totally unconsciously. In the United States, in contrast to many foreign counries, men avoid excessive touching. Regular business is conducted at distances such as 5 feet to 8 feet; highly personal business, 18 inches to 3 feet—not 2 or 3 inches.

In the United States, it is perfectly possible for an experienced executive to schedule the steps of negotiation in time and space so that most people feel comfortable about what is happening. Business transactions progress in stages from across the desk to beside the desk, to the coffee table, then on to the conference table, the luncheon table, or the golf course, or even into the home—all according to a complex set of hidden rules which we obey instinctively.

Even in the United States, however, an executive may slip when he moves into new and unfamiliar realms, when dealing with a new group, doing business with a new company, or moving to a new place in the industrial hierarchy. In a new country the danger is magnified. For example, in India it is considered improper to discuss business in the home on social occasions. One never invites a business acquaintance to the home for the purpose of furthering business aims. That would be a violation of sacred hospitality rules.

LANGUAGE OF THINGS

Americans are often contrasted with the rest of the world in terms of material possessions. We are accused of being materialistic, gadget-crazy. And, as a matter of fact, we have developed material things for some very interesting reasons. Lacking a fixed class system and having an extremely mobile population, Americans have become highly sensitive to how others make use of material possessions. We use everything from clothes to houses as a highly evolved and complex means of ascertaining each other's status. Ours is a rapidly shifting system in which both styles and people move up or down. For example:

The Cadillac ad men feel that not only is it natural but quite insightful of them to show a picture of a Cadillac and a well-turned out gentleman in his early fifties opening the door. The caption underneath reads, "You already know a great deal about this man."

Following this same pattern, the head of a big union spends an excess of $100,000 furnishing his office so that the president of United States Steel cannot look down on him. Good materials, large space, and the proper surroundings signify that the people who occupy the premises are solid citizens, that they are dependable and successful.

The French, the English, and the Germans have entirely different ways of using their material possessions. What stands for the height of dependability and respectability with the English would be old-fashioned and backward to us. The Japanese take pride in often inexpensive but tasteful arrangements that are used to produce the proper emotional setting.

Middle East businessmen look for something else—family, connections, friendship. They do not use the furnishings of their office as part of their status system; nor do they expect to impress a client by these means or to fool a banker into lending more money than he should. They like good things, too, but feel that they, as persons, should be known and not judged solely by what the public sees.

One of the most common criticisms of American relations abroad, both commercial and governmental, is that we usually think in terms of material things. "Money talks," says the American, who goes on talking the language of money abroad, in the belief that money talks the *same* language all over the world. A common practice in the United States is to try to buy loyalty with high salaries. In foreign countries, this maneuver almost never works, for money and material possessions stand for something different there than they do in America.

LANGUAGE OF FRIENDSHIP

The American finds his friends next door and among those with whom he works. It has been noted that we take people up quickly and drop them just as quickly. Occasionally a friendship formed during schooldays will persist, but this is rare. For us there are few well-defined rules governing the obligations of friendship. It is difficult to say at which point our friendship gives way to business opportunism or pressure from above. In this we differ from many other people in the world. As a general rule in foreign countries friendships are not formed as quickly as in the United States but go much deeper, last longer, and involve real obligations. For example:

It is important to stress that in the Middle East and Latin America your "friends" will not let you down. The fact that they personally are feeling the pinch is never an excuse for failing their friends. They are supposed to look out for your interests.

Friends and family around the world represent a sort of social insurance that would be difficult to find in the United States. We do not use our friends to help us out in disaster as much as we do as a means of getting ahead— or, at least, of getting the job done. The United States systems work by means of a series of closely tabulated favors and obligations carefully doled out where they will do the most good. And the least that we expect in exchange for a favor is gratitude.

The opposite is the case in India, where the friend's role is to "sense" a person's need and do something about it. The idea of reciprocity as we know it is unheard of. An American in India will have difficulty if he attempts to follow American friendship patterns. He gains nothing by extending himself in behalf of others, least of all gratitude, because the Indian assumes that what he does for others he does for the good of his own psyche. He will find it impossible to make friends quickly and is unlikely to allow sufficient time for friendships to ripen. He will also note that as he gets to know people better, they may become more critical of him, a fact that he finds hard to take. What he does not know is that one sign of friendship in India is speaking one's mind.

LANGUAGE OF AGREEMENTS

While it is important for American businessmen abroad to understand the symbolic meanings of friendship rules, time, space, and material possessions, it is just as important for executives to know the rules for negotiating agreements in various countries. Even if they cannot be expected to know the details of each nation's commercial legal practices, just the awareness of and the expectation of the existence of differences will eliminate much complication.

Actually, no society can exist on a high commercial level without a highly developed working base on which agreements can rest. This base may be one or a combination of three types:

1. Rules that are spelled out technically as law or regulation.
2. Moral practices mutually agreed on and taught to the young as a set of principles.
3. Informal customs to which everyone conforms without being able to state the exact rules.

Some societies favor one, some another. Ours, particularly in the business world, lays heavy emphasis on the first variety. Few Americans will conduct any business nowadays without some written agreement or contract.

Varying from culture to culture will be the circumstances under which such rules apply. Americans consider that negotiations have more or less ceased when the contract is signed. With the Greeks, on the other hand, the contract is seen as a sort of way station on the route to negotiation that will cease only when the work is completed. The contract is nothing more than a charter for serious negotiations. In the Arab world, once a man's word is given in a particular kind of way, it is just as binding, if not more so, than most of our written contracts. The written contract, therefore, violates the Moslem's sensitivities and reflects on his honor. Unfortunately, the situation is now so hopelessly confused that neither system can be counted on to prevail consistently.

Informal patterns and unstated agreements often lead to untold difficulty in the cross-cultural situation. Take the case of the before-

and-after patterns where there is a wide discrepancy between the American's expectations and those of the Arab:

In the United States, when you engage a specialist such as a lawyer or a doctor, require any standard service, or even take a taxi, you make several assumptions: (a) the charge will be fair; (b) it will be in proportion to the services rendered; and (c) it will bear a close relationship to the "going rate."

You wait until after the services are performed before asking what the tab will be. If the charge is too high in the light of the above assumptions, you feel you have been cheated. You can complain, or can say nothing, pay up, and take your business elsewhere the next time.

As one would expect in the Middle East, basic differences emerge which lead to difficulty if not understood. For instance, when taking a cab in Beirut it is well to know the going rate as a point around which to bargain and for settling the charge, which must be fixed before engaging the cab.

If you have not fixed the rate *in advance*, there is a complete change and an entirely different set of rules will apply. According to these rules, the going rate plays no part whatsoever. The whole relationship is altered. The sky is the limit, and the customer has no kick coming. I have seen taxi drivers shouting at the top of their lungs, waving their arms, following a redfaced American with his head pulled down between his shoulders, demanding for a two-pound ride ten Lebanese pounds which the American eventually had to pay.

It is difficult for the American to accommodate his frame of reference to the fact that what constitute one thing to him, namely, a taxi ride, is to the Arab two very different operations involving two different sets of relationships and two sets of rules. The crucial factor is whether the bargaining is done at the beginning or the end of the ride! As a matter of fact, you cannot bargain at the end. What the driver asks for he is entitled to!

One of the greatest difficulties Americans have abroad stems from the fact that we often think we have a commitment when we do not. The second complication on this same topic is the other side of the coin, i.e., when others think we have agreed to things that we have not. Our own failure to recognize binding obligations, plus our custom of setting organiza-tional goals ahead of everything else, has put us in hot water far too often.

People sometimes do not keep agreements with us because we do not keep agreements with them. As a general rule, the American treats the agreement as something he may eventually have to break. Here are two examples:

Once while I was visiting an American post in Latin America, the Ambassador sent the Spanish version of a trade treaty down to his language officer with instructions to write in some "weasel words." To his dismay, he was told, "There are no weasel words in Spanish."

A personnel officer of a large corporation in Iran made an agreement with local employees that American employees would not receive preferential treatment. When the first American employee arrived, it was learned quickly that in the United States he had been covered by a variety of health plans that were not available to Iranians. And this led to immediate protests from the Iranians which were never satisfied. The personnel officer never really grasped the fact that he had violated an iron-bound contract.

Certainly, this is the most important generalization to be drawn by American businessmen from this discussion of agreements: there are many times when we are vulnerable *even when judged by our own standards.* Many instances of actual sharp practices by American companies are well known abroad and are giving American business a bad name. The cure for such questionable behavior is simple. The companies concerned usually have it within their power to discharge offenders and to foster within their organization an atmosphere in which only honesty and fairness can thrive.

But the cure for ignorance of the social and legal rules which underlie business agreements is not so easy. This is because:

The subject is complex.

Little research has been conducted to determine the culturally different concepts of what is an agreement.

The people of each country think that their own code is the only one, and that everything else is dishonest.

Each code is different from our own; and the farther away one is traveling from Western Europe, the greater the difference is.

But the little that has already been learned about this subject indicates that as a problem it is not insoluble and will yield to research. Since it is probably one of the more relevant and immediately applicable areas of interest to modern business, it would certainly be advisable for companies with large foreign operations to sponsor some serious research in this vital field.

A CASE IN POINT

Thus far, I have been concerned with developing the five check points around which a real understanding of foreign cultures can begin. But the problems that arise from a faulty understanding of the silent language of foreign custom are human problems and perhaps can best be dramatized by an actual case.

A Latin American republic had decided to modernize one of its communication networks to the tune of several million dollars. Because of its reputation for quality and price, the inside track was quickly taken by American company "Y."

The company, having been sounded out informally, considered the size of the order and decided to bypass its regular Latin American representative and send instead its sales manager. The following describes what took place.

The sales manager arrived and checked in at the leading hotel. He immediately had some difficulty pinning down just who it was he had to see about his business. After several days without results, he called at the American Embassy where he found that the commercial attaché had the up-to-the-minute information he needed. The commercial attaché listened to his story. Realizing that the sales manager had already made a number of mistakes, but figuring that the Latins were used to American blundering, the attaché reasoned that all was not lost. He informed the sales manager that the Minister of Communications was the key man and that whoever got the nod from him would get the contract. He also briefed the sales manager on methods of conducting business in Latin America and offered some pointers about dealing with the minister.

The attaché's advice ran somewhat as follows:

1. "You don't do business here the way you do in the States; it is necessary to spend much more time. You have to get to know your man and vice versa.

2. "You must meet with him *several times* before you talk business. I will tell you at what point you can bring up the subject. Take your cues from me. [Our American sales manager at this point made a few observations to himself about 'cookie pushers' and wondered how many payrolls had been met by the commercial attaché.]

3. "Take that price list and put it in your pocket. Don't get it out until I tell you to. Down here price is only one of the many things taken into account before closing a deal. In the United States, your past experience will prompt you to act according to a certain set of principles, but many of these principles will *not* work here. Every time you feel the urge to act or to say something, look at me. Suppress the urge and take your cues from me. This is very important.

4. "Down here people like to do business with men who *are* somebody. In order to be somebody, it is well to have written a book, to have lectured at a university, or to have developed your intellect in some way. The man you are going to see is a poet. He has published several volumes of poetry. Like many Latin Americans, he prizes poetry highly. You will find that he will spend a good deal of business time quoting his poetry to you, and he will take great pleasure in this.

5. "You will also note that the people here are very proud of their past and of their Spanish blood, but they are also exceedingly proud of their liberation from Spain and their independence. The fact that they are a democracy, that they are free, and also that they are no longer a colony is very, very important to them. They are warm and friendly and enthusiastic if they like you. If they don't, they are cold and withdrawn.

6. "And another thing, time down here means something different. It works in a different way. You know how it is back in the States when a certain type blurts out whatever is on his mind without waiting to see if the situation is right. He is considered an impatient bore and somewhat egocentric. Well, down here, you have to wait much, much longer, and I really mean *much, much* longer, before you can begin to talk about the reason for your visit.

7. "There is another point I want to caution you about. At home, the man who sells takes the initiative. Here, *they* tell you when they are ready to do business. But, most of all, don't

discuss price until you are asked and don't rush things."

The Pitch

The next day the commercial attaché introduced the sales manager to the Minister of Communications. First, there was a long wait in the outer office while people kept coming in and out. The sales manager looked at his watch, fidgeted, and finally asked whether the minister was really expecting him. The reply he received was scarcely reassuring, "Oh yes, he is expecting you but several things have come up that require his attention. Besides, one gets used to waiting down here." The sales manager irritably replied, "But doesn't he know I flew all the way down here from the United States to see him, and I have spent over a week already of my valuable time trying to find him?" "Yes, I know," was the answer, "but things just move much more slowly here."

At the end of about 30 minutes, the minister emerged from the office, greeted the commercial attaché with a *doble abrazo*, throwing his arms around him and patting him on the back as though they were long-lost brothers. Now, turning and smiling, the minister extended his hand to the sales manager, who, by this time, was feeling rather miffed because he had been kept in the outer office so long.

After what seemed to be an all too short chat, the minister rose, suggesting a well-known café where they might meet for dinner the next evening. The sales manager expected, of course, that, considering the nature of their business and the size of the order, he might be taken to the minister's home, not realizing that the Latin home is reserved for family and very close friends.

Until now, nothing at all had been said about the reason for the sales manager's visit, a fact which bothered him somewhat. The whole setup seemed wrong; neither did he like the idea of wasting another day in town. He told the home office before he left that he would be gone for a week or ten days at most, and made a mental note that he would clean this order up in three days and enjoy a few days in Acapulco or Mexico City. Now the week had already gone and he would be lucky if he made it home in ten days.

Voicing his misgivings to the commercial attaché, he wanted to know if the minister really meant business, and, if he did, why could they not get together and talk about it? The com-

mercial attaché by now was beginning to show the strain of constantly having to reassure the sales manager. Nevertheless, he tried again:

"What you don't realize is that part of the time we were waiting, the minister was rearranging a very tight schedule so that he could spend tomorrow night with you. You see, down here they don't delegate responsibility the way we do in the States. They exercise much tighter control than we do. As a consequence, this man spends up to 15 hours a day at his desk. It may not look like it to you, but I assure you he really means business. He wants to give your company the order; if you play your cards right, you will get it."

The next evening provided more of the same. Much conversation about food and music, about many people the sales manager had never heard of. They went to a night club, where the sales manager brightened up and began to think that perhaps he and the minister might have something in common after all. It bothered him, however, that the principal reason for his visit was not even alluded to tangentially. But every time he started to talk about electronics, the commercial attaché would nudge him and proceed to change the subject.

The next meeting was for morning coffee at a café. By now the sales manager was having difficulty hiding his impatience. To make matters worse, the minister had a mannerism which he did not like. When they talked, he was likely to put his hand on him; he would take hold of his arm and get so close that he almost "spat" in his face. As a consequence, the sales manager was kept busy trying to dodge and back up.

Following coffee, there was a walk in a nearby park. The minister expounded on the shrubs, the birds, and the beauties of nature, and at one spot he stopped to point at a statue and said: "There is a statue of the world's greatest hero, the liberator of mankind!" At this point, the worst happened, for the sales manager asked who the statue was of and, being given the name of a famous Latin American patriot, said, "I never heard of him," and walked on.

The Failure

It is quite clear from this that the sales manager did not get the order, which went to a Swedish concern. The American, moreover, was never able to see the minister again. Why did the minister feel the way he did? His reasoning went somewhat as follows:

"I like the American's equipment and it makes sense to deal with North Americans who are near us and whose price is right. But I could never be friends with this man. He is not my kind of human being and we have nothing in common. He is not *simpatico*. If I can't be friends and he is not *simpatico*, I can't depend on him to treat me right. I tried everything, every conceivable situation, and only once did we seem to understand each other. If we could be friends, he would feel obligated to me and this obligation would give me some control. Without control, how do I know he will deliver what he says he will at the price he quotes?"

Of course, what the minister did not know was that the price was quite firm, and that quality control was a matter of company policy. He did not realize that the sales manager was a member of an organization, and that the man is always subordinate to the organization in the United States. Next year maybe the sales manager would not even be representing the company, but would be replaced. Further, if he wanted someone to depend on, his best bet would be to hire a good American lawyer to represent him and write a binding contract.

In this instance, both sides suffered. The American felt he was being slighted and put off, and did not see how there could possibly be any connection between poetry and doing business or why it should all take so long. He interpreted the delay as a form of polite brush-off. Even if things had gone differently and there had been a contract, it is doubtful that the minister would have trusted the contract as much as he would a man whom he considered his friend. Throughout Latin America, the law is made livable and contracts workable by having friends and relatives operating from the inside. Lacking a friend, someone who would look out for his interests, the minister did not want to take a chance. He stated this simply and directly.

CONCLUSION

The case just described has of necessity been oversimplified. The danger is that the reader will say, "Oh, I see. All you really have to do is be friends." At which point the expert will step in and reply:

"Yes, of course, but what you don't realize is that in Latin America being a friend involves much more than it does in the United States and is an entirely different proposition. A friendship implies obligations. You go about it differently. It involves much more than being nice, visiting, and playing golf. You would not want to enter into friendship lightly."

The point is simply this. It takes years and years to develop a sound foundation for doing business in a given country. Much that is done seems silly or strange to the home office. Indeed, the most common error made by home offices, once they have found representatives who can get results, is failure to take their advice and allow sufficient time for representatives to develop the proper contacts.

The second most common error, if that is what it can be called, is ignorance of the secret and hidden language of foreign cultures. In this article I have tried to show how five key topics —time, space, material possessions, friendship patterns, and business agreements—offer a starting point from which companies can begin to acquire the understanding necessary to do business in foreign countries.

Our present knowledge is meager, and much more research is needed before the businessman of the future can go abroad fully equipped for his work. Not only will he need to be well versed in the economics, law, and politics of the area, but he will have to understand, if not speak, the silent languages of other cultures.

Overseas Sales Grow for American Firms Peddling Door-to-Door

JOHN A. PRESTBO

At a mud-hut settlement in Nigeria, village wives purchase Tupperware plastic food containers at a "home party" staged by a traveling saleslady. In Italy, an Encyclopaedia Britannica salesman takes an order from a businessman who doesn't speak English; he's been convinced the books will help his children in their studies of the language.

Such direct-selling efforts abroad by American companies were relatively feeble only a few years ago. But now door-to-door sellers headquartered in the U.S. have salesmen pounding pavements in some 50 foreign lands, racking up ever-increasing sales of everything from lipstick to pots and pans.

Last year some two dozen U.S. direct sellers grossed around $130 million from door-bell-ringing overseas, compared with roughly $80 million in 1960 and about $10 million a decade earlier, when only a half-dozen companies were selling abroad. Sales are rising sharply again this year, industry sources say, as new concerns get a foot in the door of foreign markets and established ones expand.

Fuller Brush Co., whose salesmen are familiar to millions of American housewives, set up an international division last year with instructions to build up foreign sales as quickly as possible. Fuller Brush has previously done a small amount of export business "but not in a serious way and it didn't amount to much," says an executive. Other companies recently entering foreign markets include Sarah Coventry, Inc., which began selling costume jewelry in Britain late in 1963, and Studio Girl-Hollywood, a cosmetics subsidiary of Helene Curtis Industries, Inc., which intensified overseas efforts last fall.

BOOKS, COSMETICS AND KITCHENWARE

They have joined such established foreign sellers as Avon Products, Inc., Encyclopaedia Britannica, Inc., and Tupperware Home Parties, owned by Rexall Drug & Chemical Co. Avon began foreign efforts in 1954; today it has sales organizations in seven countries and plans to enter three more next year. Foreign sales of cosmetics and toiletries climbed 46% to $47.8 million last year, accounting for 16% of the company's total volume. Britannica, selling in 20 countries, had foreign sales of more than $37 million.

Operating in 26 countries, Tupperware is mining a particularly rich sales bonanza in Japan, where it claims 90% of the market in plastic kitchen containers after less than two years of work. Some 4,000 Japanese saleswomen, prim in kimonos, push the company's products at parties while invited housewives sip green tea and munch rice crackers. Tupperware originally expected sales of about $15 per party, but average volume quickly hit $40 and inventories vanished; high food costs in Japan motivate housewives there to be more saving of leftovers, and Tupperware filled the need.

◆ SOURCE: Reprinted by permission from *The Wall Street Journal* (Dow Jones & Company, Inc.), April 15, 1965.

The company will go into full production of containers at a new plant in Japan later this year. Several other companies are also building factories overseas to help satisfy rising demand, ease distribution problems and gain more favorable tax positions.

TOKEN OPPOSITION

United States direct sellers say they are meeting only token opposition in foreign lands from door-to-door concerns based there. They note that most such companies don't sell many of the products U.S. firms offer.

But companies have had to make some changes both in their products and their sales techniques when selling in other countries, in recognition of local customs and conditions. Britannica sells most of its encyclopedias abroad in English, but does offer for some Latin American customers. Tupperware is considering designing a new plastic container for fish, a staple in Japanese diets.

U.S. companies also find that the husband makes all the major financial decisions in households in many countries. Says one sales executive: "In the U.S., we know we can sell the wife and depend on her to wrestle her husband into paying for it." Salesmen in Italy have learned to avoid calling on housewives while their husbands are at work. It's unacceptable there for a man to be alone with someone else's wife, particularly in the woman's own home. Direct sellers almost always use foreign nationals as salesmen, because of their familiarity with such taboos and customs and fluency in the language.

Unfamiliar with many products and practices of U.S. concerns, housewives overseas sometimes tend to be skeptical. Wear-Ever Aluminum, Inc., a subsidiary of Aluminum Co. of America, finds it's wiser to demonstrate its pots and pans to wary South American customers by cooking a full dinner in them and offering a taste when it's finished. The company doesn't need to go this far in the U.S.

Do's and Don'ts in Selling Abroad

ARTHUR C. NIELSEN, JR.

Marketing men who sell abroad, or who are contemplating it, will acquire a fresh viewpoint from this 15-point discussion of marketing hazards in foreign countries.
The President of the A. C. Nielsen Company discusses some of the dangers in foreign marketing that discourage the uninitiated, harass the misinformed, and gall the ill advised. But with his warnings are suggestions for positive action to avoid the hazards.

The relentless forward thrust of science plus the productive genius of the modern business executive have resulted in a surplus of goods and services in many places.

Yet the needs and wants of modern economic man are virtually insatiable. And two-thirds of the world's population is in dire need of the basic necessities of life.

Such great marketing opportunities exist that those who profit most will be the men and organizations who best master the complex business of selling abroad.

NEED FOR RESEARCH APPROACH

The main problems in selling abroad stem from the very real differences which exist between the home markets and the various foreign markets. Oftentimes a manufacturer's initial investigation discloses so many similarities between the foreign markets and his home markets that he feels confident of ultimate success, if he can recruit capable associates who will diligently pursue the same policies which have proved successful at home.

When initial rebuffs occur, he often feels that the difficulties are due either to a reluctance of consumers to change to his superior product, or from some deep-seated, unconscious distrust of foreigners (Americans). The true reasons for the trouble may involve factors far more

basic—such as low purchasing power, lack of refrigeration, inadequate advertising media, attitudes of trade associations. Consequently, entirely different approaches may be needed.

Those remarkable companies which seem to prosper under almost any flag use the "research approach." In doing so, they assume that they know *nothing* about a new market. They do not accede to the very human tendency of oversimplification and assume that people everywhere are basically the same. True, people are similar in many respects; but there are wide differences when it comes to what they will or will not buy. So, it is through use of a research approach that costly errors in foreign marketing can be avoided.

FIFTEEN RULES AND WARNINGS

Adapt the Product to the Market

The most basic of a number of common errors is the failure to adapt the product to the market.

In other words, attempts are made to sell the home-market product in other places without *knowing*—as opposed to just hoping or believing—that it is the best product that can be designed to meet foreign needs. Often a slight and easily made modification will greatly enhance results. For example, the typical U.S. product is too costly for many foreign markets, and a scaled-down version will usually produce better sales and profits.

In this respect, historical data on established

◆ SOURCE: Reprinted by permission from *Journal of Marketing* (National Quarterly Publication of the American Marketing Association), Vol. 23, No. 4, April 1959, pp. 405–411.

competitive items sold within a foreign country—showing the trends of sales by types, sizes, and price lines, as well as the relative amounts of sales and advertising effort placed behind each—can be most illuminating.

Gauge the Impact of Custom and Tradition

If a product differs in any essential respect from those most widely accepted, the marketer must be on his guard against another error. This is the failure to gauge the underlying impact of custom, tradition, and racial and religious differences.

These factors, among the most subtle, can be the most costly. It is difficult to "get them out into the open" because people are either unaware of their influence or inarticulate when it comes to defining them. Even then, once defined, some obstacles of this type may take a generation or more to change. In fact, they might be impossible to change, regardless of the efforts of even a group of manufacturers.

Consider the preferences in French Canada for "fizz-type" beverages, which extend far beyond the soft-drink classification. Other favorites there are perfumed toilet soap, bran cereals, and home remedies. Preferences of this type will tenaciously withstand a barrage of sales and advertising effort.

A research approach would establish the fact that such preferences exist, and their degree and trends. Research would ascertain the reasons for the preferences. It would weigh the possibility of overcoming the resistance at a reasonable cost within an acceptable period of time.

Exploit Markets in Proper Sequence

Before "casting the die" and committing resources to developing a business in any *one* country, it is well to examine with equal care other likely markets, and thus avoid a third error. This is failure to exploit markets in the proper sequence.

In order to avoid this error, both budget and timetable should be adequate to permit detailed investigations to be carried out and priorities assigned. Such studies would permit the marketer to avoid temporarily countries where excessive production facilities already exist. Efforts would surely be met with depressing price cuts or tariff restrictions, or both.

Remain Politically Tolerant

Another common error is a failure to enter potentially profitable markets due to a personal repugnance toward political institutions.

Some of the most profitable markets are often ruled out solely on their record of unstable governments or political institutions alien to a particular philosophy. However, it is well to remember that in virtually every country the economic rules must be written so that the average man can make an average living. Consequently, with a better product and skillful marketing, results are likely to be rewarding.

Build a Strong Local Management

Following a decision as to the country or countries to be developed, there arises the question of who will manage the business. Undoubtedly opinions differ, but in marketing management the error may be one of failure to build a strong management of nationals.

This often has caused considerable disappointment. To avoid this, headquarters personnel can be used to train local people in the essentials of the business, and then either moved on to a new country or returned home. Most men, and their wives, are happier living in their own country than for protracted intervals in foreign and remote lands. Furthermore, the cost to the company is less since a wage premium must usually be paid to induce headquarters personnel to pull up stakes.

Beware of Language Barriers

In addition, most men must live in a country a long while before they can avoid the error: failure to appreciate differences in the connotation of words.

This error prevails regardless of whether the same language or a translation is involved. Countless anecdotes have warned us to "beware of literal translations." But how well do we learn? Experienced marketing men, whether in Montreal or Brussels, Havana or Mexico City, Copenhagen or Stockholm, can regale a visitor with story after story of how literal translations, whether on a label or in advertising copy, can lose both friends and money. Dangers that are almost equally forbidding even lurk where different versions of the same language are involved (such as Australian and American ideas of English).

This also is true of the very words used in communicating with foreign representatives or foreign-branch personnel. Every industry has its own technical jargon. Many of the terms sprang originally from colloquialisms spiced with humor and abbreviated down to single-syllable words for ease of handling. Although their true meaning may not even be found in the dictionary, they can be vital to any meeting of minds in business.

Study Differences in Advertising

Since word power has grown to be such a vital force in selling goods and services, it is often difficult in marketing abroad to escape another error: failure to understand differences in advertising.

Rules as to what advertising can claim vary from country to country. Often it is a matter of possessing a "feel" as to how the rules are interpreted, rather than a clear dictum. This is one of the reasons that absentee advertising management can find itself at a competitive disadvantage.

With mass communication playing a vital role, media importance varies sharply with such factors as literacy levels, restrictive taxation, and other forms of governmental interference. Last year's appraisal will not do, as demonstrated by the development of television advertising in the United Kingdom, in Canada, and other countries. Methods and systems differ in many respects; in fact, the basic approach is by no means uniform.

Identify the Company with the Local Scene

Important public-relations tasks in a foreign country are the identification of the company in the buyer's mind with the local scene. Otherwise, the danger is great that the company and its products will commit the error: failure to achieve a domestic personality.

No detail can be overlooked here, including such factors as the corporate name, label, package style, the design found on trucks, the architectural plan of offices and plant. They will not be overlooked by those with an aversion toward foreigners and their products.

Above all, it is important to avoid creating the impression that our country or ways of doing things are different or superior. On the other hand, we must keep up to date. Many who are willing to concede that change is the order of the day in their home markets continue to apply methods to foreign markets based on impressions which they may have gained five or ten years ago.

Know the Trade Channels

To those especially concerned with distribution, the next error is of vital importance. It is the failure to understand and weigh correctly the relative importance of the various types of retailers in the distribution of the product.

If there is any subject on which hearsay evidence is unreliable, this is probably it. Even those manufacturers well established in foreign countries often have no reliable facts as to the relative importance of the various types of retailers, because they may sell their goods largely to a multitude of varying types of wholesale organizations. They are unable to trace the redistribution of their products among retailers.

The typical U.S. grocery manufacturer, for example, selling a half or more of his output directly to a handful of large retailers and often relying on a highly skilled brokerage force, is poorly equipped to develop and manage a sales organization which can thread its way successfully through a maze of overlapping wholesalers and other intermediaries. Trade channels vary perhaps more from country to country than any other major marketing factor. For this reason, even a thorough knowledge of conditions in one country helps little when selling in another. If profitable results are to be obtained, the number, type, location, and importance of all classes of distributors—together with profit margins and fees received—must be carefully determined country by country, commodity by commodity.

Understand the Consumer's Views of Price and Quality

Another common error in foreign marketing is the failure to grasp the consumer's attitudes on the relationship between price and quality.

This pitfall varies in size and deceptiveness for each product category within each country for a whole host of reasons. Some are obscure, and some obvious. Much seems to depend on how much buyers can afford to spend. But a great deal also depends on where the people of a country place their values as between quality and price, in reference to a specific product.

There seems to be no firm relationship, and certainly no rule of thumb, which can be relied upon in a matter like this. The fact that consumers resist substandard quality does not necessarily mean that they will be able to buy and pay for extra-fancy quality. They may be fussy about some aspects of food handling, but unwilling to pay for superior or more sanitary packaging.

Many have learned that it is risky to rely on replies to questions when setting price policies. After all, it costs the respondent nothing to assure the interviewer that, of course, he will buy the higher-priced item. The true nature of competitive price relationships can be determined only after the product has been freely offered for sale under normal circumstances at prices on which a profit can be earned. Yet, if consumer reaction to price cannot be reduced to a generalized formula in other countries, this is no different from experiences in the United States. Specific study within each product category is needed both at home and abroad.

Appraise the Degree of Acceptance of Free Enterprise

Discussion of price leads to the next error: the failure to appraise properly the degree of acceptance of the competitive-economy principle.

Actually the virtues of free enterprise are by no means widely accepted. Industry-controlled output and price fixing are the more commonly encountered business forms. These are usually allied with strongly entrenched wholesale and retail trade interests.

Consequently, reprisals visited upon a new or overly aggressive competitor are sometimes very subtle but very effective. Of course, conditions vary widely from industry to industry and from country to country. Nevertheless, experience suggests that it is well to appraise these conditions in advance rather than to ignore them.

Explore Government Regulations

Trade practices are often effectively buttressed and even cloaked in respectability through laws. Consequently, special-interest laws, as well as traditions and attitudes of the government toward business, must be studied most carefully because another common error is failure to pay due attention to the various government regulations involved.

In some countries an outside manufacturer is not permitted to engage in business at all until he has obtained permission from several government agencies. It is essential to explore every form of government control. Foreign marketers should make sure that the necessary permits, machinery, labor, materials, housing, and in-and-out-of-the-country foreign exchange will be available.

Insulate Against Restrictive Legislation

Rules laid down by governments can and do change from time to time, which leads to the error: failure to insulate the business from arbitrary acts of government.

When anticipating the possibility of foreign marketing, the first thought of most sellers is simply to ship abroad the surplus production of their domestic plants. This procedure can and often does run into difficulties when foreign governments raise restrictive tariffs or impose arbitrary quotas. Such discriminatory actions are usually visited upon an importer just when his success in capturing a worthwhile market seems assured.

For these reasons, long-term efforts should in most cases be directed toward building a sufficient volume of business in a country to warrant construction of a local factory. With a production facility established, costs are usually lower—an important factor itself in building a franchise.

Of even greater significance is the fact that the company is now an employer of domestic labor. This refutes one of the major political arguments justifying restrictive legislation against the concern.

Invest for the Long Pull

While more and more producers now recognize the desirability of marketing products made locally, some fail to realize full benefit due to failure to invest for the long pull.

This usually takes one or both of two forms. Either the item is over-priced, or there is unwillingness to "plow back" a sufficient number of sales dollars into advertising. In either case, efforts to broaden acquaintance and acceptance are inhibited. Under present conditions, if political or other risks appear to be of such magnitude that invested capital must be fully recovered in less than five years, it is probably better to forget the market for most widely distributed consumer items.

Interchange Information Between the Home Office and the Foreign Office

Once a foreign business has been established on a profitable basis, there may be a tendency on the part of management to forget about it and to turn its attention to other countries and problems. This can lead to the error: failure to provide for an adequate flow of information both to and from the parent company.

Executives of the headquarters company are in far greater need of continuous, detailed information on a subsidiary operating in another country than on their domestic business with which they are more intimately familiar through years of observation and study.

They do not have the day-to-day feel of competitive conditions and trends of the foreign country. For this reason, they need continuous facts regarding the competitive progress of the subsidiary, thus permitting them to provide necessary assistance derived from their long years of practical experience. Too often, gradual year-to-year sales gains are permitted to cover up the fact that the company is slipping competitively. When finally these untoward conditions are reflected in unfavorable earnings, it may be too late for key executives at home to correct this situation, because they have been out of touch for years with the market and its peculiarities. For this reason, it is particularly important that essential marketing information concerning the operations of foreign subsidiaries be continuously sent into headquarters.

WHY SELL ABROAD?

Possibility of Profit

Considering all of these problems, why try to sell abroad? Additional profits are, of course, the almost universal objective of marketing abroad. Whether more profit could be produced by devoting to domestic markets the capital and the management effort expended in foreign development is a moot question. The answer depends on many factors, including the degree of saturation which has been attained in the home market.

When the home markets have been fully developed, the company must either stagnate or seek further growth through entry into new fields. It may be more profitable and less risky to grow by marketing in foreign countries the products for which a successful production and marketing pattern has been established at home than to enter new fields in the home market.

Either method necessarily involves risks. But the foreign route does not necessarily involve the greater risk.

Diversification of Risk

The possibility of increased profits, however, is only one of several benefits to be derived from marketing abroad. In many cases, diversification of risk is equally important. Even when a management firmly believes that its own country offers the most stable and dependable future economic conditions, it should be recognized that future conditions in various countries cannot be predicted with a high degree of accuracy. Competitive, legislative, or other obstacles may arise at any time in any country and do serious or even fatal damage to a business.

Many a company, at one time or another, has gone through very difficult periods in its home country, while its foreign subsidiaries continued to prosper, thus maintaining the entire enterprise in sound and prosperous condition.

Development of Management Personnel

Development of management personnel is another advantage usually derived from ventures abroad. Since no one country has a monopoly on brains and ability, it is almost inevitable that a comprehensive international operation will reveal some unusually capable management talent.

Furthermore, nothing develops executive talent quite so rapidly and soundly as an opportunity to manage a complete business. In an international operation, this opportunity can be granted to a considerable number of men. Obviously, possession of an unusually good supply of top-management personnel affords important protection for a company's future.

Improved Products and Methods

It is inevitable that a well-managed international organization will develop improved products and methods. The variety of obstacles encountered stimulates thought and develops more ingenuity; and men of widely different backgrounds are likely to develop a greater number and variety of products and methods.

Better products and services to customers are an almost inevitable consequence of the wider experience derived from conducting business on an international basis.

Selling the Tropical African Market

EDWARD MARCUS

The stepped-up tempo of economic development in Tropical Africa is opening new sales opportunities for American business. But for most companies the area is still a marketing "Dark Continent"; other than the large oil companies, few have ventured in on any sizable basis.
This article discusses the potentials and the problems involved in tapping the market. It also offers suggestions to cope with the anticipated difficulties.

The political turmoil that is characteristic of tropical Africa in its march to self-government should not obscure the area's economic potentiality as a market for American products. In fact, it is this very eruption that is signaling its coming of age, economically, socially, and politically. In the next few years current development plans will be boosting local consumption standards, bringing markets that eventually will reach double or triple current levels.

ESTIMATING THE MARKET

Tropical Africa can be defined as that part of the African continent south of the Sahara, north of the Rhodesian "white belt," and stretching from the Atlantic Ocean in the West to the Indian Ocean to the East. See Figure 1. It includes British East and West Africa, French West and Equatorial Africa, Portuguese Africa, the former Belgian Congo, Northern Rhodesia, Nyasaland, and Liberia. It is a uniformly poor area, but holds great promise of improvement.

As an indication of its market potential, a comparison with a more prosperous member—Ghana—is helpful. This cocoa-rich country imports about $40 per capita annually; as an agricultural producer, almost all its manufactured capital and consumers goods must come from abroad. Nigerian annual imports per cap-

◆ SOURCE: Reprinted by permission from *Journal of Marketing* (National Quarterly Publication of the American Marketing Association), Vol. 25, No. 5, July 1961, pp. 25–31.

ita, in contrast, are barely a third the Ghanaian level, while for the minerals-rich Belgian Congo the figure was about $22 in the year before independence. If the current development programs succeed in improving local living standards sufficiently to raise Tropical Africa's per capita imports to the Ghanaian figure—admittedly low by Western standards—aggregate imports would rise by some $4 billion, or an increase of 133⅓ per cent.

The prospects for American trade are even greater, although a word of caution about the market potential should be sounded. The area is "statistics poor"; even population estimates may be as much as 25 per cent in error. Hence, available sources give scanty or no firm figures about the consumption of specific commodities. Only a few broad clues can give an approximate indication. For example, the area imported somewhat more than $2.5 billion in 1959; the United States supplied some 6 per cent of this total, while the then "mother" countries—Great Britain, France, Belgium, and Portugal—supplied 47 per cent of the total. Our share, however, can be expected to rise as the loosening of political ties also weakens the economic relationships with the former European rulers. German and Japanese traders have already begun to make inroads, while many of our own exporters indicate having received a marked rise in trade inquiries.

If we include Liberia—important because of ship sales—1959 U.S. exports to the area were $204 million, compared with our over-all total of $17.4 billion. In no major commodity class —the eleven basic breakdowns given by U.S.

Customs—did Tropical Africa take more than 1 per cent of the group, other than the aforementioned ships, in which Liberia accounted for 36 per cent.

With sufficient effort, our exporters could achieve a larger share of the expected much greater total; in the Congo, for example, the American share of imports has ranged between 10 and 20 per cent of the total, two to three times the proportion for all of Tropical Africa. And there is also some evidence that profit margins are somewhat better than average—although such closely held data are notoriously difficult to obtain, for secrecy is a characteristic of the trade since its opening to the Western maritime powers some five centuries ago.

THE AFRICAN CONSUMER

In a market as changing as the African one, it becomes extremely important to keep in constant contact with the final consumer and to follow the impact of income changes on his tastes for material goods. Only a few organizations, such as the giant petroleum distributors, can afford to have their own African out-

Figure 1   Tropical Africa.

lets, with frequent visits by head-office people checking on sales trends. But if the foreign firm is to keep—and increase—its share of African spending, some such approach is necessary. In this respect, a local sales representative is often deficient; located in the large coastal cities, he tends to think in terms of the urban tastes of his immediate surroundings, and this reflects the more sophisticated and more prosperous African community. The much larger market in the rural villages and surrounding farms represents Africans who have emerged much more slowly into the modern world, or indeed are first putting cash income to spend on consumer products. In these areas the type of purchase reflects a much simpler and poorer African, though in aggregate these Africans may spend more than those in the few urban centers.[1]

Furthermore, the representative may not bother to send back customer reactions to the product, assuming he even notices them. For example, the alert personnel of the giant United Africa Company—Unilever's trading subsidiary that virtually dominates West African trade—discovered a new appeal for its carbolic soap product. Its use as fish bait had stepped up the African's catch of "giwa ruwa" in the Benue (Nigeria) area. On learning this, UAC soon capitalized on the product's new use and widened the market for the soap throughout the region. It would be unlikely that the ordinary agent would discover such a peculiarity, considering how many different products he had and how little of his time could be devoted to following the use pattern associated with each.

DISTINCTIVENESS OF AFRICAN MARKET

The emphasis on closeness to the final African market reflects the recognition of African selectivity—that it is not the beads, trinkets, and beer market depicted in lurid movies. The African is, by any standard, a sophisticated buyer, often ignoring the superficial appeal of fashion for the more basic and practical qualities of the product.

He can be exasperatingly fussy, too. The fez, for example, is only a red cap without a

brim to the average American, but the African will distingiush among the shapes, the material from which it is made, the thickness of the material, the color shadings, the extent and composition of the embroidery, as well as the particular design. He is also loyal to a brand that he has found satisfactory, thus making it difficult to sell him a "just-as-good" substitute.

There are also certain peculiarities of the African market that require product modifications. Picks and shovels must be adapted to the African's physical attributes, and even the tractor seats must be altered, for the African's posterior is generally smaller than the American's or European's.

The desire for European (that is, white) type products is probably more pronounced in West Africa than in East Africa, for the former has been in contact with Western influences for a much longer period. The African in the East has been slower to emerge into the new economy, and therefore his tastes have developed more slowly. Inasmuch as the resident European is looked to as the "upper class," he is imitated both in dress and manner.

TRADE CHANNELS

Trade in Tropical Africa is handled at three levels—characteristic to a large extent of the participation of the three main racial groups. There are the large European units whose major operation is importing the country's needs and exporting its produce; in addition they are usually secondary distributors, selling to the smaller wholesalers and retails shops, as well as to the final consumer (mainly the foreign resident group). At the next level are the smaller wholesalers, quite often Levantines in West Africa and Indians in East Africa; they serve as the link between the import stage and the final petty retailer. This last level, wherein most African (native) enterprise lies, serves the final consumer and also taps the rural sectors. Of course, this racial demarcation is only a generalization. In Ghana, Nigeria, and Sierra Leone the African women "mammy traders" often do so great a volume of business that they assume wholesale functions by selling to (and financing) petty or "penny" mammy traders rather than dealing directly with the final consumer. Also, particularly in British East Africa, the small Indian duka (or shop) services African clientele directly, especially in the more remote back-country or "bush."

These various traders perform both buying

[1] For examples of differences in buying patterns, see "Merchandise Trade in British West Africa," United Africa Company *Statistical and Economic Review*, No. 6 (September, 1950), pp. 1–40, at pp. 20–21.

and selling functions. The petty retailer may not only sell his goods, but probably also buys raw produce from the farmers in the area—produce that will ultimately enter into the export market. Sometimes these two functions merge into one transaction; the local customer barters his wares (ground nuts, for example) for cloth or hardware. Similarly the wholesaler sells consumer goods to the petty retailer, and buys the latter's combined lots of farm produce, gathering the supplies of many such retailers into larger bundles. Ultimately, the large European firms will amass these bundles of produce—now reaching large quantities—and export them; they will also break down the bulk import purchases into smaller lots for sale to the wholesaler.

In general, prices are not fixed, haggling between the buyer and seller being the accepted way of doing business at every level. Apparently the sociability that goes with such bargaining is one of the fringe benefits of the trading occupation. Only the few large stores catering primarily to the local European population go in for fixed prices, and these, it might be noted, rarely put on clearance or other sales featuring drastic price reductions.[2]

BREAKING INTO THE MARKET

Although there is no outright prohibition on a foreign product's entry into the African market, certain institutional difficulties operate at a disadvantage. In a few countries, especially French Africa, there are tariff or foreign exchange preferences favoring goods from the same currency area, for example, the franc. (Much of Equatorial Africa, however, is covered by the Congo Basin treaties which forbid tariff discrimination.) The national development plans are government administered, so that their citizens comprise the technical staff; inasmuch as their experience has usually been with supplies made in their own country or that of the former ruler—England, France, or Belgium—the chances are that the particular goods ordered will be those with specifications more readily met by producers in the mother country.

Fortunately, there are smaller aggressive

firms which are always eager to take on new lines, hoping thereby to break into the lucrative markets now dominated by the larger established houses. What they lack in size they often make up in "push"; coupled with good sales-promotion assistance from the foreign suppliers they can often make satisfactory and profitable inroads into the existing market structure and make their attempts pay off. And, of course, even the largest firms are willing to take on completely new products that do not compete with items they already handle.

SALES REPRESENTATION

Probably the most important consideration for an exporter or manufacturer seeking a trading connection in Tropical Africa as his sales agent is the selection of one who is honest and has a sense of responsibility. Too many local dealers have foundered because, faced with inadequate capital, they have over-reached themselves, either by undertaking too great a volume of operations or by giving unwise extensions to slow-paying or dishonest customers. With so vast a hinterland to flee to, it is not difficult for the unsuccessful African or Asian to melt away into the "bush," perhaps hundreds of miles from the site of his coup, and start business life anew.

Moreover, there are few "old-line" houses in any one trading community, and these are often already allied with competing manufacturers' items. While an alternative is to deal with a non-European, his influence is limited, and this factor must be weighed against the usually heavily entrenched position of the white middlemen.

A more costly method of reaching the market would be to establish a branch in the Tropical African country from which shipments would be made directly to the distributor. These units could serve as storage centers and, in addition, even some local fabrication could be undertaken. However, experience seems to indicate that even if the eventual market is large enough to justify such an operation, losses will probably be suffered for the first three-to-five years.

USE OF ITINERANT SALESMAN

A possible and practical compromise might be the employment of traveling salesmen whose duty would be to call on the many local

[2] For a more detailed description of the retail level, see Mildred Rendl Marcus, "Merchandise Distribution in Tropical Africa," *Journal of Retailing*, Vol. 35, No. 4 (Winter 1959–1960), pp. 197–201.

dealers—or as many as feasible—assisting the agent in obtaining orders, offering sales pointers to the retailer, and getting their opinions in return. To prevent any conflict it would undoubtedly be necessary to credit the company's agent with any orders the salesmen did book, since their primary function would be to obtain information about the market's changing tastes. The lowest sales level that could be realistically approached would be the small store—the duka—since by African standards even these are not miniscule; only the street peddler and wandering merchants would be ignored since they are hard to locate.

A good representative would become an intelligence outpost. He would get to know the peculiarities of the territory, enlighten the supplier with market data, and smooth the way for necessary modifications in either the product or the sales appeals. He could also transmit information about prospective economic trends and thus highlight factors affecting credit repayments.

SELECTION OF SALES PERSONNEL

In the selection of personnel a problem to be solved is whether to use nationals of the manufacturer's country or a native of the territory to be served. The advantage of the former is that it is easier to select someone who is likely to be technically qualified.

To find satisfactory Africans means looking for men in an unfamiliar country with different standards of work and perhaps totally unacquainted with either the product or the principles of sales promotion. The African's asset, on the other hand, would be his greater ability to gain access to the local outlets, since the alien stigma would be absent. He would also be more likely to speak the local dialect. And, though by no means a minor consideration, his wage cost would be appreciably lower, since living standards are so much below the American's plus the fact that relocation and special overseas allowances would be unnecessary. Of course, if the volume of business permits, a two-man team would be the appropriate compromise, one a foreign (company) man with the desired technical know-how, the other a capable African to do the actual interviewing.

A by-no-means unimportant advantage of such a staff would be realized if the manufac-

turer decided to change agents or even to set up his own local distributing branch. He would know where his products had been sold, which retailers had carried his line, and he would have some idea of the sales peculiarities and obstacles of the various local markets. Thus he would not have to start afresh if he were to drop his agent.

NEED FOR SALES-PROMOTION AIDS

Obviously the local distributor must receive help in selling, since he is not familiar with the product's specific sales qualities. Whether or not an auxiliary sales force is employed, the overseas manufacturer would still have to help with the local advertising and point-of-purchase promotion, although gearing them to the peculiarities of the market. The use of dogs in advertisements displayed in regions that despise these animals and the use of white models in a color-conscious region can be quite damaging to future sales. Particularly popular are sales-promotion campaigns in which trinkets, such as miniatures of the product, paper caps advertising the brand names, and similar free items are distributed. Belga cigarettes in the southeastern Belgian Congo popularized its brand by designing all its trucks to look like the cigarette package.

The advertising and sales-promotional appeals must be modified if the area is low in literacy, a common deficiency especially in rural Africa. Symbols and pictures become more significant than words and themes. To "play" on words may misfire because the African's knowledge of the language is often limited. Singer Sewing Machines, for example, has developed a wordless instruction book to cope with this problem.

Even the product's container may play a pivotal role in closing the sale. Petroleum drums when empty have multiple other uses in the interior; these could be resold and provide a supplementary source of income to the oil consumer. When the petroleum companies changed over to bulk deliveries by truck they reduced their customer's well-being. (Manufacturers who have placed a baby's picture on their food packages have discovered that the native frequently believes that the product is just that—a ground-up baby!)

Given a satisfactory product, an initial sale can usually result in repeat sales. Brand loyalty, as already mentioned, is a characteristic of the African market. And, of course, the local distributor can be influenced to make a greater effort on behalf of the manufacturer's product if he obtains a gross margin larger than that received on other products. Many an additional sale can be won by the extra persuasiveness of the seller rather than by any inherent virtue in the product itself.

INVENTORY AND DELIVERY PROBLEMS

Another problem which must be resolved is the size of inventories the agent is to carry. His desire, naturally, is to minimize this stock, for it represents so much tied-up capital that could be used for trade in other items. Physical inventory also takes up space, thus adding to warehouse costs, and it must also be looked after in order to prevent spoilage, theft, misplacement, and obsolescence. Possible price declines could result in losses severe enough to cause bankruptcy.

Yet he must carry sufficient stocks to fill orders without too great a delay. New deliveries from abroad take long in arriving and this prevents reliance on the foreign source for quick refills. As already implied, this is particularly important for machinery, where a lack of spare parts can render the item useless.

A possible compromise would be for the manufacturer to continue carrying the local inventory, perhaps in a bonded warehouse, if there is one locally. (Unfortunately, often only transit sheds are available with penalties on goods stored longer than the "free" period.[3]) Payment would be made only as the goods were released to the distributor. Thus, both the financial and physical burden could be shared between the two.

TRANSPORT OBSTACLES

The importance of transport time for Africa cannot be exaggerated. Only the very high-value items can be flown in: most goods must still go by water, and this is slow. Moreover, handling charges at the African ports are quite high; a study some years ago showed that they added 15 per cent to transport costs.[4]

Since the African-based representative is so far removed from his source of supply, he is forced to place a great importance on the manufacturer's reliability. He cannot pick up the telephone to correct an error. A wrong shipment cannot be replaced immediately, and defective merchandise cannot be exchanged quickly.

In gauging the extent of ultimate sales, it is unwise to assume that one outlet can serve a wide territory, for example, all Tropical Africa, or even only West or East Africa. Land transport routes do not permit easy passage of goods from one country to another, local air transport is expensive, and coastal boats often are slower than freighters from the head office abroad. A shipment from Mombasa on the Kenya east coast to Freetown on the bulge of West Africa could well take longer than the faster and more frequent freight service operating directly from New York and London. Even within the country more than one distribution center may be necessary; a Nairobi (Kenya) site, for example, would find it almost impossible to service adequately the Mwanza region on the Tanganyika side of Lake Victoria, only several hundred miles away, although both are in British East Africa.

SERVICING AIDS

For technically complicated items, such as heavy equipment, service and repair are most important. No one wants an idle machine awaiting some necessary adjustment; yet the local sales agent may have neither the machine tools nor the "know-how" to maintain such facilities. Because of the slowness of deliveries and the distance from the head office, new parts tend to be a costly source of delay, and flying in a serviceman is too expensive. Moreover, the original overseas supplier is often the only man who has the needed replacement part, because other manufacturers usually design their equipment to different specifications. As a result, it may be necessary for the manufacturer to train an employee of the distributor specifically for this service task.

The shortage of skilled help is so acute throughout Africa that most companies are forced to train raw help in order to solve this

[3] "Port Capacity and Shipping Turnaround in West Africa," United Africa Company *Statistical and Economic Review*, No. 12 (March, 1957), pp. 1–50, at pp. 16–17, 28.
[4] "Surf Port Operations in the Gold Coast,"

United Africa Company *Statistical and Economic Review*, No. 5 (March, 1950), pp. 45–52, at pp. 45–46.

need for mechanics. It may even be good policy for the overseas manufacturer to pay part of the repairman's wage in order to insure his being available, thus assuring the ultimate consumer that he need not worry about the possibility of an idle machine.

CREDIT

The local African distributor is also inevitably influenced by the supplier's credit terms since he cannot afford to tie up much capital for too long a time. Inventory turnover may often exceed a year on the average. Quite frequently the local distributor cannot pay the supplier until he has resold his product, and, in turn, received payment from his customers, who, in turn, may also have to wait until they have completed the entire transaction, that is, the sale and the subsequent payment. Yet this last vital link may be the farmer who cannot get cash to discharge his obligations until he has sold his crops.

As a result, the availability of ample credit may be *the* determining factor in obtaining an alliance with a local agent, since in the more remote sectors this credit cycle may stretch out as long as three years. Regardless of price, if the middleman cannot get the necessary financing—and reliance on the local banks must necessarily be for only limited amounts—he must depend on his own capital, a limitation which would certainly cripple any widespread operation not supplemented by credit extended by the supplier.

CONCLUSION

Like any new opportunity, the potential African market has many and complex problems. This is inherent in any growth and profit situation. But the magnitude of its challenge is also a measure of the possible gain.

Obviously so vast a plum is not to be had for the asking; merchants now in the area will fight to preserve their foothold while eager interlopers from all over will strive to break in. The seller who combines a good product with a keen insight into the dynamic African market may well realize a new profit potential that could form a welcome addition to his current operation. Even now the larger trading units are expanding the size of their investment in the area, as they get ready to take an even bigger bite of the growing pie.

CASES

Distribution Channels in an Overseas Market —Italy
(Procter & Gamble—B)

Late in 1962, the Procter & Gamble Company revamped its overseas organization into four new operating divisions in a move to expand and strengthen its international business organization. The four new divisions included the international division for Asia and Latin America, headquartered in Cincinnati; the international division for Britain, Canada, and Scandinavia, also headquartered in Cincinnati; the international division for the European Common Market, headquartered in Brussels, Belgium; and the international division for export and special operations, headquartered in Geneva, Switzerland. These divisions co-ordinated their activities by reporting to a vice president-group executive in the company's General Offices in Cincinnati.

The vitality of the Common Market in Europe offered opportunities for rapid growth in detergent sales. In a ten-year period from the early 50's to the early 60's, sales made in the six Common Market nations expanded from a nominal amount to more than 20 per cent of the company's total business outside the United States. The total volume of heavy-duty synthetic detergents sold in the Common Market by all companies (including Procter & Gamble subsidiaries) amounted to more than 60 million cases per year in the early part of the 60's and the favorable trend pointed to continued expansion.

Procter & Gamble had established separate subsidiary companies in France, West Germany, Italy, and Belgium to satisfy the requirements of this growing volume of business. The organization in Belgium served Holland and Luxemburg as well as Belgium. Each company was staffed to handle buying, manufacturing, selling, advertising, accounting, and product and market research. Products were manufactured in the company's own plants in Belgium, France, and Italy. Some products were produced by contractual arrangements with local manufacturing establishments in Germany and Belgium.

Although the Common Market was rapidly becoming a unified market, important national

◆ SOURCE: Reprinted by permission from The Procter & Gamble Company, © 1961.

differences continued to exist which required local policies within the separate companies. Language differences and social customs indicated a need for varied approaches in sales, advertising, and promotion. Local habits such as the method of washing clothes, as well as the extent of ownership of washing machines and types of machines, necessitated significant variations among washing products offered to the consumer.

In Italy, the administrative office was located in an expanding commercial section in the southern suburban area of Rome. The manufacturing facilities were situated in Pomezia, a new industrial development south of Rome. This plant was located beyond the boundary line which the national Italian government had established to divide north and south Italy for the purposes of a national industrial development program for the south. Industries located below the boundary benefited from tax advantages and incentives for industrial development.

The administrative organization included such functions as sales, advertising, buying, public relations, product and market research, and accounting. Extensive market and advertising research was conducted to determine product preferences and to measure advertising effectiveness in the Italian market. Test market procedures, including store audits, were employed following a pattern already adopted in United States markets. Advertising was placed in magazines and in broadcast media. Newspaper advertising was not used because of the relatively low readership of newspapers by women, and also because Italian newspapers did not feature week-end retail grocery advertising as is traditional in the United States.

Procter & Gamble products which had been introduced into the Italian market included Tide, Camay, Dreft (in liquid form for washing dishes), Spic and Span, and Monsavon, a toilet soap which had previously been introduced by the French company into its market.

Distribution of these products had been accomplished by means of a selling agent who had a national organization which reached all parts of the Italian market. This selling agent handled other non-competitive products in the proprietary drug area and in the grocery classification. Salesmen in the agent's organization called on wholesalers as well as retailers. Procter & Gamble maintained only a small sales organization to work with representatives of the selling agent and to perform some limited merchandising activity. Salesmen of the agent took orders in the customary fashion, with delivery made from strategically located warehouses at eleven important distribution points.

The wholesalers from whom the agent's salesmen obtained orders provided an important service in the Italian distribution system because of the predominance of small retail outlets. In some cases, delivery was by the wholesaler's truck. Sometimes, salesmen of the wholesalers filled the orders from their own cars. In most cases, however, wholesalers operated on a very small scale without salesmen, taking orders by telephone and making delivery later in their own private automobiles or small trucks. It was customary for the wholesaler to extend credit to the retailer as an aid in financing his purchases.

Almost all retailers selling soap and related products were small, and for the most part were located in densely populated urban areas on narrow streets characteristically clogged with vehicles of all descriptions—from bicycles, scooters, motorcycles, small passenger cars, to small trucks, buses, and sometimes larger transport trucks—which inevitably produced bottlenecks and traffic jams.

The system of retailing with the many small shops was in keeping with the mode of living and the social customs existing in the country. A large percentage of families in Italy had residences in apartment buildings, with a consequent high density of population in the urban areas and a high concentration of dwellings in the smaller towns and villages. In each of the apartment districts there were numerous small shops to serve the residents. Purchases of everyday necessities were made frequently and in small quantities, and there was an absence of the week-end shopping pattern so familiar in the United States. Transactions for the most part were on a cash basis but many merchants did encourage credit buying to build volumes with some customers. The many small establishments made merchandise of a wide variety available within walking distance and in this manner effected a "convenience" in the pattern of retailing. In the United States, the pattern, by contrast, developed to offer a convenience to those shopping by automobile.

The retail system in Italy, furthermore, had displayed a resistance to change which had not been so true for other Common Market countries. This rigidity was due at least in part to a system of licensing. Each merchant was required to have a license for the operation of a store and also separate licenses for the sale of many classifications of merchandise handled. Separate licenses, for example, were needed for the sale of fruit, canned goods, milk, fresh meat, smoked meat, and wine. In the clothing category, licenses were for such detailed classifications as men's shirts and men's underwear. The authorities in this way were able to protect the merchants already in business from new establishments or from new merchandise lines added to existing establishments. In the pharmaceutical classification, license granting was especially rigid and with regulations still patterned from the time drugs were prepared primarily by the pharmacist.

No specific licenses were needed for the sale of soap or detergents, but these products could be handled by merchants already licensed to sell other items. In some areas, merchants engaged in the sale of food items also sold soap; in other areas they did not. Bar toilet soap could be found in food stores, pharmaceutical stores, cosmetic stores, some clothing stores, and tobacco shops. In addition, washing powders were sometimes available in hardware stores, fuel stores, and paint stores. Finally,

there were a few of the larger department store type outlets, supermarkets, and consumer cooperatives where soaps and detergents could be purchased. As examples of the variation in approach by localities, it can be pointed out that these products were sold by bread stores in Rome, a practice not generally true in other parts of the country; in Florence, bars serving Espresso coffee, vermouth, liquor and soft drinks were important outlets for soap products; in Naples, tobacco stores were principal outlets for bar toilet soap.

In spite of this diversity, an attempt has been made in the table below to itemize the number of licenses authorizing the sale of a variety of merchandise with which soap and detergents might be sold in Italy. According to the best estimates available, approximately 215,000 of the license holders actually handled soaps and detergents and another 40,000 handled toilet soap only.

In addition to depicting the licensing system in terms of merchandise categories, the table also brings into focus the relatively small numbers of the large type merchandising operations such as department stores and supermarkets. The table lists only 40 supermarkets and 241 department-type stores. As indicated

Merchandise Category	Number of Licenses, 1959
Bread, Grocery, Coffee, Candy	219,360
Vegetables, Fruit	50,969
Smoked Meats	33,399
Other Foods	5,725
Total Food Stores	309,453
Sanitary and Chemical Articles	4,006
Perfumes, Toilet Articles	11,285
Drugs	11,153
Total Drugs and Related Products Stores	26,444
Hardware, Utensils, Plumbing Supplies	18,836
Paint, Building Supplies	11,514
Fuel	29,007
Total Hardware, Household Materials & Supplies Stores	59,357
Tobacco Stores	52,616
Supermarkets	40
Variety Stores	162
Department Stores	79
Consumer Cooperatives	4,517
Total Miscellaneous Merchandise Stores	57,414
Total Licenses, Mdse. Categories Related to Soap Products	452,668

earlier, this small number is explained by the modes of living and the licensing system. The importance of these forms of retailing outlets, however, was greater than numbers alone indicate; it indicates the changes taking place and shows the beginning of a developing trend in retailing. Whereas in 1959 there were licenses for only 40 supermarkets, private estimates in 1963 placed the number in excess of 400. In 1956, there were only two supermarkets in Italy.[1]

The slow start but the rapid gains following 1956 would suggest that the numbers of these larger stores would continue to mount. The total number of supermarkets in 1959 was still small in relation to the 17,000 existing in Germany, and even the 1,500 in France. The self-service method of operation, a basic principle in supermarket merchandising, was practiced in less than one per cent of the stores in Italy, compared with 12 per cent in Germany and Norway and four per cent in England.[2] Italy had no self-service stores in 1948. In all of Europe there were only 34. But by 1958, when Italy had only 106 self-service stores, the number in the rest of Europe had expanded to 22,922. Observers of the marketing scene in Italy were quite confident that the trends in self-service merchandising and expansion of supermarkets would persist.

There was also a belief that there would be an increase in the number of larger departmentized stores handling broader classifications of merchandise. Two organizations in Italy, "Standa" and "Upim," were actively planning expansion and an increased number of stores in their respective chains. Furthermore, the voluntary chain type of organization had been adopted in the form of buying groups of retailers in a few of the larger cities.

The continuation of the trend toward larger scale retailing might also be anticipated as a part of the social changes associated with higher standards of living and with increased ownership of automobiles. In the period from 1950 to 1959, the gross domestic product for Italy increased from 7,630 million lire to 15,413 million lire.[3] Population during the same interval grew from about 46.5 million in 1950 to 49.7 million in 1959. The greater proportionate gain in product as contrasted with population was reflected in a substantially higher product per capita. This per capita product gain was more than enough to offset inflation represented by a rise in the consumer price index from 86 in 1950 to 113 in 1959. The greatest amount of inflation came in one year, 1951, after which prices remained fairly steady.

In 1948, only 218,500 automobiles were registered in Italy. By 1959, automobile ownership had increased to 1,644,206. The gain of seven times contrasts with an increase in the United States during the same period of only 78 per cent, from 33,350,000 vehicles in 1948 to 59,567,000 in 1959. In 1948, there was one automobile for each 200 persons in Italy. By 1959 there was one for each 30 persons, and estimates indicated one for each 21 persons in 1963. It is likely that this trend will continue (in 1963 there was one car for each nine persons in Torino). Although the shopping facilities in 1963 had not changed sufficiently to accommodate this rising number of automobiles and provide for "shopping on wheels," the pressure for change was certainly present. An increased number of stores or shopping centers with ample parking space appeared to be a reasonable expectation along with the trend toward larger scale retailing.

The growth of the middle class was another social change which could have an effect on the pattern of retailing. Higher wage levels and increased opportunities in other fields of employment reduced the supply of domestic servants; at the same time, the rising cost of domestic help reduced the demand. As related to retailing, this social change was quite significant because many housewives had formerly relied on domestic help to do the family shopping. As long as this was true, the inconvenience of supplying the family's needs from a variety of small shops by means of a time-consuming process was not of major importance. But as the responsibility for the family buying shifted to the housewife, convenience and "one stop" shopping rapidly assumed greater significance. As was true in other countries, many housewives were gainfully employed and were anxious therefore to reduce the time required for shopping.

[1] "Le Libre Service en Europe," Organization Europeene de Cooperation Economique, 1960.
[2] "Appunti Di Tecnica Della Distribuzione," Prof. Carlo Fabrizi.
[3] United Nations Statistical Yearbook, 1961.

QUESTIONS

1. In view of the social and economic trends in Italy—particularly as they influenced the

pattern of retail distribution—what changes, if any, would you recommend that the company make in its policies relative to personal selling? Why?

2. If you believe changes are necessary in the personal selling policies presently employed by Procter & Gamble in the Italian market, how would you implement these changes?

3. If you have recommended no change in policy, what kind of "alarm system" do you propose which will indicate when some change is needed?

Expansion of International Markets—Japan
(*Procter & Gamble—C*)

The International Divisions of the Procter & Gamble Company are a well-established segment of the company's marketing operation, and executives of the Divisions are constantly alert to possibilities for extension of business abroad. The company began to develop international markets around the turn of the century, and intensified this activity after World War II. By 1962, P&G products were available in more than one hundred countries throughout the free world, from Canada, Mexico, Venezuela, and other Latin American countries in the Western Hemisphere, to England, Belgium, France, Switzerland, Germany, Italy, in Europe, and to the Philippines and Australia in the Far East. In the annual report for the fiscal year ending in 1962 the company reported net earnings from international operations of $20 million, which represented eighteen per cent of total company net earnings of $109 million.

In developing international markets, the company used one of four approaches or a combination of more than one. Initially, products from United States processing plants were exported to foreign markets, and, with the aid of agents, distributed to wholesalers and retailers within the countries abroad. In 1962 this practice was still followed in many parts of the world.

A second approach was that of arranging with foreign manufacturers to produce P&G products locally (contract manufacture). In these instances, P&G production personnel supervised the manufacturing processes in order to insure that the products conformed to the company's high standards of quality.

◆ SOURCE: Reprinted by permission from The Procter & Gamble Company, © 1961.

Usually one of the smaller manufacturers would be selected for this purpose rather than the country's leading producer of the type of product being introduced. In Australia, for example, Procter & Gamble products are manufactured and distributed by a local firm according to a contract with P&G. Although manufacturing is carried out by the Australian company, trained production personnel from P&G supervised the installation of the processing machinery and the production process.

In some of the countries to which the company originally exported, the growth of the market often justified a third approach; that is, P&G would build manufacturing facilities within the country. Also, in some instances, because of the large size or potential of a market, the company would establish its own production facilities at the outset. In 1962 the company had manufacturing installations in a number of countries, such as Canada, Mexico, Great Britain, Belgium, France, and the Philippines, among others.

Eventually, a fourth approach grew out of the third: products would be imported into foreign countries from factories which had previously been established abroad. For example, Camay soap sold in Australia was shipped initially from the P&G plant in England.

The type of approach adopted in any particular market and at any particular time, of course, was dependent upon a number of variables: tariff regulations; import restrictions; regulations relative to the installation of manufacturing facilities; financing availability and arrangements; the size of the market; and, finally, governmental attitudes toward such business operations.

Exports were made from the United States to the respective countries whenever possible, but distance and/or import restrictions precluded this practice in a growing number of markets. In larger countries such as Great Britain, France, West Germany, and Italy, a sufficient sales potential existed to make manufacturing installations feasible. In the smaller markets of the developing countries, however, plant investments could not be justified and the company was faced with the necessity of arranging for local manufacture, or the withdrawal of P&G products from the market. Countries representative of this category included Iran, Colombia, Morocco, and Thailand.

Because of these circumstances, the share of

total international business supplied from United States manufacturing facilities had been restricted. In the ten-year period previous to 1962, less than ten per cent of the business overseas represented goods manufactured in the United States and exported to foreign markets.

The development of manufacturing facilities abroad had been carried out to a considerable extent through the process of re-investing earnings from overseas operations and through substantial foreign borrowing. The policy of re-investing overseas earnings in foreign based facilities delayed the repatriation of funds. In the case of Canada, as an example, the first investment was made in 1915 but no dividends were returned to the parent company in the United States until 1939. By 1962, however, the total return on foreign investments resulted in a net inflow to the parent company. In the five years previous, $9 million had been invested abroad but $48 million had been returned to the United States.

Headquarters for all overseas activities were maintained in Cincinnati. However, active direction for marketing products for the European Common Market came from a division headquartered in Belgium, and certain export activities and special international opportunities were handled from a division headquartered in Switzerland. The location in Switzerland benefited from excellent banking facilities in that country and an active Swiss market for practically all types of currencies. A business-minded Swiss Government was interested in promoting the nation as a profitable location from which international business might be transacted.

In 1962 P&G was handling the marketing operation in about 75 countries from the Swiss base. Approximately half of the total sales represented products manufactured in the United States and the other half those products manufactured in facilities abroad. Shipments into foreign markets from domestic processing plants or from foreign processing locations depended on a number of considerations, including relative costs, historical trade patterns, transportation facilities, and currency restrictions.

In the complex of world markets, Japan in 1962 represented a special situation. The importance of the Japanese market, its size, and rapid growth following World War II made it a logical nation for consideration as an important potential marketing area, but political considerations as well as certain market characteristics were a matter of concern to the international executives.

Procter & Gamble had exported to Japan on a limited basis for some time, partly in order to protect the registration in that market of several P&G trade-marks, including Camay, Cheer, Dreft, Ivory, Tide, Zest, Crisco, and Crest. Any aggressive penetration of the market, however, awaited a major decision on whether it would be most desirable to: (1) set up an active import program involving the use of a local distributor; (2) contract for production by a local manufacturer; or (3) invest capital funds in production and distribution facilities.

Any type of entry would necessitate approval of the Japanese Government and conformity with a rather rigorous set of governmental regulations. Should the decision be to contract with a Japanese manufacturer or to establish manufacturing facilities within Japan, the complexities for governmental clearance might require more than a year of time-consuming negotiations. The Japanese Government had taken a very active role in the regulation of business activities, feeling that such a policy was needed to protect the many small manufacturers in that country. Seventy-seven per cent of Japanese workers were employed in firms having 50 or fewer employees, as opposed to less than twenty per cent in the United States. With the exception of a few large trusts, a "cottage type" factory operation predominated.

Foreign investments or technological agreements with Japanese firms required governmental "validation." This approval for operation within prescribed limits was sometimes difficult to obtain because of the intent of Japanese regulations in prohibiting any threat to established Japanese industry, and because of a desire to encourage only those enterprises likely to increase the supply of foreign exchange so badly needed for Japan's import requirements. Once validation had been obtained, however, profits would be protected and remittances would be assured.

Without validation from the appropriate Japanese authorities, any investment or operation in Japan would be subject to considerable risk on a number of points, among the most important of which would be the future convertibility of the Japanese currency and the restrictions on remittances. In 1962, neither Unilever nor Colgate, the two principal competitors of Procter & Gamble in world markets, had arranged for validation to permit an active operation in the Japanese market. A number of United States firms, however, had received such validation, one of which was the Otis Elevator Company. The nature of that company's business was such that the Japanese Government had permitted 100 per cent outside ownership, but after this arrangement was secured, Otis found it expedient to provide for Japanese participation to the extent of 20 per cent. This was a voluntary move by Otis designed to establish a closer rapport with the Japanese community. It was successful in improving relations with Government and other factors in the Japanese economy, and in greatly improving the morale of the workers. Japanese labor is accustomed to strongly paternalistic treatment and immediately felt more secure when Otis acquired some Japanese ownership.

It is far more difficult for a Westerner to set up independent operations in Japan than in any other large country of comparable development (all of whom, unlike Japan, are Western). In addition to direct governmental discouragement of independent foreign ventures, there are equally important, although less tangible, obstacles to be found in the areas of understanding the Japanese mind and in overcoming the ingrained apprehension of strangers. Prior to completion of negotiations with governmental officials, it was impossible for P&G to anticipate the extent of Japanese participation, if any, which would be required for validation.

Import restrictions imposed by the Japanese were in the form of an ad valorem duty based on a wholesale price established in the normal course of operations in the markets of the country of origin. To this wholesale price would be added any expenses incurred in shipping to the port of export and loading on the vessel, plus freight and insurance up to arrival of the merchandise at the port of import. According to the schedule of import duties, the classification of toilet soap, laundry soap, medicated soap, and detergents was subject to a 20 per cent ad valorem duty except for perfumed soaps, in which case the duty was 30 per cent.

In appraising the potential of the Japanese market, the executives of the International Divisions had the benefit of certain basic statistical information. The population of Japan was 93.0 million. Income per capita was slightly less than two-thirds of that for Italy and approximately one-third of that for France. Washing products consumed, on a per capita basis, were about one-half of those for France and about two-thirds of those for Italy. Per capita income was less than 15 per cent of that enjoyed in the United States, but the volume of washing products consumed per person was almost 40 per cent of the average in the United States. With almost twice as many people, Japan represented a market for washing products about equal to that of France. In the postwar period, the economy of Japan had enjoyed a tremendous and vigorous growth rate which surpassed that of most of the major nations in the world.

Executives in the International Divisions also noted that almost one billion pounds of washing products had been produced by Japanese manufacturers in 1961. Of this amount, roughly 67 per cent represented soap products and 33 per cent represented detergents. The proportion of the detergent products in the market had been increasing, as was true in most other markets where both soaps and detergents were available. In the soap category, about half of the total amount produced was laundry bar soap; a little less than a quarter was soap powders; a little less than a quarter was toilet bar soap.

From available information, it is indicated

Soap and Detergent Production in Japan (in metric tons)

Year	Soap				Soap Total	Detergents Total	Total Soap & Detergents
	Toilet	Laundry	Powder	Other			
1957	59,223	184,899	63,355	12,395	319,872	24,447	344,319
1958	60,348	192,735	81,846	11,692	346,621	30,551	377,172
1959	65,127	202,237	99,405	13,282	380,051	48,417	428,468
1960	67,203	170,392	94,518	15,175	347,288	86,280	433,568
1961	70,077	141,502	71,874	15,273	298,726	150,486	449,212

SOURCE: Japanese Ministry of International Trade and Industry.

that the production of detergents had expanded six times in the five year period from 1957 through 1961. In contrast, soap production dropped about seven per cent during the same period. A rise in output of soap products up to 1959 was offset by a decline after that date. More specifically, the downturn in soap production was in the laundry bar and soap powder classifications. Output of toilet soap continued to register small gains each year.

The bulk of clothes washing in Japan in 1962 was done outside the home in climatic conditions roughly comparable to those in the United States. Because of the soft water, soap products produced satisfactory suds. There were washing machines in 37 per cent of the urban homes. An urbanized population, crowded into the valleys of the country, resulted in a density ratio of 650 per square mile. This compares with 56 per square mile for the United States. Communities of more than 30,000 population each accounted for about one-half of the total Japanese population.

Japan enjoys an exceptionally high literacy rate which has prompted a wide circulation of newspapers and magazines. In 1962 three national daily newspapers reached 43 per cent of the market, with 96 per cent of the circulation being home delivered. Thirty weekly magazines with a combined circulation of 8.0 million provided a medium for additional advertising coverage. A number of radio stations and 46 television stations afforded a growing broadcast medium for consumer goods. It was estimated that $300 million was spent for advertising in Japan in 1958, of which about half went into newspapers. The second most important advertising medium was the outdoor medium, which accounted for 20 per cent of advertising volumes. Radio accounted for 15 per cent, television another 10 per cent, and magazine advertising the remaining 5 per cent. About 90 per cent of the Japanese homes had radios but only 16 per cent had television sets.

In studying the system of physical distribution of grocery and related products, it was noted that the retail structure was characterized by many small-scale service retailers supplied by agents (wholesalers). It was the practice of these small-scale outlets to solicit orders from homes in the morning and to make delivery in the afternoon. In 1962, the large self-service store had not become a major factor in the retail structure of the country. About 500 wholesalers serviced approximately 100,000 small-scale retailers. In the distribution of soap and related products, wholesalers operated on a gross margin of 5 to 10 per cent and retailers operated on a margin of from 15 to 25 per cent. Although subject to some fluctuation, the following retail prices were found to be representative: a 21 ounce heavy-duty soap powder similar to Duz sold for the equivalent of 28¢; a 16 ounce heavy-duty synthetic product similar to Tide sold for 28¢; and a bar of toilet soap, comparable in size to Camay, sold for 8¢.

A number of Japanese manufacturers were engaged in the production of washing products and related items:

1. *The Kao Soap Company, Ltd.*, made all types of soaps and synthetics. The principal manufacturing plant was located at Osaka, but the company had two additional plants as well as two sales offices located in other parts of the country. The principal products included a heavy-duty synthetic washing powder branded Wonderful; a light-duty synthetic product branded Amahm; and Wonderful K, a liquid detergent packaged in a lacquered can. The Kao Company, as the largest soap company in the field, was also one of the fastest growing.

2. *The Lion Fat and Oil Company* marketed a heavy-duty packaged soap branded Lion; a light-duty packaged synthetic branded Lipon; a Lion bar soap packaged in a foil wrapper; and a liquid synthetic packaged in a lacquered can and branded Lipon F. Organized as a joint stock company, Lion had as one of its major shareholders the Lion Dentifrice Company, Ltd., the oldest and largest Japanese producer of tooth powder and toothpaste.

3. *The Shiseido Company, Ltd.*, was primarily a producer and a distributor of cosmetics, but it also manufactured and distributed a line of soaps, detergents, toothpaste, and toothbrushes. The company operated 73 affiliated sales companies which provided a wholesale service network of retail outlets for the products of its productive facilities. The principal soap products included a heavy-duty powdered soap branded Hakusen, a light-duty packaged synthetic branded AP, Olive bar soap packaged in a cardboard box, and a liquid synthetic in a lacquered can branded Cleana.

4. *The Migishi Oil and Fat Company, Ltd.*, although representing less volume in the soap business, produced edible oils, shortening, oleomargarine, fatty acids, and related products.

In total volume of business, this company probably ranked somewhere between the Kao Company and the Lion Company.

Other concerns having an influence in the industry included the Nippon Oils and Fats Company, Ltd., a leading producer of paints and explosives; the Ashai Electro Chemical Company, Ltd., an important producer of electrolytic caustic soda and liquid chlorine; the Nikka Yushi Company, Ltd., a refiner and processor of vegetable oils; the Yoshihai'a Oil Mills, Ltd., also engaged in the processing of oils and fats; the Daiichi Kozyo Seigahu Company, Ltd., a smaller concern which manufactured soap and synthetics under the name of Genbu and Monogen; and, finally, the Marumiya Company, Ltd., a concern dating back to 1860 which started as a dealer in novelties and cosmetics but had been producing and selling a toilet soap since the 1890's.

Several of these Japanese companies were represented in the United States by Toyomenka, Inc., of New York City. This firm acted as an agent to facilitate entry of products of United States firms into the Japanese and other markets of the Far East. The Toyomenka Company undoubtedly could be an important source of information and consulting services available to the Procter & Gamble executives in their effort to determine the most feasible approach in studying the Japanese market.

QUESTIONS

1. You have been retained as a consultant by Procter & Gamble. Your job is to look into the various ways personal selling activity could take place in the Japanese market. During your discussion with Procter & Gamble, you obtained the information presented in the case. What tentative conclusions can you reach from this information?

2. What type of P&G sponsored personal selling activity would you recommend if a decision was made to:

   a) "Set up an active import program involving the use of a local distributor"?

   b) "Contract for production by a local manufacturer"?

   c) "Invest capital funds in production and distribution facilities"?

PART

V

Ethical Considerations in Personal Selling

Lamentations over the lack of "ethics" in personal selling have been frequent and sustained throughout history. The widening scope of personal responsibility of salesmen in the modern business world is likely to stimulate these views and indeed increase the cry of critics. What seems to be needed in this area is for the matter to be brought into the open for examination by sales people and non-sales people alike. The following articles represent the major portion of the literature which presently exists in this area.

Walton explores the trilogy "Ethical Theory, Societal Expectations, and Marketing Practices" in his inquiry into "what *ought* and *ought not* to be done by the market; what should we *like* the market to do beyond the ethical imperatives; and what *is* the market actually doing."

In "Sales Ethics: Truth and Taste Needed?" the problem of sales ethics is clearly stated with areas of abuse spelled out. According to the article what is needed in dealing with the problem is a three-pronged approach, "combining clear-cut policy statements by top management, indoctrination of salesmen and meticulous controls."

The approach of Schwartz in this matter of ethics involves "Salesmanship and Professional Standards." Attention is given to a specific code of ethics for salesmen.

Russell, Beach, and Buskirk discuss "Ethical Problems in Selling" which center around "customer relations," "employers," and "competitors." While the discussion is not intended to provide an absolute code of selling ethics, it does suggest some of the consequences of dealing with ethics problems universally.

Ethical Theory, Societal Expectations, and Marketing Practices

CLARENCE C. WALTON

A market—manned by millions of wholesalers, retailers, advertisers, warehousers and the like, and servicing hundreds of millions of consumers both here and abroad—is bound to generate an occasional uneasiness over its performance. Seizing upon its deficiencies, the critics have mounted a rather sustained attack. If, at times, the criticisms have been lacking in logic they have never been found wanting in temerity of conclusions. "Waste-makers," "hidden persuaders," "hucksters," are not terms calculated to raise the merchant to any high level of public esteem. Are these descriptions adequate? Is the marketing man's consciousness conscienceless? Are high and low positions in marketing peopled by greedy and grubby denizens? Or have we evolved market institutions that perform economic functions with a high degree of efficiency? And are these functions carried out in what can be fairly described as "ethical" ways? Perhaps on close examination there may be seen in the market a magnificently intricate and symmetrical mechanism which keeps customers supplied with need, businessmen excited by profits, and the total society satisfied with its merits.

It may be fairly conceded that the attractions and motivations of the marketplace are not found in high moral ideals; indeed marketing institutions and practices may be developed in a morally neutral climate to satisfy material wants. Yet, these institutions and practices must not collide with other values in the social system. And when they promote concern over higher values, then marketing practices can be said to contribute to a more just and humane society.

A self-adjusting market, isolated from the rest of the community and operating under its own exclusive autonomy, may have been the ideal of the nineteenth century. It is not the reality of the twentieth century. There is a range for greater judgment and greater choice which are primary ingredients of an ethical act. The assignment is to discover where moral guidelines are to be sought: in the Church? In business itself? In philosophical inquiry?

INTRODUCTION

Philosophers' condemnations of man's cupidities and theologians' fulmination against human frailties are as old as Plato's *Republic* and as new as Rabbi Finkelstein's now-famous *Fortune* blast against the current business ethos.[1] To concede that material affluence is not moral influence, that power is not probity, or economic security the equivalent of safety is to germinate a paradox. The paradox begins to press home when we are told that television has turned the high art of polity into the low cult of personality, and that the marketplace has despoiled judgment, debased tastes, invaded individual sovereignties, and eroded moral fibre.[2] If, indeed, these are the ample

◆ SOURCE: Reprinted by permission from *The Social Responsibilities of Marketing*, edited by William D. Stevens, Proceedings of the Winter Conference of the American Marketing Association, December 1961, pp. 7–24.

[1] Louis Finkelstein, "The Businessman's Moral Failure," *Fortune*, September, 1958, pp. 116 ff.

[2] Vance Packard's name and particularly *The Hidden Persuaders* (London: Longmans, Green, & Co., 1957) come immediately to mind. More devastating criticisms have come from Eric Fromm, *The Sane Society* (New York: Rinehart & Co., 1955), and Will Herberg, *Judaism and Modern Man* (New York: Farrar, Strauss, & Young, 1951), esp. pp. 16–23. The phenomenon is not unique to the United States. Viewing the French scene, Reverend Joseph Thomas bemoaned: "*Materialisation des hommes, materialisation du corps social, tel est le jugement qu'on doit porter sur notre societe quand on l'etudie objectivement.*" "*Le mieux-etre materiel est-il le tout de la vie d'un peuple?*" *Chefs d'Entreprise* V (Octobre, 1961), p. 15.

symptoms of the working out of a Gresham's law of ethics, then Marx's prophesies of the eventual doom of free-market economies appear readied for fulfillment.[3]

Yet for all its alleged weaknesses, no less an authority than Reinhold Niebuhr holds firmly that the economic realm, above all else, has become the "strategic testing ground of the adequacy and relevance of a religio-moral worldview."[4] The significance of the observation is the more striking when it is realized that traditional religious attitudes reveal an anti-economic bias. "The careful, calculating, economizing way of life is neither prophetic nor poetic. It counts the costs; it asks for reward; it has no fine frenzies; it is humdrum, commonplace, even a little sordid"[5]—yet the economic way of life becomes the stage where the drama of Everyman is to be worked out. If Neibuhr's observation is correct then the relationship of the business order to society's total value structure—always relevant—becomes crucially important.

The modest objective of this inquiry is to explore such relationships from a general and theoretical framework.[6] Although involved with three basic notions which have been identified as *ethical criteria, societal expectations,* and *marketing practices,* respectively, it is patent that each concept has its own solar system. The following questions are most germane:—what *ought* and *ought not* to be done by the market; what should we *like* the market to do beyond the ethical imperatives; and what *is* the market actually doing. The range moves from the obligatory to preference systems to actual practices. The trilogy, while suggestive of focus, fails to penetrate the heart of the matter which is the interplay of values in a pluralistic society. Involved is the total *social system* by which is meant the observable structure and organiza-tion through which basic human needs are satisfied. These needs relate to man's religious, political, cultural, sexual and economic life, and the activities carried out according to socially acceptable norms in order to achieve certain objectives. Since norms embody values, it is evident that the social system is "held together by its internal agreement about the sacredness of certain fundamental moral stand-ards."[7]

As thus construed, the system is geared to accomplish the social good—defined by New-man as less the pursuit of a theoretical absolute and more a choice among warring alternatives. To understand and to achieve the good impose the necessity for effective dialogue between men of different intellectual persuasions but of equal good wills. It assumes that peace and liberty, equity and security constitute the good society.[8] What are our sacred and fundamental values? How are they determined and expressed? What priorities prevail when value systems clash? How are refinements made without injury to the polity?

Three broad categories can be usefully employed to treat of such questions and they may be classified as (1) theological norms, (2) philosophical ethics, and (3) the business *ethos.* The first class involves the Church where matters of faith and sectarian allegiance influence and guide human behavior; the second category looks to values that can be rationally discovered by all men; and the third embraces a host of commitments and expectations which characterize an advanced industrialized society. While the classifications are less than fully satisfactory, they have merit in permitting the development of important distinctions between the supernatural and the secular orders; otherwise, there is the real danger of developing something akin to social monophysitism.[9]

---

[3] *Manifesto* (New York: New York Labor News Co., 1933), p. 15.

[4] *An Interpretation of Christian Ethics* (New York: Meridian Books, 1956), p. 165.

[5] Kenneth Boulding, "Religious Foundations of Economic Progress," *Harvard Business Review,* Vol. XXX (May–June, 1952), pp. 33–41.

[6] Reliance on the generalist view carries an important caveat for it means that in this short treatise certain details will be insufficiently treated —a weakness common to the macro approach. When the occasion warrants, therefore, the author assumes a risk in expressing opinions on trends for which supporting empirical data may be presently inadequate. In such cases note will be made that it is an informed opinion and not an established judgment.

[7] "In an inchoate, dimly perceived, and seldom explicit manner, the central authority of an orderly society, whether it be secular or ecclesiastical, is acknowledged to be the avenue of communication with the realm of sacred value." Edward Shils and Michael Young, "The Meaning of the Coronation," from the collection edited by Seymour M. Lipset and Neil Smelser, *Sociology: The Progress of a Decade* (Englewood Cliffs: Prentice-Hall, Inc., 1961), p. 232.

[8] Terence Kenny, *The Political Thought of John Henry Newman* (London: Rutledge, 1957), pp. 77–88.

[9] An ancient Christological heresy which held that the divine and human natures of Christ fused to form a distinct third nature even as gold and silver combine to form electrum.

THE BASIC TERMS: LEVELS
FOR VALUES

Theological norms—may be roughly described as standards for conduct which flow from those basic views of Deity and of man and which are often derived from Revelation; from the point of view of the communicant, such standards remain above the realm of debate. They are fixed values and hold the highest priority because they reflect God's will. Exchange of views is difficult, even when undertaken, because each religion clothes its most subtle values within an elaborate ritual [10] which has profound significance to the adherent and is often meaningless to the outsider. Perhaps Plato was right when he declared flatly in the VIIth Epistle that the really profound insights are not communicable; hence poetry, allegory and myth are always necessary. The religions of the Bible are convinced that their roles in the American Commonwealth are "vastly more than a subordinate sociological datum performing an increasingly peripheral function in society. The religions want to be a source of culture, determining its nature from a point of reference beyond it." [11] Whether the Churches are achieving such an objective is difficult to say in view of the conflicting nature of the data and the contradictory opinions held by theologians themselves. For example, Gerhard Lenski's studies of Detroit offer substantial evidence that religion colors the daily behavior of men at both the personal and social levels. Installment buying, savings, attitudes toward work, and political preferences are influenced by the socio-religious group to which one belongs.[12] Yet others, like Rabbi Finkelstein and John Courtney Murray, are far from persuaded that religion has any appreciable influence on American social behavior or institutions.[13] Two factors suggest support for the former view. In the first place there is evidence that business practices are being conditioned by religion and the efforts of Quaker businessmen associated with Walter Lamb is a case in point.[14] Secondly there are clear signs that the Churches are taking a more positive and direct position on contemporary mercantile issues. [15] There are even small signs of reciprocal interests by the business community. Perhaps it is unlikely that anything will develop to approximate the sixteenth century experience of Tomas de Mercado, a theologian at Salamanca, who was earnestly requested by the Seville merchants (then engaged in making the town the trading center for all the Spanish-American possessions) to provide them with a primer in business morality,[16] but it is worth noting that the committee on business ethics set up under the aegis of the Commerce Department does include clergymen. Looking ahead a decade, businessmen might reflect nostalgically on the easy homiletics of the *Organization Man*—and with a wish to return to the conformities which characterized the fifties.

What conclusions may be drawn so far as religious influences on the market? Clearly, Churches are reaching into the marketplace to make known religious views as they relate to a variety of business problems, including wages and working conditions, Sunday shopping and sympathy strikes, competition and advertising.[17]

[10] See Lyman Bryson *et al.*, eds., *Symbols and Values: An Initial Study* (New York: Harper and Brothers, 1954), esp. Chs. 4, 5, 7, 10 and 12.
[11] William Lee Miller, "Religion and the American Way of Life," *Religion and the Free Society* (New York: The Fund for the Republic, 1958), p. 4.
[12] *The Religious Factor* (New York: Doubleday Co., 1961). Support of this view is given in the two new volumes edited by James Ward Smith and A. Leland Jamison, *Religion in American Life* (Princeton: Princeton University Press, 1961).
[13] Finkelstein, *loc. cit.*, and John Courtney Murray, *We Hold These Truths* (New York: Sheed and Ward, 1960).

[14] T. H. Blum, "Social Audit of the Enterprise," *Harvard Business Review*, Vol. XXXVI (March–April, 1958), p. 77 and esp. the now-celebrated article by O. A. Ohmann, "Skyhooks: With Special Implications for Monday Through Friday," *loc. cit.*, Vol. XXXIII (May–June, 1955), pp. 1–9. The most recent attempt to develop empirical data has been reported in part by Rev. R. C. Baumhart, "How Ethical Are Businessmen?," *Harvard Business Review*, Vol. XXXIX (July–August, 1961), esp. p. 168.
[15] See, for example, the report on the 1959–60 steel strike from the Special Committee of the National Council of Churches of Christ in the U.S.A., *In Search of Maturity in Industrial Relations* (New York: 475 Riverside Drive, 1961), and the sharp critique by James Kuhn, "Piety and Maturity in Labor Management Relations," *Christianity and Crisis*, Vol. XXI (March 6, 1961). This difference of opinion within the "Protestant family" has not paralleled the acerbity of the quarrel over *Mater et Magistra* between liberal Catholics (represented by the Jesuit editors of America) and the conservative Catholics of William Buckley's persuasian as reflected in *The National Review*.
[16] The primer was written in 1569 and entitled *Suma de Tratos y Contratos*. See Bernard Dempsey, *Interest and Usury* (Chicago: Loyola University Press, 1960), for a critical commentary, p. 126.
[17] Encyclicals like *Rerum Novarum* and *Mater et*

If this development expands, the market faces discipline from external forces for the first time in the century—a development not to be taken lightly by either minister or marketer.[18]

Philosophical ethics—is here employed to denote the nature of right and wrong, good and evil as clarified by analysis and discussion. It can employ with equal effect either the deductive or inductive methods but its essential characteristic—as distinguished from religious ethics—is its complete reliance on human reason working with human materials: man's nature and man's institutions. However one views the intricate technical debates between absolutists and relativists,[19] between natural-law theorists and pragmatists, or between those who lament or ignore the decline of a public philosophy,[20] one is driven inexorably to fall back to an image or "model of man" as the ultimate arbiter of such differences.[21]

Now the model of man depends largely on three assessments as these touch on (*1*) his capability for rational judgment, (*2*) his capacity for exercising free options among defined alternatives, and (*3*) his basic motivations. Ever since Freud the whole thrust of psychology has been into examinations of man's irrational impulses. Herbert Simon assures us that "however adaptive the behavior of organisms in learning and choice situations, the adaptiveness falls far short of the ideal of maximizing postulated in economic theory. Evidently, organisms adapt well enough to 'satisfice'; they do not, in general, 'optimize.'"[22] The evidence is, however, far from conclusive[23] to suggest abandonment of a theory which, flowing from scholastic thought through classical economic theory, underpins representative government, personal responsibility, consumer sovereignty, and the Western legal system.[24] There is postulated therefore, as the first attribute of an ethical act, the capacity for rational decision by seller and buyer on the market; business practices which help or hinder rational choice are tinged with philosophical implications of an ethical nature.

When attention turns to the second problem, the area of individual freedom, the assessment is more difficult. Thirty years ago, John Dewey felt that "personal motives hardly count as productive causes in comparison with impersonal forces"[25] and that the range for individual initiative and action was indeed narrowing to the point of insignificance. Even with this stricture, Dewey allows more latitude than the classical market concept with its assumption of automatic governance by the impersonal forces of supply and demand.[26] There

---

Magistra, and the studies sponsored by the Federal Council of Churches are clearly concerned with matters that cannot be viewed as strictly related to dogma. See G. C. Tracy, S. J., ed., *Five Great Encyclicals* (New York: The Paulist Press, 1939), for the earlier papal encyclicals. The America Press of New York published in 1961 the English text of *Mater et Magistra.* The Protestant study was summarized by Marquis Childs and Douglass Cater, *Ethics in a Business Society* (New York: The New American Library, 1954).

[18] This is said because there are substantial differences in ethical approaches to social problems. The differences are brilliantly developed in succinct form by Norman St. John-Stevas, *Life, Death and the Law* (Bloomington: Indiana University Press, 1961), Ch. 1. A longer treatment but of equal competence is by Edward Duff, *The Social Thought of the World Council of Churches* (London: Longmans, Green, 1953), esp. pp. 93–106.

[19] That all is not relative in human affairs is argued persuasively by R. L. Humphreys, "Human Nature in American Thought," *Political Science Quarterly,* Vol. XIX (June, 1954), pp. 266–271. We agree with this position.

[20] See Walter Lippman, *Essays in the Public Philosophy* (New York: The New American Library, 1955), and David Truman, "The American System in Crisis," *Political Science Quarterly,* Vol. LXXIV (Dec., 1959), pp. 481–493, for contrary views. The nub of the matter in Lippman's view is that institutions in Western society are unworkable without relevance to a natural law. "Alexander had discovered empirically what Zeno was to formulate theoretically—that a large plural society cannot be governed without recognizing that, transcending its plural interests, there is a rational order with a superior common law," p. 83.

[21] See Richard Bendix, "The Image of Man in the Social Sciences: The Basic Assumptions of Present-

Day Research," *Commentary,* Vol. II (1951), pp. 187–192.

[22] Herbert Simon, *Models of Man: Social and Rational* (New York: John Wiley & Sons, Inc., 1957), p. 261.

[23] See Arnold M. Rose, "A Study of Irrational Judgments," *The Journal of Political Economy,* Vol. LXV (October, 1957), pp. 394–402. "True intransitivity (irrationality) in making choice or judgments appears to be a very rare phenomenon, if it exists at all," p. 401. See also Warren J. Bilkey, "The Vector Hypothesis of Consumer Behavior," *The Journal of Marketing,* Vol. XVI (October, 1951), pp. 137–151.

[24] See Anthony Downs, *An Economic Theory of Democracy* (New York: Harper & Brothers, 1957).

[25] John Dewey, *Individualism: Old and New* (New York: Minton, Balch & Co., 1930), pp. 35–6.

[26] See Edward Mason, "The Apologetics of Managerialism," *Journal of Business,* Vol. XXX (Jan.,

is postulated as the second characteristic of an ethical act freedom to choose. The practical issue is the measure of freedom accorded to producer and to consumer on today's markets.

The third and final problem to be touched upon relates to the purposes of human actions. Is human destiny fulfilled by service to others or to the self? The medievalists put the emphasis on the supernatural order. Man's gaze was firmly fixed on heaven even as his tired eyes and tortured back bent to search the earth's fruit. The Renaissance ruptured this ideal and, later, John Locke and Adam Smith erected a new intellectual structure designed to emancipate man from religious or governmental bondage.[27] If Locke was the forerunner of laissez-faire and Adam Smith its most eloquent spokesman, both were urging a hedonism at variance with the earlier views. Self-interest rather than service was the keyword but the real achievement was the equation of self-interest with public good. Economic justice was to be served in the new dominion not by ethical precept but by impersonal laws of supply and demand.

Yet it must be observed that in the whole school of English classical economics self-interest becomes a dominant factor *only* in economic transactions. What is often forgotten in our concern with the classic *Wealth of Nations* is that Smith earlier rejected the notion that self-interest was the primary determinant of historical progress [28]—a conviction shared by Ricardo and John Stuart Mill.[29] What the classicists asserted, therefore, was that a whole range of interests and motives—such as charity or social service—transcended the marketplace but that economic justice was so uniquely promoted by market mechanisms that no outside intervention by either Church or State was necessary.

In the nineteenth century people as intellectually apart as Marx and Leo XIII challenged the beneficences of the market. Marx

denounced self-interest as the "most violent, mean, and malignant passion of the human breast." [30] And Leo XIII, in the 1891 encyclical on labor, felt equally that self-interest had run rampant. Shared in common was a rejection of Smith's invisible hand as the deft manipulator of a just society. Thus was joined the historic debate between those who placed a primacy on self-interest and those who placed emphasis on service, between those who counted the gains and others who measured the cost, between men who relied on self-adjusting market and others who would put constraints upon it. While the classical position of strict laissez-faire has been substantially modified there remains the conviction that a more-or-less freely operating market is preferable if the other extreme involves centralized control over prices, wages, and production. This leads directly to the question: can such a market promote justice? Before responding to the question there is required some rough working definition of justice itself.

Now justice, even in the most mechanistic terms, involves two elements: *equality* and *proportionality*. Equality (exchange of equivalents) has traditionally been the kind of justice to which the market could and should make a major contribution; proportionality or equity (allocating fair shares) has been variously assigned to private philanthropy and to the government. It is the contention here that the market should continue to focus on the former and that equity is not a primary purpose in the exchange function.

The argument, summarily stated, rests on the premise that the market is not exclusively an impersonal and automatic mechanism; that it not only permits but relies on human judgment and choice; and that the market judgment and choice should be properly directed to exchange justice (sic, a transactionalistic ethic) and not to problems of social justice.

Business ethos—It is clear, then, that the transactionalistic ethic limits moral responsibility in the market to "the most fundamental relationship in the business world"—that which prevails solely between buyer and seller.[31]

1958), pp. 1–11, and Karl Polany, *The Great Transformation* (Boston: Beacon Press, 1957).
[27] See C. A. Czajkawski, *The Theory of Private Property in John Locke's Political Philosophy* (South Bend: Notre Dame Press, 1941), and Eli Ginzberg, "The Pleasures and Pains of Economic Man," Bryson, *op. cit.*, pp. 427–432.
[28] Adam Smith, *The Theory of Moral Sentiments*, Part VII, pp. 542–611.
[29] A. A. Young, "The Trend of Economics," *Quarterly Journal of Economics*, Vol. XXXIX (Spring, 1953), esp. pp. 175–181.

[30] *Capital*, Vol. I, Introduction, p. 15. For good interpretation see M. M. Bober, *Karl Marx's Interpretation of History* (Cambridge: Harvard University Press, 1948), Ch. 4. See also the encyclical *On the Condition of Labor* in G. C. Treacy, *op. cit.*, pp. 1–39.
[31] Frank Sharp and P. G. Fox, *Business Ethics: Studies in Fair Competition* (New York: Appleton

Even within this narrow spectrum, exchange justice was frequently denied its vital principle by total reliance on ruthless competition and rugged individualism. The real danger now is that in attributing a new dynamic quality of personal freedom and responsibility to the exchange function we expect too much. The full range of justices demanded by a complex, twentieth-century, industrialized economy cannot be met by the market; therefore, what might be called market ethics and what is often termed business ethics are not identical and never will be. The business ethic is primarily a problem for management as it seeks to discharge obligations to a variety of claimants such as stockholders, workers, consumers, suppliers, local communities, and to the public at large.[32]

An ethos will embrace value systems and expectations that have been reasonably well defined and soundly approved. An affluent society may suggest as reasonable expectations fulfillment of ambition to own one's own home, to have quality and variety in clothing, to be able to join a social club or two. A technological society may face problems of chronic unemployment or depressed areas where the ethos will impose upon management responsibilities for retraining workers, or for assuring job security even at the cost of increased profits. In a word, the ethos shifts markedly with time and circumstances and is concerned, more and more, with equity.

The point can be illustrated in terms of business power. How internal disciplines are to be developed and managed provided a spacious arena for debate. Some see in the self-perpetuating oligarchies the emergence of the corporate conscience which presumably would make the new lords temporal, the guardians of the larger society.[33] Some see the emergence of ethical behavior less in terms of ennobled business motives and more in structural changes within the business order itself.[34] Some would go even further to institutionalize both corporate conscience and corporate structure into a formally organized government pattern.[35]

Since it is patent that a whole host of values is being transformed it may be appropriate to suggest wider use of a concept called the *marginalist ethic*.[36] According to this notion, traditional criteria are challenged vigorously when a society enters a period of dynamic change. Thus, in the nineteenth century, employers who provided for workers beyond market wages soon found themselves at a competitive disadvantage with producers who did not. Soon they refused to accept such responsibilities. Such a development represented a decline in business morality from the older acceptance of trusteeship. But the change can be constructive. Accommodating values to affluence may improve traditional ethical standards by according to workers greater participation in decisions affecting the work life, or by providing relief from long hours of fatiguing toil. What is involved in marginalistic ethics, of course, is no ethical standard but a device for appraising change in the value systems of society. It seeks to relate the continuum to change: to insist on certain minimum absolute values while allowing wide scope for pragmatic assessment.

SOCIETAL EXPECTATIONS

At a level lower than ethical imperatives and lower than the ethos is a substratum of somewhat inchoate ambitions which can be called *societal expectations*. More specifically, these expectations are generated by knowledge that the traditional theory of scarcity has been modified by affluence, that buy-now-pay-later can be economically prudent (something absolutely alien to the Puritan mentality), that thrift is not always a virtue, that leisure may indeed be more humanly constructive than work, and that property no longer allows untrammeled personal control over its use. Like

Century Company, 1937), p. 13. Peter Drucker goes beyond this but carefully limits managerial authority to business performance. *The Practice of Management* (New York: Harper & Brothers, 1954).

[32] Manley Howe Jones, *Executive Decision Making* (Homewood: Richard D. Irwin Co., 1957), is philosophically oriented in its treatment of social objectives for business. He is concerned with the company's ideological, political and legal environment and not simply with more narrowly conceived economic ends. See pp. 280–298.

[33] A. A. Berle, *The Twentieth Century Capitalist Revolution* (New York: Harcourt, Brace, 1954).

[34] Courtney Brown, *The Businessman of the Future*. Address to Life Insurance Office Management Assoc. (Chicago, Nov. 10, 1961).

[35] Earl Latham, "The Anthropomorphic Corporation," *Amer. Econ. Review*, Vol. XLVII (May, 1957), *Proceedings*, pp. 303–31.

[36] Goetz Briefs claims to have first developed the idea in *Untergang des Abendlandes, Christentum and Socialismus* (Freiburg: Herder Publishing Company, 1920); fuller and more systematic treatment is found in Werner Schoellgen, *Grenzmoral* (Dusseldorf: Bastion Publishing Co., 1946).

Gompers' old formula for labor unions, the American consumer wants more.

These expectations have begun to thrust upon the country some disturbing contradictions. We demand efficiency and competition but are uncertain that the traditional alliance between the two is a sound one; indeed, a determination of what constitutes monopoly and what constitutes competition is based less on economic and more on legal criteria.[37] The fact that a high value has been attached to competition does not mean that the concept of itself is an ethical one. While we have not gone nearly so far as Learned Hand who argues that "as a principle of universal application competition defeats itself" since it always leaves the "group worse off than it would be without it," there is a clear ambivalence in our current thinking.[38] Perhaps in basic conviction we are moving toward the Italians who, according to Professor Vito, never rated competition "highly in the general opinion and conviction." [39]

Or let us turn to the contrary pulls imposed on business by a commitment to full employment, and the expectation that the private business sector would assume primary responsibility for its implementation. To achieve full employment involves a per capita increase in Gross National Product which, in turn, can be achieved through increased government expenditures, increased net export, and increased domestic consumption. In a society already at high levels of consumption this means aggressive salesmanship to sell more and more goods if the private sector is to contribute to steady employment. And yet this takes the market perilously close to accepting the wisdom of ultra-special pressure campaignings in adver-

tising and in public relations. It is related to the oft-stated criticism that the market is immoral because it urges man to increase his desires rather than concentrate on his needs.

There is also the expectation of improved products due to technological innovation. Some may see in this expectation a rationale for what Schumpeter called "creative destruction" and still others may feel that the response is planned obsolescence where the product's life is deliberately shortened and the consumer asked—and unethically in this view—to pay hidden costs. The advance of science has proceeded so intensively of late that property and work—the two pillars of economy—have "at length fallen" with consequence for the traditional morality. The problem, we are told, may be to "find people qualified to consume the increasing abundance of goods produced by a declining number of workers" and the "traditional morality," like the "conventional wisdom" appears inadequate for the assignment.[40] And finally, there is a growing expectation that business has financial responsibilities to schools, to hospitals and to community projects in a manner reminiscent of those once assumed by the medieval *casa*. Here, literally, the consumer is being taxed for philanthropies he may actually disapprove of.

The foregoing catalog is more suggestive than exhaustive. Yet, it illustrates some of the basic contradictions being foisted upon the business community and helps to explain why any application of simplistic ethical formula to the market is misleading and why the new business ethos is still so amorphous.

MARKETING PRACTICES

Thus far, two major conclusions may be drawn. The first holds that while the Churches are urging their views upon business with greater vigor than ever before, there is not great likelihood of early agreement among theologians on any practical moral code for business. Even if agreement were reached there is little evidence to suggest a willingness on the part of business to abide by such norms. The second conclusion relates to the business sector itself. In the face of contradictory demands by society there is grave doubt that the business community will effectively develop a satis-

[37] Irston Barnes, "Competitive Mores and Legal Tests in Merger Cases: The du Pont-General Motors Decision," *The Georgetown Law Journal*, Vol. XLVI (Summer, 1958), pp. 564–632. As Barnes points out, the Supreme Court itself tried the case as a violation of the Sherman Act for eight years before turning—almost as an afterthought—to section 7 of the Clayton Act.
[38] Learned Hand, *The Spirit of Liberty* (New York: Vintage Books, 1959), p. 29. Even Alfred Marshall admitted that perfect functioning of competitive markets would not yield automatically ethically acceptable results. *Principles of Economics* (London: Macmillan, 1948), p. 29 of eighth edition.
[39] E. H. Chamberlin, ed., *Monopoly, Competition and Their Regulation: Papers and Proceedings of a Conference Held by the International Economic Association* (London: Macmillan Company, 1954), p. 57.

[40] Gerard Piel, *Consumers of Abundance* (New York: Center for the Study of Democratic Institutions, 1961), pp. 3, 5 and 7.

factory ethos on the basis of industry codes, adjustments in federal statutes, advertising or selling practices. To say this is not to deny the possibility of a more rational or ethical ordering of marketing institutions. The question here is simply where initiative for guideposts can be secured.

Yet recent anti-trust cases, congressional hearings on the drug industry, and efforts by a distinguished committee of experts to draft a code of business ethics remind us constantly that the market is being assessed by criteria that transcend the sheer profit-and-loss calculus. So the problem essentially is to give greater logic and clarity to these criteria and it is submitted that philosophical ethics has much to offer. Indeed, as an initial basis for inquiry and assessment, one might ask if the market today is encouraging more rational decision-making and more rational consumer behavior? Is it encouraging greater freedom of choice for seller and buyer—even recognizing that gains for one of these parties may mean losses for the other? Is it promoting the growth of hedonistic culture or is the push for greater consumption justified by need to maintain, for example, high levels of employment and growth? If a judgment must be rendered it is the contention that, on the whole, the ethical dimension is being expanded by current market practices. The conclusion beggars support.

If a simple model of the economy embraces the production and sale of goods and services, and their purchase and consumption,[41] it is evident that marketing is concerned with the selling and buying aspects only.[42] Yet the dynamic aspect, missing from such a definition, can be supplied by considering marketing practices as the production of customers (especially regular ones) just as manufacturing is the production of goods. Thus a product improvement designed to attract new customers is a marketing practice. So is a new store, or

air conditioning, or a new product or service. Greater convenience in purchasing, and better terms of payment, communication which enhances the customer's knowledge of the product and perception of its value, also fall within this definition.

It should be noted carefully that such marketing practices seek customers who, by definition, are freely choosing agents not coerced into buying. Indeed the distinction between customer and consumer is an important one for the latter suggests recognition of the ethical element of freedom of choice.

But what of those marketing practices which are allegedly designed to blunt judgment and literally "force" a choice? Here advertising becomes the *bete noir*. The advertising fraternity defends itself on grounds that it promotes economic growth and sales while the critics argue that current advertising promotes too much sale of the wrong goods at the wrong prices. Yet both plaintiff and defense rest their cases on what may be a false assumption, namely, the power of advertising itself. This sense of power is overdrawn. A more realistic view suggests that advertising is akin to casting in a stream when the fish are biting. It does not lure fish into hitherto uninhabited waters. Industrial, retail-store, and mail-order house advertising are geared to market receptivity. Only in cosmetics, remedy goods, and so-called luxury items is advertising effective in creating demand but expenditures in this area are only a small amount of the total expenditures for advertising purposes. Viewed in this context there is not really much room for the "hidden persuaders." And since there are luxury items are they not in the area where less careful calculus of the costs is ethically permissible? And is not the responsibility here more the purchaser's than the vendor's?[43] If one adds the realities of modern life (small suburban homes located some considerable distances from the place of work) it would appear that the American male has neither room nor time for extensive luxury purchases. And even the American woman, after completing expenditures on necessary food and clothing items for herself and children, is not likely to be an overly gullible creature.

If attention is shifted from customer to mar-

---

[41] William A. Kovisto, *Principles and Problems of Modern Economics* (New York: John Wiley & Sons, Inc., 1957), p. 53.

[42] Theodore Beckman, Harold Maynard, William Davidson, *Principles of Marketing* (New York: The Ronald Press, 1957), p. 4, sixth edition. Marketing "covers all business activities necessary to effect transfers in ownership of goods and to provide for their physical distribution. It embraces the entire group of services and functions performed in the distribution of merchandise from producer to consumer, excluding only operations relating to changes in the form of goods normally regarded as processing or manufacturing operations."

[43] One of the most thoughtful studies on this aspect has recently been completed by Thomas Garrett, *Some Ethical Problems of Modern Advertising* (Rome: The Gregorian University, 1961), especially Ch. 8.

keter we note a major development in forecasting that holds promise for greater ethical performance within the market. Forecasting techniques have improved substantially over the past decades and this means ultimately more effective predicting and satisfying of real demand, better control over inventories, and less pressure to create artificial demand or to tamper erratically with prices. From this point one could go on to assert that reasonable expectations make for a more ethical and orderly society and the farther removed marketing practices are from the "oriental bazaar" mentality the more efficaciously does the market perform.[44]

If there is emerging a healthy "plus" factor for believing that both sellers and customers are operating in an institutional framework where rational decision-making is more, rather than less, likely, what of the second ethical criterion—the element of free choice? At the consumer level it would be hard to argue that such choice does not, in fact, exist in an affluent society. Of all the cruel prisons to freedom none is worse than the dungeon of poverty. In terms of range of goods, in terms of possibilities for knowing the range, the American customer is really a monarch by contrast to other times and other societies.

The most persistent charge of violation in this regard is in terms of "planned obsolescence." But there is a waste factor built into every dynamic process and some of it is deliberately contrived to achieve other goals. "Built-for-life" is not always a blessing as some of the antiquated dwellings along Riverside Drive amply demonstrate. If product change and product design are part of the culture then some measure of obsolescence is tolerable and necessary. This strikes cruelly at the folklore of thrift and frugality but it is one of the prices society is asked to pay to achieve other things. Given a choice between full employment with a planned rapid turnover of products versus the older ethos of thrift and frugality at the cost of unemployment, there is little doubt what option the American people will select.

Now this does not mean a defense of marketing practices which deceive the customer but such offenses can be corrected by guaran-

tees adjusted to the life of the product. If a customer knows that one television set will last five years and a second will last fifteen for double the price, there is no assurance whatever that it is to his best interest to buy the latter—given the state of modern technology and the fashions of modern life.

Finally, what of motivations? Are they basically moving away from narrow self-interest toward a loftier plane? The present state of the question is so murky that the best that can be expected are a few reasoned opinions. Plausible arguments have been developed for holding that "Adam Smith's recognition of self-interest as a perennial and durable spring of human conduct is as true today as it was in his time";[45] that the marketplace responds to the ring of coin and not to moralistic preachment. Yet here again institutional changes of first magnitude are in the making. For example, marketing research is showing first signs of losing its special functional identity as it seeks to relate demand to production. If this develops then the marketing specialist becomes less concerned with his specialty and more concerned with the total process. As a generalist he will tend to relate parts to the whole—to be concerned with the totality. And one of the primary attributes of ethical behavior is precisely this kind of view and this kind of concern. Clearly, there is no necessary connection between an "overview" and more ethical behavior but in the context of business today there is sufficient grounds for holding that such a relationship will in fact prevail.

Nor is this the full story. Ours is an "organization life" and in the economic order group life is being influenced more significantly by that large association known as the corporation. By definition, the corporation is a voluntary association and so long as it remains true to its origins it can survive only as it holds the allegiances of a wide variety of clients. Unlike the seller in Adam Smith's view, the corporation looks to a life eternal and its objective tempers and restrains temptations to shortcut either morals or mores. It relies spatially on mass markets and the very impersonality of this market demands stability in pricing, quality of goods and servicing. Hit-and-run tactics are effective with the pirate's ship but impos-

---

[44] Paul Lazarsfeld points out that the "empirical study of individual choices or decisions . . . has remained largely undeveloped." *Social Science Research on Business: Product and Potential* (New York: Columbia University Press, 1959), p. 103.

[45] E. G. Nourse, *Price Making in a Democracy* (Washington: The Brookings Institute, 1944), p. 449.

sible for the citadel, and the corporation is the citadel in the modern economy.

CONCLUSIONS

Lamentations over the decline of a "traditional morality" which emphasized thrift and labor not infrequently ignore another aspect of the older ethic; namely the conviction that economic practices operated exclusively under their own laws and, hence were immune to, and unaffected by, other ethical considerations. Glorified was the individual with his immediate self-interest. But the glories have been tarnished and many of the old realities dissipated. Corporations, with long-term interest in society at large, have replaced the small seller and the corporation must be, like Caesar's wife, above suspicion. Corporate leaders would agree that "the economic objective of competitive policy in a market economy is to promote good performance—good in the sense that resources are used efficiently (if not ideally), that progress through technological change is encouraged, and the economic activity contributes to, or at least does not interfere with, the achievement of equally important social and political goals . . . "[46] Motivations may still be largely self-centered and hence "conscience alone, whether of public trustees or of Christian businessmen, is not enough."[47] But the institutional mechanisms are changing to provide wider latitude for personal responsibility. It is a hard skeptic indeed who, given prevailing market conditions, would not view the widening scope for personal responsibility with greater enthusiasm than the old iron law of supply and demand. Then, too, history has a long and grim verdict to pass on the ethical planes which prevailed in poverty-ridden societies. Affluence brings its problems but also its opportunities. Finally, improvements in pricing, forecasting and distribution suggest strongly a more effective and more efficient satisfying of consumer demands. The ideal moral economy of the Ralph Barton Perry's vision[48] may not be realized but surely Professor Henry Oliver is correct when he peceives some major "trends toward a new moral philosophy for Business."[49]

[46] Almarin Phillips, "Policy Implications of the Theory of Interfirm Organization," *American Economic Review: Proceedings*, Vol. LI (May, 1961).

[47] William C. Frederick, "The Growing Concern Over Business Responsibility," *California Management Review*, Vol. II (Summer, 1960), p. 61. See also Reinhold Niebuhr, *Interpretation of Christian Ethics*, p. 165.

[48] *The Moral Economy* (New York: Charles Scribner's Sons, 1909). See also Robert Bartels, *Business Ethics: Compliance or Conviction* (Los Angeles: University of Southern California, 1961).

[49] *Business Horizons*, Vol. 1 (Spring, 1958), pp. 33–43.

Sales Ethics: Truth and Taste Needed?

Sales ethics has come up out of the swamp, but it still has a long swim ahead. Areas of most concern to responsible businessmen are price-cutting, conflict of interest and antitrust. All are critical, but concentration on any one of them, at the expense of a general sales-ethics policy, is fundamentally wrong.

A purchasing agent in Omaha leaned over his desk last week and opened a sports magazine to a page he had marked. "Here she is," he said to the salesman across the desk from him, pointing to an expensive imported shotgun. "I know you're not a sportsman yourself, but I just thought 'I'd show it to you in case you were wondering what to get me for Christmas."

On a train headed for Atlanta, another salesman was toting up his expense statement for a three-day trip. He paused at the end of the column as he did a quick mental calculation, then entered 20 per cent of the day's total in the "entertainment" box.

A few days before, in the bar of a hotel in Denver, three salesmen came to a friendly agreement not to cut each other's prices—an agreement they all knew they would probably be forced to break within the next month.

In all three of these cases the salesmen involved were costing their companies money—money that would have to come directly out of profits. But perhaps even more important, they were undermining both the reputation and the basically sound marketing and advertising programs which their companies had built up to help them sell.

THE PROBLEM

Advertising ethics has come under heavy fire in recent years. Sales ethics, because it directly affects only the few individuals involved and isn't apparent to the mass audiences reached by advertising, has managed to keep out of the limelight for the most part. But recent government actions now are bringing sales ethics out of the shadows—notably the

◆ SOURCE: Reprinted by permission from *Printers' Ink*, Vol. 279, No. 9, June 1, 1962, pp. 25–28.

Congressional investigation into, and the Federal Trade Commission action against, three major manufacturers of electrical equipment for price collusion in bids for government contracts.

These actions are forming a pattern, and the pattern is repeating itself on a less spectacular scale and in many other places besides Washington. New York City had its own price-fixing scandal the winter of 1960–61, for example—involving companies selling salt to the city sanitation department for cleaning streets. A few months later a Federal grand jury indicted a major automaker and three dealers' associations of conspiring to prevent the sale of their cars below list price. Hardly a week goes by without several such actions being taken against some area of the sales function.

Clearly a great deal of ethical malpractice exists in the sales-management area, and the public—as represented by the government and law-enforcement agencies—is getting fed up with it. So are many corporate officers, who realize that most ethical malpractices undermine their marketing programs and usually take sizable bits out of tight-squeezed profits.

This doesn't mean that sales ethics is getting worse. Most executives agree that it has improved, because of tighter government regulation, and the increasing awareness of the importance of public relations and reputation in business. "There are still abuses, but we've come a long way from the darkest days around 1955," an auto executive said.

But even though sales ethics isn't getting worse, by and large, it isn't getting better fast enough to please a great many top corporate officials. There is a growing awareness that a tremendous problem still exists, and that something must be done about it.

AREAS OF ABUSE

Moreover, there are strong indications that this awareness is growing particularly fast. Some examples:

An interest survey that Research Institute of America, New York, conducted among sales managers showed a high level of interest in sales ethics. Another RIA study, this one conducted on all levels, from managers down to rank-and-file salesmen, posed hypothetical problems in ethics, brought forth much more thoughtful replies than expected. "Before this year, we'd never elicited any inkling of interest in sales-ethics problems," said Jack Tarrant, director of RIA's development division.

A three-day American Management Assn. personnel conference this fall devoted a full panel discussion to the subject of business ethics. The panel was headed by Theodore V. Purcell, S.J., associate professor of psychology and industrial relations at Loyola University, Chicago. An increasing number of such seminars on ethics have been cropping up in business conventions lately.

Last summer the *Harvard Business Review* surveyed 1,700 of its readers—mostly top management men—on the subject of ethics, found about half of them believe that "the American business executive tends to ignore the great ethical laws as they apply immediately to his work. He is preoccupied chiefly with gain." Four out of five executives affirmed the presence in their industry of unethical practices, many of them directly related to sales, such as bribes, excessive gifts, call girls, price discrimination, price fixing.

National Industrial Conference Board polled top executives of 130 manufacturing firms on the subject of business ethics, found that most of them believe conflict of interest is the major problem area. This is a question that frequently affects upper sales-management levels, as when, e.g., a sales executive holds a large stock interest in a supply or customer firm. NICB found an increasing concern with this problem among the executives polled. One out of three companies represented in the survey now has a written policy statement on the subject of conflict of interest. Last year, when a similar study was made, the ratio was only one to ten. One metals company has even set up a special "conflict-of-interest committee," made up of three board members, to

review and recommend action on conflict-of-interest cases.

A PRINTERS' INK survey of corporate executives found a widespread belief that many unethical sales practices are on the increase. Specifically:

misrepresentation of merchandise—judged on the rise by 45 per cent of respondents
demands for kickbacks—named by 38 per cent
price gouging—32 per cent
abuse of co-op advertising—25 per cent
income-tax maneuvering—19 per cent
excessive demands for entertainment—16 per cent
padded expense accounts—six per cent.

Some of the comments these executives appended showed concern verging on disgust with present sales ethics, and a conviction that the situation is getting steadily worse. "It seems many more people accept less than the highest ethics in business," said Robert Graham, sales education director at Diebold Inc. Some other comments:

"The percentage of market is important to a company; when this percentage drops, the company will occasionally 'cut a corner' "—Glen Palmer, national sales manager of the Lustra Corp. "Today most businesses are primarily interested in the immediate sale or profit. Services, prestige and goodwill seem to be passé"—Francis Esmay, sales manager, New York Telephone Co., Albany.

Another recent PRINTERS' INK survey found that 45 per cent of a group of sales executives condemned the widespread practice of sales reciprocity (demanding that a supplier also buy from your firm) as unethical, and 80 per cent thought it was bad salesmanship.

There has been an increasing number of public attacks on sales immorality by such well-known business figures as George Romney, president of American Motors (until he resigned to seek the Michigan governorship); Lee Bristol, board chairman of Bristol-Myers Co.; T. "Jeff" Wood, vice-president of Procter & Gamble.

VULNERABLE SALES

Business immorality is by no means limited to the sales function, all of these men have pointed out. But sales is particularly vulnerable for several reasons. Sales impinges on the highly sensitive antitrust areas of price-fixing, for example. It's an axiom (to be taken with a grain of salt) that whenever two salesmen get together they are bound to discuss prices.

The very fuzziness of federal legislation invites violation in some cases—or at least careless behavior by sales personnel. One company president told the National Industrial Conference Board, "There are many areas of business which are covered by ambiguous and even conflicting laws. As a result, a manager cannot get a precise answer to the question, 'What is legal?' To obey one law is to break another. Under these circumstances a manager can only do the best he can, and hope for the best."

Another company president—in the chemical industry—said, "Even a mature executive with high business ethics can run afoul of the law unknowingly if he does not have adequate legal counsel and judgment enough to know when to use it. The law, particularly with regard to antitrust provisions, is far from clear, and the wise executive will call in an experienced 'pilot' to steer the ship through such unfamiliar waters."

The salesman and sales executive are constantly plunged into such "gray" regions, where it's next to impossible to decide what is right. Research Institute of America's Jack Tarrant described one such situation that arises occasionally in almost every company. A price change is coming up and the information leaks to salesmen before the official announcement. A customer of long standing and close friendship, tipped off by rumors, asks a salesman, frankly, if there's a price change coming. "In this situation, the salesman looks like a heel no matter what he says," Tarrant said. "If he spills the news he's betraying his own company. But if he doesn't, he'll look like a traitor to his customer a few weeks later when the price does change."

There are particular ethical pitfalls in sales, also because salesmen handle sizable amounts of travel- and entertainment-expense money— and are constantly engaged in confidential dealings involving much larger merchandise orders. Add to this the pressure of stiff competition in most industries, and almost any sales job becomes a potential ethical trap.

In some industries ethical malpractices are practically endemic—especially in the retail field. There are supermarket operators who cheerfully admit that their profit all comes from rakeoffs on cooperative advertising—their actual food operations barely break even.

Profit-taking on co-op may not be illegal, due to the spread between local ad rates (which the supermarket operator pays) and national rates (at which he bills the manufacturer); but the ethical status of this practice is open to question—and possible eventual legislation.

It's also well known that kickbacks to buyers are widespread in supermarkets and other types of retail stores. A Cleveland chain-store merchandising manager was amazed recently when he walked into one of his company stores and stood face to face with an end-aisle display he'd never authorized. A grocery *clerk* (not even a manager) innocently revealed that a salesman had offered him a new wristwatch to put the display up. *He didn't even realize he was taking a bribe.*

The relationship between manufacturers and dealers or distributors are strewn with enticements. The manufacturer's control over dealer conduct is extremely tenuous, especially in the automobile field. Under present legislation it's difficult for a manufacturer to cut off a dealer because he chisels on service or treats customers unethically in other respects.

Another ethical pitfall exists for many old companies, because legislation and sales ethics may have changed considerably since the companies' early policies were formulated. An executive in the National Industrial Conference Board study pointed out, "Many procedures which were perfectly legal and ethical 15 or 20 years ago would not be legal today."

BLAME AT THE TOP?

The answer to many of these problems lies in a firm policy statement by top management. The NICB study shows that written policy statements are becoming more common, not only in the area of conflict of interest but also in order to cover such potential antitrust matters as price-fixing.

The top-level policy statement is valuable, first, because it sets a guide and an example for ethical conduct. But more important, it takes the salesman off the hook. About the only valid answer to a buyer's request for a kickback or valuable "Christmas present" is, "Sorry, but we have a firm company policy against that. You can understand how fast it would run us into bankruptcy if we bought everyone we deal with a present like that."

The dilemma facing the salesman in the case of an information leak concerning an imminent price change is clearly top management's fault.

The only valid solution to this dilemma is for top management not to leak the information in the first place.

In view of the repeated temptations that salesmen are bound to face in these areas, any company that does not formulate firm top-management policies is cutting the ground out from under its sales force. There's danger in limiting these statements to the touchy areas of conflict-of-interest and price-fixing, too.

"Several executives note that the only actions that most companies have taken in the field of business ethics have dealt specifically with either possible conflicts of interest or adherence to antitrust laws—usually in reaction to the over-publicized mistakes of a few," the National Industrial Conference Board study points out. "These executives often share the belief of one chemical company president who suggests that 'an elaborate defense is being built up against a specific problem, whereas trouble is most apt to occur in another quarter in the future.'"

Policy statements in any case are only the beginning—control is an even more crucial problem, as is graphically illustrated by some of the remarks of General Electric chairman Ralph Cordiner, in the wake of the antitrust actions brought against GE, Westinghouse Electric and Allis-Chalmers last year.

Without trying to dodge top management's responsibility in the price-fixing case, Cordiner pointed out, "It would be impossible for any of us to have knowledge of the prices of the hundreds of different product lines offered at the marketplace by the company. There are 3-million catalog numbers, representing the available variations of our many product lines. Each product department . . . has hundreds or thousands of items offered at different prices, and I would not expect to monitor all those individual prices or the day-to-day transaction involved . . .

"Equally, I am unaware of the suggested retail price in Chicago for a 15-cubic-foot General Electric refrigerator. . . . The suggested retail price is the responsibility of the General Electric distributor serving the dealers in Chicago.

"The officers of the company, of course, have the general function of seeing that customers continue to receive good value and service. . . . But the basic responsibility to see that such values and service do in fact exist for a particular customer must remain with those to whom the responsibility has been delegated. . . . I cannot recall a single instance, since I ceased to have operating responsibility . . . many years ago, when on my own initiative I originated or quoted a price to a customer."

And, Cordiner pointed out, the price-fixing that prompted last year's charges took place in the face of a firm, written company policy of many years' standing, expressly prohibiting any understandings on prices with competitors, or any other actions that violate antitrust legislation. This is one of only six mandatory policies in effect at GE.

THREE-WAY APPROACH

An effective attack on the problem of sales ethics requires a three-pronged approach, combining clear-cut policy statements by top management, indoctrination of salesmen and meticulous controls. All three of the electrical apparatus manufacturers involved in the recent price-fixing case have taken strong steps in all three areas.

Westinghouse Electric revised and reissued its Management Guide on Legal and Ethical Conduct—a one-page statement spelling out the company's policy "to comply with all laws governing its operations and to conduct its affairs in keeping with the highest moral, legal and ethical standards." The guide specifies the penalties for infraction—"which may include reprimand, probation, suspension, reduction in salary, demotion or dismissal—depending on the seriousness of the offense. Clear-cut price-fixing or bid-rigging acts, or illegal activities with competitors to divide or allocate markets or customers, will result in dismissal."

A six-page memo explains just how this policy is to be enforced, and where responsibility for it lies.

Even before these steps were taken, Westinghouse had mapped out a program of rigid controls. Division and department managers are obliged to investigate all prices being quoted, bid or charged, to determine that they were not arrived at collusively—and file certificates with the general counsel's office that they had done this.

A second set of certificates must be signed and filed by salesmen each time they attend a meeting (including civic organizations such as chambers of commerce), stating that no discussion of price-fixing took place. A third set of certificates is filed by certain individuals with pricing responsibilities, after each *phone conversation* with personnel of competitors.

Westinghouse is also stressing ethics in its sales training. The field-training program includes three conferences devoted to business ethics and laws. The Westinghouse sales-personnel development workshop also carries lectures and discussions in an "intensive two-day program aimed at stimulating personal development and high moral standards."

General Electric took similar steps, instituted tighter legal reviews of operations, new auditing techniques designed to turn up clues to malpractices, intensified teaching and instruction by the legal-services department. Executives all down the line were urged to develop more effective controls.

The drug industry—another area that has come under governmental fire for actual and alleged malpractices in sales—is less eager to talk about the subject of sales ethics. Most companies reportedly give their salesmen careful instruction, taking special pains to see that the salesmen don't misrepresent the capabilities of drugs, and many of these companies have high ethical reputations. But sales abuses are still widespread in many areas, drug officials allow.

And most executives agree that sales abuses are still common in most other industries. The significant development in recent months is the widespread awakening of management desire to control these abuses. Sales ethics—along with business ethics—is moving out of the area of sermonizing and into the area of scientific control and management—along with all other aspects of successful marketing.

Salesmanship and Professional Standards

DAVID J. SCHWARTZ

CRITERIA OF A "PROFESSION"

There can be no absolute or unqualified answer to the question, "Is personal selling a professional activity?" Rather, this question can be answered only in terms of the degree to which personal selling, as practiced today, meets the generally accepted criteria established to designate a "profession." Five such criteria of professional practice were used for purposes of this study.

Intellectual Preparation

Formal preparatory education is generally considered a primary criterion of a professional activity. Generally this criterion is met only with accepted prescribed knowledge obtained in colleges and universities. Ministers, teachers, medical doctors, and architects obviously qualify in this regard. Salesmen generally do not. While an increasing number of companies require sales applicants to have earned a college degree, more often than not no specific degree is made mandatory. Many companies appear to place just as much value on a liberal arts degree as on a degree in business administration.

Continuous Learning and Development

A mark of a profession is *emphasis on further learning and development* above and beyond formal educational preparation. This learning and development takes on many

◆ SOURCE: Reprinted by permission from *Atlanta Economic Review,* September 1961, pp. 15–19.

forms, such as postgraduate study, seminars and conferences, reading of literature in the field, and creative research. This criterion is quite subjective. Many salesmen meet this test. However, many others appear to make no effort to become better informed and more proficient.

Service Attitude

From long-standing tradition, professional activities have specified the *"service first"* attitude. Two marketing authorities sum up this criterion as it pertains to salesmen:

The opportunity to benefit mankind generally, or specifically one's clients or one's patients, is in many cases a more dominant motive than is financial return. Many salesmen are so motivated; many are not. The test comes to the salesman just as it does to the physician, the accountant or the attorney when he knows that by giving incomplete, vague, or perhaps inaccurate advice, his fee or commission might be larger than if he told the whole truth. Some salesmen meet the test; others fail.

Adherence to Accepted Ethical Standards or Codes

A fourth characteristic of a professional activity is adherence to a set of accepted guideposts which define *ethical practices*. These codes generally spell out matters pertaining to compensation for services rendered, such as split fees, competition with other members of the profession, soliciting work, use of advertising, and related items. No industry-wide codes of ethics are found in selling today.

Public Recognition and Respect

A final criterion of a professional activity is the *attitude of the public* toward that activity. In order to be "professional," a group engaged in an activity must be recognized as a profession by people outside their activity. Salesmen as an occupational group do not meet this test.

EVIDENCE OF LESS-THAN-PROFESSIONAL SELLING

There is evidence that much personal selling is conducted on a less-than-professional basis. The following examples illustrate unprofessional conduct in selling: [1]

1. The salesman who suggests to a purchasing agent that he can make some extra money if he places his purchases in the right places. Sharing the commission with the person who is doing the buying.
2. The salesman who attempts to pry information from purchasing agents regarding bids submitted by competing companies.
3. Misrepresentation of actual price of product. Quoting one price at order time and billing another price at invoice time.
4. Discussing business affairs of other companies with customer.
5. Trickery used to obtain interview with prospect, such as, "I'm just making a survey and I'd like to have your opinion."
6. Taking orders and promising delivery on dates known to be impossible.
7. Failure to take the responsibility for errors made in shipment.
8. Telling customer that competitor is dishonest or no good.
9. Purposely overselling an account, that is, selling more than the customer logically needs.
10. Adding items to a given order without a customer's knowledge or consent.
11. Calling on customers when lacking the technical information needed to provide service.
12. Begging for business. Making appeals based on personal handicap or under charitable organization sponsorship.
13. Quoting prices on last year's model when customer thinks the price refers to this year's model.

[1] These are some of the practices revealed by statements made by salesmen attending sales seminars conducted by the author.

14. Neglecting to find out what customers really need and continuing to sell on the basis of assumptions of what they need.
15. Calling secretaries or other office employees to find out competitive quotes that have been submitted.

Lack of Dignity in Selling

The personal behavior of many salesmen attests to nonprofessionalism—for example: [2]

1. The use of slang, profanity, or off-color stories in the sales interview.
2. Wearing gaudy, loud, or distasteful clothing.
3. Chewing gum, smoking cigarettes, eating candy or peanuts in the presence of customers.
4. Eating onions, garlic, or drinking alcoholic beverages before calling on customers.
5. Failure to dress properly or, specifically, being sloppily dressed.
6. Boisterousness—loud jokes.
7. Exhibitionism. Dressing in such a way as to be an "attention-getter."
8. Romeoism—the salesman who must stop by desk of each girl in the office to "charm" her.
9. Know-it-all—the salesman who is never wrong and appears to be an expert on everything.
10. Lack of sincerity—not really believing in what one sells.

Illegal Marketing Activities

Most investigations of the Federal Trade Commission are concerned with various marketing practices. These violations, while not always involving salesmen directly, do nevertheless reflect on the behavior of salesmen. Insofar as business practices are concerned, it seems that much more "cheating" is associated with marketing than with any other business function.

False advertising, misrepresentation, misbranding, and false labeling are examples of the many violations of the Federal Trade Commission legislation. Unquestionably, such violations of legislation pertaining to fair competition does much to lower public acceptance of personal selling.

[2] *Ibid.*

Salesmen Often Not Sold on Selling

Part of the reason behind low public acceptance of selling can be traced directly to salesmen themselves.

In a summer-1960 survey of 6,000 members of the National Association of Women's and Children's Apparel Salesmen—men who averaged twenty-three years in outside commission selling and who had an average compensation of $9,600 before income tax deductions—half of the 2,000 respondents were not particularly enthusiastic about selling as a career.

In a survey, recently published, salesmen were asked to rank fifteen different occupations in terms of ethical conduct. Four categories of salesmen were included in the list—those selling to business and industry, those selling for resale, door-to-door salesmen, and automobile salesmen.

The results show that salesmen rate other salesmen low on the scale. Further, it is interesting to note that two other categories of marketing personnel—retailers and advertising personnel—also were rated very low. (See Table 1.)

Table 1. How Salesmen Compare Themselves with Members of Other Occupations in Terms of Ethical Conduct

Cumulative Rankings
(Most Ethical to Least Ethical)

1. Engineers
2. Teachers
3. University Professors
4. Doctors
5. Salesmen to Business and Industry
6. Corporation Top Management
7. Lawyers
8. Editors and Publishers
9. Salesmen Selling for Resale
10. Production Workers
11. Government Officials
12. Retailers
13. Advertising Men
14. Door-to-Door Salesmen
15. Automobile Salesmen

SOURCE: Based on confidential responses to the American Salesmen's national salesmen's panel as reported in *The American Salesman*, January 1961, pp. 48–53. Reproduced here with permission of *The American Salesman*.

EFFECTS OF UNPROFESSIONAL STATUS

Damage resulting from unprofessional status is twofold. First, unprofessional status appears to discourage talented people from entering selling. Second, because the best human resources are not attracted to the selling occupation, total output of the economy is lowered.

Unprofessional Status Harms Recruitment

The fact that selling is widely regarded as an unprofessional activity has two negative influences on recruitment of individuals. First, young people put selling way down on their list of occupational choices. Much potential sales talent therefore never enters the field of selling. Second, many people who harbor prejudices toward selling enter the field much later in life than is desirable. Often a person with, say, an accounting background or an engineering education initially wants no part of selling but later finds that this occupational choice is a much more direct avenue toward job success.

The impact of a professional regard for a job classification cannot be taken lightly in terms of recruitment. The young individual contemplating a career in medicine knows before he begins that society—his friends, his relatives, teachers, neighbors, and others—will have a high opinion of his job choice. This is not true of selling. Individuals contemplating a career in this activity are aware that many in their social group will not be impressed by their career choice. In fact, there will be some in the social group who will feel that the individual is a failure.

Unprofessional Status Produces Economic Loss

Most executives, economists, and educators agree that one of the principal tasks of our economy is to discover ways to put more goods and services in the hands of the ultimate consumer. To the extent that the marketing arm of industry is weakened because of insufficiently capable and qualified sales personnel, all industry suffers.

It has been estimated that the field of selling needs one million new and qualified individuals to help perform the demand-creation function.

In this connection, the following observations are pertinent:

But even more important than mere numbers is the need for nearly a million *top caliber* salesmen who can persuade consumers to buy if the nation is to enjoy a $150-billion increase in its national product.

That's the stark fact that leads sales and marketing executives queried by *Printer's Ink* to agree unanimously there is indeed a *crisis in talent* facing sales. For instance, Tom McCall, a Chicago employment agency head who specializes in sales recruiting, says that for the average industrial selling job paying between $8,000 and $12,000, he now finds only six to eight qualified applicants out of every 400 who apply. Another example: the personnel head of a large company says they regularly fill only 90 per cent of their sales-job openings. Reason: there just aren't enough qualified men.

That's the heart of the problem. No one doubts that sales could get its million more men. But it doesn't want "people who can't do anything else" and turn to sales. It wants capable, persuasive men who want to sell and will be effective salesmen.[3]

OBSTACLES TO PROFESSIONALIZING SELLING

Lack of Acceptable Definition of "Selling"

One factor which complicates efforts made to professionalize selling is the lack of an acceptable definition of selling. All people who sell bear the title of "salesmen." One might liken it to saying that anyone who works in the field of medicine is a doctor, or that anyone that helps build a house is an engineer. No provision in the customary definitions of selling is made for different grades or levels of selling. There appears to be as much difference between a salesman selling door-to-door and a salesman selling advertising for a large agency as there is between a hospital orderly and a surgeon. Since retail salespeople and door-to-door salespeople are much more frequently exposed to the public, the typical young person tends to think of a salesman as someone in a store or someone pushing the doorbell.

[3] *Printers' Ink*, March 27, 1959.

New terminology. There is much reason to believe that many people fear the word "salesman" and what it stands for. As a result, many companies hope to disarm prospective buyers by calling their salesmen something other than "salesmen," such as educational consultants, field editors, financial consultants, representatives, account executives, and media representatives. The public forms its impressions of salesmen by their deeds and actions—their behavior —rather than the terminology printed on their business card.

Vague Requirements for Professional Education

Earlier in this paper it was stated that a principal requirement of a profession is intellectual preparation. There is virtually no agreement as to what constitutes the proper intellectual preparation for a career in selling. In fact, there is no agreement as to the proper curriculum for a career in the *general* field of business.

Lack of Encouragement by Salesmen's Unions

Unions generally rely on the contracts made with employers to spell out what constitutes minimum standards of performance. No provision is made which calls for members to do their best to treat customers fairly, to advance themselves professionally, and to strengthen the reputation of selling. Unions might well attempt to raise the performance standards of their members and to upgrade the members' thinking with regard to their responsibilities to customers and to employers.

FAVORABLE TRENDS IN PROFESSIONALIZING SELLING

Some positive actions have been taken which are intended to elevate selling to a higher status.

Pi Sigma Epsilon

There is only one professional college fraternity devoted to professionalizing selling—Pi Sigma Epsilon, founded at Georgia State College in 1951.

The rapid growth in chapters and membership of this professional fraternity can be interpreted as evidence of a definite need for such an organization in American colleges and universities.

The objective of Pi Sigma Epsilon can be summed up in three words "Develop Professional Salesmen." One of the operational goals of Pi Sigma Epsilon is to bring the advantages of selling to the attention of young college men. On most college campuses there is virtually no effort made to explain the pros and cons of a selling career to college students.

Code of Ethics

A second example of efforts underway to make selling a truly professional activity is found in codes of ethics adopted by various salesmen's groups.

The nation's largest organized body of organized outside salesmen, the National Association of Women's and Children's Apparel Salesmen, has developed a code of ethics for its 12,000 members. This group, composed of independent contractor salesmen, functions as a trade association. It lists as one of its principal objectives obtaining "adherence to the NAWCAS Code of Ethics."

The progressive leadership of this association is aware that unethical practices of one member cast a negative reflection on other members. Therefore, policing of its membership to ferret out unethical practices is regarded as a continuing responsibility.

The code of ethics adopted and enforced by this association is provided below.

THE NAWCAS CODE OF ETHICS

This long needed code for our industry can only become 100% effective when all manufacturers recognize the need for NAWCAS, and when, they, too, subscribe to the same high standards which NAWCAS has set for all its members to follow:

1. Honest performance of salesman's duties and the obligation of the salesman to perform a full and complete day's work.
2. Intelligent, truthful and conscientious representation of his product.
3. Diligent effort at all times to bolster the reputation of his firm, refraining from derogatory remarks.
4. Create goodwill in order to promulgate a better relationship between salesman, manufacturer and buyer.

5. Notification to employer of termination of employment in sufficient time for replacement.
6. Fair notice to the manufacturer on termination of contract during the season.
7. Return all samples within a reasonable time.
8. Refrain from promises to buyers that the firm will not be able to fulfill.
9. Carry additional lines only with the full knowledge of his employer.
10. Honor and fulfill any agreements made between himself and his employer.[4]

Professional Designations

Possibly the most outstanding example of action taken to elevate selling to professional status is the C.L.U. professional designation program developed by the life insurance industry.

The need and background for this program is explained as follows:

If practiced as it should be, life underwriting meets all the requirements of the professional concept. As a calling, it is so fundamentally useful to society and so inherently noble in its purpose as to inspire the practitioner to make it his full-time life's work. It also involves a deep science and in its practice an expert knowledge of that science. Life underwriters can be of inestimable service to clients by way of counsel and guardianship.

The day is passing when the underwriter is content to know only the technique of salesmanship and to rely on motivation of his prospects by subtle appeals to their emotions. Instead, he is stressing the intelligent analysis of human problems and the extending of professional advice of a high order.

The efficient underwriter needs a broad business education—including economics, business finance, personal finance, social problems, taxation, business and insurance law, law of wills, trusts and estates—in addition to life and health insurance fundamentals—if his services are to be of maximum value to his clients. The Chartered Life Underwriter program covers these subjects.

The C.L.U. designation is therefore a professional one. It does more than denote that the holder of it has met certain academic standards by passing a series of examinations. Primarily,

[4] Reproduced here with permission of the National Association of Women's and Children's Apparel Salesmen.

it serves to indicate that the underwriter has spent time and effort in preparing himself to render a high type of service to the public and will continue to merit the confidence of the public by keeping abreast of the times.[5]

The C.L.U. designation program involves a specific curriculum or program of studies.

The C.P.C.U. designation. The success of the C.L.U. program provides encouragement for a professional designation for salesmen engaged in property and casualty insurance underwriting.

The designation Chartered Property Casualty Underwriter (C.P.C.U.) can be awarded only to those career persons who furnish satisfactory evidence of meeting the professional concept. For this purpose the American Institute has established and will enforce high qualifying standards of moral character, education and experience. The C.P.C.U. recognition, therefore, signifies that the holder has met not only the educational qualifications, but also fulfilled an experience requirement.[6]

Other Favorable Trends

Several other indications that selling is becoming more professional can be mentioned. Chief of these are: (1) The trend toward knowledge as a requirement for selling. More and more companies now provide some form

[5] American College of Life Underwriters Catalogue, 1960–61, p. 10.
[6] American Institute for Property and Liability Underwriters Announcement, 1960–61, p. 9.

of formalized training than at any time in the past. (2) The upgrading of requirements for entering selling. Many companies today will not employ anyone in a sales capacity who is not a college graduate. (3) The licensing requirements now in effect in many states for persons selling real estate, insurance, and securities.

SUMMARY

There is much evidence that, generally, present-day selling does not meet professional standards. This evidence is based on numerous examples of unprofessional conduct, behavior patterns of many salesmen, much illegal marketing activity, and lack of respect for selling by salesmen themselves.

The unprofessional status of much personal selling is a serious obstacle to recruitment of qualified young people for this activity. Further, because many of the most capable young people do not enter selling, the over-all marketing effort of our economy appears weakened.

Raising selling to professional status is hampered because of the sweeping definition given selling and because the educational requirements for a selling career have not been established.

Despite the general lack of professionalism in present-day selling, several favorable trends are in evidence. These include development of fraternal organizations to encourage professional selling, establishment of codes of ethics by trade groups, and development of professional designation programs in the insurance industry.

Ethical Problems in Selling

*When you do it, it's unethical;
when I do it, it's competition.*—ANON

*But 'twas a maxim he had often tried, that right was right,
and there he would abide.*—GEORGE CRABBE

Webster gives us, among others, this definition of ethics: "Moral principles, quality, or practice; the morals of individual action or practice."

Doctors and lawyers have codes of professional ethics. Do salesmen have such a code? Some cynics (and some salesmen) might scoff at the notion. Indeed, from early days the ethical behavior of salesmen has been roundly condemned by honest folk who considered them little more than swindlers and thieves. Even today their conduct is subject to steady criticism by the trade press, by government agencies, by buyers, and by each other. Beyond question, this is a live and troublesome problem.

The philosophers distinguish between absolute ethics and relative ethics, the former being inflexible and always applicable, while the latter are somewhat flexible and adaptable to differing situations. The salesman usually operates under a system of relative ethics, for it is virtually impossible to develop a single code that would cover a significant segment of the situations that arise and still take into account the problems peculiar to each industry and type of selling activity. Practices condemned in one industry are considered permissible in another. Different companies lay down quite varying rulings for their salesmen's guidance.

Therefore, the purpose of this selection is not to provide an absolute code of selling ethics, but rather to introduce the reader to some of the ethical problems that salesmen

◆ SOURCE: Reprinted by permission from *Textbook of Salesmanship* by F. A. Russell, F. H. Beach, and R. H. Buskirk (McGraw-Hill Book Company, 1963), pp. 523–540.

meet and to suggest some of the consequences of dealing with them unwisely.

There seems to be no one simple test or rule that can be applied to all acts of salesmen to determine which is right and which is wrong. Experience indicates, however, that some standards are more widely applicable than others. For example, a salesman may evaluate the ethical status of an act by answering the question, "Is this sound from a long-run viewpoint?" Other standards are set by the way a man answers such questions as: "Would I do this to a friend?" "Is society harmed or benefited by this practice?" "Who will be injured if I do this?" "Am I willing to have this done to me?" (Golden Rule) "If other people learn of this act, what will be their reactions?" "Will I be ashamed to tell about this?"

The man who is guilty of some unethical act usually knows it; he has inner qualms about it because he is not comfortable with some of the answers he must make to such questions as those above.

But sometimes the pressure on a salesman is almost irresistible; he feels that his personal interests or those of his firm are at stake. He may revert to the code of the jungle, which decrees that survival may be purchased at any price; ethical considerations are forgotten. It is easy to be ethical when it involves no hardship, and most salesmen prefer to play it that way as long as they can. The real problems arise when it costs something to stick to the right.

ETHICAL PROBLEMS INVOLVED IN CUSTOMER RELATIONS

These comprise a large portion of the salesman's ethical problems. In the long run it usually pays to deal ethically with one's customers, as most salesmen find it profitable to build up a large and loyal clientele.

Keeping Confidences

Industrial salesmen, as well as many selling to retail outlets, call on accounts that are competing with each other. The salesman naturally learns much vital, confidential information which could be of great value to a competitor, such as plans for new products, volume of sales in various lines and territories, marketing campaigns in preparation, contemplated changes in personnel, and other facts which the executives would dislike to have broadcast.

Naturally, should the salesman violate such confidences, he will never receive any more and might not even be welcome to call on that account in future. It would seem that only the worst and weakest of gossips would succumb to the temptation of telling one customer any facts about a competitor which had been given him under seal of secrecy, but the problem is not that simple. Sometimes the poor salesman is subjected to severe pressure to divulge critical information as the price he must pay for a firm's patronage.

The sales manager of a chemical company was keenly interested in learning the sales volume of a certain chemical compound sold by a competitor, the only other seller of that product. He was haunted by the suspicion that the other firm was outselling him, so he figured out what he thought was a clever scheme to get this information. One of the ingredients in the compound was purchased by both firms from the same source, a refiner of corn syrup. So he pressured the corn syrup salesman to find out how many carloads of the ingredient his competitor bought each year. He hinted that, if the salesman failed to come across with this information, he would buy from another corn products refiner. Naturally, no salesman wants to lose a large-volume account, so these threats were taken seriously. The salesman promised to see what he could do, but he stated clearly that such information was not available to the sales force and he might find it hard to obtain. Later he reported back that the other account was handled by a different salesman, who flatly refused to tell him what he wanted to know, and that the office sharply informed him that it was none of his business and that, if he valued his job, he had better keep things that way. Thus he

avoided offending his customer and losing the account, but not all salesmen can evade the issue so smoothly, for the customer may know that they do have the facts that are wanted.

Some salesmen prefer to meet such requests firmly with, "If your competitor asked me to give him the same information about you, what would you want me to do? If I told you what you just asked for, you should throw me out of this plant, for you could no longer trust me. If I would tell *you*, how could you ever feel sure that I wouldn't tell your competitors your secrets? One thing you can be sure of in dealing with me is that your secrets stay secret. I tell *no one*, not my boss or my colleagues or my family. That's one rule of the game I'll never break."

This ethical attitude is not always maintained. In fact, in certain industries it is not expected, and executives are careful not to reveal to salesmen anything they do not want repeated.

Clearly, such ethics are relative, not absolute. But the smart salesman will bear in mind that, where any doubt exists, silence is golden.

Be silent and safe—silence never *betrays you.*
—JOHN BOYLE O'REILLY

Bribes

An unpleasant fact of selling life is the existence of bribery. Not that bribery does not thrive in other areas of activity, for it does. It is sometimes called by nicer names, such as "reward" or "in appreciation for services rendered," and is regarded as standard procedure in some circles. But in selling it is not standard.

However, some firms and some salesmen have found that it is effective, at least in the short run. A small businessman selling an item to oil well drillers took an active part in private meetings where field prices were established, all firms selling this standard product at identical list prices. He said, "Everything is billed out at the agreed price, but I manage to get a fair hunk of it back to them under the table to the right men who won't spill the beans."

In other cases buyers request bribes of some sort. The sales manager for a regional paint manufacturer related that he had this problem with a large aircraft company. He said, "They had a purchasing agent who was on the take. He was rather open about it and

Table 1

What Form Does "Chiseling" Usually Take?	Per Cent
Fictitious price bids to lower your price	47
Suggestions that you give special price or handling (in violation of Robinson-Patman Act)	38
Misrepresenting your competitors' products	31
Suggestions for elaborate gifts or entertainment	18
Requests for kickbacks	15
Blackmail	2
Other (extra free goods, reciprocity, threats to cancel orders, play one quote against another)	11

SOURCE: *The American Salesman,* November, 1961, p. 56.

made it clear that if we wanted any of their business, he had to be paid off. We just won't do business that way, so we pulled out of bidding and stopped calling on them. One day the big brass in the east stumbled onto the fact that the region's largest paint manufacturer was not bidding for their business. I got a call from their Executive VP who asked me why we hadn't submitted bids lately. I told him exactly the reason. Now we do business with a new purchasing agent. But I know there are still some buyers out there who are on the take."

One survey of salesmen made on the subject of "chiseling purchasing agents" concluded, "98% of those responding are confronted with a minority of buyers who sometimes try to 'chisel.' " [1] "The proportion . . . who try to 'chisel' in some way varies all the way from ½ of 1% to 50%." Table 1 presents the frequency of replies to the question, "What form does 'chiseling' usually take?"

Table 2 records what the salesmen say they reply to these requests.

Few purchasing agents are so clumsy as to ask for outright bribes. Instead, some offer veiled hints that they are in need of something or other. The salesman for one electronics firm recalls the time an executive of a potential account mentioned that his family had been pressuring him for a new stereo set, a prod-

uct which one division of the salesman's firm "just happened" to make.

However, far more clever are the purchasing agents who say nothing of their larcenous inclinations but manage to patronize the perceptive salesman who senses their bent. These buyers, while not openly soliciting bribes and preferential treatment, nevertheless bestow their business on the firms that are most generous.

One sales manager admonishes his salesmen to start looking for a bribe or personal friendship somewhere in the background if they cannot understand why some other firm is getting an account's business. He says, "In our industry buyers have good reasons for buying from the sources they do. If none of the usual business reasons are present in a certain situation, then I immediately start looking for the existence of personal friendships, family ties, or bribes. It makes no sense for one of our salesmen to beat his head against a stone wall trying to sell a purchasing agent who is in the control of one of our competitors. Once we find this to be the situation, we simply stop calling on him."

It would be nice if there were some easy answers to this problem, but unfortunately there are none. A salesman will encounter buyers who want to be bribed and competitors who are willing to do so. How he handles the situation depends to such a large extent upon the conditions peculiar to the industry and the situation that it is impossible to provide any meaningful rule for action. There are many salesmen and many firms that refuse under any circumstances to be parties to commercial bribery not only on legal grounds, but also on

Table 2

How Do You Handle Requests from P.A.'s Which You Consider Out of Line?	Per Cent
Refuse point-blank	51
Ignore	36
Pass off as a joke	29
Go along with them	9
Other (demand proof of competitor's price, pass on to home office, explain company policy and law)	27

SOURCE: *The American Salesman,* November, 1961, p. 56.

[1] "Sales Panel Reports on Buyers' Ethics," *The American Salesman,* November, 1961, pp. 56–58.

moral ones. Likewise, there are some firms and some salesmen who will not hesitate if they feel that a bribe will gain them what they want.

Gifts

Closely akin to bribes is the practice of giving gifts, particularly at Christmastime. The practice has become so widespread in industry that outcries are being heard from many sectors of the business community complaining of their general ineffectiveness and meaninglessness. Clearly, the dividing line between a gift and a bribe is rather arbitrary at best. Some firms have declared that their executives may not accept gifts over a certain nominal value, thus in effect saying that articles under that amount are gifts while items over it constitute bribes. Salesmen, as frequent bearers of gifts, are caught in the middle of this confusion of top management over the role of the gift in business. One psychologist is quoted [2] as saying, "We train children from infancy to be generous, to share, to show appreciation. It's part of the way people reach each other. What we need in business is to reduce gift-giving again to the level of generosity, where a gift is a nice gesture, an extension of self."

Fortunately, there are a few guideposts which have been erected to keep the salesman from making too many serious errors in his gift-giving. One purchasing agent for a large oil company warned, "Never give us a gift *before* we have done business with you. Use sales ability, not thirty pieces of silver."

A psychologist claims that the way in which a man gives is probably tied in with his personality. He says,[3] "The best salesmen do it with finesse. They give unobtrusively; they never talk about it, and they never show signs of expecting a return. If a salesman feels queasy about a gift, it's probably a sign that he doesn't have the right motive and ought to be careful."

According to one buyer, only 5 per cent of business gift-giving is done deftly enough to benefit salesmen. What are the mistakes that reduce the effectiveness of gifts? The experts list the following common mistakes made in gift-giving: [4]

[2] Velma A. Adams, "What's Hidden in Your Christmas Gifts?" *The American Salesman*, November, 1961, p. 43.
[3] *Ibid.*, p. 44.
[4] *Ibid.*, p. 45.

(1) Any gift that puts the recipient at a disadvantage is in bad taste and a mistake. When it appears to be given from a selfish and monetary point of view, a gift may make a man feel threatened. But if it is clearly symbolic of appreciation, no strings attached, the gift has a good effect. (2) If it is so extravagant as to approach bribery or if it is blatant advertising, it is in bad taste. (3) If an item can be misinterpreted, a wrong connotation put on it, it's dangerous. For example, one man never gives another grooming aids. (4) Another mistake is to overestimate the effect of barroom humor. Just because you think nude figures on the inside of beer glasses are amusing doesn't mean your best customer will. You have to know the man. (5) In most cases good taste prohibits the giving of gifts to the purchasing agent's wife, but gifts to his children are fine and may be especially effective.

The timing of a gift may be particularly critical to its effectiveness. Another box of candy at Christmastime gets lost in the deluge, but the same gift at another time of year—say, the purchasing agent's wedding anniversary—may be deeply appreciated. Many of the most effective gift programs in business are not routinized to the point of boredom, but instead are administered by salesmen who attempt to send only appropriate gifts to the right people at the right time. A pair of tickets to a football game may be far more effective in creating good will than an expensive portable television set.

Entertainment

The problem of entertainment is in much the same category as bribes and gift-giving. It can be an attempt by the salesman to influence the buyer on a basis other than the merits of his proposition. Nonetheless, it is a widespread practice, and most salesmen must decide who should be entertained and to what extent.

Naturally, there are problems connected with entertainment. A large portion of the salesman's expense money is devoted to it. If he does not spend it wisely, if he wastes it on prospects with little potential, his productivity will be seriously impaired and his costs of selling out of line. Indeed, in many industries one of the key factors in a salesman's success is his ability to know who is the right person to entertain and what the nature of the entertainment should be. It is a mistake to assume that all entertainment takes the form of eating and drinking. In many circumstances unusual forms of entertainment are far more effective. One book representative was particularly effective in his entertainment by inviting prospects to go skiing with him—he would pay for the tow tickets, a modest amount in comparison with a night of winning and dining. His philosophy of entertaining was to do something a little different. He tried to determine what the prospect best liked to do and then treated him to it. An invitation to play golf at some swank country club is highly appreciated by the avid golfer.

One psychologist [5] who carefully investigated the phenomena of business entertainment put forth a few suggestions for making it psychologically sounder and thus more effective. He said:

"Salesmen shouldn't be in too big a hurry to entertain. Invitations extended on impulse may be taken lightly. As a general rule, it is far better to withhold the more lavish entertainment until after the first order, when it becomes a psychological 'reward,' and may help build a permanent relationship. On his early calls, the salesman may make it a point not to invite the prospect to lunch just when it seems he is going to do so. Then when the invitation comes, it may mean something. Of course, there are exceptions. If a buyer hints broadly that he wants to be taken to lunch to get away from the office for an hour or so, then the thing to do is to invite him on the spur of the moment. But to retain the upper hand, the salesman should assure him that no business will be discussed—and stick to it.

"It's a mistake to take away from the prospect's dearly protected freedom of choice. A salesman shouldn't assume the buyer or purchasing agent wants to go to a most expensive restaurant, or even that he wants a drink. It's better to ask, and a good salesman should have the social skill necessary to determine whether the answer is sincere or not.

"Salesmen should be careful about doing actual selling during entertainment, especially at meals. Whenever feasible, it's better to talk about subjects other than business, giving the prospect the confidence that he is an enjoyable person.

[5] Daniel Brower, "A Psychologist Looks at Business Entertainment," *The American Salesman*, July, 1960, pp. 90–96.

"Salesmen ought to try to understand their own reasons for entertaining. They should ask themselves such searching questions as: Was it necessary to impress this particular customer? Was I afraid I wouldn't make the sale otherwise? What would have happened on this if I had not taken the prospect to dinner?"

One survey of salesmen disclosed that they entertain not to earn a specific order but for long-term awards. Various quotes from the salesmen were:

"A friend is always more useful than a cold business contact in getting hold of some business."

"I like to get better acquainted with customers so that negotiations can be conducted on a warmer, personal basis."

"Selling would be a lonesome life without entertainment."

"It's a courtesy that is expected and a natural way to do business."

"Away from the prospect's office, the salesman can add color to what is sometimes a concise presentation. At the same time, he can learn more about the customer's problems."

"To get the buyer out from behind his desk and find out what he likes to talk about."

These surveyed salesmen pointed out that too great a dependence on entertainment works against the salesman. "If it's done to buy business, someone can always bid higher."

"It's like price-cutting. Anyone influenced by me can be wined away by another."

"It's no substitute for product and service."

"Some salesmen entertain because they want to be big operators. They get carried away."

Seventy-four per cent of the men said they streamline their entertaining to fit the type of customer and the potential volume of the account. In their own words here's how they make up their minds:

"If a potential is not there, I cannot spend the time."

"I don't entertain customers without social inclinations."

"Some buyers don't expect or don't want to be entertained; others wouldn't respond to entertainment."

"Company policies may prohibit buyers from being entertained."

"Depends on the personality of the customer and how big the account is—from buying a coat to a trip to the Kentucky Derby."

The following is a list of the most frequently

mentioned results the salesmen expected to accomplish with entertainment: [6]

1. To get better acquainted, make friends. (This purpose was mentioned three times more than any other purpose.)
2. Good will.
3. Get orders, increase business.
4. Avoid interruptions, get purchasing agent out of his office.
5. Acquaint buyers with salesmen in his company.
6. Show appreciation.
7. Please customers who expect it.
8. Nothing.
9. Break down price objection.
10. Reciprocate.
11. Prospecting for referrals.
12. Introduce product to prospect.
13. Sell himself.
14. Increase sales time.
15. Create setting for persuasion.
16. Cement relations.

In conclusion, business entertainment is definitely a part of the work of most salesmen. And if he is to use it effectively, the salesman must learn the niceties of the art. He must know who should be entertained and what diversions should be offered. He should allocate his entertainment budget properly among accounts according to their potential and the anticipated effectiveness of the expenditures. It might be unwise for a salesman to spend large sums of money on the purchasing agent of a prospective account that is firmly locked to another firm on the basis of reciprocity. Finally, he must learn how to behave during entertainment to avoid offending the sensibilities of the prospect, for there is a right and wrong time to talk business. This does not mean to imply that a salesman can never discuss business matters during social respites, for many men like to talk business while relaxing socially.

Reciprocity

Some firms maintain a policy of reciprocity; they give preference in buying to firms that buy from them. Similarly, some sales departments attempt to use the reciprocity appeal in selling to companies from which they are buying. It is not unknown for a salesman, with

the approval of his manager, to hint that unless an order is forthcoming, the prospect's sales to his firm may suffer.

Obviously, this is a form of commercial blackmail. In theory a purchasing agent should buy the right product without regard to the seller's purchasing policies, but in many competitive situations there is little difference between the products offered by competing concerns. Hence, competition comes down to various differentiating factors, among which reciprocity may be won. In some industries, such as oil, reciprocity is widely practiced. The drilling contractor automatically uses lubricants from the company for which he is drilling. Where reciprocity is a matter of standard practice, purchasing agents may attempt to split their business among all competitors, thereby making it easier for their sales forces to sell to all concerns.

However, great care must be exercised in using a reciprocity appeal even if it is ethically permissible in the existing competitive environment. Should the salesman lean too heavily on reciprocity and fail to do a good job of selling and servicing, he will lose the account, reciprocity or no. When reciprocity is not considered ethical, the salesman who relies upon it is walking on rather thin ice. Many executives will rebel strongly at any hint of such blackmail and will regard it not only as an affront to their integrity but also as a sign that the salesman and his proposition have little merit. A good salesman with a worthy proposition does not need to rely heavily on reciprocity.

Conflicts of Interest

In some cases a salesman may be faced with a conflict of interests in handling an account. One salesman selling to an electronics firm proved to all parties his high ethical standards by withdrawing from the account on the grounds that his brother-in-law was the president of a competing firm. He preferred to avoid a position in which he might be suspected of passing along to his brother-in-law information gained from servicing a competitors' account.

A salesman may have interests in firms in conflict with those of customers or his employer. The ethical, professional salesman will take great pains to make his exact position clear to all parties concerned, lest his interests

[6] "Salesmen View Business Entertainment," *The American Salesman*, August, 1961, pp. 12–19.

be misinterpreted at some later date when they are discovered—as they usually will be.

ETHICAL PROBLEMS CONNECTED WITH EMPLOYERS

A salesman's relationships with his employer are even closer than those with his customers and give rise to just as many, if not more, ethical problems.

Changing Jobs

There usually comes a time when a salesman considers changing jobs and must weigh certain ethical considerations.

In some industries the ethical code is so strict that it precludes the salesman from going to work for a direct competitor lest that firm benefit by information and knowledge obtained by the man from his first employer. However, this is the exception.

More commonly, it is considered unethical for a competitor to initiate negotiations with the salesman in trying to lure him away from his present employer. However, usually a dissatisfied salesman may ethically initiate contacts with competitors. Needless to say, in some industries open piracy of men is considered perfectly ethical and is practiced by all.

The salesman is faced with the ethical problem of how much notice he should give his employer, because in many instances it is difficult to replace him immediately. It may take several months to train the replacement, and in the meantime the company may be severely damaged should it not have a representative in that territory. Clearly, the ethical man would not want to place his employer in such a position by leaving without notice. He would try to reach an amicable agreement on the date of severance.

In severance situations there arises the problem of the salesman's present accounts. Should he attempt to take them with him to the new employer? In some cases accounts have been known to follow the salesman rather than stay with the house; however, that usually happens in competitive environments in which there is little difference between products, and the accounts have been buying the salesman's services rather than the firm's wares. One survey of appliance dealers made by Philco directly asked dealers if they would switch lines if their favorite salesman changed houses. The dealers unanimously claimed they would not follow

any salesman to another distributor but would stick with the lines they were selling. Many salesmen have been deluded into thinking they had a clientele loyal to them only to be rudely shocked when they discovered that their previous customers had been buying products, not personalities.

Sometimes a firm will lure away key salesmen of successful competitors for the knowledge they may have of important operational details. Naturally, it is difficult to control the information a salesman gives his new employer, but there are limits beyond which a salesman's behavior is clearly unethical. One man resigned as a salesman to accept the sales managership of a smaller competitor. He managed to get into the files before leaving and take with him important marketing research information and data on the firm's customers. Needless to say, the president of the firm was quite disturbed at this unethical behavior, but there was little he could do about it. Most employers take precautions to protect themselves against this risk.

Expense Accounts

The salesman's handling of his expense account naturally encompasses many ethical considerations. For the moment, let's ignore the situation in which the company encourages fictional expense accounts and assume that accurate statements of legitimate sales expenses are desired.

The ethical problems connected with expense accounts are not concerned with whether or not the salesman should abide by his employer's wishes, for that is rather clear-cut ethically. But many little problems arise which are seemingly quite innocent. Suppose the employer has set limits on what can be spent for certain activities. For example, he will pay only 7 cents a mile for automobile expenses. Yet the salesman, in all honesty, has computed his operating costs at 10 cents a mile. Now he may be tempted to pad his mileage to make up for the difference between the 7 and 10 cents. In his own mind he may try to justify his actions on the basis that the money was actually spent for business purposes and that the spirit of the expense account was not being violated. The salesman faces the ethical problem: Should he manipulate the expense account in order to protect himself from the niggardly policies of his management, thereby recovering money honestly spent on the solicitation of business for his firm? Or should the salesman strenuously attempt to get the policies changed, and failing that, change employers rather than commit what he believes to be unethical acts? What are the dangers of such manipulation? Quite simple! Once a salesman finds he can manipulate figures with ease for honest amounts, does this not encourage him to manipulate a bit more and increase his earnings? Just where can he draw the line at manipulation?

There is an old story about a salesman who lost his Stetson while making a sales call. He thought the company should compensate him for the loss of his hat since it was in the pursuit of business. He put at the bottom of his next expense account, "New Stetson hat to replace one damaged while calling on customer: $20." The auditor disallowed his claim. The next week he put it in again and, once again, it was disallowed. The third week at the bottom of his expense account was the notation, "O.K., Wise Guy. It's in there. Just try to find it."

Suppose a company allows $7 a night for lodging. Should the salesman average out one night which cost $9 with another which cost only $5 by recording both as $7 nights? Should he put overages on one account into others? For example, suppose it cost him $3 more for lodging than is allowable, should he take his $3 from the entertainment fund?

It is a mistake to assume that all salesmen cheat on their expense accounts. One outstanding book salesman and a customer took a long trip in the salesman's car to a football game in which they both were interested. It would have been easy for the salesman to charge a good portion of the expenses of both himself and the customer to the employer, but he did not. Because of the customer's interest in the subject of expense accounts, the two got into a rather long discussion concerning them. The salesman said, "I made up my mind a long time ago that I was not going to cheat my boss out of a dime. I like this job, and he's been very good to me. There's nobody in this world I'd rather work for, and I decided that I would be a fool to cheat him and jeopardize our relationship. It's not so much that he would ever find out or even suspect. But I would know that I was cheating him, and this would affect my relationship with him. As it is, I honestly feel that I am the best employee he has, and when it comes time for promotion, I will have nothing on my conscience." Incidentally, the same salesman frequently entertained

certain customers and prospects at poker parties. While he was kidded about not charging his losses to the expense account, he replied, "I don't expect my boss to pay for my poor judgment of cards, just as I wouldn't expect him to benefit by any streak of luck which I might have." This man has since become sales manager.

Most unethical expense account practices evolve when the salesman can rationalize them because of some niggardly policies of his employer. If a salesman is able to justify his actions to himself by thinking that the amounts he steals on the expense account are justly due him, stealing becomes much easier. It is quite similar to the situation in which the underpaid bank clerk embezzles, rationalizing that it was due him.

So far, we have been dicussing situations in which the employer does not condone the manipulation of expense accounts. Unfortunately, there are many cases in which the salesman is directly encouraged by his superiors to file inaccurate expense claims. Many such policies have been forced upon the sales management organization by some unwise policies of the accountants. The district managers for one large industrial equipment manufacturer openly instruct their salesmen on how to fill out expense accounts in order to avoid conflict with the auditors. An autonomous accounting department has imposed upon them certain limits on the money they can spend for entertainment in any one day or on any one account. The salesmen are told that if they go over those limits to spread the amounts into other categories or to report that they worked days they didn't and file expense accounts for them.

The managers justify this practice as simply being an internal convenience to keep peace within the family. In this manner the sales department gets what it wants and is able to spend money as it deems necessary, and the accountants are happy because they are deluded into thinking the sales force is abiding by their rules. But is such conduct ethical, even assuming that it is legal?

When these deceptions involve violating the Internal Revenue laws, other ethical considerations come into the picture. For example, the Internal Revenue Service takes a dim view of expenditures for bribes or large gifts. Should a salesman, at the direction of his manager, hide such gifts in other categories? Obviously, the action might be illegal, but so might be other things a salesman does. He never knows when some action of his might be declared an unfair business practice or a violation of some other law. Clearly, the salesman has an ethical problem which may become more serious as the Internal Revenue Service continues to clamp down on certain practices.

Moonlighting

In some situations a salesman can quite easily carry additional lines of merchandise other than those furnished by his principal employer. One representative for a manufacturer of women's high-priced dresses without the approval of his employer carried lines of underwear, lingerie, and sportswear. His employer had clearly disapproved of such moonlighting activities when he had fired a salesman in Texas for exactly the same practice. The employer's reasoning was that the men were making good money, about $30,000 a year, selling his line and that they should devote their entire attention to it. The dress salesman justified his moonlighting by saying, "It's true that my principal line is making me sufficient money presently. But in this business it is 'here today and gone tomorrow.' While the market is buying our styles in large quantities today, I've got to look ahead because I never know when this line will go sour. So I take on these other lines of merchandise to keep in with my accounts. I don't want to become too identified with one line, so that when it goes bad, the buyers won't look at anything else from me. In this industry you have to take care of yourself. I don't know who they (the management) think they're kidding, for they pay us on a straight commission basis, and we pay all of our own expenses. We have no fringe benefits; really I don't see how we are employees of the company, for they certainly don't treat us that way. We even have to pay our own way back to pick up our samples in New York City. I'm really in business for myself."

Thus, the ethical dilemma is neatly posed.

Fellow Salesmen

One's relationships with his fellow salesmen are fraught with ethical problems. Although most companies endeavor to minimize conflicts between their men by assigning specific territories and accounts, ample room still exists for misunderstandings. What about the account that is a personal friend of the salesman, and is located in another salesman's territory? What about the prospect a fellow salesman fails to sell? When is it ethical for another to call upon him? Should permission be asked of the first salesman? Does a salesman owe a split commission for leads furnished by others? Firms do set policies to handle a few of such problems, but naturally they cannot cover all contingencies.

When salesmen are turned loose in an area without territorial assignments, conflicts arise. Suppose a prospect contacts a realty firm in January about a house, and Salesman Jones shows him around but fails to close a deal. In September the prospect contacts Salesman Smith, who closes a deal on a house first shown him by Salesman Jones. Obviously, troubles will arise when Jones learns of this. It is for this reason that real estate men have established boards to judge these matters and have set forth fairly clear-cut rules governing such situations. However, in other fields this type of regulation is not available.

Personal Use of Company Assets

One of the unique attributes of the salesman's position is that corporate assets are entrusted to him. Frequently cars, expensive samples, or equipment are furnished. Most managers establish policies governing the use of the company cars. A few firms allow the salesman to use the company car just as if it were his own, with the company paying the costs, but this is the exception. More commonly, the salesman may use the car for his personal needs, but he must pay so much a mile to cover direct costs. Some concerns severely limit personal use. Some insist that he not take *long* personal trips, while a few restrict *all* personal usage. Whatever the company's policies on these matters, the salesman has ample opportunity for violating them.

On the other hand, a slightly different problem arises in the case of samples and equipment. There have been numerous cases in which salesmen have sold samples for personal gain, claiming that they lost them or that they had been given to some customer in furtherance of a sale. Some firms instruct salesmen to sell their samples when they become shopworn or damaged. The result—opportunity for questionable practices. Minnesota Mining and Manufacturing salesmen are sometimes faced with an ethical problem in picking up old stock on dealers' hands and writing it off. Top management does not want outdated stock shipped back to the factory; the quicker it is junked, the less expense is involved with it. Hence, authority is vested at very low levels for writing the stock off as a complete loss. Some salesmen have been known to take such stock home and sell it later for personal gain. This is particularly true with Christmas tapes the company uniformly picks up after each Yuletide. This behavior is not only unethical but also illegal, but it is mentioned to illustrate that these problems do exist.

Contests

Contests, and other managerial tools, frequently pose ethical problems for the salesman because the opportunistic operator can take advantage of loopholes in the rules. For example, one man was able to win a large monthly contest by withholding orders taken during the last 10 days of the previous month and filing them with those taken during the contest month, thereby significantly enlarging his sales volume. While this is clearly unethical, a salesman might defend it because management established the situation which fostered it.

And what of the contest that is designed to promote tremendous volume production? Does it not tempt the salesman to overload his customers or dealers to a degree that is unethical? What about the contest that offers great rewards for selling a certain product? Does it not encourage some salesmen to sell it to prospects despite the fact that it might not be the best product for them? These are problems that the salesman must work out for himself.

ETHICAL PROBLEMS CONNECTED WITH COMPETITORS

When a salesman is accused of unethical behavior, the chances are that those accusations are being made by a competitor. If any particular tactics or tricks were used to gain the victory, the loser is tempted to yell "Foul." However, this does not automatically make it unethical, for the very essence of competition involves certain sharp practices. All too often the price-cutter is called unethical. Yet genuine competition usually involves price variation. The industrial salesman who persuades a customer's engineering department to establish certain specifications which favor his firm may be accused by a competitor of being unethical, but others would merely consider him an ex-

cellent salesman. A competitor may claim that it is unethical for one to sell direct to a certain account at a lower price. Yet, is not this just a matter of business policy under our competitive system?

There are some competitive practices, however, that are clearly unethical. At one time a business machines manufacturer had his salesmen drop sand in competing machines whenever they could. The practice became so bad that finally the Federal Trade Commission issued a cease-and-desist order against this firm, which is in effect today. The order specifically orders the company's salesmen not to drop sand in competitors' equipment.

Many salesmen admit that if they are forced to make a demonstration against the leading competitor's equipment, they can always make it look bad in comparison to their own. One favorite tactic of a vacuum cleaner salesman is to clean a rug with the owner's present machine first and then reclean it with his own to show the superiority of his cleaner. Just how far can a salesman go in adroitly disparaging the competition? Should he even agree to such tests?

Naturally, these are questions that cannot be answered categorically, for they depend upon the circumstances. In many situations the salesman must agree to a test demonstration against all the competitive equipment if the prospect demands it. In some instances the competitive equipment may have disadvantages which should be pointed out to the prospect, but the salesman must remember that if he goes too far, the word will get back to the competition. A victory gained by an unethical tactic may cost the salesman dearly in the future as competitors retaliate.

There is one area in selling where competition is particularly vicious and unethical practices are common. The merchandisers calling upon supermarkets have gotten into dog fights over the shelf space allotted to them. This is understandable because sales volume in a supermarket is almost directly proportional to shelf space. Hence, a salesman's productivity is directly correlated with the amount and quality of display space he can obtain. One baby-food salesman told of his success in stealing baskets away from a competitor. He explained that when he took over the territory the major competitor had about 90 per cent of the market. Where his firm would be granted only about 4 or 5 baskets for its baby food, the competitor would have 20 to 25. In the larger, more significant supermarkets he would manage to call at a time when he knew that the baskets would be empty; he had observed the restocking schedules of his customers. He would combine the contents of two or three of the competitor's almost empty baskets into one and fill the now free baskets with his own brand. Supermarket managers can become angry with quarreling salesmen and may throw both of them out, for they do not like to spend their time refereeing such disputes between squabbling salesmen.

Bread salesmen may steal space from competitors, burying some of their merchandise at the same time. Salesmen have ruined the goods of competitors deliberately, hoping to make the accounts unhappy with that source of supply. Naturally, all of this behavior can backfire very badly on a salesman, should he be too aggressive; but he must take care of himself against competing salesmen eager to steal his space, if that is the nature of the business.

CASES

Acme Furniture Company

Acme Furniture Company is a manufacturer of school and institutional furniture. The company produces a medium-priced line of classroom furniture and a quality line of church, scientific, dormitory, and library furniture.

The company was founded in the early 1900's as a small, family-owned enterprise. Today Acme is an affiliate of one of the country's largest furniture manufacturers. The main plant of Acme Furniture is located in Brandhill, Michigan. About nine hundred people earn more than $3,000,000 per year in hourly wages at Acme. The sales force consists of twenty-seven men who cover the Northeastern United States. However, there is national distribution through complete dealer organization.

In the past, the prices of Acme Furniture Company have been consistently higher than those of other similar product manufacturers. The company justifies this difference in price by stressing quality and service.

Covering twenty-six counties in one of the eastern states is a man who has been working for Acme for approximately fifteen years, Paul Huntley. Paul entered military service after two years of college. Following his tenure with "Uncle Sam," he became regional director of the Boy Scouts of America. Dissatisfied with that, he entered Chamber of Commerce work

for a brief period; then he went to work for Acme.

Paul obtains prospects by personal observations and use of the Hodge reports. This publication deals with various construction projects contemplated and underway. He calls on school superintendents, church directors, college business managers, and college presidents.

One of the real problems Paul encounters exists in the selling of scientific, library, and dormitory furniture. Projects of this nature are awarded through a state centralized purchasing office, based on competitive bidding. Contracts are awarded on the basis of what is judged to be the best value for the purposes intended. The procedure to be followed presents a problem for Paul because of the red tape involved.

For example, the procedure to be followed by a school superintendent in the acquisition of school laboratory furniture would be as follows:

1. Any item(s) which will result in an expenditure of $2,000 or more will be requisitioned through a centralized purchasing office known as the State Division of Purchase and Contracts.
2. It shall be the responsibility of the superintendent to requisition items based on need, purposefulness, and value.
3. The Division of Purchase and Contracts, based on what is requisitioned, will draw up general specifications on a Request for Bids form. Public notice is given and Request for Bids are distributed to approved companies.
4. These bids are evaluated by the Purchase and Contracts Division, canvassed by the Board of Awards, and contracts are awarded to the successful bidder.
5. The Purchase and Contracts Division will notify the successful company and the school superintendent who then has the authority to issue a confirming purchase order.
6. After the equipment is installed, it will be inspected by a state inspector to see that it conforms to the accepted specifications as set forth in the contract and spelled out in a specifications and standards manual. If the project passes inspection, the Division will notify the superintendent of fulfillment of the contract and authorize payment.

In July of 1966, Acme Furniture Company received two Request for Bids forms from the Purchase and Contracts Division for the installation of laboratory furniture in two high school science laboratories in the same school district. Since these two schools, Brownview and Orangeburg High Schools, were in Paul Huntley's territory, Acme management forwarded the requests to him for completion. Using the state's General Standards and Specifications for Science Furniture as a guideline, Paul filled in his company's prices.

Acme's bids, along with the bids of other competing companies, were reviewed by the Purchase and Contracts Division, and the contracts were awarded by the Board of Awards. Acme Company was the successful bidder on the Orangeburg High School project. However, Baker Company, a newcomer in the laboratory furniture field, was the successful bidder on the Brownview project.

The contracts were awarded the last of July with the completion deadline set for September 1.

The projects were completed and were accepted by a state inspector on September 1. The superintendent of schools received notice of acceptance and was authorized to make payment. Wanting a firsthand look, the superintendent inspected both projects and was shocked at the visible differences in quality of the Baker Company installation compared to the installation of Acme. Because of his dissatisfaction and in order to have some visible record of the condition which led to this dissatisfaction, he took colored slides of the Brownview project.

The superintendent, desiring further evidence of the difference in quality, asked Paul Huntley, with whom he had become acquainted during the Orangeburg project, to inspect the Brownview project and prepare a report of any discrepancies that were evident.

The superintendent informed Paul that he was a member of the Board of Awards of the State's Purchase and Contracts Division, having been appointed to the eight-member Board as an "at-large" member. He indicated that he wanted some proof to send to other members regarding the poor workmanship of Baker Company.

Exhibit 1 contains excerpts from the report which resulted from Paul's examination of the Brownview project.

QUESTIONS

1. After preparing the report of discrepancies found in Baker Company's installation work, Paul Huntley is having second thoughts about the propriety of giving the superintendent this information.
   a) If you were Paul Huntley, would you deliver the inspection report to the superintendent?
   b) What reasons prompt you to make this decision?
   c) In what way do you expect this decision to benefit you and your company at the present time?
   d) In what way do you expect this decision to benefit you and your company in the long-run?
2. Assume that you have become aware of the contents of the report cited in this case, who prepared it, and the reason for which it was prepared. What would be your reactions if you were:
   a) The territorial salesman for Baker Company?
   b) The president of Baker Company?
   c) The president of Acme Furniture Company?
   d) A member of the Board of Awards?

EXHIBIT 1

Inspection Report Prepared by Paul Huntley on Laboratory Equipment Installation at Brownview High School by Baker Furniture Company

The equipment was first inspected to determine the compliance of each individual item of equipment with the equipment schedule and drawings. The discrepancies noted as follows:

Item No.	Remarks
1	Two locks missing on each of the two desks
3	One faucet leaking
5	One hose connection missing from faucet

Item No.	Remarks
7	Stainless steel corners on base mould missing in both rooms
8	Veneer on shelving top is cracking
10	Bottom board of cupboard missing
13	Stainless steel corners on base mould missing
—	—
—	—

The next phase of the inspection was devoted to checking the project and casework in general to determine any deviations from the general specifications that were included as a part of the bid invitation. Following is a comparison between the bid specifications and the actual equipment installed. The paragraph numbers refer to specifications:

Paragraph Number	Specifications	Equipment Installed
4:01	All major structural joints shall be mortised and tenoned, securely glued and screwed.	Sides of horizontal division frames not tenoned into ends and not glued.
4:04	Welded fibre tops to be 1¼″ thick. Tops shall be fastened to casework with heavy metal fasteners constructed to allow for expansion and contraction.	Welded fibre tops are 1⅛″ thick. A light weight fastener furnished that does not permit expansion and contraction.
4:08	Case ends to be ⅞″ plywood, with hardwood core.	Case ends are ¾″ with fir plywood core.
4:09	Horizontal division frames to have security and dust panels.	No panels furnished.
5:03	Hinges shall be institutional type, 2½″ high, solid brass, .095″ thick.	Hinges are institutional type, 2½″ high, *steel*, approximately .068 to .075.
5:04	Each sink shall be provided with lead combination stopper-strainer.	Sinks provided only with lead stopper.
8:01	Casework finish shall be a chemical resistant varnish, with qualities listed in specifications.	Casework finish appears to be a *lacquer* coating, with little or no chemical resistant qualities.
—	—	—
—	—	—

SUMMARY

Although several of the discrepancies listed above are of a minor nature, there are several major discrepancies that will reduce the durability of this equipment. In summary, we wish to point out and remark, concerning several of the more major items as follows:

1. A simple test was performed on the casework finish, and due to the complete deterioration of the finish, it is assumed that a lacquer base type finish has been utilized. The lacquer finish will have little or no chemical resistant qualities, and is readily attacked by most solvents. Due to the possibility of spillage and the corrosive atmosphere in laboratories, it is almost imperative that the casework be finished with a chemical resistant varnish.

2. Almost without exception, the drawers in this casework had extremely poor dovetail joints. From the appearance of the joints, it appears that evidently this company's

dovetail machine is not functioning properly, and the wood had been torn around the dovetails. The resultant joints between the drawer fronts, backs and sides were very poor, since it was necessary that these joints be filled with a plastic wood. This is a very serious aspect; due to the softness of the plastic wood, it is felt that these joints will fail after very little usage.

3. The sample submitted by this manufacturer to the Division of Purchase and Contracts had a cupboard door fabricated with a five-ply construction, with a hardwood core. The doors furnished on this project are of a three-ply constuction with the core of a relatively soft particle board. This is a very unacceptable door construction, and not only are the doors subject to excessive warpage, but due to the softness of the core, it is felt that the hinge screws will work loose in a period of time.

4. Relatively poor workmanship was evidenced both in the casework, and in the installation of the equipment. The poor workmanship in the casework could be noted on several of the sliding door cases, drawers and cabinet interiors. The poor installation workmanship could be noted primarily by the manner in which the base mould had been installed, and in the manner in which the cupboard sink bottom boards were cut to accommodate plumbing.

5. Although not covered by your specifications, it is a common practice in the laboratory equipment industry to make a splined joint where two pieces of top material join. None of the tops on this project were splined, and in several instances the joint between the tops had not even been filled with an adhesive. This practice will permit all spillage to run down into the casework.

6. The plywood selection on this project was relatively poor. This is especially true on several of the cupboard doors, where very dark plywoods were mixed with lighter woods.

7. In general, the inexperience of this manufacturer in the fabrication of equipment that will withstand the abuse to which institutional furniture is subjected, and in particular science equipment, has resulted in a number of major and minor discrepancies that will seriously affect the durability of the over-all installation. We would classify this equipment on the grade of good millwork, but certainly not equal to the laboratory equipment casework being manufactured by the recognized manufacturers in the laboratory equipment industry.

City of Centerville
(*National Aluminum Corporation—B*)

According to Jack West, the City of Centerville had been a constant friend and customer of National Aluminum for 20 to 25 years.

In 1951, Jack sold the City of Centerville three primary substation structures for their electrical distribution system. At that time National Aluminum handled most of the orders from the City of Centerville directly rather than through a distributor. Due to a change in company policy, the City of Centerville account had been turned over to Cranston Corporation, the local distributor. At that time the City and Cranston got along very well, and Na-

tional Aluminum continued to get its fair share of the business.[1]

In 1954, a gentleman who was engaged in a supply business in the City of Centerville was elected mayor. It occurred to him that he should expand his business and include in it electrical conductor and wiring products of the type manufactured by National Aluminum. He asked for the National Aluminum line. After much deliberation, Jack's sales manager instructed him to tell the mayor that his company had a contract with Cranston Corporation which read to the effect that Cranston Corporation would represent it exclusively in the state.[2] Jack explained to him that Cranston

◆ SOURCE: Reprinted by permission from Bennett and Reeves, *op. cit.* Case prepared by Walter Gorman.

[1] "Fair Share" of the market meant about 25 percent which was the national share.
[2] Deliberation consisted of an examination of the market area which determined that the particular area would not support two agencies.

Corporation had been the agent of National Aluminum for many years and that Cranston had always done a good job for National Aluminum. He explained further that there were other sufficient reasons to cause the company to reach a decision that it could not offer its line of equipment to him on an agency basis.

This refusal thoroughly vexed the mayor of Centerville, and he let Jack know in no uncertain terms that he felt that Cranston Corporation had undermined him and that Cranston had been the cause of his not getting the contract.

The City of Centerville stopped buying National Aluminum products through the Cranston Corporation. When National Aluminum Supply, a totally-owned subsidiary of the National Aluminum Corporation, opened in an adjoining state, the City of Centerville began purchasing National Aluminum products through this new distributor.

The City of Centerville was reassigned to Jack West as a customer to be handled through the Cranston Corporation. He made an initial call on the City of Centerville and found the mayor and other key personnel to be still very friendly toward National Aluminum and him personally. He was of the opinion that he could get business from the City of Centerville. However, in order for him to get credit for the business on his quota, it would be necessary for the business to be handled through the Cranston Corporation rather than through National Aluminum Supply.

QUESTIONS

1. Explain the relationship of the National Aluminum salesman to the distributor?
2. What is the role of the salesman in selling industrial goods?
3. Was National Aluminum correct in refusing to give the mayor of Centerville a contract?
4. Should Jack West try to take the Centerville business away from the subsidiary?

Cranston Corporation
(*National Aluminum Corporation—C*)

Cranston Corporation was the exclusive distributor handling regular accounts in the dis-

♦ SOURCE: Reprinted by permission from Bennett and Reeves, *op. cit.* Case prepared by Walter Gorman.

trict of the National Aluminum Corporation. It was essential that Jack West, the missionary sales engineer for the National Aluminum Corporation, become first completely acquainted with the distributor's sales setup, and second gain the complete confidence of the personnel in the Cranston Corporation organization. The Cranston Corporation had in the field eight salesmen who were directed by the electrical equipment sales manager. It was determined in the beginning that Jack would call on the customers of the company only with the electrical equipment sales manager or one of the eight salesmen. Over the first eight months of Jack West's new assignment, he had gained the confidence of the individual salesmen and the management personnel of the Cranston Corporation by traveling with these men and living with them week in and week out.

Cranston Corporation had one territory covered by a young man who was very aggressive and described as "sharp." He was extremely eager to learn about the products manufactured by the National Aluminum Corporation. One of the main responsibilities of Jack West was to educate the individual salesman on the products and services offered by National Aluminum Corporation. This particular young man by the name of James Jackson had applied himself vigorously to the proposition of learning everything that he could about National Aluminum Corporation's products and people. He had been selected to take a two-week refresher course in the National Aluminum Corporation's headquarters and had applied himself very well. He made a good impression on the National Aluminum Corporation people and came back highly complimented as being a young agency salesman destined to succeed.

James Jackson's territory had been one of the outcast type of territories in which Cranston Corporation had not received very much business over the previous ten years. James Jackson had gone in and built up the accounts and had started getting orders. In Jack West's travels with James Jackson, he found that the customers liked him and were, in some cases, very anxious to see him succeed.

James Jackson with Jack West's help had no problem in building up this territory.

The only problem which existed was that James Jackson was the type of young man who had not matured personally. He was in constant marital trouble and was on the verge of divorce. He had received several citations for reckless driving and speeding. He was the type of young man known as a "hard worker and hard player." The only thing wrong was that his playing was getting in the way of his productive capacity.

James had confided in Jack with respect to his troubles. Part of this was by accident due to the fact that they lived together in motels. James received calls from his lawyer, and he discussed these matters in the presence of Jack. Jack West had not tried to inject himself into the personal life of James Jackson.

Jack West did not consider the direction of the Cranston Corporation to be his responsibility and he wished to stay out of this area as far as possible. However, as personal matters affect the over-all business, then Jack West felt that he had some obligation to discuss the matter with Cranston management. Jack West found himself in the position of knowing more about James Jackson's personal operation than did the Cranston management. James had asked Jack not to report him to Cranston Corporation's management. Jack had explained to James that this put him in a very bad situation, and therefore Jack had tried to help James with his problems in an effort to get him straightened out. It was evident, however, that James would not accept the good advice and was not straightening out. James Jackson was still getting business and the volume was still high. Jack believed that this business was in danger of drying up due to James Jackson's extracurricular activities.

QUESTION

1. How should the salesman handle this situation? What are the problems?

Ace Paint and Varnish Company
(*Dow Chemical Company—B*)

On October 10, Ralph Davis, coatings salesman assigned to the San Francisco Sales Office, made his regular monthly call on the Ace Paint and Varnish Company of San Francisco, California.

◆ SOURCE: Reprinted by permission from Bennett and Reeves, *op. cit.*

The Ace Paint and Varnish Company was a manufacturer of paints and varnishes with an annual sales volume of $25,000,000. The company employed 5,000 people. Ace purchased latexes, toluene, and Dowicides from Dow at an annual volume of approximately $75,000. Dow's Great Western Division purchased about $8,000 of Ace paint in the last fiscal year for the plant at Pittsburgh.

Lester M. Surl was the purchasing agent for Ace. He was young, very smart, and got along well with Davis. He did not like to be put on the spot, but was willing to face facts. He was motivated in purchasing by price, quality, and service.

Robert G. Basil, vice-president and in charge of Ace's purchasing, was a tough man. He used any method to do business and wasn't afraid to step on anyone's toes.

Soon after Davis presented his card to the receptionist, he was called into the purchasing agent's office. Before Davis could say anything, Surl said, "We've got a problem; and unless you can come up with the right answer, Ace is going to reduce all purchases from Dow." Surl said he was bringing the matter up at the insistence of Mr. Basil, but did not agree with the reasoning behind it. Surl explained that Basil felt that for some reason or other, Ace had not been able to sell the other divisions of Dow. Further, the purchases by Ace from Dow had been very high in the past, but business from the Great Western Division was not large enough to make it attractive to continue purchasing from Dow at the same level. Basil wanted Davis to do something about increasing Ace's sales to Dow. If nothing was done, Ace would purchase a greater portion of its raw materials elsewhere, rather than from Dow.

QUESTIONS

1. What is the problem in this case?
2. What can the salesman do about the problem?
3. Is reciprocity ethical?
4. Is reciprocity legal?
5. When prices and quality are equal, how can reciprocity be avoided?

PART
VI

Research in Selling and Sales Management

Generally, research in personal selling has been lacking. Reports of three studies are included in this section in the hope that it will provide more thought and direction for future research efforts.

In one of the first mathematically-oriented studies within selling, Professor Nordin, in "Spatial Allocation of Selling Expense," suggests a method for such allocation. A comparison with others that have been used for the same purpose is provided.

Shuchman, in the following article, notes that the use of Markov Chain Theory can give sales management several types of information. An application of this theory is provided in detail.

The final article, by Hughes, is an essay "describing an experiment that measured a central aspect of effective salesmanship, namely the prospective buyer's changes in awareness and attitudes as he is exposed to personal selling."

Spatial Allocation of Selling Expense

J. A. NORDIN

The purpose of this paper is to suggest a method for the allocation of selling effort among sales districts, and to compare it with others that have been used for the same purpose.[1]

The actions the business planner may take can be divided into groups among which there are complicated interactions. One convenient division is into actions pertaining to selling, production, and maintenance of inventory, respectively. If a new plan of selling is contemplated, the planner must realize that there will be repercussions through the rearrangement of sales in time. This change must be met by alterations in the schedule of production, or inventory, or both.

There are also intertemporal relations among selling activities and sales. In general the variations in sales of two time intervals can be expected to be inverse, since some of the added sales of the first of the two periods may be simply anticipated replacement. However, sales effort can be devoted either to fitting the presentation of product to the customer, or to fitting the customer to the type of product the salesman wants him to buy. If money is spent in making a very careful study of the requirements of the customer, the increased purchasing of the first interval may be matched by later reorders induced by the satisfaction given by the original goods. On the other hand, if the

selling effort is directed toward selling the customer unsuitable goods, he may later refuse to buy at all.

There are also many ways of expending a given total amount of selling expense within a given period. For instance, the planner must allocate money between advertising and hiring salesmen. If the marginal results of a given period could be divorced from the marginal effects of all other periods, he ought to equate marginal receipts per dollar of selling effort of all kinds for the given period.

Such is the general picture. But analysis from this point must be partial, since the interrelations are so complex that the analyst would be lost in tracing the results of a given course of action. The statement of the requirements of an equilibrium situation is not difficult, but it is couched in terms of criteria not available to the planner. Therefore, it is desirable to concentrate on just one detail, under assumptions sufficiently simple so that the nature of a particular adjustment can be studied. Then, when the planner is confronted with a particular situation, he will have a guide for action after he shall have noted the way in which the factors to be held constant in this analysis affect the results suggested.

Concretely the following assumptions will be made to bring into relief the problem of allocation of selling effort among districts:

1. There is one product, sold in two districts.
2. The time during which the planner expects to be interested in the affairs of his business is to be thought of as divided into a number of periods. He is to plan for the first period, on the supposition that the sales of

◆ SOURCE: Reprinted by permission from *Journal of Marketing* (National Quarterly Publication of the American Marketing Association), Vol. 7, No. 3, January 1943, pp. 210–219.

[1] For criticism and suggestions, I am indebted to Professor H. R. Wellman and Professor G. M. Kuznets of the Giannini Foundation.

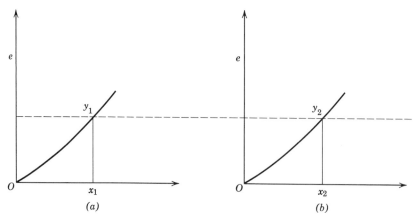

Figure 1

every subsequent period are independent of the sales within the period selected for analysis.

3. The analysis will be carried on as though the facts of the period just concluded were expected to continue unchanged. Although the planner will expect certain changes in the external conditions to which his efforts are subject, it will be convenient to use the past facts as a background. In many cases there will be no other important guide, and in any case anticipations can easily be substituted for the past facts as guides for action.

4. In order that the substitutions among selling plans may be isolated, assume that all adjustments are subject to the condition that they shall leave unchanged the total selling expense in the two districts taken together. Thus, the object of making adjustments is to maximize the total sales of the two districts taken together, while maintaining the constant total of selling expense.[2]

5. The only form of selling expense is the salaries of salesmen.[3] Salary per man is constant, and the salesmen are completely interchangeable. Moreover, whichever district a man works in, his personal efficiency is the same. That is, his response to each of a sufficiently wide range of stimuli is the same as that of each other salesman, and is independ-

[2] The analysis could have been carried out on the assumption that the total sales are to be maintained constant while the total selling expense is to be reduced. The rationale of adjustment is essentially the same in both cases.
[3] Thus only variable selling cost is considered. However, this is not a serious departure from reality, since there is a wide range of selling problems in which no discontinuation of branch offices is contemplated.

ent of the selection of the district in which he works.

6. Although actually the determination of a price policy is a pressing problem, it is separable from the allocation of selling effort given the price. Therefore, let it be assumed that the price is known, and is the same for both the districts.

7. The problem of deciding the optimum selling expense for the given period will not be considered. It will be assumed in accordance with assumption (4) above that the sole task is that of increasing sales without increasing the total selling cost of the two districts. While such a movement seems desirable, consideration of the whole plan of operation might dictate an increase in selling expense in each of the districts.

On the basis of the assumptions made, how shall the planner proceed to realize the goal that has been suggested? Consider first the analysis appropriate if the planner knows all the relevant facts about both districts. It may be expected that each additional unit of product sold in a given district will encounter greater sales resistance than the last preceding unit, so that the sale of each additional unit will require an increasing amount of effort. This in turn means that the marginal selling expense entailed by the selling of additional units is an increasing function of the total amount of sales. In Figure 1, the amount of product is shown on each horizontal axis, and the marginal selling expense on each vertical axis. Since only variable costs are considered, the curves go through the origin.

In Figure 1A each ordinate represents the cost of making an addition to the total sales.

At the origin there are no sales; at x_1 the total variable selling expense is the sum of all the ordinates between $x_1 = 0$ and $x_1 = x_1$. If y_1 can be written as $f(x_1)$ the sum of the selling expenses can conveniently be written as

$$\int_0^{x_1} f(x_1) \, dx_1.^4$$

Similarly, if $y_2 = g(x_2)$, the variable selling expenses entailed by the sale of x_2 units in district 2 is

$$\int_0^{x_2} g(x_2) \, dx_2.$$

The planner's task is thus seen to be that of maximizing $x_1 + x_2$, while preserving the condition

$$\int_0^{x_1} f(x_1) \, dx_1 + \int_0^{x_2} g(x_2) \, dx_2 = K,$$

where K is the total selling expense available for allocation between the two districts.

Assume that the planner knows the exact shapes of the marginal selling expense curves; that is, knows their equations. Then the desired adjustment is achieved by equating the marginal selling expenses in the two districts. The reason why this is so may be indicated as follows: $y_1 = y_2$. Let a "unit" of product be thought of as the width of an ordinate. If a unit is added to the sales in district one, the marginal sales expense required will be greater than y_1, since added units are sold under conditions of diminishing returns to selling. It would not do to take the unit from district two, for doing so would only free the selling expense $y_2 = y_1$. The same considerations disqualify the reverse movement, and therefore the adjustment that equates y_1 and y_2 maximizes the sales to be made with the constant selling expense.[5]

If y_1 is less than y_2, selling effort ought to be diverted from district two to district one. If both curves are continuous—that is, contain no breaks—then just to the right of the present y_1 there is an ordinate whose height is between y_1 and y_2.[6] If the selling expense

y_2 is transferred, one "unit" of product is lost in district two, but y_2 more than suffices to sell the next unit to the right of the point x_1.

Three observations are appropriate in this connection. In the first place, the records of the planner run not in terms of marginal selling expense, but rather in terms of the past variable selling expense totals and past sales. Some way must be found to use the existing records.

In the second place, the analysis to this point does not point out a course of action. If the marginal selling expense is greater in district two than in district one, the planner will know that he ought to spend more money in district one. But how much more? There will be some shift slight enough so that the planner will be sure it will not make y_1 greater than y_2; but is the planner condemned to groping even if he has the complete factual knowledge supposed?

In the third place, the planner will not know the marginal selling expense functions exactly; it will be necessary for him to approximate them. In what follows it is shown that an approximation making no unreasonable demands on the planner will indicate at once a selling expense division that will approximate the optimum.

The nature of the required approximation is this: the planner must assume $y_1 = a \cdot x_1^\alpha$ and $y_2 = b \cdot x_2^\alpha$, where a and b need not be assumed, but α must be assumed. In view of the kind of approximations that must constantly be used in the conduct of a modern business, this seems a rather modest demand. Probably in most cases assuming that the curves are straight lines will suffice to bring about an improvement. If there is reason to think that the rate of increase of marginal selling effort increases as x increases, α can be made slightly greater than one, and the opposite adjustment can be made if the planner thinks that the increase in the difficulty of selling decreses as selling proceeds. Past records will help in the determination of a and b, as appears below. By varying them is it possible to show two rather different curves, even though α is the same for both.

Even without determining a and b, the planner can decide whether his allocation is the optimum. Let P_1 be the total variable selling

<hr />

[4] This expression is simply shorthand for the area under the marginal selling expense curve from $x_1 = 0$ to $x_1 = x_1$.

[5] A proof of this statement is contained in the Mathematical Appendix.

[6] y_2 is equal to some height on the y_1 curve, and between two points on a continuous curve there is always another point. Since the marginal selling

expense curves rise throughout, this third point will be higher than y_1 but not as high as y_2.

expense in district one, and P_2 the corresponding figure for district two.

$$P_1 = a \cdot \int_0^{x_1} x_1{}^\alpha dx_1 = \frac{a \cdot x_1{}^{\alpha+1}}{\alpha + 1} \cdot \quad (1)$$

The ratio of P_1 to x_1 is

$$\frac{a \cdot x_1{}^\alpha}{\alpha + 1} = \frac{y_1}{\alpha + 1} \cdot \quad (2)$$

This is the ratio of variable selling expenses to sales for the first district, and the same ratio for the second district is $y_2/\alpha + 1$. Thus if $P_1/x_1 = P_2/x_2$, $y_1 = y_2$, and the desired balance has been attained. The planner ought to strive for an adjustment in which the ratio of variable selling expense to sales is the same for both districts. If the ratio is low for one district, effort ought to be diverted to that district.

But how much money ought to be so diverted? Fortunately, the record for any representative recent period can be used to determine exactly the optimum allocation, subject to the degree of error introduced by using α. Suppose that during a given preceding period, say the last one, the actual variable selling expense in district one was $P_1{}'$, and the sales $x_1{}'$. From (2) above,

$$P_1{}'/x_1{}' = \frac{y_1{}'}{\alpha + 1}. \text{ Therefore, } y_1{}' = (\alpha + 1) \cdot \frac{P_1{}'}{x_1{}'}.$$

If the results of the given past period are not thought to deviate significantly from the equation $y_1 = a \cdot x_1{}^\alpha$, then

$$a \cdot x_1{}'^\alpha = (\alpha + 1) \cdot \frac{P_1{}'}{x_1},$$

or

$$a = \frac{(\alpha + 1) \cdot P_1{}'}{x_1{}'^{\alpha+1}},$$

and similarly

$$b = \frac{(\alpha + 1) \cdot P_2{}'}{x_2{}'^{\alpha+1}} \cdot$$

If it is not thought advisable to place so much confidence in the representativeness of the results of any one past period, several periods can be used, and the values of a and b respectively can be averaged over all the trials.[7]

The last stage in the approximation process has now been reached. In equilibrium, $y_1 = y_2$, so that

$$ax_1{}^\alpha = bx_2{}^\alpha. \quad (3)$$

From (1) above,

$$P_1 = \frac{ax_1{}^{\alpha+1}}{\alpha + 1},$$

and a similar calculation would show that

$$P_2 = \frac{bx_2{}^{\alpha+1}}{\alpha + 1} \cdot K = P_1 + P_2.$$

Thus K can be expressed in terms of x_1 and x_2. But from (3) above, x_1 can be expressed in terms of x_2. Thus it is possible to solve for x_2. Since P_2 is in terms of x_2, it is finally possible to determine that

$$P_2 = \frac{K}{(b/a)^{1/\alpha} + 1} \cdot \quad (4)$$

Similarly, the correct value of P_1 is

$$\frac{K}{(a/b)^{1/\alpha} + 1} \cdot$$

If the selling expense is allocated in accordance with (4), the maximum possible sales total is approximated to a degree determined by the appropriateness of α. It is possible to set up equations for some cases in which the two marginal selling expense curves may be different types of function. However, the simplicity of equation (4) is helpful; moreover, the planner's information will frequently be so meager that the use of complicated functions would be over-precise.

A summary of the method advocated:

1. Estimate α in the marginal selling expense curves $y_1 = ax_1{}^\alpha$ for district one and $y_2 = bx_2{}^\alpha$ for district two. This step amounts to deciding on the general nature of the curves. In many cases it will be sufficient to let $\alpha = 1$, so that the marginal selling expense curves will be thought of as straight lines.

2. Select some representative past period, whose total variable selling expenses are $P_1{}'$ for district one and $P_2{}'$ for district two. Divide each P' by the sales for its district. Multiply the quotient by $\alpha + 1$. The result is the marginal selling effort for the given district in the given past period. Since one y and one x are known for each district, $y_1 = ax_1{}^\alpha$ and $y_2 = bx_2{}^\alpha$ can be solved for a and b respectively.

3. When a, b, and α have been determined, the proper amounts to spend on selling in the two districts are respectively

$$P_1 = \frac{K}{(a/b)^{1/\alpha} + 1}$$

and

$$P_2 = \frac{K}{(b/a)^{1/\alpha} + 1} \cdot$$

4. This allocation approximates the optimum. That is, it gives approximately the maxi-

---

[7] This qualification represents a deviation from the strict application of assumption 3 above.

mum possible total sales with the constant total of variable selling expense. The inaccuracy of the method is due to the fact that α is not likely to be a perfectly appropriate exponent for both equations, and to the unpredictable change of underlying forces over time.

Consider next a method that has gained considerable support as a theoretically correct manner of solving the same problem. It has been stated that selling effort ought to be allocated among districts in accordance with the distribution of "potential" for the commodity. In general terms potential has been defined as the capacity of a market to buy a commodity, and it has been stated that the definition may be framed in terms of either dollars or physical units.[8]

For the purpose of the allocation problem, Professor L. O. Brown considers the sales potential the maximum amount that the firm in question could possibly sell in a given district.[9] For the same problem, Dr. Donald R. G. Cowan deals with a consumption potential, which does not make adjustments for the state of competition.[10] The first thing to be noted is

that neither of these leading exponents of the use of potential defines potential with reference to price. Since price is assumed constant for the present analysis, it is not necessary to introduce a separate convention; but it is clear that the concept of capacity to buy in terms of physical units depends on the price. The capacity to buy in terms of dollar sales depends on the price also, unless it be assumed that the elasticity of demand for the product is unity throughout.

In the second place, the amount that can be sold, with or without adjustment for the effect of competition, depends on the amount of selling effort. Perhaps no violence will be done to the meanings of Brown and Cowan if the potential, $\bar{s}$, is defined as $\lim_{E \to \infty} s(E)$, where E is the total variable selling expense in a district, and s is the total volume of sales in that district.

Both Brown and Cowan support the idea that balance has been achieved, with respect to the allocation of selling effort, when $E_1/\bar{s}_1 = E_2/\bar{s}_2$.[11] Consider first the version in which the potential has been adjusted for the state of competition. In Figure 2, E represents the total variable selling effort, so that the e of Figure 1 is the first derivative of E with respect to the amount of sales. As before, s is the total sales in a district. Figure 2 has been drawn so that $E_1/\bar{s}_1 = E_2/\bar{s}_2$, i.e., so that the condition proposed by Brown is satisfied. The "$\bar{s}$"s are limits, so they must be approached by the sales curves; but this fact gives no information about the slope of either curve at any point, except that both slopes will be positive.

It has been shown above that the balance condition is equivalent to the condition $e_1 = e_2$.[12] In the case of Figure 2 the slopes of the two curves ought to be equal. However, there is no reason to think that they would be equal, nor can the true state of affairs be regarded as

[8] L. O. Brown, "Quantitative Market Analysis: Scope and Use," *Harvard Business Review* 15 No. 2, p. 236, n. 4. "Sales or Market Potential—an estimate of the capacity of any market to buy a commodity."

[9] L. O. Brown, "Comments on 'The Distribution of Selling Effort Among Geographical Areas' by H. R. Wellman," *Journal of Marketing* 3 No. 4, p. 395. Professor Brown asserts that Professor Wellman errs in neglecting the fact that potential ought to be used in the sense suggested in the text.

[10] Dr. Cowan enumerates four factors that determine the index of possible sales: (1) consumption data, such as the age and income distributions of the population, (2) competition, (3) effort factors, such as the quantity of advertising and salesmanship, (4) price. (Donald R. G. Cowan, *Sales Analysis from the Management Standpoint*, Chicago, 1938, University of Chicago Press, p. 86.) He then asks which of the factors ought to be considered in connection with the problem, and decides that only the first ought. "These estimates of consumption may be used by management in appraising its present distribution of selling and advertising effort, and in apportioning that effort in closer relationship to market possibilities" (p. 89). ". . . Comparisons with a consumption index imply that, if necessary, effort could be redistributed, while comparisons with a sales index infer that the regional amounts of effort are fixed and only their qualitative application may be improved" (p. 95). Elsewhere Dr. Cowan makes a statement that is difficult to connect with his previous analysis: "Apparently . . . the allocation

of effort in proportion to market possibilities is quite sound, but whether the amount of allocation is profitable or not is a matter for management to decide." ("In Answer to Professor Wellman," *Journal of Marketing* 3 No. 3, p. 241.) Does this statement mean more than that the theoretical results must be checked with experience, since they are based on necessarily partial analysis?

[11] L. O. Brown, "Quantitative Market Analysis: Scope and Uses," *Harvard Business Review* 15 No. 2, p. 236. Donald R. G. Cowan, *Sales Analysis from the Management Standpoint*, Chicago, 1938, University of Chicago Press, pp. 86 ff.

[12] See above, p. 316.

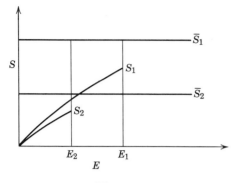

Figure 2

being approximated by the condition of equality.

The choice between the "potential" method and that suggested above is based partly on this highly significant fact. The latter yields an approximate solution, whereas there is no predictable relation between the optimum solution and that indicated by the use of the ratio of sales to potential.

But there is another weighty reason for deciding against the method proposed by Brown. It is impossible to find a numerical measure of the ability of a particular concern to sell its goods in any district, even if potential can be defined rigorously. Consider the method Brown advocates for determining potential. The actual sales in both districts for a number of past periods are correlated with other series that appear to have logical connections with the making of sales. A regression equation is set up to "predict" the past sales from a knowledge of the past values of the related series. The exact nature of the regression is determined by the condition that it must minimize deviations of the "predictions" from the actual sales.[13] Suppose that the sales series in question is that of low-priced cars. Suppose further that a regression equation can be found to enable the analyst to predict past sales almost perfectly from a knowledge of past

labor income, when the labor income series is lagged by six months. If the planner knows the total labor income for the present six months' period he can predict the car sales for the next six months. If there is no lag in the relation, the situation is not so favorable, for the car sales cannot be predicted until the planner shall know the labor income for the same period. However, even in this case the method may be useful if for any reason labor income can be predicted more easily than car sales. The sales history of just one firm can be used if the firm has wide market coverage and intensive exploitation.[14]

Consider the philosophy of this method. The income represents the external situation in which sales effort is put to work. The relation between past incomes and past sales is determined by the nature and extent of the selling effort. If the selling effort is essentially unchanged in the future, then the relation between income and sales will be essentially unchanged. Consequently when the external cause (this period's income) is known, the planner can predict the next period's sales, on the assumption that the nature and extent of selling effort remain unchanged.

As a part of a budget procedure this system has much merit. It is recognized practice to avoid the assumption that there will be a sudden change in the effectiveness of selling. But what of the usefulness of the procedure for the present purpose? Is the objective that of predicting actual sales in each district, assuming no change in the nature and extent of selling effort? Manifestly it is not. Potential is the amount that could be sold with a very great expenditure of selling effort, and presumably with a high level of efficiency. Thus the nature and extent of the present plan would have to be modified very drastically—at least it would be wrong to assume a continuation of present selling arrangements. If labor income remains constant, then, according to Brown's method, potential equals past sales, no matter how serious the previous selling plan's deficiencies.[15]

[13] "The first step in using multiple correlation for estimating sales potential is to set up a control series in the form of sales data for a number of markets." ("Quantitative Market Analysis-Multiple Correlation: Accuracy of the Methods," *Harvard Business Review* 16 No. 1, p. 62.) "The use of the multiple correlation method of quantitative analysis rests on the fundamental assumption that the only scientific basis for measuring market power is our knowledge of the amount of power which markets have shown in the past under differing conditions." (*Ibid.*, p. 63.)

[14] *Ibid.*, p. 62.
[15] Brown does suggest that small variations between actual and potential are to be expected on the basis of imperfections of allocations of selling effort and imperfections of selling actions. But this statement merely sets up a "blind bogey" for the minimization process. Moreover, what is the assurance that the errors of allocation of resources are small?

Brown obtains only relative measures of potential

Thus the correlation procedure is strictly worthless for the determination of potential.

The foregoing examination of what seems to be the most widely used method of determining potential indicates that it is impossible to arrive at a meaningful figure. This fact militates powerfully against the use of potential in allocating sales effort between districts.

If potential is considered as making no allowance for competitive conditions, the situation is still more serious. When the condition suggested by Cowan has been attained, too much money may have been spent in a district where very little money would have sufficed to make practically all the sales that could be made. On the other hand, the market may be so antagonistic to the products of the given company that it ought not to be invaded at all. The analysis of potential without reference to competition will not disclose either of these conditions.

Certain statements by Brown indicate that he has another way of allocating resources. "After the sales potential has been set, there arises a fundamental question of policy . . . Should a company concentrate its efforts in the markets in which it has shown the poorest performance relative to potential?" [16] This question suggests that Brown is considering an equilibrium adjustment in which the ratio of sales to potential is the same for both districts. He illustrates the proposal by comparing for two districts the penetration ratios, which he has defined as $s/\bar{s}$, where s is the actual sales and $\bar{s}$ the potential that allows for the effect of competition.[17] In enumerating the "qualifications" to be borne in mind when using quantitative market analysis, he concludes that the comparison of the penetration ratios does not lead to the determination of a policy. The ratio

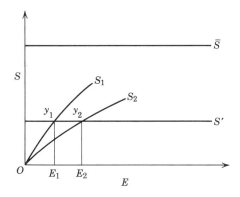

Figure 3

may be high because the particular market is adapted to the sale of the product of a given concern, and perhaps that market ought to be exploited more fully before a more resistant market is even entered.[18]

In Figure 3, the use of the axes is the same as that in Figure 2. Suppose that the potential is $\bar{s}$, the same in both districts. Let Os_1 be the sales curve for district one, and Os_2 for district two. If the amount of sales is s' in each of the districts, then there is balance, according to the method considered by Brown. However, the fact that the limit of both curves is $\bar{s}$ does not indicate anything about the rates at which the curves approach their limits. The slopes at the points y_1 and y_2 may differ widely. If they do, the system is out of balance, according to the analysis developed above. Yet consideration of the penetration ratio cannot reveal that fact.[19]

(*op. cit.*, p. 68). This is strange, since his own definition of potential mentions the *capacity* of a market, not the relative capacity. It is noteworthy that if the absolute values of sales were used, and absolute values of potentials were to be estimated, a peculiar restriction would have to be imposed on the multiple correlation process. Since potential is the maximum amount that can be sold in a district, actual sales must not be greater than estimated sales. If the standard error of estimate or the average deviation were to be minimized, there would be both positive and negative deviations from expectation; Brown's analysis would be subject to the restriction that the estimate would always have to be at least equal to be observed.

[16] *Market Research and Analysis,* New York, 1937, Ronald Press, p. 419.

[17] *Ibid.,* p. 412.

[18] Perhaps it is unfair to attribute the method to Professor Brown. However, his readers seem to be invited to infer that (1) the penetration ratio is a proper tool for analyzing the allocation of resources, and (2) little confidence can be placed in the results secured by its use.

[19] Professor H. R. Wellman repeated in substance Brown's own statement that no decision could be based on the use of the penetration ratio. (H. R. Wellman, "The Distribution of Selling Effort Among Geographical Areas," *Journal of Marketing* 3 No. 4, p. 230.) Brown replied that Wellman had ignored the fact that the potential ought to be adjusted for the effect of competitive conditions. However, it is clear from what has been said in the text above that this answer is inadequate. Cowan answered the statement of Wellman by writing: "The question of varying penetration of the market mentioned by Professor Wellman is not a serious complication. Those with marketing experience know that if salesmen or advertising are withdrawn following market penetration, it is not long before that penetration ceases." ("In

In summary, the best method examined for allocating selling expense among districts attempts to equate the ratio of variable selling cost to sales, for both districts. Facts possessed by the sales manager suffice for approximating the allocation that will bring about the maximum sales total with a given variable expense. Formula (4) above makes the use of the method relatively simple, although the algebra used in establishing the formula may seem abstract. The chief rival method requires that selling expense be made proportional to the maximum amount of sales the given competitor can hope to make in a district. In the first place, this method does not yield an approximation, for it rests on the assumption that the slopes of the marginal selling expense curves are equal at points determined by the establishment of the proportionality condition, although nothing in the nature of the curves or of the adjustment indicates any predictable relation between the slopes at the selected points. In the second place, there is reason to doubt that a useful meaning can be attached to the term "potential."

If potential is interpreted without reference to the strength of competition, the method is worse still. Finally, the penetration ratio is useless in allocating selling expense. The method of equating the ratio of variable sales cost to sales appears to give a reasonable approximation to the solution of one of the partial problems of management.

Answer to Professor Wellman," *Journal of Marketing* 3 No. 3, p. 241.) Clearly this observation is irrelevant to Wellman's objection. The question involved is this: What would happen to total sales if some of the selling effort were taken from one district and used in another district?

MATHEMATICAL APPENDIX

Using the notation of the text, let

$$F(x_1, x_2) = \int_0^{x_1} f(x_1) dx_1$$

$$+ \int_0^{x_2} g(x_2) dx_2 - K = 0. \quad (1)$$

The sum $x_1 + x_2$ is to be maximized, so it is appropriate to maximize

$$h(x_1, x_2, \lambda) = x_1 + x_2 + \lambda \cdot F(x_1, x_2) \quad (2)$$

where λ is a LaGrange multiplier. Differentiating (2) partially,

$$\frac{\partial h}{\partial x_1} = 1 + \lambda \cdot \frac{\partial F}{\partial x_1} = 0 \quad (3)$$

and

$$\frac{\partial h}{\partial x_2} = 1 + \lambda \cdot \frac{\partial F}{\partial x_2} = 0 \quad (4)$$

$$\frac{\partial F}{\partial x_1} = f(x_1), \quad (5)$$

and

$$\frac{\partial F}{\partial x_2} = g(x_2). \quad (6)$$

Except in the trivial case in which there is no selling expense in the first district, $f(x_1) \neq 0$, and so $\partial F/\partial x_1 \neq 0$. Therefore, it is possible to obtain from (3),

$$\lambda = -\frac{1}{\partial F/\partial x_1}.$$

When this expression is substituted in (4),

$$0 = 1 - \frac{\partial F/\partial x_2}{\partial F/\partial x_1}, \quad \text{or} \quad \frac{\partial F}{\partial x_1} = \frac{\partial F}{\partial x_2}.$$

Thus from (5) and (6) above, $f(x_1) = g(x_2)$, or, finally, $y_1 = y_2$.

The Planning and Control of Personal Selling Effort Directed at New Account Acquisition: A Markovian Analysis

ABRAHAM SHUCHMAN

In a paper published in 1962, Cyert, Davidson, and Thompson [4:287–303] provided a transition probability Markov Chain description of accounts receivable behavior. They noted that the techniques of their work "are obviously applicable to many other kinds of problems." The problems they had in mind, however, were those that "can be characterized as 'inventory' problems in which we consider items produced and stored in inventory [which] eventually . . . leave the inventory either by being 'sold' or by 'spoiling.'" This paper describes a possible application to a problem which is not at all related to the storage and spoilage or obsolescence of commodities.

One of the important unsolved problems of sales management is the allocation of salesmen's calls among accounts and prospects. In the main, this problem is now solved almost entirely by heuristic and intuitive methods, if any attempt at solution is made at all [6:96–98; 3]. More rational and formal methods have been applied in at least three cases, but each of these has involved a strictly ad hoc attack on the problem [7; 2; 1]. Moreover, two of these cases were concerned only with the allocation of sales calls among existing accounts

◆ SOURCE: Reprinted by permission from *New Research in Marketing* (Institute of Business and Economic Research, University of California, Berkeley, 1965), by the Regents of the University of California, Berkeley, pp. 111–120.

while the third was concerned only with allocation between existing accounts and prospective customers. No reports have dealt with the problem of allocation within the prospect group. The structure of this problem suggests that the methods employed by Cyert, Davidson, and Thompson may provide a rational basis for planning and controlling the personal selling effort devoted to the opening of new accounts.

THE MODEL

Consider a salesman's list of prospects at time i. The prospects can be segregated then, or at any subsequent time, into $n + 1$ categories. For a group of prospects at time i, let:

G_0 = number of prospects on the list who have not yet been called on;

G_1 = number of prospects on the list who have been called on only once;

G_j = number of prospects on the list who have been called on j times;

.
.
.

G_{n-1} = number of prospects on the list who have been called on $n - 1$ times;

G_n = number of prospects on the list who have been called on n times.

We are thus classifying prospects into "age" groupings based upon the number of calls that have been made. G_n, the last category, depends on some rule for dropping a prospect from the list. It is the cut-off point beyond which policy dictates that there shall be no further investment of effort directed toward converting the prospect to customer status.

Now consider a prospect on the list as of time i at the next later time period $i + 1$. At time $i + 1$, the prospect can be classified in two ways, according to the age or call frequency category from which he came and according to the "age" category in which he now is. In general, we will let G_{jk} equal the number of prospects in category k at time $i + 1$ who came from category j at time i.

This two-way classification cannot account at time $i + 1$, however, for all the prospects at time i. A complete accounting requires two additional age categories. One, denoted by subscript s, corresponds to a prospect who has been sold and hence has been transferred from the prospect list to a customer list. The second, denoted by the subscript d, corresponds to a prospect who has been eliminated from the salesman's list because he is no longer regarded as being worth further effort.

With this system of classification, prospects can be described, in general, by an $n + 3$ square matrix G, which we will call the "prospect matrix." In this prospect matrix the individual entries G_{jk} represent the number of prospects in "age" category j at time i who have moved to age category k at time $i + 1$.

$$G = \begin{bmatrix} G_{ss} & G_{sd} & \cdots & G_{sk} & \cdots & G_{sn} \\ G_{ds} & G_{dd} & \cdots & G_{dk} & \cdots & G_{dn} \\ \cdots & \cdots & \cdot & \cdot\cdot & \cdot & \cdots \\ G_{js} & G_{jd} & \cdots & G_{jk} & \cdots & G_{jn} \\ \cdots & \cdots & \cdot & \cdot\cdot & \cdot & \cdots \\ G_{ns} & G_{nd} & \cdots & G_{nk} & \cdots & G_{nn} \end{bmatrix}$$

From this $n + 3$ prospect matrix, G, it is possible to develop an $n + 3$ matrix of transition probabilities, P. The entries in P measure the likelihood that prospects in a particular category at time i will move to another category during the time interval $(i + 1) - i$. It is assumed that this transition probability is measured over the same period of time that is used for the classification of the prospects.

The transition probability, P_{jk}, is defined, in general, as the probability that a prospect in age category j at time i will move to age category k by time $i + 1$. In terms of the entries of the prospect matrix, G_{jk}, the transition probabilities are defined by:

$$P_{jk} = \frac{G_{jk}}{\sum\limits_{s}^{n} G_{jk}} \quad (k = s, d, 0, 1, \cdots, n)$$

The model assumes that the matrix of transition probabilities is constant over time and independent of the initial age distribution of the prospects. To be sure, this condition is not likely to be perfect, for seasonal and cyclical changes in transition probabilities may occur. Whether changes constitute a gross and heavily damaging violation of the assumption of constant transition probabilities depends on their magnitude. Before the model is utilized, actual changes in transition probabilities and their effect on the results generated by the model should be investigated carefully.

The model also assumes that all prospects on a list are of equal value to the salesman (or firm). This assumption is patently invalid, but the implied difficulty can be handled by stratifying prospects on the basis of potential purchases and estimating the limiting probabilities for each stratum separately.

Finally, it is assumed that each prospect on the salesman's list is visited once and only once during each period. This assumption, too, is troublesome. For salesmen of many different kinds of goods and services, however, if a period is defined as a relatively short time interval—say one or two weeks—the assumption should conform very closely to reality. Nevertheless, the assumption does limit applicability of the model.

With these assumptions in view, we may now complete the description of the model. What remains to be noted is that the matrix of transition probabilities has several special characteristics. First, any prospect entering the s (sold) category cannot move to another category since he ceases to be a prospect. He remains in the sold category. From this it follows that

$$P_{ss} = 1.00; P_{sd} = 0; P_{s0} = 0; P_{s1} = 0;$$
$$\cdots; P_{sk} = 0; P_{sn} = 0.$$

Similarly, any prospect reaching the d (dropped) category remains there; he, too, is no longer regarded as a prospect. As a consequence

$$P_{ds} = 0; P_{dd} = 1.00; P_{d0} = 0; P_{d1} = 0;$$
$$\cdots; P_{dk} = 0; \cdots; P_{dn} = 0.$$

Finally, the third assumption signifies that a prospect in age category j at time i cannot move beyond age category $j + 1$ at time i

+ 1. Hence all entries in the diagonals of the transition matrix above the one beginning with P_{12} are zero. Thus, taken together, the special characteristics of the matrix of transition probabilities establish that many of the probabilities in the matrix are zero.

By this time the reader has probably recognized that the model comprises a Markov Chain process with $n + 3$ states and a transition matrix given by P. Moreover, the process is a Markov Chain with two absorbing states. Both the sold and dropped categories are absorbing states and it is possible to reach one of these two absorbing states from every non-absorbing state. Thus, the theorems and corollaries of Markov Chain Theory, both those that are generally known and those derived by Cyert, Davidson, and Thompson, can be applied to generate results which, appropriately interpreted, provide information useful in planning and controlling sales effort directed toward new account acquisition.

More specifically, the use of Markov Chain Theory can give sales management the following information: (1) the proportion of prospects in each age category at a given time i which should end up as sold and the proportion which should end up as dropped; (2) the composition of each salesman's work load in terms of the distribution of prospects by age category; (3) the efficiency in terms of prospects converted or number of sales made to new accounts of various policies with respect to the cut-off point or maximum number of calls to be made on any individual prospect.

APPLICATION OF MARKOV CHAIN THEORY

Proofs of the elements of Markov Chain Theory which will be utilized are available either in textbooks [5] or in the article by Cyert, Davidson, and Thompson [4]. As we have seen, the matrix of transition probabilities P is square and of the order $n + 3$. This matrix may be recast into canonical form by reordering the states (age categories) so that the first is the absorbing state s, the second is the absorbing state d, and the remaining states, all transient, are the age categories 0, 1, . . . , n. We may then partition this matrix P so that we have

$$P = \frac{I \mid 0}{R \mid Q}$$

where I is the 2×2 identity matrix, 0 is a $2 \times n + 1$ zero matrix; R is an $n + 1 \times 2$ matrix; and Q is an $n + 1 \times n + 1$ matrix. Since it always exists, it is then possible to obtain the matrix

$$N = (I - Q)^{-1} = I + Q + Q^2 + Q^3 + \cdots + Q^n,$$

which is known as the fundamental matrix of the absorbing Markov Chain. Each of the rows of this matrix N gives the proportion of prospects in the stipulated state (age category) at the beginning of the period which will receive 0, 1, 2, . . . n calls. If we total the first row of this matrix and divide the resulting sum into the number of prospects the salesman is to contact during each period, we obtain the average number of new prospects entering the salesman's list each period.

Having obtained the matrix N, we may now form the $n + 1 \times 2$ matrix NR. This matrix furnishes estimates of the probabilities of absorption in each of the absorbing states s and d. The entries in the first column of NR represent the probabilities of converting to customer status the prospects in the corresponding age categories; the entries in the second column represent the probabilities of dropping the prospects in the corresponding age categories.

In order to exercise rational control over salesmen's new account development activities, estimates are also needed of the total number of conversions that can be expected in each period and the variance of this estimate. Markov Chain Theory provides this information. Suppose that the number of prospects in each age category at time i is given by the $n + 1$ component vector

$$G_i = [G_{i0}, G_{i1}, \cdots, G_{in}].$$

Then the entries of the two-component vector $G_i NR$ give the expected number of prospects sold and the expected number dropped from the total in age distribution vector, G_i.

But before we can obtain the variances of these sold and dropped expectancies we must define an additional matrix and some additional matrix operations. If we let g be the total number of prospects included in the vector G_i, then $\pi = (1/g)G_i$ is a vector whose components represent the proportion of total prospects in each age category. It should be noted that vector π has non-negative components with sum to one; hence, it is a probability vector. Moreover, as the movement of each prospect may be assumed to be independent of that of any other prospect, vector π may be regarded as the initial vector for the Markov Chain. And if Z is any matrix, we define Z_{sq} as the matrix obtained by squaring each entry in Z, and Z_{rt} as the matrix obtained by taking the square root of each entry in Z. Using these definitions, we then find that the variances of number of prospects sold and number of prospects dropped are given by the components of

$$Z = g[\pi NR - (\pi NR)_{sq}]$$

and the components of Z_{rt} give the standard deviations of these same numbers.

We have to this point taken the age distribution of prospects as given and fixed. In each period, however, some prospects are sold and some are dropped. To replace them, the salesman adds new prospects to his list. Thus the age distribution of the salesman's prospect list varies from period to period, making it impossible to establish a value for new accounts obtained which could serve as a standard of performance over time and greatly complicating control over the process of new account development. If we assume, however, that the number of prospects added to the salesman's list each period is precisely equal to the number sold and dropped, we know from Markov Chain Theory that after some determinate and finite number of periods an age distribution of prospects will arise which will persist thereafter. This persisting distribution is the *steady-state* age distribution of prospects. For the next step in our analysis, we therefore need to determine the number of prospects in each age category in the steady state together with the variances of these numbers, and the expected numbers of prospects sold and dropped in each period after the steady-state distribution has been reached and the variances of these expectancies.

component column vector with all components equal to one. Then, utilizing these definitions, we have the following: First, the components of vector CN give the number of prospects in each age category in the steady-state while the variances of these numbers are given by the formula

$$V = c[\eta N - \sum_{k=0}^{\infty} (\eta Q^k)_{sq}],$$

and the standard deviations are given by V_{rt}. Second, the number CN gives the total number of prospects on the salesman's list in the steady state and the variance of this number can be obtained from

$$v = c[\eta N\xi - \sum_{k=0}^{\infty} (\eta Q^k \xi)_{sq}],$$

while the standard deviation is v_{rt}. Third, the two-component vector CNR gives steady-state values for the number of prospects sold and the number dropped in each time period, while

$$W = c[\eta NR - \sum_{k=0}^{\infty} (\eta Q^k R)_{sq}]$$

gives the variances of these values and W_{rt} gives the standard deviations. Finally, CN^2R gives the expected number of prospects on a given period's list who will eventually be converted to customers as well as the expected number on this list who will eventually be dropped. The variance of these numbers is given by $t[\pi NR - (\pi NR)_{sq}]$, where $t = CN\xi$ and $\pi = (1/t)CN$. The variance formulas for age distribution, total number of prospects, and prospects sold and dropped cited in this paragraph involve unsummed series. As Cyert, Davidson, and Thompson note, lower-bound estimates of these variances can be obtained by taking a few terms of each series. Upper-bound estimates can be secured from these formulas

$$V \leq c[\eta N - \eta_{sq}N^*], \text{ where } N^* = (I - Q_{sq})^{-1};$$
$$v \leq V\xi \leq c[\eta N - \eta_{sq}N^*]\xi; \ W \leq c[\eta NR - \eta_{sq}N^*R_{sq}].$$

Suppose that a number c of new prospects are added to the salesman's list each period and that we represent the age distribution of these prospects by the vector:

$$C = [C_0, C_1, \cdots, C_n],$$

where every component except C_0 is zero. In addition, let us define the vector $\eta = (1/c)C$. This vector, n, is a probability vector and can be regarded as the initial vector of the Markov Chain. Finally, let us define vector ξ as an n-

USING THE RESULTS IN PLANNING AND CONTROL

The model which has been developed describes the behavior of a salesman's prospects. We have seen that, given a matrix of transition probabilities and a vector of new prospects, it is possible to generate these results: (1) estimates of the number of prospects sold and the number dropped by age categories; (2) an estimate of the total number of prospects who will be sold each period; (3) an estimate of the number of prospects at any given time who will eventually be converted to customers; (4) the steady-state age distribution of the prospects; (5) variances for the estimates in (2), (3), and (4).

These results constitute a foundation for much more rational planning and control of the new business activities of a sales force than has heretofore been available. Let us examine first the potential usefulness of our results in controlling the new account development activities of the sales force. Given the expected value and variance of conversions (prospects sold) in each period for each salesman, the sales manager possesses a standard for evaluating the performance of his men. With this information, the sales manager is in a position to apply well-known control chart procedures to detect performance which deviates significantly from standard and therefore requires investigation.

Similarly, the expected values and variances of the number of prospects in each age category represent a standard which may be used in controlling the number and composition of calls the salesman makes. This information, too, enables the sales manager to apply control chart procedures and to detect significant deviations. It may also have diagnostic utility, for it may point to the cause of a typical performance in effecting conversions. At the very least, however, the detection of significant deviations from the "norm" may serve to cue the sales manager to the need for remedial action.

From the point of view of planning, the important question is: How much effort should be invested in a prospect? It would be highly beneficial if a policy could stipulate the maximum number of calls that should be made. This policy should lead to maximization of the number of conversions made per period for a fixed total number of calls by the salesman. This optimum policy can be identified through

use of the expected value of conversions in the steady-state which is obtained by means of the analysis described above. Given the total number of salesman calls per period, we can determine both the age distribution of his prospects and the expected number of conversions in the steady-state. Both the age distribution and expected number of conversions vary with the cut-off point for calls. It is clearly possible, however, to compute the expected number of conversions for each feasible cut-off point; and by comparing all these expectancies we can identify the cut-off that, on the average, produces the maximum number of conversions. Thus by comparison of the expected outcomes of various policies the optimum policy can be determined.

In all, then, the analysis presented here may be useful to sales managers in three ways. First, it may be used in conjunction with control chart procedures to generate signals needed for control over the process of new account development. Second, when performance falls below standard, the results may be used as a diagnostic tool. And, finally, the results may be used to determine that call frequency policy which optimizes the allocation of effort. Lack of this kind of information has heretofore greatly impeded rational decision making in the area of new account development through personal selling.

SAMPLE APPLICATION

The computations involved in and the nature of the information obtained from a Markovian analysis of call frequency are elaborated below.

Suppose we have examined the call reports of a salesman who has been contacting 30 prospects per week. We have found that he never calls on one prospect more than six times ($n = 6$) and that his calls are always confined to one in each week. The transition matrix for this salesman is:

		s	d	0	1	2	3	4	5	6
	s	1	0	0	0	0	0	0	0	0
	d	0	1	0	0	0	0	0	0	0
	0	0	0	0	1	0	0	0	0	0
	1	.05	.05	0	0	.9	0	0	0	0
$P =$	2	.10	.10	0	0	0	.8	0	0	0
	3	.15	.05	0	0	0	0	.8	0	0
	4	.15	.05	0	0	0	0	0	.8	0
	5	.10	.10	0	0	0	0	0	0	.8
	6	.05	.95	0	0	0	0	0	0	0

where the states (age categories) have already been arranged so that the absorbing states appear first. The matrix is, thus, in canonical form. Inspection of this matrix, P, indicates that:

$$
R = \begin{matrix} 0 & 0 \\ .05 & .05 \\ .10 & .10 \\ .15 & .05 \\ .15 & .05 \\ .10 & .10 \\ .05 & .95 \end{matrix} \quad \text{and } Q = \begin{matrix} 0 & 1 & 0 & 0 & 0 & 0 & 0 \\ 0 & 0 & .9 & 0 & 0 & 0 & 0 \\ 0 & 0 & 0 & .8 & 0 & 0 & 0 \\ 0 & 0 & 0 & 0 & .8 & 0 & 0 \\ 0 & 0 & 0 & 0 & 0 & .8 & 0 \\ 0 & 0 & 0 & 0 & 0 & 0 & .8 \\ 0 & 0 & 0 & 0 & 0 & 0 & 0 \end{matrix}
$$

Having identified matrix, Q, we can now obtain the fundamental matrix:

$$
(I\text{-}Q)^{-1} = N = \begin{matrix} 1 & 1 & .9 & .72 & .576 & .4608 & .36864 \\ 0 & 1 & .9 & .72 & .576 & .4608 & .36864 \\ 0 & 0 & 1 & .8 & .64 & .512 & .4096 \\ 0 & 0 & 0 & 1 & .8 & .64 & .512 \\ 0 & 0 & 0 & 0 & 1 & .8 & .64 \\ 0 & 0 & 0 & 0 & 0 & 1 & .8 \\ 0 & 0 & 0 & 0 & 0 & 0 & 1 \end{matrix}
$$

Then summing across the top row of fundamental matrix N and dividing the number so obtained, 5.02544, into the total number of prospects seen each period, 30, we get the average number of prospects entering the salesman's list in each period, 5.97. Thus, the steady-state vector of new prospects, C, becomes:

$$C = [5.97, 0, 0, 0, 0, 0, 0].$$

It follows from this that the number of prospects in each age category in the steady-state is:

$$
CN = [5.97, 0, 0, 0, 0, 0, 0] \begin{matrix} 1 & 1 & .9 & .72 & .576 & .4608 & .36864 \\ 0 & 1 & .9 & .72 & .576 & .4608 & .36864 \\ 0 & 0 & 1 & .8 & .64 & .512 & .4096 \\ 0 & 0 & 0 & 1 & .8 & .64 & .512 \\ 0 & 0 & 0 & 0 & 1 & .8 & .64 \\ 0 & 0 & 0 & 0 & 0 & 1 & .8 \\ 0 & 0 & 0 & 0 & 0 & 0 & 1 \end{matrix}
$$

$$ = [5.970, 5.970, 5.373, 4.298, 3.439, 2.751, 2.201].$$

Using this result to calculate CNR, we obtain:

$$
CNR = [5.970, 5.970, 5.373, 4.298, 3.439, 2.751] \begin{matrix} 0 & 0 \\ .05 & .05 \\ .10 & .10 \\ .15 & .05 \\ .15 & .05 \\ .10 & .10 \\ .05 & .95 \end{matrix} = [2.381, 3.589]
$$

which represents the expected number of prospects sold and the expected number dropped during each period in the steady-state.

In order to determine whether a cut-off policy of six calls is optimal (maximizes the number of conversions per period), we use the same procedure as above to calculate CNR for other policies in the neighborhood of six calls. Assuming that the proportion of conversions on the seventh call is identical to the proportion on the sixth call, the results obtained are:

Cut-off policy	Number of prospects entering list each period	Expected number of conversions per period	Expected number of drops per period
4 calls	7.149	2.391	4.758
5 calls	6.442	2.451	3.991
6 calls (Calculated above)	5.970	2.381	3.589
7 calls	5.639	2.322	3.317

These results indicate that the optimum cut-off point is five calls and that in the long run this policy will produce three more conversions per year than will a four-call policy and three-and-one-half more conversions per year than will a six-call policy. If the maximum number of conversions per period is desired, the five-call policy should be instituted.

Having selected the five-call policy, we can now combine the information about the expected number of conversions per period, which we already have, with information about the variance or standard deviation of this number. Thus we can set up a control mechanism. To obtain the variance, we compute

$$N^* = (I - Q_{sq})^{-1} = \begin{bmatrix} 1 & 1 & .81 & .5184 & .33178 & .11234 \\ 0 & 1 & .81 & .5184 & .33178 & .11234 \\ 0 & 0 & 1 & .64 & .4096 & .26214 \\ 0 & 0 & 0 & 1 & .64 & .4096 \\ 0 & 0 & 0 & 0 & 1 & .64 \\ 0 & 0 & 0 & 0 & 0 & 1 \end{bmatrix}$$

$$\eta = (1, 0, 0, 0, 0, 0)$$

$$NR = \begin{bmatrix} 1 & 1 & .9 & .72 & .576 & .4608 \\ 0 & 1 & .9 & .72 & .576 & .4608 \\ 0 & 0 & 1 & .8 & .64 & .512 \\ 0 & 0 & 0 & 1 & .8 & .64 \\ 0 & 0 & 0 & 0 & 1 & .8 \\ 0 & 0 & 0 & 0 & 0 & 1 \end{bmatrix} \begin{bmatrix} 0 & 0 \\ .05 & .05 \\ .10 & .10 \\ .15 & .05 \\ .15 & .05 \\ .10 & .90 \end{bmatrix} = \begin{bmatrix} .38048 & .61952 \\ .38048 & .61952 \\ .36720 & .63270 \\ .33400 & .66600 \\ .23000 & .77000 \\ .10000 & .90000 \end{bmatrix}$$

$$\eta NR = (1, 0, 0, 0, 0, 0) \begin{bmatrix} .38048 & .61952 \\ .38048 & .61952 \\ .36720 & .63270 \\ .33400 & .66600 \\ .23000 & .77000 \\ .10000 & .90000 \end{bmatrix} = [.38048, .61952]$$

$$\eta_{sq} N^* = (1, 0, 0, 0, 0, 0) \begin{bmatrix} 1 & 1 & .81 & .5184 & .33178 & .11234 \\ 0 & 1 & .81 & .5184 & .33178 & .11234 \\ 0 & 0 & 1 & .64 & .4096 & .26214 \\ 0 & 0 & 0 & 1 & .64 & .4096 \\ 0 & 0 & 0 & 0 & 1 & .64 \\ 0 & 0 & 0 & 0 & 0 & 1 \end{bmatrix}$$

$$= [1, 1, .81, .5184, .33178, .11234].$$

$$\eta_{sq} N^* R_{sq} = [1, 1, .81, .5184, .33178, .11234] \begin{bmatrix} 0 & 0 \\ .0025 & .0025 \\ .0100 & .0100 \\ .0225 & .0025 \\ .0225 & .0025 \\ .0100 & .8100 \end{bmatrix}$$

$$= [.0309, .1112].$$

The variance of the components of CNR (expected values of conversions and drops) may then be estimated by the following upper bounds:

$$W \leq c\,[\eta NR - \eta_{sq}' N^* R_{sq}]$$
$$\leq 6.442\,[(.38048, .61952) - (.0309, .1112)]$$
$$= (2.25, 3.27).$$

The corresponding standard deviations are 1.5 and 1.8 for number of conversions and number of drops respectively.

The analysis has afforded an optimum call policy (five calls), the expected number of conversions per period under this policy (2.451), and the standard deviation of conversions per period (1.5). Clearly, we are in position to apply standard control chart procedures and in this way maintain close surveillance over the process of new account development.

REFERENCES CITED

1. Ackoff, R. L. "Determining Optimum Allocation of Sales Effort," *Proceedings, Operations Research Conference, September 29–30, 1955.* Society for Advancement of Management.
2. Brown, A. A., Hulsurt, F. T., and Kettelle, J. D. "A Study of Sales Operations," *Operations Research,* 4, No. 3, June 1956.
3. Canfield, Bertrand R. *Sales Administration; Principles and Problems,* 4th ed. Englewood Cliffs, N. J.: Prentice-Hall, 1961.
4. Cyert, R. M., Davidson, H. J., and Thompson, G. I. "Estimation of the Allowance for Doubtful Accounts by Markov Chains," *Management Science,* 8, No. 3, April 1962.
5. Kemeny, J. G., and Snell, L. J. *Finite Markov Chains.* New York: Van Nostrand, 1959
6. Loen, R. O. "How Many Sales Calls Is Any Given Account Worth?," *Industrial Marketing,* January 1962.
7. Magee, J. F. "The Effect of Promotional Effort on Sales," *Journal of the Operations Society of America,* 1, No. 2, February 1953.

The Measurement of Changes in Attitude Induced by Personal Selling[1]

G. DAVID HUGHES

The degree to which a discipline has matured is determined by the precision with which it can observe and measure the variables with which it deals. In marketing, personal selling is of great importance; yet hitherto little has been done to measure the components of a sale. This essay makes a contribution to such a study by describing an experiment that measured a central aspect of effective salesmanship, namely the prospective buyer's changes in awareness and attitudes as he is exposed to personal selling. These measurements were then used to establish interim goals for salesmen, and to identify weakness in the marketing mix.

What is the contribution of personal selling to the buying process?

How can selling goals be identified with this process?

Answers to these questions are of interest to marketing theorists and marketing managers alike. The study described here attempts to answer these questions.

But first we must identify the basic elements of the buying process in order to make it possible for us even to raise the questions. The question to be answered immediately is. "What *is* the buying process?" But we cannot stop here. We must determine what properties are inherent in this process and how they can best be observed and measured.

ELEMENTS OF THE BUYING PROCESS

In identifying the elements of the buying process, we discover a very simple thing: that the interaction between the salesman and the buyer is a learning process for both. The salesman learns the needs of the buyer and then thinks of how his products can meet these needs. On the other hand, the buyer who attempts to make a rational decision has a substantial learning process. This can be classified into three stages. Initially, he must learn the present state of his needs, then he must consider his present means for meeting these needs, and finally he must weigh the merits of the product being offered against other alternatives. In short, the rational buying process is hard work.

Of these two distinct learning processes, the buyer's is the more important because it lies at the very heart of a sale. If the salesman is to achieve his ultimate goal, i.e., a sale, he must direct this learning process. Sales management texts wrongly focus on the *salesman's* learning process when they recommend that salesmen be evaluated by testing their knowledge of products or applications. This is not to say there is no correlation between the sales-

◆ SOURCE: Reprinted by permission from *Toward Scientific Marketing*, edited by Stephen A. Greyser, Proceedings of the Winter Conference of the American Marketing Association, December 1963, pp. 175–185.

[1] The experiment described here is presented fully in the author's dissertation, "The Measurement of Changes in Attitude Induced by Personal Selling," (unpublished Ph.D. dissertation, University of Pennsylvania, 1963). Resources for field work and stenographic services were made available by the Graduate School of Business and Public Administration, Cornell University. Tabulating and computing facilities were donated by the Cornell Computing Center. The author gratefully acknowledges these resources.

men's knowledge and their sales, for there certainly is. But salesmen's knowledge may not lead to a sale for reasons such as the salesman's inability to communicate his knowledge, or factors beyond his control, e.g., weaknesses in the product or promotional mix, the strong efforts of competitors, and so forth. Clearly, the correlation between a salesman's knowledge and his sales would be greater than it is, if more emphasis were placed on his ability to communicate, and if weaknesses in the product and promotional mix were eliminated.

Since the buyer's learning process lies at the heart of many of the problems of sales management, it is important that we not exclude it from analysis by focusing on the salesman instead of the buyer. Psychologists tell us that the learning process is composed of changes in an individual's awareness and attitudes. If this be so, and if the interaction of the seller and the buyer is one of learning, we might deduce that the buying process consists of a change in a buyer's awareness and attitudes toward his present needs, his present means for meeting these needs, and the products or services being offered. In order to determine whether or not a salesman could bring about a measurable change in prospects' awareness and attitudes towards the components of a purchase, it was necessary to conduct a controlled experiment, a description of which is the subject of the remainder of this paper.

Inasmuch as awareness and attitudes are key concepts in this paper, they must be defined precisely. It will be easier to define awareness if an attitude is defined first. Guilford describes the latter as ". . . a personal disposition common to individuals, but possessed to different degrees, which impels them to react to objects, situations or propositions in ways that can be called favorable or unfavorable." [2] The phrase *level of attitude* in this study was represented by the median attitude of the respondents within the group studied. Changes in attitude were limited to changes in direction, i.e., the sign of the change. For later analysis, these were expressed as a percentage of the sample making such a change.

Attitudes were measured with scaling devices, which will be described in further detail shortly. Each scale was equipped with a phrase such as "No information," for those un-

informed respondents who refused to express an attitude about the concept being measured. If after promotional stimuli, a respondent was willing to express an attitude, he was classified as having gained *awareness.* Thus, *awareness* was said to be present when a prospect had a sufficient amount of information about a concept, a company, or a product, to have an opinion about it. No attempt was made to identify degrees of awareness. The phrase *level of awareness* represented the number of respondents, expressed as a percentage of the total sample, who had reached a state of awareness about a particular concept, or variety of companies and their products. Thus, awareness and attitudes were measured with one scaling device.

Measuring Awareness and Attitudes

One of the greatest problems in the measurement of attitudes is choosing from a wide range of scaling devices which have been developed by psychologists. In this study a rational choice of a scaling device rested on the device's ability to meet four criteria. Expressed in question form, did the device have: (1) an acceptable scaling rationale? (2) ease of construction? (3) a reasonable interview length? and (4) an ability to measure changes in attitudes? A brief explanation of each criterion is in order.

1. A scaling technique was considered consistent with scaling rationale when it placed the respondents' attitudes along a psychological continuum. This requirement was necessary in order to measure a change in attitude.

2. Ease of construction was necessary in order to minimize the costs of implementing the techniques developed, so that large-scale commercial application would be feasible. Precisely because the buying process is composed of a large number of attitudes, the cost of individual scale construction should be kept at a minimum.

3. The scale selected had to suggest the construction of a questionnaire that could be completed during a short interview and also have the potential of being used as a mail questionnaire. This criterion not only reduced the cost of measuring attitudes, but also elicited respondents' cooperation; so necessary since repeated measurements were required in order to detect a change in attitude.

[2] Joy P. Guilford, *Psychometric Methods* (New York: McGraw-Hill Book Co., Inc., 1954), pp. 456-7.

4. The technique had to demonstrate, on the basis of previous studies, that it had sufficient sensitivity to detect a change in attitude. The use of a scale that had not demonstrated this ability could lead to an indefinite conclusion, since, if changes were not detected, the fault could be either the lack of sufficient stimuli, or the lack of sensitivity of the scaling device.

With the needs of this study in mind, a search of the scaling literature yielded three techniques that met the necessary criteria. They were the Thurstone, the semantic differential, and the check-list scales.[3] A priori, there was no basis for the selection of a single scale, so the three techniques were included in the questionnaire. This inclusion necessarily brought forth the question, "What is the best measuring device for this problem?" The data from this study were used to answer this adjunct question.

THE STUDY ITSELF

Identifying Relevant Attitudes

The adding machine buying process was selected for study because this product is common to most businesses, thus simplifying the sampling procedure. In identifying the attitudes that were important to the purchase of an adding machine, an extensive preliminary investigation was conducted. The investigation included an examination of both the advertising literature of twelve adding machine manufacturers, and the sales manuals of three manufacturers, as well as unstructured interviews with salesmen and present users of adding machines. At the conclusion of this investigation, 67 variables, selected for their relevance to the buying process, were included in the questionnaire. These attitudes were classified as follows: (1) the prospect's sense of his need for a new adding machine, (2) his image of the adding machine companies, (3) his image of adding machine salesmen in general, (4) his evaluation of adding machine features, and (5) his attitudes toward economic conditions that may affect the purchase of such equipment. The economic variables were eliminated during the analysis stage for it became apparent that they had no influence on these small

purchases. Thus, the number of variables to be examined was reduced to 59.

Gathering and Analyzing the Data

When the questionnaire was submitted to a pretest, several weaknesses were revealed. Modifications were made in some of the adjectives in the semantic differential. A more important modification was the provision for respondents who lacked information and therefore were not in a position to express an attitude. A forced choice scale, such as the Thurstone or the semantic differential, makes no provision for conditions of "No information," but instead instructs respondents to check the midpoint of the scale if they consider the concept irrelevant.[4] This modification made it possible to measure awareness and attitudes with a single scaling device, for it was assumed that respondents who moved from "No information" to a point along the scale after the salesmen called, had been made *aware* by the sales stimulus. The ability to distinguish between changes in awareness and changes in attitudes proved valuable during the analysis of the data.

The experimental design for this study consisted of an experimental and a control group, each containing 85 randomly selected persons who represented business firms that could be prospects for an adding machine. If the effect of the first measurement on the respondents' perception of subsequent stimuli is important, an additional control must be added.

The steps of the experiment were as follows:

1. The awareness and attitudes of both groups were measured.

2. The salesmen from the cooperating company for this experiment called on the respondents in the experimental group. During this call they left literature describing a new adding machine and reported that they would return in a few weeks to demonstrate it.

The attitudes of both groups were measured for a second time, and the changes in awareness and the direction of the changes in attitudes that had occurred since the first measurement were recorded. After comparing the proportion of respondents who had changed in

[3] For a description of these techniques, see Hughes, *op. cit.*, pp. 13–30.

[4] Charles E. Osgood, George J. Suci, and Percy H. Tannenbaum, *The Measurement of Meaning* (Urbana, Illinois: University of Illinois Press, 1957), p. 83.

the experimental group with that of the control group, it was concluded that *the salesmen had been unable to induce changes* that could be regarded as statistically significant.

3. The next time around, the salesmen demonstrated the equipment. Sales resistance was apparent, for the sample of this test dropped to 33. This smaller sample was used as a basis for analysis because the experiment was designed not to evaluate the salesmen, but to test measuring devices. Had the evaluation of salesmen been the purpose of this study, the sample of 85 would have had to be used, since only this sample would have reflected the salesmen's ability to overcome sales resistance.

The awareness and attitudes of the respondents in both groups were measured for the third and final time. Changes in awareness and the direction of the changes in attitudes since the second measurement were computed. Because changes in attitudes are a complicated process, only the direction of the change and not the extent of the change was examined during the analysis of the data.

4. The proportion of the respondents in both the experimental and control groups who had demonstrated changes in awareness and attitudes were compared. The salesmen were said to have induced the change when the proportion of the respondents in the experimental group who had changed exceeded those in the control group by an amount that was greater than could occur by chance at the .05 level.

The combination of these two calls was considered effective because 24 per cent of the scales detected a change at this .05 level. The answer to the question, "What is the contribution of personal selling to the buying process?" is found in the data dealing with *changes* in awareness and attitudes. From these data we discover that the contribution of personal selling to the buying process is its ability to induce a change in the prospect's awareness and attitudes toward the relevant components of the purchase.

Interim Goals for Personal Selling

To seek information on the second question, "How can selling goals be identified with this process?" we must take a long look at the data concerned with the *levels* of awareness and attitudes. The levels analyzed below were computed from the first measurements of the total sample, i.e., a total of 170 respondents. These measurements were obtained before the experimental group received the first sales stimulus.

Levels of attitudes, it will be recalled, were the median attitudes of the groups being examined. In order to make these levels representative of those encountered by the salesmen, the sample was divided according to the sales territories of the cooperating Company A. These were designated as Cities X, Y, and Z. Within each city, the respondents' levels of attitudes toward Companies A, B, C, and D were compared. These comparisons revealed the favorable and unfavorable corporate images that were unique to individual territories. For example, respondents in City Y had a favorable image of Company A, which was to be expected, inasmuch as the company had a plant there and maintained excellent community relations. However, in City X the respondents did not know that Company A was active in the adding machine field. The sales manager could translate this fact into a personal selling goal by instructing the salesman in City X to "Raise prospects' awareness of our activity in the adding machine field from 45 per cent to 55 per cent within the next three months." Such individual goals should be more stimulating to salesmen than the old familiar one, "Make five more calls per week."

A common way of designating sales territories is by industrial classification. Therefore the 170 respondents were divided into four classifications that included manufacturing, wholesaling-retailing, financial, and the service industries. Among these groups the attitudinal levels toward corporate images and applications for adding machines were compared. This comparison revealed that Company A's image was weak among the respondents in the manufacturing industries, while it was strong in the financial industry. In contrast, the chief competitor, Company B, had a good image in the manufacturing industry, but was second to Company A in the financial industry. The product mix of these companies provided a possible explanation of these contrasting images, since the products of Company A were better suited to the financial industry than those of Company B.

With the respondents still divided according to industrial classifications, their attitudes toward 14 applications for adding machines were compared in order to test the ability of these measuring devices to detect differences among market segments. Based on the respondents' evaluation of the importance of these applications, the market segments classified as manufacturing and wholesaling-retailing were identified as the best prospects for adding machines. Salesmen's observations confirmed this finding.

After examining the results of these comparisons of the *levels* of attitudes, we must conclude that the measuring devices used here demonstrated an ability to detect valid differences among territories. This conclusion permits us to answer the question, "How can selling goals be identified with this process?" by stating that interim selling goals, defined in terms of levels of awareness and attitudes, can be used to relate the selling effort directly to the buying process.

Reallocating Marketing Effort

No attempt was made in the study to use measurements of awareness and attitudes to predict a sale, because the link between a person's attitude and his behavior remains vague. The record of predictions of behavior from attitudinal data has not been impressive. Research examining this link is needed; the buying process might well be a rewarding area in which learning theorists could experiment.

Since we do not have this link between behavior and attitudes, we cannot identify the level of attitudes that are needed to produce a sale. However, a comparison of prospects' levels of attitudes with selected benchmarks can be useful to the location of weak spots in the product and promotional mix. Such a comparison was made during this study by comparing the attitudes of prospects who scaled that they had a low probability of buying an adding machine with those who scaled that they had a high probability of such a purchase. This comparison suggested that some concepts were underpromoted while others were overpromoted. A concept was classified as underpromoted when the attitudes of the low probability prospects were considerably below the high probability prospects. A concept was classified as overpromoted when the attitude of the low probability prospects exceeded those of the high probability prospects. Observing such phenomena, the sales manager may decide to reallocate the effort of personal selling by suggesting changes in the content of the sales message that would result in less emphasis on the overpromoted concepts and more effort on the underpromoted concepts.

APPLICATIONS AND IMPLICATIONS

For Marketing Management

The techniques described here have applications that extend beyond the management of the sales force into the broader problems of marketing management, because the results of this study suggest that the goals of personal selling and advertising can be defined in common and measurable terms. Thus, after experimentation, it would be possible to approximate the least cost combination of these promotional stimuli.

One may ask the question, "Are the techniques used here too expensive for commercial application?" The cogency or applicability of such a question depends upon the nature of the product and the usual buying process that accompanies it. For consumer goods or impulse items, less expensive measurement techniques would probably be sufficient. However, for capital goods with an extended buying process, these measurements would provide a valuable feedback that may not be available from any other source. Under such conditions, the costs of these measurements may seem very reasonable.

The need to minimize the cost of implementing the techniques described here was reflected in the criteria used to select scaling devices. It will be recalled that one criterion required that a scale be completed during short interviews and have the potential of being used in a mail questionnaire. In this experiment, the average length of the interviews was twenty minutes. Since, according to respondents' reports, the scales were easy and interesting to complete, these methods probably could be used in a mail questionnaire. If the interim goals of several departments, e.g., advertising, public relations, and personal selling, were defined in terms of awareness and attitudes, it might be feasible to perform one study that would provide feedback for the entire communication mix, thereby lowering the cost to any one department.

The usefulness of these techniques to marketing management could be enhanced if research were conducted to answer the following questions: (1) *"What attitudes should be examined?"* There is no procedure for the selection of the appropriate attitudes prior to the development of the questionnaire. Judgment must be used to select attitudes from those collected during the extensive preliminary investigation. (2) *"What is the importance of each attitude to the final decision?"* This question must be answered before attitudes can be used to predict behavior. (3) *"How are attitudes related to behavior?"* Until more is known about this relationship, the techniques described here will be limited in their contribution to marketing.

You will remember that the questionnaire was composed of three scaling techniques. Now for a study such as the one just described, was it possible at the completion of the experiment to determine whether the Thurstone, the semantic differential, or the check-list scale was the most suitable? Upon examining the test-retest reliability, the sensitivity, and the respondents' preference for each scale, the Thurstone scale was eliminated from future consideration. The semantic differential had the highest reliability and sensitivity, but it was second to the check-list scale in respondents' preference. However, after respondents used the questionnaire for the third time, they became familiar with the semantic differential and the percentage of them preferring this scale and the check-list scale were almost identical. Thus, the semantic differential would be the first choice of this researcher for future studies of the type described here.

For Marketing Theory

It is hoped that the contribution of this study will extend beyond the problems of sales management and demonstrate the importance of measurement to the development of both management techniques and a science of marketing. With regard to the latter, the history of the sciences has demonstrated that a descriptive discipline must be able to measure its variables with precision before it can develop into a science in the true sense of the term. The procedures used in performing these measurements are arduous tasks, but are justified by the contributions they make to a discipline.

CASES

Wade Weeks, Inc.

Wade Weeks, Inc., is a wholesale tobacco distributor with main offices in Richmond, Virginia. The company has franchises for various brands of cigars which are distributed in North Carolina and a good portion of Virginia and South Carolina. The company has one salesman working in West Virginia and one working in Tennessee, but their territory covers only a small portion of these two states. Thirty-two salesmen represent the company in the North Carolina, South Carolina, and Virginia territory.

Wade Weeks carries a full line of tobacco accessories such as pipes and lighters. They also carry such items as ladies' stockings, inexpensive wrist watches, watchbands, sunglasses, razor blades, and ball point pens. They publish a wholesale catalog containing these and many other items from which customers can order. The only exclusive franchises handled by Wade Weeks are in the cigar lines. In other words, they do not carry any cigar brands which a dealer can purchase from sources other than Wade Weeks. Consequently, large retailers and wholesalers are forced to purchase from Wade Weeks if they want to carry these franchised brands.

Thomas Sutton of Landville, North Carolina, has been employed as a salesman for Wade Weeks for eight years. He has approximately 550 customers in his territory. The principal cities in his territory are: Landville and Bern, which have about 100 customers each; Capital City, with about 75; and Brookgreen, with about 50 customers. Mr. Sutton handles exclusive franchises for seventeen different brands of cigars, but his most important brands are El Producto, Muriel, Blue Ribbon, and Nurica.

He works Monday through Friday of each week and calls on any retailer in his territory whom he believes he can sell in profitable volume, since the selection of prospective firms is left to his discretion. He spends the night at home if he is working a town within twenty miles of Landville; otherwise, he stays at motels and is reimbursed for his expenses. Mr. Sutton submits a weekly expense account for truck expenses and food and lodging while on the road.

In addition to his retail customers, Mr. Sutton calls on all wholesale houses in his territory.

He sell them cigars for four per cent less than the price quoted to most of his retail accounts since wholesalers buy in much larger quantities. These wholesalers sell cigars to some of the small stores which Sutton does not visit and also to some of Sutton's retail accounts when they run out of a particular brand. However, most of the stores Sutton calls on will buy in sufficient quantities to last them until he returns on his next trip since the wholesalers charge ten to fifteen cents more for a box of cigars than does Mr. Sutton.

By calling on fifteen customers a day, it takes Mr. Sutton eight weeks to get around his entire territory. Recently Wade Weeks informed Sutton that he should reduce this time to five weeks. The company gave several reasons for this new requirement.

The first was that the salesman could give the customer better service. The company also felt that by reducing the time to five weeks, Sutton could keep his stock fresher and in general could obtain more business from each customer by calling on them every five weeks.

The company also felt that competition was getting keener and by getting around every five weeks, the salesman would be better equipped to meet competition.

According to Mr. Sutton, he does not have too much trouble with competition now; but he says that he has noticed that it has increased in the last few years. In getting around his territory so seldom, he finds that his competitors move his cigar brands to the back of the dealers' shelves, which, of course, hurts sales of his products. He recognizes that if he got around more often, he could keep his brands in a better position on the dealers' shelves.

Another reason suggested by the company for the change in policy is that most customers charge their purchases instead of paying cash. The company does not send these customers statements, but requires the salesmen to collect for the goods on their next visit to each customer. Initially, the reason behind this was to encourage the customer to buy more merchandise. The reasoning has been that the customer will have sold the merchandise by the time of the second call and thus will have recovered his money from the sale of the product. By getting around the territory three weeks faster, the company feels that it would cut down by three weeks accounts receivable outstanding.

Mr. Sutton is concerned over this new policy. He knows that all of his customers do not give him large orders. Many orders are around $25 to $30, while others run as high as $200. However, he does not want to cut out these smaller accounts, as the manufacturers of the franchised brands insist that he obtain as broad a coverage as possible on their cigar brands in his territory in order to keep the franchise. Also, he fears that his territory might be cut by the company in the future; and, therefore, he will need these smaller accounts to keep his sales volume up. Furthermore, he does not want to cut down on the time which he spends with each customer, since he feels that by doing so, his sales volume will drop. Consequently, he is extremely concerned over what to do about getting around his territory in five weks instead of the eight which it now takes him.

In order to determine what he did with his time during a "routine" day on the road, Sutton hired a neighbor's son, a senior in the School of Business of North State College, to time his activities.

On Thursday, the student spent the day charting the activities of Thomas Sutton. Sutton spent the previous night at home, in order to load his truck since the weekly shipment of merchandise from Richmond, Virginia, was received in Landville every Wednesday afternoon. Exhibit 1 is a summary of the activities noted by the student.

QUESTIONS

1. Do you believe the salesman is managing his own time properly? If you do not, what specific changes would you suggest?
2. Evaluate the reasons given by the home office for reducing the amount of time the salesman uses to cover his territory.
3. What should the salesman do?

EXHIBIT 1

Call No. 1 is a large service center in Landville, N.C. that the customer requested the salesman call on that particular day. He left home at 8:07. Travel time to the first call was 3 minutes.

Time entered establishment	8:10
Conversation	3 min
Write up order and check stock	15 min
Get merchandise from truck	5 min
Sell a sundry item ($3 card of corncob pipes)	3 min
Conversation	3 min
Put up stock	12 min
Total sale—$165.15 Total time	41 min

There was no collection, as this customer mails his check to the company office at the end of the month.

Call No. 2 is a general store in Shower, N.C. Travel time is 66 minutes.

Time entered establishment	9:57
Conversation	1 min
Check store and clean shelf	16 min
Write up order	5 min
Get merchandise from truck	4 min
Put up stock	4 min
Collect for past bill	15 min
Sell a sundry item (tried and failed to sell sunglasses and ballpoint pens on promotion)	8 min
Total sale—$52.32 Total time	53 min

The reason for the long collection time was because the owner was waiting on customers.

Call No. 3 is a service station in Besthaven, N.C. Travel time is 30 minutes.

Time entered establishment	11:20
Collect for past bill	4 min
Write up order	6 min
Sell a sundry item ($12 card of pipes)	4 min
Get merchandise from truck	4 min
Put up stock	2 min
Conversation	3 min
Total sale—$23.36 Total time	23 min

Call No. 4 is a grocery in Besthaven, N.C. Travel time is 5 minutes.

Time entered establishment	11:48
Conversation	2 min
Write up order	4 min
Get merchandise from truck	2 min
Collect for past bill	3 min
Total sale—$29.40 Total time	11 min

He does not have to put the merchandise on the dealer's shelf here.

We left call No. 4 at 11:59 and arrived at a restaurant at 12:05. We ate lunch until 12:54.

Call No. 5 is a cafe in Besthaven, N.C. Travel time is 1 minute from the restaurant where we ate lunch.

Time entered establishment	12:55
Conversation	3 min
Write up order	3 min
Sell a sundry item (took a special order from the catalog which the customer had picked out)	3 min
Picked up merchandise (customer had a broken watch that had to be sent back to the factory for repairs)	4 min
Get merchandise from truck	2 min
Put up stock	2 min
Collect for past bill	4 min

Delivered sales—$21.00   Total time   21 min
Catalog order   39.00

Total sale $60.00

Call No. 6 is a service station in Besthaven, N.C. Travel time is 1 minute.

Time entered establishment	1:17
Wait for owner who was waiting on customers	7 min
Write up order	2 min
Wait for owner who was waiting on customers	4 min
Picked up merchandise (customer had $17.08 in stale cigars)	8 min
Get merchandise from truck	7 min
Put up stock	3 min
Sell a sundry item (took a special order from the catalog which the customer had picked out)	2 min
Collect for past bill	5 min
Sell a sundry item (tried and failed to sell sunglasses on promotion)	4 min

Delivered sales—$34.85   Total time   42 min
Catalog order   16.80

Total sale $51.65

Call No. 7 is a small grocery in Besthaven, N.C. Travel time is 2 minutes. This establishment had gone out of business since the previous time the salesman called. The owner lived across the street from the grocery, and his bill of $36.75 was collected in full in 15 minutes.

Call No. 8 is a drugstore in Besthaven, N.C. Travel time is 4 minutes.

Time entered establishment	2:20
Conversation	3 min
Check stock and clean shelf	3 min
Write up order	8 min
Get merchandise from truck	5 min
Collect for past bill	3 min
Put up stock	19 min
Conversation	1 min

Total sale—$39.94   Total time   42 min

Call No. 9 is a service station in Besthaven, N.C. Travel time is 5 minutes.

Time entered establishment	3:07
Check stock and clean shelf	3 min
Write up order	4 min
Get merchandise from truck	1 min
Put up stock	1 min
Collect for past bill	10 min
Sell a sundry item (sold sunglasses on promotion)	8 min

Delivered sales—$17.60   Total time   27 min
Sunglass order   72.00

Total sale $89.60

Call No. 10 is a wholesaler in Besthaven, N.C. Travel time is 6 minutes. This wholesaler usually sends his order in direct to the home office. However, the salesman calls on him anyway, because he receives credit for orders the wholesaler sends in and this maintains goodwill. He spent 7 minutes here and exchanged four boxes of cigars. No cash was involved.

Call No. 11 is a restaurant/grill in Besthaven, N.C. Travel time is 8 minutes.

Collect for past bill	6 min

Total time 6 min

The owner could not pay his whole bill, and the company has a policy which prohibits the salesman from selling any more merchandise to a customer who cannot pay his entire bill.

Call No. 12 is a service station in Vertigo, N.C. Travel time is 9 minutes.

Time entered establishment	4:10
Conversation	4 min
Collect for past bill	3 min
Write up order	15 min
Get merchandise from truck	9 min
Put up stock	12 min
Sell a sundry item (sold sunglasses on promotion)	4 min
Conversation	4 min

Delivered sales—$127.32   Total time   51 min
Sunglass order   61.00

Total sale $188.32

Call No. 13 is a service station in Capital City, N.C. Travel time is 39 minutes. He took 2 minutes here to get gas.

Time entered establishment	5:42
Conversation	3 min
Write up order	15 min
Get merchandise from truck	13 min
Collect for past bill	2 min
Put up stock	25 min
Conversation	5 min

Total sale $168.97   Total time   63 min

We left Capital City, N.C. and arrived back at Landville, N.C. at 7:15.

Sealright, Incorporated

Sealright, Incorporated, of Tupelo, New York, manufactures and distributes containers for liquid and semi-liquid products. They also manufacture and lease the machines that package products in these containers. Grady Morgan is the Sealright sales representative for Virginia, North Carolina, and South Carolina. His principal customers are dairies that buy containers for the packaging of milk, ice-cream, and milk by-products.

Sealright has recently developed a flat-top liquid container which they believe will "revolutionize" milk packaging. The container differs from containers presently on the market by virtue of its flat-top as opposed to a gable top, and its plastic coating as opposed to wax coating. A general consensus in the container industry indicates that within twelve months plastic will replace wax on all liquid containers.

With this new flat-top, plastic coated container Sealright hopes to gain a marked advantage over its principal competitor, Pure-Pak. The new container will be available in one-half pint and one-quart sizes. One-half gallon containers will be provided by the "twin-pak" arrangement—an arrangement whereby two one-quart containers are sealed together side by side and a handy carrying handle attached. Sealright believes this one-half gallon package will be widely accepted since the two quarts can be separated and opened one at a time, thus enabling one quart to remain sealed and fresh.

Recently, Grady Morgan met with his sales manager, Avery Rodgers, to select the company within Morgan's territory which would first be asked to adopt these new containers. They decided to introduce the new containers to Malon Milk and Ice Cream Company in New Town, North Carolina. They further decided that the visit to Malon Milk be made in July so that they could push for installation prior to school opening, the peak season for dairy products.

Morgan arranged an interview with the following Malon personnel: John L. Dixon, purchasing agent; L. C. Beck, general sales manager; A. M. Stuart, assistant sales manager. At the meeting, Morgan showed samples of the new containers and explained how they differed from his competitor's product. He pointed out the advantages of the flat-top carton in saving storage space and the fact that the containers were plastic coated. He stressed the idea that wax tended to flake off and fall into the milk, causing customer dissatisfaction.

After being assured by Morgan that the new product would be the "future" container and that they would be the first milk processor in the area to have the container, Mr. Beck agreed to submit the idea to the President and Vice-President for approval. Morgan was told that final approval of the containers would probably be made within a week. At this point Morgan assured Mr. Beck that Sealright engineers would be in New Town within seven days after he received the order for the packaging machinery and equipment to be installed. Morgan wrote up the order and indicated that he would return the following Monday to confirm it.

On his return the next week, Morgan was interviewed by Mr. McCutcheon, plant manager; Mr. Baker, plant supervisor; and Mr. Beck. They expressed an interest in obtaining a few more facts about the size and operation of the Sealright packaging machine. After a two-hour session. Morgan was asked to wait about one hour while they had a conference with the President and Vice-President. Shortly, Mr. Beck returned to inform Morgan that they had decided to install the new equipment. He indicated that they had made a decision to use the new containers in fifty per cent of the production of one-half pints of milk and fifty per cent of the production of one-half gallons of milk.

The installation of the new machines was completed by the fifteenth of August. During the installation period, Morgan made numerous visits to the milk company to see that installation was going according to schedule.

The conversion to the new type of container was made on August 18. Morgan paid a visit to Malon Milk Company on August 20 to see how things were going with the new containers. He was informed immediately that the President of the company, Mr. Walker Jenkins, had been trying to get in touch with him for the last two days. Morgan went directly to Mr. Jenkins's office. Mr. Jenkins related the following occurences related to the new containers:

1. The packaging machine had broken down and after a three-hour delay was repaired by the plant electrician.

2. The top of the new carton had a one-half inch indenture. When a drop of water with dust in it settled and dried, it left an ugly dark spot on the top of the white container.

3. When the two quarts were glued together to make one-half gallon, they did not fit tight enough in the crates to hold together until the glue dried, thereby binding them together.

In an attempt to resolve the problems associated with these situations the president noted that he had called a meeting of the following individuals:

L. C. Beck, General Sales Manager
McCutcheon, Plant Manager
John L. Dixon, Purchasing Agent
A local retailer friend.

The president further stated that the meeting was scheduled to take place in about thirty minutes from now, and that, since Morgan would probably have some explaining to do, he should also attend.

Role for Walker Jenkins, President, Malon Milk & Ice Cream Company

You have called a meeting of several people to discuss the problems incurred with the new container.

The problems as you see them are: the packaging equipment must be operative; if the container appears to be dirty the consumer won't buy; if the half-gallon "twin-pak" won't bind together then it doesn't serve as a half-gallon container.

Arising out of these basic problems, are other problems which are proving to be annoying to you. Yesterday a leading retailer called and stated that he was having all sorts of customer complaints regarding the new container and he had only had them in his dairy case for one day. Since he is a good friend of yours, you have invited him to express his problems before some of your key personnel at the meeting this afternoon.

The problems have got to be ironed out today. Either some solutions must be seen or else we will have to return to one hundred per cent production with the old container. You are still unable to understand how this whole ridiculous set of problems could have occurred anyway.

Role for L. C. Beck, General Sales Manager, Malon Milk & Ice Cream Company

You enter this meeting with mixed emotions. You have sent out promotional material, advertised in newspapers and on television, and pointed a good deal of marketing effort to the introduction of this new container. Therefore you hate to see all of this concerted effort and financial outlay go down the drain.

On the other hand, you have received eighteen calls in the last 48 hours regarding complaints and difficulties retail accounts were having with the new container. In addition, your truck drivers on routes were upset about the "twin-pak" arrangement and the additional delivery time required because of them separating.

For an idea which you figured would permit your marketing team to "scoop" other milk companies it has caused a lot of headaches in a short time. You really can't understand how the Sealright people and Mr. McCutcheon could have allowed this situation to happen in the first place.

Role for Avery Rodgers, Sales Manager, Sealright, Incorporated

You have not been back to Malon Milk Company since your visit with Grady Morgan in July. You had assumed from correspondence and progress reports from Morgan that he was squarely on top of the Malon job.

You received a call from your home office last evening to report to Malon Milk Company in New Town, North Carolina, for a meeting this afternoon regarding problems they were having with the new Sealright container.

You have been trying, unsuccessfully, to get in touch with Morgan since last evening.

You have driven all morning to get to this meeting. You are wondering about the nature of the Malon problems. You suspect that they are fairly major since the telegram was marked *urgent*.

Role for John L. Dixon, Purchasing Agent, Malon Milk & Ice Cream Company

The first you heard about these problems with the new container was this morning. You're quite surprised that anything like this could happen, especially since no one had even voiced objections to the partial shift to the new container.

You were so pleased with everyone's favorable inclination toward the new Sealright container, that on several occasions you made a special effort to call to everyone's attention the most favorable supplier relationship you had experienced in past dealings with Sealright. You wish now you hadn't made these statements.

Role for McCutcheon, Plant Manager, Malon Milk & Ice Cream Company

You know that all sorts of problems are happening in regard to this new container. Certainly, it has been a headache, as far as you are concerned for the last two days. You believe that if it hadn't been for the good electrician you recently hired the packaging machine would probably still be inoperative.

You're amazed at the fact that Sealright wasn't able to know about the problem before. At least you didn't sell the old packaging machine. You're satisfied that it can be installed again, even though this will require about six days. You can work the other packaging line on an overtime basis in order to meet production requirements.

Next time you'll be a little more inquisitive when people start talking about new marketing "gimmicks."

Role for Local Retailer

You operate the largest supermarket in New Town. You have been buying Malon milk products for fifteen years. You called Walker Jenkins yesterday to tell him what some of your customers were saying about the dark smudges on the new container and the trouble customers were having by dropping one half of the improperly bound "twin-paks."

You are concerned about your sales of milk dropping off because of this. You are equally concerned with the problems your friend Walker Jenkins must be having. Both of these reasons prompted you to accept Walker's invitations to sit in on this meeting of theirs.

QUESTIONS

1. Supply the "role" for Grady Morgan, Salesman, Sealright, Incorporated.
2. What actions should Grady Morgan take at this meeting?

Best-Yet Cake Mix Company

You are Carl Sanders, a salesman for Best-Yet Cake Mix Company of Richmond, Virginia. Your company manufactures and markets an extensive line of cake mixes, pie-crust and pie-filling mixes, and cookie mixes. Some fifty-eight items are included in your line.

The company operates primarily in states along the Eastern shore of the United States.

While the manufacturing plant is located in Richmond, regional warehouses are maintained in Charlotte, North Carolina, and Atlanta, Georgia. The company owns a fleet of trucks to facilitate transportation of goods to regional warehouses and some large customers. Delivery to smaller accounts is usually handled by common carriers.

You are thirty-two years old and have been employed as a salesman in the Eastern Region of the North Carolina Sales Division for the past two years. Before joining Best-Yet Cake Mix Company, you were employed by your father-in-law in his pickle-processing company in Raleigh, North Carolina, as Personnel Director. Prior to that you attended State University, where you earned an A.B. degree in business administration.

As indicated in the partial organization chart shown in Exhibit 1, you are one of five salesmen in the Eastern Region. Your sales manager is Mr. A. T. Cole who has offices in Raleigh. Your territory includes three counties in Eastern North Carolina. Your job requires you to make regular calls on grocery wholesalers in this area. In addition to your duties of keeping these wholesalers adequately stocked with Best-Yet Cake Mixes, you must provide them with information regarding new products, special promotions, pricing, methods of keeping stock rotated to insure freshness, and so on. Furthermore, one of your prime responsibilities is making calls on retail grocery stores for the purpose of helping them to move Best-Yet products. In doing this "missionary" work, you frequently take orders for Best-Yet products and in turn give credit for the order to the wholesaler who usually services the retail account.

It is 9:30 A.M., Wednesday, May 12, 1965. You and your wife have just returned from a ten-day vacation in Nassau, a company-sponsored trip you won by having the greatest percentage increase in annual sales within the Eastern Region. This is the first day you have been in your office, which is located in your home in Greenwood, since May 1. You have already helped your wife unload the luggage and you are in your office. You have just started to look over materials that have arrived during your absence. At 10:40 this morning you have an appointment to meet with the representative of an architectural firm regarding plans for building a small office adjacent to your home. This afternoon you and the architects have an appointment with the Zoning Com-

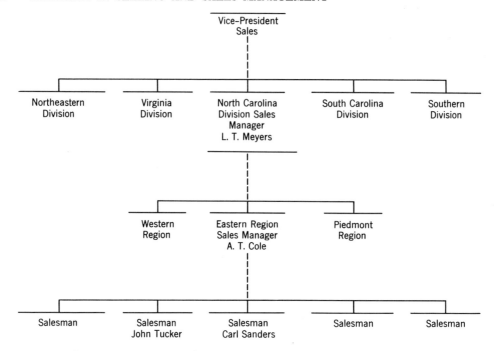

EXHIBIT 1   Best-Yet Cake Mix Company, Partial Organization Chart.

mittee of the Greenwood City Council regarding permission to construct an office in an area zoned residential. You expect these meetings to take the remainder of the day. You have completed preparations for these meetings.

Make notes regarding what disposition, if any, you wish to make concerning the correspondence and rough out any letters, messages, etc., you might wish to send. Your wife serves as your secretary.

SUTTON WHOLESALE HOUSE

1106 Railroad Avenue   Kingston, North Carolina

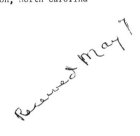

Mr. Carl Sanders
204 Lord Ashley Drive
Greenwood, North Carolina

Dear Sir:

You received a letter from me dated March 22, 1965 referring to Best-Yet cake goods being constantly damaged on arrival at my firm, the Sutton Wholesale House. Your reply to the above mentioned letter said that you would correct the situation immediately.

The three orders I received during April arrived in sound condition. Therefore, I thought the shipping problem had been cleared up.

However, the last order placed on April 26 arrived with most of the goods damaged and unsellable.

Unless this problem is corrected immediately, the Sutton Wholesale House will have no choice but to completely curtail relations with your firm.

Sincerely,

Ben Sutton, Jr.

343

B E S T - Y E T   C A K E   M I X   C O M P A N Y

North Carolina Division

Office of Sales Manager

To all Salesmen:

There was a typographical error on the recent
wholesaler price list you received

Cake mixes #371, 372, 374, 378 were priced
$5.17 too low per case. Please inform your whole-
salers of this error and thus the increased amount
on their invoices before the shipments are made on
May 17.

Sincerely,

L. T. Meyers
Division Sales Manager

EGGERTON GROCERY, INC.   Milan, North Carolina

Sales Representative
Best-Yet Cake Mix Company
Greenwood, North Carolina

Dear Sir:

    Please send me a copy of your latest suggested
retail selling price list on cake mixes.

               Sincerely,

               Joseph Eggerton
               Owner-Manager

```
              H E A R T   F U N D
```

Municipal   Greenwood
Building   North Carolina

Dear Mr. Sanders:

    The businessmen of Greenwood have made their
Heart Drive a success every year by contributing
as much as $50. Since you are associated with Best-
Yet Cake Mix Company, I know you would be glad to
help this worthy cause. If you contribute $25 or
more your name and your company will appear in the
Greenwood paper May 19, 1965.

    Thanks for your cooperation.

               Sincerely,

               William Greene
               Executive Chairman

P. S. We must have your response one week prior to
     the paper's going to press on the 19th.

```
                  T E L E G R A M
```

```
Mr. Carl Sanders
204 Lord Ashley Drive
Greenwood, North Carolina


Could you join Mr. Meyers and me for dinner here in
Raleigh 6:00, May 13.  Plan to discuss plans for
East coast promotion.

                        A. T. Cole
```

S E L L M O R E   104 East Haven
                                                      Greenwood
S U P E R M A R K E T   North Carolina

Received May 3

Mr. Carl Sanders
Greenwood
North Carolina

Dear Mr. Sanders:

    For the third consecutive year Sellmore Supermarket is
sponsoring a promotion in conjunction with "National Cake-
Mix Week" May 17-22. We think this will be the best year
yet for the widely accepted display.

    A large space will be available where all brands of
the cake mixes we carry can be set up in whatever fashion
is deemed best. An expense account will be made available
for any materials, etc., that are needed.

    Because of your relationship with us as a representa-
tive of Best-Yet, as well as a friend we would like for you
to arrange and control the display. You will be needed at
the store from 2-4 p.m. every day during this week to talk
"cake mixes" with the customers. You will receive $10 per
hour for all the time you spend concerning the display.

    Please notify us as soon as possible concerning your
decision as to this matter.

                              Sincerely,

                              Abbot Greene
                              President

John Tucker
Sales Representative
Best-Yet Cake Mix Company

Received May 8

Dear Carl:

Could you possibly call on a few of my customers in the Snow
Hill area on Thursday, May 13, 1965. The other day a car pulled
out in front of me and we collided. The doctors here at Goldsboro
Memorial say it will probably be ten days to three weeks before I
can be up and around.

If you can possibly do this favor for me, it will be appreciated. I have taken care of the remainder of my customers, but
these twelve customers, as you know, are quite a bit off my regular route and closer to you than any of the other salesmen.

Enclosed is a list of the twelve customers and an old invoice
on each one so you will know about what he buys. You can see that
three of these boys are among the largest accounts in our region,
so naturally I am anxious that someone call on them on the regularly scheduled visit. (This room rate is enough to make anybody
anxious. Ha!)

If you can do this for me it will be appreciated. Just send
the orders in with your regular orders. Unless I hear something
different, I'll assume you can handle this for me. Maybe I can
return the favor sometime, but I hope that it won't be under the
same circumstances.

Sincerely,

John Tucker

Enclosure

cc. Mr. A. T. Cole

CROSSROADS   GROCERS,

INCORPORATED

Camp Level   North Carolina

Representative
Best-Yet Cake Mix Company
Greenwood, North Carolina

Dear Sir:

    Recently we have had trouble keeping an adequate
supply of your products on hand to meet our demands.
We purchase your products from Brown Wholesale of Kingston, North Carolina who has been sending a salesman by
our stores on a weekly basis. During the past two months
a Brown's salesman has called only twice.

    Since we have had no previous trouble with Brown,
we feel that there has been a mix up in sales territory
or the salesman has overlooked our store. It is imperative that we have an adequate supply of your products
if they are to be displayed properly.

    Your prompt attention to this matter will be greatly
appreciated.

              Yours truly,

              Allen Baker
              President

Greenwood Wholesale Supply
Greenwood
North Carolina

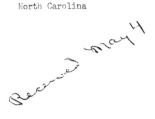

Mr. Carl Sanders
Greenwood
North Carolina

Dear Carl:

The local grocery wholesalers are having their annual "Wholesale-
Retailer Supper" on May 19. As chairman of the supper committee,
I was asked to select a guest speaker for the night. Would it be
possible for you to speak to us then? There will be about 100 to
125 people present at the Holiday Inn at 7:00 p.m.

I am sure I'll see you in the next week or so; but if something
comes up that you cannot be with us, just leave word with my
secretary.

We look forward to having you with us.

                Sincerely,

                Melvin Lakely

P.S. Any aspects regarding wholesaler-retailer relationships
would be a good topic, but you have complete freedom in selecting
a topic.

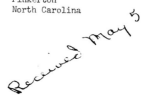

Best-Yet Cake Mix Company
204 Lord Ashley Drive
Greenwood, North Carolina

Dear Sir:

We, the Keller Wholesale Company, for the past two years, have
been supplying Best-Yet cake mixes to the retailers in our area,
as you know.

One particular retailer, the Big Giant Grocery, in Pinkerville,
North Carolina, has complained that our cake mixes were damaged
and nonsaleable when they opened them to put them out for display.

The Keller Wholesale Company has its own delivery service, and
we know that the goods were not damaged by us.

Associated Transport Company delivered the goods to us, but they
say they did not damage them and will not make any adjustment to
us.

Will you inquire into this matter further and help us to get some
kind of adjustment.

                    Sincerely,

                    Abraham Collier
                    Treasurer

Colvin Wholesale Grocery Company
Powtown
North Carolina

Received May 11

Best-Yet Cake Mix Company

North Carolina

Dear Sir:

Please inform me immediately concerning the order of ten
cases of "Best-Yet" cake mix that I ordered from you on
May 3, 1965. You promised me that I would receive the
cake mix by May 10, 1965, so that I could promote and prepare for the national cake mix sale.

You will find an enclosed copy of the order that I placed.
If you cannot see that the ten cases are at the store by
the morning of May 13, 1965, cancel the order because it
will be too late to prepare for pushing, etc.

    Sincerely,

    R. V. Colvin